RUNNING

Microsoft®
Access 2000

John Viescas

PUBLISHED BY
Microsoft Press
A Division of Microsoft Corporation
One Microsoft Way
Redmond, Washington 98052-6399

Library of Congress Cataloging-in-Publication Data
Viescas, John L., 1947-
   Running Microsoft Access 2000 / John L. Viescas.
      p.   cm.
   Includes index.
   ISBN 1-57231-934-8
   1. Microsoft Access. 2. Database management. I. Title.
  II. Title: Running Microsoft Access two thousand.
QA76.9.M3V54 1999
005.75'65--dc21   98-50599
                                        CIP

Printed and bound in the United States of America.

15 16 QWT 7 6 5 4 3

Distributed in Canada by H.B. Fenn and Company Ltd.

A CIP catalogue record for this book is available from the British Library.

Microsoft Press books are available through booksellers and distributors worldwide. For further information about international editions, contact your local Microsoft Corporation office or contact Microsoft Press International directly at fax (425) 936-7329. Visit our Web site at www.microsoft.com/mspress. Send comments to *mspinput@microsoft.com*.

Acquisitions Editor: Christey Bahn
Project Editor (Microsoft Press): Sandra Haynes
Project Editor (Siechert & Wood): Carl Siechert

For Suzanne—again, and always.

Chapters at a Glance

Table of Contents

Acknowledgments

The Microsoft Access development team has produced yet another substantial release just in time for Millennium celebrations. Without the team's dedicated efforts, authors like me wouldn't have anything new to write about. Special thanks to Dave Gainer for his leadership and support in the beta test effort.

This book wouldn't have happened without the outstanding efforts of Carl Siechert, my manuscript and project editor, and Blake Wesley Whittington, the excellent technical editor on the book. Thanks also to the entire team at Siechert & Wood Professional Documentation—I know lots of other folks worked hard behind the scenes to get a quality product out on time. I also wish to send my warm regards to the family of the late Stan DeGulis. Stan was the original manuscript editor, and he provided me with lots of critical and excellent feedback in the early stages of this book project.

Special thanks to Ray McCann of RM Productions for graciously allowing me to use a major portion of his scheduling database for many of the advanced examples in the book. He actually uses a much-enhanced version of this database to run his business.

Thanks also to Sandra Haynes, the project editor at Microsoft Press, and to Jim Buyens, author of *Running Microsoft FrontPage*, who provided invaluable assistance on the "Publishing Data on the Web" chapter.

Last, but certainly not least, special thanks to all my family members for putting up with what seems like my nonstop writing on this project. Special thanks to Ann for baby-sitting our cats while we trucked off to Europe (and I wrote some chapters!) last summer and to Mary and Beth for understanding my hiding away to work on the book during several visits with them in Texas. Thanks also to Beth's husband, Gary, who gave me key technical advice about networking issues. And, of course—and again—thanks to my wonderful wife, Suzanne, who must think my laptop is grafted onto my hands.

John Viescas
Kirkland, Washington
February, 1999

Using the Companion CD

Bound into the back of this book is a CD-ROM disc. The companion CD contains all of the sample databases discussed in this book as well as additional sample spreadsheet, bitmap, icon, Web page, and text files to be used with various exercises in this book. Also included on the companion CD is a tour of Microsoft MapPoint 2000. MapPoint allows Microsoft Office users to easily find and illustrate points on a map, integrate maps into their Office documents, and quickly identify business trends on the map using their own data. See MapPoint Guided Tour Readme.doc, in the Mappoint folder, for more information.

Installing the Sample Files

You can use the book's sample files for hands-on exploration or as templates for your own work. You can either install the sample files on your hard disk or access them directly from the companion CD.

To install the sample files on your hard disk, be sure the companion CD is in your CD-ROM drive. Choose Run from the Start menu, and then type *d:\setup.exe* (where *d* is the drive letter of your CD-ROM drive). Then follow the instructions for installation as they appear.

If you prefer, you can use the sample files directly from the CD without installing them on your hard disk. Note, however, that you cannot create any new objects or update any of the sample databases directly on the CD. If you want to make changes to the data, first use the setup program to copy the samples onto your hard disk.

Notes About Sample File Location

All four main sample databases (Entertainment Scheduling, Microsoft Press Books, Golf Tournament, and Wedding List) have startup properties defined to use the three icon files supplied (Notes.ico, Books.ico, Golf.ico, and Wedbell.ico) when you run the applications. These icon files must be in the same folder as the databases; otherwise, you won't see these custom icons when you start the applications. Also, the sample data access pages and Active Server Pages are designed to execute with the sample database installed in the default C:\Running Access 2000 Samples folder. If you choose to install the samples in another folder, you will have to alter the connection properties of these files in order to run them successfully. *See Chapter 19, "Publishing Data on the Web," for details.* Finally, to be able to open the client/server version of the Microsoft Press Books database (BooksCS.adp), you must first attach the BooksSQL files to your local installation of Microsoft Data Engine (MSDE). *See Chapter 25, "After Completing Your Application," for details.*

Most of the files you'll need for the exercises in this book are located in the main installation folder. You can find author pictures and biographical information used to load information into the Microsoft Press Books sample database in the Authors subfolder. The BookCovers subfolder contains bitmap images of the book covers for many of the books in the Microsoft Press Books database. The Documents subfolder contains text descriptions of the books, table of contents files for the books in Microsoft Word format, and the design templates mentioned in Chapter 4. The Pictures subfolder contains miscellaneous bitmaps and icons used throughout the sample applications.

In the Web Pages subfolder, you can find all the files and additional folders required for the FrontPage Web described in Chapter 19. If you have installed Microsoft FrontPage, you can open this subfolder from FrontPage to edit the Web files.

Additional Information

If you have comments, questions, or ideas regarding this book or the companion CD, please write to Microsoft Press, Attn: Running Series Editor, One Microsoft Way, Redmond, WA 98052-6399. You can also send feedback to Microsoft Press via electronic mail at mspinput@microsoft.com. Please note that product support is not offered through this e-mail address.

Introduction

Microsoft Access 2000 is the fifth full release of the product since its original introduction in 1992. Microsoft has sold more than 75 million copies of Microsoft Office (all versions), and more than 45 million copies of Office 97 (by Microsoft's count). Since a significant percentage of Office 97 sales included Microsoft Access, this certainly gives Access reasonable claim to being the most popular desktop database in the world. As further testament, I've seen overflowing Access sessions at conferences worldwide; I've taught oversold seminars about the product, from introductory to advanced levels; and I've seen everyone from novice end users to developers of advanced database applications make productive use of Access. The high volume of activity on the Access forum on CompuServe and the Microsoft Access user newsgroups on the Internet are further examples of the high interest in the product.

Access is just one part of Microsoft's overall data management product strategy. Like all good relational databases, it allows you to link related information easily—for example, customer and order data that you enter. But Access also complements other database products because it has several powerful connectivity features. As its name implies, Access can work with data from other sources, including many popular PC database programs (such as dBASE and Paradox) and many SQL (structured query language) databases on the desktop, on servers, and on minicomputers and mainframes. Access also fully supports Microsoft's ActiveX technology, so an Access application can be either a client or a server to applications such as Microsoft Word, Microsoft Excel, Microsoft PowerPoint, and Microsoft Outlook.

Access provides a very sophisticated application development system for the Microsoft Windows operating system. This helps you build applications quickly, whatever the data source. In fact, you can build simple applications by defining forms and reports based on your data and linking them with a few Visual Basic statements; there's no need to write complex code in the classic programming sense. Because Access uses Visual Basic, you can use the same set of skills with other applications in Microsoft Office or with Microsoft Visual Basic.

For small businesses (and for consultants creating applications for small businesses), Access is all that's required to store and manage the data used to run the business. Access coupled with Microsoft SQL Server—on the desktop or on a server—is an ideal way for many medium-size companies to build new applications for Windows quickly and inexpensively. For large corporations with a big investment in mainframe relational database applications as well as a proliferation of desktop applications that rely on PC databases, Access provides the tools to easily link mainframe and PC data in a single Windows-based application.

Microsoft Access can also act as a direct source of information published on an intranet or the World Wide Web. Access 2000 includes a new feature—data access pages—that lets you quickly create and deploy intranet applications using pages that you create directly from Access much like you would create an Access application form. Data access pages can retrieve and update data stored either in an Access database or in Microsoft SQL Server.

About This Book

If you're developing a database application, this book gives you a thorough understanding of "programming without pain" using Access. It provides a solid foundation for designing databases, forms, and reports and getting them all to work together. You'll learn that you can quickly create complex applications by linking design elements with Access's powerful macro facilities or with Visual Basic. Even if someone else has built most of the application for you, you'll find this book useful for understanding how to use an Access application and for learning how to extend that application to suit your changing needs.

Running Microsoft Access 2000 is divided into six major parts.

■ Part I provides a thorough overview of Access. Chapter 1 describes how Access fits in the world of personal computer database systems; Chapter 2 describes how you might use Access; and Chapter 3 takes you on a tour of Access, introducing you to the basic concepts and terminology. Chapter 3 also provides summaries of key features.

■ Part II teaches you how to design, define, and modify database definitions in Access. Starting with a good design is the key to building easy-to-use applications. Chapter 4 explains a simple technique that you can use to design a good relational database application with little effort. Even if you're already familiar with Access or creating database applications in general, getting the table design right is so important that it's a "must read" for everyone. Chapter 5 teaches you how to create databases and tables, and Chapter 6 shows you the ins and outs of modifying tables even after you've already begun to load data and build other parts of your application.

■ Part III focuses on working with data. Here you'll learn how to add, update, delete, and replace data in an Access database as well as how to design queries to work with data from multiple tables, calculate values, or update many records using one command. Chapter 10 explains how Access can work with data in other popular databases, spreadsheets, and text files. Chapter 11 includes a comprehensive look at the SQL database language that underlies Access's graphical user interface and that Access uses to manage and update its data.

■ Part IV is all about forms. Chapter 12 introduces you to forms—what they look like and how they work. The remaining chapters in Part IV provide an extensive tutorial on designing, building, and implementing simple and complex forms, including use of the Form Wizard feature.

■ Part V provides detailed information about the publishing your data—either in a report or on the Internet. Chapter 16 leads you on a guided tour of reports and explains their major features. Chapters 17 and 18 teach you how to design, build, and implement both simple and complex reports in your application. Chapter 19 covers the basic architectures for working with Access data on the Web and shows you how to publish static data from Access or build Web pages that can update your Access data.

■ Part VI shows you how to use the programming facilities in Access—macros and Visual Basic—to integrate your database objects and make your application "come alive." First you'll learn how to create Access macros and how to use them to link forms and reports in an application. Then you'll learn the basics of Visual Basic. The last two chapters show you how to complete your applications. The final chapter takes you beyond the basic application development topics with an overview of replication, Access security, and upsizing your database to link directly to Microsoft SQL Server.

Throughout this book, you'll see examples from four sample Access applications.

■ **Wedding List (Wedding.mdb and WeddingVB.mdb).** A simple database to track invitees to a wedding. One version uses only macros to automate the application. The second version is identical in function but uses Visual Basic instead of macros.

■ **Golf Tournament (GolfTournament.mdb).** A more complex database built primarily with the help of wizards to schedule golf tournaments, enter golfer scores, and report the winners by round and by tournament.

■ **Entertainment Scheduling (Entertain.mdb).** A sophisticated application for running a business that arranges contracts between entertainment groups and nightclubs.

■ **Microsoft Press Books (Books.mdb).** An Internet-enabled application that shows you how to limit access to signed-on users while allowing them to create personal orders for their favorite books.

You can find these databases on the companion CD provided with this book. *See page xxv, "Using the Companion CD," for details.* Please note that the invitee names, golfer names, entertainment groups, and club names in these databases are fictitious. The book and author information is actual information obtained from Microsoft Press, but the customer names and addresses (except my own) are fictitious.

This book also includes an appendix that provides instructions for installing Access, shows you how to define and manage data source connections using Open Database Connectivity (ODBC), and explains how to convert version 1.*x*, version 2, version 7 (Microsoft Access for Windows 95), or version 8 (Microsoft Access 97) databases to version 9 (Microsoft Access 2000).

NOTE

In case you're wondering why the numbers skip from version 2 to version 7, Microsoft synchronized the version numbers of all Office applications in Office for Windows 95. Because the highest previous version number for any Office application was Microsoft Word version 6, all of the applications "jumped" to version 7 in Office for Windows 95.

The examples in this book assume you have installed Office 2000, not just Access 2000. Several examples also assume that you have installed all optional features of Access through the Office 2000 setup program. If you have not installed these additional features, your screen might not match the illustrations in this book or you might not be able to run the samples from the companion CD. A list of the additional features you will need to run all the samples in this book is included in the appendix. The dialog boxes illustrated in this book assume that the Office Assistant has been turned off.

PART I

Understanding Microsoft Access

Microsoft Access Is a Database and More

If you're a serious user of a personal computer, you've probably been using word processing or spreadsheet applications to help you solve problems. You might have started a long time ago with character-based products running under MS-DOS but subsequently upgraded to software that runs under the Microsoft Windows operating system. You might also own some database software, either as part of an integrated package such as Microsoft Works or as a separate program.

Database programs have been available for personal computers for a long time. Unfortunately, many of these programs have been either simple data storage managers that aren't suitable for building applications or complex application development systems that are difficult to learn and use. Even many computer-literate people have avoided the more complex database systems unless they have been handed a complete, custom-built database application. The introduction of Microsoft Access, however, represented a significant turnaround in ease of use. Many people are drawn to it to create both simple databases and sophisticated database applications.

Now that Access is in its fifth release and has become an even more robust product in the third edition designed for 32-bit versions of Windows, perhaps it's time to take another look at how you work with your personal computer to get the job done. If you've previously shied away from database software because you felt you needed programming skills or because it would take you too much time to become a proficient user, you'll be pleasantly surprised at how easy it is to work with Access. But how do you decide whether you're ready to move up to a database system such as Access? To help you decide, let's take a look at the advantages of using database application development software.

What Is a Database?

In the simplest sense, a *database* is a collection of records and files that are organized for a particular purpose. On your computer system, you might keep the names and addresses of all your friends or customers. Perhaps you collect all the letters you write and organize them by recipient. You might have another set of files in which you keep all your financial data—accounts payable and accounts receivable or your checkbook entries and balances. The word processor documents that you organize by topic are, in the broadest sense, one type of database. The spreadsheet files that you organize according to their uses are another type of database. Shortcuts to all your programs in your Windows Start menu are a kind of database. Internet shortcuts organized in your Favorites folder are a database.

If you're very organized, you can probably manage several hundred spreadsheets or shortcuts by using folders and subfolders. When you do this, *you're* the database manager. But what do you do when the problems you're trying to solve get too big? How can you easily collect information about all customers and their orders when the data might be stored in several document and spreadsheet files? How can you maintain links between the files when you enter new information? How do you ensure that data is being entered correctly? What if you need to share your information with many people but don't want two people to try updating the same data at the same time? Faced with these challenges, you need a *database management system (DBMS)*.

Relational Databases

Nearly all modern database management systems store and handle information using the *relational* database management model. The term *relational* stems from the fact that each record in the database contains information related to a single subject and only that subject. If you study the relational database management model, you'll find the term *relation* applied to a set of rows about a single subject. Also, data about two classes of information (such as customers and orders) can be manipulated as a single entity based on related data values. For example, it would be redundant to store customer name and address information with every order that the customer places. In a relational database system, the information about orders contains a field that stores data, such as a customer number, which can be used to connect each order with the appropriate customer information.

In a relational database management system, sometimes called an *RDBMS,* the system manages all data in *tables.* Tables store information about a subject (such as customers or products) and have columns that contain the different kinds of information about the subject (for example, customers' addresses or book titles) and rows that describe all the attributes of a single instance of the subject (for example, data on a specific customer or book). Even when you *query* the database (fetch information from one or more tables), the result is always something that looks like another table.

You can also *join* information on related values from multiple tables or queries. For example, you can join author information with book information to find out which authors wrote which books. You can join employee information with contract information to find out which salesperson should receive a commission.

Some Relational Database Terminology

- **Relation.** Information about a single subject such as customers, orders, golfers, golfer scores, or entertainment groups. A relation is usually stored as a table in a relational database management system.

- **Attribute.** A specific piece of information about a subject, such as the address for a customer or the dollar amount of a contract. An attribute is normally stored as a data column, or field, in a table.

- **Relationship.** The way information in one relation is related to information in another relation. For example, customers have a *one-to-many relationship* with orders because one customer can place many orders, but any order belongs to only one customer. Entertainment groups might have a *many-to-many relationship* with night clubs because each group is interested in working for multiple clubs, and each club will book several groups over time.

- **Join.** The process of linking tables or queries on tables via their related data values. For example, customers might be joined to orders by matching customer ID in a customers table and an orders table.

Database Capabilities

An RDBMS gives you complete control over how you define your data, work with it, and share it with others. The system also provides sophisticated features that make it easy to catalog and manage large amounts of data in many tables. An RDBMS has three main types of capabilities: data definition, data manipulation, and data control.

- **Data definition.** You can define what data will be stored in your database, the type of data (for example, numbers or characters), and how the data is related. In some cases, you can also define how the data should be formatted and how it should be validated.

- **Data manipulation.** You can work with the data in many ways. You can select which data fields you want, filter the data, and sort it. You can join data with related information and summarize (total) the data. You can select a set of information and ask the RDBMS to update it, delete it, copy it to another table, or create a new table containing the data.

- **Data control.** You can define who is allowed to read, update, or insert data. In many cases, you can also define how data can be shared and updated by multiple users.

All this functionality is contained in the powerful features of Microsoft Access. Let's take a look at how Access implements these capabilities and compare them to what you can do with spreadsheet or word processing programs.

Microsoft Access as an RDBMS

Microsoft Access is a fully functional RDBMS. It provides all the data definition, data manipulation, and data control features you need to manage large volumes of data.

Data Definition and Storage

While you're working with a document or a spreadsheet, you generally have complete freedom to define the contents of the document or each cell in the spreadsheet. Within a given page in a document, you might include paragraphs of text, a table, a chart, or multiple columns of data displayed with multiple fonts. Within a given column on a spreadsheet, you might have text data at the top to define a column header for printing or display, and you might have various numeric formats within the column, depending on the function of the row. You need this flexibility because your word processing document must be able to convey your message within the context of a printed page, and your spreadsheet must store the data you're analyzing as well as provide for calculation and presentation of the results.

This flexibility is great for solving relatively small, well-defined business problems. But a document becomes unwieldy when it extends beyond a few dozen pages, and a spreadsheet becomes difficult to manage when it contains more than a few hundred rows of information. As the amount of data grows, you might also find that you exceed the data storage limits of your word processing or spreadsheet program or of your computer system. If you design a document or spreadsheet to be used by others, it's difficult (if not impossible) to control how they will use the data or enter new data. For example, on a spreadsheet, even though one cell might need a date and another a currency value to make sense, a user might easily enter character data in error.

Some spreadsheet programs allow you to define a "database" area within a spreadsheet to help you manage the information you need to produce the desired result. However, you are still constrained by the basic storage limitations of the spreadsheet program, and you still don't have much control over what's entered in the rows and columns of the database area. Also, if you need to handle more than number and character data, you might find that your spreadsheet program doesn't understand such things as pictures or sounds.

An RDBMS allows you to define the kind of data you have and how the data should be stored. You can also usually define rules that the RDBMS can use to ensure the integrity of your data. In its simplest form, a *validation rule* might ensure that you can't accidentally store alphabetic characters in a field that should contain a number. Other rules might define valid values or ranges of values for your data. In the most sophisticated systems, you can define the relationship between collections of data (usually tables or files) and ask the RDBMS to ensure that your data remains consistent. For example, you can have the system automatically check to ensure that every order entered is for a valid customer.

With Access, you have complete flexibility to define your data (as text, numbers, dates, times, currency, Internet links, pictures, sounds, documents, and spreadsheets), to define how Access stores your data (string length, number precision, and date/time precision), and to define what the data looks like when you display or print it. You can define simple or complex validation rules to ensure that only accurate values exist in your database. You can request that Access check for valid relationships between files or tables in your database.

Because Access is a state-of-the-art application for Microsoft Windows, you can use all the facilities of *Dynamic Data Exchange (DDE)*, *ActiveX* objects, and *ActiveX* custom controls. DDE lets you execute functions and send data between Access and any other Windows-based application that supports DDE. You can also make DDE connections to other applications using macros or Microsoft Visual Basic. ActiveX is an advanced Windows capability that, in part, allows you to link objects to or embed objects in your Access database. Objects include pictures, graphs, spreadsheets, and documents from other Windows-based applications that also support ActiveX. Figure 1-1 shows embedded object data from the sample Northwind Traders database that ships with Access. You can see a product category record that not only has the typical name and descriptive information but also has a picture to visually describe each category. Access 2000 can also act as an ActiveX *server,* allowing you to open and manipulate Access database objects (such as tables, queries, and forms) from other Windows-based applications.

FIGURE 1-1.

The Categories form in the Northwind Traders sample database.

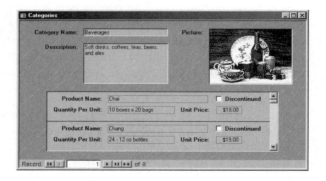

Within your Access forms and reports, you can include ActiveX custom controls to enhance the operation of your application. ActiveX controls provide sophisticated design objects that allow you to present complex data in a simpler, more graphical way. Most ActiveX controls provide a rich set of "actions" (called *methods* in object terminology) that you can call from a procedure and properties you can set to manage how the control looks and behaves. For example, you might want to let your user enter a date by selecting from a calendar picture. You could laboriously build a "calendar" form that has sets of boxes arranged in rows of seven columns and write lots of code to let the user "scroll" to the "next" or "previous" month and then click in a box to pick the date. Access 2000 comes with a standard ActiveX calendar control that takes care of all the details for you. This control is used in the Contracts form in the Entertainment Scheduling database that is included with this book. You can see this form in Figure 1-2.

FIGURE 1-2.

Choosing a date using the ActiveX calendar control.

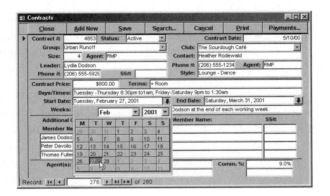

The user can type in contract start and end dates or click a down-arrow button to reveal the ActiveX calendar control. The user can choose a different month or year from the drop-down boxes on the control, and the control displays the appropriate month. When the user clicks a date on the calendar control, the control passes the date back to the form to update the date field in the record. If you purchase Microsoft Office 2000 Developer, you will have several additional ActiveX controls available to use in your applications. Many third-party software vendors have built libraries of ActiveX controls that you can purchase for use with Microsoft Access.

Access can also understand and use a wide variety of other data formats, including many other database file structures. You can export data to and import data from word processing files or spreadsheets. You can directly access Paradox, dBASE III, dBASE IV, Microsoft FoxPro, and other database files. You can also import data from these files into an Access table. In addition, Access can work with most popular databases that support the *Open Database Connectivity (ODBC)* standard, including Microsoft SQL Server, Oracle, DB2, and Ingres.

Data Manipulation

Working with data in a word processing or spreadsheet program is very different from working with data in an RDBMS. In a word processing document, you can include tabular data and perform a limited set of functions on the data in the document. You can also search for text strings in the original document and, with ActiveX, include tables, charts, or pictures from other applications. In a spreadsheet, some cells contain functions that determine the result you want, and in other cells you enter the data that provides the source information for the functions. The data in a given spreadsheet serves one particular purpose, and it's cumbersome to use the same data to solve a different problem. You can link to data in another spreadsheet to solve a new problem, or you can use limited search capabilities to copy a selected subset of the data in one spreadsheet to use in problem-solving in another spreadsheet.

An RDBMS provides you with many ways to work with your data. You can, for example, search a single table for information or request a complex search across several related tables or files. You can update a single field or many records with a single command. You can write programs that use RDBMS facilities to read and update your data. Many systems provide data entry and report generation facilities.

Access uses the powerful SQL database language to process data in your tables. (SQL is an acronym for Structured Query Language.) Using SQL, you can define the set of information that you need to solve a particular problem, including data from perhaps many tables. But Access simplifies data manipulation tasks. You don't even have to understand SQL to get Access to work for you. Access uses the relationship definitions you provide to automatically link the tables you need. You can concentrate on how to solve information problems without having to worry about building a complex navigation system that links all the data structures in your database. Access also has an extremely simple yet powerful graphical query definition facility that you can use to specify the data you need to solve a problem. Using point and click, drag and drop, and a few keyboard strokes, you can build a complex query in a matter of seconds.

Figure 1-3 shows a complex query under construction in Access. You can find this query in the Entertainment Scheduling sample database on the companion CD included with this book. Access displays field lists from selected tables in the upper part of the window; the lines between field lists indicate the automatic links that Access will use to solve the query.

To create the query, you simply select the fields you want from the upper part of the window and drag them to the design grid in the lower part of the window. Choose a few options, type in any criteria, and you're ready to have Access select the information you want.

FIGURE 1-3.

A query to retrieve club and contract information from the Entertainment Scheduling database.

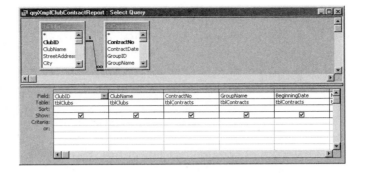

Figure 1-4 shows an example of an SQL statement that Access automatically creates from your specifications in the design grid. You don't need to be an expert to correctly construct the SQL syntax you need to solve your problem, but as you'll learn in Chapter 11, "Advanced Query Design—SQL," you can specify the SQL yourself for certain advanced types of queries. Figure 1-5 shows the result of running the query.

FIGURE 1-4.

The SQL statement for a query to retrieve club and contract information.

```
SELECT tblClubs.ClubID, tblClubs.ClubName, tblContracts.ContractNo, tblContracts.GroupName,
tblContracts.BeginningDate, tblContracts.NumberOfWeeks, [NumberOfWeeks]*[ContractPrice] AS
ContractAmount, tblContracts.Status
FROM tblClubs INNER JOIN tblContracts ON tblClubs.ClubID = tblContracts.ClubID
WHERE (((tblContracts.Status)="A" Or (tblContracts.Status)="Pd"));
```

FIGURE 1-5.

A list of clubs and their contracts.

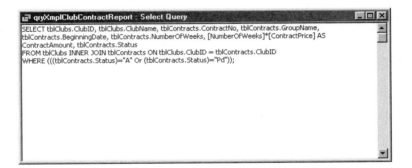

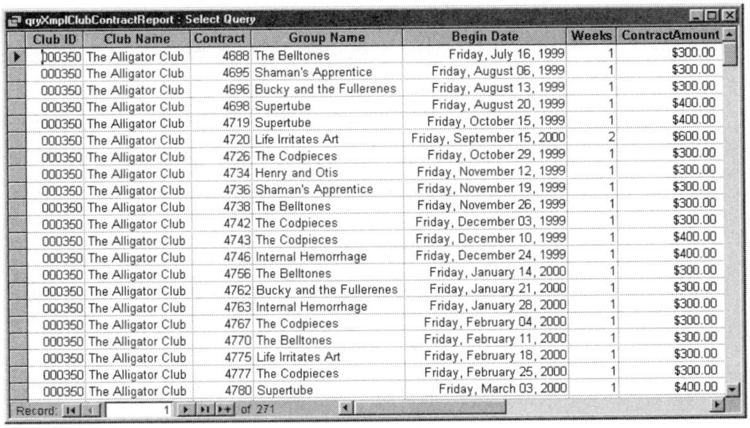

Data Control

Spreadsheets and word processing documents are great for solving single-user problems, but they are difficult to use when more than one person needs to share the data. Spreadsheets are also useful for providing templates for simple data entry, but they don't do the job well if you need to perform complex data validation. For example, a spreadsheet works well as a template for an invoice for a small business with a single proprietor. But if the business expands and a number of salespeople are entering orders, you need a database. Likewise, a spreadsheet can assist employees with expense reports in a large business, but the data eventually must be captured and placed in a database for corporate accounting.

When you need to share your information with others, true relational database management systems allow you to make your information secure so that only authorized users can read or update your data. An RDBMS that is designed to allow data sharing also provides features to ensure that no two people can change the same data at the same time. The best systems also allow you to group changes (a series of changes is sometimes called a *transaction*) so that either all of the changes or none of the changes appear in your data. For example, while entering new order information for a customer, you probably want to know that all items are recorded or, if you encounter an error, that none of the changes are saved. You probably also want to be sure that no one else can view any part of the order until you have entered all of it.

Access is designed to be used either as a stand-alone RDBMS on a single workstation or in a shared client/server mode across a network. Access can also act as the database server for data displayed on Web pages on your company intranet. Because you can share your Access data with other users, Access has excellent data security and data integrity features. You can define which users or groups of users can have access to objects (such as tables, forms, and queries) in your database. Access automatically provides locking mechanisms to ensure that no two people can update an object at the same time. Access also understands and honors the locking mechanisms of other database structures (such as Paradox, FoxPro, and SQL databases) that you attach to your database. In addition, Access lets you create multiple copies of a "master" database through a process called *replication*. Several remote users can have their own copies of the database, and they can each use utilities built into Windows and Access to periodically synchronize their copies.

Microsoft Access as Something More

Being able to define exactly what data you need, how it should be stored, and how you want to access it solves the data management part of the problem. However, you also need a simple way to automate all of the common tasks you want to perform. For example, each time you need to enter a new order, you don't want to have to run a query to search the Customers table, execute a command to open the Orders table, and then create a new record before you can enter the data for the order. And once you've entered the data for the new order, you don't want to have to worry about scanning the table that contains all your products to verify the order's sizes, colors, and prices.

Advanced word processing software lets you define templates and macros to automate document creation, but it's not designed to handle complex transaction processing. In a spreadsheet, you enter formulas that define what automatic calculations you want performed. If you're an advanced spreadsheet user, you might also create macros or Visual Basic procedures to help automate entering and validating data. If you're working with a lot of data, you've probably figured out how to use one spreadsheet as a "database" container and use references to selected portions of this data in your calculations.

Although you can build a fairly complex "application" using spreadsheets, you really don't have the debugging and application management tools you need to easily construct a robust data management application. Even something as simple as a wedding guest invitation and gift list is much easier to handle in a database. (See the Wedding List sample database included with this book.) Database systems are specifically designed for application development. They give you the data management and control tools that you need and also provide facilities to catalog the various parts of your application and manage their interrelationships. You also get a full programming language and debugging tools with a database system.

Developing Application Logic

When you want to build a more complex database application, you need a powerful relational database management system *and* an *application development system* to help you automate your tasks. Virtually all database systems include application development facilities to allow programmers or users of the system to define the procedures needed to automate the creation and manipulation of data. Unfortunately, many database application development systems require that you know a programming language, such as C or Xbase, to define procedures. Although these languages are very rich and powerful, you must have experience before you can use them properly. To really take advantage of some database systems, you must learn programming, hire a programmer, or buy a ready-made database application (which might not exactly suit your needs) from a software development company.

Fortunately, Microsoft Access makes it easy to design and construct database applications without requiring that you know a programming language. Although you begin in Access by defining the relational tables and the fields in those tables that will contain your data, you will quickly branch out to defining actions on the data via forms, reports, data access pages, macros, and Visual Basic.

You can use forms and reports to define how you want the data displayed and what additional calculations you want performed—very much like spreadsheets. In this case, the format and calculation instructions (in the forms and reports) are separate from the data (in the tables), so you have complete flexibility to use your data in different ways without affecting the data. You simply define another form or report using the same data.

When you want to automate actions in a simple application, Access provides a macro definition facility to make it easy to respond to events (such as clicking a button to open a related report) or to link forms and reports together. When you want to build something a little more complex (like the Microsoft Press Books database included with this book), you can quickly learn how to create simple Visual Basic event procedures for your forms and reports. If you want to create more sophisticated applications, such as order entry or scheduling systems (see the Entertainment Scheduling sample database), you can employ more advanced techniques using Visual Basic and module objects.

 Access 2000 introduces a new facility to make it easy to provide access to your data over your company's local intranet. You can create data access pages that allow users to view and browse the data in your Access database from Microsoft Internet Explorer (version 5 and later).

Access provides advanced database application development facilities to process not only data in its own database structures but also information stored in many other popular database formats. Perhaps Access's greatest strength is its ability to handle data from spreadsheets, text files, dBASE files, Paradox and FoxPro databases, and any SQL database that supports the ODBC standard. This means you can use Access to create a Windows-based application that can process data from a network SQL server or from a mainframe SQL database.

 New in Access 2000 for advanced developers is the ability to create an Access application that links directly to Microsoft SQL Server (version 6.5 and later). You store your tables and queries (as views or procedures) directly in SQL Server and create forms, reports, and data access pages in Access directly bound to SQL Server.

Deciding to Move to Database Software

When you use a word processing document or a spreadsheet to solve a problem, you define both the data and the calculations or functions you need at the same time. For simple problems with a limited set of data, this is an ideal solution. But when you start collecting lots of data, it becomes difficult to manage in many separate document or spreadsheet files. Adding one more transaction (another contract or a new investment in your portfolio) might push you over the limit of manageability. It might even exceed the memory limits of your system or the data storage limits of your software program. Because most spreadsheet programs must be able to load an entire spreadsheet file into memory, running out of memory will probably be the first thing that forces you to consider switching to a database.

If you need to change a formula or the way certain data is formatted, you might find you have to make the same change in many places. When you want to define new calculations on existing data, you might have to copy and modify an existing document or create complex links to the files that contain the data. If you make a copy, how do you keep the data in the two copies synchronized?

Before you can use a database such as Microsoft Access to solve problems that require a lot of data or that have complex and changing requirements, you must change the way you think about solving problems with word processing or spreadsheet applications. In Access, you store a single copy of the data in the tables you design. Perhaps one of the hardest concepts to grasp is that you store only your basic data in database tables. For example, in a database, you would store the quantity of items ordered and the price of the items, but you would not usually store the extended cost (a calculated value). You use a query, a form, or a report to define the quantity-times-price calculation.

You can use the query facility to examine and extract the data in many ways. This allows you to keep only one copy of the basic data, yet use it over and over to solve different problems. In a book sales database, you might create one form to display individual books and their authors. You can create another form to enter orders for these books. You can use a report defined on the same data to graph the sales of books by author during specified time periods. You don't need a separate copy of the data to do this, and you can change either the forms or the report independently, without destroying the structure of your database. You can also add new book or sales information easily without having to worry about the impact on any of your forms or reports. You can do this because the data (tables) and the routines you define to operate on the data (queries, forms, reports, macros, or modules) are completely independent of each other. Any change you make to the data via one form is immediately reflected by Access in any other form or query that uses the same data.

If you're wondering how you'll make the transition from word processing documents and spreadsheets to Access, you'll be pleased to find features in Access to help you out. You can use the import facilities to copy the data from your existing text or spreadsheet files. You'll find that Access supports most of the same functions you have used in your spreadsheets, so defining calculations in a form or a report will seem very familiar. Within the Help facility, the Office Assistant can suggest

---

Reasons to Switch to a Database

Reason 1: You have too many separate files or too much data in individual files. This makes it difficult to manage the data. Also, the data might exceed the limits of the software or the capacity of the system memory.

Reason 2: You have multiple uses for the data—detailing transactions (invoices, for example), summary analysis (such as quarterly sales summaries), and "what if" scenarios. Therefore, you need to be able to look at the data in many different ways, but you find it difficult to create multiple "views" of the data.

Reason 3: You need to share data. For example, numerous people are entering and updating data and analyzing it. Only one person at a time can update a spreadsheet or a word processing document, but many people can simultaneously share and update a database table. Also, databases ensure that people reading the data see only committed updates.

Reason 4: You must control the data because different users access the data, because the data is used to run your business, and because the data is related (such as data for customers and orders). This means you must secure access to data and control data values, and you must ensure data consistency.

solutions quickly. Help also includes "how do I" topics that walk you through key tasks you need to learn to begin working with a database and "tell me about" and reference topics that enhance your knowledge. In addition, Access provides powerful wizard facilities to give you a jump start on moving your spreadsheet data to an Access database, such as the Import Spreadsheet Wizard and the Table Analyzer Wizard to help you design database tables to store your old spreadsheet data.

Take a long look at the kind of work you're doing today. The sidebar on the facing page summarizes some of the key reasons why you might need to move to Access. Is the number of files starting to overwhelm you? Do you find yourself creating copies of old files when you need to answer new questions? Do others need to share the data and update it? Do you find yourself exceeding the limits of your current software or the memory on your system? If the answer to any of these is *yes,* you should be solving your problems with a relational database management system like Microsoft Access.

In the next chapter, "The Uses of Microsoft Access," you'll read about some uses of the Access application development system in different professional settings. Then, in Chapter 3, "Touring Microsoft Access," you'll open the Entertainment Scheduling sample database to explore some of the many features and functions of Access.

CHAPTER 2

The Uses of Microsoft Access

Microsoft Access has all the features of a classic relational database management system (RDBMS)—and more. Access is not only a powerful, flexible, and easy-to-use RDBMS, it is also a complete database application development facility. You can use Access to create and run under the Microsoft Windows operating system an application tailored to your data management needs. Access lets you limit, select, and total your data by using queries. You can create forms for viewing and changing your data. You can also use Access to create simple or complex reports. Both forms and reports "inherit" the properties of the underlying table or query, so in most cases you need to define such things as formats and validation rules only once. You can create data access pages bound to your data to make it easy to share your information over your company's intranet.

Among the most powerful features of Access are the wizards that you can use to create tables and queries and to customize a wide variety of forms, reports, or data access pages simply by selecting options with your mouse. Access also includes wizards that help you analyze your table design, import spreadsheet or text data, improve database performance, or build and customize one of many types of applications using built-in templates. Access includes a comprehensive programming language, Microsoft Visual Basic, that you can use to create very robust "production" applications that can be shared by many users.

Finally, you get all of these development facilities not only for working with an Access database but also to attach to and work with data stored in many other popular formats. You can build an Access application to work directly with dBASE files, with Paradox and Microsoft FoxPro databases, and with any SQL database that supports the Open Database Connectivity (ODBC) standard. You can also easily import and export data as text, word processing files, or spreadsheet files.

This chapter describes five scenarios, in which Access is used to meet the database and application development needs of the owner of a small business, a PC application developer or consultant, the marketing department in a company, a management information systems (MIS) coordinator in a large corporation, and a home computer user.

In a Small Business

If you're the owner of a small business, you can use the simple yet powerful capabilities of Microsoft Access to manage the data you need to run your business. In addition, you can find dozens of third-party Access-based applications that will add to your productivity and make running your business much simpler. Because Access's application design facilities are so simple to use, you can be confident in creating your own applications or in customizing applications provided by others for your specific needs.

Throughout much of the rest of this book, you'll read about the design and creation of a database application for an entertainment booking agency, RM Productions. This company is an actual small business in western Washington state, owned by a friend who not only handles the booking for many nightclub acts but also is an accomplished musician in his own right.

RM Productions is like many small businesses. The owner, Ray McCann, realized many years ago that a personal computer system could potentially help him run his business more efficiently. At a minimum, he could keep a readily searchable list of all the clubs and groups that hired him as their booking agent, rather than depend on a manual card file. His first personal computer ran on something called CP/M (we won't ask him how long ago that was), and he eventually found a simple little database program that would let him keep track of the clubs and groups and print out contracts.

Even as his business grew, Ray hung on to his old CP/M database program. He even went so far as to install a special emulation card in his

PC so that he could still run the program after he had upgraded to MS-DOS and Windows. As his entertainment booking business grew, Ray needed more sophisticated ways to send out mailings and keep track of clubs and groups that had open future dates. He got pretty creative dumping comma-separated data into an MS-DOS-based word processing program, but he quickly realized that he needed something better.

Ray spent some time in early 1993 taking a look at several new Windows-based database systems. He settled on Microsoft Access. Even though he had virtually no database programming experience, it didn't take Ray long to learn how to import his club and group information into an Access database and create simple queries and mailing labels. Ray contacted me to help him expand his database to run his entire booking business. Figure 2-1 shows the central contract booking form from that application. In this book, we'll explore many of the key elements of this database. A major portion of Ray's database application is on the companion CD included with this book.

FIGURE 2-1.

The Contracts data entry form in the Entertainment Scheduling database.

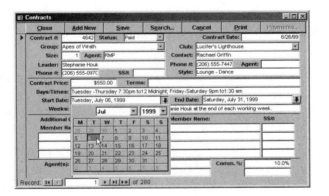

The bottom line? It's true that Ray was already pretty comfortable working with a personal computer. But without Access, he would still be struggling with his outdated database and word processing system. Now he has the database he needs for his growing business. If you're a small business owner who understands that computers should be able to do more than word processing and spreadsheet programs can do, perhaps Access is for you too. You'll find a lot of computer consultants ready and able to put together an Access-based application for you in a short time and at low cost. Even if someone has constructed your database for you, you'll want to know more about Access so that you can take advantage of its native features.

In Contract Work

In today's highly competitive consulting marketplace, the developer who can deliver custom applications quickly and inexpensively will win the lion's share of the business. If you're a PC application developer or consultant, you'll find that the query, form, and report features of Microsoft Access allow you to create applications for your clients in record time. You can also take advantage of Visual Basic, which is built into Access, to satisfy unique requirements and produce truly custom applications. Because this is the same Visual Basic that you can use in all the other Microsoft Office products, you'll find the Access application development features very familiar.

If you're a consultant building applications for a vertical market, you'll especially appreciate how Access makes it easy to build your core application and modify the application for each client's needs. You can create add-on features that you can price separately. Whether you're building a custom application from scratch or modifying an existing one, your clients will appreciate the fact that you can sit down with them and use Access to prototype the finished application so that they can see exactly what they'll get.

You can scale your application to your clients' needs because Access can connect to and work with other database management systems. For smaller clients, you'll find the native Access database system more than adequate. For larger clients, you can connect your application to Microsoft SQL Server or other host databases without having to change any of the forms, reports, macros, or modules in your application.

Imagine that your local golf club uses a database to help track and total tournament scores. Suppose the database system was built by you several years ago using an Xbase product. The golf club would like to upgrade the system by converting it to run under the latest Microsoft Windows operating system. The club would also like to connect the database system to the current golfer information that is kept in an SQL Server database. The club wants the new database system to make it easy to schedule upcoming tournaments, to track golfer scores as a tournament is in progress, to post results on their internal intranet, and to calculate golfer raw scores, handicaps, and final scores.

Access is a perfect solution. You can use the existing Xbase data or convert it easily to Access format. You can also connect the new application to the existing SQL Server golfer data. Creating forms to enter data and data access pages or reports to examine results is a snap. Figure 2-2 shows the main menu and the form to enter information about the golf course and tee statistics. All of the forms, reports, and data access pages in this sample application (which you can find on the companion CD) were created with the help of the wizards built into Access.

FIGURE 2-2.

Entering golf course information in the Golfing sample database.

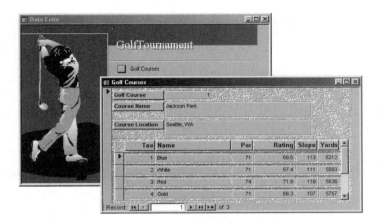

As a Sales and Marketing Tool

As you might expect, Microsoft Corporation takes full advantage of its database tools to provide applications for its field marketing and sales force. I have worked on several application projects at Microsoft using Access. On one project, I built an Access database to manage a large catalog of Microsoft PowerPoint slides used for marketing presentations. Using this database, a sales representative can enter criteria for an upcoming presentation, including products of interest, type of audience, and maximum time allowed for the presentation. The application then builds a core presentation from the available slides and suggests some optional slides that the representative might want to include.

On another project, I built a database to provide Microsoft marketing representatives with information about leading systems and network integrators around the country. When the representatives work with a customer, they can use this tool to quickly search for local companies that might be available to help implement a new system. The representatives can also use the information to provide integrators in their area with information about upcoming products or seminars.

Throughout the rest of this book, you can find many examples that use another sort of sales and marketing database. The Microsoft Press Books database, included on the companion CD, contains information about many of the books offered by Microsoft Press and about the authors who have written the books. Included is an extensive search capability as well as an option to identify yourself as a customer and create an order for the books you find of interest. Figure 2-3 shows you a book search in progress in this sample database. You can print out your order and take it to your local bookstore—there's even a list of stores that stock Microsoft Press books and a search capability to help you locate the nearest store. If you have an Internet browser installed on your computer, there's also a hyperlink to the Microsoft Press home page for the latest information as well as hyperlinks to many of the bookstores' Web sites.

FIGURE 2-3.

Looking for a book of interest in the Microsoft Press Books database.

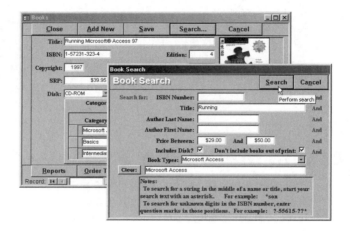

SEE ALSO

See Chapter 25, "After Completing Your Application," for details about Office 2000 Developer.

Although Microsoft Press doesn't currently distribute this database to potential customers (except by way of the sample included with this book), you can imagine how easy it would be to include the complete catalog to send to stores or computer users who might be interested in these books. If you own Office 2000 Developer, you can package a marketing database application so that even a computer user who doesn't own a copy of Microsoft Access can use the application.

In a Large Corporation

Today all companies recognize that one of the ways to remain competitive is to use computer-stored data for more than just day-to-day operations. Creative managers are constantly looking for ways to "turn data into information." As a result, companies no longer have "data processing" units; they have vast MIS departments charged with the care and feeding of the company's valuable computer-stored information.

Nearly all corporations start by building operational data processing systems. These systems collect and process the individual transactional data required to run the business on a day-to-day basis. Examples of transactional data include the following.

- Checks cleared and money withdrawn and deposited in a banking demand deposit system

- Incoming inventory and items sold in a retail system

- Raw materials ordered and received and finished goods shipped in a manufacturing system

- Energy consumed, raw product delivered, and service connection/disconnection data in a utility system

These systems are relatively simple to design and implement with respect to the data input, the processes required on this data, and the data output. They are also easy to justify financially because they can reduce clerical tasks and, at the same time, handle rapidly growing volumes of data. (Imagine trying to post 10 million checks to accounts manually.)

After operational systems are in place and management becomes aware of the vast amounts of data being collected, management often begins to examine the data to better understand how the business interacts with its customers, suppliers, and competitors—to learn how to become more efficient and more competitive. Information processing in most MIS departments usually begins quite innocently as an extension of operational systems. In fact, some information processing almost always gets defined as part of an operational application system design. While interviewing users of a system during the systems analysis phase, the system designer usually hears requests such as, "When the monthly invoices are produced, I'd also like to see a report that tells me which accounts are more than 90 days past due." Printing the invoices is not information processing. Producing the report is.

On the surface, it would seem simple to answer a question about delinquent accounts, given the data about all accounts receivable. However, the operational system might require only 30 days of "current" data to get the job done. The first information request almost always begins to put demands on the data processing systems, and these demands far exceed the data and processing power needed to merely run the business. At some point, the MIS organization decides to reserve additional data storage and processing capability to meet the growing need for information.

This need for information has led companies to build vast networks of departmental systems, which are in turn linked to desktop systems on employees' desks. As more and more data spreads through the corporation, the data becomes more difficult to manage, locate, and access, as Figure 2-4 makes clear. Multiple copies of the same data proliferate, and it becomes hard to determine who has the most current and accurate data.

Why do so many copies exist? Many copies of data exist because the vast majority of tools aren't designed to work with data in more than one format or to connect to data from multiple sources. Employees must resort to obtaining a copy of the data they want and then converting it to the format understood by their tool of choice.

FIGURE 2-4.

The typical corporate computing environment, in which data can spread and become difficult to manage, locate, and access.

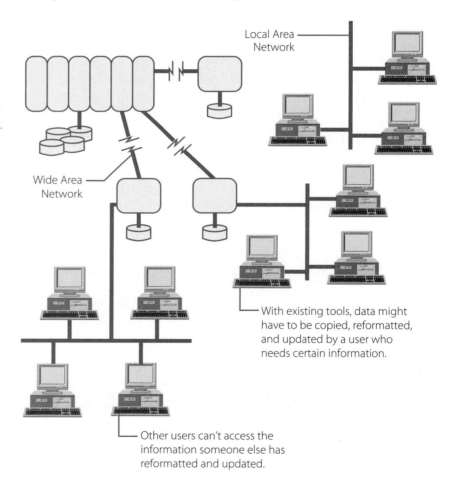

Local Area Network

Wide Area Network

With existing tools, data might have to be copied, reformatted, and updated by a user who needs certain information.

Other users can't access the information someone else has reformatted and updated.

One major strength of Microsoft Access in a corporate environment is the ability to link to a variety of database formats on the workstation, on database servers, or on host computers. A manager trying to solve a problem no longer has to figure out how to get copies of data from several different sources to plug into a spreadsheet-based graph for analysis. Using Access, the manager can connect directly to the source data, build a query to extract the necessary information, and create a report with an embedded graph—all with one tool. When a corporation has implemented an intranet, authorized users can access this same information in published data access pages. The ability to retrieve data from multiple sources, combined with ease of use, makes Access a powerful tool for creating information processing systems.

Workgroup Applications

Large corporations find Access especially well suited for creating the workstation portion of client/server applications. Unlike many other Windows-based client application development systems, Access uses its knowledge of the application data and structure to simplify the creation of forms, reports, and data access pages. (Data access pages are a new feature in Access 2000 that make it easy to design and deploy Access-based web applications on a company intranet.) Applications developed using Access can be made available to users at all levels of the corporation. And with Access it's easy to design truly "user-friendly" applications that fully utilize the investment in employee workstations.

Because Access can link to and share data in many different database formats, it's ideal for creating workgroup applications that maintain data on local departmental servers but need to periodically use data from applications in other departments or upload data to corporate servers. For smaller workgroup applications, local data can be stored and shared across the workgroup using native Access database files. For larger applications, a true database server, such as SQL Server, can be used to store the data, with Access as the workstation client. When data must be shared with other workgroups or corporate servers, the Access-based application can use the ODBC standard to execute queries that read or update data that is stored in any of several database formats.

? SEE ALSO
See Chapter 15, "Advanced Form Design" for more details about forms. See Chapter 19, "Publishing Data on the Web," for more details about data access pages. See Chapter 10, "Importing, Linking, and Exporting Data," for more details about ODBC.

Information Processing Systems

Perhaps a more common use for Access in a corporate environment is as the front-end tool for information processing systems. Many corporations create Executive Information System (EIS) applications using Access so that knowledgeable executives can create their own "drill down" queries, graphs, and reports. MIS departments find that Access is also a great tool for creating the end-user interface for information processing applications.

In recent years, Ray McCann's business has grown by leaps and bounds. He now keeps track of dozens of entertainment groups and more than 100 nightclubs. Although he doesn't run a large corporation, his information processing needs have grown to the point that he often needs sophisticated search tools to find the perfect match between entertainment groups and clubs. The Entertainment Scheduling sample database now contains the sort of "drill down" search mechanism that you might implement in a corporate information processing system.

Figure 2-5 shows a complex search in progress. The initial search screen generates a filtered list of groups (the Group Search Summary) when more than a few groups meet the criteria entered. A double-click on a specific group in the filtered list lets Ray display the full details for that group.

FIGURE 2-5.

A "drill down" search in progress in the Entertainment Scheduling sample database.

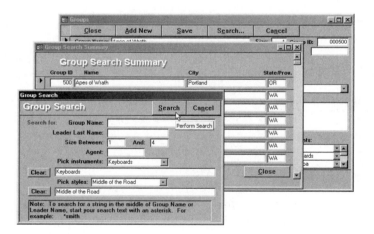

As a Personal RDBMS

Last, but certainly not least, Microsoft Access is a great tool for managing personal information on your home computer. If you're one of the millions of PC users who has a home computer system that runs Microsoft Windows, you can use Access to help you be more productive.

You might want to build a database application to manage your investment portfolio, or create a directory containing the addresses, birthdays, and anniversaries of all your friends. If you like to cook, a recipe database could be useful. Perhaps you'd like to keep track of your collection of movies or books. I have a friend who uses Access to keep track of his athletic training. The Database Wizard in Access shows you how to quickly build and customize an assortment of personal databases.

When one of our daughters got married a few years ago, I created a small Access application to keep track of the wedding guest list. You can see the form that I designed for this purpose in Figure 2-6. This was one of the very first Access databases that I created, and it's automated completely with macros. You can find it on the companion CD.

FIGURE 2-6.

Keeping track of wedding guests and gifts.

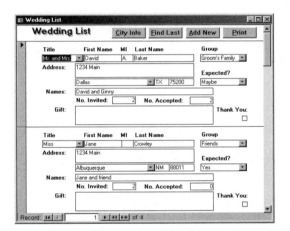

We also used the database to keep track of who had accepted the invitation. It was a snap to produce a summary report by groom's family, bride's family, or friends. After the wedding, we used the form to keep track of the gifts received and thank-you notes written.

Because Access makes it so easy to create forms and reports and link them together with macros or with Visual Basic, you can create small personal applications in a jiffy. Access also supports ActiveX, so you can get very creative with your applications. Imagine embedding sound snippets from your favorite albums in the database you use to catalog your CD collection. The possibilities are endless.

Typical Uses for Microsoft Access

Here are just a few of the ways Access can fulfill the needs of a wide range of users.

Small Business

- Accounting
- Order entry
- Customer tracking
- Contact management

Consulting

- Vertical market applications
- Cross-industry applications

Sales and Marketing

- Product promotion
- Sales information resource
- Order processing

Large Corporation

- Workgroup applications
- Information processing systems
- Intranet publishing

Personal Use

- Address book
- Investment management
- Cookbook
- Collections—recordings, books, movies

In the next chapter, you'll learn more about Access's many features as we take a quick tour of the product.

CHAPTER 3

Touring Microsoft Access

Before you explore the many features of Microsoft Access, it's worth spending a little time looking it over and "kicking the tires." This chapter helps you understand the relationships between the main components in Access and shows you how to move around within the database management system.

Windows Features

Access takes advantage of the many easy-to-use features of the Microsoft Windows operating system. If you've used other Windows-based products, such as Microsoft Excel or Microsoft Word, you'll be right at home with the menus, toolbars, and drop-down lists in Access. Even if you're new to Windows, you'll discover that the techniques you need to work with Access are easy to learn. When working with data, you'll find familiar cut, copy, and paste capabilities for moving and copying data and objects within Access. In addition, Access supports useful drag-and-drop capabilities to assist you in designing queries, forms, reports, and macros. For example, you can select a field in a table and then drag the field, dropping it where you want that data to appear in a report. You can also drag any form or report that you use frequently and drop it on your desktop for easy access.

Access uses a Multiple Document Interface (MDI) to allow you to work on multiple objects at one time. This means that you can work with a number of tables, forms, reports, macros, or modules simultaneously. If you've used some of the other products included in the Microsoft Office 2000 package, you already know how to open multiple Microsoft Excel spreadsheets or graphs, or Microsoft PowerPoint slide presentations within a single application window. As an example,

Key Features in Access 2000

Here's a list of important features in Access 2000.

- Outlook-like Database window

- Long filename support

- Ability to create desktop shortcuts to Access objects

- Ability to create custom object groups within the Database window

- Ability to set database startup properties such as Application Title, Application Icon, and initial display form

- Ability to create a replica of your database and use the Briefcase to keep the replica objects and data synchronized with the master

- Database Wizard to provide a "jump start" on creating more than 20 common types of applications

- Name AutoCorrect option to propagate field name changes in tables to queries, forms, and reports

- Ability to manipulate Access objects from other Windows-based applications via Automation

- Support for hyperlinks throughout the product

- Ability to create dynamic HTML data access pages to publish your data on your local intranet

- Integration with the Office Assistant help facility

- Compact On Close option to keep your database size to a minimum

- Ability to specify the number of databases you want to see on your recently used list

- Ability to create an Access project file (adp extension) that links directly to views and tables in an SQL Server database on your local machine or on a network

Figure 3-1 shows you an Access session with the Group Search Summary and Groups forms open at the same time.

FIGURE 3-1.

Two forms open simultaneously within Access.

Click and drag a window title bar to move a window.

Click here to maximize the window to fill the entire application workspace.

Click here to minimize the Access application to a button on the taskbar.

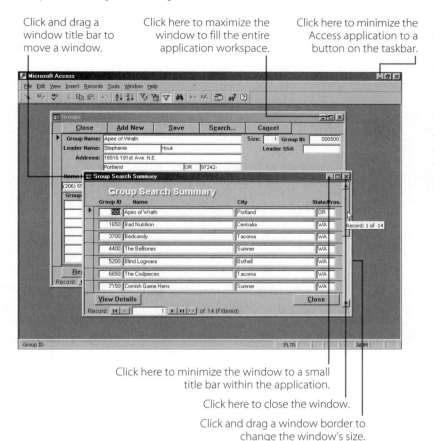

Click here to minimize the window to a small title bar within the application.

Click here to close the window.

Click and drag a window border to change the window's size.

🟠 **TIP**

You can ask Access to show all visible open objects on the Windows taskbar to make it easy to switch from one window to another within Access. Choose Options from the Tools menu. On the View tab, select the Windows In Taskbar option.

Access also fully supports object linking and embedding (part of Microsoft's ActiveX technology). This means that you can embed (in your tables, queries, forms, and reports) objects from other applications, such as pictures, word processing documents, spreadsheets, graphs, sounds, and more. You can use an *ActiveX control* to enhance the way your forms work. ActiveX controls are a broad class of custom controls that can be used in Office applications as well as for pages designed for use on the Internet. You'll learn how to use ActiveX objects and ActiveX controls in an Access database later in this book.

The Architecture of Microsoft Access

Microsoft Access calls anything that can have a name an *object*. Within an Access database, the main objects are tables, queries, forms, reports, data access pages, macros, and modules.

If you have worked with other database systems on desktop computers, you might have seen the term *database* used to refer to only those files in which you store data. In Access, however, a database also includes all the major objects related to the stored data, including objects you define to automate the use of your data. Here is a summary of the major objects in an Access database.

- **Table.** An object you define and use to store data. Each table contains information about a particular subject, such as customers or orders. Tables contain *fields* (or *columns*) that store different kinds of data, such as a name or an address, and *records* (or *rows*) that collect all the information about a particular instance of the subject, such as all the information about an entertainment group named The Belltones. You can define a *primary key* (one or more fields that have a unique value for each record) and one or more *indexes* on each table to help retrieve your data more quickly.

- **Query.** An object that provides a custom view of data from one or more tables. In Access, you can use the graphical query by example (QBE) facility or you can write SQL statements to create your queries. You can define queries to select, update, insert, or delete data. You can also define queries that create new tables from data in one or more existing tables.

- **Form.** An object designed primarily for data input or display or for control of application execution. You use forms to customize the presentation of data that your application extracts from queries or tables. You can also print forms. You can design a form to run a *macro* or a Visual Basic *procedure* (see the sections on macros and modules below) in response to any of a number of events—for example, to run a procedure when the value of data changes.

■ **Report.** An object designed for formatting, calculating, printing, and summarizing selected data. You can view a report on your screen before you print it.

 ■ **Data Access Page.** An object that includes an HTML file and supporting files to provide custom access to your data from Microsoft Internet Explorer. You can publish these files on your company intranet to allow other users on your network who also have Office 2000 and Internet Explorer version 5 or later to view, search, and edit your data.

■ **Macro.** An object that is a structured definition of one or more actions that you want Access to perform in response to a defined event. For example, you might design a macro that opens a second form in response to the selection of an item on a main form. You might have another macro that validates the content of a field whenever the value in the field changes. You can include simple conditions in macros to specify when one or more actions in the macro should be performed or skipped. You can use macros to open and execute queries, to open tables, or to print or view reports. You can also run other macros or Visual Basic procedures from within a macro.

■ **Module.** An object containing custom procedures that you code using Visual Basic. Modules provide a more discrete flow of actions and allow you to trap errors—something you can't do with macros. Modules can be stand-alone objects containing functions that can be called from anywhere in your application, or they can be directly associated with a form or a report to respond to events on the associated form or report.

Figure 3-2 on the next page shows a conceptual overview of how objects in Access are related. Tables store the data that you can extract with queries and display in reports or that you can display and update in forms or data access pages. Notice that forms, reports, and data access pages can use data either directly from tables or from a filtered "view" of the data created by using queries. Queries can use Visual Basic functions to provide customized calculations on data in your database. Access also has many built-in functions that allow you to summarize and format your data in queries.

SEE ALSO

For a list of events on forms and reports, see Chapter 20, "Adding Power with Macros."

Events on forms and reports can "trigger" either macros or Visual Basic procedures. What is an event? An *event* is any change in state of an Access object. For example, you can write macros or Visual Basic procedures to respond to opening a form, closing a form, entering a

FIGURE 3-2.

Main objects and their relationships in Access.

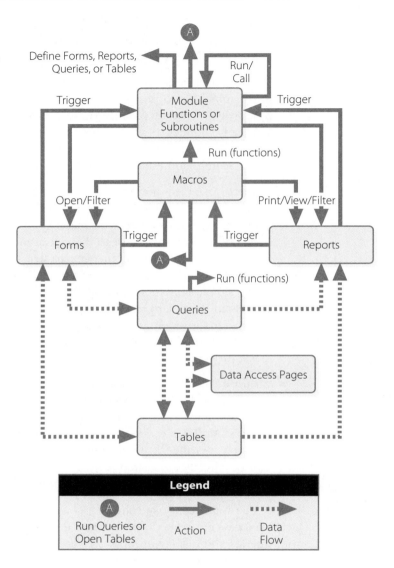

For more information about using Visual Basic within Access, see Chapter 22, "Visual Basic Fundamentals," and Chapter 23, "Automating Your Application with Visual Basic."

new row on a form, or changing data either in the current record or in an individual *control* (an object on a form or report that contains data). You can even design a macro or a Visual Basic procedure that responds to the user pressing individual keys on the keyboard when entering data!

Using macros and modules, you can change the flow of your application; open, filter, and change data in forms and reports; run queries; and build new tables. Using Visual Basic, you can create, modify, and delete any Access object; manipulate data in your database row by row or column by column; and handle exceptional conditions. Using module code you can even call Windows Application Programming Interface (API) routines to extend your application beyond the built-in capabilities of Access.

Exploring the Entertainment Scheduling Database

Now that you know a little bit about the major objects that make up a Microsoft Access database, a good next step is to spend some time exploring the Entertainment Scheduling database (Entertain.mdb) that comes with this book. First, follow the instructions at the beginning of this book for copying the sample databases to your hard drive. When you start Access, it shows you the opening choices dialog box, shown in Figure 3-3.

FIGURE 3-3.

The opening choices dialog box in Access.

Select the Open An Existing File option, and click OK to see the Open dialog box, shown in Figure 3-4 on the next page. In the Open dialog box, select the file Entertain.mdb from the folder to which you copied the sample databases, and then click Open. You can also double-click the filename to open the database. (If you haven't set options in Windows Explorer to show filename extensions for registered applications, you won't see the mdb extension for your database files. In Windows 98 or Windows 95 with Internet Explorer 4.0 or later installed, choose Folder Options from the View menu in Windows Explorer. In other versions of Windows, choose Options from the View menu. Select the View tab and deselect the option to hide file extensions.) The Entertainment Scheduling application will start, and you'll see the main switchboard form with buttons for Groups, Contracts, Clubs, Maintenance, Reports, and Exit. Click Exit to close the application and return to the Database window for the Entertainment Scheduling database, as shown in Figure 3-5. (Note: If you hold down the Shift key while you open a database, the application won't start, and you can view just the Database window.)

FIGURE 3-4.

The Open dialog box for databases.

Double-click here to open the Entertain.mdb database.

Microsoft Access Project Files

Microsoft Access 2000 introduces an advanced facility that allows you to create a project file (with an adp extension) that contains only your forms, reports, data access pages, macros, and modules. When you create a new project file, you can specify a Microsoft SQL Server database to support the project. You can connect your project file to a Microsoft SQL Server version 6.5 database on a server or to a version 7.0 or later database on a server or on your desktop. You will see available tables in the server database as table objects in your project. You will also see views and procedures as query objects. Access 2000 includes special table and view editors to allow you to work directly with the objects in SQL Server.

You can use all the techniques you learn in this book for creating forms, reports, data access pages, macros, and modules in Microsoft Access project files. For more details about creating and working with project files, see the *Microsoft Access 2000 Developer's Handbook*.

FIGURE 3-5.

The Database window for the Entertainment Scheduling sample database.

Tables button selected

Name of the database

List of tables in the database

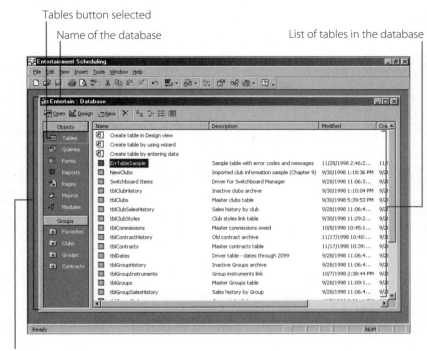

Database window

For an existing database, the Database window always remains where you last placed it on your screen. The title bar of the window shows the name of the database that you have open. As you'll learn later in this book, you can set options in the database to change the title bar of the main Access window to show the name of your application instead of "Microsoft Access." Although you can have only one Access database open at a time within a single copy of Microsoft Access, you can connect an open database (and its forms, reports, data access pages, macros, and modules) to tables in other Access databases, to data in Paradox or dBASE files, or to data in SQL Server databases.

Notice in Figure 3-5 that Access makes available most of the buttons on the toolbar after you open a Database window. To see what a particular toolbar button on either the main Access toolbar or the toolbar in the Database window does, place the mouse pointer over the button but *don't* click it. In about a half-second, Access pops up a ScreenTip that describes the button's function, as shown on the next page.

Understanding Access

As you explore Access, you'll see that it provides more than a dozen built-in toolbars. Normally, Access shows you the toolbar most appropriate for the work you're doing. However, you can control which toolbars are active, and you can customize which buttons appear on which toolbars. You can define custom toolbars and menu bars that display all the time. You can also open and close toolbars from macros or modules. In fact, the Entertainment Scheduling application includes a custom form toolbar and a custom menu bar that are open for all the forms in the application. *You'll learn how to build a custom form toolbar in Chapter 14, "Customizing Forms." Chapter 24, "The Finishing Touches," shows you how to construct a custom menu bar.*

Down the side of the Database window are buttons that allow you to choose one of the seven major object types: tables, queries, forms, reports, data access pages, macros, and modules. You can also collect shortcuts to objects in groups that you create to help organize how you work. You'll see how to work with groups at the end of this chapter.

Tables

When you first open the Database window, Microsoft Access selects the Tables button and shows you the list of tables in the database, as shown in Figure 3-5. At the upper left corner of the Database window are three toolbar buttons. One allows you to create a new table, and the other two allow you to open a table in one of two available views.

 Clicking this button opens a Table window in Datasheet view, which lets you view and update the data in the table.

 Clicking this button opens a Table window in Design view, which lets you view and modify the table's definition.

 Clicking this button gives you the option to define a new table by entering its data (much like creating a new spreadsheet), to create a new table from scratch, or to start one of the table wizards.

When the Database window is active, you can choose any of these command buttons from the keyboard by pressing the first letter of the button name while holding down the Alt key. The Database window also contains three special icons, shown below, that provide shortcuts for creating a new table. Double-click any of these icons to begin defining a new table.

 Create table in Design view

Create table by using wizard

Create table by entering data

NOTE

You can remove the new-object shortcuts from the Database window by choosing Options from the Tools menu, and then clearing the New Object Shortcuts option on the View tab.

You can also open a table in Datasheet view by double-clicking the table name in the Database window; or you can open the table in Design view by holding down the Ctrl key and double-clicking the table name. If you right-click a table name, Access displays a *shortcut menu,* as shown in Figure 3-6, that lets you perform a number of handy operations on the item you selected. Simply choose one of the options on the shortcut menu, or left-click anywhere else in the Access window to dismiss the menu.

FIGURE 3-6.

A shortcut menu for a table in the Database window.

Understanding Access

Key Table Features in Access 2000

Here's a list of important table features in Access 2000.

- Ability to define a table by entering its data

- Table wizards

- Performance Analyzer to help make table designs and relationships more efficient

- Datasheet formatting options

- Ability to define default field-display controls for most fields

- Automatic combo boxes in table datasheets for fields related to other tables (if the Display Control property is set to Combo Box or List Box)

- Subdatasheets in Datasheet view that let you see information from re-lated tables

- Ability to set the default data type for table design mode

- Datasheet scroll bar "thumb tips" that display the relative record loca-tion

- AutoNumber data type with Random option

- Support for the Hyperlink data type

- Ability to use table data as a direct source for HTML pages (data access pages)

- Row-level locking

- Support for Unicode character sets for international languages

---

Table Window in Design View

When you want to change the *definition* of a table (the structure or de-sign of a table, as opposed to the data in a table), you must open the Table window in Design view. With the Entertainment Scheduling data-base open, right-click the table named tblClubs and choose Design from the shortcut menu; this opens the tblClubs table in Design view, as shown in Figure 3-7. Notice that the Database window appears behind the active Table window. You can click in any part of the Database win-dow to bring it to the front and make it active. You can also press F11 to make the Database window active. (Press Alt+F1 on keyboards with only 10 function keys.)

 TIP

> If you choose the option to use the Windows taskbar for each document (choose Options from the Tools menu, and then choose View), you can switch between the Database window and the table window by clicking the window buttons on the taskbar.

FIGURE 3-7.

A table open in Design view.

Each row defines a field in the table.

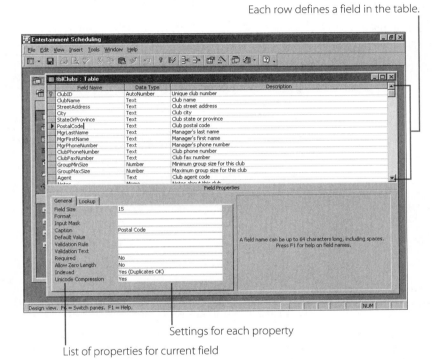

List of properties for current field

Settings for each property

? SEE ALSO

You'll learn about creating table definitions in Chapter 5, "Building Your Database in Microsoft Access."

In Design view, each row in the top portion of the Table window defines a different field in the table. You can use the mouse to select any field that you want to modify. You can also use the Tab key to move left to right across the screen from column to column, or Shift+Tab to move right to left.

Use the up and down arrow keys to move from row to row in the field list. As you select a different row in the field list in the top portion of the window, you can see the property settings for the selected field in the bottom portion of the window. Press F6 to move between the field list and the field property settings portions of the Table window in Design view.

Access has many convenient features. Wherever you can choose from a limited list of valid values, Access provides a drop-down list box to assist you in selecting the proper value. For example, when you tab to the Data Type column, a down arrow button appears at the right of the column. Click the button or press Alt+down arrow to see the list of valid data types, as shown in Figure 3-8.

FIGURE 3-8.

The Data Type drop-down list box.

Click the down arrow button
to see a list of data types.

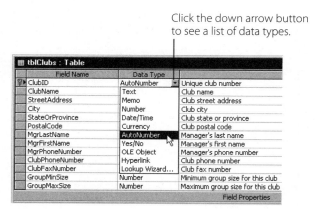

You can open as many as 254 tables (fewer if you are limited by your computer's memory). You can minimize any of the windows to an icon by clicking the Minimize button in the upper right corner of the window, or you can maximize the window to fill the Access workspace by clicking the Maximize/Restore button in that same corner. If you don't see a window you want, you can select it from the list of active windows on the Window menu and bring the window to the front. If you choose the option to use the Windows taskbar for each document, you can select the window you want by clicking the window's button on the taskbar. You can choose the Hide command on the Window menu to make selected windows temporarily disappear, or choose the Unhide command to make visible any windows that you've previously hidden. Figure 3-9 shows an example of multiple open windows. Choose the Close command from the File menu or click the window's Close button to close any window.

FIGURE 3-9.

Working in multiple windows in Access.

Choose this command to reveal a hidden window.

Select a window, and then choose this command to hide it.

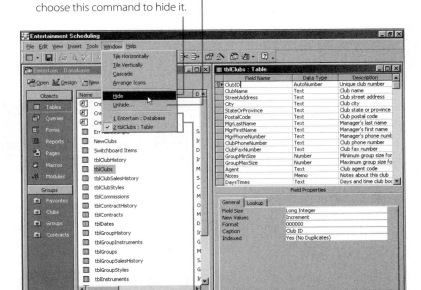

List of open, unhidden windows (the Table window has the focus).

 NOTE

Microsoft Access 2000 uses "smart" menus that display only the most commonly or recently used items when you first open a menu. For this reason, you may not see some of the menu options mentioned in this book right away. If you hover over the menu for a few seconds, it will display all available options. (You can display the seldom-used commands immediately by clicking the down arrow at the bottom of the menu.) If you want to turn off this delay, choose Customize from the Tools menu, click the Options tab, and clear the Menus Show Recently Used Commands First option.

Table Window in Datasheet View

 SEE ALSO

You'll read more about working with data in Datasheet view in Chapter 7, "Using Datasheets."

To view, change, insert, or delete data in a table, you can use the table's Datasheet view. A datasheet is a simple way to look at your data in rows and columns without any special formatting. You can open a table's Datasheet view by selecting the name of the table you want in the Database window and clicking the Open button. When you open a table in Design view, such as the tblClubs table shown in Figure 3-7 on page 43, you can switch to the Datasheet view of this table, shown in Figure 3-10, by clicking the View button on the toolbar. Likewise, when you're in Datasheet view, you can return to Design view by clicking the View button. You can also list the available views by clicking the small down arrow button to the right of the View button and then choosing the view you want by clicking its name.

FIGURE 3-10.

A Table window in Datasheet view.

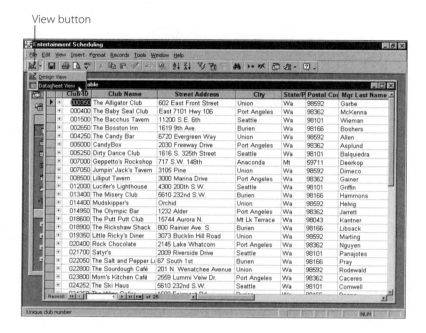

As in Design view, you can move from field to field in the Table window in Datasheet view using Tab, and you can move up and down through the records using the arrow keys. You can also use the scroll bars along the bottom and on the right side of the window to move around in the table. To the left of the bottom scroll bar, Access shows you the current record number and the total number of records in the currently selected set of data. You can select the record number with your mouse (or by pressing F5), type a new number, and then press Enter to go to that record. As shown in Figure 3-11, you can use the arrows on either side of this record number box to move up or down one record or to move to the first or last record in the table. You can start entering data in a new record by clicking the New Record button on the right.

FIGURE 3-11.

Using the record selectors in Datasheet view to move to different records.

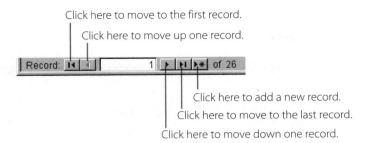

Click here to move to the first record.

Click here to move up one record.

Click here to add a new record.

Click here to move to the last record.

Click here to move down one record.

Close the tblClubs table now by clicking the window's Close button or by choosing the Close command from the File menu. You should now be back in the Database window for the Entertainment Scheduling database.

Queries

You probably noticed that the Datasheet view of the tblClubs table gave you all the fields and all the records in the table. But what if you want to see only the club names and addresses? Or maybe you'd like to see in one view information about groups and all of their outstanding contracts. To fill these needs, you can create a query. Click the Queries button in the Database window to see the list of queries available in the Entertainment Scheduling database, as shown in Figure 3-12 on the next page.

At the upper left corner of the Database window are three toolbar buttons.

 Clicking this button opens a Query window in Datasheet view, which lets you view and possibly update the data gathered by the query. (You might not be able to update all of the data in a query.) If the query is an action query, clicking this button runs the query.

 Clicking this button opens a Query window in Design view, which lets you view and modify the definition of the query.

 Clicking this button gives you the option to create a new query from scratch or to start one of the query wizards.

FIGURE 3-12.

A list of queries in the Entertainment Scheduling database.

Queries button selected

You can see the Large Icon view by clicking the Large Icons button in the top of the Database window.

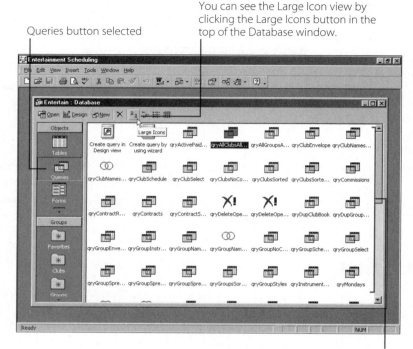

List of queries in the database

When the Database window is active, you can choose any of these command buttons from the keyboard by pressing the first letter of the button name while holding down the Alt key.

The Database window also contains two special icons, shown below, that provide shortcuts for creating a new query. Double-click either of these icons to begin defining a new query.

Create query in   Create query by
Design view   using wizard

SEE ALSO

Chapters 8, 9, and 11 contain details about creating queries.

You can also open a query in Datasheet view by double-clicking the query name, or you can open the query in Design view by holding down the Ctrl key and double-clicking the query name. You can also right-click a query name and choose an option from the shortcut menu.

> **Key Query Features in Access 2000**
>
> Here's a list of important query features in Access 2000.
>
> - Query wizards
> - Performance Analyzer to help make queries more efficient
> - Datasheet formatting options
>
> - Subdatasheets in Datasheet view that let you see information from related tables
> - Ability to define the field-display control property for most fields
> - Automatic combo boxes in query datasheets for fields related to other tables (if the Display Control property is set to Combo Box or List Box)
> - Ability to apply sort and filter criteria in Datasheet view
> - Datasheet scroll bar "thumb tips" that display the relative record location
> - Support for hyperlinks
>
> - Ability to use queries as a direct source for HTML pages (data access pages)
> - A high level of compatibility with the ANSI SQL database language standard

Query Window in Design View

When you want to change the definition of a query (the structure or design, as opposed to the data represented in the query), you must open the query in Design view. Take a look at one of the more complex queries in the Entertainment Scheduling query list by scrolling to the query named qryContracts. Hold down the Ctrl key and double-click the query name to see the query in Design view, as shown in Figure 3-13 on the next page.

In the upper part of a Query window in Design view, you can see the field lists of the tables or other queries that this query uses. The lines connecting the field lists show how Access links the tables to solve your query. If you define relationships between tables in your database design, Access draws these lines automatically. *See Chapter 5, "Building Your Database in Microsoft Access," for details.* You can also define relationships when you build the query by dragging a field from one field list and dropping it on another field list.

FIGURE 3-13.

A Query window in Design view showing data from three tables being linked.

Link between tables

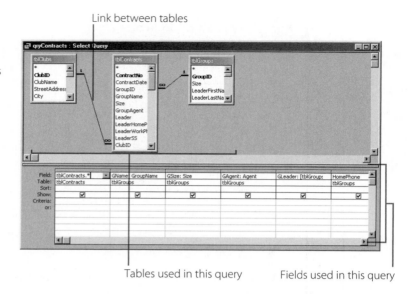

Tables used in this query   Fields used in this query

In the lower part of the Query window, you can see the design grid. The design grid shows fields that Access uses in this query, the tables or queries from which the fields come (when the Table Names command on the View menu has a check mark next to it), any sorting criteria, whether fields show up in the result, and any selection criteria for the fields. You can use the horizontal scroll bar to bring other fields in this query into view. As in the Design view of tables, you can use F6 to move between the top and bottom portions of the Query window.

You can learn how to build this type of complex multiple-table query in Chapter 7, "Using Datasheets." You will build a similar query in Chapter 15, "Advanced Form Design," and you can find this query used in the Entertainment Scheduling database as the source of data for the frmContracts form.

Query Window in Datasheet View

Click the Query Run button on the toolbar to run the query and see the query results in Datasheet view, as shown in Figure 3-14.

The Query window in Datasheet view is similar to a Table window in Datasheet view. Even though the fields in the query datasheet shown in Figure 3-14 are from three different tables, you can work with the fields as if they were in a single table. If you're designing an Access application for other users, you can use queries to hide much of the complexity of the database and make the application much simpler to

FIGURE 3-14.
Datasheet view of the qryContracts query.

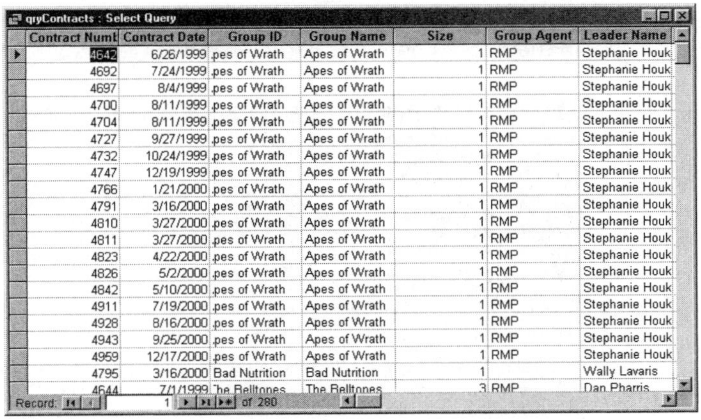

Contract Numb	Contract Date	Group ID	Group Name	Size	Group Agent	Leader Name
4642	6/26/1999	pes of Wrath	Apes of Wrath	1	RMP	Stephanie Houk
4692	7/24/1999	pes of Wrath	Apes of Wrath	1	RMP	Stephanie Houk
4697	8/4/1999	pes of Wrath	Apes of Wrath	1	RMP	Stephanie Houk
4700	8/11/1999	pes of Wrath	Apes of Wrath	1	RMP	Stephanie Houk
4704	8/11/1999	pes of Wrath	Apes of Wrath	1	RMP	Stephanie Houk
4727	9/27/1999	pes of Wrath	Apes of Wrath	1	RMP	Stephanie Houk
4732	10/24/1999	pes of Wrath	Apes of Wrath	1	RMP	Stephanie Houk
4747	12/19/1999	pes of Wrath	Apes of Wrath	1	RMP	Stephanie Houk
4766	1/21/2000	pes of Wrath	Apes of Wrath	1	RMP	Stephanie Houk
4791	3/16/2000	pes of Wrath	Apes of Wrath	1	RMP	Stephanie Houk
4810	3/27/2000	pes of Wrath	Apes of Wrath	1	RMP	Stephanie Houk
4811	3/27/2000	pes of Wrath	Apes of Wrath	1	RMP	Stephanie Houk
4823	4/22/2000	pes of Wrath	Apes of Wrath	1	RMP	Stephanie Houk
4826	5/2/2000	pes of Wrath	Apes of Wrath	1	RMP	Stephanie Houk
4842	5/10/2000	pes of Wrath	Apes of Wrath	1	RMP	Stephanie Houk
4911	7/19/2000	pes of Wrath	Apes of Wrath	1	RMP	Stephanie Houk
4928	8/16/2000	pes of Wrath	Apes of Wrath	1	RMP	Stephanie Houk
4943	9/25/2000	pes of Wrath	Apes of Wrath	1	RMP	Stephanie Houk
4959	12/17/2000	pes of Wrath	Apes of Wrath	1	RMP	Stephanie Houk
4795	3/16/2000	Bad Nutrition	Bad Nutrition	1		Wally Lavaris
4644	7/1/1999	he Belltones	The Belltones	3	RMP	Dan Pharris

use. Depending on how you designed the query, you might also be able to update some of the data in the underlying tables simply by typing in new values in the Query window as you would in a Table window in Datasheet view. Close the Query window to see only the Database window.

Forms

Datasheets are useful for viewing and changing data in your database, but they're not particularly attractive or simple to use. If you want to format your data in a special way or automate how your data is used and updated, you need to use a form. Forms provide a number of important capabilities.

- You can control and enhance the way your data looks on the screen. For example, you can add color and shading or add number formats. You can add controls such as drop-down list boxes and check boxes. You can display ActiveX objects such as pictures and graphs directly on the form. And you can calculate and display values based on data in a table or a query.
- You can perform extensive editing of data using macros or Visual Basic procedures.
- You can link multiple forms or reports by using macros or Visual Basic procedures that are run from buttons on a form. In addition, you can customize the menu bar by using macros associated with your form.

Click the Forms button in the Database window to see the list of forms in the Entertainment Scheduling database, shown in Figure 3-15.

FIGURE 3-15.

A Forms list in the Database window in Small Icon view.

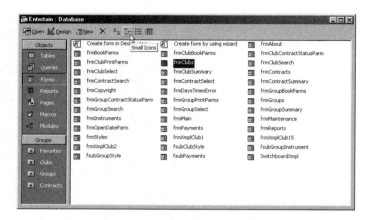

At the upper left corner of the Database window are three toolbar buttons.

 Clicking this button opens a Form window in Form view, which lets you view and update your data through the form.

 Clicking this button opens a Form window in Design view, which lets you view and modify the definition of the form.

 Clicking this button opens a dialog box in which you can choose to build a form from scratch or activate any of the available form wizards to help you out.

 SEE ALSO

You'll learn more about form design in Chapter 12, "Form Basics"; Chapter 13, "Building Forms"; and Chapter 15, "Advanced Form Design."

When the Database window is active, you can choose any of these command buttons from the keyboard by pressing the first letter of the button name while holding down the Alt key. The Database window also contains two special icons, shown below, that provide shortcuts for creating a new form. Double-click either of these icons to begin defining a new form.

 Create form in Design view
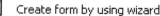 Create form by using wizard

You can also open a form in Form view by double-clicking the form name in the window, or you can open the form in Design view by holding down the Ctrl key and double-clicking the form name. Finally, you can right-click a form name and choose a command from the shortcut menu.

Key Form Features in Access 2000

Here's a list of important form features in Access 2000.

- AutoFormat command to design and apply custom form styles
- Ability to define custom ScreenTips for all controls
- Image control to efficiently display static pictures
- ActiveX control properties that are available via the standard Design property sheet
- Etched, Shadowed, and Chiseled special effects for controls
- Formatting toolbar and Format Painter to make it easier to set the control format
- Ability to change a control type without having to redefine it

- Ability to group/ungroup controls
- Ability to select multiple items in a list box control

- Option to allow changing properties from Form view to make designing forms easier
- Chart and PivotTable Wizards
- Query By Form and Filter By Selection features
- More efficient form performance when the form has no code

- Ability to define conditional formatting of controls based on values in the current row without writing any Visual Basic code or macros

- Ability to directly assign a Recordset object defined in code directly to the form Recordset property
- Option to create a Visual Basic procedure as the default to respond to form events
- Custom programmable command bars (toolbars and menu bars)
- Support for hyperlinks

Form Window in Design View

When you want to change the definition of a form (the structure or design, as opposed to the data represented in the form), you generally must open the form in Design view. As you'll learn in Chapter 14, you can also set a form property to allow you to make changes from Form view while you are designing the form. Take a look at the frmClubs form in the Entertainment Scheduling database. (To open the form, scroll through the list of forms in the Database window and then hold down the Ctrl key and double-click the frmClubs form.) This form, shown in Figure 3-16, is designed to display all data from the tblClubs table and related classification data from the tblClubStyles table. Don't worry if what you see on your screen doesn't exactly match Figure 3-16. In this figure, a few items have been moved around and several options have been selected so that you can see all the main features of the Form window in Design view.

FIGURE 3-16.

The frmClubs form in Design view.

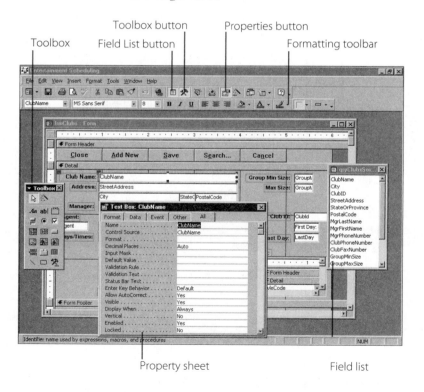

When you first open this form in Design view, you should see the toolbox in the lower left area of the screen. If you don't see it, choose the Toolbox command from the View menu or click the Toolbox button (the crossed hammer and wrench symbol) on the toolbar. This is the action center of form design; you'll use the tools here to add the controls you want, to display data, and to trigger macros or Visual Basic procedures.

In the lower right of the window shown in Figure 3-16, you can see a field list labeled *qryClubsSorted*. This query selects all of the fields in the tblClubs table and then sorts the rows by club name and city. You might see the field list near the top of the Form window when you first open the form. If you don't see the field list, choose the Field List command from the View menu or click the Field List button (the mini-datasheet symbol) on the toolbar. You can move the field list by dragging its title bar. When you read about form design in Chapter 13, "Building Forms," you'll see that you can choose a tool from the toolbox and then drag a field from the field list to place a field-display control on the form.

? SEE ALSO

You'll learn how to customize a form in Chapter 14,"Customiz-ing Forms."

After you place all the controls on a form, you might want to customize some of them. You do this by opening the property sheet, which is shown in the lower center of Figure 3-16. To see the property sheet, choose the Properties command from the View menu or click the Properties button (a datasheet with a pointing-finger symbol) on the toolbar. The property sheet always shows the property values for the control selected in the Form window. Click the tabs at the top of the property sheet to display all properties or to display only properties for formats, data, or events. In the example shown in Figure 3-16, the text box named ClubName, near the top of the form, has been selected. If you scroll down the list of properties for this text box, you can see the wide range of properties you can set to customize this control. As you learn to build applications using Access, you'll soon discover that you can customize the way your application works by simply setting form and control properties—you don't have to write any code.

If you scroll to the bottom of the property list, or click the Event tab, you'll see a number of properties that you can set to define the macros or Visual Basic procedures that Access will run whenever the associated event occurs on this control. For example, you can use the Before Update event property to perform additional validation before Access saves any changes typed in this control. You can use the On Click or On Dbl Click event properties to cause "magic" to happen if the user clicks the control. If you need to, you can even look at every individual character the user types in a control with the On Key event properties. As you'll discover later, Access provides a rich set of events that you can detect for the form and all controls on the form.

You might have noticed that Access made available all of the boxes and buttons on the Formatting toolbar when you selected the ClubName control. When you select a text box on a form in Design view, Access enables the drop-down list boxes on this toolbar to make it easy to select a font and font size, and it also enables buttons that let you set the Font Weight, Font Italic, and Font Underline properties. To the right of these buttons are three buttons that set text alignment: Align Left, Center, and Align Right. You can also set the foreground, background, and border colors; border width; and special effects from buttons on this toolbar.

If all of this looks just a bit too complex, don't worry! Building a simple form is really quite easy. In addition, Access provides form wizards that you can use to automatically generate a number of standard form layouts based on the table or query you choose. You'll find it simple to customize a form to your needs once the form wizard has done most of the hard work.

Form Window in Form View

To view, change, insert, or delete data via a form, you can use Form view. Depending on how you've designed the form, you can work with your data in an attractive and clear context, have the form validate the information you enter, or use the form to trigger other forms or reports based on actions you take while viewing the form. You can open a form in Form view by selecting the form's name in the Database window and then clicking the Open button. Because you have the frmClubs form open in Design view, you can go directly to Form view by clicking the View button on the toolbar.

Figure 3-17 shows a complex form that brings together data from three tables into a display that's easy to use and understand. This form includes all the fields from the tblClubs table. You can tab or use the arrow keys to move through the fields. You can experiment with the Filter By Form and Filter By Selection toolbar buttons to see how easy it is to select only the records you want to see. For example, you can click in the State field and then click the Filter By Selection button to display records only for the current state.

FIGURE 3-17.

The frmClubs form in Form view.

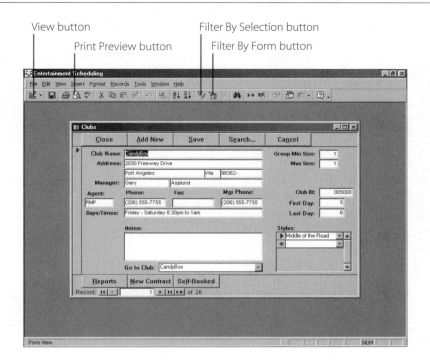

View button

Print Preview button

Filter By Selection button

Filter By Form button

> **NOTE**
>
> The frmClubs form is the only form in the Entertainment Scheduling database that you can open to see a built-in form view menu bar and toolbar. All of the other forms in the Entertainment Scheduling sample database have form properties set to use a custom menu bar and toolbar.

There are two other ways to look at a form: in Datasheet view and in Print Preview. You can select Datasheet View from the View button drop-down list to see all of the fields in the form arranged in a datasheet—similar to a datasheet for a table or a query. You can click the Print Preview button on the toolbar to see what the form will look like on a printed page. You'll read more about Print Preview in the next section. For now, close the frmClubs window so that only the Database window is visible on your screen.

Reports

If your primary need is to print data, you should use a report. Click the Reports button to see the list of reports available in the Entertainment Scheduling database, as shown in Figure 3-18 on the next page.

FIGURE 3-18.

A list of reports in the Database window in List view.

Reports button selected   List button

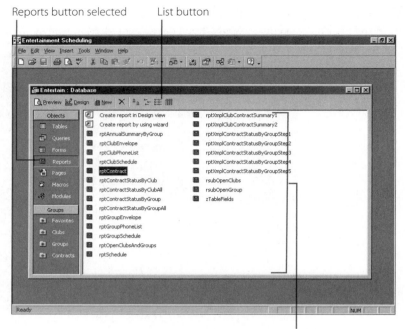

List of reports in the database

Although you can print information in a datasheet or a form, neither of these formats provides the flexibility that reports do when you need to produce complex printed output (such as invoices or summaries) that might include many calculations and subtotals. Formatting in datasheets is limited to sizing the rows and columns, specifying fonts, and setting the colors and gridline effects. You can do a lot of formatting in a form, but because forms are designed primarily for viewing and entering data on the screen, they are not suited for extensive calculations, grouping of data, or multiple totals and subtotals in print.

At the upper left corner of the Database window are three toolbar buttons.

Clicking this button initiates the Print Preview command, which lets you see how the selected report will look on a printed page.

Clicking this button opens a Report window in Design view, which lets you view and modify the definition of the report.

Clicking this button opens a dialog box in which you can choose to build a new report from scratch or activate any of the available report wizards to help you out.

When the Database window is active, you can choose any of these command buttons from the keyboard by pressing the first letter of the button name while holding down the Alt key. The Database window also contains two special icons, shown below, that provide shortcuts for creating a new report. Double-click either of these icons to begin defining a new report.

   Create report in Design view

Create report by using wizard

You can also view the report in Print Preview by double-clicking the report name in the window, or you can open the report in Design view by holding down the Ctrl key and double-clicking the report name. Finally, you can right-click any report name and choose Design from the shortcut menu.

Key Report Features in Access 2000

Here's a list of important report features in Access 2000.

- AutoFormat command to design and apply custom report styles
- Image control to efficiently display static pictures
- ActiveX control properties that are available via the standard Design property sheet
- Etched, Shadowed, and Chiseled special effects for controls
- Formatting toolbar and Format Painter, which make it easier to set the control format
- Ability to change a control type without having to redefine it
- Ability to group/ungroup controls
- Ability to output subreport data to text and spreadsheet files
- Chart and Label Wizards
- Print Preview Zoom capabilities
- Ability to define conditional formatting of controls based on values in the current row without writing any Visual Basic code or macros.
- More efficient report performance when the report has no code
- Custom programmable command bars (toolbars and menu bars)
- Support for hyperlinks

Report Window in Design View

? SEE ALSO

When you read about report design in Chapter 17,"Constructing a Report,"you'll see that you can choose a tool from the toolbox and then drag a field from the field list to place the field-display control on the report.

When you want to change the definition of a report, you must open the report in Design view. In the report list for Entertainment Scheduling, hold down the Ctrl key and double-click the rptContract report to see the design for the report, as shown in Figure 3-19. Don't worry if what you see on your screen doesn't exactly match Figure 3-19. In this figure a few things have been moved around and several options have been selected so that you can see all the main features of the Report window in Design view.

This report is designed to display all the information about contracts between clubs and groups, bringing together information from several tables. You can see that the Design view for reports is similar to the Design view for forms. (For comparison, see Figure 3-16 on page 54.) Reports provide additional flexibility, allowing you to group items and to total them (either across or down). You can also define header and footer information for the entire report, for each page, and for each subgroup on the report.

FIGURE 3-19.

The rptContract report in Design view.

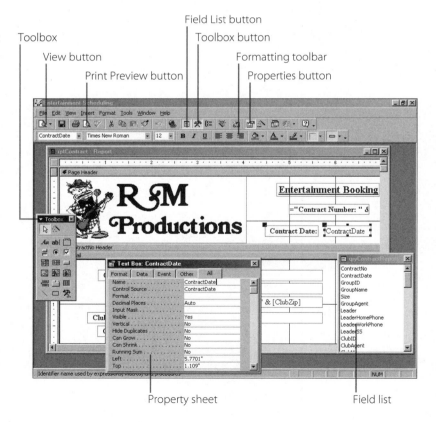

Toolbox

View button

Print Preview button

Field List button

Toolbox button

Formatting toolbar

Properties button

Property sheet

Field list

When you first open this report in Design view, the toolbox should appear in the lower left area of the screen. If you don't see the toolbox, choose the Toolbox command from the View menu or click the Toolbox button on the toolbar.

In the lower right of Figure 3-19, you can see a window titled qryContractReport. This is a field list containing all the fields from the tblContracts table and related fields from the tblClubs and tblGroups tables that provide the data for this report. You might see this list near the top of the report's Design view when you first open it. If you don't see the field list, choose the Field List command from the View menu or click the Field List button on the toolbar. You can move the field list by dragging its title bar.

After you place all the controls on a report, you might want to customize some of them. Do this by opening the property sheet, which you can see in the lower center of Figure 3-19. To see the property sheet, choose the Properties command from the View menu or click the Properties button on the toolbar. The property sheet always shows the property settings for the control selected in the Report window. In the example shown in Figure 3-19, the text box named ContractDate is selected. You can see that Access displays the ContractDate field from the tblContracts table as the control source (input data) for this control. You can also specify complex formulas that calculate additional data for report controls.

? SEE ALSO

You'll learn how to customize a report in Chapter 17, "Constructing a Report," and in Chapter 18, "Advanced Report Design."

You might have noticed that Access made available some additional list boxes and buttons on the Formatting toolbar when you selected the ContractDate control. When you click a text box in a report in Design view, Access enables drop-down list boxes on the Formatting toolbar that make it easy to select a font and font size. Access also enables buttons that let you set the Font Weight, Font Italic, and Font Underline properties. To the right of these buttons are three buttons that set text alignment: Align Left, Center, and Align Right. You can also set the foreground, background, and border colors; border width; and special effects from buttons on this toolbar.

Reports can be even more complex than forms, but building a simple report is really quite easy. Access provides report wizards that you can use to automatically generate a number of standard report layouts based on the table or query you choose. You'll find it simple to customize a report to suit your needs after the report wizard has done most of the hard work.

Report Window in Print Preview

Reports do not have a Datasheet view. To see what the finished report looks like, click the Print Preview button (shown in Figure 3-19) on the toolbar when you're in the Report window in Design view. From the Database window, you can also select the report name and then click the Preview button or right-click the report name and choose Print Preview from the shortcut menu. Figure 3-20 shows a Report window in Print Preview.

FIGURE 3-20.

The rptContract report in Print Preview.

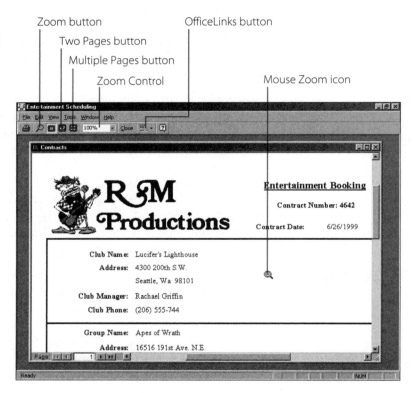

Access initially shows you the upper left corner of the report. To see the report centered in full-page view in Print Preview, click the Zoom button on the toolbar. To see two pages side-by-side, click the Two Pages button. This gives you a reduced picture of two pages, as shown in Figure 3-21, and an overall idea of how Access arranges major areas of data on the report. Unless you have a large monitor, however, you won't be able to read the data. Click the Multiple Pages button to see more than two pages. When you move the mouse pointer over the window in Print Preview, the pointer changes to a magnifying glass icon. To zoom in, place this icon in an area that

FIGURE 3-21.

Two pages of the rptContract report in Print Preview.

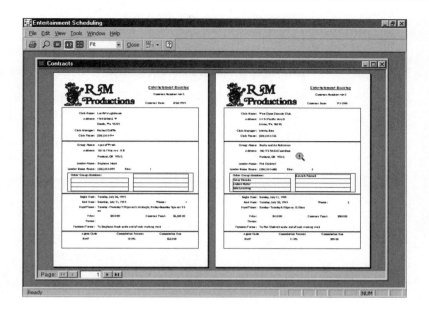

you want to see more closely and then press the left mouse button. You can also click the Zoom button on the toolbar again to see a close-up view of the report and then use the scroll bars to move around in the magnified report. Use the Zoom Control on the toolbar to magnify or shrink your view. Access also provides an OfficeLinks button on the standard Print Preview toolbar to let you output the report to Microsoft Word or Microsoft Excel.

Close the Report window to return to the Database window.

Data Access Pages

An exciting new feature in Access 2000 is the ability to easily "publish" your data as Web pages on your company's intranet as data access pages. Click the Pages button to see the list of data access pages available in the Entertainment Scheduling database, as shown in Figure 3-22 on the next page.

In Microsoft Access 97 (version 8), you could publish static data views from tables and queries by saving them as HTML objects. *See Chapter 19, "Publishing Data on the Web," for an example.* You could also save a form as an active server page that could both browse and update data, but you had to install the correct database drivers on your Web server and define the correct links to your database file on the server. Data

FIGURE 3-22.

A list of data access pages in the Database window in Details view.

Pages button selected

Details button

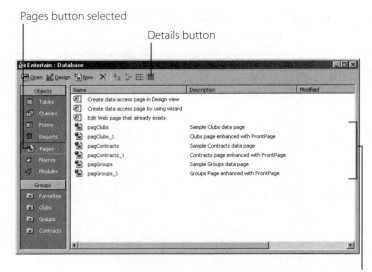

List of data access pages in the database

access pages in Access 2000 let you publish active data without having to worry about all the details. As long as your Web users have Office 2000 installed, they can open your data access pages directly from their client machines. The Web server handles the HTML, but the database access is controlled by the client Microsoft Office software.

At the upper left corner of the Database window are three toolbar buttons.

Click this button to view a previously defined data access page within your Access application. This lets you view the page as your users will see it from Internet Explorer version 5 or later.

Click this button to open a Data Access Page window in Design view, which lets you view and modify the definition of the page.

Click this button to open a dialog box in which you can choose to build a new data access page from scratch or activate any of the available data access page wizards to help you out.

When the Database window is active, you can choose any of these command buttons from the keyboard by pressing the first letter of the button name while holding down the Alt key.

The Database window also contains three special icons, shown below, that provide shortcuts for editing a data access page definition. Double-click any of these icons to begin work on a data access page.

Create data access page in Design view

Create data access page by using wizard

Edit Web page that already exists

You can also view the data access page in Page view by double-clicking the data access page name in the window, or you can open the data access page in Design view by holding down the Ctrl key and double-clicking the data access page name. Finally, you can right-click any data access page name and choose Design from the shortcut menu.

Key Data Access Page Features in Access 2000

Here's a list of important data access page features in Access 2000.

- Format command to apply a custom Web template to your data access page

- Web-specific controls to make it easy to define image "hotspots" or add animation objects to your Web page

- ActiveX control properties that are available via the standard Design property sheet

- Expanded field list to make it easy to add any field from any table or query to your page

- Formatting toolbar that makes it easy to set control formats

- Sorting and grouping specifications to provide "drill down" capabilities in your page

Data Access Page Window in Design View

When you want to change the definition of a data access page, you must open the page in Design view. In the page list for Entertainment Scheduling, hold down the Ctrl key and double-click the pagContracts page to see the design for the page, as shown in Figure 3-23 on the next page. Don't worry if what you see on your screen doesn't exactly match Figure 3-23. In this figure, a few things have been moved around and several options have been selected so that you can see all the main features of the Page window in Design view.

FIGURE 3-23.

The pagContracts data access page in Design view.

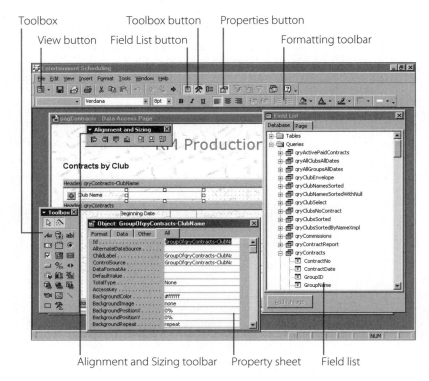

This page is designed to display information about contracts for each club, bringing together information from several tables. You can see that the Design view for pages is similar to the Design view for forms and reports. (For comparison, see Figure 3-16 on page 54 and Figure 3-19 on page 60.) Like a form, you can allow users to edit your data using Microsoft Internet Explorer. Like a report, you can group and sort data and make it easy for users to "drill down" into details about a particular topic. On the pagContracts page, users can browse through the information by Club, and then click the expand button (the plus sign next to the Club Name label) to see details about contracts for the club they choose.

When you first open this page in Design view, the toolbox should appear in the lower left area of the screen. If you don't see the toolbox, choose the Toolbox command from the View menu or click the Toolbox button on the toolbar.

Understanding Access

 CAUTION

Data access pages are "hard wired" to the location of your database file. If you move the database file, you must also change the Connection properties of the data access page. For example, if you do not install the sample files for this book to "C:\Running Access 2000 Samples," the data access page examples will not work. See Chapter 19, "Publishing Data on the Web," for details about changing the Connection properties.

In the lower right of Figure 3-23, you can see the Field List window. In this window, you can choose any table or query in the database that provides data for this page and drag any field onto the page to show the data. If you choose a field that's not in a table related to the data already shown on the page, the page may display a confusing result. To see the field list, choose the Field List command from the View menu or click the Field List button on the toolbar. Click the plus sign next to the database name to see the Tables and Queries folders. Click the plus sign next to the Queries folder to see the list of queries. You can move the field list by dragging its title bar.

After you place all the controls on a page, you might want to customize some of them. You do this by opening the property sheet, which you can see in the lower center of Figure 3-23. To see the property sheet, choose the Properties command from the View menu or click the Properties button on the toolbar. The property sheet always shows the property settings for the control selected in the Data Access Page window. In the example shown in Figure 3-23, the text box named GroupOfqryContracts-ClubName is selected. You can see that the Control Source property specifies that the ClubName field provides the data that the data access page will display in the ClubName100 control. You can also specify complex formulas that calculate additional data for page controls.

You might have noticed that Access made available some additional list boxes and buttons on the Formatting toolbar when you selected the ClubName100 control. When you click a text box in a page in Design view, Access enables drop-down list boxes on the Formatting toolbar that make it easy to select a font and font size. Access also enables buttons that let you set the Font Weight, Font Italic, and Font Underline properties. To the right of these buttons are three buttons that set text alignment: Align Left, Center, and Align Right. You can also set the foreground, background, and border colors; border width; and special effects from buttons on this toolbar. You can right-click any toolbar and choose Alignment And Sizing to open the Alignment And Sizing toolbar, which you can use to resize and align controls with each other.

SEE ALSO

You'll learn how to design data access pages in Chapter 19, "Publishing Data on the Web."

Data access pages can be even more complex than forms or reports, but building a simple page is really quite easy. Access provides data access page wizards that you can use to automatically generate a number of standard page layouts based on the table or query you choose. You'll find it simple to customize a page to suit your needs after the data access page wizard has done most of the hard work.

Data Access Page Window in Page View

To see what the finished page looks like, click the View button (shown in Figure 3-23) on the toolbar when you're in the Data Access Page window in Design view. From the Database window, you can also select the page name and then click the Open button, or right-click the page name and choose View from the shortcut menu. Figure 3-24 shows a Data Access Page window in Page view.

FIGURE 3-24.

The pagContracts data access page in Page view.

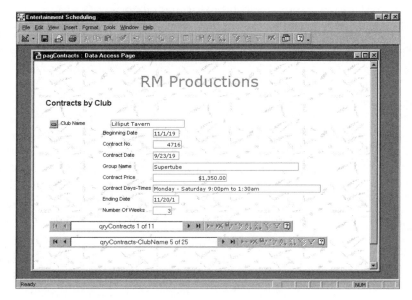

You can experiment with this page to see how it works. When you first open this page you will see only club names near the top of the page. Use the navigation buttons just below the names to move to the row you want. Note that you can also click in the club name and then click options on the record navigation bar to sort or filter what you see. When you find a club you want, click the plus sign button next to the club name to "drill down" into the contracts for the club, as shown in Figure 3-24. This also opens up a second record navigation bar so you can move through contracts for the selected club and sort or filter fields.

You can also test this page to see how it works in Internet Explorer. Close Microsoft Access and find the pagContracts.htm file in your Running Access 2000 Samples folder in Windows Explorer. Double-click the file to open it in Internet Explorer. Internet Explorer might prompt you for a user ID and file open method. Click OK to sign on as user Admin with read/write ability. You should see a result, as shown in Figure 3-25.

FIGURE 3-25.

The pagContracts data access page displayed in Internet Explorer.

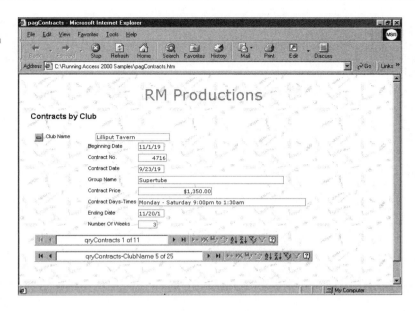

Close Internet Explorer and reopen the Entertainment Scheduling database in Microsoft Access to continue the tour.

 NOTE

> If you work with any objects in the Entertainment Scheduling database in Design view, Access locks the database so no other user or program can reference or change the data or object designs. If you try to display any of the sample data access pages in Internet Explorer while Access is still open, you will see no data because Access has the data locked.

Macros

You can make working with your data within forms and reports much easier by triggering a macro action. Microsoft Access provides more than 40 actions that you can include in a macro. They perform tasks such as opening tables and forms, running queries, running other macros, selecting options from menus, and sizing open windows. You can even start other applications that support Dynamic Data Exchange (DDE), such as Microsoft Excel, and exchange data from your database with that application. You can also group multiple actions in a macro and specify conditions that determine when each set of actions will or will not be executed by Access.

In the Database window, click the Macros button to see the list of macros in the Entertainment Scheduling database, shown in Figure 3-26.

FIGURE 3-26.

The macros in the Entertainment Scheduling database.

Macros button selected   List of macros in the database

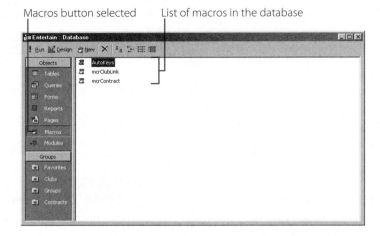

At the upper left corner of the Database window are three toolbar buttons.

 Clicking this button lets you execute the actions in the macro selected in the Database window. A macro object can consist of a single set of commands or multiple named sets. If you select a macro object from the Macros list and then click the Run button, Access runs the first macro in the object. You can also choose Macro from the Tools menu to open a dialog box that lets you select a specific macro within a macro object to run.

 Clicking this button opens a Macro window in Design view, which lets you view and modify the definition of the macro.

 Clicking this button lets you define a new macro.

When the Database window is active, you can choose any of these command buttons from the keyboard by pressing the first letter of the button name while holding down the Alt key. You can also run a macro by double-clicking the macro name in the window, or you can open the Macro window in Design view by holding down the Ctrl key and double-clicking the macro name. Finally, you can right-click a macro name and choose Run or Design from the shortcut menu.

One of the most useful functions of a macro is to test and set data entered on a form. For example, take a look at the BeforeInsert macro in the mcrContract macro object in the Entertainment Scheduling database. Scroll the Database window until you see this macro object name, select it, and then click the Design button. You'll see a window similar to the one shown in Figure 3-27.

FIGURE 3-27.

The mcrContract macro object in the Entertainment Scheduling database.

Macro name

Condition that must be true
to execute the action

Action name

Macro actions listed in the
sequence that Access will execute

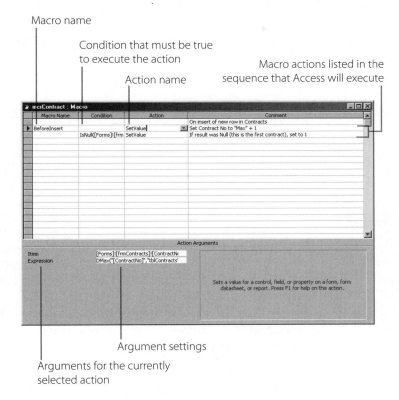

Arguments for the currently
selected action

Argument settings

SEE ALSO
Chapter 20, "Adding Power with Macros," and Chapter 21, "Automating Your Application with Macros," provide detailed discussions of macros.

Each contract in the database must have a unique contract number. You could have Access automatically generate a number by using a special data type called *AutoNumber. See Chapter 5 for details.* However, once you start to create a new contract, Access assigns a number to the contract and will never reuse it even if you decide not to save the contract. Ray McCann will often start a new record for a potential contract while talking with a group or club on the phone. However, he won't save the record if the booking date isn't confirmed. He doesn't want to skip any contract numbers, so the application is designed (using this macro) to generate new numbers. It does this by calling a function (DMax) that finds the previous highest contract number and adds one to that number. If there are no contracts, the DMax function returns a special Null value. The macro tests for this on the second line and sets the value of the contract number to 1 if this is the case. Close the Macro window to return to the Database window.

Key Macro Features in Access 2000

Here's a list of important macro features in Access 2000.

- SetMenuItem action to gray/ungray, check/uncheck, or hide/unhide custom menu entries
- Save action to save the definition of any Access object
- Printout action to print any datasheet, form, report, or module
- Converter tool for forms and reports to convert macros to Visual Basic event procedures

---

Modules

You might find that you keep coding the same complex formula over and over in some of your forms or reports. Although you can easily build a complete Microsoft Access application using only forms, reports, and macros, some actions might be difficult or impossible to define in a macro. If that is the case, you can create a Visual Basic procedure that performs a series of calculations and then use that procedure in a form or report.

If your application is so complex that it needs to deal with errors (such as two users trying to update the same record at the same time), you must use Visual Basic. Since Visual Basic is a complete programming language with complex logic and the ability to link to other applications and files, you can solve unusual or difficult programming problems by using Visual Basic procedures.

Version 2 of Access introduced the ability to code Basic routines in special modules attached directly to the forms and reports that they support. You can create these procedures from Design view for forms or reports by requesting the Code Builder in any event property. You can make Visual Basic the default for form and report events by choosing Options from the Tools menu. You can also edit this "code behind forms" by choosing Code from the View menu in Design view for forms and reports. *See Chapter 22, "Visual Basic Fundamentals," and Chapter 23, "Automating Your Application with Visual Basic," for details.* In fact, once you learn a little bit about Visual Basic, you may find that coding small event procedures for your forms and reports is much more efficient and convenient than trying to keep track of many macro objects. You'll also soon learn that you can't fully respond to some sophisticated events, such as KeyPress, in macros because macros can't "see" special additional parameters (such as the value of the key pressed) generated by the event. You can fully handle these events only in Visual Basic.

Click the Modules button in the Database window to display the list of modules in the Entertainment Scheduling database, as shown in Figure 3-28 on the next page. The Entertainment Scheduling database has several module objects that contain procedures that can be called from any query, form, report, or other procedure in the database. The modMedian module contains a function to calculate the median value of a column in any table or query. The modUtility module contains several functions that you might find useful in your applications.

Key Visual Basic Features in Access 2000

Here's a list of important Visual Basic features in Access 2000.

- Visual Basic—a 32-bit engine that is compatible with all other Microsoft Office products that use Basic

- Visual Basic Editor that is shared with all Microsoft Office applications

- Color-coded syntax that allows you to easily distinguish keywords, variables, comments, and other language components as you type them

- Long lines of code that can be continued to new lines

- An Object Browser that lets you see all supported methods and properties for any object

- Debugging facilities, including the ability to "watch" variables or expressions

- Ability to define code segments that compile conditionally

- Ability to define procedures with optional parameters

- Inline syntax help

- Ability to create a compiled database that contains no source code

FIGURE 3-28.
The Visual Basic modules in the Entertainment Scheduling database.

From the Database window, you can create a new module by clicking the New button or you can open the design of an existing module by clicking the Design button. You can run a module function from a macro, a form, or a report. You can also use functions in expressions in queries and as validation functions from a table or a form.

? SEE ALSO

Chapter 22, "Visual Basic Fundamentals," and Chapter 23, "Automating Your Application with Visual Basic," introduce coding with modules.

Select the modUtility module and click the Design button to open the Visual Basic Editor window containing the Visual Basic code in the module. Use the Procedure drop-down list box (in the upper right of the Code window) or choose the Object Browser command from the View menu to look at the procedure names available in the sample. One of the functions in this module, IsLoaded, checks all forms open in the current Access session to see whether the form name, passed as a parameter, is one of the open forms. This function is useful in macros or in other modules to direct the flow of an application based on which forms the user has open. You can see this function in Figure 3-29.

Note that the Visual Basic Editor runs in an entirely different application window from Microsoft Access. Click the Return to Microsoft Access button on the far left of the toolbar to easily return to the Access window.

Organizing Your Objects

Although you may not have created any objects yet yourself, it's useful to know that you can create special groups in your database to help you organize related tables, queries, forms, reports, data access pages, macros, and modules. You can save shortcuts in each of these groups that are pointers to the objects in the group.

FIGURE 3-29.

The IsLoaded function.

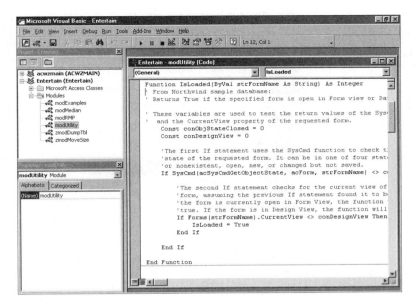

In the Entertainment Scheduling sample database, you can find groups defined for each of the main subjects in the database: the clubs that book entertainment, the groups that perform for the clubs, and the contracts that book the groups into the clubs. Click the Clubs group button to see all of the shortcuts to objects related to clubs, as shown in Figure 3-30.

FIGURE 3-30.

Shortcuts to all objects related to Clubs.

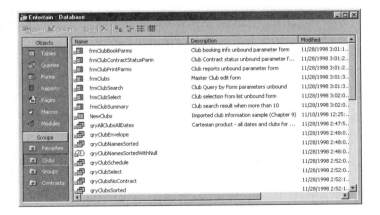

To add an object to a group, find the object you want in the Database window. Right-click the object to display the shortcut menu, as shown in Figure 3-31 on the next page. Choose Add To Group in the shortcut menu, and then select the group or choose New Group to define a

FIGURE 3-31.
Adding a shortcut to
the Clubs group.

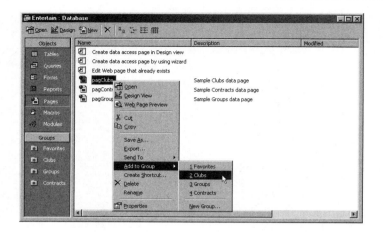

new group of shortcuts. Once you have defined groups, you can also drag an object from an object listing onto one of the group names in the lower left of the Database window to add a shortcut to the object to the group.

Now that you've had a chance to look at the major objects in the Entertainment Scheduling sample database, you should be feeling comfortable with Access. Perhaps the most important aspect of building an application is designing the database that will support your application. The next chapter describes how you should design your database application and its data structures. Building a solid foundation makes creating the forms and reports for your application easy.

PART II

Building a Database

CHAPTER 4

Designing Your Database Application

You could begin building a database in Microsoft Access much as you might begin creating a simple single-sheet solution in a spreadsheet application such as Microsoft Excel—by simply organizing your data into rows and columns and then throwing in formulas where you need calculations. If you've ever worked extensively with a database or a spreadsheet application, you already know that this unplanned approach works in only the most trivial situations. Solving real problems takes some planning; otherwise, you end up building your application over and over again. One of the beauties of a relational database system such as Access is that it's much easier to make midcourse corrections. However, it's well worth spending time up front designing the tasks you want to perform, the data structures you need to support those tasks, and the flow of tasks within your database application.

You don't have to go deeply into application and database design theory to build a solid foundation for your database project. You'll read about the fundamentals of application design in the next section, and then you'll apply those fundamentals in the succeeding sections, "An Application Design Strategy" and "Data Analysis." The section "Database Design Concepts" teaches you a basic method for designing the tables you'll need for your application and for defining relationships between those tables.

Application Design Fundamentals

Methodologies for good computer application design were first devised in the 1960s by recognized industry consultants such as James Martin, Edward Yourdon, and Larry Constantine. At the dawn of modern computing, building an application or fixing a broken one was so expensive that the experts often advised spending 60 percent or more of the total project time getting the design right before penning a single line of code.

Today's application development technologies make building an application much cheaper and faster. An experienced user can sit down with Microsoft Access on a PC and build in an afternoon what used to take months to create on an early mainframe system (if it was even possible). It's also easier than ever to go back and fix mistakes or to "redesign on the fly."

Today's technologies also give you the power to build very complex applications. And the pace of computing is several orders of magnitude faster than it was just a decade ago. But even with powerful tools, creating a database application (particularly a moderately complex one) without first spending some time determining what the application should do and how it should operate invites a lot of expensive time reworking the application. If your application design is not well thought out, it will also be very expensive and time-consuming later to track down any problems or to add new functionality.

The following is a brief overview of the typical steps involved in building a database application.

Step 1: Identifying Tasks

Before you start building an application, you'll probably have some idea of what you want it to do. It is well worth your time to make a list of all the major tasks you want to accomplish with the application—including those that you might not need right away but might want to implement in the future. By "major tasks," I mean application functions that will ultimately be represented in a form or a report in your Access database. For example, "Enter customer orders" is a major task that you would accomplish by using a form created for that purpose, while "Calculate extended price" is most likely a subtask of "Enter customer orders" that you would accomplish by using the same form.

Step 2: Charting Task Flow

To be sure your application operates smoothly and logically, you should lay out the major tasks in topic groups and then order those tasks within groups on the basis of the sequence in which the tasks must be performed. For example, you probably want to separate employee-related tasks from sales-related ones. Within sales, an order must be entered into the system before you can print the order or examine commission totals.

You might discover that some tasks are related to more than one group or that completing a task in one group is a prerequisite to performing a task in another group. Grouping and charting the flow of tasks helps you discover a "natural" flow that you can ultimately reflect in the way your forms and reports are linked in your finished application. Later in this chapter, you'll see how I laid out the tasks performed in one of the sample applications included with this book.

Step 3: Identifying Data Elements

After you develop your task list, perhaps the most important design step is to list the data required by each task and the changes that will be made to that data. A given task will require some input data (for example, a price to calculate an extended amount owed on an order); the task might also update the data. The task might delete some data elements (remove invoices paid, for example) or add new ones (insert new order details). Or the task might calculate some data and display it, but it won't save the data anywhere in the database.

Step 4: Organizing the Data

After you determine all the data elements you need for your application, you must organize the data by subject and then map the subjects into tables and queries in your database. With a relational database system such as Access, you use a process called *normalization* to help you design the most efficient and most flexible way to store the data. *See the section "Database Design Concepts" later in this chapter for a simple method of creating a normalized design.*

Step 5: Designing a Prototype and a User Interface

After you build the table structures needed to support your application, you can easily mock up the application flow in forms and tie the forms together using simple macros or Visual Basic event procedures. You can build the actual forms and reports for your application "on screen," switching to Form view or Print Preview periodically to check your progress. If you're building the application to be used by someone else, you can easily demonstrate and get approval for the "look and feel" of your application before you write any complex code that's needed to actually accomplish the tasks. (Parts IV and V of this book show you how to design and construct forms and reports; Part VI shows you how to use macros and Visual Basic to link forms and reports to build an application.)

Step 6: Constructing the Application

For very simple applications, you might find that the prototype *is* the application. Most applications, however, will require that you write code to fully automate all the tasks you identified in your design. You'll probably also need to create certain linking forms that facilitate moving from one task to another. For example, you might need to construct switchboard forms that provide the navigational road map to your application. You might also need to build dialog forms to gather user input to allow users to easily filter the data they want to use in a particular task. You might also want to build custom menus for most, if not all, of the forms in the application.

Step 7: Testing, Reviewing, and Refining

As you complete various components of your application, you should test each option that you provide. As you'll learn in Part 6 of this book, you can test macros by stepping through the commands you've written, one line at a time. If you automate your application using Visual Basic, you'll have many debugging tools at your disposal to verify correct application execution and to identify and fix errors.

If at all possible, you should provide completed portions of your application to users so that they can test your code and provide feedback about the flow of the application. Despite your best efforts to identify tasks and lay out a smooth task flow, users will invariably think of new and better ways to approach a particular task after they've seen your application in action. Also, users often discover that some features they asked you to include are not so useful after all. Discovering a required change early in the implementation stage can save you a lot of time reworking things later.

The refinement and revision process continues even after the application is put into use. Most software developers recognize that after they've finished one "release," they often must make design changes and build enhancements. For major revisions, you should start over at step 1 to assess the overall impact of the desired changes so that you can smoothly integrate them into your earlier work.

Typical Application Development Steps

1 Identifying tasks

2 Charting task flow

3 Identifying data elements

4 Organizing the data

5 Designing a prototype and a user interface

6 Constructing the application

7 Testing, reviewing, and refining

An Application Design Strategy

The two major schools of thought on designing databases are *process-driven design* (also known as *top-down design*), which focuses on the functions or tasks you need to perform, and *data-driven design* (also known as *bottom-up design*), which concentrates on identifying and organizing all the bits of data you need. The method used here incorporates ideas from both philosophies.

This method begins with you identifying and grouping tasks to decide whether you need only one database or more than one database. (This is a top-down approach.) As explained previously, databases should be organized around a group of related tasks or functions. For each task, you choose the individual pieces of data you need. Next you gather all the data fields for all related tasks and begin organizing them into subjects. (This is a bottom-up approach.) Each subject forms the foundation for the individual tables in your database. Finally, you apply the rules you will learn in the "Database Design Concepts" section of this chapter to create your tables.

The examples in the rest of this chapter are based on the Microsoft Press Books sample database application from the companion CD. Later in this book, you'll learn how to build various pieces of the application as you explore the architecture and features of Microsoft

II

Building a Database

Access. The Microsoft Press Books application is somewhat more complex than the Northwind Traders application that is included with Access. The Microsoft Press Books application also employs many techniques not found in the product documentation.

Oh No! Not Another Order-Entry Example!

You might have noticed that when you study database design—whether in a seminar, reading a book, or examining sample databases—nearly all the examples (including the one presented here) seem to be order-entry applications. There are several good reasons why you encounter this sort of example over and over again.

1 A large percentage of business-oriented database applications use the common order-entry model. If you build a database, it's likely to use this model.

2 Using the order-entry model makes it easy to demonstrate good database design techniques.

3 At the core of the model, you'll find a "many-to-many" relationship example. (An order may be for many products, and any one product can appear in many orders.) Many-to-many relationships are common to most database applications yet often trip up even the most seasoned computer user.

You might argue, "Wait a minute, I'm building a hospital patient tracking system, not an order-entry system!" Or perhaps you're creating a database to track seminar attendees. Aren't you "selling" hospital beds to patients? Isn't registering a student for a seminar "selling" a seminar seat to a customer? If you take a look at your business applications from this viewpoint, you'll be able to compare your project to the order-entry example with ease. Even if you're writing a personal application to keep track of your wine collection, you're "selling" a rack position in your cellar to your latest bottle purchase, and you're probably also tracking the "supplier" of your purchases.

The concept of data subjects related to each other in a "many-to-many" fashion is important in all but the simplest of database applications. This type of data relationship can be found in nearly all business or personal database applications. A particular patient may need many different medications, and any one medication is administered to many patients. A movie in your home collection has many starring actors, and any one actor appears in many movies. As you'll discover, a well-designed order-entry database contains several many-to-many relationships.

Analyzing the Tasks

Let's assume that you've been hired by the Information Technology Group (ITG) at Microsoft to design a book catalog and order entry database for Microsoft Press. The database application must allow authorized users to enter and update book and author data. Potential customers who receive this catalog must be able to search for books of interest, select ones they want to order, search for nearby stores that carry Microsoft Press books, and print out an order that they can take to the store.

The first design step you should perform is to list all the major tasks that this database application must automate. The list would include the following.

- Enter book data

- Enter author data

- Link books with authors

- Capture customer information

- Enter store information

- Perform a book search

- Perform an author search

- Create a new order

- Add selected books to an open order

- Search for a nearby store

- Print an open order

Figure 4-1 on the next page shows a blank application design worksheet that you should fill out for each task.

Consider the task of ordering a book. For this task, the customer might need to search for a book of interest by author, book category, or price. At a minimum, the customer would need to be able to select from a list of available books on an order form. Related tasks that would need to precede book ordering might include capturing the customer information, entering author information, entering book information, and linking books and authors. You should fill out one worksheet for each related task, and then you need to begin to determine what data you need.

II

Building a Database

FIGURE 4-1.

An application design worksheet for describing tasks.

APPLICATION DESIGN WORKSHEET #1 - TASKS			
Task Name:			
Brief Description:			
Related Tasks:			
Data Name	Usage	Description	Subject

NOTE

You can find the Application Design Worksheet #1 in the \Running Access 2000 Samples\Documents\Design folder of the companion CD, in the file Chap4-01.doc. Worksheet #2 is in the file Chap4-02.doc.

Data or Information?

You need to know the difference between data and information before you proceed any further. This bit of knowledge makes it easier to determine what you need to store in your database.

The difference between data and information is that *data* is the set of static values you store in the tables of the database, while *information* is data that is retrieved and organized in a way that is meaningful to the person viewing it. You *store* data and you *retrieve* information. The distinction is important because of the way that you construct a database application. You first determine the tasks that are necessary (what *information* you need to be able to retrieve), and then you determine what must be stored in the database to support those tasks (what *data* you need in order to construct and supply the information).

Whenever you refer to or work with the structure of your database or the items stored in the tables, queries, macros, or code, you're dealing with data. Likewise, whenever you refer to or work with query records, filters, forms, or reports, you're dealing with information. The process of designing a database and its application becomes clearer once you understand this distinction. Unfortunately, this is another set of terms that people in the computer industry have used interchangeably. But armed with this new knowledge, you're ready to go on to the next step.

Selecting the Data

After you identify all the tasks, you must list the data items you need in order to perform each task. On the task worksheet, you enter a name for each data item, a usage code, and a brief description. In the Usage column, you enter one or more usage codes—I, O, U, D, and C—which stand for input, output, update, delete, and calculate. A data item is an *input* for a task if you need to read it from the database (but not update it) to perform the task. For example, a customer name and address are some of the inputs needed to create an order. Likewise, data is an *output* for a task if it is new data that you enter as you perform the task or that the task calculates and stores based on the input data. For example, the quantities of items you enter for an order are outputs; the shipping address and phone number you provide for a new order are outputs as well.

You *update* data in a task if you read data from the database, change it, and write it back. A task such as recording a customer's change of address would input the old address, update it, and write the new one back to the database. As you might guess, a task *deletes* data when it removes the data from the database. In the Books database, you might have a task to remove a book from an order if the customer decides not to order that book after all. Finally, *calculated* data creates new values from input data to be displayed or printed but not written back to the database.

In the Subject column of the task worksheet, you enter the name of the Access object to which you think each data item belongs. For example, an address might belong to a Customers table. A completed application design worksheet for the Order a Book task might look like the one shown in Figure 4-2.

FIGURE 4-2.

A completed worksheet for the Order a Book task.

APPLICATION DESIGN WORKSHEET #1 - TASKS			
Task Name:	Order a book		
Brief Description:	Search for book desired		
	Add book to outstanding order for signed-on customer		
Related Tasks:	Customer add / edit		
	Customer sign-on		
	Book add / edit		
Data Name	Usage	Description	Subject
OrderID	O	Unique ID for the order	Orders
CustomerID	I, O	ID of the customer for the order	Customers
StoreID (optional)	I, O	ID of the store filling the order	Stores
OrderDate	O	Today's Date	Orders
LastName	I	Customer last name	Customers
FirstName	I	Customer first name	Customers
MiddleInit	I	Customers middle initial	Customers
ShipName	O	Name for shipment (Default customer Name)	Orders
Address	I	Customer Address	Customers
ShipAddress	O	Ship address (Default customer Address)	Orders
City	I	Customer City	Customers
ShipCity	O	Ship city (Default customer City)	Orders
PostalCode	I	Customer postal code	Customers
ShipPostalCode	O	Ship Postal Code (Default customer Postal Code)	Orders
Country	I	Customer Country	Customers
ShipCountry	O	Ship country (Default customer Country)	Orders
PayBy	I	Customer normal payment method	Customers
PayBy	O	Order Payment method (Default customer PayBy)	Orders
CCNumber	I	Customer credit card number	Customers
CCNumber	O	Order credit card number	Orders
ISBN	I	Book ID	Books
ISBN	O	Book ID for the order	Order Details
Quantity	O, U	Quantity wanted	Order Details
Discount	O	Potential Discount	Order Details

Organizing Tasks

You should use task worksheets as a guide in laying out an initial structure for your application. Part of the planning you do on these worksheets is to consider usage—whether a piece of data might be needed as input, for updating, or as output of a given task. Wherever you have something that is required as input, you should have a *precedent* task that creates that data item as output.

For example, for the worksheet shown in Figure 4-2, you must gather book and author data and customer data before you can record a book order. Similarly, you need to create the book category data in some other task before you can use that data (or update it) in this task. Therefore, you should have a task for gathering the book and author data, a task for gathering basic customer data, and a task for recording search categories for books. It's useful to lay out all of your defined tasks in a relationship diagram. The relationships among the tasks in the Microsoft Press Books database are shown in Figure 4-3. Optional precedent tasks are shown with dashed lines. (In other words, a customer might know the ISBN [the book's ID number] and name of a book, making it possible to order it without performing a criteria search.)

II

Building a Database

FIGURE 4-3.

The relationships among tasks in the Microsoft Press Books database.

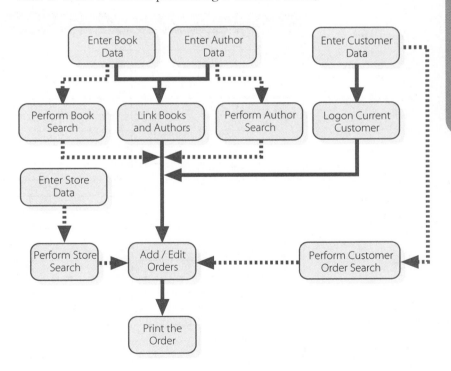

Data Analysis

Now you're ready to begin a more thorough analysis of your data and to organize the individual items into data subjects. These subjects become candidates for tables in your database design.

Choosing the Database Subjects

If you've been careful in identifying the subject for each data item you need, the next step is very easy. You create another worksheet, similar to the worksheet shown in Figure 4-4, to help you collect all the data

FIGURE 4-4.

An application design worksheet for identifying related subjects.

APPLICATION DESIGN WORKSHEET #2 - SUBJECTS			
Subject Name:			
Brief Description:			
Related Subjects:	Name	Relationship	
Data Name	Data Type	Description	Validation Rule

items that belong to each subject. In the top part of the worksheet, you list the related subjects that appear in any given task and indicate the kind of relationship—one-to-many or one-to-one. For example, a book might have several authors, and an author might have written more than one book. A completed worksheet for the Orders subject is shown in Figure 4-5.

FIGURE 4-5.

A completed worksheet for the Orders subject.

APPLICATION DESIGN WORKSHEET #2 - SUBJECTS			
Subject Name:			
Brief Description:	Information about orders		
Related Subjects:	**Name**	**Relationship**	
	Customers	One	
	Stores	One	
	Order details	Many	
Data Name	Data Type	Description	Validation Rule
OrderID	AutoNumber	Order identifier	Required (P Key)
CustomerID	Number (long)	Customer identifier	Required
StoreID (optional)	Number (long)	Store identifier	
OrderDate	Date/Time	Date order was placed	Required - 99/99/00 (Default today)
ShipName	Text (50)	Ship-to person name (Default customer Name)	Required
ShipAddress	Text (255)	Ship-to address	Required
ShipCity	Text (50)	Ship-to city	Required
ShipStateOrProvince	Text (20)	Ship-to state or province	
ShipPostalCode	Text (20)	Ship-to postal code	Required
ShipCountry	Text (50)	Ship-to country	Required
ShipPhoneNumber	Text (30)	Ship-to phone	Req. - (999) 000-0000
PayBy	Number (Integer)	Payment method (code)	Between 1 and 6
CCNumber	Text (20)	Credit card	1st digit of CCNumber must match PayBy if PayBy>2. Input mask dependent on PayBy
Printed	Yes/No	Order has been printed	

II

Building a Database

It's important to understand these relationships because they have a significant effect on the database structure and on how you use certain types of objects in Access. You'll learn more about these relationships later in this chapter.

As you copy each data item to the subject worksheet, you designate the data type (text, number, currency, memo, and so on) and the data length in the Data Type column. You can enter a short descriptive phrase for each data item in the Description column. When you create your table from the worksheet, the description is the default information that Access will display on the status bar at the bottom of the screen whenever the field is selected on a datasheet or in a form or a report.

Finally, in the Validation Rule column, you might make a note of any validation rules that should always apply to the data field. Later, you can define these rules in Access, and Access will check each time you create new data to ensure that you haven't violated any of the rules. Validating data can be especially important when you create a database application for other people to use.

Mapping Subjects to Your Database

After you fill out all of the subject worksheets, each worksheet becomes a candidate to be a table in your database. For each table, you must confirm that all the data you need is included. You should also be sure that you don't include any unnecessary data.

For example, if any customers need more than one line for an address, you should add a second data field. If you expect to have more than one type of book category (audience, software application, book type), you should create a separate table for category classes that contains records for each classification. In the next section, you'll learn how to use four simple rules to create a flexible and logical set of tables from your subject worksheets.

Database Design Concepts

When using a relational database system such as Microsoft Access, you should begin by designing each database around a specific set of tasks or functions. For example, you might design one database for customers and orders that contains data about each customer, the products available for sale, the orders for each customer, and the product sales history. You might have another database that handles human resources for your company. It would contain all relevant data about the employees and their dependents, such as names, job titles, employment histories, departmental assignments, insurance information, and the like.

At this point, you face your biggest design challenge: How do you organize data within each task-oriented database so that you take advantage of the relational capabilities of Access and avoid inefficiency and waste? If you followed the steps outlined earlier in this chapter for analyzing application tasks and identifying database subjects, you're well on your way to creating a logical, flexible, and usable database design. But what if you just "dive in" and start laying out your tables without first analyzing tasks and subjects? The rest of this chapter shows you how to apply some rules to transform a makeshift database design into one that is robust and efficient.

Waste Is the Problem

A table stores the data you need for the tasks you want to perform. A table is made up of columns, or fields, each of which contains a specific kind of data (such as a customer name or a credit rating), and rows, or records, that collect all the data about a particular person, place, or thing. You can see this organization in the Customers table in the Microsoft Press Books database, as shown in Figure 4-6.

FIGURE 4-6.
The Customers table in Datasheet view.

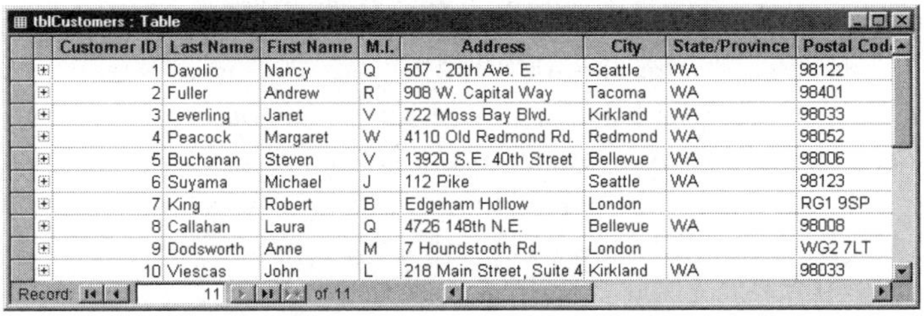

tblCustomers : Table

Customer ID	Last Name	First Name	M.I.	Address	City	State/Province	Postal Cod
1	Davolio	Nancy	Q	507 - 20th Ave. E.	Seattle	WA	98122
2	Fuller	Andrew	R	908 W. Capital Way	Tacoma	WA	98401
3	Leverling	Janet	V	722 Moss Bay Blvd.	Kirkland	WA	98033
4	Peacock	Margaret	W	4110 Old Redmond Rd.	Redmond	WA	98052
5	Buchanan	Steven	V	13920 S.E. 40th Street	Bellevue	WA	98006
6	Suyama	Michael	J	112 Pike	Seattle	WA	98123
7	King	Robert	B	Edgeham Hollow	London		RG1 9SP
8	Callahan	Laura	Q	4726 148th N.E.	Bellevue	WA	98008
9	Dodsworth	Anne	M	7 Houndstooth Rd.	London		WG2 7LT
10	Viescas	John	L	218 Main Street, Suite 4	Kirkland	WA	98033

Record: 11 of 11

For the purposes of this design exercise, let's say you want to build a new database (named Books) for creating book orders without the benefit of first analyzing the tasks and subjects you'll need. You might be tempted to put all the data about the task you want to do—keeping track of customers and the books they order—in a single Customer Orders table, whose fields are represented in Figure 4-7 on the next page.

There are many problems with this technique. For example:

- Every time a customer adds another order, you have to duplicate the Customer Name and Customer Address fields in another record for the new order. Repeatedly storing the same name and

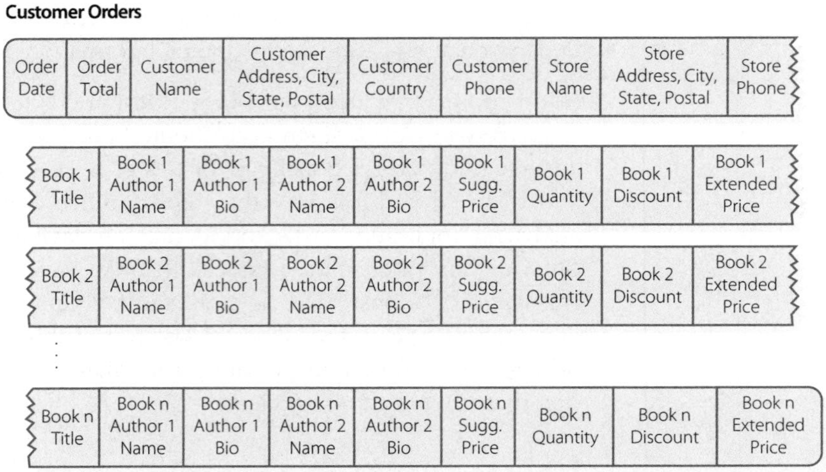

FIGURE 4-7.

The design for the
Books database using
a single Customer
Orders table.

Customer Orders

Order Date	Order Total	Customer Name	Customer Address, City, State, Postal	Customer Country	Customer Phone	Store Name	Store Address, City, State, Postal	Store Phone

Book 1 Title	Book 1 Author 1 Name	Book 1 Author 1 Bio	Book 1 Author 2 Name	Book 1 Author 2 Bio	Book 1 Sugg. Price	Book 1 Quantity	Book 1 Discount	Book 1 Extended Price

Book 2 Title	Book 2 Author 1 Name	Book 2 Author 1 Bio	Book 2 Author 2 Name	Book 2 Author 2 Bio	Book 2 Sugg. Price	Book 2 Quantity	Book 2 Discount	Book 2 Extended Price

Book n Title	Book n Author 1 Name	Book n Author 1 Bio	Book n Author 2 Name	Book n Author 2 Bio	Book n Sugg. Price	Book n Quantity	Book n Discount	Book n Extended Price

address in your database wastes a lot of space—and you can easily make mistakes if you have to enter basic information about a customer more than once.

■ You have no way of predicting how many titles will be ordered in any given order. If you keep track of each order in a single record, you have to guess the largest number of titles and leave space for Book 1, Book 2, Book 3, and so on, all the way to the maximum number. Again you're wasting valuable space in your database. If you guess wrong, you'll have to change your design just to accommodate an order that has more than the maximum number of titles. And later, if you want to find out which books were sold to what customers, you'll have to search each Book Name field in every record.

■ You have to waste space in the database storing data that can easily be calculated when it's time to print a report. For example, you'll certainly want to calculate the total order amount for each order, but you do not need to keep the result in a field.

■ Designing one complex field to contain all the parts of simple data items (for example, lumping together Street Address, City, State, and Postal Code) makes it difficult to search or sort on part of the data. In this example, it would be impossible to sort on customer postal code because that piece of information might appear anywhere within the more complex single address field.

Normalization Is the Solution

You can minimize the kinds of problems noted above (although it might not always be desirable to eliminate all duplicate values), by using a process called *normalization* to organize data fields into a group of tables. The mathematical theory behind normalization is rigorous and complex, but the tests you can apply to determine whether you have a design that makes sense and that is easy to use are quite simple—and can be stated as rules.

Rule 1: Field Uniqueness

Since wasted space is one of the biggest problems with an unnormalized table design, it makes sense to remove redundant fields from a table. So the first rule is about field uniqueness.

Rule 1: Each field in a table should represent a unique type of information.

This means that you should break up complex compound fields and get rid of the repeating groups of information. In this example, the complex address fields should be separated into simple fields and new tables designed to eliminate the repeating book information. When you create separate tables for the repeating data, you include some "key" information from the main table to create a link between the new tables and the original one. One possible result is shown in Figure 4-8.

FIGURE 4-8.

A design for the Books database that eliminates redundant fields.

Customer Orders

Order Date	Customer Name	Customer Address	Customer City	Customer State or Province	Customer Postal Code	Customer Country	Customer Phone	Order Total

Store Name	Store Address	Store City	Store State or Province	Store Postal Code	Store Phone

Order Details

Order Date	Customer Name	Book Title	Book Quantity	Book Price	Book Discount	Book Extended Price

Books

Book Title	Sugg. Price	Copyright Year	Edition	Pages	Liner Notes	Disk

Book - Authors

Book Title	Author First Name	Author Middle Name	Author Last Name	Author Bio	Author E-mail

II

Building a Database

These tables are much simpler because you can process one record per book ordered. Also, you don't have to reserve room in your records to hold a large number of books per order. And, if you want to find out what book has the highest price, you can now search the separate Books table, where key information about each book is recorded only once.

The duplicate data problem is now somewhat worse, however, because you are repeating the Order Date and Customer Name fields in each Order Details record. The potentially long Book Title field is also redundant in the Books, Book-Authors, and Order Details tables. This "duplicate" data is necessary, however, to maintain the links between the tables. You can solve this problem by following the second rule.

Rule 2: Primary Keys

In a good relational database design, each record in any table must be uniquely identified. That is, some field (or combination of fields) in the table must yield a unique value for each record in the table. This unique identifier is called the *primary key*.

Rule 2: Each table must have a unique identifier, or primary key, that is made up of one or more fields in the table.

Whenever possible, you should use the simplest data that "naturally" provides unique values. Nearly all books published in the world have a relatively short (12 character) International Standard Book Number—or ISBN—that uniquely identifies each book. This makes the ISBN field a good "natural" primary key for the Books table. Although it appears that you've created duplicate data with the book ISBN field in three of the tables, you've actually significantly reduced the total amount of data stored. The lengthy book title data is stored only once for each book in the Books table and not for each detail line in an order. You've duplicated only a small piece of data, the ISBN field, which allows you to *relate* the order detail and author data to the appropriate book data. Relational databases are equipped to support this design technique by giving you powerful tools to bring related information back together easily. *You'll take a first look at some of these tools in Chapter 8, "Adding Power with Select Queries."*

Whenever you build a table, Access always recommends that you define a primary key for that table. For many tables, you might need to create an artificial unique value to act as the primary key. The Books application will probably generate a unique order number or Order ID for each new order entered. (You'll see in the next chapter that Access provides a special data type, called AutoNumber, that generates a unique number for every new row in a table.) In the case of Order Details, the combination of the Access-generated Order ID and the book ISBN is most likely unique for each row in the table (you're not likely to create more than one order detail line for a particular title in a single order). The result of adding primary keys is shown in Figure 4-9.

FIGURE 4-9.

The Books database tables with primary keys defined.

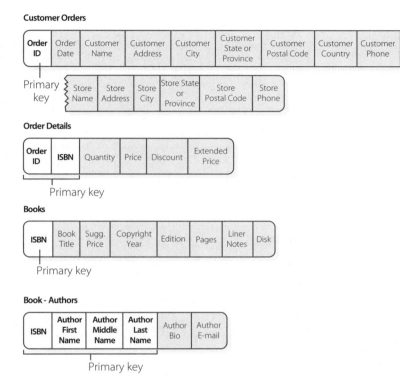

Rule 3: Functional Dependence

After you define a primary key for each table, you can check to see whether you included all the data relevant to the subject of the table. In other words, you should check to see whether each field is *functionally dependent* on the primary key that defines the subject of the table.

Rule 3: For each unique primary key value, the values in the data columns must be relevant to, and must completely describe, the subject of the table.

This rule works in two ways. First, you shouldn't have any data in a table that is not relevant to the subject (as defined by the primary key) of the table. For example, although customer information is required for each order, customers are in fact a separate subject and should have their own table. Likewise, an author may write more than one

II

Building a Database

book, so creating a separate table for authors makes sense. Second, the data in the table should completely describe the subject. For example, books in an order may be shipped to a person and location different from the customer who is buying the books (perhaps as a gift). Adding shipping information to the Orders table makes that information more complete. The result is shown in Figure 4-10.

FIGURE 4-10.

Creating additional subject tables in the Books database to ensure all fields in a table are functionally dependent on the primary key of the table.

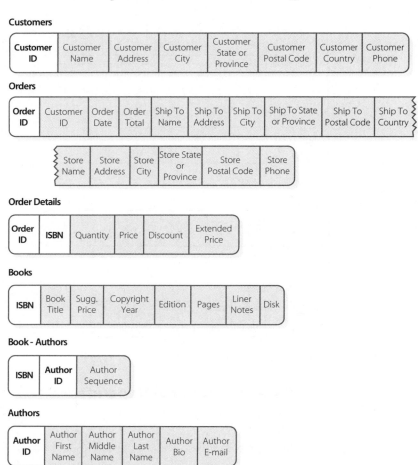

Rule 4: Field Independence

The last rule checks to see whether you'll have any problems when you make changes to the data in your tables.

Rule 4: You must be able to make a change to the data in any field (other than a field in the primary key) without affecting the data in any other field.

Take a look again at the Orders table in Figure 4-10. As we applied the second and third rules, we left Store information with the Orders information because it seems reasonable that you need Store information to complete an order. Note that if you need to correct the spelling of a store name, you can do so without affecting any other fields in that record. If you misspelled the same store name for many orders, however, you might have to change many records. Also, if you entered the wrong store (the order is actually for Powell's Technical Bookstore, not University Bookstore), you can't change the store name without also changing that record's address and phone data. The Store Name, Store Address, and Store Phone fields are not independent of one another. In fact, Store Address, Store City, Store State or Province, and Store Phone are functionally dependent on Store Name. (See Rule 3.) Although it wasn't obvious at first, Store Name describes another subject that is different from the subject of orders. You can see how carefully applying this fourth rule helps you identify changes that you perhaps should have made when applying earlier rules. This situation calls for another table in your design: a separate Stores table, as shown in Figure 4-11 on the next page.

Now, if you've misspelled a store name, you can simply change the store name in the Stores table. Also, instead of using the Store Name field (which might be 40 or 50 characters long) as the primary key for the Stores table, you can create a shorter Store ID field (perhaps a five-digit number) to minimize the size of the relational data you need in the Order table.

Note also that the Order Total field has been removed from the Orders table and the Price and Extended Price fields have been removed from the Order Details table. Because the price of a book rarely changes, it makes little sense to carry the price in both the Books table and the Order Details table. As you'll see later when you learn about building queries, it's a simple matter to link the Order Details table with the Books table in a query to retrieve the price and calculate the extended price for each book. Likewise, Order Total is removed from the Orders table because any change to a price, order quantity, or discount will cause a change in the total. It's better to calculate the total order value when the order is complete—perhaps as part of the report that prints the order.

An alternative (but less rigorous) way to check for field independence is to see whether you have the same data repeated in your records. In the previous design, whenever you created an order for a particular store, you had to enter the store's name, address, state or province,

FIGURE 4-11.

A design for the Books
database that follows
all the design rules.

Customers

Customer ID	Customer Name	Customer Address	Customer City	Customer State or Province	Customer Postal Code	Customer Country	Customer Phone

Orders

Order ID	Customer ID	Order Date	Ship To Name	Ship To Address	Ship To City	Ship To State or Province	Ship To Postal Code	Ship To Country	Store ID

Order Details

Order ID	ISBN	Quantity	Discount

Stores

Store ID	Store Name	Store Address	Store City	Store State Or Province	Store Postal Code	Store Phone

Books

ISBN	Book Title	Sugg. Price	Copyright Year	Edition	Pages	Liner Notes	Disk

Book - Authors

ISBN	Author ID	Author Sequence

Authors

Author ID	Author First Name	Author Middle Name	Author Last Name	Author Bio	Author E-mail

postal code, and phone number in the order record. With a separate
Stores table, if you need to correct a spelling or change an address, you
have to make the change only in one field of one record in the Stores
table. If you entered the wrong store in an order, you have to change
only the Store ID in the Orders table to fix the problem.

The actual Microsoft Press Books sample database includes ten tables,
which are all shown in the Relationships window in Figure 4-12. Notice
that additional fields were created in each table to fully describe the
subject of each table and that other tables were added to support some
of the other tasks identified earlier in this section. For example, fields
were added to the Orders table to capture payment method and credit
card number. New tables were added to provide a means to designate

book categories and category classes, such as Intermediate (a category) and Book Audience (a class).

FIGURE 4-12.

Tables in the Microsoft Press Books sample database shown in the Relationships window.

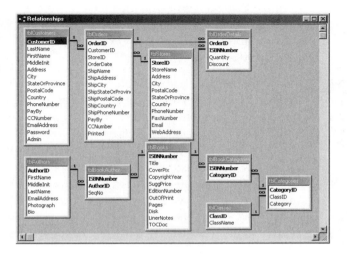

The Four Rules of Good Table Design

Rule 1: Each field in a table should represent a unique type of information.

Rule 2: Each table must have a unique identifier, or primary key, that is made up of one or more fields in the table.

Rule 3: For each unique primary key value, the values in the data columns must be relevant to, and must completely describe, the subject of the table.

Rule 4: You must be able to make a change to the data in any field (other than a field in the primary key) without affecting the data in any other field.

Efficient Relationships Are the Result

When you apply good design techniques, you end up with a database that efficiently links your data. You probably noticed that when you normalize your data as recommended, you tend to get many separate tables. Before relational databases were invented, you had to either compromise your design or manually keep track of the relationships between files or tables. For example, you had to put customer data in your Orders table or write your program to first open and read a record from the Orders table and then search for the matching record in the Customers table. Relational databases solve these problems. With a good design you don't have to worry about how to bring the data together when you need it.

II

Building a Database

Foreign Keys

You might have noticed as you followed in the Microsoft Press Books example that each time you created a new table, you left behind a field that could link the old and new tables, such as the Customer ID and the Store ID fields in the Orders table. These "linking" fields are called *foreign keys*.

 SEE ALSO

For details about refer-
ential integrity and
defining indexes, see
Chapter 5, "Building
Your Database in
Microsoft Access."

In a well-designed database, foreign keys result in efficiency. You keep track of related foreign keys as you lay out your database design. When you define your tables in Access, you link primary keys to foreign keys to tell Access how to join the data when you need to retrieve information from more than one table. As you'll learn in Chapter 5, you can add indexes to your foreign key fields to improve performance. You can also ask Access to maintain the integrity of your table relationships—for example, Access will ensure that you don't create an order for a product that doesn't exist. When you ask Access to maintain this *referential integrity,* Access automatically creates indexes for you.

One-to-Many and One-to-One Relationships

In most cases, the relationship between any two tables is one-to-many. That is, for any one record in the first table, there are many related records in the second table, but for any record in the second table, there is exactly one matching record in the first table. You can see several instances of this type of relationship in the design of the Microsoft Press Books database. For example, each customer might have several orders, but a single order record applies to only one customer.

Occasionally, you might want to break down a table further because you use some of the data in the table infrequently or because some of the data in the table is highly sensitive and should not be available to everyone. For example, you might want to keep track of certain customer data for marketing purposes, but you don't need access to that data all the time. Or you might have data about credit ratings that should be accessible only to authorized people. In either case, you can create a separate table that also has a primary key of CustomerID. The relationship between the original Customers table and the Customer Info or Customer Credit table is one-to-one. That is, for each record in the first table, there is exactly one record in the second table.

Creating Table Links

The last step in designing your database is to create the links between your tables. For each subject, identify those for which you wrote *Many* under "Relationship" on the worksheet. Be sure that the corresponding relationship for the other table is *One*. If you see *Many* in both places, you must create a separate *intersection table* to handle the relationship. (Access won't let you define a many-to-many relationship directly between two tables.) In the example of the Order Books task, a customer may have an order for "many" books, and a book can appear in many orders. The Order Details table in the Microsoft Press Books database is an intersection table that clears up this many-to-many relationship between orders and books. Book-Authors is another table that works as an intersection table because it has a one-to-many relationship with both Authors and Books. (A book can have more than one author, and an author might write more than one book.)

After you straighten out the many-to-many relationships, you need to create the links between tables. To complete the links, place a copy of the primary key from the "one" tables in a field in the "many" tables. For example, by looking at the worksheet for Orders shown in Figure 4-5 on page 91, you can surmise that the primary key for the Orders table, OrderID, also needs to be a field in the Order Details table.

When to Break the Rules

As a starting point, for every application that you build, you should always analyze the tasks you need, decide on the data required to support those tasks, and create a well-designed (also known as *normalized*) database table structure. After you have a design that follows all the rules, you might discover changes that you need to make either to follow specific business rules or to make your application more responsive to the needs of your users. In every case for which you decide to "break the rules," you should know the specific reason for doing so, document your actions, and be prepared to add procedures to your application to manage the impact of those changes. The following sections discuss some of the reasons why you might need to break the rules.

Improving Performance of Critical Tasks

The majority of cases for breaking the rules involve manipulating the design to achieve better performance for certain critical tasks. For example, although modern relational database systems (like Microsoft Access) do a good job of linking many related tables back together to perform complex tasks, you might encounter situations in which the performance of a multiple-table link (also called a *joined query*—see Chapter 8 for details) is not fast enough. Sometimes if you "denormalize" selected portions of the design, you can achieve the required performance. For example, instead of building a separate table of book classification codes that requires a link, you might place the classification descriptions directly in the book categories table. If you choose to do this, you will need to add procedures to the forms you provide to edit these categories to make sure that similar descriptions aren't duplicate entries.

Another case for breaking the rules is the selective inclusion of calculated values in your database. For example, if a critical management report needs the calculated totals for all orders, but the data is retrieved too slowly when calculating the detailed values for thousands of order detail records, you might want to add a field for order total in the Orders table. Of course, this also means adding procedures to your order-entry forms to ensure that any change in an order detail record is reflected in the calculated order total. Your application will spend a few extra fractions of a second processing each order so that month-end totals can be obtained quickly.

Capturing Point-In-Time Data

Sometimes you need to break the rules to follow known business rules. In the previous design exercise, we removed the Price field from the Order Details table because it duplicated the price information in the Books table. However, if your business rules say that the price of a book (or any product) can change over time, you may need to include the price in your order details to record the price at the *point in time* that the order was placed. If your business rules dictate this sort of change, you should add procedures to your application to automatically copy the "current" price to any new order detail row.

You can see a similar case in the Microsoft Press Books database. Some of the shipping name and address information in the Orders table may duplicate information in the Customers table. If you examine the way the Microsoft Press Books database works, you'll find some code that copies the customer information to the shipping information when you create a new order. The user is free, however, to change the shipping information as required by the order.

There's another example in the Entertainment Scheduling database. In this database, the user creates new contracts that specify the commitment of an entertainment group to perform at a specific club on a specific date. The information about clubs remains fairly constant, but groups change their name and membership all the time. If you look at the database design for the Entertainment Scheduling database, shown in Figure 4-13, you'll see what looks like lots of duplicate information in the Contracts table. For example, the club manager who arranged the contract is copied to the contract (the manager might be different next week!). In addition, all the information about the group (Group Name, Leader Name, and Member Names) is copied to the contract to capture the information at the point in time that the contract was signed.

FIGURE 4-13.

The design for the Entertainment Scheduling database includes "duplicate" point-in-time group information in the tblContracts table.

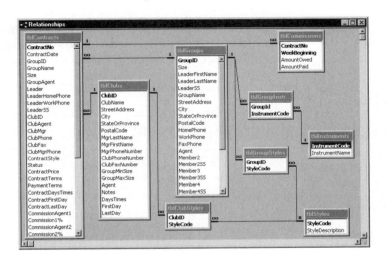

In many cases, the group leader may not decide what "sidemen" to bring to the "gig" until the actual performance date. The member information may appear to be unnormalized in both the tblGroups table and the tblContracts table. However, Ray McCann uses the member information in the Groups table only to track long-term members of the group. In the Contracts table, he fills in the member names only when the club insists that certain performers make up the group booked. It would be more work than necessary to try to keep track of all potential performers in a separate table—Ray is only interested in the information about the group leader who can sign the contracts! If you look in the Entertainment Scheduling sample database, you'll find lots of code in the contract edit form (frmContracts) to copy any available information about group members automatically.

Report Snapshot Data

One additional case for breaking the rules involves accumulating data for reporting. As you'll see in Chapter 18, "Advanced Report Design," the queries required to collect data for a complex report can be quite involved. If you have a lot of data required for your report, running the query could take an unacceptably long time, particularly if you need to run several large reports from the same complex collection of data. In this case, it's acceptable to create temporary but "rule-breaking" tables that you load once with the results of a complex query in order to run your reports. I call these tables "snapshots" because they capture the results of a complex reporting query for a single moment in time. You can look in Chapter 9, "Modifying Data with Action Queries," for some ideas about how to build action queries that save a complex data result to a temporary table. If you use the resulting "snapshot" data from these tables, you can run several complex reports without having to run long and complex queries more than once.

Now that you understand the fundamentals of good database design, you're ready to do something a little more fun with Access—building a database. The next chapter, "Building Your Database in Microsoft Access," shows you how to create a new database and tables; Chapter 6, "Modifying Your Database Design," shows you how to make changes later if you discover that you need to modify your design.

CHAPTER 5

Building Your Database in Microsoft Access

After you design the tables for your database, defining them using Microsoft Access is incredibly easy. This chapter shows you how it's done. You'll learn how to:

- Create a new database application using the Database Wizard

- Create a new empty database for your own custom application

- Create a simple table by entering data directly in the table

- Get a jump start on defining custom tables by using the Table Wizard

- Define your own tables from scratch

- Select the best data type for your fields

- Set validation rules for your fields and tables

- Tell Access what relationships to maintain between your tables

- Optimize data retrieval by adding indexes

- Print a table definition

Creating a New Database

When you first start Microsoft Access, you see the opening choices dialog box shown in Figure 5-1. In this dialog box you specify whether you want to create a brand-new empty database, to use the Database Wizard to create a database application using any of the several database application templates that come with Access, or to open an existing database (mdb) file. If you've previously opened other databases, such as the Northwind Traders sample database that is included with Access, you'll also see a "most recently used" list of up to nine database selections in the Open An Existing File section of the dialog box. If you have Microsoft Office installed, when you open Access for the first time you'll also see the Microsoft Office Assistant in the lower right corner of your screen (as shown in Figure 5-11 on page 115). If this is the first time you've used Access, choose Start Using Microsoft Access in the Office Assistant. You'll learn about using the Office Assistant and Access online help in more detail later in this chapter.

FIGURE 5-1.
The Access opening choices dialog box.

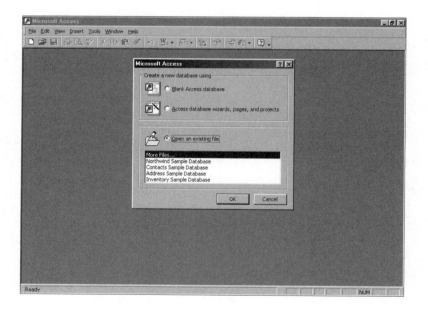

Using the Database Wizard

Just for fun, let's explore the Database Wizard first. If you're a beginner, you can use the Database Wizard to work with any of the several database application templates included with Access without needing to know anything about designing database software. You might find that the application the wizard builds meets most of your needs right off the bat. As you learn more about Access, you can build on and customize the basic application design and add new features.

Even if you're an experienced developer, you might find that the application templates save you lots of time in setting up the basic tables, queries, forms, and reports for your application. If the application you need to build is covered by one of the templates, the wizard can take care of many of the simpler design tasks.

When you start Access, you can select the Database Wizard option in the opening choices dialog box and then click OK to open the dialog box shown in Figure 5-2. Or, if you have already started Access, you can choose New Database from the File menu. You work with all of the templates in the Database Wizard in the same way. This example will show you the steps that are needed to build an Asset Tracking database.

FIGURE 5-2.

Some of the Database Wizard templates.

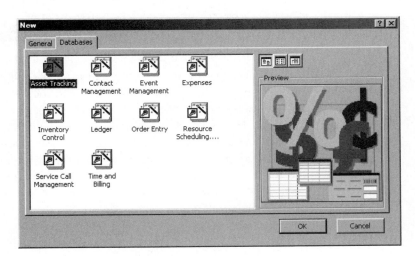

Scan the list of available templates under the Databases tab of the New dialog box. When you click a template icon, Access shows a preview graphic to give you another hint about the purpose of the template. You start the Database Wizard by selecting a template and then clicking OK. You can also double-click a template icon. Access opens the File New Database dialog box and suggests a name for your new database file. You can modify the name and then click Create to launch the wizard.

The wizard takes a few moments to initialize and to create a blank file for your new database application. The wizard first displays a screen with a few more details about the capabilities of the application you are about to build. If this isn't what you want, click Cancel to close the wizard and delete the database file. You can click Finish to have the

II

Building a Database

wizard quickly build the application with all the default options. Click Next to proceed to a window that provides options for customizing the tables in your application, as shown in Figure 5-3.

FIGURE 5-3.

Selecting optional fields in the Database Wizard.

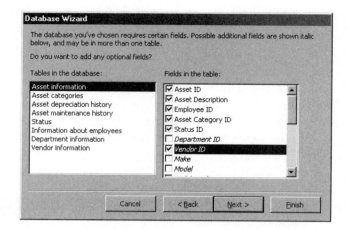

In this window, you can see the names of the tables the wizard plans to build. As you select each table name in the list on the left, the wizard shows you the fields it will include in that table in the list on the right. For many of the tables, you can have the wizard include or exclude certain optional fields (which appear in *italic*). In the Asset Tracking application, for example, you might be interested in keeping track of the vendor for each asset. When you click the optional Vendor ID field in the Asset information table, you'll be able to relate assets to vendors. Click Next when you finish selecting optional fields for your application.

In the next window, shown in Figure 5-4, you select one of several styles for the forms in your database. As you recall from Chapter 3, "Touring Microsoft Access," forms are objects in your database that are used to display data on your screen. Some of the styles, such as Expedition or Ricepaper, are quite whimsical. The Standard style has a very businesslike gray-on-gray look.

After you select a form style, click Next to proceed to the window shown in Figure 5-5. You use this window to select a report style. You might want to select Bold, Casual, or Compact for personal applications. Corporate, Formal, and Soft Gray are good choices for business applications. Select an appropriate report style, and then click Next.

In the window shown in Figure 5-6, you specify a title that will appear on the Access title bar when you run the application. You can also ask

FIGURE 5-4.

Selecting a style for forms in the Database Wizard.

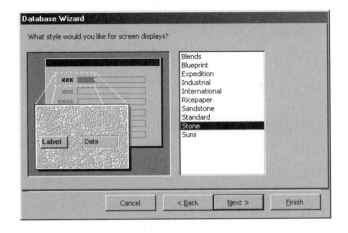

FIGURE 5-5.

Selecting a report style in the Database Wizard.

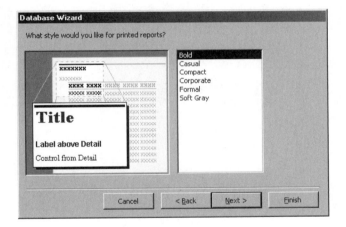

FIGURE 5-6.

Naming your database in the Database Wizard.

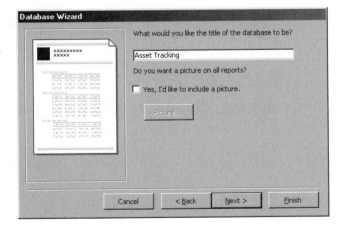

to include a picture file in your reports. This picture file can be a bitmap, a Windows metafile, or an icon file. Click Next after you supply a title for your application.

In the final window, you can choose to start the application immediately after the wizard finishes building it. You can also choose to open a special set of help topics to guide you through using a database application. *See the section titled "Using Microsoft Access Help" later in this chapter for details about special help features in Access.* Select the Yes, Start The Database option and click Finish to create and then start your application. Figure 5-7 shows the opening "switchboard" form for the Asset Tracking database application.

FIGURE 5-7.

The switchboard form for the Asset Tracking database application.

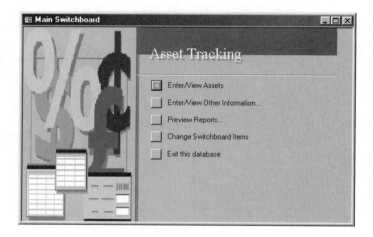

> **2000 NOTE**
>
> All new forms you create in Microsoft Access 2000 have a new option set to allow design changes from Form view. You will see the form design toolbars and may see several form design windows open when you view your new Asset Tracking switchboard. *See Chapter 13, "Building Forms," for details about changing the form's Allow Design Changes property.*

Creating a New Empty Database

To begin creating a new empty database when you start Access, select Blank Access Database in the opening choices dialog box shown in Figure 5-1 on page 108. (If you have already started Access, you can choose the New command from the File menu and then double-click the Database icon on the General tab in the New dialog box.) This opens the File New Database dialog box, shown in Figure 5-8. Select the drive and folder you want from the Save In drop-down list. In this example, the My Documents folder of the current drive is selected. Finally, go to the File Name text box and type the name of your new database. Access appends an mdb extension to the filename for you. (Access uses a file with an mdb extension to store all your database objects, including tables, queries, forms, reports, data access pages, macros, and modules.) For this example, create a new sample database named Kathy's Wedding List to experiment with one way to create a database and tables. Click the Create button to create your database.

FIGURE 5-8.

The File New Database dialog box.

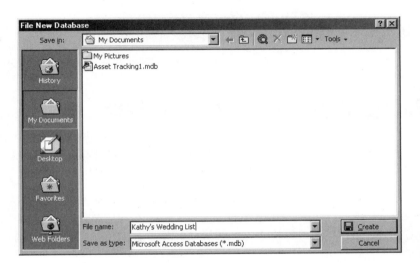

TIP

You can create a new database either by choosing the New command from the File menu or by clicking the New button on the toolbar. The New Database button is the first button at the left end of the toolbar.

Access takes a few moments to create the system files in which to store all the information about the tables, queries, forms, reports, data access pages, macros, and modules that you might create. When Access completes this process, it displays the Database window for your new database, shown in Figure 5-9 on the next page.

When you open a database (unless the database includes special startup settings), Access selects the object button you last chose in the Database window for that database. The button displays the available objects of that type. Because this is a new database and no tables or special startup settings exist yet, you see an empty Database window.

II

Building a Database

FIGURE 5-9.
The Database window for a new database.

Using Microsoft Access Help

Access provides several ways to obtain help. To explore these, open the Help menu, shown in Figure 5-10. If you have turned off the Office Assistant (see later in this section for details), you can click Microsoft Access Help to open Help with an index list displayed. If the Assistant is active, it will help you locate the help topic you need based on where you are in Access at the moment. Choose Show The Office Assistant if you have turned it off and want to turn it back on. (If you have rejected help from the Assistant several times in a row, it will offer to turn itself off.) Choose What's This? to turn your mouse pointer into a question mark. You can then click an item of interest to see a pop-up definition of the item. If you have an Internet browser on your computer, choose Office On The Web to see a list of links to Web sites that provide product information and support.

FIGURE 5-10.
Choosing Microsoft Access Help from the Help menu.

 **TIP**

You can see a short description of any toolbar button by placing your mouse pointer over the button (without clicking the button) and waiting a second. Below the button, Access displays a small label, called a *ScreenTip*, that contains the name of the button. If you can't see ScreenTips, choose the Toolbars command from the View menu while you have a database open, and then choose the Customize command from the submenu. Under the Options tab of the Customize dialog box, make sure the Show ScreenTips On Toolbars check box is selected.

Just about anywhere within Access, you can find an Office Assistant button at the far right of the toolbar. Clicking this button is the same as choosing Microsoft Access Help from the Help menu or pressing F1 anywhere in the product. The Office Assistant is a feature in all the Microsoft Office 2000 products. It provides "intelligent" context-sensitive access to help topics and tutorials and is linked to your choice of entertaining and informative "characters" that guide you on your search for information. (For those of you who thought Microsoft Bob was an unsuccessful product, the technology lives on in this more efficient and useful tool within the Microsoft Office products!) You probably noticed the assistant the first time you started Microsoft Access 2000, as shown in Figure 5-11.

FIGURE 5-11.

You are introduced to the Office Assistant when you start Access for the first time.

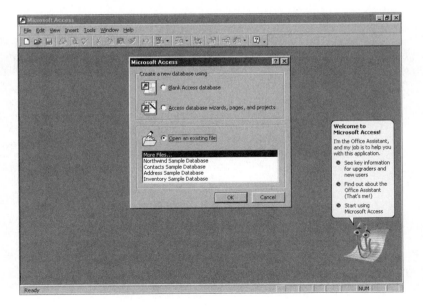

Anytime the Office Assistant is open, you can right-click the character to open a shortcut menu that lets you set options for how the Office Assistant works. You can see the options settings for the Office Assistant in Figure 5-12. Table 5-1 provides a summary of what the various options can do for you.

FIGURE 5-12.

Customizing the way the Office Assistant works.

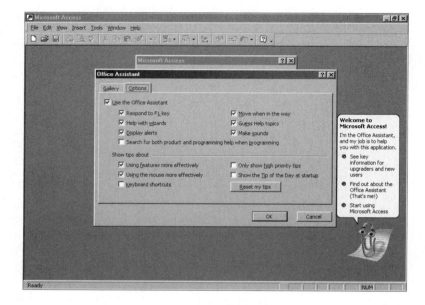

TABLE 5-1. **Option Settings for the Office Assistant**

Option	Usage
Respond to F1 key	Select this option if you want the Office Assistant to appear instead of the normal help window when you press the F1 (help) key. Some of the property sheets in Microsoft Access do not activate the Office Assistant even if you choose this option.
Help with wizards	Choose this option to get additional step-by-step help from the Office Assistant when you're running a wizard.
Display alerts	When you select this option, any messages from Access or your application are displayed in the Office Assistant window if you have the window open.
Move when in the way	Select this option to have the Office Assistant try to move out of the way when you're typing or when a message appears on the screen. With this option selected, the Office Assistant automatically shrinks if more than 5 minutes elapse without use.

TABLE 5-1. *continued*

Option	Usage
Guess Help topics	Choose this option to have the Office Assistant automatically guess what topics you might need based on what you're doing in Access. The Office Assistant also tracks topics you use frequently and offers those first.
Make sounds	If you have a sound card and speakers installed, you can select this option to hear humorous (or sometimes annoying) sounds from the Office Assistant as it does its work.
Search for both product and programming help when programming	With this option selected, the Office Assistant includes related product help topics when you invoke help from within a programming area.
Show tips about	
Using features more effectively	Select this option to see tips about more efficient alternative ways to perform a given task.
Using the mouse more effectively	Select this option to see occasional tips about how to use your mouse.
Keyboard shortcuts	When you select this option, the Office Assistant will highlight alternative keyboard shortcuts.
Only show high priority tips	Select this option to include only time-saving tips in suggested help topics.
Show the Tip of the Day at startup	Choose this option to see a randomly selected tip each time you start Microsoft Access.

If you don't like the standard Clippit character, you can click the Gallery tab to choose from nearly a dozen options, as shown in Figure 5-13 on the next page. Each character has a slightly different "personality." Clippit, Dot, and Rocky can be a bit hyperactive. F1 and The Genius are a bit more sober and straightforward. Mother Nature is calm and soothing. I chose a character named Links—an animated, yet adorable cat. Oh, by the way, each character comes with a distinctive set of sounds and animations. Perhaps I chose Links because she makes my real cats crazy when she purrs and meows through my computer speakers!

FIGURE 5-13.
Choosing your Office
Assistant.

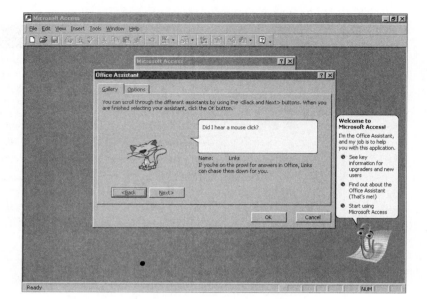

If you didn't select the option under Office Tools to install all of the Assistant characters, choosing a new character may result in a prompt to insert your Office CD-ROM.

Although the Office Assistant might seem a bit whimsical at first blush, it's really a very useful (as well as entertaining) tool. In addition to providing context-sensitive help at the click of a button, it can also respond to questions you might have as you perform various tasks. Let's say you're about to create your first new table. Click the Office Assistant button on the toolbar to open the Office Assistant together with a pop-up message box, as shown in Figure 5-14. (The Guess Help Topics option has been turned off for this figure.) If the Office Assistant is already open, click the Office Assistant to open the message. You're

FIGURE 5-14.
Asking the Office Assistant a question.

interested in learning how to create a table in your new database, so type *Create a table* or *How do I build a new table* or some similar request in the box labeled "What Would You Like To Do?"

You don't have to be too specific with your request, but the more "key" words that you give the assistant to work with (verbs such as "build," "create," or "define," or nouns such as "table," "form," or "report"), the more likely that the assistant will find the most relevant help topics or tutorials. Once you have phrased a request that you think will do the trick, click the Search button. In this case, the phrase "Create a New Table" returned at least five topics that may be related to what you want to do, as shown in Figure 5-15.

FIGURE 5-15.

The results of the Office Assistant's search.

NOTE

The topics you see in the Office Assistant when you ask for help to "Create a new table" may be different than what you see in Figure 5-15. The Assistant tracks what you have been doing in Access and help topics you have visited recently, so it tries to present solution topics that are relevant to the way you use Access.

It looks like the "Create a new table…" topic should do the trick. Click that selection to see the beginning panel from the tutorial about creating tables, as shown in Figure 5-16 on the next page. If you don't see a topic listed that you think is relevant to what you want to do, the Office Assistant will often offer a See More button to look at other topics. You can also rephrase your request and click Search again.

Building a Database

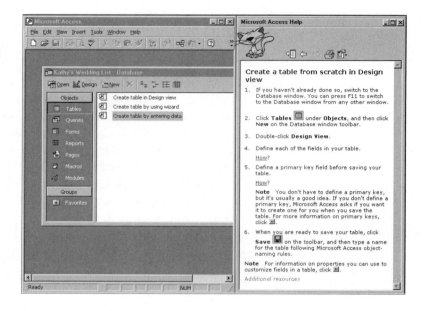

FIGURE 5-16.
The beginning panel
from the Help tutorial
about creating data-
base tables.

You may notice that opening the Office Help window causes the Access window to shrink to one side. The Help window then appears docked to the other
side in the remaining screen space. If you would like to have the Help window
not exhibit this behavior, open the window and then "undock" it by grabbing
its title bar with your mouse and moving it away from the edge of your screen.
You can now resize the window to your liking. The next time you open Office
Help, it will not resize your Access window.

Creating Your First Simple Table

If you've been following along to this point, you should still have your
new Kathy's Wedding List database open with an empty Database window, as shown in Figure 5-9 on page 113. (You can also follow these
steps in any open database.) Make sure the Tables button in the Database
window is selected, and then click the New button in the Database window to open the New Table dialog box, shown in Figure 5-17.

For details about en-
tering an expression in
a query, see Chapter 8,
"Adding Power with
Select Queries."

Select Datasheet View in the list, and then click OK to get started.
(You can also double-click Datasheet View in the list.) What you see
next is an empty datasheet, which looks quite similar to a spreadsheet.
You can enter just about any type of data you want—text, dates, numbers, currency. But unlike in a spreadsheet, in a datasheet you can't
enter any calculated expressions. As you'll see later in the chapters

FIGURE 5-17.
The New Table dialog
box.

about queries, you can easily display a calculated result using data
from one or more tables by entering an expression in a query.

Since we're starting a list of wedding invitees, we'll need columns containing information such as title, first name, middle initial, last name,
street address, city, state, postal code, number of guests invited, number
of guests confirmed, gift received, and a gift acknowledged indicator. Be
sure to enter the same type of data in a particular column for every row.
For example, enter the city name in the same column for every row.

You can see some of the data entered for the wedding invitee list in
Figure 5-18. When you start to type in a field in a row, Access displays
a pencil icon on the row selector at the far left to indicate that you're
changing data in that row. Use the Tab key to move from column to

FIGURE 5-18.
Creating a table by
entering data.

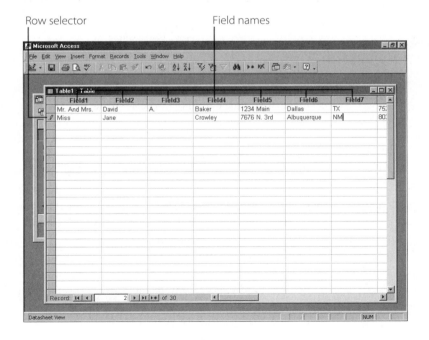

II

Building a Database

column. When you move to another row, Access saves what you typed. If you make a mistake in a particular row or column, you can click the data you want to change and type over it or delete it.

If you create a column of data that you don't want, click anywhere in the column and choose Delete Column from the Edit menu. If you want to insert a blank column between two columns that already contain data, click anywhere in the column to the right of where you want to insert the new column and then choose Column from the Insert menu. To move a column to a different location, click the field name at the top of the column to highlight the entire column, and then click again and drag the column to a new location. You can also click an unselected column and drag your mouse pointer through several adjacent columns to highlight them all. You can then move the columns as a group.

You probably noticed that Access named your columns Field1, Field2, and so forth—not very informative. You can enter a name for each column by double-clicking the column's field name. You can also click anywhere in the column and then choose Rename Column from the Format menu. In Figure 5-19, two of the columns have been renamed.

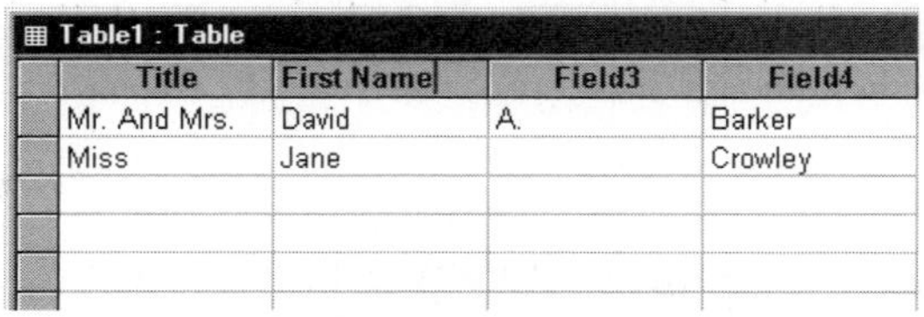

FIGURE 5-19.

Renaming a column in Datasheet view.

Title	First Name	Field3	Field4
Mr. And Mrs.	David	A.	Barker
Miss	Jane		Crowley

After you enter several rows of data, it's a good idea to save your table. You can do this by clicking the Save button on the toolbar or by choosing Save from the File menu. Access displays a Save As dialog box, as shown in Figure 5-20. Type an appropriate name for your table, and then click OK. Access displays a message box warning you that you have no primary key defined and offering to build one for you. If you accept the offer, Access adds a field called ID and assigns it a special data type named AutoNumber that automatically generates a unique number for each new row you add. *See the section titled "Field Data Types" later in this chapter for details about AutoNumber.* If one or more of the data columns you entered would make a good primary key, click No in the message box. But in this case, click Yes to build a field called ID that will serve as the primary key. In Chapter 6, "Modifying Your Database Design," you'll learn how to use the Design view of the table to define your own primary key(s) or to change the definition of an existing primary key.

FIGURE 5-20.

Saving your new table.

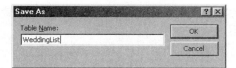

Using the Table Wizard

If you look in the Wedding List sample database (Wedding.mdb) included with this book, you'll find it very simple, with one main table and a few supporting tables for data such as titles, cities, and postal codes. Most databases are usually quite a bit more complex. For example, the Microsoft Press Books and Entertainment Scheduling sample databases each contain more than a dozen tables. If you had to create every table "by hand," it could be quite a tedious process. Fortunately, Microsoft Access comes with a Table Wizard to help you build many common tables. For this exercise, create a new blank database and give it the name Books And Authors, as shown in Figure 5-21. We'll use this database to start building tables like some of those you saw in Chapter 4.

FIGURE 5-21.

Creating a blank database named Books And Authors.

To build a table using the Table Wizard, go to the Database window, click the Tables button, and then click the New button. In the New Table dialog box (see Figure 5-17 on page 121), select Table Wizard

II

Building a Database

from the list and click OK. You'll see the opening window of the wizard, shown in Figure 5-22.

FIGURE 5-22.

The opening window
of the Table Wizard.

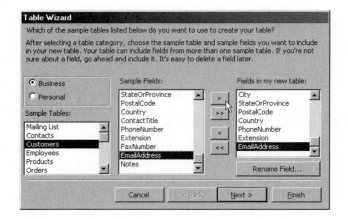

Toward the middle left of the window are two option buttons—Business (to select business-oriented tables) and Personal (to select personal tables). You can find an entry for a Customers sample table in the Business category. Scroll down the Sample Tables list until you see Customers. When you select it, the wizard displays all the fields from the Customers sample table in the Sample Fields list. (You will change the table you create now in Chapter 6, "Modifying Your Database Design," so that it is more like the final tblCustomers table in the Microsoft Press Books database.)

To select a field, click its name in the Sample Fields list, and then click the single right arrow (>) button to move it to the Fields In My New Table list. (You can also select a field by double-clicking its name.) You define the sequence of fields in your table on the basis of the sequence in which you select them from the Sample Fields list. If you add a field that you decide you don't want, select it in the Fields In My New Table list and click the single left arrow (<) button to remove it. If you want to start over, you can remove all fields by clicking the double left arrow (<<) button.

Many of the fields in the Customers sample table are fields you'll need in the Customers table for the Books And Authors database. You can pick CustomerID, BillingAddress, City, StateOrProvince, PostalCode, Country, PhoneNumber, Extension, and EmailAddress directly from the Customers sample table, as shown in Figure 5-22.

In the Books And Authors database, customers are individual people, not companies, so you need to find some name fields in another sample table to use in your new Customers table. Scroll up the Sample Tables list, and select the Employees sample table. Click the CustomerID field in the Fields In My New Table list to indicate that you want to insert a field after CustomerID. Add the FirstName, MiddleName, and LastName fields from the Employees table, as shown in Figure 5-23. The BillingAddress field in the finished table needs to be named simply "Address," so select that field, click the Rename Field button, and name it Address (the name you'll find in the original tblCustomers table in the Microsoft Press Books database). As you can see, it's easy to mix and match fields from various sample tables and then rename the fields to get exactly what you want.

FIGURE 5-23.

Choosing fields from different sample tables and renaming fields.

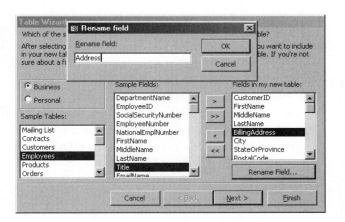

Click the Next button to see the window shown in Figure 5-24 on the next page. In this window, you can specify a new name for your table. You can also ask the wizard to set a primary key for you, or you can define your own primary key. In most cases, the wizard chooses the most logical field or fields to be the primary key. If the wizard can't find an appropriate field to be the primary key, it creates a new Primary Key field that uses a special data type called AutoNumber. As you'll learn later in this chapter, the AutoNumber data type ensures that each new row in your table will have a unique value as its primary key. For this example, let the wizard set the primary key for you. Because your table includes the primary key from the Customers sample table, a single field called CustomerID, the wizard will choose CustomerID to be the primary key for your new table.

FIGURE 5-24.
Specifying a table
name and selecting a
primary key option in
the Table Wizard.

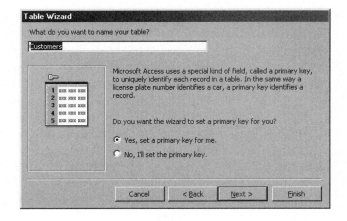

Click the Next button to move to the next window. If you have other
tables already defined in your database, the Table Wizard shows you a
list of those tables and tells you whether it thinks your new table is
related to any of the existing tables. If the wizard finds a primary key
in another table with the same name and data type as a field in your
new table (or vice versa), it assumes that the tables are related. If you
think the wizard has made a mistake, you can tell it not to create a relationship (a link) between your new table and the existing table.
You'll learn how to define your own relationships between tables later
in this chapter.

Because this is the first and only table in this database, you won't see
the Relationships window in the Table Wizard. Instead, the wizard
shows you a final window in which you can choose to see the table in
Table Design view, open it as a datasheet, or call the AutoForm Wizard
to create a simple form to let you begin entering data. (See Figure 5-25.)

FIGURE 5-25.
Selecting final options
in the Table Wizard.

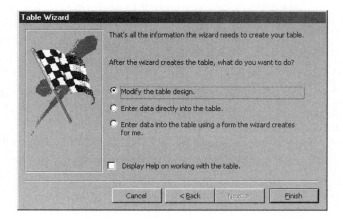

Select the Modify The Table Design option and click Finish to let the wizard build your table. The table will open in Design view, as shown in Figure 5-26. In the next chapter, you'll learn how to modify this table in Design view to exactly match the tblCustomers table in the Microsoft Press Books database. For now, close the Table window so that you can continue building other tables that you need.

FIGURE 5-26.

The Customers table built using the Table Wizard.

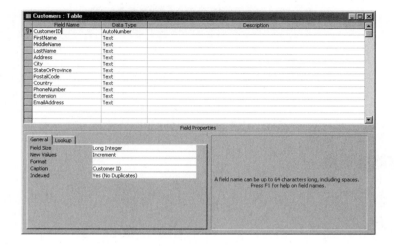

Creating a Table in Design View

You could continue to use the Table Wizard to build some of the other tables in the Books And Authors database. For example, you could use the Orders table from the Business samples or the Books or Authors table in the Personal sample tables. However, you'll find it very useful to learn the mechanics of building a table from scratch, so now is a good time to explore Design view and learn how to build tables without using the Table Wizard. You'll also see many additional features that you can use to customize the way your tables (and any queries, forms, or reports built on these tables) work.

If you want to design a new table in a database, the Database window (shown in Figure 5-9 on page 114) must be active. Click the Tables button (the topmost Objects button), and then click the New button. Access shows you the New Table dialog box you saw in Figure 5-17 on page 121. Select Design View and click OK. Access displays a blank Table window in Design view, as shown in Figure 5-27 on the next page.

II

Building a Database

FIGURE 5-27.

A blank Table window in Design view.

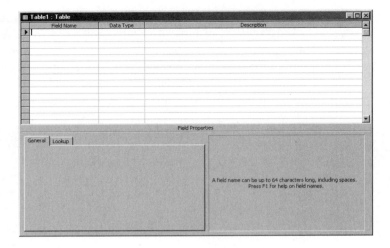

 **TIP**

> You can also open a blank Table window in Design view by selecting Table from the New Object toolbar button's drop-down list, and then selecting Design View in the New Table dialog box.

In Design view, the upper part of the Table window displays columns in which you can enter the field names, the data type for each field, and a description of each field. After you select a data type for a field, Access allows you to set field properties in the lower left area of the Table window. In the lower right area of the Table window is a box in which Access displays information about fields or properties. The contents of this box change as you move from one location to another within the Table window.

Defining Fields

? SEE ALSO

For details about data type values, see "Field Data Types" later in this chapter.

Now you're ready to begin defining the fields for the Orders table. Be sure the insertion point is in the first row of the Field Name column, and then type the name of the first field, *OrderID*. Press the Tab key once to move to the Data Type column. A button with a down arrow appears on the right side of the Data Type column. Here and elsewhere in Microsoft Access, this type of button signifies the presence of a drop-down list. Click the down arrow or press Alt+Down arrow to open the list of data type options, shown in Figure 5-28. In the Data

Type column, you can either type a valid value or select from the list of values in the drop-down list. Select AutoNumber as the data type for OrderID. Tab down to the next line, enter *CustomerID* as a field name, and then choose Number as the data type. If you recall the design exercise in Chapter 4, this will be the linking field to identify which customer placed this order.

FIGURE 5-28.

The drop-down list of data type options.

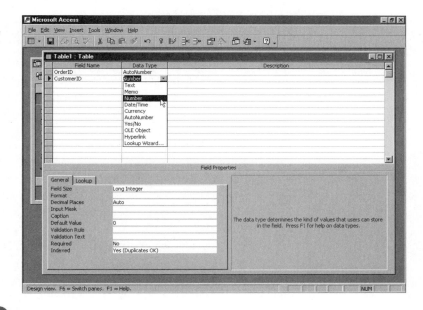

? SEE ALSO

For details about the various property settings for each property box, see the section titled "Field Properties" later in this chapter.

After you select a data type, Access displays some property boxes in the Field Properties area in the lower part of the Table window. These boxes allow you to set properties and thereby customize a field. The boxes Access shows you depend on the data type you selected; they appear with some default properties in place, as shown in Figure 5-28.

In the Description column for each field, you can enter a descriptive phrase. Access displays this description in the status bar (at the bottom of the Access window) whenever you select this field in a query in Datasheet view or in a form in Form view or Datasheet view. As you can imagine, paying careful attention to what you type in the Description field can later pay big dividends as a kind of "mini help" on the status bar for the users of your database. Also, since this data propagates automatically, you probably don't want to type something nonsensical or silly. Typing *I don't have a clue what this field does* is probably not a good idea—it will show up later on the status bar!

II

Building a Database

Field Data Types

Access supports nine types of data, each with a specific purpose. These data types are described in Table 5-2. Access also gives you a tenth option, Lookup Wizard, to help you define the characteristics of foreign key fields that link to other tables. You'll learn how to use the Lookup Wizard in the next chapter.

Choosing Field Names

Microsoft Access gives you lots of flexibility when it comes to naming your fields. A field name can be up to 64 characters long, can include any combination of letters, numbers, spaces, and special characters except a period (.), an exclamation point (!), an accent grave ('), and brackets ([ ]); however, the name cannot begin with a space, and cannot include control characters (ANSI values 0 through 31). In general, you should give your fields meaningful names and should use the same name throughout for a field that occurs in more than one table. You should avoid using field names that might also match any name internal to Microsoft Access or Visual Basic. For example, all objects have a Name property, so it's a good idea to qualify a field containing a name by calling it CustomerName or ClubName. You should also avoid names that are the same as built-in functions, such as Date, Time, Now, or Space. See Microsoft Access help for a list of all the built-in function names.

Although you can use spaces anywhere within names in Access, you should try to create field names and table names *without* embedded spaces. Most SQL databases to which Access can attach do not support spaces within names. If you ever want to move your application to a true client/server environment and store your data in an SQL database such as Microsoft SQL Server or Oracle, you'll have to change any names in your database tables that have an embedded space character. As you'll learn later in this book, table field names propagate into the queries, forms, reports, and data access pages that you design using these tables. So any name you decide to change later in a table must also be changed in all your queries, forms, reports, and data access pages.

You can choose a new option in Access 2000 called Track Name AutoCorrect that asks Access to track and correct field name references in queries, forms, and reports. If you choose Options from the Tools menu and then select this option on the General tab, Access maintains a unique internal ID number for all field names. When you change a field name in a table, Access automatically propagates the name change. However, this requires some additional overhead in all your tables, queries, forms, and reports, so carefully choosing names as you design your tables is a good idea.

TABLE 5-2. Access Data Types

Data Type	Usage	Size
Text	Alphanumeric data	Up to 255 characters
Memo	Alphanumeric data— sentences and paragraphs	Up to 64,000 characters
Number	Numeric data	1, 2, 4, or 8 bytes (16 bytes for ReplicationID and Decimal)
Date/Time	Dates and times	8 bytes
Currency	Monetary data, stored with 4 decimal places of precision	8 bytes
AutoNumber	Unique value generated by Access for each new record	4 bytes (16 bytes for ReplicationID)
Yes/No	Boolean (true/false) data	1 bit
OLE Object	Pictures, graphs, or other ActiveX objects from another Windows-based application	Up to about 1 gigabyte
Hyperlink	A link "address" to a document or file on the World Wide Web, on an intranet, on a local area network (LAN), or on your local computer	Up to 2048 characters

II

Building a Database

For each field in your table, select the data type that is best suited to how you will use that field's data. For character data, you should normally select the Text data type. You can control the maximum length of a Text field by using a field property, as explained later. Use the Memo data type only for long strings of text that might exceed 255 characters or that might contain formatting characters such as tabs or line endings (carriage returns).

When you select the Number data type, you should think carefully about what you enter as the Field Size property because this property choice will affect precision as well as length. (For example, integer numbers do not have decimals.) The Date/Time data type is useful for calendar or clock data and has the added benefit of allowing calculations in minutes, seconds, hours, days, months, or years. For example, you can find out the difference in days between two Date/Time values.

Use the Date/Time data type to store any date, time, or date and time value. It's useful to know that Access stores the date as the integer portion of the Date/Time data type and the time as the fractional portion—the fraction of a day, measured from midnight, that the time represents, accurate to seconds. For example, 6:00:00 AM internally is 0.25. The day number is actually the number of days since December 30, 1899 (there will be a test on that later!) and can be a negative number for dates prior to that date. When two Date/Time fields contain only a date, you can subtract one from the other to find out how many days are between the two dates.

 Always use the Currency data type for storing money values. Currency has the precision of integers, but with a fixed number of decimal places. When you need to store a precise fractional number that's not money, use the Number data type and choose the Decimal field size.

The AutoNumber data type is specifically designed for automatic generation of primary key values. Depending on the Field Size and New Values properties you choose for an AutoNumber field, you can have Access create a sequential or random long integer. You can include only one field using the AutoNumber data type in any table.

Use the Yes/No data type to hold Boolean (true or false) values. This data type is particularly useful for flagging accounts paid or not paid or orders filled or not filled.

The OLE Object data type allows you to store complex data, such as pictures, graphs, or sounds, that can be maintained by a dynamic link to another Windows-based application. For example, Access can store and allow you to edit a Microsoft Word document, a Microsoft Excel spreadsheet, a Microsoft PowerPoint presentation slide, a sound file (wav), a video file (avi), or pictures created using the Paint or Draw application.

The Hyperlink data type lets you store a simple or complex "link" to an external file or document. This link can contain a Uniform Resource Locator (URL) that points to a location on the World Wide Web or on a local intranet. It can also contain the Universal Naming Convention (UNC) name of a file on a server on your local area network (LAN) or on your local computer drives. The link can point to a file that is in Hypertext Markup Language (HTML) or in a format that is supported by an ActiveX application on your computer.

Field Properties

You can customize each field by setting specific properties. These properties vary according to the data type you choose. Tables 5-3 and 5-4 describe all of the possible properties for a field in a table.

TABLE 5-3. Field Properties on the General Tab

Data Type	Options, Description
Field Size property	
Text	Text can be from 0 through 255 characters long, with a default length of 50 characters.
Number	**Byte.** A single-byte integer containing values from 0 through 255.
	Integer. A 2-byte integer containing values from −32,768 through +32,767.
	Long Integer. A 4-byte integer containing values from −2,147,483,648 through +2,147,483,647.
	Single[1]. A 4-byte floating-point number containing values from -3.4×10^{38} through $+3.4 \times 10^{38}$.
	Double[1]. An 8-byte floating-point number containing values from -1.797×10^{308} through $+1.797 \times 10^{308}$.
	Replication ID[2]. A 16-byte Globally Unique Identifier (GUID).
	Decimal. A 16-byte integer with an assumed decimal precision containing values from -10^{28} through $+10^{28}$. The default precision is 0 and the default scale is 18.
Format property	
Text, Memo	You can specify a custom format that controls how Access displays the data. *For details about custom formats, see "Setting Control Properties" in Chapter 14 or the Access Help topic "Format Property—Text and Memo Data Types."*

1. Single and Double field sizes use an internal storage format called floating point that can handle very large or very small numbers, but which is somewhat imprecise. If the number you need to store contains more than 7 significant digits for a Single or more than 15 significant digits for a Double, the number will be rounded. For example, if you try to save 10,234,567 in a Single, the actual value stored will be 10,234,570. Likewise, 10.234567 stores as 10.23457 in a Single. If you want absolute fractional precision, use Decimal field size or Currency data type instead.

2. In general, the Replication ID field size should be used only in a database that is managed by the Replication Manager. *See Chapter 25, "After Completing Your Application," for details.*

(continued)

TABLE 5-3. *continued*

Data Type	Options, Description
Format property *continued*	
Number (except Replication ID), Currency, AutoNumber	**General Number** (default). No commas or currency symbols; decimal places shown depend on the precision of the data.
	Currency. Currency symbol (from Control Panel Regional Settings) and two decimal places.
	Euro. Euro currency symbol (regardless of Control Panel settings) and two decimal places.
	Fixed. At least one digit and two decimal places.
	Standard. Two decimal places and separator commas.
	Percent. Percentage (moves displayed decimal point two places to the right).
	Scientific. Scientific notation (for example, 1.05E+06 represents 1.05×10^6).
Date/Time	**General Date** (default). Combines Short Date and Long Time format (for example, 4/15/95 5:30:10 PM).
	Long Date. Uses Long Date Style from Regional Settings Properties in Windows Control Panel (for example, Saturday, April 15, 1995).
	Medium Date. 15-Apr-95.
	Short Date[3]. Uses Short Date Style from Regional Settings Properties (for example, 4/15/95).
	Long Time. Uses Time Style from Regional Settings Properties (for example, 5:30:10 PM).
	Medium Time. 5:30 PM.
	Short Time. 17:30.
Yes/No	**Yes/No** (default).
	True/False.
	On/Off.
Decimal Places property	
Number (except Replication ID), Currency	You can specify the number of decimal places that Access displays. The default specification is Auto, which causes Access to display two decimal places for the Currency, Fixed, Standard, and Percent formats and the number of decimal places necessary to show the current precision of the numeric value for General Number format. You can also request a fixed display of decimal places ranging from 0 through 15.

3. To help alleviate Y2K problems, I recommend that you use the new Use Four-Digit Year Formatting option in Access. Choose Options from the Tools menu, and then click the General tab to find this option. You should also change Short Date Style in Regional Settings Properties to a four-digit year.

TABLE 5-3. *continued*

Data Type	Options, Description
Input Mask property	
Text, Number (except Replication ID), Date/Time, Currency	You can specify an editing mask that the user sees while entering data in the field. For example, you can have Access provide the delimiters in a date field such as __/__/__, or you can have Access format a U.S. phone number as (###) 000-0000. *See the section titled "Defining Input Masks" later in this chapter for details.*
Caption property	
All	You can enter a more fully descriptive field name that Access displays in form labels and in report headings. (Note: If you create field names with no embedded spaces, you can use the Caption property to specify a name that includes spaces for Access to use in labels and headers associated with this field in queries, forms, and reports.)
Default Value property	
Text, Memo, Date/Time, Hyperlink	You can specify a default value for the field. The default for Default Value is Null.
Number, Currency	Default value is 0.
Yes/No	Default value is False.
Validation Rule property	
All (except OLE Object, Replication ID, and AutoNumber)	You can supply an expression that must be true whenever you enter or change data in this field. For example, *<100* specifies that a number must be less than 100. You can also check for one of a series of values. For example, you can have Access check for a list of valid cities by specifying *"Chicago" Or "New York" Or "San Francisco."* In addition, you can specify a complex expression that includes any of the built-in functions in Access. *See the section "Defining Simple Field Validation Rules" later in this chapter for details.*
Validation Text property	
All (except OLE Object, Replication ID, and AutoNumber)	You can have Access display text whenever the data entered does not pass your validation rule.

II

Building a Database

(continued)

TABLE 5-3. *continued*

Data Type	Options, Description
Required property	
All (except AutoNumber)	If you don't allow a Null value in this field, set this property to Yes.
Allow Zero Length property	
Text, Memo	You can set the field equal to a zero-length string ("") if you set this property to Yes. *See the sidebar titled "Nulls and Zero-Length Strings" on page 137 for more information.*
Indexed property	
Text, Number, Date/Time, Currency, AutoNumber, Yes/No	You can ask that an index be built to speed access to data values. You can also require that the values in the indexed field always be unique for the entire table. *See the section titled "Adding Indexes" later in this chapter for details.*
Unicode Compression property	
Text, Memo	You can ask Access to compress double-byte characters into single-byte when you do not need to store complex international characters in the field. The default for new tables is Yes in all countries where the standard language character set does not require two bytes to store all the characters.

TABLE 5-4.   Properties on the Lookup Tab

SEE ALSO
For details about lookup properties, see Chapter 6, "Modifying Your Database Design."

Property	Options, Description
Display Control	Specifies the default control type for displaying this field in datasheets, forms, and reports. For most fields, select Text Box. If the field is a foreign key *(see Chapter 4, "Designing Your Database Application")* that points to another table, you can select List Box or Combo Box to display meaningful values from the related table. You can also select List Box or Combo Box if this field must always contain one of a specific list of values.

TABLE 5-4. *continued*

Property	Options, Description
Row Source Type	When you select List Box or Combo Box for Display Control, set this property to indicate whether the list of valid values comes from a Table/Query, a Value List that you enter, or a Field List of names of fields from another table.
Row Source	If Row Source Type is Table/Query or Field List, specify the table or query providing the values for the list. If Row Source Type is Value List, enter the values, separating them by semicolons.
Bound Column	Specify which column in a multiple-column list provides the value that sets this field. If the Row Source is a single column, enter *1*.
Column Count	Enter the number of columns of information provided by the Row Source.
Column Heads	If Yes, the list displays the Caption for each column from the Row Source.
Column Widths	Enter the display width of the columns, separated by semicolons. If you do not want to display a column, enter a width of 0. For example, if this field is a code value, you might not want to display the code that you need to set the value, but you should display the description of the codes being supplied by another table or list. If Display Control is Combo Box, Access shows the value from the first nonzero-width column when the list is closed.
List Rows	When Display Control is Combo Box, specifies the number of rows to display in the combo box's list.
List Width	When Display Control is Combo Box, specifies the width of the combo box's list. The default value of Auto opens a list as wide as the combo box. If the width of the combo box is not wide enough to display all the values in the list, enter a specific value here to make sure the opened list displays all columns.
Limit To List	For combo boxes, if the field can contain only values supplied by the list, enter Yes. If you can enter values not contained in the list, enter No. (Note: If you don't display the bound column value as the first column, the combo box behaves as though you specified Yes for Limit To List.)

Completing the Fields in the Orders Table

You now know enough about field data types and properties to finish designing the Orders table in this example. (You can also follow this example using the tblOrders table from the Microsoft Press Books sample database.) Use the information listed in Table 5-5 to design the table shown in Figure 5-29.

Nulls and Zero-Length Strings

Relational databases support a special value in fields, called a *Null,* that indicates an unknown value. Nulls have special properties. A Null value cannot be equal to any other value, not even to another Null. This means you cannot join (link) two tables on Null values. Also, the test "A = B," when A, B, or both A and B contain a Null, can never yield a true result. Finally, Null values do not participate in aggregate calculations involving such functions as *Sum* or *Avg.* You can test a value to determine whether it is a Null by comparing it to the special keyword NULL or by using the *IsNull* built-in function.

In contrast, you can set Text or Memo fields to a *zero-length string* to indicate that the value of a field is known but the field is empty. You can join tables on zero-length strings, and two zero-length strings will compare to be equal. However, for Text, Memo, and Hyperlink fields, you must set the Allow Zero Length property to Yes to allow users to enter zero-length strings. Otherwise, Access converts a zero-length or all-blank string to a Null before storing the value. If you also set the Required property of the Text field to Yes, Access stores a zero-length string if the user enters either "" or blanks in the field.

Why is it important to differentiate Nulls from zero-length strings? Here's an example: Suppose you have a database that stores the results of a survey about automobile preferences. For questionnaires on which there is no response to a color-preference question, it is appropriate to store a Null. You don't want to match responses based on an "unknown" response, and you don't want to include the row in calculating totals or averages. On the other hand, some people might have responded "I don't care" for a color preference. In this case, you have a known "nothing" answer, and a zero-length string is appropriate. You can match all "I don't care" responses and include the responses in totals and averages.

Another example might be fax numbers in a customer database. If you store a Null, it means you don't know whether the customer has a fax number. If you store a zero-length string, you know the customer has no fax number. Access gives you the flexibility to deal with both types of "empty" values.

TABLE 5-5.   Field Definitions for the Orders Table

Field Name	Data Type	Description	Field Size
StoreID	Number	Optional store for Purchase Order	Long Integer
OrderDate	Date/Time	Date order was entered	
ShipName	Text	Ship-to name	50
ShipAddress	Text	Ship-to address	255
ShipCity	Text	Ship-to city	50
ShipStateOr Province	Text	Ship-to state/ province	20
ShipPostalCode	Text	Ship-to postal code	20
ShipCountry	Text	Ship-to country	50
ShipPhoneNumber	Text	Ship-to phone	30
PayBy	Number	1 = Cash, 2 = Check, 3 = American Express, 4 = Visa, 5 = MasterCard, 6 = Discover	Integer
CCNumber	Text	Credit card number	20
Printed	Yes/No	Order has been printed	

II

Building a Database

FIGURE 5-29.
The fields in the Orders table and a validation rule on the PayBy field.

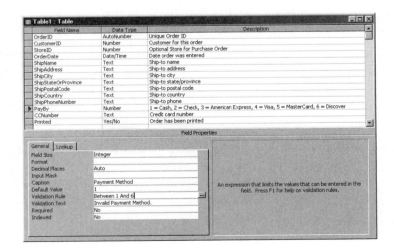

Defining Simple Field Validation Rules

To define a simple check on the values that you allow in a field, enter an expression in the Validation Rule property box for the field. Access won't allow you to enter a field value that violates this rule. Access performs this validation for data entered in a Table window in Datasheet view, in an updateable query, or in a form. You can specify a more restrictive validation rule in a form, but you cannot override the rule in the table by specifying a completely different rule in the form.

In general, a field validation expression consists of an operator and a comparison value. If you do not include an operator, Access assumes you want an "equals" (=) comparison. You can specify multiple comparisons separated by the Boolean operators OR and AND.

You should always enclose text string values in quotation marks. If one of your values is a text string containing blanks or special characters, you must enclose the entire string in quotation marks. For example, to limit the valid entries for a City field to the two largest cities in the state of California, enter *"Los Angeles" Or "San Diego"*. If you are comparing date values, you must enclose the date constants in pound sign (#) characters, as in *#01/15/95#*.

You can use the comparison symbols to compare the value in the field to a value or values in your validation rule. Comparison symbols are summarized in Table 5-6. For example, you might want to check that a numeric value is always less than 1000. To do this, enter *<1000*. You can use one or more pairs of comparisons to check that the value falls within certain ranges. For example, if you want to verify that a number is in the range of 50 through 100, enter either *>=50 And <=100* or *Between 50 And 100*. In the example in Figure 5-29 on the previous page, the *PayBy* code must be an integer value *Between 1 And 6*. That is, the code must be greater than or equal to 1 and less than or equal to 6.

Another way to test for a match in a list of values is to use the IN comparison operator. For example, to test for states surrounding the U.S. capital, enter *In ("Virginia", "Maryland")*.

If you need to validate a Text, Memo, or Hyperlink field against a matching pattern (for example, a postal code or a phone number), you can use the LIKE comparison operator. You provide a text string as a comparison value that defines which characters are valid in which

TABLE 5-6.   Comparison Symbols Used in Validation Rules

Operator	Meaning
<	Less than
<=	Less than or equal to
>	Greater than
>=	Greater than or equal to
=	Equal to
<>	Not equal to
IN	Test for "equal to" any member in a list; comparison value must be a list enclosed in parentheses
BETWEEN	Test for a range of values; comparison value must be two values (a low and a high value) separated by the AND operator
LIKE	Test a Text or Memo field to match a pattern string

positions. Access understands a number of *wildcard characters,* which you can use to define positions that can contain any single character, zero or more characters, or any single number. These characters are shown in Table 5-7.

TABLE 5-7.   LIKE Wildcard Characters

Character	Meaning
?	Any single character
*	Zero or more characters; used to define leading, trailing, or embedded strings that don't have to match any specific pattern characters
#	Any single digit

You can also specify that any particular position in the Text or Memo field can contain only characters from a list that you provide. To define a list of valid characters, enclose the list in brackets ([ ]). You can specify a range of characters within a list by entering the low value character, a hyphen, and the high value character, as in *[A-Z]* or *[3-7]*. If you want to test a position for any characters *except* those in a list, start the list with an exclamation point (!). Some examples of validation rules using LIKE are shown on the next page.

II

Building a Database

Validation Rule	Tests For
LIKE "#####" or LIKE "#####-####"	A U.S. ZIP Code
LIKE "[A-Z]#[A-Z] #[A-Z]#"	A Canadian postal code
LIKE "Smith*"	A string that begins with *Smith*
LIKE "*smith##*"	A string that contains *smith* followed by two numbers, anywhere in the string
LIKE "??00####"	An eight-character string that contains any first two characters followed by exactly two zeros and then any four digits
LIKE "[!0-9BMQ]*####"	A string that contains any character other than a number or the letter B, M, or Q in the first position and ends with exactly four digits

Defining Input Masks

To assist you in entering formatted data, Access allows you to define an *input mask* for any type of field except AutoNumber, Replication ID, Memo, OLE Object, Hyperlink, and Yes/No data types. You can use an input mask to do something as simple as forcing all letters entered to be uppercase or as complex as adding parentheses and dashes to phone numbers. You create an input mask by using the special mask definition characters shown in Table 5-8. You can also embed strings of characters that you want displayed for formatting or stored in the data field.

An input mask consists of three parts, separated by semicolons. The first part defines the mask string using mask definition characters and embedded fixed data. The optional second part indicates whether you want the formatting characters stored in the field in the database. Set this second part to 0 to store the characters or to 1 to store only the data entered. The optional third part defines the single character that Access uses as a placeholder to indicate positions where data can be entered. The default placeholder character is an underscore (_).

Perhaps the best way to learn to use input masks is to take advantage of the Input Mask Wizard. In the Orders table of the Books And Authors database, the ShipPhoneNumber field could benefit from the use of an input mask. Click the ShipPhoneNumber field in the upper part of the Table window in Design view, and then click in the Input Mask property box in the lower part of the window. You should see a small button with three dots on it (called a Build button) to the right of the property box, as shown in Figure 5-30 on page 144.

TABLE 5-8.   Input Mask Definition Characters

Mask Character	Meaning
0	A single digit must be entered in this position.
9	A digit or a space can be entered in this position. If the user skips this position by moving the cursor past the position without entering anything, Access stores nothing in this position.
#	A digit, a space, or a plus or minus sign can be entered in this position. If the user skips this position by moving the cursor past the position without entering anything, Access stores a space.
L	A letter must be entered in this position.
?	A letter can be entered in this position. If the user skips this position by moving the cursor past the position without entering anything, Access stores nothing.
A	A letter or a digit must be entered in this position.
a	A letter or a digit can be entered in this position. If the user skips this position by moving the cursor past the position without entering anything, Access stores nothing.
&	A character or a space must be entered in this position.
C	Any character or a space can be entered in this position. If the user skips this position by moving the cursor past the position without entering anything, Access stores nothing.
.	Decimal placeholder (depends on the setting in the Regional Settings section of Windows Control Panel).
,	Thousands separator (depends on the setting in the Regional Settings section of Windows Control Panel).
: ; - /	Date and time separators (depends on the settings in the Regional Settings section of Windows Control Panel).
<	Converts to lowercase all characters that follow.
>	Converts to uppercase all characters that follow.
!	Causes the mask to fill from right to left when you define optional characters on the left end of the mask. You can place this character anywhere in the mask.
\	Causes the character immediately following to be displayed as a literal character rather than as a mask character.
"literal"	You can also enclose any literal string in double quotation marks rather than use the \ character repeatedly.

II

Building a Database

FIGURE 5-30.

The Build button for the Input Mask property.

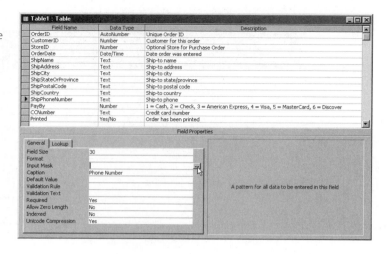

Click the Build button to start the Input Mask Wizard. If you haven't already saved the table, the wizard will insist that you do so. Save the table and name it "Orders." When Access warns you that you have not defined a primary key, and asks if you want to create a primary key now, click No. We'll define a primary key in the next section. In the first window, the wizard gives you a number of choices for "standard" input masks that it can generate for you. In this case, click the first one in the list—Phone Number. You'll see a dialog box like the one shown in Figure 5-31. Note that you can type something in the Try It box below the Input Mask selection box to try out the mask.

FIGURE 5-31.

Selecting an input mask in the Input Mask Wizard.

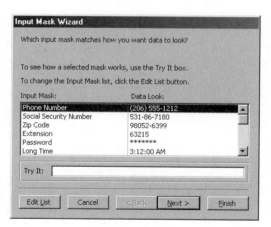

Click the Next button to go to the next window. In this window, shown in Figure 5-32, you can see the mask name, the proposed mask string, a drop-down list from which you select the placeholder character, and another Try It box. The default underscore character (_) works well as a placeholder character for phone numbers.

FIGURE 5-32.

Selecting the placeholder character in the Input Mask Wizard.

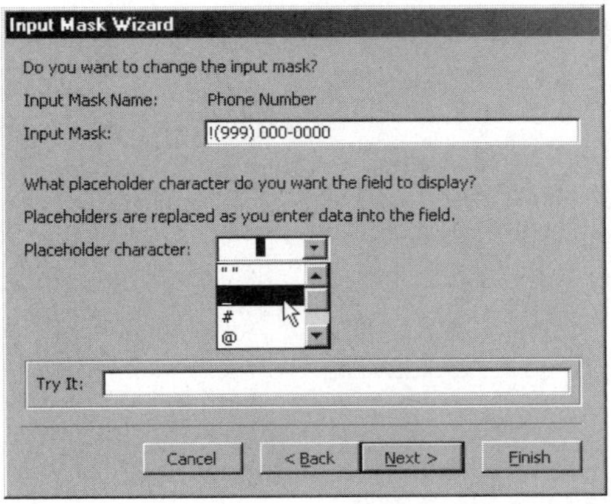

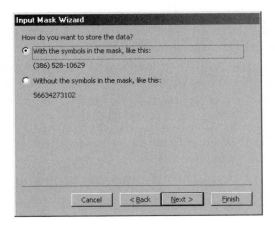

Click Next to go to the next window, where you can choose whether you want the data stored without the formatting characters (the default) or stored with the parentheses, spaces, and dash separator. In Figure 5-33, the data is going to be saved with the formatting characters. Click Next to go to the final window, and then click the Finish button in that window to store the mask in the property setting. Figure 5-34 on the next page shows the mask resulting in the ShipPhoneNumber field. You'll find this same mask handy for any text field that is meant to contain a U.S. phone number (such as the PhoneNumber field in the Customers table).

FIGURE 5-33.

Opting to store formatting characters.

Input Mask Wizard

How do you want to store the data?

○ With the symbols in the mask, like this:

(386) 528-10629

○ Without the symbols in the mask, like this:

56634273102

Cancel   < Back   Next >   Finish

FIGURE 5-34.

The field input mask for ShipPhoneNumber.

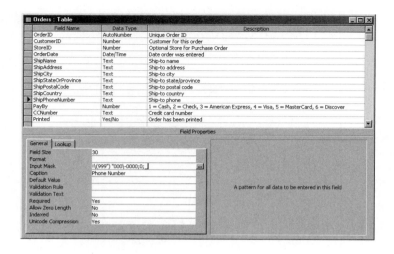

Defining a Primary Key

Every table in a relational database should have a primary key. If you use the procedure outlined in Chapter 4, "Designing Your Database Application," you should know what fields must make up the primary key for each of your tables.

Telling Microsoft Access how to define the primary key is quite simple. Open the table in Design view, and then select the first field for the primary key by clicking the row selector to the left of that field's name. If you need to select multiple fields for your primary key, hold down the Ctrl key and click the row selector of each additional field you need.

After you select all the fields you want for the primary key, click the Primary Key button on the toolbar or choose the Primary Key command from the Edit menu. Access displays a key symbol to the left of the selected field(s) to acknowledge your definition of the primary key. *To eliminate all primary key designations, see the section titled "Adding Indexes" later in this chapter.* When you've finished creating the Orders table for the Books And Authors database, the primary key should be the OrderID field, as shown in Figure 5-35.

Be sure to click the Save button on the toolbar to save this latest change to your table definition.

FIGURE 5-35.

The Orders table with a primary key defined.

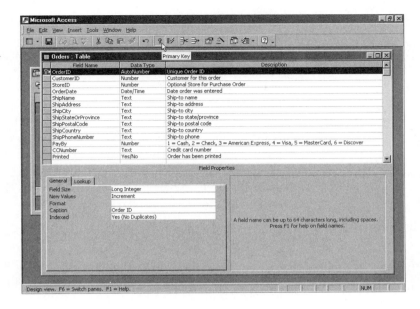

Defining a Table Validation Rule

The last detail to define is any validation rules that you want Microsoft Access to apply to any fields in the table. Although field validation rules get checked as you enter each new value, Access checks a table validation rule only when you save or add a row. Table validation rules are handy when the values in one field are dependent on what's stored in another field. You need to wait until the entire row is about to be saved before checking one field against another. To define a table validation rule, be sure that the table is in Design view, and then click the Properties button on the toolbar or choose the Properties command from the View menu to open the Table Properties window, shown in Figure 5-36.

FIGURE 5-36.

Defining a table validation rule.

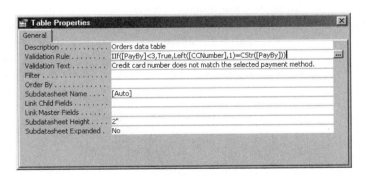

In the Table Properties window, you can enter a description of the table on the first line. On the second line, you can enter any valid comparison expression. In the Orders table in your Books And Authors database (or the tblOrders table in the Microsoft Press Books sample database), the code in the PayBy field serves as a validation check against the credit card number entered. If the value of PayBy is 1 (cash) or 2 (check), no further check of the credit card number need be made. If payment is by credit card, the leading digit of the credit card number should match the PayBy code. (I bet you didn't realize that all American Express cards start with the digit 3, Visa with 4, MasterCard with 5, and Discover with 6! This provides a simple cross-check between the code and the card number.)

To refer to a field name, enclose the name in brackets ([ ]), as shown in Figure 5-36 on the previous page. You'll use this technique whenever you refer to the name of an object anywhere in an expression. In this case, we're using several built-in functions in the table validation rule to perform the test on PayBy and CCNumber fields. First there's a handy built-in function named *Immediate If* (or *IIF* for short) that can evaluate a test in the first argument and then return the evaluation of the second argument if the first argument is true or the evaluation of the third argument if the first argument is false. Note that I said *evaluation of the argument*—this means I can enter additional tests, even another IIF, in the second and third arguments.

? SEE ALSO

To learn more about expressions, see the sections "Using the Expression Builder" in Chapter 8. You can learn more about expressions by asking the Office Assistant about "building an expression."

So, the first argument uses IIF to evaluate the expression *[PayBy] < 3*—is the value in the field named PayBy less than 3? If this is true, IIF will return the evaluation of the second argument. Since we're not interested in performing any other test if PayBy is 1 or 2, returning True in the second argument causes the entire validation rule to evaluate to True—and there's no error. If PayBy is 3 or greater, IIF evaluates the third argument: is the first digit of the CCNumber field equal to what's in the PayBy field? There's another handy built-in function, Left, that can return any number of characters from the left of a text field. We need only the first character from CCNumber, hence *Left([CCNumber], 1)*. The Left function returns text, but PayBy is a number. To get a valid comparison, we need to either convert the one text character from CCNumber to a number or convert PayBy to text (also known as a string). I chose to use a built-in function named CStr (Convert to String) to make sure I'm comparing "apples" to "apples"—to see if the first character of the credit card matches the PayBy value. As you might imagine, once you become more familiar with building expressions and with the available built-in functions, you can create very sophisticated table validation rules.

? **SEE ALSO**

For a list of all the available built-in functions, see the topic "Functions Reference" in Access Help.

On the third line in the Table Properties window, enter the text that you want Access to display whenever the table validation rule is violated. Additional table properties you can define include Filter and Order By. Filter lets you predefine criteria to limit the data displayed in the Datasheet view of this table. *You'll learn more about filters in Chapter 7, "Using Datasheets."* You can use Order By to define one or more fields that define the default display sequence of rows in this table when in Datasheet view. If you don't define an Order By property, Access displays the rows in primary key sequence.

Defining Relationships

After you have defined two or more related tables, you should tell Microsoft Access how the tables are related. If you do this, Access will be able to link all your tables when you need to use them in queries, forms, data access pages, or reports.

To define relationships, you need to return to the Database window by closing any Table windows that are open and then clicking in the Database window to make it active. Then choose the Relationships command from the Tools menu. If this is the first time you have defined relationships in this database, Access opens a blank Relationships window and opens the Show Table dialog box, shown in Figure 5-37.

FIGURE 5-37.

The Show Table dialog box.

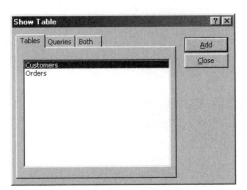

In the Show Table dialog box, select each table and click the Add button in turn. Click Close to dismiss the Show Table dialog box. Your Relationships window should now look like the one shown in Figure 5-38 on the next page.

FIGURE 5-38.
The Customers and Orders database tables in the Relationships window.

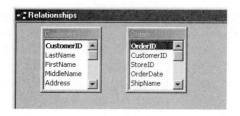

Defining Your First Relationship

If you remember the design work you did in Chapter 4, "Designing Your Database," you know that a customer can have several outstanding orders, but any order can apply to only one customer. This means that customers have a one-to-many relationship with orders. You can see that for the CustomerID primary key in the Customers table, there is a matching CustomerID foreign key in the Orders table. To create the relationship you need, click in the CustomerID field in the Customers table and drag it to the CustomerID field in the Orders table, as shown in Figure 5-39.

FIGURE 5-39.
Dragging the linking field from the "one" table (Customers) to the "many" table (Orders).

When you release the mouse button, Access opens the Edit Relationships dialog box, shown in Figure 5-40.

FIGURE 5-40.
The Edit Relationships dialog box.

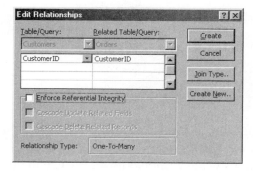

You'll notice that Access has filled in the field names for you. If you need to define a multiple-field relationship between two tables, use the additional blank lines to define those fields. Because you probably don't want any orders lying around for nonexistent customers, click the Enforce Referential Integrity check box. When you do this, Access ensures that you can't add an order for an invalid CustomerID. Also, Access won't let you delete any records from the Customers table if they have orders outstanding.

Note that after you click the Enforce Referential Integrity check box, Access makes two additional options available: Cascade Update Related Fields and Cascade Delete Related Records. If you select Cascade Delete Related Records, Access deletes child rows (the related rows in the "many" table of a one-to-many relationship) when you delete a parent row (the related row in the "one" table of a one-to-many relationship). If you decide to remove a customer from the database, it's probably a good idea to remove the customer's orders. If you select Cascade Delete Related Records, Access will remove the orders for you. In this database design, the CustomerID field has the AutoNumber data type, so it cannot be changed once it is set. However, if you build a table with a primary key that is Text or Number (perhaps a ProductID field that could change at some point in the future), it might be a good idea to select Cascade Update Related Fields. This option requests that Access automatically update any foreign key values in "child" tables (the "many" table in a one-to-many relationship) if you change a primary key value in a "parent" table (the "one" table in a one-to-many relationship).

You probably noticed that the Show Table dialog box, shown earlier in Figure 5-37, gives you the option to include queries as well as tables. Sometimes you might want to define relationships between tables and queries or between queries so that Access knows how to join them properly. You can also define what's known as an *outer join* by clicking the Join Type button in the Relationships dialog box and selecting an option in the Join Properties dialog box. With an outer join, you can find out, for example, which customers have no orders or which books haven't been sold.

? SEE ALSO

For details about outer joins, see the section titled "Outer Joins" in Chapter 8.

After you click the Create button to finish your relationship definition, Access draws a line between the two tables to indicate the relationship. Notice that when you ask Access to enforce referential integrity, Access displays a 1 at the end of the relationship line, next to the "one" table, and an infinity symbol (∞) next to the "many" table. If you want to delete the relationship, click the line and press the Delete key.

II

Building a Database

If you want to edit or change the relationship, double-click the line to open the Relationships dialog box again. Figure 5-41 shows the Relationships window for all the main tables in the Microsoft Press Books sample database.

FIGURE 5-41.

The Relationships window showing all the main tables in the Microsoft Press Books database.

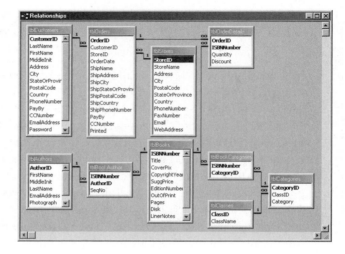

Note that once you define a relationship, you can delete the table or query field lists from the Relationships window without affecting the relationships. To do this, click the table or query list header and press the Delete key. This can be particularly advantageous in large databases that have dozens of tables. You can also display only those tables that you're working with at the moment. To see the relationships defined for any particular table or query, include it in the Relationships window by using the Show Table dialog box, and then click the Show Direct Relationships button on the toolbar or choose Show Direct from the Relationships menu. To redisplay all relationships, click the Show All Relationships button on the toolbar or choose Show All from the Relationships menu.

When you close the Relationships window, Access asks whether you want to save your layout changes. Click Yes to save the relationships you've defined. That's all there is to it. Later, when you use multiple tables in a query in Chapter 8, "Adding Power with Select Queries," you'll see that Access builds the relationships among tables based on these relationships.

NOTE

> You can right-click any table in the Relationships window and then choose Table Design from the shortcut menu to open that table in Design view. You can also choose Print Relationships from the File menu while viewing the Relationships window to create a report that prints what you have laid out in the window.

Adding Indexes

The more data you include in your tables, the more you need indexes to help Microsoft Access search your data efficiently. An *index* is simply an internal table that contains two columns: the value in the field or fields being indexed and the location of each record in your table that contains that value. Let's assume that you often search your Customers table by city. Without an index, when you ask Access to find all the customers in the city of Bellevue, Access has to search every record in your table. This search is fast if your table includes only a few customers but very slow if the table contains hundreds of customer records collected over many years. If you create an index on the City field, Access can use the index to more rapidly find the records for the customers in the city you specify.

Single Field Indexes

Most of the indexes you'll need to define will probably contain the values from only a single field. Access uses this type of index to help narrow down the number of records it has to search whenever you provide search criteria on the field—for example, *City = Redmond* or *PostalCode = 98052*. If you have defined indexes for multiple fields and provided search criteria for more than one of the fields, Access uses the indexes together (using a technology called Rushmore from Microsoft FoxPro) to find the rows you want quickly. For example, if you have created indexes on City and LastName and you ask for *City = Redmond* and *LastName = "Viescas",* Access uses the rows in the City index that equal *Redmond* and matches those with the rows in the LastName index that equal *Viescas*. The result is a small set of pointers to the records that match both criteria.

Creating an index on a single field in a table is easy. Open the table in Design view, and select the field for which you want an index—in this case, StateOrProvince. Click the Indexed property box in the lower part of the Table window, and then click the down arrow to drop down the list of choices, as shown in Figure 5-42 on the next page.

II

Building a Database

FIGURE 5-42.

Using the Indexed property box to set an index on a single field.

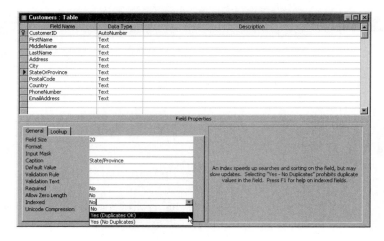

When you create a table from scratch (as you did earlier in this chapter for the Orders table), the default Indexed property setting for all fields except the primary key is No. If you use the Table Wizard to create a table (the Customers table in this chapter), the wizard indexes fields that might benefit from an index. If you followed along earlier using the Table Wizard to build the Customers table, you will find that the wizard built indexes for the EmailAddress, LastName, and PostalCode fields. You can find this table saved as *CustomerWiz* in the Books And Authors sample database.

If you want to set an index for a field, Access offers two possible Yes choices. In most cases, a given field will have multiple records with the same value—perhaps you have multiple customers in a particular state or province or multiple books published in the same year. You should select Yes (Duplicates OK) to create an index for this type of field. By selecting Yes (No Duplicates) you can use Access to enforce unique values in any field by creating an index that doesn't allow duplicates. Access always defines the primary key index with No Duplicates because, as you learned in Chapter 4, all primary key values must be unique.

> **NOTE**
>
> You cannot define an index using a Memo or OLE Object field.

Multiple Field Indexes

If you often provide multiple criteria in searches against large tables, you might want to consider creating a few multiple field indexes. This helps Access narrow the search quickly without having to match values from two separate indexes. For example, suppose you often perform a search for customers who have a particular last name, first name, and middle name. If you create an index that includes all of these fields, Access can satisfy your query more rapidly.

To create a multiple field index, you must open the Table window in Design view and open the Indexes window (shown in Figure 5-43) by clicking the Indexes button on the toolbar or by choosing the Indexes command from the View menu. You can see the primary key index and the index that you defined on StateOrProvince in the previous section. Each of these indexes comprises exactly one field.

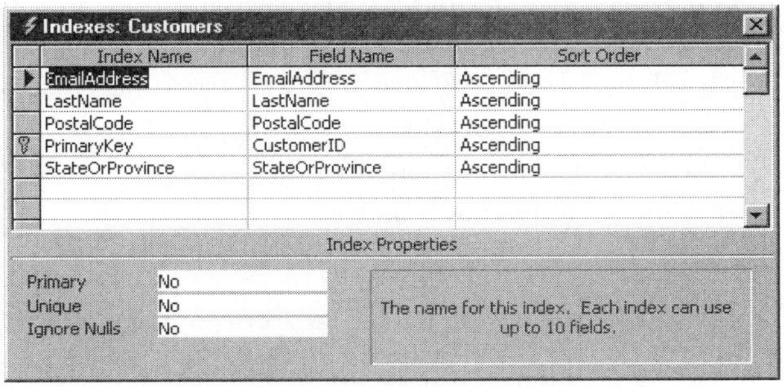

FIGURE 5-43.

The indexes for the Customers table shown in the Indexes window.

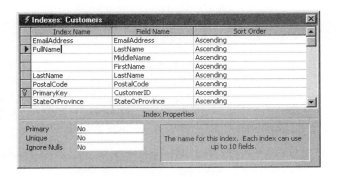

To create a multiple field index, move the cursor to an empty row in the Indexes window and type a unique name. In this example, you want a multiple field index using the LastName, FirstName, and MiddleName fields, so *FullName* might be a reasonable index name. Select the LastName field in the Field Name column of this row. To add the other fields, simply skip down to the next row and select another field without typing a new index name. When you're done, your Indexes window should look like the one shown in Figure 5-44.

FIGURE 5-44.

The FullName index includes the LastName, FirstName, and MiddleName fields.

NOTE

> You can remove an existing index by simply highlighting the row (by clicking the row selector) that defines the index and then pressing the Delete key. Any indexes you define, change, or delete are saved when you save the table definition.

Access can use a multiple field index in a search even if you don't provide search values for all the fields, as long as you provide search criteria for consecutive fields starting with the first field. Therefore, in the multiple field index shown in Figure 5-44 on the previous page, you can search for last name; for last name and first name; or for last name, first name, and middle name. There's one additional limitation on when Access can use multiple field indexes: only the last search criterion you supply can be an inequality, such as >, >=, <, or <=. In other words, Access can use the index shown in Figure 5-44 when you specify searches such as this:

LastName = "Smith"

LastName > "Franklin"

LastName = "Buchanan" And FirstName = "Steven"

LastName = "Viescas" And FirstName >= "Bobby"

But Access will not use the index shown in Figure 5-44 if you ask for

LastName > "Davolio" And FirstName > "John"

because only the last field in the search (FirstName) can be an inequality. Access also will not use this index if you ask for

FirstName = "John"

because the first field (LastName) is missing from the search criterion.

Printing a Table Definition

After you create several tables, you might want to print out their definitions to provide a permanent paper record. You can do this by choosing Analyze from the Tools menu and then choosing Documenter from the submenu. Microsoft Access displays several options in the Database Documenter dialog box, as shown in Figure 5-45.

You can select not only the type of object you want to document but also which objects you want to document. Click the Options button to select what you want reported. For example, you can ask for the properties, relationships, and permissions for a table; the names, data types, sizes, and properties for fields; and the names, fields, and prop-

FIGURE 5-45.

The Database
Documenter dialog
box.

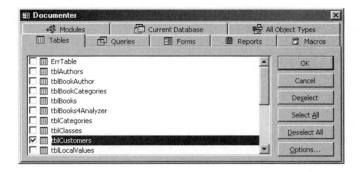

erties for indexes. Click OK in the Database Documenter dialog box to
produce the report and view it in Print Preview.

Database Limitations

As you design your database, you should keep in mind the following
limitations.

- A table can have up to 255 fields.

- A table can have up to 32 indexes.

- A multiple field index can have up to 10 columns. The sum of
  the lengths of the columns cannot exceed 255 bytes.

- A row in a table, excluding memo fields and ActiveX objects,
  can be no longer than approximately 4 kilobytes.

- A memo field can store up to 2 gigabytes, but you can't display
  a memo larger than 64 kilobytes in a form or a datasheet.

- An ActiveX object can be up to 2 gigabytes in size.

- There is no limit on the number of records in a table, but an Access database cannot be larger than 2 gigabytes. If you have several large tables, you might need to define each one in a
  separate Access database and then attach them to the database
  that contains the forms, reports, macros, and modules for your
  applications. *See Chapter 10, "Importing, Attaching, and Exporting Data," for details.*

Now that you've started to get comfortable with creating databases and
tables, you can read the next chapter to learn how to make modifications to tables in an existing database.

II

Building a Database

CHAPTER 6

Modifying Your Database Design

N o matter how carefully you design your database, you can be sure that you'll need to change it at some later date. Here are some of the reasons you might need to change your database.

- You no longer need some of the tables.

- You need to perform some new tasks that require not only creating new tables but also inserting some linking fields in existing tables.

- You find that you use some fields in a table much more frequently than others, so it would be easier if those fields appeared first in the table design.

- You no longer need some of the fields.

- You want to add some new fields that are similar to fields that already exist.

- You discover that some of the data you defined would be better stored as a different data type. For example, a field that you originally designed to be all numbers (such as a U.S. ZIP Code) must now contain some letters (as in a Canadian postal code).

- You have a number field that needs to hold larger values or needs a different number of decimal places than you originally planned.

- You can improve your database design by splitting an existing table into two or more tables using the Table Analyzer Wizard.

- You discover that the field you defined as a primary key isn't always unique, so you need to change the definition of your primary key.

- You find that some of your queries take too long to run and might execute faster if you add an index to your table.

This chapter takes a look at how you can make these changes easily and relatively painlessly with Microsoft Access. If you want to follow along with the examples in this chapter, you should first create the Books And Authors database described in Chapter 5, "Building Your Database in Microsoft Access."

> **NOTE**

> You might have noticed that the Customers table you defined for the Books And Authors database in Chapter 5 is different from the tblCustomers table in the Microsoft Press Books database on the companion CD that comes with this book. In this chapter, you'll modify the Customers table you built in Chapter 5 so that it is more like the one on the companion CD. You'll also learn how to use the Table Analyzer Wizard to help you "normalize" an existing table that contains data from several subjects.

Before You Get Started

Microsoft Access makes it easy for you to change the design of your database, even when you already have data in your tables. You should, however, understand the potential impact of any changes you plan and take steps to ensure that you can recover your previous design if you make a mistake. Here are some things to consider before you make changes.

- Access does not automatically propagate changes that you make in tables to any queries, forms, reports, macros, data access pages, or modules. You must make changes to dependent objects yourself, or choose Options from the Tools menu and then select the option on the General tab to ask Access to autocorrect table field name changes for you. *See "Changing Field Names" in this chapter for more details.*

You can determine which objects use the tables or fields you plan to change by using the Database Documenter. (Choose Analyze from the Tools menu, and then choose Documenter from the submenu.)

- You cannot change the data type of a field that is part of a relationship between tables. You must first delete the relationship, and then change the field's data type and redefine the relationship.

- You cannot change the definition of any table that you have open in a query, a form, a data access page, or a report. You must close any objects that refer to the table you want to change before you open that table in Design view. If you give other users access to your database over a network, you won't be able to change the table definition if someone else has the table (or a query or form based on the table) open.

Before committing any changes that permanently alter or delete data in your database, Access always prompts you for confirmation and gives you a chance to cancel the operation.

Making a Backup Copy

The safest way to make changes to the design of your database is to make a backup copy of the database before you begin. If you expect to make extensive changes to several tables in your database, you should also make a copy of the mdb file that contains your database by using a utility such as Windows Explorer.

If you want to change a single table, you can easily make a backup copy of that table right in your database. Use the following procedure to copy any table structure (the contents of the Table window in Design view), table data (the contents of the Table window in Datasheet view), or the structure and the data together.

1 Open the database containing the table you want to copy. If the database is already open, click the Tables button in the Database window.

2 Select the table you want to copy by clicking the table's name or icon in the Database window. The table name will be highlighted.

II

Building a Database

3 Choose the Copy command from the Edit menu (as shown in Figure 6-1), or click the Copy button on the toolbar. This copies the entire table (structure and data) to the Clipboard.

FIGURE 6-1.
Using the Copy command to copy a table from the Tables list.

4 Choose the Paste command from the Edit menu, or click the Paste button on the toolbar. Access opens the Paste Table As dialog box, shown in Figure 6-2. Type in a new name for your table. (When naming a backup copy, you might simply add *Backup* and the date to the original table name, as shown in Figure 6-2.) The default option is to copy both the structure and the data. You also have the option of copying only the table's structure or of appending the data to another table.

FIGURE 6-2.
The Paste Table As dialog box.

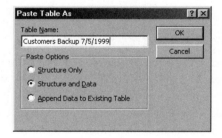

Deleting Tables

You probably won't need to delete an entire table very often. However, if you set up your application to collect historical information—for example, total book sales by year—you'll eventually want to delete information that you no longer need. You also might want to delete a table if you've made extensive changes that are incorrect and it would be easier to delete your work and restore the table from a backup.

To delete a table, select it in the Database window and press the Delete key (or choose the Delete command from the Edit menu). Access opens the dialog box shown in Figure 6-3, which asks you to confirm or cancel the delete operation. Even if you mistakenly confirm the deletion, you can immediately select the Undo command from the Edit menu to get your table back.

FIGURE 6-3.

This dialog box gives you the option of canceling the deletion of a table.

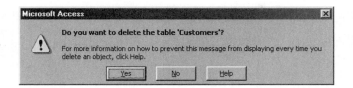

 **TIP**

You can use the Cut command on the Edit menu or the Cut button on the toolbar to delete a table. Both of these methods place a copy of the table on the Clipboard. After you close the database in which you've been working, you can open another database and paste the table that's on the Clipboard.

If the warning dialog box doesn't look exactly like Figure 6-3, it might be because you turned on features in the Microsoft Office Assistant. If you have the Office Assistant open and you chose the option to have it display alerts *(see Figure 5-12 and Table 5-1 in Chapter 5)*, the Office Assistant will respond with any Access warning message, as shown in Figure 6-4. In this message, the Links character stuck its nose forward and purred at me as part of its animation.

FIGURE 6-4.

The Office Assistant displaying the same table deletion warning as shown in Figure 6-3.

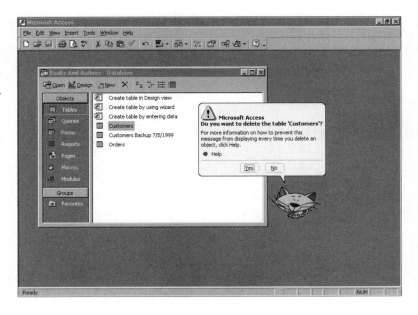

If you have defined relationships between the table you want to delete and other tables, Access displays another dialog box that alerts you and asks whether you want to also delete the relationships. If you click Yes, Access deletes all relationships between any other table and the table you want to delete and then deletes the table. Even at this point, if you find you made a mistake, you can immediately choose Undo from the Edit menu to restore both the table and all its relationships.

Renaming Tables

If you keep transaction data (such as receipts, deposits, or checks written), you might want to save that data at the end of each month in a table with a unique name. One way to save your data is to rename the existing table (perhaps by adding a date to the name). You can then create a new table (perhaps by making a copy of the backup table's structure) to start collecting information for the next month.

To rename a table, select it in the Database window and choose the Rename command from the Edit menu. Access places the name in edit mode in the Database window so that you can type in a new name, as shown in Figure 6-5. Type in the new name, and press Enter to save it.

FIGURE 6-5.

Renaming a table in the Database window.

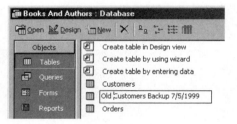

You can also place the name of an object in edit mode by selecting it in the Database window, waiting a second, and then clicking the name again. This works just like it would in Windows Explorer.

If you enter the name of a table that already exists, Access displays a dialog box that asks whether you want to replace the existing table, as shown in Figure 6-6. If you click Yes, Access deletes the old table before performing the renaming operation. Even if you replace an existing table, you can undo the renaming operation by immediately choosing the Undo command from the Edit menu.

FIGURE 6-6.

This dialog box asks whether you want to replace an existing table with the same name.

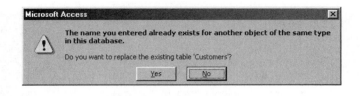

 **TIP**

You can use the techniques you just learned for copying, renaming, and deleting tables to copy, rename, and delete queries, forms, reports, data access pages, macros, or modules.

Changing Field Names

Perhaps you misspelled a field name when you first created one of your tables. Or perhaps you've decided that one of the field names isn't descriptive enough. You won't want the hassle of giving the field a caption every time it appears in a query, a form, or a report. Fortunately, Microsoft Access makes it easy to change a field name in a table—even if you already have data in the table.

 NOTE

The next several examples in this chapter show you how to change the Customers table that you created in the previous chapter to more closely match the tblCustomers table in the Microsoft Press Books sample database.

Assume that you created the first draft of the Customers table by using a wizard. Now you need to make a few changes so that it will hold all the data fields that you need for your application. You bypassed your chance in the wizard to rename all sample fields when you originally selected them, but now you decide to rename one of the fields before beginning work on the rest of your application.

Renaming a field is easy. For example, you chose the field "MiddleName" in the wizard, but you've decided that you need only the customer's middle initial in this database. It makes sense to change the field name to reflect the actual data you intend to store in the field. (Later in this chapter, you'll see how to shorten the length of the field.) Open the Customers table in the Books And Authors database in Design view, and then move the cursor to the MiddleName field. Use the mouse to highlight the characters "Name" at the end of the field name, and then type *Init*. You can also click in the field name, use the arrow keys to position the cursor just before the letter *N*, press the Delete key to remove the characters you don't want, and type in the new ones. While you're at it, press F6 to jump down to the Field Properties area of the window and change the field caption. Your result should look something like Figure 6-7.

FIGURE 6-7.

Changing a field name and a field caption in Design view.

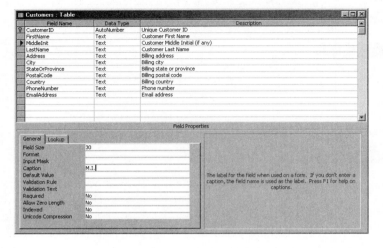

 NOTE

If you have any queries, forms, reports, modules, or macros that use a field you've renamed, you must also change the field name in those other objects. You can determine which objects use this field by running the Database Documenter (choose Analyze from the Tools menu, and then choose Documenter from the submenu) for your forms, reports, and queries. If you save the Database Documenter reports, you can use the search capabilities of most text editors to find references to the old name. You can also turn on the Name AutoCorrect feature in Access to track field name changes and auto-matically correct the name in your queries, forms, and reports. Using this fea-ture, however, does not fix all uses of the name in expressions.

You might not be concerned about changing field names as you create the initial design for your tables, but changing a field name after you have designed dozens of queries, forms, or reports can be a big prob-lem. Before Access 2000, you had to track down all uses of the field and make each change by hand. Access 2000 introduces a new feature to help propagate any change you make to the name of a field in a table to all objects that use that field. This Name AutoCorrect feature finds and changes any simple use of a field in queries, forms, and re-ports. In some cases, Name AutoCorrect also finds and corrects field names used in expressions in calculated fields. *For more information about expressions, see Chapter 8, "Adding Power with Select Queries."*

To turn on the Name AutoCorrect features, choose Options from the Tools menu. Click the General tab to see the Name AutoCorrect feature options, as shown in Figure 6-8. Select Track Name AutoCorrect Info to turn on the tracking facility. You must turn on this option before you make any field changes for Name AutoCorrect to work. Select the Perform Name AutoCorrect option to correct any field name changes when you save the table. Select the Log Name AutoCorrect Changes option to ask Access to create a table called "Name AutoCorrect Log" where you can verify the changes made by this feature.

FIGURE 6-8.

Choosing Name AutoCorrect options.

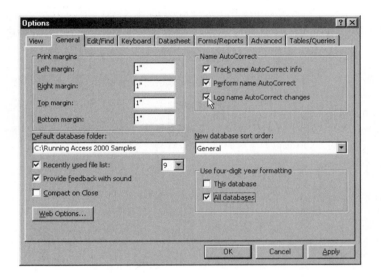

II

Building a Database

> **NOTE**

Although many options in the Options dialog box apply to your use of Access in general, the Name AutoCorrect options apply only to the database you currently have open. If you want to turn on AutoCorrect in another database, you must first open the database, and then set the options again.

Inserting Fields

Perhaps one of the most common changes you'll make to your database is to insert a new field in a table. In the preceding exercise, you changed the field name MiddleName in the Customers table to MiddleInit. If you compare this table to the tblCustomers table in the Microsoft Press Books sample database, you can see that a few more fields are needed. Now you're ready to insert fields to store the customer payment method and a credit card number, a sign-on password field, and a Yes/No field indicating whether users have "admin" status. (As you'll see later when we explore the application, an admin user can update book and author data.)

First, you must select the row or move your cursor to the row that defines the field *after* the point where you want to insert the new field. In this case, if you want to insert fields for the payment method and credit card number between the PhoneNumber and EmailAddress fields, place the cursor anywhere in the row that defines the EmailAddress field or select the entire row (by using the arrow keys or by clicking the row selector). Next, choose the Rows command from the Insert menu (as shown in Figure 6-9) or click the Insert Row button on the toolbar.

FIGURE 6-9.

The Insert Rows command inserts a new row above a selected row or above the row in which the cursor is located.

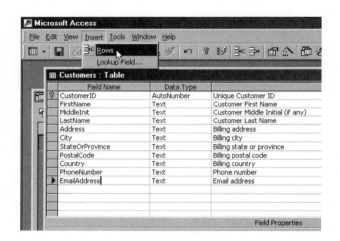

Microsoft Access adds a blank row that you can use to define your new field. Type in the definition for the PayBy field. Choose the Number data type, and set the Field Size property to Integer. Move down to the EmailAddress field again, and insert another row above it. Enter a CCNumber field that has the Text data type with a field size of 20. Move down to the blank row beyond EmailAddress, and insert rows for a Password field that is text with a length of 16 and an Admin field that has the Yes/No data type. You can also type in field descriptions if you want to (note that the wizard didn't supply them). When you finish, your Table window in Design view should look something like the one shown in Figure 6-10. Don't worry about setting other properties just yet.

⭐ **TIP**

You can move the cursor between the upper part and the lower part of any Table or Query window in Design view by pressing F6.

FIGURE 6-10.

The Customers table with additional fields inserted.

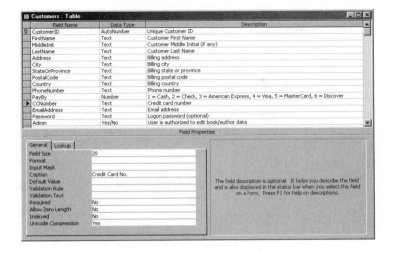

Copying Fields

As you create table definitions, you might find that several fields in your table are similar. Rather than enter each of the field definitions separately, you can enter one field definition, copy it, and then paste it as many times as necessary.

There's only a single field for the street address in the tblCustomers table in the Microsoft Press Books database. However, you might decide to add an optional second-line address field to handle more complex business addresses. You could certainly insert a new row and type in all the properties as you just did in the previous section, but why not copy a field that is similar?

CAUTION

If you choose the Paste command when a row containing data is selected, the copied row will *replace* the selected row. Should you make this replacement in error, choose the Undo command from the Edit menu to restore the original row.

For this exercise, select the row for the Address field definition by clicking the row selector at the far left of the row. Choose the Copy command from the Edit menu, or click the Copy button on the toolbar, as shown in Figure 6-11 on the next page. Move the insertion point to the row that should follow the row you'll insert. (In this case, move the insertion point to the City field, which should follow your new field.) Insert a blank row by choosing Rows from the Insert menu or by clicking the Insert Row button on the toolbar. Select the new row by clicking the row selector. Choose the Paste command from the Edit menu (or click the Paste button on the toolbar) to insert the copied row, as shown in Figure 6-12 on the next page. You can use the Paste command repeatedly to insert a copied row more than once. Remember to change both the name and the description of the resulting field or fields before you save the modified table definition. In this case, it's a simple matter to change the name of the copied row from Address to Address2. Note that this procedure also has the benefit of copying any formatting, default value, or validation rule information.

FIGURE 6-11.

The address field is selected and copied.

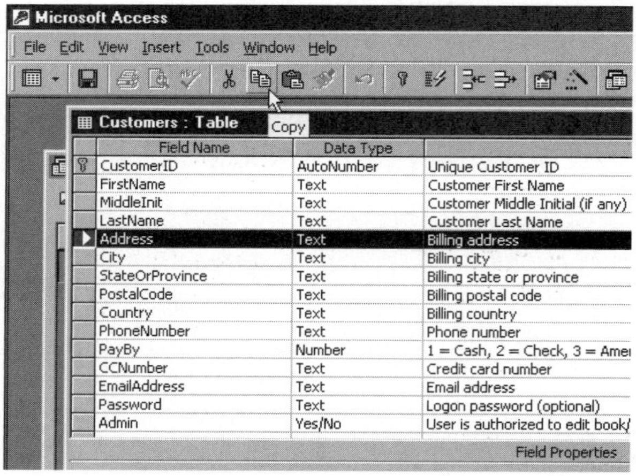

FIGURE 6-12.

The copied Address field can be pasted into a new blank row.

Deleting Fields

Removing unwanted fields is easy. With the Table window open in Design view, select the field that you want to delete by clicking the row selector. You can extend the selection to multiple contiguous fields by holding down the Shift key and using the up and down arrow keys to select multiple rows. You can also select multiple contiguous rows by clicking the row selector of the first row and, without releasing the mouse button, dragging up or down to select all the rows you want. After you select the appropriate fields, choose Delete or Delete Rows from the Edit menu or press the Delete key to delete the selected fields.

If a table contains one or more rows of data (in Datasheet view), Access displays a warning message when you delete field definitions in Design view, as shown in Figure 6-13. Click No if you think you made a mistake. Click Yes to proceed with the deletion of the fields and the data in those fields. (Again, if you have the Office Assistant open and you asked it to handle alerts, you'll see this message in an Office Assistant window.)

FIGURE 6-13.

This dialog box asks you to confirm a field deletion.

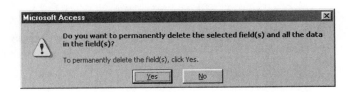

Moving Fields

You might want to move a row in a table definition for a number of reasons. Perhaps you made an error as you entered or changed the information in a table. Or perhaps you've discovered that you're using some fields you defined at the end of a table quite frequently in forms or reports, in which case it would be easier to find and work with those fields if they were nearer the beginning of your table definition.

You can use the mouse to move one or more rows. Simply follow these steps.

1 To select a row you want to move, click its row selector.

If you want to move multiple contiguous rows, click the row selector for the first row in the group and scroll until you can see the last row in the group. Hold down the Shift key and click the row selector for the last row in the group. The first and last rows and all rows in between will be selected. Release the Shift key.

2 Click and drag the row selector(s) for the highlighted row(s) to a new location. A small shaded box attaches to the bottom of the mouse pointer while you're dragging, and a highlighted line will appear, indicating the position to which the row(s) will move when you release the mouse button.

In the design for the tblCustomers table in the Microsoft Press Books database, the MiddleInit field appears between the FirstName and LastName fields. Let's assume you want the LastName field to appear first by default in all datasheets. Select the LastName field by clicking its row selector. Click the row selector again, and drag up until the line between the CustomerID field and the FirstName field is highlighted, as shown in Figure 6-14.

FIGURE 6-14.

The LastName field is being dragged to its new position between the CustomerID and FirstName fields.

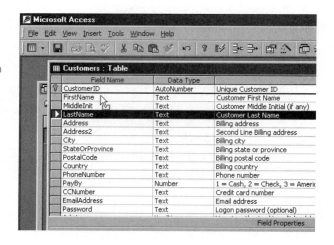

When it comes to moving fields, you might find it easier to use a combination of mouse and keyboard methods. Use the mouse to select the row or rows you want to move. Then activate Move mode by pressing Ctrl+Shift+F8, and use the arrow keys to position the row(s). Press Esc to deactivate Move mode. As you experiment with Access, you'll discover more than one way to perform many tasks, and you can choose the techniques that work the best for you.

In Figure 6-15, the fields are positioned correctly.

FIGURE 6-15.

The LastName field is now correctly placed.

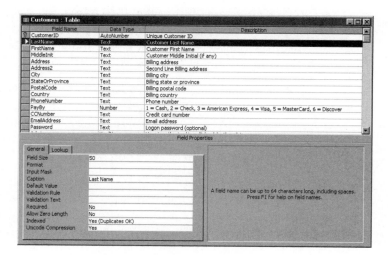

Changing Data Attributes

As you learned in the previous chapter, Microsoft Access provides a number of different data types. These data types help Access work more efficiently with your data and also provide a base level of data validation; for example, you can enter only numbers in a Number or Currency field.

When you initially design your database, you should match the data type and length of each field to its intended use. You might discover, however, that a field you thought would contain only numbers (such as a U.S. ZIP Code) must now contain some letters (perhaps because you've started doing business in Canada). You might find that one or more number fields need to hold larger values or a different number of decimal places. Access allows you to change the data type and length of many fields, even after you've entered data in them.

Changing Data Types

Changing the data type of a field in a table is simple. Open the table in Design view, click in the data type column of the field definition you want to change, click the down arrow button at the right to see the available choices, and select a new data type. You cannot convert an OLE Object or a ReplicationID to another data type. With a few limitations, Access can successfully convert every other data type to any other data type. Table 6-1 shows you the possible conversions and potential limitations.

TABLE 6-1.   Limitations on Converting One Data Type to Another

Convert To	Limitations
Convert from Text	
Memo	Access deletes indexes that include the text field.
Number	Text must contain only numbers and valid separators. The number value must be within the range for the Field Size.
Date/Time	Text must contain a recognizable date and/or time, such as 11-Nov-95 5:15 PM.
Currency	Text must contain only numbers and valid separators.
AutoNumber	Not possible if table contains data.

(continued)

Building a Database

II

TABLE 6-1. *continued*

Convert To	Limitations
Convert from Text *continued*	
Yes/No	Text must contain only one of the following values: Yes, True, On, No, False, or Off.
Hyperlink	Text must contain an optional description, link address (URL or UNC format), and optional subaddress separated by the "#" character. (Note: Access allows conversion of any text to Hyperlink, but the link won't work properly if it's not in the correct format.)
Convert from Memo	
Text	Access truncates text longer than 255 characters.
Number	Memo must contain only numbers and valid separators. The number value must be within the range for the Field Size.
Date/Time	Memo must contain a recognizable date and/or time, such as 11-Nov-95 5:15 PM.
Currency	Memo must contain only numbers and valid separators.
AutoNumber	Not possible if table contains data.
Yes/No	Memo must contain only one of the following values: Yes, True, On, No, False, or Off.
Hyperlink	Memo must contain an optional description, link address (URL or UNC format), and optional subaddress separated by the "#" character. (Note: Access allows conversion of any memo to Hyperlink, but the link won't work properly if it's not in the correct format.)
Convert from Number, except ReplicationID	
Text	No limitations.
Memo	No limitations.
Number (different precision)	Number must not be larger or smaller than can be contained in the new precision.
Date/Time	Number must be between −657,434 and 2,958,465.99998843.
Currency	No limitations.
AutoNumber	Not possible if table contains data.
Yes/No	Zero or Null = No; any other value = Yes.

TABLE 6-1. *continued*

Convert To	Limitations
Hyperlink	Possible, but Access converts the number to a text string in the form *[number]#http://[number]*, where *[number]* is the text conversion of the original numeric value; the result is probably not a valid link address.

Convert from Date/Time

Text	No limitations.
Memo	No limitations.
Number	If the Field Size is Byte, the date must be between April 18, 1899, and September 11, 1900. If the Field Size is Integer, the date must be between April 13, 1810, and September 16, 1989. For all other Field Sizes, there are no limitations.
Currency	No limitations, but value might be rounded.
AutoNumber	Not possible if table contains data.
Yes/No	12:00:00 AM or Null = No; any other value = Yes.
Hyperlink	Possible, but Access converts the date/time to a text string in the form *[date/time]#http://[date/time]*, where *[date/time]* is the text conversion of the original date or time value; the result is probably not a valid link address.

Convert from Currency

Text	No limitations.
Memo	No limitations.
Number	Number must not be larger or smaller than can be contained in the Field Size.
Date/Time	Number must be between –$657,434 and $2,958,465.99.
AutoNumber	Not possible if table contains data.
Yes/No	Zero or Null = No; any other value = Yes.
Hyperlink	Possible, but Access converts the currency value to a text string in the form *[currency]#http://[currency]*, where *[currency]* is the text conversion of the original currency value; the result is probably not a valid link address.

II

Building a Database

(continued)

TABLE 6-1. *continued*

Convert To	Limitations
Convert from AutoNumber	
Text	No limitations except ReplicationID.
Memo	No limitations.
Number	The number value must be within the range for the Field Size.
Date/Time	Value must be less than 2,958,466.
Currency	No limitations.
Yes/No	All values evaluate to Yes.
Hyperlink	Possible, but Access converts the number to a text string in the form *[number]#http://[number]*, where *[number]* is the text conversion of the original autonumber; the result is probably not a valid link address.
Convert from Yes/No	
Text	Yes = "Yes"; No = "No".
Memo	Yes = "Yes"; No = "No".
Number	Yes = −1; No = 0.
Date/Time	Yes = 12/29/1899; No = 12:00:00 AM.
Currency	Yes = −$1; No = 0.
AutoNumber	Not possible.
Hyperlink	Possible, but Access converts the yes/no to a text string in the form *[yes/no]#- http://[yes/no]*, where *[yes/no]* is the text conversion of the original yes ("−1") or no ("0") value; the result is probably not a valid link address.
Convert from Hyperlink	
Text	May lose some data if the hyperlink string is longer than 255 characters.
Memo	No limitations.
Number	Not possible.
Date/Time	Not possible.
Currency	Not possible.
AutoNumber	Not possible.
Yes/No	Not possible.

Changing Data Length

For text and number fields, you can define the maximum length of the data that can be stored in the field. Although a text field can be up to 255 characters long, you can restrict the length to as little as 1 character. If you don't specify a length for text, Access normally assigns a default length of 50 characters. Access won't let you enter text field data longer than the defined length. If you need more space in a text field, you can increase the length at any time; but if you try to redefine the length of a text field so that it's shorter, you will get a warning message (like the one shown in Figure 6-16) stating that Access will truncate a number of the data fields when you try to save the changes to your table.

TIP

You can change the default data type for a new field and the default length of new text and number fields by choosing Options from the Tools menu and then clicking the Tables/Queries tab of the Options dialog box.

FIGURE 6-16.
This dialog box informs you of possible data truncation problems.

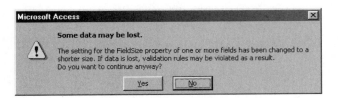

Sizes for numeric data types can vary from a single byte (which can contain a value from 0 through 255) to 2 or 4 bytes (for larger integers), 8 bytes (necessary to hold very large floating-point or currency numbers), or 16 bytes (to hold a unique ReplicationID or Number, Decimal). Except for ReplicationID, you can change the size of a numeric data type at any time, but you might generate errors if you make the size smaller. Access also rounds and truncates numbers when converting from floating-point data types (Single or Double) to integer or currency values.

Conversion Errors

When you try to save a modified table definition, Access always warns you if any changes to the data type or length will cause conversion errors. For example, if you change the Field Size property of a Number field from Integer to Byte, Access warns you if any of the records contain a number larger than 255. (Access deletes the contents of any field it can't convert.) If you examine Table 6-1, you'll see that you should

II

Building a Database

expect some data type changes to always cause problems. For example, if you change a field from Hyperlink to Date/Time, you can expect all data to be deleted. You'll see a dialog box similar to the one shown in Figure 6-17 warning you about fields that Access will set to a Null value if you proceed with your changes. Click the Yes button to proceed with the changes. You'll have to examine your data to correct any conversion errors.

FIGURE 6-17.

This dialog box informs you of conversion errors.

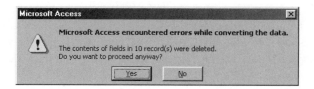

If you click the No button, Access opens the dialog box shown in Figure 6-18. If you deleted any fields or indexes, added any fields, or renamed any fields, Access will save those changes. Otherwise, the database will be unchanged. You can correct any data type or length changes you made, and then try to save the table definition again.

FIGURE 6-18.

This dialog box appears if you decide not to save a modified table definition.

Reversing Changes

If you make several changes and then decide you don't want any of them, you can close the Table window without saving it. When you do this, Access opens the dialog box shown in Figure 6-19. Simply click the No button to reverse all of your changes. Click the Cancel button to return to the Table window without saving or reversing your changes.

FIGURE 6-19.

This dialog box gives you the option of reversing unsaved changes to a table.

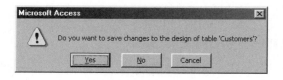

You can always reverse the last change you made by immediately choosing the Undo command from the Edit menu.

Using the Table Analyzer Wizard

Even if you follow all the recommendations in Chapter 4, "Designing Your Database Application," and build a normalized database, you might not arrive at the best design. In fact, you often cannot fully evaluate a database design until you use the database and store data. Access contains a Table Analyzer Wizard that can examine data in your tables (or data you import from another source) and recommend additional refinements and enhancements to your database design.

You'll recall from Chapter 4 that one of the key elements of good database design is the elimination of redundant data. The Table Analyzer Wizard is particularly good at scanning data in your tables, identifying data repeated in one or more columns, and recommending alterations to your design that break out the redundant data into separate "lookup" tables. You can find an example of such redundant data in the Microsoft Press Books database. Imagine that you downloaded a file containing book category information. Sounds like a good, easy place to start collecting book information. However, when you open the file, you see that most books are listed several times because the original data was sorted by category. You'll find just such a table, saved as tblBooks4Analyzer, in the Microsoft Press Books sample database.

You can see how the Table Analyzer Wizard works by using it on the tblBooks4Analyzer table. First, hold down the Shift key as you open the Microsoft Press Books database. This keeps Access from starting the application. *You'll learn more about startup properties in Chapter 24, "The Finishing Touches."* If you open the database in the normal way, you can return to the Database window by clicking the Exit button on the main switchboard form.

Choose Analyze from the Tools menu and then choose Table from the submenu. Access starts the Table Analyzer Wizard and displays the first window, shown in Figure 6-20 on the next page.

This first window is one of two introductory windows that explain what the wizard can do. Click the Show Me buttons to get a better understanding of the kinds of problems the wizard can solve and to see how the wizard works. Click Next twice to get to the first "action" window in the wizard, shown in Figure 6-21 on the next page.

FIGURE 6-20.

The opening window
of the Table Analyzer
Wizard.

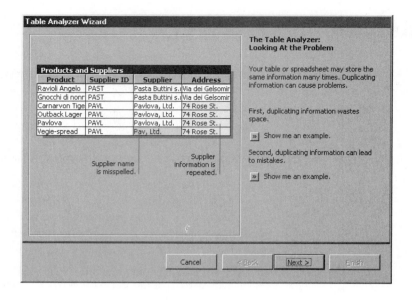

FIGURE 6-21.

Selecting the table
you want to analyze.

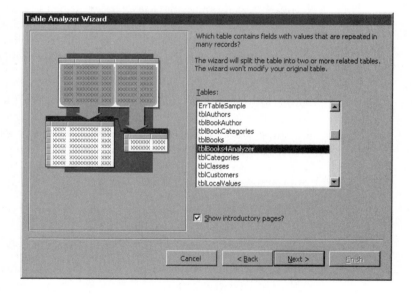

In this window, you select the table you want to analyze. For this exercise, select the tblBooks4Analyzer table. (Note that you have an option in this window to continue to show the two introductory windows each time you start the wizard. If you think you understand how the wizard works, you can clear the check box to skip the introductory windows the next time you start the wizard.) Click Next.

In the next window, the wizard asks if you want to rearrange the fields in the target table or if you want the wizard to decide the arrangement for you. If you know which fields contain redundant data, you can make the decision yourself. Because the wizard handles all the "grunt work" of splitting out lookup data, you might choose the latter option in the future to further normalize tables in your application. For now, select the Yes, Let The Wizard Decide option to see how effective it is. Click Next to start the analysis of your table. Figure 6-22 shows the result of the wizard's analysis. (I've shifted the contents of this figure to fit the result in a single window.)

FIGURE 6-22.

The initial recommendation of the Table Analyzer Wizard.

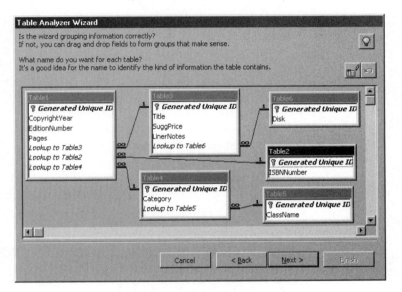

In this case, the wizard splits out the ISBNNumber, Title (along with SuggPrice and LinerNotes), Disk, Category, and ClassName fields into separate lookup tables. It does this because it sees lots of duplicated values in the sample data for these fields, but the wizard is not quite smart enough to see that any particular ISBNNumber always has the same Title, SuggPrice, and LinerNotes. The wizard did a good job by identifying Category as a separate lookup table, with ClassName as a lookup table related to Category rather than to the original data.

If you remember from the database design exercise in Chapter 4, all the basic book information belongs in one table, the Category information should be in another table, and you need a linking table between Books and Categories because these two tables have a many-to-many relationship. In this example, Table1 should end up as the linking table. You can use Table2 as the foundation for the Books table. Move all the information related to ISBNNumber to Table2 by dragging the Title, SuggPrice, and LinerNotes fields from Table3 and the Disk field from Table6 (Table3 and Table6 will disappear when you do this), and then CopyrightYear, EditionNumber, and Pages from Table1.

Once you have adjusted the way the wizard split your tables, the next step is to give each of the new tables a new name. To rename a table, first click the table name and then click the Rename Table button in the upper part of the window. (You can also double-click the table's title bar.) The wizard opens a dialog box in which you can enter a new name. You should change Table1 to BookCategories, Table2 to Books, Table4 to Categories, and Table5 to Classes. Click Next when you are finished.

The next window asks you to verify the primary key fields for these tables. You can select new fields for the primary key of each table or add fields to the primary key. You should click the ISBNNumber field in the Books table and click the Set Unique Key button (because we know that ISBNNumber is a good unique value for each book). Access removes its *Generated Unique ID* when you do this. Figure 6-23 shows the result of moving fields, assigning new names to the tables, and changing the primary key. Click Next to accept the settings and go on to an analysis of duplicate values in the lookup tables.

FIGURE 6-23.
The result after moving fields and renaming the new tables.

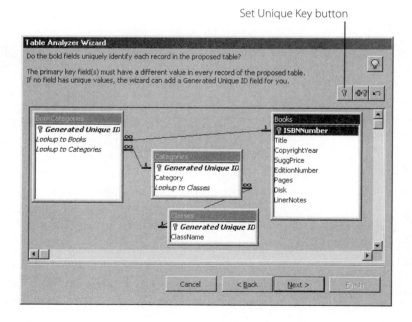

The Table Analyzer Wizard looks at values in any new lookup tables to try to eliminate any possible duplicates created by typing errors. Figure 6-24 shows part of the result of this analysis on the sample table. Because the wizard sees the word *Windows* in multiple rows, it suggests that some of these values might, in fact, be the same. You can use this window to tell the wizard any correct values for actual mistyped duplicates. The wizard will store only unique values in the final code table. In this case, you should tell the wizard to use the original value for all the values listed as duplicates by selecting the (Leave as is) option as shown in Figure 6-24. Click Next when you are finished to go on to the next window.

FIGURE 6-24.

Looking at potentially duplicate lookup values.

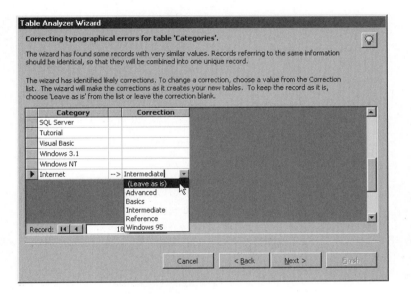

Finally, the wizard offers to create a new query that has the same name as the original table. (See Figure 6-25 on the next page.) If you've already been using the old table in queries, forms, reports, and data access pages, creating a new query that integrates the new tables into the original data structure means you won't have to change any other objects in your database. In most cases, the new query will look and operate just like the original table. Old queries, forms, reports, and data access pages based on the original table will now use the new query and won't know the difference.

Click Finish to build your new tables. The wizard also creates relationships among the new tables to make sure you can easily re-create the original data structure in queries. Figure 6-26 on the next page shows the four new tables built by the wizard. You may want to make one

FIGURE 6-25.

The final window of
the Table Analyzer
Wizard.

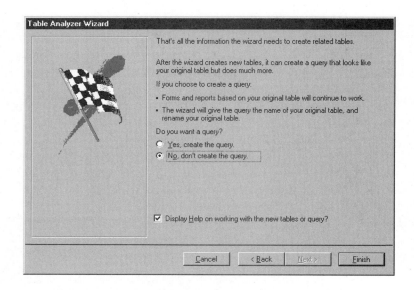

final adjustment to remove the ID field from BookCategories and use
the combination of ISBNNumber and Categories_ID for the primary
key, similar to the actual design from Chapter 4. *See the section titled
"Changing the Primary Key" later in this chapter to see how to do this.*
As you'll see in the next section, the final design for the
BookCategories table uses a special feature of table design to pull in
this lookup data whenever you use this table.

FIGURE 6-26.

The tables produced
by the Table Analyzer
Wizard.

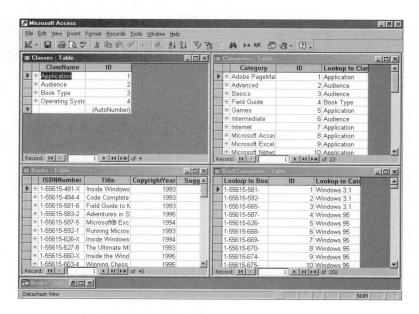

Taking Advantage of Lookup Properties

In the previous section, you learned how to use the Table Analyzer Wizard to break out redundant data into more efficient lookup tables. The end result stores a space-efficient code number in the original table. However, when you look at the main data, you probably want to see the original meaning of the code, not the code number. You can take advantage of lookup properties on code fields to make this happen automatically.

To see how this works, open the tblBookCategories table in the Microsoft Press Books database in Design view. (You might want to make a backup copy of the table and work with the copy.) You can modify the existing lookup property by following these steps. (Note that the sample table already has lookup properties defined; following this procedure will redefine those properties.) Click the Data Type column for the ISBNNumber field, click the down arrow, and then select Lookup Wizard from the drop-down list, as shown in Figure 6-27.

FIGURE 6-27.

Starting the Lookup Wizard for the ISBNNumber field.

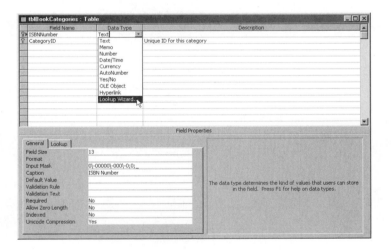

The purpose of the Lookup Wizard is to help you set the lookup properties of any code field in a table so that you see meaningful values from the lookup table whenever you use the main table—either in Datasheet view, in a query, or in a form or a report. Once you get the hang of it, you can set the lookup values without using the wizard. It's helpful to use the wizard the first few times to become familiar with how lookup properties work.

In the first window, shown in Figure 6-28 on the next page, the wizard asks whether you want to look up the values in another table or query

FIGURE 6-28.

The first window of the Lookup Wizard.

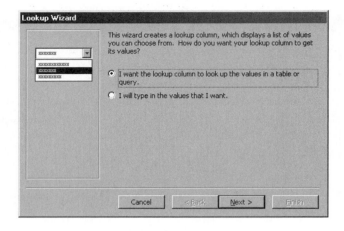

or type in a list of values. In this example, you know that the book titles are in another table, so select the first option. Click Next to go on to the next step.

In the next window, select the table named tblBooks. This is where the lookup values are stored in the Microsoft Press Books database. Choose Next to go on. The next window asks you to select the fields from the lookup table that you want to include for the code field in the current table. (See Figure 6-29.) The code value will be included automatically. In addition, you can select one or more descriptive fields that will be displayed when you view the code field in the original table. In this case, you need the ISBNNumber field and at least the book title. The book edition number might also be useful to help distinguish books for different versions of the same software product. Click Next to go on.

FIGURE 6-29.

Selecting fields from the lookup table.

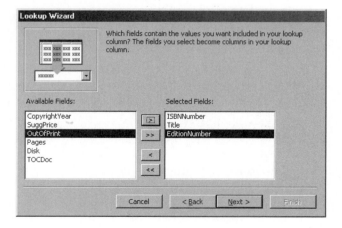

After you select the fields, the wizard shows you how it might display them, as shown in Figure 6-30. You can alter the width of the display column by clicking the right edge of the column heading and dragging it. Since you don't really need to see the code values, the wizard hides them. Click Next to go on.

FIGURE 6-30.

Adjusting the width of the display columns.

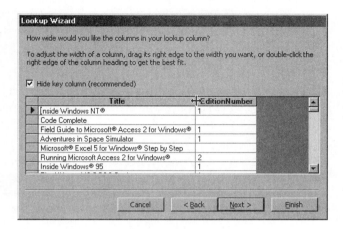

In the final window, the wizard asks you to name the code field in the original table. This "name" actually sets the caption property of the field, which is the name you'll see on datasheets and in labels for the field in forms and reports. Since the list will now show book titles and edition numbers (and not the ISBN number), you might want to change the displayed name to something like "Book Information."

Figure 6-31 shows the lookup properties set by the wizard after you click Finish in the final window. The wizard chooses a special type of

FIGURE 6-31.

The resulting lookup properties.

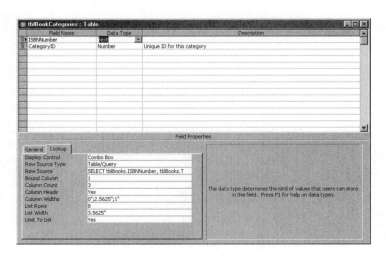

II

Building a Database

display control called a combo box to let you see the original code value for the field or to let you select a new one from a drop-down list. The wizard also creates a query to pull in the descriptive values from the lookup table automatically.

Table 6-2 gives you a quick overview of what the lookup settings set by the wizard mean. When you study combo box controls later, in Chapter 13, "Building Forms," you'll see how you can also use lookup properties to display lists from related tables in a form.

Save the table design, and switch to Datasheet view to see the result, as shown in Figure 6-32. Instead of a code number, you can now see the matching descriptive value from the lookup table. You can open the drop-down list and select a new value to set the code in the table.

TABLE 6-2. Lookup Properties Set by the Wizard

Lookup Property	Setting	Meaning
Display Control	Combo Box	The value displays in a box with a drop-down list from which you can select a new value.
Row Source Type	Table/Query	A table or query supplies the information for the list you see when you open the list.
Row Source	<SELECT statement>	The text of the query (in SQL) that provides the list when you open the list. *See Chapter 11 for details about SQL.*
Bound Column	1	When you select a value in the list, the first column in the query sets the value of the field.
Column Count	3	Only the first 3 columns from the table or query specified in Row Source should be used.
Column Heads	Yes	Display the field name at the top of any displayed column when you open the list.
Column Widths	0";2.565";1"	The data in the first column in the Row Source doesn't display when you open the list because the width is zero. The second and third values specify the width of the two displayed columns.

TABLE 6-2. *continued*

Lookup Property	Setting	Meaning
List Rows	8	When you open the list, it will show up to 8 rows. If more rows are available, you can scroll through them.
List Width	3.5625"	Specifies the width of the list when you open it.
Limit To List	Yes	You can't pick a value that's not on the list.

FIGURE 6-32.

The lookup column in Datasheet view.

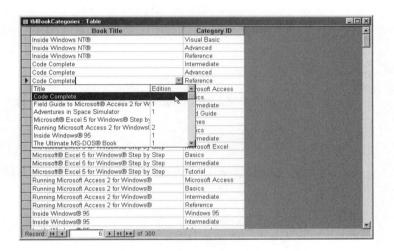

II

Building a Database

Changing the Primary Key

Chapter 4, "Designing Your Database Application," discussed the need to have one or more fields that provide a unique value to every row in your table. This field with unique values is identified as the *primary key*. If a table doesn't have a primary key, you can't define a relationship between it and other tables, and Microsoft Access has to guess how to link tables for you. Even if you define a primary key in your initial design, you might discover later that it doesn't actually contain unique values. In that case, you might have to define a new field or fields to be the primary key.

Using the Books And Authors database as an example, suppose you discover after using the Table Analyzer Wizard to design the

BookCategories table that the ISBNNumber and Categories_ID together are unique. You don't need the generated ID field as the primary key. To solve this problem, you must remove the ID field as the only field in the primary key and redefine the key to include the ISBNNumber and Categories_ID fields. Access provides several ways for you to accomplish this task. You could open the Indexes window (as you learned in Chapter 5), delete the primary key definition, and build a new one. A simpler way is to highlight the new fields you want as the primary key, and then click the Primary Key button on the toolbar, as shown in Figure 6-33.

Access won't let you delete an index if the table has relationships defined with other tables. First, use the Relationships window to remove the table's relationships, and then use the Indexes window to remove the index.

FIGURE 6-33.
Highlighting new fields that will become the primary key.

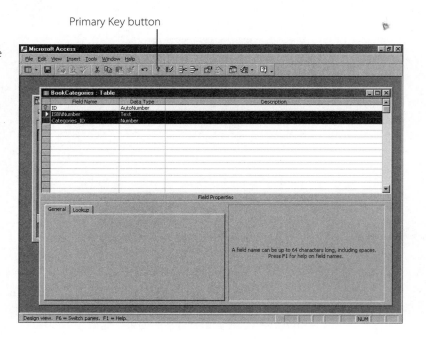

Next, highlight the old ID field and press the Delete key to remove it. When you save the table, Access creates a new index that includes both the ISBNNumber and Categories_ID fields as the primary key.

Compacting Your Database

As you delete old database objects and add new ones, the space within your mdb file can become fragmented. The result is that, over time, your database file can grow larger than it needs to be to store all your definitions and data.

To remove unused space, you should compact your database periodically. No database can be open when you run the compact utility. Also, no other users should be accessing the database you intend to compact. To execute the compact utility, close all databases, choose Database Utilities from the Tools menu in the Access window, and then choose the Compact And Repair Database command from the submenu. Access opens the dialog box shown in Figure 6-34.

FIGURE 6-34.

The dialog box for specifying a database to compact.

II

Building a Database

Select the database you want to compact, and then click Compact. Access asks you for a name for the compacted database. You can enter the same name as the database you are compacting, or you can use a different name. If you use the same name, Access warns you that the original database of the same name will be replaced. If you proceed, Access compacts your database into a temporary file. When compaction is successfully completed, Access deletes your old database and gives its name to the new compacted copy.

NOTE

You can also choose an option to compact the database each time you close it. Choose Options from the Tools menu, click the General tab, and select Compact On Close. If multiple users are sharing the same database, Access will compact the database when the last user closes it.

You now have all the information you need to modify and maintain your database table definitions. In the next chapter, you'll explore working with the data in your tables.

PART III

Working with Data

Using Datasheets

The simplest way to look at your data is to open a table in Datasheet view. Although when you build your application you'll probably work with your data mostly through forms that you design, studying datasheets is useful because it improves your understanding of basic concepts such as viewing, updating, inserting, and deleting data. Microsoft Access performs these functions in the same way regardless of whether you're using a datasheet or a specially designed form to work with your data. On some forms, you might decide to embed a Datasheet view of data to make it easy to look at several rows and columns at once. After you've built an application to work with your data, you'll find that Datasheet view is often useful for verifying data at the basic table level.

Throughout this chapter, you'll look at examples of operations using the tblStores, tblOrders, and tblBooks tables in the Microsoft Press Books sample database included with this book. Take a moment now to make a copy of the tblStores, tblOrders, and tblBooks tables. Open the Microsoft Press Books database, and then click Exit on the main switchboard form to return to the Database window. *The copying procedure is described in Chapter 6, "Modifying Your Database Design."* Name your copies *tblStoresBackup, tblOrdersBackup,* and *tblBooksBackup,* respectively.

Viewing Data

To look at data in one of your tables in Datasheet view, do the following.

1   Open your database. By default, Microsoft Access displays the list of tables in the database within the Database window. If you opened the Microsoft Press Books database without holding down the Shift key, click Exit on the main switchboard form to return to the Database window.

2   Double-click the name of the table you want to see. If you prefer to use the keyboard, press the Up or Down arrow key to move to the table you want, and then press Enter or Alt+O.

Figure 7-1 shows the Datasheet view of the tblStores table and identifies some key elements. (Note the change in the toolbar buttons when you view a table in Datasheet view.) Open this table now. If you like, you can make the datasheet fill the workspace by clicking the Maximize button near the upper right corner of the Table window. You can also press Alt+hyphen to open the Control menu and then press *X* to choose the Maximize command.

The subdatasheet selector is a new feature in Access 2000. *See "Working with Subdatasheets" later in this chapter for details.*

Moving Around

Changing the display to show different records or fields is simple. You can use the horizontal scroll bar to scroll through a table's fields, or you can use the vertical scroll bar to scroll through a table's records.

In the lower left corner of the table in Datasheet view, you can see a record number box, as shown in Figure 7-2. The record number box shows the *relative record number* of the current record (meaning the number of the selected record in relation to the current set of records, also called a *recordset*). You might not see the current record in the window if you've scrolled the display. The number to the right of the record number box shows the total number of records in the current recordset. If you've applied a filter against the table *(see the section titled "Searching for and Filtering Data" later in this chapter)*, this number might be less than the total number of records in the table.

FIGURE 7-1.

The Datasheet view of the tblStores table.

Row selector

Subdatasheet selector

Sort Descending button

Sort Ascending button

Filter By Selection button

Filter By Form button

Apply Filter button

Find Button

Field name or caption

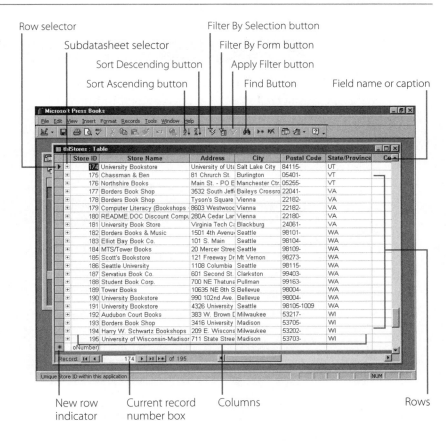

New row indicator

Current record number box

Columns

Rows

FIGURE 7-2.

The record number box.

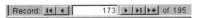

You can use the record number box to quickly move to the record you want. As you'll read a bit later in this chapter, you'll usually select some data in a record in order to change it. You can also choose the Go To command from the Edit menu to move to the first, last, next, or previous record, or to move to a new, empty record. You can make any record current by clicking anywhere in its row; the number in the record number box will change to indicate the row you've selected.

Keyboard Shortcuts

You might find it easier to use the keyboard rather than the mouse to move around in a datasheet, especially if you're typing in new data. Table 7-1 on the next page lists the keyboard shortcuts for scrolling in a datasheet. Table 7-2, also on the next page, lists the keyboard shortcuts for selecting data in a datasheet.

III

Working with Data

TABLE 7-1. **Keyboard Shortcuts for Scrolling in a Datasheet**

Keys	Scrolling Action
Page Up	Up one page
Page Down	Down one page
Ctrl+Page Up	Left one page
Ctrl+Page Down	Right one page

TABLE 7-2. **Keyboard Shortcuts for Selecting Data in a Datasheet**

Keys	Selecting Action
Tab	Next field
Shift+Tab	Previous field
Home	First field, current record
End	Last field, current record
Up arrow	Current field, previous record
Down arrow	Current field, next record
Ctrl+Up arrow	Current field, first record
Ctrl+Down arrow	Current field, last record
Ctrl+Home	First field, first record
Ctrl+End	Last field, last record
F5	Record number box
Ctrl+Spacebar	Select the current column
Shift+Spacebar	Select the current record
F2	Switch between selecting all data in the field and single character edit mode

Modifying the Datasheet Format

You can make a number of changes to the appearance of a datasheet. You can change the height of rows or the width of columns, rearrange or hide columns, set the display or printing font, and decide whether you want to see gridlines. You can make most of these changes from the Format menu, shown in Figure 7-3.

FIGURE 7-3.

The Format menu of a Table window in Datasheet view.

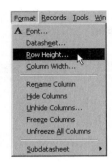

Changing Row Height and Column Width

Access initially displays all the columns and rows using a default width and height. The standard column width (approximately 1 inch) is probably wider than it needs to be for columns that contain a small amount of data, but it's not wide enough for columns with a large amount of data. For example, the default width is wider than it needs to be for the State/Province column in the tblStores table to display the state abbreviations in the field. The Store Name and Address columns, however, are not wide enough to display the data contained in them.

One way to adjust the width of a column is to select any value in the column and then choose the Column Width command from the Format menu. In the Column Width dialog box, shown in Figure 7-4, you can type in a new value for the width (in number of characters). The standard width, approximately 1 inch when printed, can vary depending on the current font selection. If you click the Best Fit button, Access sets the column width to accommodate the longest currently displayed data value in this column. In other words, Access adjusts the column width to show the widest data in the current display window. It does not search all available data. (You probably wouldn't want it to do this, anyway, on a table with thousands of rows!)

FIGURE 7-4.

The Column Width dialog box.

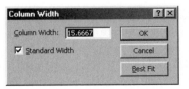

You can also modify column widths directly on the datasheet by placing the mouse pointer on the line between two column names at the top of the Table window. (See Figure 7-5 on the next page.) When you do this, the mouse pointer becomes a vertical bar with arrows pointing to the left and right. By dragging the column boundary, you can adjust the size of the column.

FIGURE 7-5.

Using the mouse to adjust the column width.

If you plan to print your datasheet, you might want to increase the height of the rows to create some space between records on the report. Choose the Row Height command from the Format menu to open the Row Height dialog box, shown in Figure 7-6. The row height is measured in points—units of $1/72$ inch (approximately $1/28$ centimeter). To allow space between rows, Access calculates a standard height that is approximately 30 percent taller than the current font's point size. You can enter a new height in the Row Height text box. If you specify a number that is shorter than the font size, your rows will overlap when you print the datasheet. You can also change the row height by dragging the row boundary between two row selectors, in the same way that you changed the column width using the mouse. (See Figure 7-5.) Note that changing the row height applies to all rows in the datasheets.

FIGURE 7-6.

The Row Height dialog box.

Arranging Columns

The default order of fields from left to right in Datasheet view is the order in which the fields were defined in the table. You can easily change the column order for viewing or printing. Select the column you want to move by clicking the field selector (the field name bar at the top of the column). Access highlights the entire column. You can select multiple columns by dragging across several columns in either direction before you release the mouse button. You can also click a field selector and extend the selection by holding down the Shift key while pressing the Left or Right arrow key to expand the highlighted area.

To move the selected columns, drag the columns' field selectors to the new location. (See Figure 7-7.) To move the selected columns using the keyboard, press Ctrl+Shift+F8 to turn on Move mode. Access displays *MOV* in one of the areas on the status bar. Shift the columns to the left or right using the arrow keys. Press Esc to turn off Move mode.

FIGURE 7-7.

You can move a column by selecting it and then dragging the field selector.

Hiding and Showing Columns

By default, Access displays all of the table's columns in Datasheet view, although you might have to scroll to see some of them. If you're not interested in looking at or printing all these fields, you can hide some of them. One way to hide a column is to drag the right column boundary to the left (from within the field selector) until the column disappears. You can also select one or more columns and choose the Hide Columns command from the Format menu.

To reveal hidden columns or to hide additional ones, choose the Unhide Columns command from the Format menu to open the Unhide Columns dialog box, shown in Figure 7-8 on the next page. Select the check box next to a column name to display the column. The checked columns are already showing. Click Close to close the dialog box.

FIGURE 7-8.

The Unhide Columns dialog box.

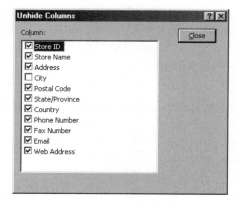

Freezing Columns

Sometimes you might want to keep one column displayed on the screen while scrolling left or right through the other columns. For example, you might want to keep the Store Name column displayed as you scroll to the right to see the Phone Number column. You can freeze one or more contiguous columns by selecting them and then choosing the Freeze Columns command from the Format menu. (If you want to freeze multiple noncontiguous columns, you need to select and then freeze each column in turn.) Access moves the selected columns to the far left and freezes them there. These fields do not scroll off the left of the window when you scroll right. To release frozen columns, choose the Unfreeze All Columns command from the Format menu. (Note that Unfreeze All Columns does not return the columns to their original sequence.) Figure 7-9 shows the Store Name column frozen at the left, with the rest of the display scrolled right to show the city, postal code, state or province, country, and phone number.

Removing Gridlines

Datasheet view normally displays gridlines between the columns and rows. Access also includes these gridlines if you print the datasheet. You can customize the look of the cells in your datasheet by choosing Datasheet from the Format menu. In the Datasheet Formatting dialog box, shown in Figure 7-10, you can select options to display horizontal or vertical gridlines and select the color of the gridlines and the background color of the cells. You can also select a special sunken or raised effect.

FIGURE 7-9.

A datasheet with a frozen column (Store Name).

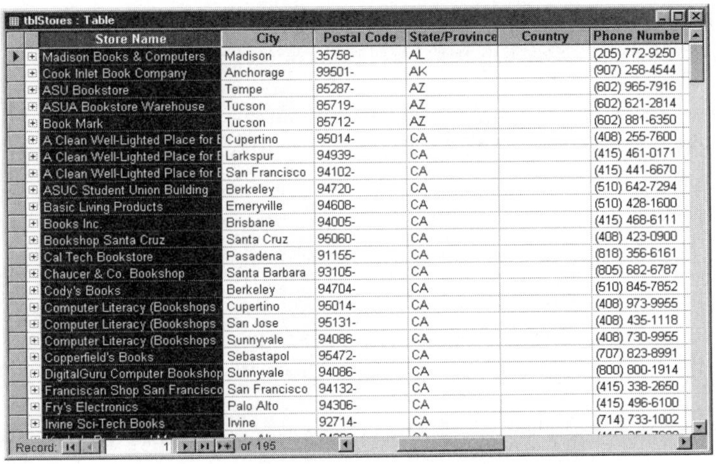

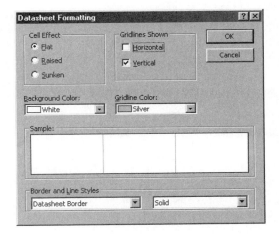

FIGURE 7-10.

Setting the look of datasheet cells in the Cells Effects dialog box.

Figure 7-11 on the next page shows the datasheet from Figure 7-9 without the horizontal gridlines. Notice that a line is present to indicate that the Store Name column is frozen. Access includes this line if you print a report with frozen columns, even if you have turned off vertical gridlines.

To print a datasheet without the frozen column line, choose the Unfreeze All Columns command from the Format menu before printing the datasheet.

III

Working with Data

FIGURE 7-11.

A datasheet without horizontal gridlines. The line to the right of the Store Name column indicates that this column is frozen.

Selecting Fonts

Another thing you can do to customize the look of a datasheet is to select a different font. Choose the Font command from the Format menu to see the dialog box shown in Figure 7-12.

FIGURE 7-12.

The Font dialog box.

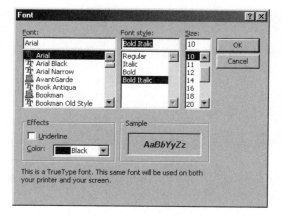

In the Font list box at the upper left of the dialog box, you can see all the fonts that are installed in your Microsoft Windows operating system. You can scroll down the list box and select the font name you want. The icon to the left of the font name indicates whether the font is a PostScript or printer font (printer icon) or a TrueType font (TT icon) that you can use for both screen display and printing. If there is no icon to the left of the font name, the font is a screen font.

If you select a printer font, Access uses the closest matching screen or TrueType font to display the datasheet on your screen. If you select a screen font, Access uses the closest matching printer or TrueType font when you print. In either case, your printed result might look different from the image on your screen. If you select a TrueType font, it should look the same on your screen as on the printed page.

When you select a font, Access shows you a sample of the font in the Sample box. Depending on which font you select, you might also see a wide range of font styles (such as italic or bold) and font sizes. Select the Underline check box if you want all the characters underlined. You can also select a color for the characters. Click OK to set the new font for the entire datasheet. Click Cancel to dismiss the dialog box without changing the font.

You can also set the default font for all datasheets. To do this, choose the Options command from the Tools menu. On the Datasheet tab of the Options dialog box (see Figure 7-13), you can set the default font name, size, and weight (light, normal, or bold), and select italic and underline. You'll also find options here to set colors, horizontal and vertical gridlines, default column width, cell effects, and an option to display the animations that accompany certain actions in Access.

FIGURE 7-13.
Setting new default options for all datasheets.

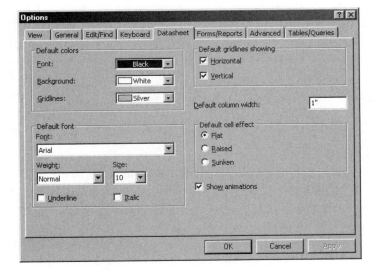

Saving Datasheet Formatting

After you have the datasheet formatted the way you want it, you don't have to lose your work when you close the table. Choose the Save command from the File menu to save the format of the datasheet. Access also asks whether you want to save formatting changes when you try to close a table.

III

Working with Data

🄰 Working with Subdatasheets

Microsoft Access 2000 introduces a new feature that lets you display information from multiple related tables in a single datasheet. In the design we developed in Chapter 4 for the Microsoft Press Books sample database, Customers can have multiple Orders, and Orders can have many Order Details (books that were ordered). Wouldn't it be nice to be able to open the Orders table and also see the books for that order in one datasheet?

Open the Microsoft Press Books sample database. If you didn't hold down the Shift key as you opened the database (to prevent the application from starting), click the Exit button on the first window you see to return to the Database window. Click the Tables button, select the tblOrders table, and open it in Datasheet view. Click the plus sign next to the first row to open the subdatasheet as shown in Figure 7-14.

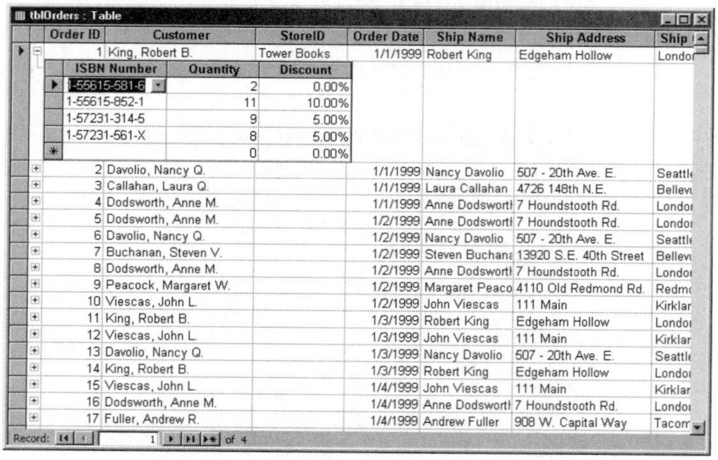

FIGURE 7-14.

Viewing the order details for the first order in a subdatasheet.

Access automatically built this subdatasheet when I defined the relationship between tblOrders and tblOrderDetails. *See "Defining Relationships" in Chapter 5.* In the subdatasheet window, you can see the four books that were ordered in order number 1.

You can click the plus sign next to each order row to see the order detail information for that order. If you want to expand or collapse all of the subdatasheets, choose Subdatasheet on the Format menu, and select the option you want as shown in Figure 7-15.

FIGURE 7-15.

The Subdatasheet menu allows you to easily expand all subdatasheets, col-lapse all subdata-sheets, or remove the currently displayed subdatasheet.

The information from the related tblOrderDetails table is interesting, but it doesn't show the book title or pricing information. If you want to see additional details, you can define a query that uses both tblOrderDetails and tblBooks as the source for the subdatasheet. To do this, first remove the existing subdatasheet. Choose Subdatasheet from the Format menu, and select the Remove option on the submenu to remove the current subdatasheet on the tblOrders table. Next, choose Subdatasheet on the Insert menu to see the dialog shown in Figure 7-16.

FIGURE 7-16.

Choosing a query to display more informa-tion in a subdatasheet.

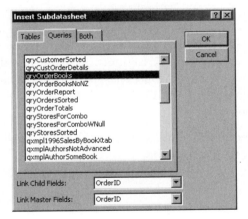

The Microsoft Press Books sample database includes a query that dis-plays all of the columns from tblOrderDetails as well as related title and pricing information from tblBooks. You will learn how to create this type of query in the next chapter. Click the Queries tab in the In-sert Subdatasheet dialog box and scroll down until you see qryOrderBooks. Note that when you click this query, Access figures out that it needs to link the OrderID field in tblOrders with the

OrderID field included in the query. Click OK to define the new subdatasheet based on the query.

When you return to the tblOrders Datasheet window, choose Subdatasheet from the Format menu and select the option on the submenu to Expand All. You will now see more useful information about each book ordered as shown in Figure 7-17.

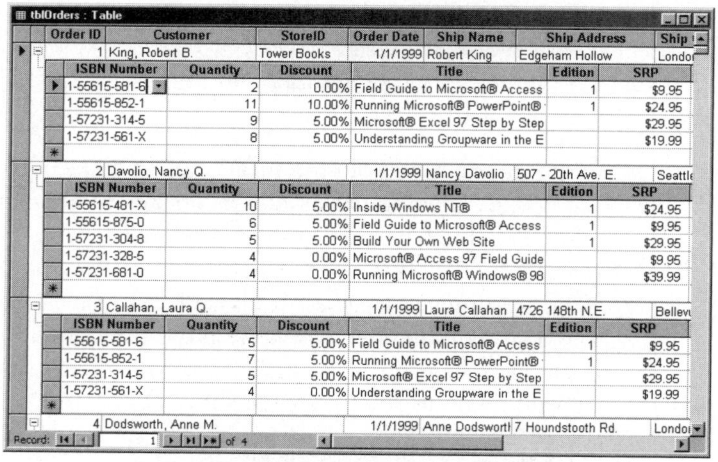

FIGURE 7-17.

Reviewing all order detail information from the subdatasheet on the tblOrders table.

Note that you can search and edit the fields in the subdatasheet just like you can in the main datasheet. In the next section, you'll learn more about editing data in Datasheet view. You can use these editing techniques equally with the main datasheet as well as with any expanded subdatasheet.

Close the tblBooks table and open the tblStores table to follow the examples in the next section.

Changing Data

Not only can you view and format data in a datasheet, you can also insert new records, change data, and delete records.

Record Indicators

You might have noticed as you moved around in the datasheet that occasionally icons appeared on the row selector at the far left of each row. (See Figure 7-1.) These *record indicators* and their meanings are listed on the next page.

Indicates that this is the current row.

 Indicates that you are making or have made a change to one or more entries in this row. Microsoft Access saves the changes when you move to another row. Before moving to a new row, you can press Esc once to undo the change to the current value or press Esc twice to undo all changes in the row. If you're updating a database that is shared with other users through a network, Access locks this record when you save the change so that no one else can update it until you're finished. (See the last indicator below.)

 Indicates a blank row at the end of the table that you can use to create a new record.

 Indicates that another user might be changing this record. You'll see this icon only when you're working in a database that is shared with other users through a network. You should wait until this indicator disappears before attempting to make changes to the record.

Adding a New Record

As you build your application, you might find it useful to place some data in your tables so you can test the forms and reports that you design. You might also find it convenient sometimes to add data directly to your tables by using Datasheet view rather than by opening a form. If your table is empty, Access shows a single blank row when you open the table in Datasheet view. If you have data in your table, Access shows a blank row beneath the last record. You can jump to the blank row to begin adding a new record either by choosing the Go To command from the Edit menu and then choosing New Record from the submenu, by clicking the New Record button on the toolbar, or by pressing Ctrl+plus sign. Access places the insertion point in the first column when you start a new record. As soon as you begin typing, Access changes the record indicator to the pencil icon to show that updates are in progress. You can press the Tab key to move to the next column.

If the data you enter in a column violates a field validation rule, Access notifies you as soon as you attempt to leave the column. You must provide a correct value before you can move to another column. Press Esc, choose Undo Typing from the Edit menu, or click the Undo button on the toolbar to remove your changes in the current field.

III

Working with Data

Press Shift+Enter at any place in the record or press the Tab key in the last column in the record to commit your new record to the database. You can also choose the Save Record command from the Records menu. If the changes in your record violate the validation rule for the table, Access warns you when you try to save the record. You must correct the problem before you can save your changes. If you want to cancel the record, press Esc twice or click the Undo button on the toolbar until it turns gray. If you want to use the Edit menu to undo the current record, you must first choose Undo Typing from the Edit menu if you are in a field that contains changes; Access then changes the available Edit menu item to Undo Current Field/Record so that you can undo all changes.

Access provides several keyboard shortcuts to assist you as you enter new data, as shown in Table 7-3.

TABLE 7-3. Keyboard Shortcuts for Entering Data in a Datasheet

Keys	Data Action
Ctrl+semicolon (;)	Enters the current date
Ctrl+colon (:)	Enters the current time
Ctrl+Alt+Spacebar	Enters the default value for the field
Ctrl+single quotation mark (') or Ctrl+double quotation mark (")	Enters the value from the same field in the previous record
Ctrl+Enter	Inserts a carriage return in a memo or text field
Ctrl+plus sign (+)	Adds a new record
Ctrl+minus sign (–)	Deletes the current record

Selecting and Changing Data

When you have data in a table, you can easily change the data by editing it in Datasheet view. You must select data before you can change it, and you can do this in several ways.

- In the cell containing the data you want to change, click just to the left of the first character you want to change, and then drag the cursor to highlight all the characters you want to change.

- Double-click any word in a cell to select the entire word.

■ Click at the left edge of a cell in the grid (that is, where the mouse pointer turns into a large white cross). Access selects the entire contents of the cell.

Any data you type replaces the old, selected data. In Figure 7-18, the address value for Cook Inlet Book Company in the tblStores table is selected. In Figure 7-19, that value is changed before the record is saved. Access also selects the entire entry if you tab to the cell in the datasheet grid. If you want to change only part of the data (for example, to correct the spelling of a street name), you can shift to single-character mode by pressing F2 or by clicking the location at which you want to start your change. Use the Backspace key to erase characters to the left of the cursor and use the Del key to remove characters to the right of the cursor. Hold down the Shift key and press the Right or Left arrow key to select multiple characters to replace. You can press F2 again to select the entire cell. A useful keyboard shortcut for changing data is to press Ctrl+Alt+Spacebar to restore the data to the default value specified in the table definition.

FIGURE 7-18.

The old data is selected.

		1	Madison Books & Computers	8006-5 Madison Pike
		2	Cook Inlet Book Company	415 West Fifth Ave
		3	ASU Bookstore	Arizona State University

FIGURE 7-19.

The new data is typed in, replacing the old.

		1	Madison Books & Computers	8006-5 Madison Pike
		2	Cook Inlet Book Company	415 Fifth Ave West
		3	ASU Bookstore	Arizona State University

You can set two options to control how the arrow keys and Enter work as you move from cell to cell. Choose the Options command from the Tools menu, and click the Keyboard tab of the Options dialog box, shown in Figure 7-20 on the next page. To control what happens in a cell when you use the Right or Left arrow key, select Next Field in the Arrow Key Behavior section (selection moves to the next field in the record) or Next Character (cursor moves over one character). I prefer the Next Character option because it lets me always use the arrow keys to move one character at a time while reserving Tab for moving a field at a time.

In the Move After Enter section, you can select Next Field so that pressing Enter completes the update of the current field in the record and tabs to the next field. If you select Next Record, pressing Enter moves you to the next row on the datasheet. If you select Don't Move, pressing Enter selects the current cell.

III

Working with Data

FIGURE 7-20.

The Keyboard tab of the Options dialog box.

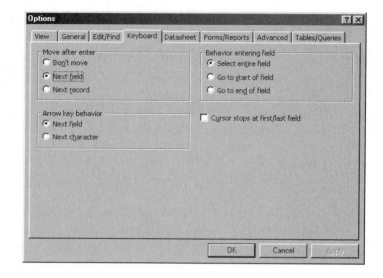

You can select the Cursor Stops At First/Last Field check box to prevent the arrow keys from moving the insertion point beyond the current record. If you leave this option unchecked, the insertion point moves to the first field in the next row when you press the Right arrow key while at the last character in a row, and moves to the last field in the previous row when you press the Left arrow key while at the first character in a row.

Replacing Data

What if you need to make the same change in more than one record? Access provides a way to do this quickly and easily. Select any cell in the column whose values you want to change (select the cell in the first row if you want to start at the beginning of the table), and then choose the Replace command from the Edit menu or press Ctrl+H to see the dialog box shown in Figure 7-21. Suppose, for example, that you suspect that the city name "Tucson" is misspelled as "Tuscon" in some rows in the tblStores table. (All the city names are spelled correctly in the sample table.) To fix this using Replace, open the tblStores table in Datasheet view, select the City field in the first row, choose the Replace command, type *Tuscon* in the Find What text box, and then type *Tucson* in the Replace With text box, as shown in Figure 7-21. Click the Find Next button to search for the next occurrence of the text you've typed in the Find What text box. Click the Replace button to change data selectively, or click the Replace All button to change all the entries that match the Find What text. Click the More button (which then changes to a Less button, as shown in Figure 7-21) to have the option to search all fields or only the current field, to exactly match the case for text searches (because searches in Access are normally case-insensitive), and to select an entry only if the Find What text matches the entire entry in the field.

FIGURE 7-21.
The Find And Replace dialog box.

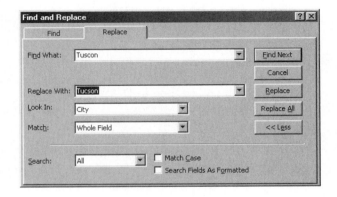

Copying and Pasting Data

You can copy or cut any selected data to the Windows Clipboard and paste this data into another field or record. To copy data, tab to the cell or click at the left edge of the cell in the datasheet grid to select the data within it. Choose the Copy command from the Edit menu or press Ctrl+C. You can also choose the Cut command from the Edit menu or press Ctrl+X to delete (cut) the data you have selected. To paste the data in another location, move the cursor to the new location (to replace data in that location, select the data you want to replace), and choose the Paste command from the Edit menu or press Ctrl+V.

 NOTE

If you select and copy to the Clipboard several items of text data, Access may show you the new Office Clipboard. Unlike the Windows Clipboard, this new facility allows you to copy several separate items, and then select them later to paste into other fields or documents. You may find this feature useful when working in a product like Microsoft Word. You can copy or cut several noncontiguous paragraphs to the Clipboard, and then paste them into another location or document.

To select an entire record to be copied or cut, click the row selector at the far left of the row. You can drag through the row selectors or press Shift+Up arrow or Shift+Down arrow to extend the selection to multiple rows. Choose the Copy command from the Edit menu or press Ctrl+C to copy the contents of multiple rows to the Clipboard. You can open another table and paste the copied rows into the table, or you can use the Paste Append command on the Edit menu to paste the rows at the end of the same table. You can paste copies of records into the same table only if the table has no primary key or if the primary key has the AutoNumber data type. When the primary key is AutoNumber, Access generates new primary key values for you.

Be aware that cutting rows from a table is the same as deleting them. (See the next section.) However, the Cut command is handy for moving to a backup table data that you don't want in an active table. You can have both tables open in Datasheet view at the same time. Simply cut the rows you want to move, switch to the backup table window, and paste the cut rows by using the Paste Append command.

Whenever you paste rows in a table, Access asks you to confirm the paste operation. (See Figure 7-22.) Click Yes to proceed, or click No if you decide to cancel the operation.

FIGURE 7-22.

The dialog box that asks whether you want to proceed with a paste operation.

> You can't change the physical sequence of rows in a relational database by cutting rows from one location and pasting them in another location. Access always pastes new rows at the end of the current display. If you close the datasheet after pasting in new rows and then open it again, Access displays the rows in sequence by the primary key you defined. *If you want to see rows in some other sequence, see the section titled "Sorting and Searching for Data" later in this chapter.*

Deleting Rows

To delete one or more rows, select the rows using the row selectors and then press the Delete key. For details about selecting multiple rows, see the previous discussion on copying and pasting data. You can also use Ctrl+minus sign to delete the current or selected row. When you delete rows, Access gives you a chance to change your mind if you made a mistake. (See Figure 7-23.) Click Yes in the dialog box to delete the rows, or click No to cancel the deletion.

After you click Yes in the confirmation dialog box, you cannot restore the deleted rows. You have to reenter them or copy them from a backup.

FIGURE 7-23.
The dialog box that appears when you delete a row.

Working with Hyperlinks

Microsoft Access 97 (also known as version 8.0) introduced the Hyperlink data type. The Hyperlink data type lets you store a simple or complex "link" to a file or document outside your database. This link pointer can contain a Uniform Resource Locator (URL) that points to a location on the World Wide Web or on a local intranet. It can also use a Universal Naming Convention (UNC) filename to point to a file on a server on your local area network (LAN) or on your local computer drives. The link may point to a file that is in HyperText Markup Language (HTML) or in a format that is supported by an ActiveX application on your computer.

A Hyperlink is actually a text field that can contain up to 2048 characters. The link itself can have up to four parts.

- An optional descriptor that is displayed when you're not editing the link. The descriptor can start with any character other than a pound sign (#) and must have a pound sign as its ending delimiter. If you do not include the descriptor, start the link address with a pound sign.

- The link address expressed as either a URL (beginning with a recognized Internet protocol name such as http: or url:) or in UNC format (a file location expressed as *server**share**path**filename*). If you do not specify the optional descriptor field, the link address is displayed in the field.

- An optional subaddress that specifies a named location (such as a cell range in a Microsoft Excel spreadsheet or a bookmark in a Microsoft Word document) within the file. Separate the link address from the subaddress with a pound sign (#).

III

Working with Data

■ An optional ScreenTip that appears when you move your mouse pointer over the hyperlink. Separate the screen tip from the subaddress with a pound sign (#).

When you have a field defined using the Hyperlink data type, you work with it differently than a standard text field. To see an example, open the tblBooks table (or your backup copy) in the Microsoft Press Books sample database. Scroll to the right, if necessary, so that you can see the Link To TOC field, and place your mouse pointer over one of the fields that contains data, as shown in Figure 7-24.

FIGURE 7-24.

Placing the mouse pointer over a Hyperlink field in Datasheet view.

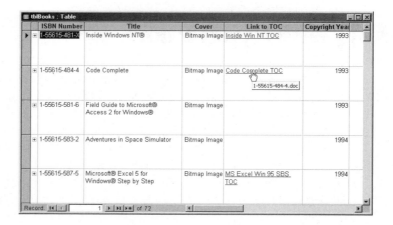

Activating a Hyperlink

Notice that the text in a hyperlink field is underlined and that the mouse pointer becomes a hand with a pointing finger when you move the pointer over the field. If you leave the pointer floating over the field for a moment, Access displays the ScreenTip. In the tblBooks table, the entries in the Link To TOC hyperlink field for many of the books contain pointers to Microsoft Word documents. These links will work as long as you do not move the documents from the folder in which they were installed from the companion CD. When you click a link field, Access starts the application that supports the link and passes the link address and subaddress to the application. If the link starts with an Internet protocol, Access starts your Web browser. In the case of the links in the tblBooks table, all are relative path UNC links to Word documents. If you click one of them, Microsoft Word should start and display the related document, as shown in Figure 7-25.

FIGURE 7-25.

The result of clicking a Word document file link in the tblBooks table.

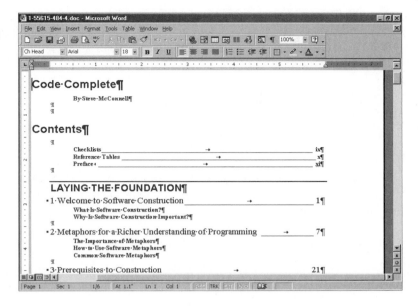

Inserting a New Hyperlink

To insert a hyperlink in an empty hyperlink field, tab to the field or click in it with your mouse. If you're confident about the format of your link, you can type it in following the rules for the four parts noted earlier. If you're not sure, choose Hyperlink from the Insert menu to see the dialog box shown in Figure 7-26.

FIGURE 7-26.

The dialog box used to insert a hyperlink; it shows a file link to the table of contents document for *Code Complete*.

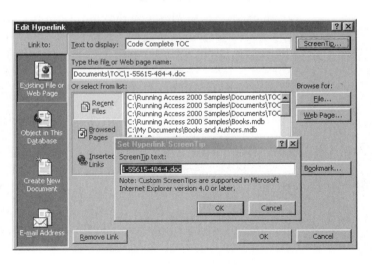

You can enter the descriptor in the Text To Display box at the top. I clicked the ScreenTip button to open the Set Hyperlink ScreenTip dialog box you see in Figure 7-26 on the previous page. You can type the document address directly into the Type The File Or Web Page Name box. If the document is in a folder relative to the current database location, you can type in just the subfolder name and file name. You can also enter a specific drive, folder, and file name, network path name, or Internet or intranet address.

Click the Recent Files, Browsed Pages, or Inserted Links buttons to choose from a list of files or Internet addresses you have recently visited. Click the File or Web Page buttons to locate any file or Web page on your local computer or on any network computer to which you're connected.

Whether you are creating a link to an Internet site or to a file, after you have chosen a link address, you can use the Bookmark button (see Figure 7-26) to specify a location within the file or Internet site document. After you click the Bookmark button, you can click the Browse button to start the target application of the link address to search for named locations. For example, in a Microsoft Word document, Bookmarks are named locations within the document.

Click OK to save your link in the field in the datasheet.

Editing an Existing Hyperlink

Changing the value of a hyperlink is a bit tricky. You can't simply click in a hyperlink field; that activates the link. What you can do is click in a field next to the hyperlink and use the Tab key to move to the link field. Then press F2 to shift to character edit mode to edit the text string that defines the link. Figure 7-27 shows you a hyperlink field after following this procedure. You can use the arrow keys to move around in the text string to change one or more parts. In many cases, you might want to add an optional descriptor at the beginning of the link text, as shown in the figure. ("Code Complete TOC" may be more readable than the name of the document: "1-55615-484-4.doc".)

You can also right-click a link field to open a shortcut menu. Choose Hyperlink from this menu to see options to open the link document, copy the link to the Clipboard, add the link to your Windows list of favorites, edit the link (which opens the dialog box shown in Figure 7-26), or change the text displayed in the field.

Close the tblBooks table and return to the tblStores table for the remainder of the examples in this chapter.

FIGURE 7-27.

Editing the text that defines a hyperlink.

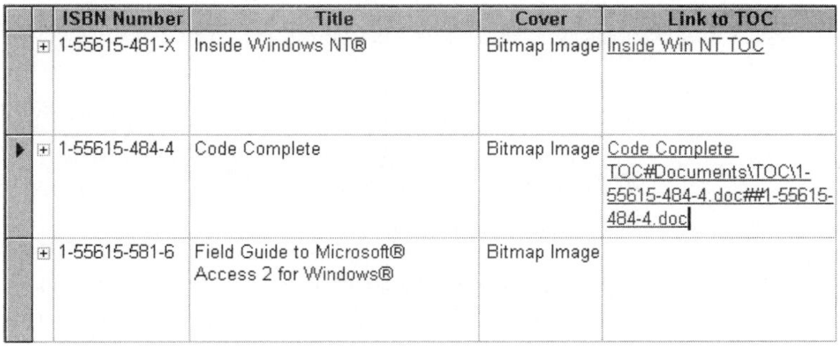

		ISBN Number	Title	Cover	Link to TOC
	⊞	1-55615-481-X	Inside Windows NT®	Bitmap Image	Inside Win NT TOC
▶	⊞	1-55615-484-4	Code Complete	Bitmap Image	Code Complete TOC#Documents\TOC\1-55615-484-4.doc##1-55615-484-4.doc
	⊞	1-55615-581-6	Field Guide to Microsoft® Access 2 for Windows®	Bitmap Image	

Sorting and Searching for Data

When you open a table in Datasheet view, Microsoft Access displays the rows sorted in sequence by the primary key you defined for the table. If you didn't define a primary key, you'll see the rows in the sequence in which you entered them in the table. If you want to see the rows in a different sequence or search for specific data, Access provides you with tools to do that.

Sorting Data

Access provides several ways to sort data in Datasheet view. As you might have noticed, two handy toolbar buttons allow you to quickly sort the rows in the table in ascending or descending order, based on the values in a single column. To see how this works, open the tblStores table, click anywhere in the State/Province column, and click the Sort Ascending button on the toolbar. Access sorts the display to show you the rows ordered alphabetically by state, as shown in Figure 7-28.

FIGURE 7-28.

Sorting stores by state or province.

	Store ID	Store Name	Address	City	Postal Code	State/Province	Co
▶ ⊞	2	Cook Inlet Book Company	415 West Fifth	Anchorage	99501-	AK	
⊞	1	Madison Books & Computers	8006-5 Madison	Madison	35758-	AL	
⊞	3	ASU Bookstore	Arizona State U	Tempe	85287-	AZ	
⊞	4	ASUA Bookstore Warehouse	850 E. 18th St.	Tucson	85719-	AZ	
⊞	5	Book Mark	5001 East Spee	Tucson	85712-	AZ	
⊞	33	The UCLA BookZone	308 Westwood	Los Angeles	90024-	CA	
⊞	22	Fry's Electronics	340 Portage Ro	Palo Alto	94306-	CA	
⊞	23	Irvine Sci-Tech Books	15333 Culver Dr	Irvine	92714-	CA	
⊞	25	Milligan News Co.	150 North Autur	San Jose	95110-	CA	
⊞	27	Opamp Technical Books	1033 N. Sycam	Los Angeles	90038-	CA	
⊞	28	Printers Inc. Bookstore	301 Castro Stre	Mountain View	94041-	CA	
⊞	29	San Diego Technical Books	4698 Convoy St	San Diego	92111-	CA	
⊞	30	Stacy's Bookstore	581 Market St.	San Francisco	94105-	CA	
⊞	21	Franciscan Shop San Francisco	1650 Holloway	San Francisco	94132-	CA	
⊞	32	Tower Books	2538 Watt Aven	Sacramento	95821-	CA	
⊞	24	Kepler's Books and Magazines	1007 Elwell Cou	Palo Alto	94303-	CA	
⊞	34	University Bookstore	Unviersity of Ca	Irvine	92717-	CA	
⊞	35	University Bookstore Q008	University of Ca	La Jolla	92093-	CA	
⊞	36	USC Bookstore/Trojan Bookstor	835 W. 36th Pla	Los Angeles	90089-	CA	
⊞	31	Stanford Bookstore Distribution	8424 Central Av	Newark	94560-	CA	
⊞	9	ASUC Student Union Building	Bancroft Way a	Berkeley	94720-	CA	
⊞	6	A Clean Well-Lighted Place for E	21269 Stevens	Cupertino	95014-	CA	
⊞	26	MTS/Tower Books	2601 Del Monte	W. Sacramento	95091-	CA	

Record: 1 of 195

You can click the Sort Descending button to sort the rows in descending order.

If you want to sort more than one field, you must use the filtering and sorting feature. Let's assume that you want to sort by State/Province, then by City within State/Province, and then by Store Name. Here's how to do it.

1 Choose Filter from the Records menu, and then choose Advanced Filter/Sort from the submenu. You'll see the Advanced Filter/Sort window (shown in Figure 7-29) with a list of fields in the tblStores table shown in the top part of the window.

FIGURE 7-29.

Selecting the StoreName field in the Advanced Filter/Sort window.

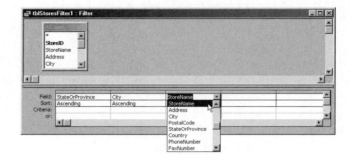

2 Access normally places the insertion point in the first column of the Field row in the lower part of the window. If you don't see the insertion point there, click in that cell.

3 Open the field list by clicking the drop-down arrow or by pressing Alt+Down arrow on the keyboard. Select the StateOrProvince field in the list. (You can also place the StateOrProvince field in this first column by finding StateOrProvince in the list of fields in the top part of the window and dragging it onto the Field row in the first column of the design grid.)

4 Click in the Sort row, immediately below the StateOrProvince field, and select Ascending from the drop-down list.

5 Add the City and StoreName fields to the next two columns, and select Ascending in the Sort row for both.

6 Click the Apply Filter toolbar button or choose Apply Filter/Sort from the Filter menu to see the result shown in Figure 7-30.

Searching For and Filtering Data

If you want to look for data anywhere in your table, Access provides several powerful searching and filtering capabilities.

FIGURE 7-30.

Sorting store records by state or province, city, and then store name.

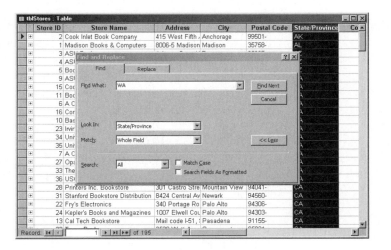

Using Find

To perform a simple search on a single field, select that field, and then open the Find And Replace dialog box (shown in Figure 7-31) by choosing the Find command from the Edit menu, by pressing Ctrl+F, or by clicking the Find button on the toolbar.

FIGURE 7-31.

Using the Find And Replace dialog box to search for data.

In the Find What text box, type the data that you want Access to find. You can include wildcard characters similar to that of the LIKE comparison operator. *See the section titled "Defining Simple Field Validation Rules" in Chapter 5 to perform a generic search.* Use an asterisk (*) to indicate a string of unknown characters of any length, and use a question mark (?) to indicate exactly one unknown character (or a space). For example, "*AB??DE*" matches "Aberdeen" and "Tab idea" but not "Lab department." If you're searching a date field for dates in January, you can specify *-Jan-* (provided that you click the Search Fields As Formatted check box and provided that the field uses the Medium Date format).

By default, Access searches the field that your cursor was in before you opened the Find And Replace dialog box. To search the entire table, select the table name from the Look In drop-down list box. By default, Access searches all records from the top of the recordset unless you change the Search drop-down list box to search down or up from the current record position. Select the Match Case check box if you want to find text that exactly matches the uppercase and lowercase letters you typed. By default, Access is case-insensitive unless you select this check box.

Select the Search Fields As Formatted check box if you need to search the data as it is displayed rather than as it is stored by Access. Although searching this way is slower, you probably should select this check box if you are searching a Date/Time field. You might also want to select this check box when searching a Yes/No field for Yes because any value except 0 is a valid indicator of Yes.

Click Find Next to start searching from the current record. Each time you click Find Next again, Access moves to the next value it finds, and loops to the top of the recordset to continue the search if you started in the middle. After you establish search criteria and you close the Find And Replace dialog box, you can press Shift+F4 to execute the search from the current record without having to open the dialog box again.

Using Filter By Selection

If you want to see all the rows in your table that match any part of a value that you can see in a row in the datasheet grid, you can use Filter By Selection. For example, to see all stores that have the word *University* in their name, find a store that has *University* in its name and highlight that word. Click the Filter By Selection button on the toolbar or choose Filter from the Records menu and then Filter By Selection from the submenu. When the search is completed you should see only university bookstores listed. To remove a filter, click the Remove Filter button on the toolbar or choose Remove Filter/Sort from the Records menu.

Alternatively, you can select a complete value in a field to see only rows that match that value. Figure 7-32 shows the value *WA* selected in the State/Province column and the result after clicking the Filter By Selection button. If the filtering data you need is in several contiguous columns, click the first column, hold down the Shift key and click the last column to select all of the data, and then click the Filter By Selection button to see only rows that match the data in all the columns you selected.

FIGURE 7-32.

The list of stores in Washington state, compiled using Filter By Selection.

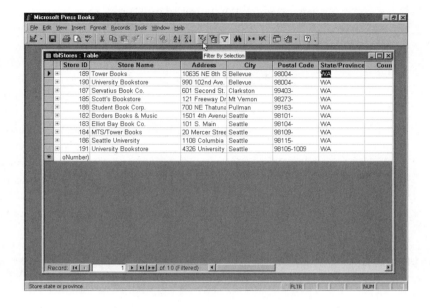

You can also add a filter to a filter. For example, if you want to see all university bookstores in the state of Texas, find a row containing the word *University* in the store name, select the word, and then click the Filter By Selection button. In the filtered list, find the value *TX* in the State/Province column, highlight it, and click the Filter By Selection button again.

 NOTE

> If you select a word at the beginning of a field and use it with Filter By Selection, you will see only rows whose value is the first word in the column. Likewise, selecting a word at the end of a field finds only rows whose column value ends in a matching value. Selecting a word in the middle of a field searches for that word anywhere in the same column.
>
> If you apply a filter to a subdatasheet, you will filter all of the subdatasheets that are open.

Using Filter By Form

Filter By Selection is great for searching for rows that match *all* of several criteria (Store Name like "*University*" *and* State/Province equals "TX"), but what if you want to see rows that meet *any* of

III

Working with Data

several criteria (State/Province equals "WA" *or* State/Province equals "CA" *or* State/Province equals "OR")? You can use Filter By Form to easily build the criteria for this type of search.

When you click the Filter By Form button on the Table Datasheet toolbar, Access shows you a Query By Form example that looks like your datasheet but contains no data. (See Figure 7-33.) If you have no filtering criteria previously defined, Access shows you the Look For tab and one Or tab at the bottom of the window. Move to each column in which you want to define criteria and either select a value from the drop-down list or enter criteria, much the same way that you did to create validation rules in Chapter 5, "Building Your Database in Microsoft Access." For example, you can enter *Like "University*"* in the Store Name field to search for the word *University* at the beginning of the name. You can use criteria such as *>5* in a numeric field to find only rows containing values greater than 5. You can enter multiple criteria on one line, but *all* of the criteria you enter on a single line must be true for a particular row to be selected.

FIGURE 7-33.

Using Filter By Form to search for one of several states.

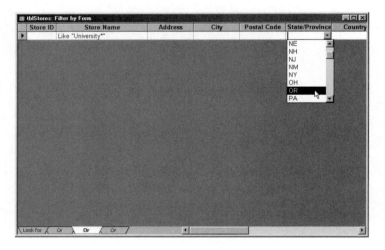

If you want to see rows that contain any of several values in a particular column (for example, rows from several states), enter the first value in the appropriate column, and then click the Or tab at the bottom of the window to enter additional criteria. In this example, *"WA"* was entered in the State/Province column on the Look For tab and *"CA"* on the first Or tab; you can see *"OR"* being selected for the second Or tab in Figure 7-33. Each tab also specifies Like "University*" for the store name. (As you define additional criteria, Access makes additional Or tabs available at the bottom of the window.) Figure 7-34 shows the result of applying this criteria by clicking the Apply Filter button on the toolbar.

FIGURE 7-34.

The stores with names starting with "University" in the states of "WA," "CA," and "OR."

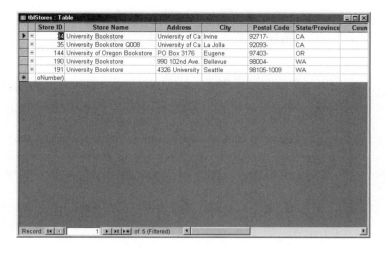

Store ID	Store Name	Address	City	Postal Code	State/Province	Coun
34	University Bookstore	Unviersity of Ca	Irvine	92717-	CA	
35	University Bookstore Q008	University of Ca	La Jolla	92093-	CA	
144	University of Oregon Bookstore	PO Box 3176	Eugene	97403-	OR	
190	University Bookstore	990 102nd Ave.	Bellevue	98004-	WA	
191	University Bookstore	4326 University	Seattle	98105-1009	WA	

Record: 1 of 5 (Filtered)

TIP

Access always remembers the last filtering or sorting criteria you defined for a datasheet. The next time you open the datasheet, click the Apply Filter toolbar button to apply the last filter you created. If you want to save a particular filter/sort definition, choose Filter from the Records menu, and then choose Advanced Filter/Sort from the submenu. Choose Save As Query from the File menu, and give your criteria a name. The next time you open the table, return to Advanced Filter/Sort, and then choose Load From Query from the File menu to find the criteria you previously saved.

? SEE ALSO

Chapter 8, "Adding Power with Select Queries," provides details about building complex filtering criteria.

You can actually define very complex filtering criteria using expressions and the Or tabs in the Filter By Form window. If you look at the Advanced Filter/Sort window, you can see that Access builds all your criteria in a design grid that looks similar to a Query window in Design view, which you'll study in the next chapter. In fact, filters and sorts use the query capabilities of Access to accomplish the result you want, so in Datasheet view you can use all the same filtering capabilities you'll find for queries.

Printing a Datasheet

You can use Datasheet view to print information from your table. If you have applied filter/sort criteria, you can limit which records Microsoft Access prints and you can define the print sequence. You can also control which fields are printed. (You cannot perform any calculations; you must create a query, a form, or a report to do that.) As

III

Working with Data

you discovered earlier in this chapter, you can format the fields you want to print, including setting the font and adjusting the spacing between columns and between rows. If you use the Caption property when defining fields in Design view, you can also customize the column headings.

To produce the datasheet layout shown in Figure 7-35 for the tblStores table, you should hide all but the columns shown, increase the row height to add space between the printed rows, and size the columns so that you can see all the information. You should also eliminate the vertical gridlines—you turn them off by choosing Datasheet from the Format menu, and then clearing the Vertical check box in the Gridlines Shown area of the Datasheet Formatting dialog box. Add the search criteria for stores beginning with "University" in Washington, California, and Oregon as you learned in the previous section.

FIGURE 7-35.

A datasheet that's ready to print.

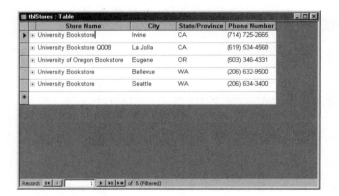

Print Preview

After you format a datasheet the way you want it, you can switch to Print Preview to verify that the data fits on a printed page. Choose the Print Preview command from the File menu (or click the Print Preview button on the toolbar) to see the display shown in Figure 7-36. Notice that the mouse pointer changes to a small magnifying glass. You can move the mouse pointer to any part of the report and click to zoom in and see the data up close. You can also click the Zoom button on the toolbar (the magnifying glass icon) to magnify the report and display the upper left corner of the current page. You can set a custom zoom percentage by using the Zoom Control drop-down box. While zoomed in, you can use the arrow keys to move around the displayed page in small increments. Press the Page Up or Page Down key to move around in larger increments. You can press Ctrl+Down arrow to move to the bottom of the page, Ctrl+Up arrow to move to the top,

Ctrl+Right arrow to move to the right margin, and Ctrl+Left arrow to move to the left margin. Ctrl+Home puts you back in the upper left corner, and Ctrl+End moves the display to the lower right corner. Click the Zoom button again or press the left mouse button to zoom out.

FIGURE 7-36.

The datasheet in Print Preview.

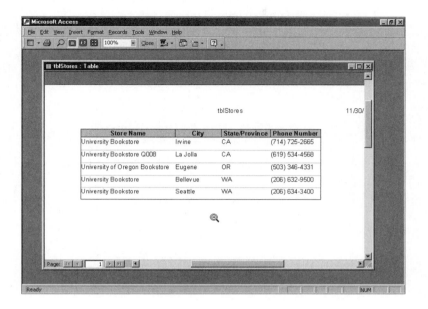

If your printed output has multiple pages, you can use the Page Up and Page Down keys while you are zoomed out to move between pages. Click the Two Pages or the Multiple Pages button on the toolbar to see the layout of multiple pages at the same time. (Unless you have a high resolution monitor and are using large fonts in your datasheet, you probably won't be able to read the data on the page in multiple page view.) Click the Close button to exit Print Preview without printing. Click the Print button to send your formatted datasheet to a printer. Choose Page Setup from the File menu to specify printer setup options, as explained in the next section. You can use the drop-down list next to the Office Links button to start the Microsoft Word Mail Merge Wizard or to export the report to Word or to Microsoft Excel (if you have these applications installed).

 NOTE

> For a datasheet that has a subdatasheet defined, if you expand the subdatasheet before you print the datasheet, you will see the related data in your request.

Page Setup

For every table, you can set default page setup attributes that you want Access to use whenever you print the datasheet. With the datasheet open, choose Page Setup from the File menu to see the dialog box shown in Figure 7-37.

FIGURE 7-37.

The Page Setup dialog box.

In this dialog box, click the Margins tab to specify the top, bottom, left, and right margins. Click the Page tab to select the paper size and a specific type of printer. In general, it's best to leave the Default Printer option selected. This provides maximum flexibility if you move the database application to another computer. Note also that you can ask Access to print the datasheet in Landscape orientation (sideways across the length of the paper). This is very handy if you want to print more fields than will normally fit across the narrower width of the printer paper.

Printing

To send the datasheet to the printer, click the Print button on the toolbar. You can also print a datasheet directly from the Database window by selecting the table you want and choosing the Print command from the File menu. When you choose the Print command, Access displays a Print dialog box similar to the one shown in Figure 7-38. (The dialog box varies depending on your printer.) If you click the Print button on one of the toolbars, Access sends the report directly to the printer without prompting you.

FIGURE 7-38.

The Print dialog box.

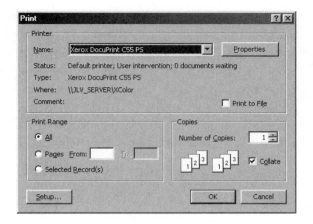

In all Print dialog boxes, you can choose to print multiple copies. You can also choose to print all pages or a range of pages. If you select the Collate check box, Access prints the first through last pages in sequence and then repeats that order for each set of pages. If you clear the Collate check box, Access prints the number of copies you requested for the first page, then the number of copies you requested for the second page, and so on. On some printers, printing uncollated is faster because each page is sent to the printer memory only once, and the printer can quickly produce multiple copies once the page is loaded. Printing collated can be slower because each copy of a page must be sent to the printer separately. You can also tell Access to send your output to a file that you can copy to your printer when you want to print it.

When you send the output to a printer, Access displays a printing progress report in a dialog box, as shown in Figure 7-39. While Access is sending pages to the print spool, you can switch to other applications to perform other tasks. Once the pages have been spooled, you can go on to other tasks in Access while Windows sends the report to your printer.

FIGURE 7-39.

The Printing dialog box, which shows the printing status.

III

Working with Data

Now that you've worked with data from single tables by using datasheets, it's time to deal with data from multiple tables and to update many rows in a table in one operation. To handle these operations, you need the power of queries, as explained in the next two chapters.

CHAPTER 8

Adding Power with Select Queries

I n the previous chapter, you learned about working with
the data in your tables in Datasheet view. Although you
can do a lot with datasheets—including browsing, sorting, filtering, updating, and printing your data—you'll find
that you often need to perform calculations on your data or
retrieve related data from multiple tables. To select a set of
data to work with, you use queries.

When you define and run a *select query* (which selects information from the tables and queries in your database, as opposed to an *action query,* which inserts, updates, or deletes
data), Microsoft Access creates a *recordset* of the selected
data. In most cases, you can work with a recordset in the
same way that you work with a table: you can browse
through it, select information from it, print it, and even update the data in it. But unlike a real table, a recordset doesn't
actually exist in your database. Access creates a recordset
from the data in the source tables of your query at the time
you run the query.

As you learn to design forms and reports later in this book,
you'll find that queries are the best way to focus on the specific
data you need for the task at hand. You'll also find that queries
are useful for providing choices for combo and list boxes, which
make entering data in your database much easier.

NOTE

> The examples in this chapter are based on the tables and data from the Entertainment Scheduling sample database (Entertain.mdb) on the companion CD included with this book.

To open a new Query window in Design view, click the Queries button in the Database window, and then click the New button in the top row of the Database window. A dialog box opens that lets you either start a new query from scratch in Design view or select a query wizard. (You'll learn about query wizards later in this chapter.)

To open an existing query in Design view, click the Queries button in the Database window (which, in this case, displays the Query list for the Entertainment Scheduling database, as shown in Figure 8-1), select the query you want, and click the Design button.

FIGURE 8-1.

Opening a Query window in Design view from the Database window.

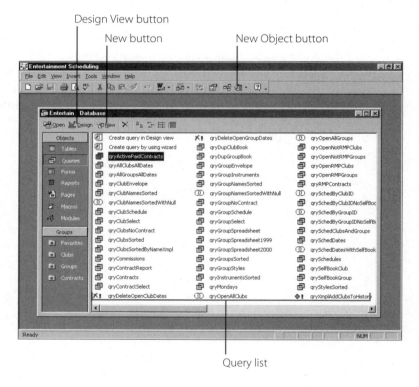

Figure 8-2 shows a query whose window has been opened in Design view. The upper part of the Query window contains field lists, and the lower part contains the design grid.

FIGURE 8-2.

A query open in
Design view.

Field lists of tables or
queries used in this query

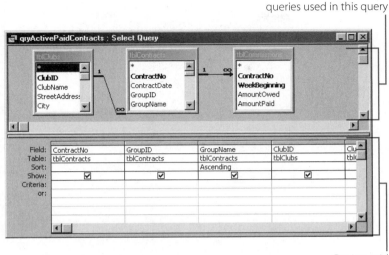

Design grid

Selecting Data from a Single Table

One advantage of using queries is that they allow you to find data easily in multiple related tables. Queries are also useful, however, for sifting through the data in a single table. All the techniques you use for working with a single table apply equally to more complex multiple-table queries, so this chapter begins by using queries to select data from a single table.

The easiest way to start building a query is to open the Database window, select the table you want, and select Query from the New Object toolbar button's drop-down list. (See Figure 8-1.) Do this now with the tblGroups table in the Entertainment Scheduling database, and then select Design View in the New Query dialog box. Click OK to open the window shown in Figure 8-3 on the next page. If you can't see the Table row in the lower part of the Query window, choose the Table Names command from the View menu.

> **NOTE**

The New Object button "remembers" the last new object type that you created. If you've created only tables up to this point, you have to use the button's drop-down list to select Query. Once you start a new query in this manner, the New Object button defaults to Query until you use the button's drop-down list to create a different type of object.

III

Working with Data

FIGURE 8-3.

The Query window in Design view for a new query on tblGroups.

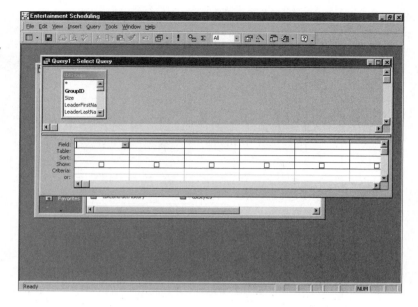

As mentioned earlier, the Query window in Design view has two main parts. In the upper part are field lists with the fields for the tables or queries you chose for this query. The lower part of the window is the design grid, in which you do all the design work. Each column in the grid represents one field that you'll work with in this query. As you'll see later, a field can be a simple field from one of the tables, a calculated field based on several fields in the tables, or a total field using one of the functions provided by Microsoft Access.

You use the first row of the design grid to select fields—the fields you want in the resulting recordset, the fields you want to sort, and the fields you want to test for values. As you'll learn later, you can also generate custom field names (for display in the resulting recordset), and you can use complex expressions or calculations to generate a calculated field.

Because you chose the Table Names command from the View menu, Access displays the table name (which is the source of the selected field) in the second row of the design grid. In the Sort row, you can specify whether Access should sort the selected or calculated field in ascending or in descending order.

> It's a good idea to select the Show Table Names option on the Tables/Queries tab of the Options dialog box (choose the Options command from the Tools menu) whenever your query is based on more than one table. Because you might have the same field name in more than one of the tables, showing table names in the design grid helps to ensure that your query refers to the field you intend it to.

In the Show row, you can use the check boxes to indicate the fields that will be included in the recordset. By default, Access includes all the fields you selected in the design grid. Sometimes you'll want to include a field in the query to allow you to select the records you want (such as the contracts for a certain date range), but you won't need that field in the recordset. You can add that field to the design grid so that you can define criteria, but you should clear the Show check box beneath the field to exclude it from the recordset.

Finally, you can use the Criteria row and the rows labeled *Or* to enter the criteria you want to use as filters. Once you understand how a query is put together, you'll find it easy to specify exactly the fields and records that you want.

Specifying Fields

The first step in building a query is to select the fields you want in the recordset. You can select the fields in several ways. Using the keyboard, you can tab to a column in the design grid and press Alt+Down arrow to open the list of available fields. (To move to the design grid, press F6.) Use the Up and Down arrow keys to highlight the field you want, and then press Enter to select the field.

Another way to select a field is to drag it from one of the field lists in the upper part of the window to one of the columns in the design grid. In Figure 8-4 on the next page, the Size field is being dragged to the design grid. When you drag a field, the mouse pointer turns into a small rectangle.

At the top of each field list in the upper part of the Query window (and also next to the first entry in the Field drop-down list in the design grid) is an asterisk (*) symbol. This symbol is shorthand for "all fields in the table or the query." When you want to include all the fields in a table or a query, you don't have to define each one individually in the design grid (unless you also want to define some sorting or selection criteria for specific fields). You can simply add the asterisk to the design grid to include all the fields from a list. Note that

III

Working with Data

you can add individual fields to the grid in addition to the asterisk in order to define criteria for those fields, but you should clear the Show check box for the individual fields so that they don't appear twice in the recordset.

FIGURE 8-4.

Dragging a field to a column in the design grid.

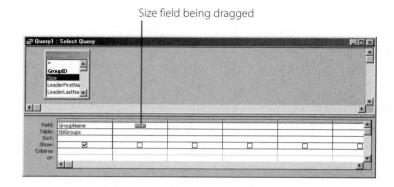

Size field being dragged

TIP

Another easy way to select all the fields in a table is to double-click the title bar of the field list in the upper part of the Query window. This highlights all the fields. Then click any of the highlighted fields and drag them as a group to the Field row in the design grid. While you're dragging, the mouse pointer changes to a multiple rectangle icon, indicating that you're dragging multiple fields. When you release the mouse button, you'll see that Access has copied all the fields to the design grid for you.

For this exercise, select GroupName, Size, City, and StateOrProvince from the tblGroups table in the Entertainment Scheduling database. If you switch the Query window to Datasheet view at this point, you'll see records containing only the fields you selected from the underlying table.

Setting Field Properties

SEE ALSO

For details about field properties, see Chapter 5, "Building Your Database in Microsoft Access."

In general, fields that are output by a query inherit the properties defined for the field in the table. You can define a different Description property (the information that is displayed on the status bar when you select that field in a Query window in Datasheet view), Format property (how the data is displayed), Decimal Places property (for numeric data), Input Mask property, and Caption property (the column heading). When you learn to define calculated fields later in this chapter, you'll see that it's a good idea to define the properties for these fields. If the field in the query is a foreign key linked to another table, you can also set the lookup properties as described in Chapter 6, "Modifying

Your Database Design." Access propagates lookup properties that you have defined in your table fields; however, you can use the properties in the Lookup tab on the query field properties to override them.

To set the properties of a field, click any row of the field's column in the design grid, and then click the Properties button on the toolbar or choose Properties from the View menu to display the Field Properties window, shown in Figure 8-5. Even though the fields in your query inherit their properties from the underlying table, you won't see those properties here. For example, the Format property for Size in tblGroups is Standard, and Decimal Places is 0, although neither value appears in the Field Properties window. Use the property settings in the Field Properties window to override any inherited properties and to customize how a field looks when viewed for this query. Try entering new property settings for the Size field, as shown in Figure 8-5.

FIGURE 8-5.

Setting properties for the Size field.

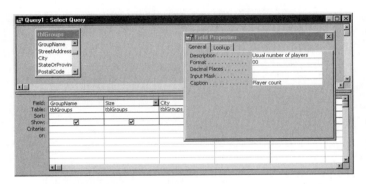

If you make these changes and switch to Datasheet view, you'll see that the Size column heading is now *Player Count,* that two digits are displayed, and that the text on the status bar matches the new description, as shown in Figure 8-6.

FIGURE 8-6.

The Size field displayed with new property settings.

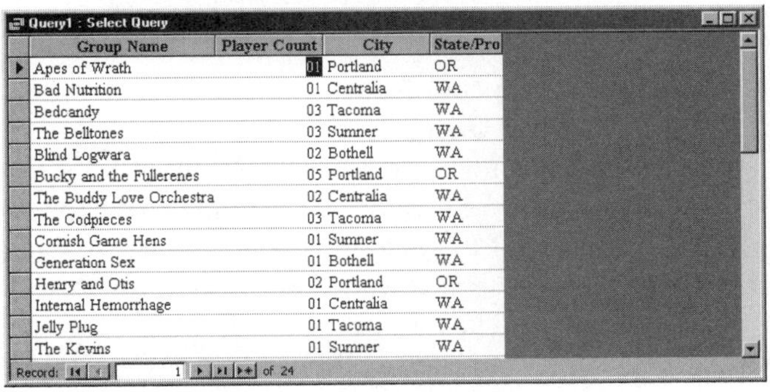

III

Working with Data

TIP

You'll notice that in Datasheet view, any new query you build using the tblGroups table will have no vertical gridlines and will use a serif font. These attributes are inherited from the table datasheet settings that you saw in the previous chapter. While you are in a query's Datasheet view, you can set the display format exactly as you would for a table in Datasheet view by using the commands on the Format menu. *See the previous chapter for details.* When you save the query, Access saves the custom query datasheet format settings.

Entering Selection Criteria

The next step is to further refine the values in the fields you want. The example shown in Figure 8-7 selects groups from the state of Washington.

FIGURE 8-7.

A design grid that specifies "WA" as a selection criterion.

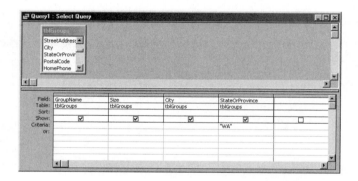

Entering selection criteria in a query is similar to entering a validation rule for a field, which you learned about in Chapter 5, "Building Your Database in Microsoft Access." To look for a single value, simply type it in the Criteria row for the field you want to test. If the field you're testing is a text field and the value you're looking for has any blank spaces in it, you must enclose the value in quotation marks. Note that Access adds quotation marks for you around single text values. (In Figure 8-7, *WA* was typed, but the field shows "WA" after Enter is pressed.)

If you want to test for any of several values, enter the values in the Criteria row, separated by the word *Or.* For example, specifying *WA Or OR* searches for records for Washington or Oregon. You can also test for any of several values by entering each value in a separate Criteria or Or row for the field you want to test. For example, you can enter *OR* in the Criteria row, *WA* in the next row (the first Or row), and so on—but you have to be careful if you're also specifying criteria in other fields, as explained below.

> You should be careful when entering criteria that might also be a Microsoft Access keyword. In the examples shown here, I specifically chose to use criteria for the two-character abbreviation for the state of Oregon ("OR") because "or," as you can see in the examples, is also a keyword. In many cases, Access is smart enough to figure out what you mean from the context. You can enter:
>
>   Or Or Wa
>
> in the criteria under State, and Access assumes that the first "Or" is criteria (by placing quotation marks around the word for you) and the second "Or" is the Boolean comparison keyword. If you want to be sure that Access interprets your criteria correctly, always place double quotation marks around criteria text.

In the next section, you'll see that you can also include a comparison operator in the Criteria row so that, for example, you can look for values less than (<), greater than or equal to (>=), or not equal to (<>) the value that you specify.

AND vs. OR

When you enter criteria for several fields, all of the tests in a single Criteria row or Or row must be true for a record to be included in the recordset. That is, Access performs a logical AND operation between multiple criteria in the same row. So if you enter *WA* in the Criteria row for StateOrProvince and *<3* in the Criteria row for Size, the record must be for the state of Washington *and* must have a group size of less than three in order to be selected. If you enter *WA Or OR* in the Criteria row for StateOrProvince and *>=2 And <=5* in the Criteria row for Size, the record must be for the state of Washington or Oregon, *and* the group size must be between two and five inclusive.

Figure 8-8 shows the result of applying a logical AND operator between any two tests. As you can see, both tests must be true for the result of the AND to be true and for the record to be selected.

FIGURE 8-8.
The result of applying the logical AND operator between two tests.

AND	True	False
True	True (Selected)	False (Rejected)
False	False (Rejected)	False (Rejected)

III

Working with Data

When you specify multiple criteria for a field and separate the criteria by a logical OR operator, only one of the criteria must be true for the record to be selected. You can specify several OR criteria for a field, either by entering them all in a single Criteria row separated by the logical OR operator, as shown earlier, or by entering each subsequent criterion in a separate Or row. When you use multiple Or rows, if the criteria *in any one of the Or rows* is true, the record will be selected. Figure 8-9 shows the result of applying a logical OR operation between any two tests. As you can see, only one of the tests must be true for the result of the OR to be true and for the record to be selected.

FIGURE 8-9.

The result of applying the logical OR operator between two tests.

OR	True	False
True	True (Selected)	True (Selected)
False	True (Selected)	False (Rejected)

> **NOTE**
>
> It's a common mistake to get *Or* and *And* mixed up when typing a compound criteria for a single field. You may think to yourself, "I want all the entertainment groups in the states of Washington *and* California," and then type: *WA And CA* in the Criteria row for the StateOrProvince field. When you do this, you're asking Access to find rows where *(StateOrProvince = "WA") And (StateOrProvince = "CA")*. Since a field in a record can't have more than one value at a time (it can't contain both the values "WA" and "CA" in the same record), there won't be any records in the output. To look for all the rows for these two states, you need to ask Access to search for *(StateOrProvince = "WA") Or (StateOrProvince = "CA")*. In other words, type *WA Or CA* in the Criteria row under the StateOrProvince field.

Let's look at a specific example. In Figure 8-10, you specify *WA* in the first Criteria row of the StateOrProvince field and *<3* in that same Criteria row for the Size field. In the next row (the first Or row), you specify *OR* in the StateOrProvince field. When you run this query, you get all the records for the state of Washington that also have a group size of less than three. You also get any records for the state of Oregon regardless of the group size.

FIGURE 8-10.

A design grid that specifies multiple AND and OR selection criteria.

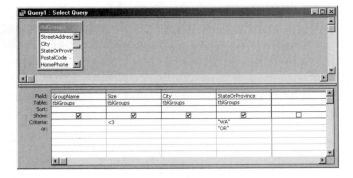

In Figure 8-11, you can see the recordset (in Datasheet view) that results from running this query.

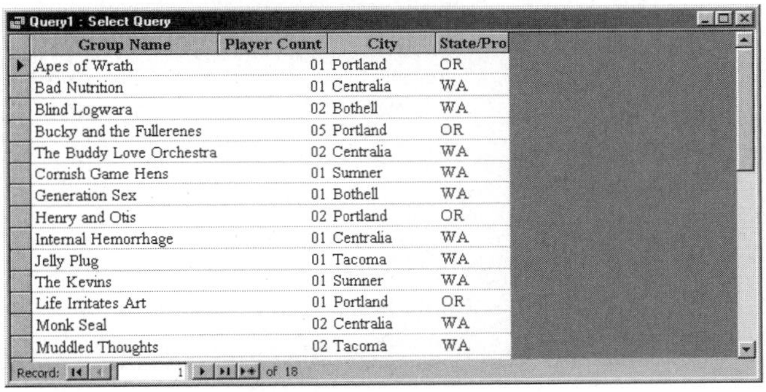

FIGURE 8-11.

The recordset of the query shown in Figure 8-10.

If you also want to limit rows from groups in Oregon to those that have a size less than three, you must specify <3 again under Size in the first Or row—that is, on the same row that filters for OR under StateOrProvince. Although this seems like extra work, this gives you complete flexibility to filter the data you want. You could, for example, include groups smaller than three members in Washington and groups smaller than five members in Oregon by placing a different criteria (<5) under Size on the row that filters for Oregon.

BETWEEN, IN, and LIKE

In addition to comparison operators, Access provides three special predicate clauses that are useful for specifying the data you want in the recordset. Table 8-1 on the next page describes these clauses.

TABLE 8-1. Predicate Clauses for Queries

Predicate	Description
BETWEEN	Useful for specifying a range of values. The clause *Between 10 And 20* is the same as specifying *>=10 And <=20.*
IN	Useful for specifying a list of values, any one of which can match the field being searched. The clause *In ("WA","CA","ID")* is the same as *"WA" Or "CA" Or "ID".*
LIKE	Useful for searching for patterns in text fields. You can include special characters and ranges of values in the LIKE comparison string to define the character pattern you want. Use a question mark (?) to indicate any single character in that position. Use an asterisk (*) to indicate zero or more characters in that position. The pound-sign character (#) specifies a single numeric digit in that position. Include a range in brackets ([ ]) to test for a particular range of characters in a position, and use an exclamation point (!) to indicate exceptions. The range *[0-9]* tests for numbers, *[a-z]* tests for letters, and *[!0-9]* tests for any characters except *0* through *9.* For example, the clause *Like "?[a-k]d[0-9]*"* tests for any single character in the first position, any character from *a* through *k* in the second position, the letter *d* in the third position, any character from *0* through *9* in the fourth position, and any number of characters after that.

Suppose you want to find all entertainment groups in the city of Tacoma or in the town of Sumner that have between two and four members and whose name begins with the letter *B*. Figure 8-12 shows how you would enter these criteria. (Note that the test for GroupName checks for names that begin either with *B* or with the word *The* followed by a name beginning with the letter *B*.) Figure 8-13 shows the recordset of this query.

FIGURE 8-12.

A design grid that uses BETWEEN, IN, and LIKE.

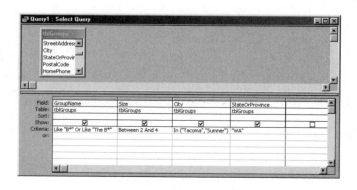

FIGURE 8-13.

The recordset of the query shown in Figure 8-12.

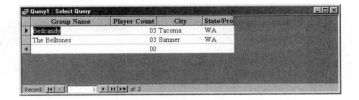

For additional examples that use the BETWEEN, IN, and LIKE comparison operators, see the section titled "Defining Simple Field Validation Rules" in Chapter 5 and the "Predicate" sections in Chapter 11.

Working with Dates and Times in Criteria

Access stores dates and times as eight-byte decimal numbers. The value to the left of the decimal point represents the day (day zero is December 30, 1899), and the fractional part of the number stores the time as a fraction of a day, accurate to seconds. Fortunately, you don't have to worry about converting internal numbers to specify a test for a particular date value because Access handles date and time entries in several formats.

You must always surround date and time values with pound signs (#) to tell Access that you're entering a date or a time. To test for a specific date, use the date notation that is most comfortable for you. For example, *#April 15, 1997#*, *#4/15/97#*, and *#15-Apr-1997#* are all the same date if you chose English (United States) from the drop-down list on the Regional Settings tab of the Regional Settings Properties window. (You can display the Regional Settings Properties window by double-clicking the Regional Settings icon in Control Panel.) Similarly, *#5:30 PM#* and *#17:30#* both specify 5:30 in the evening.

Access has several useful functions to assist you in testing date and time values. Table 8-2 on the next page explains each function and includes examples that use the BeginningDate field in the tblContracts table.

Calculating Values

You can specify a calculation on any of the fields in your table and make that calculation a new field in the recordset. You can use any of the many built-in functions that Access provides. (See the examples in Table 8-2.) You can also create a field in a query by using arithmetic operators on fields in the underlying table to calculate a value. In a contract record, for example, you might have a NumberOfWeeks field and a ContractPrice (per week) field, but not the extended price (weeks times price). You can include that value in your recordset by

TABLE 8-2. **Date and Time Functions**

Function	Description	Example
Day(*date*)	Returns a value from 1 through 31 for the day of the month.	To select records with BeginningDate values after the 10th of any month, enter *Day([BeginningDate])* as a calculated field (see the next section) and enter *>10* as the criterion for that field.
Month(*date*)	Returns a value from 1 through 12 for the month of the year.	To find all records that have a BeginningDate value of June, enter *Month([BeginningDate])* as a calculated field (see the next section) and enter *6* as the criterion for that field.
Year(*date*)	Returns a value from 100 through 9999 for the year.	To find dates in 1997, enter *Year([BeginningDate])* as a calculated field (see the next section) and enter *1997* as the criterion for that field.
Weekday (*date*)	As a default, returns a value from 1 (Sunday) through 7 (Saturday) for the day of the week.	To find business day dates, enter *Weekday([BeginningDate])* as a calculated field (see the next section) and enter *Between 2 And 6* as the criterion for that field.
Hour(*date*)	Returns a value from 0 through 23 for the hour of the day.	To find a scheduled start time before noon, enter *Hour([BeginningDate])* as a calculated field (see the next section) and enter *<12* as the criterion for that field.
DatePart (*interval, date*)	Returns a portion of the date or time, depending on the interval code you supply. Useful interval codes are *"q"* for quarter of the year (1 through 4) and *"ww"* for week of the year (1 through 53).	To select dates in the second quarter, enter *DatePart("q," [BeginningDate])* as a calculated field (see the next section), and enter *2* as the criterion for that field.
Date	Returns the current system date.	To select dates more than 30 days ago, enter *<Date() – 30* as the criterion for that field.

typing the calculation in the field of an empty column in the design grid using the NumberOfWeeks field, the multiplication operator (*), and the ContractPrice field.

You can also create a new text (string) field by concatenating fields containing text, string constants, or numeric data. You create a string constant by enclosing the text in double or single quotation marks. Use the ampersand character (&) between fields or strings to indicate that you want to concatenate them. For example, you might want to create an output field that concatenates the LastName field, a comma, a blank space, and then the FirstName field.

Table 8-3 shows some of the operators you can use in expressions.

TABLE 8-3. Operators Used in Expressions

Operator	Description
+	Adds two numeric expressions.
–	Subtracts the second numeric expression from the first numeric expression.
*	Multiplies two numeric expressions.
/	Divides the first numeric expression by the second numeric expression.
\	Rounds both numeric expressions to integers and then divides the first integer by the second integer. The result is truncated to an integer.
^	Raises the first numeric expression to the power indicated by the second numeric expression.
MOD	Rounds both numeric expressions to integers, divides the first integer by the second integer, and returns the remainder.
&	Creates an extended text string by concatenating the first text string to the second text string. If either expression is a number, Access converts it to a text string before concatenating the expressions.

Try creating a query on the tblGroups table in the Entertainment Scheduling database that shows a field containing the group name, followed by a single field containing the street address, a comma and a blank space, the city, another comma and a blank space, the state or province followed by two blank spaces, and the postal code. Your expression should look like this:

> [StreetAddress] & ", " & [City] & ", " & [StateOrProvince] & " " & [PostalCode]

The Query window in Design view for this example is shown in Figure 8-14. I clicked in the Field row of the column I wanted and then pressed Shift+F2 to open the Zoom window, where it is easier to enter the expression. Note that you can click the Font button to select a larger font that's easier to read. Once you choose a font, Access uses it whenever you open the Zoom window again.

NOTE

Access requires that all fields on the Field row in a query have a name. For single fields, Access uses the name of the field. When you enter an expression, Access generates a field name in the form *ExprN:* to be able to give the expression a name. *See the section titled "Specifying Field Names" later in this chapter for details about changing the name of fields or expressions.*

FIGURE 8-14.

Editing an expression in the Zoom window.

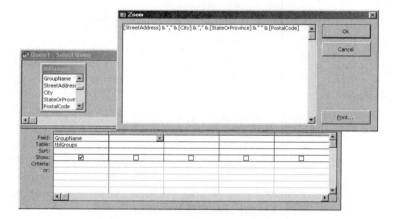

When you look at the query result in Datasheet view, you should see something like that shown in Figure 8-15.

Try typing within the Expr1 field in Datasheet view. Because this display is a result of a calculation (concatenation of strings), Access won't let you update the data in this column.

Using the Expression Builder

For more complex expressions, Access provides a utility called the Expression Builder. Let's say you want to calculate the total commission

FIGURE 8-15.

A query result with concatenated text fields.

owed for a contract in the Entertainment Scheduling database. You have to work with several fields to do this: ContractPrice, NumberOfWeeks, and Commission1%. To see how the Expression Builder works, start a new query on the tblContracts table. Click in an empty field in the design grid, and then click the Build button on the toolbar. Access opens the Expression Builder window shown in Figure 8-16.

FIGURE 8-16.

The Expression Builder window.

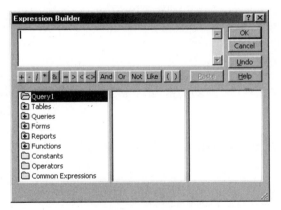

In the upper part of the window is a blank text box in which you can build an expression. You can type the expression yourself, but it's much easier to use the various expression operator buttons just below the text box to help you out. In the lower part of the window are three list boxes you can use to find field names and function names that you need to build your expression.

The basic expression you need looks something like this:

[ContractPrice] * [NumberOfWeeks] * [Commission1%]

ContractPrice is a Currency field, and NumberOfWeeks is an integer. Whenever you ask Access to evaluate an arithmetic expression, it returns a result that has a data type sufficiently complex to contain the result. As you might expect, multiplying an integer (a simple data type) with a currency field (a more complex data type) returns a currency field. So far, so good. But what do you suppose happens when you multiply the currency field by the Commission1% field, a floating-point number? Access doesn't know in advance that Commission1% contains only a simple percentage and that a Currency result would do very nicely. Access has to assume that the floating-point field could contain a very large or a very small number, so the data type of the calculation result is a floating-point number. To get the value back as Currency you'll have to ask Access to convert the data type for you. Fortunately, there's a handy built-in function called *CCur* (Convert to Currency) to do this.

As you might guess, you can use the Expression Builder to help you correctly construct this expression. Because you need to hand the expression to the CCur built-in function, double-click the Functions folder in the far left list box to expand the list to show categories of functions. As shown in Figure 8-17, the Expression Builder allows you to select any of the built-in functions or any of the user-defined functions in the Entertainment Scheduling database. Click Built-In Functions, and then select Conversion in the second list box. Select CCur in the third list box, and then click Paste to move a "skeleton" of the function to the text box in the upper part of the window. You should see CCur («expr») in the list box. Click «expr» to highlight it so you can replace it with the next part of your expression.

FIGURE 8-17.

Selecting from the Built-In Functions list in the Expression Builder window.

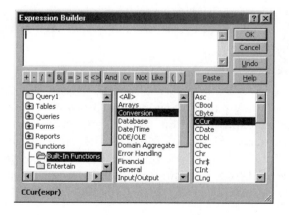

Because you need fields from the tblContracts table, double-click the Tables folder in the far left list box. The Tables folder expands to show all the table names. Scroll down in the Expression Builder window until you can see the tblContracts table. Click the tblContracts table to display the list of fields from that table in the middle list box.

To get the total commission for the contract, you need to start with ContractPrice. Click that field, and then click the Paste button to move the field to the expression area. You'll notice that Access pastes *[tblContracts]![ContractPrice]* into the expression area, not just *ContractPrice*. There are two good reasons for this. First, you should enclose all names of objects in Access in brackets ([ ]). If you designed the name without any blank spaces, you can leave out the brackets, but it's always best to include them. Second, the Expression Builder doesn't know whether you might include other tables in this query and whether some of those tables might have field names that are identical to the ones you're selecting now. The way to avoid conflicts is to *fully qualify* the field names by preceding them with the table name. When working in queries, separate the table name from the field name with a period or an exclamation point.

> **NOTE**

> As you'll learn in Chapters 20 and 22, in most cases you should separate the name of an object from the name of an object within that object (for example, a field within a table) with an exclamation point. When you build an expression in the Expression Builder, you'll usually find names separated by exclamation points. However, as you'll learn in Chapter 11, the standard for the SQL database query language uses a period between the name of a table and the name of a field within the table. To be most compatible with the SQL standard when constructing a query expression, use a period between a table name and a field name. Access accepts either an exclamation point or a period in query design.

Next, you need to multiply the price by the commission percentage. Click the small asterisk (*) button to insert a multiplication symbol, and then click «Expr». Select the Commission1% field from the tblContracts table, and then click the Paste button. Insert another multiplication symbol, click «Expr» again, and then insert the NumberOfWeeks field. Your result should look like that shown in Figure 8-18 on the next page.

Click OK to paste your result into the design grid. This should give you a nice Currency result, but remember that Currency can hold up to four decimal places. If you want to print a Currency result on an invoice, customers aren't going to be able to pay you fractions of a cent. To fix this, you need to pass the result of your calculation to one more built-in function.

 New in Access 2000 is a Round function that will serve quite nicely for this purpose. Round accepts two parameters: the expression you want to round, and an integer indicating how many decimal places you want after rounding. In this case, you want cents, so you should tell the Round function to round to 2 decimal places.

III

Working with Data

FIGURE 8-18.

The completed commission expression.

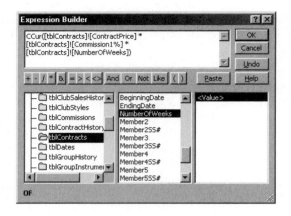

Click just to the left of the CCur function and type:

Round(

Press the End key to move the cursor to the end of your expression, and type:

, 2)

That's all there is to it! Well, almost. Once you create a complex expression like this, if you want the data to display in a specific format or with a certain number of decimal places, you must set the field properties. You should click the field expression in the design grid, and then open the Field Properties window to set the Format property of your new field to Currency.

You might also want to include in your query the ContractNo field and all the fields used in the calculation. Figure 8-19 shows a similar query I built that shows a custom Caption for the Commission1% field, the ContractPrice times NumberOfWeeks (formatted as Currency) as Expr1, the field you just created using Round (also set to Currency format) as Expr2, and the commission calculation without rounding as Expr3 (with Decimal Places set to 4). You can find this query saved as *qryXmplCalc1* in the Entertainment Scheduling Database. The point of this query is to demonstrate potentially problem values if you don't bother to round. If you open qryXmplCalc1 in Datasheet view and scroll down to contract number 4771 as shown in Figure 8-19, you'll see that the unrounded commission amount in Expr3 shows fractional cents. Note that the rounded amount in Expr2 is correct.

FIGURE 8-19.

A query with calculated fields.

Contract No.	Begin Date	Weeks	Contract Price	Ray's %	Expr1	Expr2	Expr3
4764	28-Jan-00	4	$250.00	10.0%	$1,000.00	$100.00	100
4765	28-Jan-00	1	$400.00	11.0%	$400.00	$44.00	44
4766	01-Feb-00	2	$750.00	10.0%	$1,500.00	$150.00	150
4767	04-Feb-00	1	$300.00	10.0%	$300.00	$30.00	30
4768	11-Feb-00	1	$300.00	10.0%	$300.00	$30.00	30
4769	11-Feb-00	1	$300.00	9.0%	$300.00	$27.00	27
4770	11-Feb-00	1	$300.00	11.0%	$300.00	$33.00	33
4771	14-Feb-00	7	$235.00	7.5%	$1,645.00	$123.38	123.375
4772	15-Feb-00	2	$650.00	10.0%	$1,300.00	$130.00	130
4774	16-Feb-00	20	$650.00	10.0%	$13,000.00	$1,300.00	1300
4775	18-Feb-00	1	$300.00	10.0%	$300.00	$30.00	30
4776	18-Feb-00	2	$400.00	9.0%	$800.00	$72.00	72
4777	25-Feb-00	1	$300.00	9.0%	$300.00	$27.00	27
4778	03-Mar-00	1	$250.00	10.0%	$250.00	$25.00	25
4779	03-Mar-00	1	$250.00	10.0%	$250.00	$25.00	25

Record: 120 of 282

> **NOTE**
>
> Fields in an Access database table can contain the special value Null (discussed in Chapter 5). If you ask Access to perform an arithmetic calculation on one or more fields, and any of the fields contain Null, the result of the calculation will be Null. If you suspect you might encounter a Null value in a field, you can use the Immediate If (IIf) and IsNull built-in functions or the NZ (null-to-zero) built-in function to test for Null and substitute a zero (or other appropriate non-Null value) when a field contains Null. For example, if you're using a field named [Quantity] that might contain a Null value in an expression, substitute either of the following expressions.
>
> IIf(IsNull([Quantity]), 0, [Quantity])
>
> or
>
> NZ([Quantity], 0)

Specifying Field Names

You learned earlier that you can change the caption (column heading) for a field in a query by using the field's property sheet. You might have noticed that when you create an expression in the Field row of the design grid, Access adds a prefix such as *Expr1* followed by a colon. Every field in a query must have a name. By default, the name of a field in a query is the name of the field from the source table. Likewise, the default caption for the field is either the field name or the field's original caption property.

You can change or assign field names that will appear in the recordset of a query. This feature is particularly useful when you've calculated a value in the query that you'll use in a form, a report, or another query. In the queries shown in Figures 8-15 and 8-19, you calculated a value and Access assigned a temporary field name. You can replace this name with something more meaningful. For example, in the first query you might want to use something like FullName: and FullAddress:. In the second query, ContractAmt: and RMPCommission: might be appropriate.

III

Working with Data

To change a name generated by Access, replace *ExprN* with the name you want on the Field row in query design. To assign a new name to a field, place the cursor at the beginning of the field specification and enter the new name followed by a colon. Figure 8-20 shows the second query with the field names changed.

FIGURE 8-20.

The result of changing the Expr1 and Expr2 column headings shown in Figure 8-19.

Contract No.	Begin Date	Weeks	Contract Price	Ray's %	ContractAmt	RMP Commission
4642	06-Jul-99	4	$550.00	10.0%	$2,200.00	$220.00
4643	11-Jul-99	2	$450.00	11.0%	$900.00	$99.00
4644	11-Jul-99	1	$0.00	10.0%	$0.00	$0.00
4645	13-Jul-99	3	$600.00	11.0%	$1,800.00	$198.00
4646	01-Mar-00	1	$700.00	10.0%	$700.00	$70.00
4647	30-May-00	2	$550.00	9.0%	$1,100.00	$99.00
4648	30-Nov-99	2	$550.00	10.0%	$1,100.00	$110.00
4649	07-Mar-00	2	$550.00	10.0%	$1,100.00	$110.00
4650	14-Dec-99	2	$550.00	11.0%	$1,100.00	$121.00
4651	05-Oct-99	2	$550.00	10.0%	$1,100.00	$110.00
4652	23-Jul-99	2	$300.00	11.0%	$600.00	$66.00
4654	21-Jun-00	2	$550.00	9.0%	$1,100.00	$99.00
4655	21-Jul-99	2	$550.00	11.0%	$1,100.00	$121.00
4656	03-May-00	2	$550.00	10.0%	$1,100.00	$110.00
4657	20-Oct-99	2	$550.00	10.0%	$1,100.00	$110.00

Record: 1 of 282

Sorting Data

Normally, Access displays the rows in your recordset in the order in which they're retrieved from the database. You can add sorting information to determine the sequence of the data in a query exactly as you did for tables in the previous chapter. Click in the Sort row for the field you want to sort, and select Ascending or Descending from the drop-down list. In the example shown in Figure 8-21, the query results are to be sorted in descending order based on the calculated RMPCommission field. The recordset will list the contracts paying the largest commission first. The resulting Datasheet view is shown in Figure 8-22. (You can find this query saved as *qryXmplCalc* in the Entertainment Scheduling database.)

You can also sort on multiple fields. Access honors your sorting criteria from left to right in the design grid. If, for example, you want to sort by BeginningDate and then by RMPCommission, you should include

FIGURE 8-21.

A query with sorting criteria added.

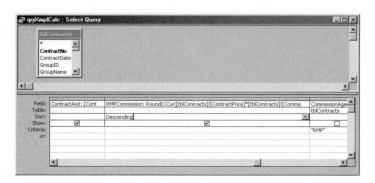

FIGURE 8-22.

The recordset of the query shown in Figure 8-21 in Datasheet view.

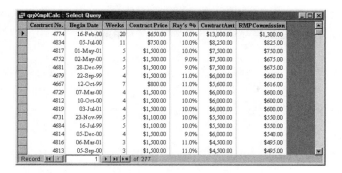

the BeginningDate field to the left of the RMPCommission field. If the additional field you want to sort is already in the design grid but in the wrong location, click the column selector box above the field to select the entire column and then click the selector box again and drag the field to its new location.

 NOTE

> When you first construct and run a query, Access might return the rows in the sequence you expect (for example, in primary key sequence of the leftmost table). However, if you want to be sure Access always returns rows in this order, you must specify sort criteria. As you later add and remove rows in your database, Access may decide to solve your query in a different way, which, in the absence of sorting criteria, might result in a different row sequence than you intended.

Total Queries

Sometimes you aren't interested in each and every row in your table. You'd rather see totals of different groups of data. For example, you might want the total contract amount for all clubs in a particular state. Or you might want to know the average of all sales for each month in the last year. To get these answers, you need a *total query*. To calculate totals within any query, click the Totals button on the toolbar in Design view to open the Total row in the design grid, as shown in Figure 8-23 on the next page.

Totals Within Groups

When you first click the Totals button on the toolbar, Access displays *Group By* in the Total row for any fields you already have in the design grid. At this point the records in each field are grouped but not totaled. If you were to run the query now, you'd get one row in the recordset for each set of unique values—but no totals. You can create totals by replacing Group By with some *total functions* in the Total row.

III

Working with Data

FIGURE 8-23.

The Total row in the design grid.

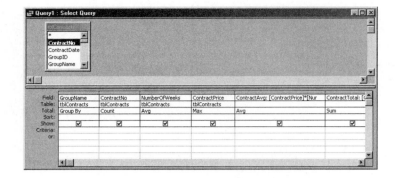

Access provides nine total functions for your use. You can choose the one you want by typing its name in the Total row in the design grid or by selecting it from the drop-down list. The available functions are shown in Table 8-4.

You can experiment with total functions by building a query similar to the one shown in Figure 8-23. Start a new query on the tblContracts table, and include the GroupName, ContractNo, NumberOfWeeks, and ContractPrice fields in the design grid. Include the expression *[ContractPrice] * [NumberOfWeeks]* twice in the design grid and name one field *ContractAvg:* and the other *ContractTotal:*. Click the Totals button on the toolbar to show the Total row. For ContractNo, select Count (to count the number of contracts for each group), select Avg for NumberOfWeeks, Max for ContractPrice, Avg for your first calculated field, and Sum for your second calculated field. Figure 8-24 shows the results when you run the query. (Again, I set some field properties to correctly format AvgOfNumberOfWeeks.)

FIGURE 8-24.

The recordset of the query shown in Figure 8-23.

Group Name	CountOfContrac	AvgOfNumberOf	MaxOfContractP	ContractAvg	ContractTotal
Apes of Wrath	19	1.84	$750.00	$1,023.68	$19,450.00
Bad Nutrition	1	2.00	$650.00	$1,300.00	$1,300.00
Blind Logwara	8	2.38	$650.00	$1,375.00	$11,000.00
Bucky and the Fu	18	1.83	$550.00	$805.56	$14,500.00
Cornish Game He	2	1.00	$300.00	$300.00	$600.00
Generation Sex	9	6.44	$1,100.00	$4,483.33	$40,350.00
Henry and Otis	10	1.70	$550.00	$855.00	$8,550.00
Internal Hemorrh	14	1.43	$400.00	$403.57	$5,650.00
Jelly Plug	8	2.00	$550.00	$406.25	$3,250.00
King Tut and the	8	2.25	$700.00	$1,262.50	$10,100.00
Life Imitates Art	10	1.70	$550.00	$740.00	$7,400.00
Monk Seal	12	2.83	$950.00	$2,241.67	$26,900.00
Muddled Thoughi	15	3.47	$1,500.00	$5,166.67	$77,500.00
Seiza Bench	1	1.00	$450.00	$450.00	$450.00
Shaman's Apprer	26	1.69	$650.00	$732.69	$19,050.00
Supertube	25	2.56	$1,350.00	$1,976.00	$49,400.00

Record: 1 of 23

In the drop-down list for the Total row in the design grid, you'll also find an Expression setting. Select this when you want to create an expression in the Total row that uses one or more of the total functions

TABLE 8-4. Total Functions

Function	Description
Sum	Calculates the sum of all the values for this field in each group. You can specify this function only with number or currency fields.
Avg	Calculates the arithmetic average of all the values for this field in each group. You can specify this function only with number or currency fields. Access does not include any Null values in the calculation.
Min	Returns the lowest value found in this field within each group. For numbers, Min returns the smallest value. For text, Min returns the lowest value in collating sequence ("dictionary" order), without regard to case. Access ignores Null values.
Max	Returns the highest value found in this field within each group. For numbers, Max returns the largest value. For text, Max returns the highest value in collating sequence ("dictionary" order), without regard to case. Access ignores Null values.
Count	Returns the count of the rows in which the specified field is not a Null value. You can also enter the special expression COUNT(*) in the Field row to count all rows in each group, regardless of the presence of Null values.
StDev	Calculates the statistical standard deviation of all the values for this field in each group. You can specify this function only with number or currency fields. If the group does not contain at least two rows, Access returns a Null value.
Var	Calculates the statistical variance of all the values for this field in each group. You can specify this function only with number or currency fields. If the group does not contain at least two rows, Access returns a Null value.
First	Returns the value for the field from the first row encountered in the group. Note that the first row might not be the one with the lowest value.
Last	Returns the value for the field from the last row encountered in the group. Note that the last row might not be the one with the highest value.

III

Working with Data

listed earlier. For example, you might want to calculate a value that reflects the range of commission percentages in the group, as in the following.

Max([Commission1%]) – Min([Commission1%])

Selecting Records to Form Groups

You might not want to include some records in the groups that form your total query. To filter out certain records from groups, you can add to the design grid the field or fields you want to use as filters. To create the filter, select the Where setting in the Total row, clear that field's Show check box, and enter criteria that tell Access which records to exclude. In the tblContracts table, Ray McCann (owner of the RM Productions booking agency) is probably most interested in contracts for which he is the commissioning agent. Or he might be interested only in contracts that have been paid. To filter out this data, add the CommissionAgent1 field to the query, set its Total row to Where, and enter *"RMP"* in the Criteria row. Also add the Status field and check for the value *"Pd"*. This example is shown in Figure 8-25.

FIGURE 8-25.

Using the CommissionAgent1 and Status fields to select the rows that will be included in groups.

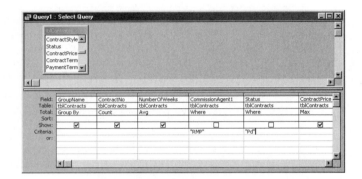

Now, when you run the query, you get totals only for paid contracts for which Ray is the commissioning agent. The result is shown in Figure 8-26. Note that because the query doesn't specify to sort by Group Name in ascending sequence, the rows might not be in strict alphabetical order by Group Name as you might expect. Add a sort criteria to see the rows ordered by Group Name.

FIGURE 8-26.

The recordset of the query shown in Figure 8-25.

Group Name	CountOfContrac	AvgOfNumberO:	MaxOfContractF	ContractAvg	ContractTotal
Apes of Wrath	8	1.75	$750.00	$950.00	$7,600.00
Blind Logwara	4	1.75	$650.00	$975.00	$3,900.00
Bucky and the Fu	11	1.64	$550.00	$736.36	$8,100.00
Generation Sex	2	1.50	$1,100.00	$1,425.00	$2,850.00
Henry and Otis	5	1.60	$550.00	$780.00	$3,900.00
Internal Hemorrh	6	1.67	$400.00	$450.00	$2,700.00
Jelly Plug	3	2.33	$550.00	$366.67	$1,100.00
King Tut and the	3	2.00	$650.00	$1,233.33	$3,700.00
Life Irritates Art	8	1.75	$550.00	$756.25	$6,050.00
Monk Seal	7	2.71	$925.00	$2,135.71	$14,950.00
Muddled Though	3	3.67	$1,500.00	$5,500.00	$16,500.00
Shaman's Apprer	13	1.69	$650.00	$569.23	$7,400.00
Supertube	12	2.42	$1,350.00	$2,008.33	$24,100.00
The Belltones	9	1.78	$600.00	$883.33	$7,950.00
The Codpieces	20	1.20	$475.00	$422.50	$8,450.00
The Kevins	1	2.00	$600.00	$1,200.00	$1,200.00

Record: 1 ▶ ▶| ▶* of 17

Selecting Specific Groups

You can also filter out groups of totals after the query has calculated the groups. To do this, enter criteria for any field that has a Group By setting, one of the total functions, or an expression using the total functions in its Total row. For example, you might want to find out which groups have more than $10,000 in total sales. To find that out, you would use the settings shown in Figure 8-25 and enter a Criteria setting of *>10000* for the ContractTotal field, as shown in Figure 8-27. This query should return three rows in the sample database. You can find this query saved as *qryXmplContractTotals* in the sample database.

FIGURE 8-27.

Entering a Criteria setting for the ContractTotal field.

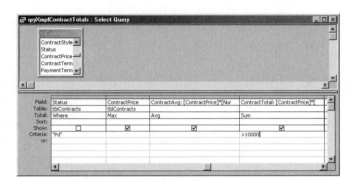

Using Query Parameters

So far you've been entering selection criteria directly in the design grid of the Query window in Design view. However, you don't have to decide at the time you design the query exactly what value you want Access to search for. Instead, you can include a parameter in the query, and Access will prompt you for the criteria each time the query runs.

To include a parameter, you enter a name or a phrase enclosed in brackets ([ ]) in the Criteria row instead of entering a value in the Criteria row. What you enclose in brackets becomes the name by which Access knows your parameter. Access displays this name in a dialog box when you run the query, so it's a good idea to enter a phrase that accurately describes what you want. You can enter several parameters in a single query, so each parameter name must be unique and informative. If you want a parameter value to also display as output in the query, you can enter the parameter name in an empty column on the field row.

You can adapt the query in Figure 8-25 so that Access will prompt for a particular month of interest each time the query runs. First, create a new calculated field to display a year and month by entering

Working with Data

III

SchedStart: and the expression *Format([BeginningDate], "yyyy mmm")* in the Field row of an empty column. (This expression uses the built-in Format function to display BeginningDate values as a four-digit year followed by a three-character month.) Enter a parameter in the Criteria row for this field, as shown in Figure 8-28.

FIGURE 8-28.

Setting a query parameter for the SchedStart field.

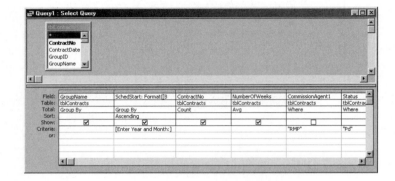

For each parameter in a query, you should tell Access what data type to expect. Access uses this information to validate the value entered. For example, if you define a parameter as a number, Access won't accept alphabetic characters in the parameter value. Likewise, if you define a parameter as a Date/Time data type, Access won't accept anything but a valid date or time value in the parameter prompt (see below). By default, Access assigns the text data type to query parameters, which is fine for our example. If you need to change a parameter's data type, choose the Parameters command from the Query menu. Access then displays the Query Parameters dialog box, as shown in Figure 8-29.

FIGURE 8-29.

The Query Parameters dialog box.

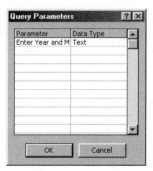

In the Parameter column, enter each parameter name whose data type you want to specify, exactly as you entered it in the design grid but without the brackets. In the Data Type column, select the appropriate data type from the drop-down list. Click the OK button when you finish defining all your parameters.

When you run the query, Access prompts you for an appropriate value for each parameter, one at a time, with a dialog box like the one shown in Figure 8-30. Because Access displays the "name" of the parameter that you provided in the design grid, you can see why naming the parameter with a useful phrase can help you enter the correct value later. In this case, *1999 Dec* is typed in the Enter Parameter Value dialog box, and the recordset is shown in Figure 8-31. (You can find this query saved as *qryXmplContractTotalsParameter* in the Entertainment Scheduling database.)

FIGURE 8-30.

The Enter Parameter Value dialog box.

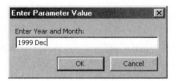

FIGURE 8-31.

The recordset of the query shown in Figure 8-28 when *1999 Dec* is typed in the Enter Parameter Value dialog box.

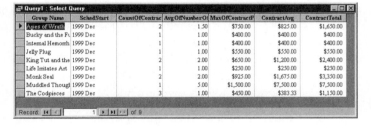

Crosstab Queries

Access supports a special type of total query called a *crosstab query* that allows you to see calculated values in a spreadsheetlike format. For example, you can use this type of query to see total sales by month for each entertainment group in the tblContracts table.

To build a crosstab query, first select the table you want in the Database window and then select New Query from the New Object toolbar button's drop-down list. Select Design View in the New Query dialog box, and then choose the Crosstab Query command from the Query menu. Access adds a Crosstab row to the design grid, as shown in Figure 8-32 on the next page. Each field in a crosstab query can have one of four crosstab settings: Row Heading, Column Heading, Value (displayed in the crosstab grid), or Not Shown.

III

Working with Data

FIGURE 8-32.

A crosstab query in Design view.

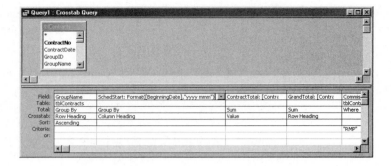

You must have at least one Row Heading in a crosstab query, and you can specify more than one Row Heading. Each Row Heading must be a grouped value or expression (and the expression can include one or more of the total functions—Count, Min, Max, Sum, and so on). The Row Heading fields form the columns down the side of the crosstab. In this example, we'll be grouping by Group Name and including the total value of each group's contracts as a second column.

You must also have one (and only one) Column Heading. This must also be a grouped or totaled value. These values form the headings of the columns across the crosstab datasheet. Because the values in the data you're selecting determine the column names when you run the query, you cannot always predict in advance the field names the query will output. In the following example, we'll be specifically formatting the Column Heading field so that the field names will be the four-digit year followed by the name of the month of the contracts.

Finally, you need one (and only one) Value. This field must be a totaled value or an expression that contains one of the total functions. The Value appears in the intersection of the Row Heading values and each of the Column Headings. In the following example, the group names will appear down the left side, the year and month names will appear as column headings across the top, and the sum of the contract value for each group for each month will appear in the intersection.

As in other types of total queries, you can include other fields to filter out values from the result. For these fields, you should select the Where setting in the Total row and the Not Shown setting in the Crosstab row and then enter your criteria. You can also enter criteria for any column headings, and you can sort any of the fields. As you'll see a bit later, Access sorts the column heading values in ascending order by default.

To build the crosstab query referred to on the previous page—one that shows contract sales by month for each group and a grand total for each group—perform the following steps.

1 Start by selecting the tblContracts table in the Database window. Select Query from the New Object toolbar button's drop-down list. Select Design View in the New Query dialog box, and then choose the Crosstab Query command from the Query menu.

2 Drag the GroupName field from the field list to the first column in the design grid. Fill in the column as shown in Figure 8-32 (with the Group By, Row Heading, and Ascending settings).

3 To generate output in the form of monthly sales columns, you can create an expression that uses one of the built-in Access functions. You can use the same expression you saw earlier in the totals parameter query example:

SchedStart: Format([BeginningDate], "yyyy mmm")

This is your column heading. Fill out the second column of the design grid as shown in Figure 8-32 (with the Group By and Column Heading settings).

4 To calculate a grand total for each group, you need another Row Heading column that sums up the subtotals of ContractPrice times NumberOfWeeks. The expression is as follows.

GrandTotal: [ContractPrice] * [NumberOfWeeks]

Enter *Sum* in the Total row and enter *Row Heading* in the Crosstab row.

5 To calculate the total for each month, you need to multiply the same two fields and call the result *ContractTotal*. Enter *Sum* in the Total row and *Value* in the Crosstab row.

6 Add Where tests to total only contracts issued by RM Productions (*CommissionAgent1 = "RMP"*).

Figure 8-33 on the next page shows the recordset of the query shown in Figure 8-32. Notice that although you didn't specify a sort sequence on the dates, the years appear left to right in ascending collating order. However, if you run the query as is, you'll get the month names in alphabetical order, not in the desired numeric order.

FIGURE 8-33.

The recordset of the query shown in Figure 8-32.

Row Heading columns

Column Headings (one column per Column Heading value)

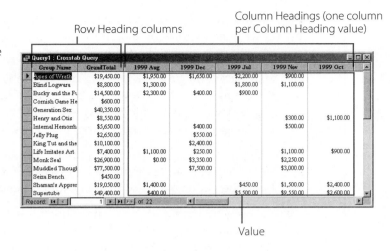

Value

Access provides a solution for this: You can specifically define the order of columns for any crosstab query by using the query's property sheet. Click in the upper part of the Query window in Design view, and then click the Properties button on the toolbar to see the property sheet, as shown in Figure 8-34.

FIGURE 8-34.

Entries in the property sheet that fix the order of column headings for the query shown in Figure 8-32.

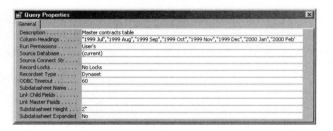

To control the order of columns displayed, enter the headings exactly as they are formatted and in the order you want them in the Column Headings row. Be sure to include all the column headings that match the result of the query. If you omit (or misspell) a column heading, Access won't show that column. When you run the query with formatted column headings, you see the recordset shown in Figure 8-35.

You can find this query, with a field added to limit the dates of the retrieved contracts, saved as *qryXmplCrossTab* in the Entertainment Scheduling database.

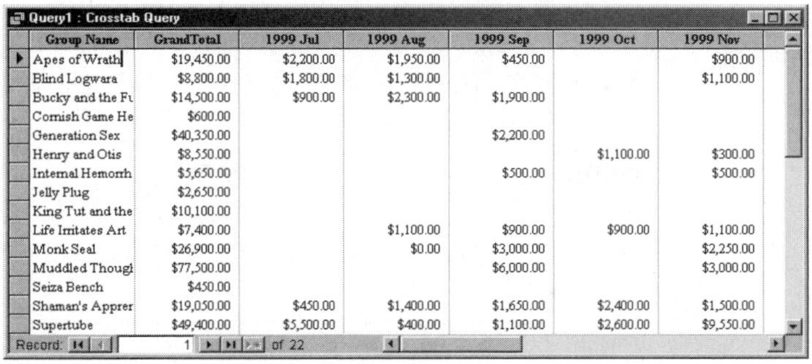

FIGURE 8-35.

A crosstab query recordset with custom headings and custom column order, as defined in Figures 8-32 and 8-34.

Group Name	GrandTotal	1999 Jul	1999 Aug	1999 Sep	1999 Oct	1999 Nov
Apes of Wrath	$19,450.00	$2,200.00	$1,950.00	$450.00		$900.00
Blind Logwara	$8,800.00	$1,800.00	$1,300.00			$1,100.00
Bucky and the Fu	$14,500.00	$900.00	$2,300.00	$1,900.00		
Cornish Game He	$600.00					
Generation Sex	$40,350.00			$2,200.00		
Henry and Otis	$8,550.00				$1,100.00	$300.00
Internal Hemorrh	$5,650.00			$500.00		$500.00
Jelly Plug	$2,650.00					
King Tut and the	$10,100.00					
Life Irritates Art	$7,400.00		$1,100.00	$900.00	$900.00	$1,100.00
Monk Seal	$26,900.00		$0.00	$3,000.00		$2,250.00
Muddled Though	$77,500.00			$6,000.00		$3,000.00
Seiza Bench	$450.00					
Shaman's Apprer	$19,050.00	$450.00	$1,400.00	$1,650.00	$2,400.00	$1,500.00
Supertube	$49,400.00	$5,500.00	$400.00	$1,100.00	$2,600.00	$9,550.00

Searching Multiple Tables

At this point, you've been through all the variations on a single theme—queries on a single table. It's easy to build on this knowledge to retrieve related information from many tables and to place that information in a single view. You'll find this ability to select data from multiple tables very useful in designing forms and reports.

Try the following example, in which you combine information about an entertainment contract and about the club where the entertainment is to be performed. Start by bringing the Entertainment Scheduling Database window to the front. Click the Queries button, and then click the New button. Select Design View in the New Query dialog box, and click OK to open a new Query window in Design view. Access immediately opens the Show Table dialog box. In this dialog box, you select tables and queries with which to design a new query. Select the tblClubs and tblContracts tables, click the Add button, and then close the dialog box.

If you defined the relationships between your tables correctly, the upper part of the Query window in Design view should look like that shown in Figure 8-36 on the next page. Access links multiple tables in a query based on the relationship information you provide when you design each table. Access shows the links between tables as a line drawn from the primary key in one table to its matching field in the other table. If you don't define relationships between tables, Access makes a best guess by linking the primary key field(s) in one table to those that have the same name and matching data type in other tables.

In this example, you want to add to the query the ContractNo, GroupID, and ClubID fields from the tblContracts table and the ClubID, ClubName, and StreetAddress fields from the tblClubs table. When you

FIGURE 8-36.

A query that selects information from the tblClubs and tblContracts tables.

Join line

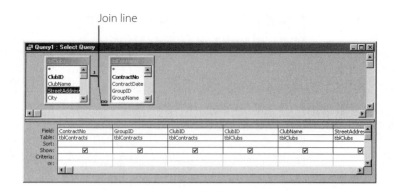

run the query, you see the recordset shown in Figure 8-37. The fields from the tblContracts table appear first, left to right. Notice the group name in the column for the GroupID field from the tblContracts table. If you check the definition of the GroupID field in the tblContracts table, you'll see a Lookup combo box defined—the query has inherited those properties. Click in a GroupID field in this query, and the combo box appears. If you choose a different group name in the drop-down list, you will update the GroupID for that contract. Likewise, the ClubID field from the tblContracts table displays the club name in a combo box, not the underlying ClubID values. You can scroll to the right to see the fields you added from the tblClubs table.

FIGURE 8-37.

The recordset of the query shown in Figure 8-36. The group information in the drop-down list comes from the lookup properties defined in the *tblContracts* table.

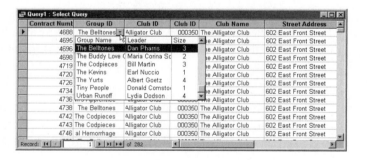

As mentioned earlier, you can do many of the things with Query windows in Datasheet view that you can do with Table windows in Datasheet view. To see club information alongside group information, you can select the columns containing club data and move them next to the Group ID column. You can also select the columns containing group information and then choose the Freeze Columns command from the Format menu. This action will lock those fields on the left side of the datasheet. You can then scroll to the right to bring the club columns into view.

One interesting aspect of queries on multiple tables is that in many cases you can update the tables from any of the columns. *See the section titled "Limitations on Using Select Queries to Update Data" later in this chapter for a discussion of when joined queries are not updateable.* For example, you can change the club name in the tblClubs table by changing the data in this query's datasheet.

Likewise, you can change the ClubID from the tblContracts table (the one on the left in this example) by choosing a different club name from the drop-down combo box, and Access will automatically update the new related club information. Try changing ClubID in the first row from "Alligator Club" to "CandyBox". (CandyBox is the first club in the drop-down list.) When you select the new value for the ClubID field in tblContracts, you should see the ClubID field from tblClubs change to 5000 and the Club Name entry change from The Alligator Club to CandyBox. Note that in this case you're changing only the linking ClubID field in tblContracts, not the name of the club in tblClubs.

Outer Joins

Most queries that you create to request information from multiple tables will show results on the basis of matching data in one or more tables. For example, the Query window in Datasheet view shown in Figure 8-37 contains the names of clubs that have contracts in the tblContracts table—and it does not contain the names of clubs that don't have contracts. This type of query is called an *equi-join query*. This means that you'll see rows only where there are *equal* values in *both* tables. What if you want to display clubs that do not have any contracts in the database? You can get the information you need by creating an *outer join*. An outer join lets you see all rows from one of the tables even if there's no matching row in the related table. When no matching row exists, Access returns the special value Null in the columns from the related table.

To create an outer join, you must modify the join properties. Look at the Design view of the query you created in Figure 8-36. Double-click the join line between the two tables in the upper part of the Query window in Design view to see the Join Properties dialog box, shown in Figure 8-38 on the next page.

The default setting in the Join Properties dialog box is the first option—when the joined fields from both tables match. You can see that you have two additional options for this query: to see all clubs and any contracts that match, or to see all contracts and any clubs that match. If you entered your underlying data correctly, you shouldn't

III

Working with Data

FIGURE 8-38.

The Join Properties dialog box with the second option selected.

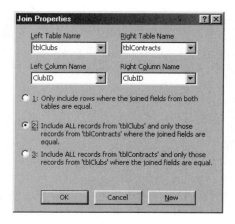

have contracts for nonexistent clubs. If you asked Access to enforce referential integrity (discussed in Chapter 5, "Building Your Database in Microsoft Access") when you defined the relationship between the tblClubs table and the tblContracts table, Access won't let you create any contracts for nonexistent clubs.

Select the second option in the dialog box. When the link between two tables involves more than one field in each table, you can click the New button to define the additional links. Click OK. You should now see an arrow on the join line pointing from the tblClubs field list to the tblContracts field list, indicating that you have asked for an outer join with all records from tblClubs regardless of match, as shown in Figure 8-39. For clubs that have no contracts, Access returns the special Null value in the columns for tblContracts. You can see only the clubs that aren't generating any business by including the Is Null test for any of the columns from tblContracts. When you run this query on the data in the Entertainment Scheduling database, you should find exactly one club (the No One Wants to Work Here club, naturally) that has no contracts, as shown in Figure 8-40. The finished query is saved as *qryXmplClubsWithNoContracts* in the Entertainment Scheduling database.

FIGURE 8-39.

You can double-click the join line between two tables in a query to open the Join Properties dialog box

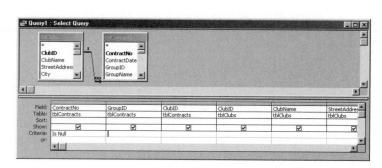

FIGURE 8-40.
The recordset that
shows clubs that have
no contracts.

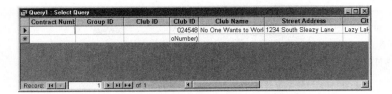

Building a Query on a Query

You might have noticed in the Show Table dialog box in the query's
Design view that you can select not only tables but also other queries
to be the input source for a new query. In fact, another way to build
queries using multiple tables is to use another query as input. To solve
certain types of problems, you must first build one query to define a
subset of data from your tables and then use that query as input to another query to get the final answer.

For example, suppose you want to find out which clubs or groups
have no bookings in a certain time period. You might guess that an
outer join using the tblContracts table will do the trick. That would
work fine if the tblContracts table contained contracts only for the time
period in question. Remember, to find clubs that aren't booked, you
have to look for a special Null value in the columns from tblContracts.
But to limit the data in tblContracts to a specific time period—let's say
December 1999—you have to be able to test real values. In other
words, you have a problem because a column from tblContracts can't
be both Null and have a date value at the same time.

To solve this problem, you must first create a query that contains only
the contracts for the month you want. As you'll see in a bit, you can
then use that query with an outer join in another query to find out
which clubs aren't booked in December 1999. Figure 8-41 on the next
page shows the query you need to start with. This example includes
both the ClubID and the GroupID fields, so you can use it to search
for either clubs or groups that aren't booked in the target month. A
simple Between criterion in the BeginningDate field ensures that this
query will return the correct rows. This query is saved as
qryXmplBookDec1999 in the Entertainment Scheduling database.

After you save the first query, select it in the Database window and select Query from the New Object toolbar button's drop-down list to start
a new query using the first one as input. In your new query, add
tblClubs to the design grid by choosing Show Table from the Query
menu and then selecting tblClubs in the Show Table dialog box. Access
should automatically link tblClubs to the query on matching ClubID

III

Working with Data

FIGURE 8-41.

A query that lists contract data for a particular month.

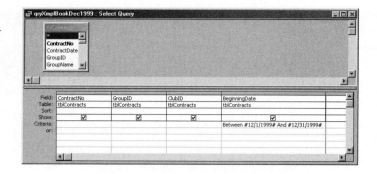

fields. Double-click the join line to open the Join Properties dialog box, and choose option 3 to see all rows from tblClubs and any matching rows from the query. The join line's arrow should point from tblClubs to the query, as shown in Figure 8-42. (When you first add tblClubs to the query grid, it appears to the right of tblContracts. I repositioned the field lists with respect to each other. You can grab either field list by its title bar with your mouse to move it.)

FIGURE 8-42.

An outer join query searching for clubs not booked in December 1999.

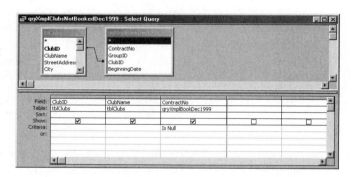

As you did in the previous outer join example, include some fields from the tblClubs table and at least one field from the query that contains contracts only from December 1999. In the field from the query, add the special Is Null criterion. When you run this query (the results of which are shown in Figure 8-43), you should find 16 clubs without bookings in December 1999—including the No One Wants to Work Here club that you found earlier. This query is saved as *qryXmplClubsNotBookedDec1999* in the Entertainment Scheduling database.

FIGURE 8-43.

The clubs without any bookings in December 1999.

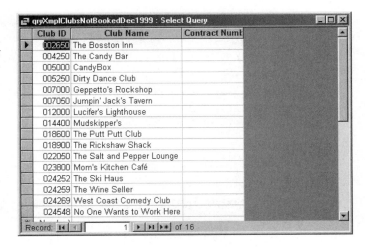

Using Multiple Tables in Total Queries

As you might suspect, you can also use multiple tables in a total query or in a crosstab query. Earlier in this chapter, you built a crosstab query to show monthly contract amounts for each group. (See Figure 8-32 on page 260.) You could do this using a single table as input because the application copies the relevant group name from the tblGroups table each time you create a new contract. In the form you use to create and edit contracts, some special Visual Basic code does this copying for you, which you'll see later in Chapter 23, "Automating Your Application with Visual Basic." However, if you want to see totals sorted by club name, you need to include tblClubs in this query so that you can use the related ClubName field to form the groups for the crosstab totals. (If you use the ClubID from tblContracts, you will see club names in the query output because a Combo Box is specified in the lookup properties of the table, but they will be sorted by the ID value, not by the name.)

Figure 8-44 on the next page shows the crosstab query with the tblClubs table added. Instead of using GroupName from the tblContracts table for the row heading, you can now use the ClubName field from the tblClubs table. The settings for the field remain the same (Group By, Row Heading, and Ascending). Figure 8-45 on the next page shows the recordset of the query, with club names instead of group names. This example is saved as *qryXmplCrossTabClubs* in the Entertainment Scheduling database.

FIGURE 8-44.

A crosstab query that uses multiple tables.

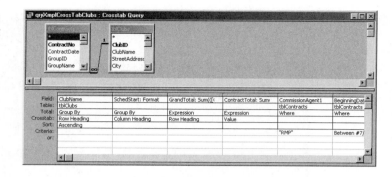

FIGURE 8-45.

The recordset of the crosstab query shown in Figure 8-44.

Club Name	GrandTotal	1999 Jul	1999 Aug	1999 Sep	1999 Oct	1999 Nov	1999
CandyBox	$3,350.00						
Dirty Dance Club	$3,600.00	$1,800.00					
Geppetto's Rockshop	$13,000.00						
Lilliput Tavern	$5,900.00					$4,050.00	$1,8
Little Ricky's Diner	$17,250.00		$2,800.00		$1,300.00	$1,200.00	$2,8
Lucifer's Lighthouse	$3,700.00	$2,200.00					
Mom's Kitchen Café	$475.00				$475.00		
Mudskipper's	$1,200.00	$600.00				$600.00	
Rock Chocolate	$3,800.00						$4
Satyr's	$2,100.00						$2
The Alligator Club	$8,500.00	$300.00	$1,000.00		$700.00	$900.00	$1,1
The Baby Seal Club	$12,100.00		$1,100.00	$2,200.00	$1,100.00	$2,200.00	$1,1
The Bacchus Tavern	$4,200.00		$450.00	$900.00	$450.00	$900.00	$6
The Bosston Inn	$1,200.00						
The Candy Bar	$250.00					$250.00	
The Misery Club	$56,640.00	$5,500.00		$9,300.00	$2,200.00	$8,500.00	$7,5
The Olympic Bar	$15,400.00	$1,100.00	$2,200.00		$2,200.00	$1,100.00	$5

Record: 1 ▶ ▶I ▶* of 23

Using a Query Wizard

Throughout this chapter, you've seen the tantalizing Query Wizard entries in the New Query dialog box. You can use query wizards to help you build certain types of "tricky" queries such as crosstab queries and queries to find duplicate or unmatched rows. For example, you could have used a query wizard to build the query shown in Figure 8-39 to locate clubs that have no outstanding contracts. Let's use a query wizard to build a query to perform the same search on groups.

To try this, click the Queries button in the Database window, and then click the New button. This time, select Find Unmatched Query Wizard in the New Query dialog box, as shown in Figure 8-46.

The wizard opens a window with a list of tables from which you can select the initial records, as shown in Figure 8-47. If you want to search in an existing query, select the Queries option. If you want to look at all queries and tables, select the Both option. In this case, you're looking for groups that have no outstanding contracts, so select the tblGroups table and then click the Next button.

FIGURE 8-46.
Selecting a query
wizard.

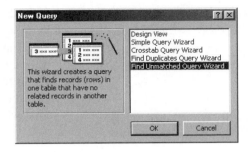

FIGURE 8-47.
The first window of
the Find Unmatched
Query Wizard.

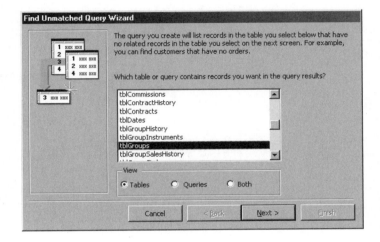

In the next window, select the table that contains the related information you expect to be unmatched. You're looking for groups that have
no outstanding contracts, so select the tblContracts table and then click
the Next button to go to the next window, shown in Figure 8-48.

FIGURE 8-48.
Defining the un-
matched link.

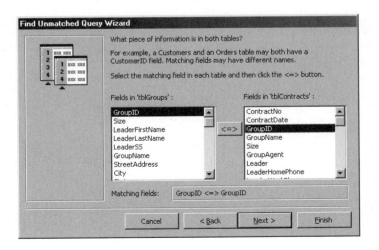

Next, the wizard needs to know the linking fields between the two tables. If you properly defined the table relationships, the wizard should select the related fields correctly. If you didn't do it properly, select the linking field in the first table (GroupID in tblGroups) in the left list box, select the linking field for the second table (GroupID in tblContracts) in the right list box, and then click the <=> button in the center to define the link. Click Next to go to the window shown in Figure 8-49.

FIGURE 8-49.

The window in which you select the fields to be displayed in a query.

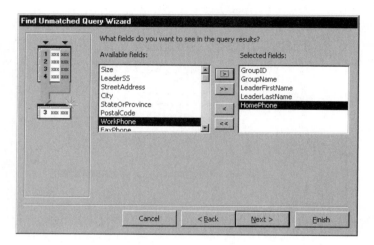

Select the fields you want to display (see Figure 8-49), and then click Next. In the next window, select Modify The Design to open the Query window in Design view, and then click Finish. Figure 8-50 shows the finished query to find groups that have no contracts.

FIGURE 8-50.

A query to find groups that have no contracts.

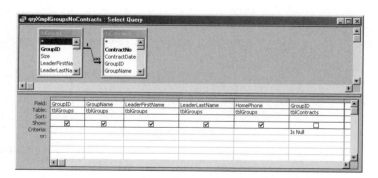

Limitations on Using
Select Queries to Update Data

The recordset that Microsoft Access creates when you run a query looks and acts pretty much like a real table containing data. In fact, in most cases you can insert rows, delete rows, and update the information in a recordset, and Access will make the necessary changes to the underlying table or tables for you.

In some cases, however, Access won't be able to figure out what needs to be changed. Consider, for example, any calculated field. If you try to increase the amount in a Total field whose value is a result of multiplying data in the Quantity field by data in the Price field, Access can't know whether you mean to update the Quantity field or the Price field. On the other hand, you can change either the Price field or the Quantity field and then immediately see the change reflected in the calculated Total field.

In addition, Access won't accept any change that might potentially affect many rows in the underlying table. For that reason, you can't change any of the data in a total query or in a crosstab query. Access can't update data in a field that has a Sum or Avg setting when the result might be based on the values in many records.

When working with a recordset that is the result of a join, Access lets you update all fields from the "many" side of a join but only the nonkey fields on the "one" side, unless you have specified Cascade Update in the relationship. Also, you cannot set or change any field that has the AutoNumber data type. For example, you can't change the ClubID in the tblClubs table or the GroupID in the tblGroups table.

The ability to update fields on the "one" side of a query can produce unwanted results if you aren't careful. For example, you could intend to assign a contract to a different club. If you change the club name, you'll change that name for all contracts related to the current club ID. What you should do instead is change the club ID in the tblContracts table, not the club name in the tblClubs table. *You'll learn techniques later in Chapter 15, "Advanced Form Design," to prevent inadvertent updating of fields in queries.*

III

Working with Data

Query Fields That Cannot Be Updated

Some types of query fields cannot be updated.

- Any field that is the result of a calculation

- Any field in a total or crosstab query

- Any field in a query that includes a total or crosstab query as one of the row sources

- AutoNumber fields

- A primary key participating in a relationship unless Cascade Update is specified

- Any field in a Unique Values query or a Unique Records query *(see "Working with Unique Records and Values" later in this chapter)*

- Any field in a UNION query *(see Chapter 11)*

Customizing Query Properties

Microsoft Access provides a number of properties associated with queries that you can use to control how a query runs. It's worth spending a moment examining these properties before going on to the next chapter. Figure 8-51 shows the property sheet that's used for select queries.

FIGURE 8-51.

The property sheet for select queries.

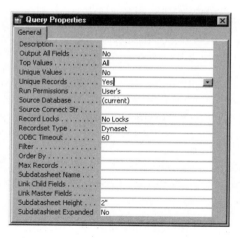

Controlling Query Output

You'll normally select only specific fields that you want returned in the recordset when you run a select query. However, if you're designing the query to be used in a form and you want all fields from all tables used in the query available to the form, set the Output All Fields property to Yes. It's a good idea to keep the default setting of No and change this option only for specific queries.

> To open the property sheet for queries, click in the upper part of a Query window in Design view outside of the field lists and then click the Properties button.

When a query is very complex, Access might need several seconds (or perhaps minutes) to find all the rows and to begin displaying information. If you're interested in only the "first" or "top" rows returned by a query, you can use the Top Values property to tell Access that you want to see information as soon as it finds the first n rows or the first $x\%$ of rows. If you enter an integer value, Access displays the result when it finds the number of rows specified. If you enter a decimal value between 0 and 1, Access displays the result when approximately that percentage of rows has been found. Note, however, that if you include sorting criteria in your query, Access might have to first retrieve all the rows and then sort them before it can find the first n rows. In this case, specifying a Top Values property does not speed up the query.

When working in a query datasheet, you can define and apply filters and specify sorting just as you can in a table datasheet. Access stores this filtering and sorting criteria in the query's Filter and Order By properties. If you are the person who created the query (or if security isn't defined on your system), Access offers to save any changes you make to filtering and sorting criteria when you close a query datasheet. When you design a query, you can use the Filter and Order By properties to define additional, but temporary, filtering and sorting criteria. Access applies these criteria when you run the query, but you can see all the rows in the query by choosing Remove Filter/Sort from the Records menu.

Working with Unique Records and Values

When you run a query, Access can often find duplicate rows in the recordset. The default in Access 2000 is to return all records. You can also ask Access to return only unique records, as shown in Figure

8-51. (This was the default for all versions of Access prior to version 8, also called Access 97). Unique records means that the identifier for each row (the primary key of the table in a single-table query or the concatenated primary keys in a multiple-table query) is unique. If you ask for unique records, Access returns only rows with identifiers that are different from each other. If you want to see all possible data (including duplicate rows), set both the Unique Values property and the Unique Records property to No. You cannot update fields in a query that has its Unique Values property set to Yes.

Setting Unique Records to Yes has no effect unless you include more than one table in your query and do not include at least one field from each table in the output. You might have this situation when you are interested in data from one table but you want to filter it based on data in a related table without displaying the fields from the related table. For example, let's assume you are interested in information about clubs but want to select clubs based on contract dates in matching rows in the tblContracts table.

To understand how the Unique Values and Unique Records settings work, create a query that includes both the tblClubs table and the tblContracts table. Include any field from tblClubs. Include the ContractDate field from tblContracts, but uncheck the Show box. Figure 8-52 shows a sample query with a date criteria that will select all rows (called *qryXmplNoUnique* in the Entertainment Scheduling sample database).

FIGURE 8-52.

A query to demonstrate setting both Unique Values and Unique Records to No using two tables.

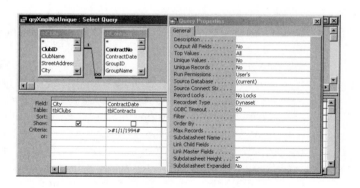

If you switch to the datasheet view, as shown in Figure 8-53, you can see that the query returns 282 rows—one for each contract that has a contract date greater than January 1, 1994 (all of them, actually).

FIGURE 8-53.

The result of retrieving all rows across a join even though the output column is from only one of the tables.

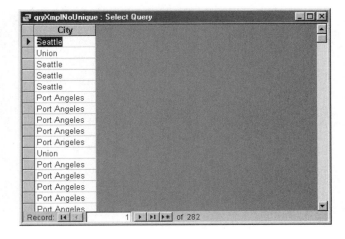

If you're really interested only in one row per club that has any qualifying contract, you can set the Unique Records property to Yes. The result is one row per Club, regardless of the number of contracts, as shown in Figure 8-54 (saved as *qryXmplUniqueRecords*).

FIGURE 8-54.

The result of retrieving Unique Records across a join, with output from one table.

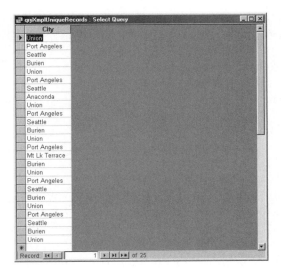

Finally, if you're interested in only what cities had entertainment scheduled after a certain date, and you want to see each city name only once, then set Unique Values to Yes. (Access automatically resets Unique Records to No.) The result is shown in Figure 8-55 on the next page (saved as *qryXmplUniqueValues*).

FIGURE 8-55.

The result of setting
Unique Values to Yes.

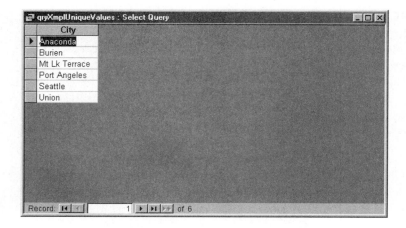

FIGURE 8-55.

The result of setting
Unique Values to Yes.

When you ask for Unique Values, you're asking Access to calculate and remove the duplicates. As with any calculated value in a query, fields in a Unique Values query can't be updated.

Other Query Properties

If you have designed your database to be shared by multiple users across a network, you might want to secure the tables and grant access to other users only through queries. The owner of the tables always has full access to the tables. You can deny access to the tables to everyone and still let authorized users see certain data in the tables. You accomplish this by setting the Run Permissions property to User's. If you want to allow users of this query to "inherit" the owner's permission to access tables when they use this query, you can set Run Permissions to Owner's. *See the section titled "Securing Your Database" in Chapter 25 for details.*

Use the Record Locks property to control the level of editing integrity for a query that is designed to access data shared across a network. The default is to not lock any records when the user opens the query. Access applies a lock only when it needs to write a row back to the source table. Select the Edited Record setting to lock a row as soon as the user begins entering changes in that row. The most restrictive setting, All Records, locks every record retrieved by the query as long as the user has the query open. Use this setting only when the query must perform multiple updates to a table and other users should not access any data in the table until the query is finished.

Four of the remaining properties—Source Database, Source Connect Str, ODBC Timeout, and Max Records—apply to attached tables. *See*

Chapter 10, "Importing, Linking, and Exporting Data," for details. Use the Subdatasheet Name property to define another table or query that provides rows for a subdatasheet. Be sure to set the Link Child Fields and Link Master Fields properties to correctly list the fields that link this query to the subdatasheet table or query. You can define the default height of the subdatasheet and whether the subdatasheet is open by default.

Now that you understand the fundamentals of building select queries with Access, you're ready to move on to updating sets of data with action queries in the next chapter.

III

Working with Data

Modifying Data with Action Queries

In Chapter 7, "Using Datasheets," you learned how to insert, update, and delete single rows of data within a datasheet. In Chapter 8, "Adding Power with Select Queries," you discovered that you can use queries to select the data you want—even from multiple tables. Now you can take the concept of queries one step further and use *action queries* to quickly change, insert, create, or delete sets of data in your database.

In this chapter, we'll use the tables and data from the Entertainment Scheduling sample database that comes with this book to explore action queries.

Updating Groups of Rows

It's easy enough to use a table or a query in Datasheet view to find a single record in your database and change one value. But what if you want to make the same change to many records? Changing each record one at a time could be very tedious.

As a normal part of business, Ray McCann (the owner of RM Productions) often creates a contract record for entertainment booking dates that are still being negotiated. When he creates a new record for a contract that hasn't been confirmed, he marks it as pending (by using a *P* as the contract status code). Over time, he accumulates anywhere from a few to perhaps dozens of such contracts in his database. He likes to keep a record of these pending contracts—at least for local clubs—but he doesn't need to have them displayed when he's looking at other active contracts.

The Status field in the tblContracts table allows the value D to indicate a deleted contract record. As you'll see later, the query that supplies the data for the main contract edit form has a filter to weed out all "D" records. Ray could go through his contracts periodically and set all the old pending contracts to deleted status by hand. But why not let Microsoft Access do the work for him with a single query?

Testing with a Select Query

Before you create and run a query to update many records in your database, it's a good idea to first create a select query using criteria that select the records you want to update. You'll see in the next section that it's easy to convert this select query to an update query or other type of action query after you're sure that Access will process the right records.

To filter out pending contracts for local clubs, you need the club city, state, and postal code information, which is not in the tblContracts table. You can join the tblClubs table with tblContracts to get this information. You could filter on postal code ranges, but in this case, searching for clubs in the state of Washington is sufficient. You also need to filter on the contract beginning date to be sure you don't throw away any current contracts. The query shown in Figure 9-1 looks for pending contracts with a proposed start date (the BeginningDate field) that is earlier than January 1, 2000. You can also use the built-in Date function to look for contracts dated prior to today's date.

FIGURE 9-1.

A select query to find old pending contracts.

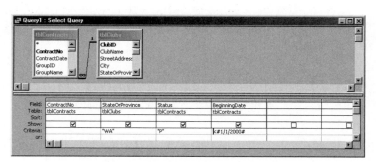

TIP

> Although Access 2000 generally interprets 21st century dates with two-digit
> years correctly, I strongly recommend that you take advantage of the new Use
> Four-Digit Year Formatting option in Access to avoid all confusion. When you
> choose this option, Access displays four-digit years in datasheets, forms, and
> reports. It also converts whatever you type in an expression (such as Criteria in
> a query) to display four digits, as you can see on the query grid in Figure 9-1.
> Choose Options from the Tools menu, and then click the General tab to set
> this option. I also recommend that you change your Regional Settings in Win-
> dows Control Panel to display a four-digit year in the Short Date Style. This will
> assist your entry and display of year values in other applications.

When you run the query, you'll see four contract records that you
want to change, as shown in Figure 9-2.

FIGURE 9-2.

The recordset of the
select query shown in
Figure 9-1.

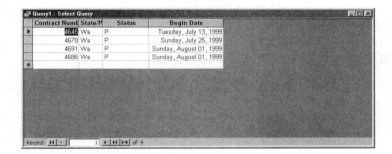

Converting a Select Query to an Update Query

Now you're ready to change the query so that it will update the table.
When you first create a query, Access creates a select query by default.
You can find commands for the four types of action queries—make-
table, update, append, and delete—on the Query menu when the query
is in Design view. You can also select one of these options from the
Query Type toolbar button's drop-down list, as shown in Figure 9-3.
Select Update Query to convert the select query to an update query.

FIGURE 9-3.

The Query Type
toolbar button's drop-
down list.

When you convert a select query to an update query, Access changes the title bar of the Query window in Design view and adds a row labeled Update To to the design grid, as shown in Figure 9-4. You use this row to specify how you want your data changed. In this case, you want to change all "P" status contracts in Washington state that originated before January 1, 2000, to "D".

FIGURE 9-4.

An update query with its Update To setting.

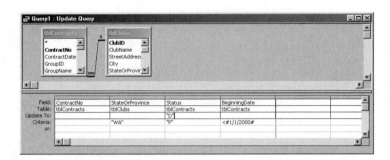

> 🌟 **TIP**
>
> You can enter any valid expression in the Update To row. You can include in the expression one or more of the fields from the source tables in the query. For example, if a particular group wants to raise its contract price for all pending contracts by 10 percent, rounded to the nearest dollar, you can include the ContractPrice field on the design grid and enter
>
>   Round(CCur(tblContracts.[ContractPrice] * 1.1), 0)
>
> in the Update To row. Note that the above formula uses the Round and CCur built-in functions discussed in the previous chapter to round the result to the nearest dollar.

Running an Update Query

If you want to be completely safe, you should make a backup copy of your table before you run an update query. To do that, go to the Database window, select the table you're about to update, and choose the Copy command from the Edit menu. Then choose the Paste command from the Edit menu, and give the copy of your table a different name when Access prompts you with a dialog box. Now you're ready to run the update query.

To run the query, choose the Run command from the Query menu or click the Run button on the toolbar. Access first scans your table to determine how many rows will change based on your selection criteria. It then displays a confirmation dialog box like the one shown in Figure 9-5.

FIGURE 9-5.

The dialog box that reports the number of rows that will be changed by an update query.

You already know that there are four old pending contract records, so you know that your update query is OK. To perform the update, click the Yes button in the dialog box. (If the number of rows indicated in the dialog box is not what you expected or if you're not sure that Access will update the right records or fields, click the No button to stop the query without updating.) After the update query runs, you can look at the table or create a new select query to confirm that Access made the changes you wanted. Figure 9-6 shows the result—old pending contracts are now marked as deleted.

FIGURE 9-6.

The updated data in the tblContracts table.

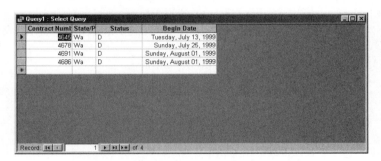

If you think you might want to perform this update again, you can save the query and give it a name. This sample query is saved in the Entertainment Scheduling database as *qryXmplUpdateOldPending*. In the Database window, Access distinguishes action queries from select queries by displaying a special icon, followed by an exclamation point, before action query names. For example, Access displays a pencil and an exclamation point next to the new update query that you just created.

> It's a good idea to include identifying fields (such as ContractNo in the above example) when you build a test select query that you plan to convert to an action query. However, Access discards any fields that do not have criteria specified or are not being updated when you save your final action query. This is why you won't see the ContractNo field in *qryXmplUpdateOldPending*.

To run an action query again, select it in the Database window and click the Open button. When you run an action query from the Database window, Access displays a confirmation dialog box similar to the one shown in Figure 9-7. Click the Yes button to complete the action query. If you want to disable this extra confirmation step, choose the Options command from the Tools menu and, on the Edit/Find tab of the Options dialog box, deselect the Confirm Action Queries check box.

FIGURE 9-7.

The dialog box that asks you to confirm an action query.

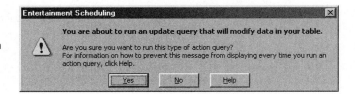

Updating Multiple Fields

When you create an update query, you aren't limited to changing a single field at a time. You can ask Access to update any or all of the fields in the record by including them in the design grid and then specifying an update formula.

You can also update one field by using a formula that is based on a different field in the record. Before Access updates a record in the underlying table or query, it makes a copy of the original record. Access applies the formulas you specify using the values in the original record and places the result in the updated copy. It then updates your database by writing the updated copy to your table. Because updates are made first to the copy, you can, for example, swap the values in a field named A and a field named B by specifying an Update To setting of [B] for the A field and an Update To setting of [A] for the B field. If Access were making changes directly to the original record, you'd need to use a third field to swap values because the first assignment of B to A would destroy the original value of A.

Creating a New Table

Sometimes you might want to save as a new table the data that you extract with a select query. If you find that you keep executing the same query over and over against data that isn't changing, it can be faster to access the data from a table rather than from the query, particularly if the query must join several tables. For example, if at the end of each week you run a series of reports that all use the same complex joined query (which may take several minutes to run for each report), you will save a lot of time if you first save the result of the complex query as a temporary table and then run your reports from that table. Saving the data selected by a query as a table is also useful for gathering summary information that you intend to keep long after you delete the detailed data on which the query is based.

Creating a Make-Table Query

Assume that at the end of each year you want to create and save a table that summarizes the sales for the year by group or by club. You might recall from the exercises in building total queries in the previous chapter that the tblContracts table contains the data you need to calculate such information as number of contracts, average number of weeks per contract, and total contract amount for each group.

As with most action queries, it's a good idea to start with a select query to verify that you're working with the right data. In this case, start with the qryXmplContractTotalsParameter query you saw in the previous chapter and make a few modifications to get it ready to store the result in a new table. First choose the Parameters command from the Query menu and delete the parameter, and then click the OK button. Next remove the SchedStart field and replace it with a field named *EntertainMonth: Format([BeginningDate], "yyyy mm")*. This gives you a month number (which is easier to sort in ascending order) instead of a month abbreviation. Add a criterion on this field to pick out all of the 1999 contracts: *Between "1999 01" and "1999 12"*. It's probably a good idea to add the GroupID field and then sort the result by EntertainMonth and GroupID. Because GroupID in tblContracts has a lookup display defined, change the Display Control of the GroupID field in the query to Text Box if you want to see the actual numeric value of the ID field rather than the group name from the lookup when you run the query. (Use the Lookup tab in the Field Properties window you learned about in the previous chapter.) Your result should look something like that shown in Figure 9-8.

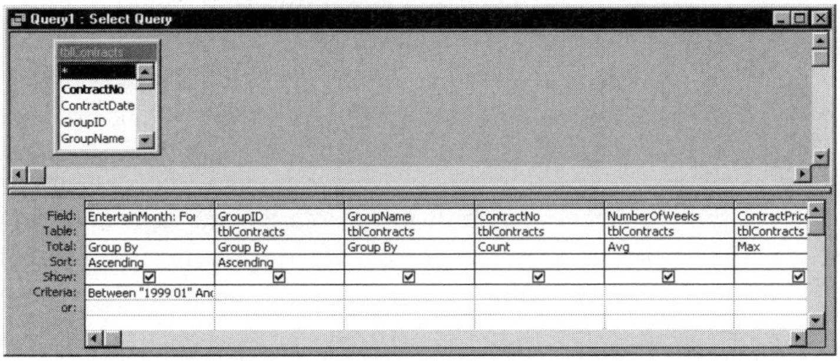

FIGURE 9-8.

A select query to calculate contract data by group for 1999.

III

Working with Data

Run this query to verify that you'll get the rows you want. Switch to Datasheet view to check the result, as shown in Figure 9-9.

To convert this select query to a make-table query, choose Make-Table Query from the Query menu. Access displays the Make Table dialog box, shown in Figure 9-10. Type in an appropriate name for the summary table you are creating, and click OK to close the dialog box.

At any time, you can change the name of the table your query creates. Choose the Properties command from the View menu whenever the query is in Design view and change the Destination Table property.

Running a Make-Table Query

After you set up a make-table query, you can run it by choosing Run from the Query menu or by clicking the Run button on the toolbar. Access creates the records that will be inserted in the new table and displays a confirmation dialog box, as shown in Figure 9-11, that informs you of how many rows you'll be creating in the new table.

Click the Yes button to create your new table and insert the rows. Switch to the Database window and click the Tables button to bring up the table list, which should include the name of your new table.

Open the table in Datasheet view to verify the information, as shown in Figure 9-12.

FIGURE 9-11.

The dialog box that asks you to confirm the preliminary results of a make-table query.

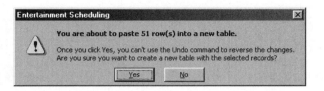

FIGURE 9-12.

The result of the *qryXmplGroup1999-SalesMakeTable* make-table query.

EntertainMontl	GroupID	GroupName	CountOfContra	AvgOfNumber	MaxOfContrac	ContractAvg
1999 07	500	Apes of Wrath	1	4	$550.00	$2,200.00
1999 07	4400	The Belltones	3	1.33333333333	$550.00	$466.67
1999 07	5300	Bucky and the F	1	2	$450.00	$900.00
1999 07	6650	The Codpieces	1	2	$300.00	$600.00
1999 07	14555	Shaman's Appre	1	1	$450.00	$450.00
1999 07	14562	Supertube	1	5	$1,100.00	$5,500.00
1999 08	500	Apes of Wrath	2	1.5	$750.00	$975.00
1999 08	5200	Blind Logwara	1	2	$650.00	$1,300.00
1999 08	5300	Bucky and the F	2	1.5	$550.00	$700.00
1999 08	14300	Life Irritates Art	1	2	$550.00	$1,100.00
1999 08	14555	Shaman's Appre	2	1.5	$550.00	$700.00
1999 08	14562	Supertube	1	1	$400.00	$400.00
1999 09	500	Apes of Wrath	1	1	$450.00	$450.00
1999 09	4400	The Belltones	1	3	$550.00	$1,650.00
1999 09	5300	Bucky and the F	2	2	$550.00	$950.00
1999 09	6650	The Codpieces	1	1	$450.00	$450.00
1999 09	8350	Generation Sex	1	2	$1,100.00	$2,200.00
1999 09	10750	Internal Hemorrh	1	2	$250.00	$500.00
1999 09	14300	Life Irritates Art	1	2	$450.00	$900.00
1999 09	14524	Monk Seal	1	4	$750.00	$3,000.00
1999 09	14536	Muddled Though	1	4	$1,500.00	$6,000.00
1999 09	14555	Shaman's Appre	2	1.5	$550.00	$825.00
1999 09	14562	Supertube	2	2	$1,100.00	$550.00

Record: 1 of 51

NOTE

One of the shortcomings of a Make Table query is it propagates only the field name and data type to the resulting table. Running the query does not set other property settings such as Caption or Decimal Places in the target table. This is why the AvgOfNumberOfWeeks field looks different in the table than it does in the query.

You might want to switch to Design view, as shown in Figure 9-13 on the next page, to correct field names or to define formatting information. As you can see, Access copies only basic field attributes when creating a new table.

At a minimum, you should create a primary key that contains the EntertainMonth and GroupID fields. You might also want to change the CountOfContractNo and AvgOfNumberOfWeeks field names (which are generated automatically by Access) to something more meaningful.

III

Working with Data

FIGURE 9-13.

The Design view of the table created by the *qryXmplGroup-1999SalesMakeTable* make-table query.

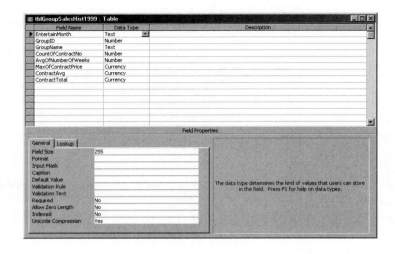

Inserting Data from Another Table

Using an append query, you can copy a selected set of information and insert it into another table. You can also use an append query to bring data from another source into your database—for example, a list of names and addresses purchased from a mailing list company—and then edit the data and insert it into an existing table. (In the next chapter, you'll learn how to import data from external sources.)

An append query, like a make-table query, provides a way to collect calculated totals and save them in a predefined target. One major advantage to using an append query is that you can fully define the fields and field properties that you want in the final result table. A disadvantage is that it's easier to run into errors either because you're trying to reinsert data that's already there (based on the primary key you defined) or because the data you're adding doesn't match the data type you defined in the table. *See the section titled "Troubleshooting Action Queries" later in this chapter for a specific discussion of potential errors. Later in this chapter, in the section titled "Example 2: Updating/Appending Rows from Imported Data," you can find an example showing you how to match and update existing data and how to insert new rows without errors.*

Creating an Append Query

In the previous example, you saw how to take one of the total queries you learned about in Chapter 8 and turn it into a make-table query. In truth, if you plan to collect such data over several months or years, you should probably design a table to hold the results and use append queries to periodically insert new sales data.

The Entertainment Scheduling database includes two tables that were created for this purpose: tblClubSalesHistory and tblGroupSalesHistory. Both tables have an EntertainMonth field to record the year and month as formatted text, a NumberOfContracts field to record the number of contracts for each club or group for each month, a ContractAvgWeek field to store the average number of weeks per contract, a HighestContractPrice field for the largest weekly contract price, a ContractAvg field for the average of all contracts, and a ContractTotal field for the sum of the contract amounts for each club or group and month. As you might expect, the tblClubSalesHistory table has ClubID and ClubName fields, and the tblGroupSalesHistory table has GroupID and GroupName fields.

You can use the qryXmplGroup1999SalesMakeTable query as a starting point for Groups because it already contains all the output fields you need. (This query is the same as the make-table query that you just studied.) Open the query in Design view, and then choose Append Query from the Query menu. Access will prompt you for the name of the table to receive the new rows; change "tblGroupSalesHist1999" to "tblGroupSalesHistory" and click OK. Access adds an Append To row to let you specify to which field in the receiving table each column in this query is to be appended. When the field names match, Access automatically fills in the name. You should specify that ContractNo (actually the Count of ContractNo) be appended to the NumberOfContracts field. Likewise, change the Append To under NumberOfWeeks to ContractAvgWeek, and point ContractPrice to HighestContractPrice. Be sure to choose Save As from the File menu to save this new query under a different name. You can find a similar query (with the field names renamed for ContractNo, NumberOfWeeks, and ContractPrice) saved as *qryXmplAppendGroupSales* in the Entertainment Scheduling database.

The query to append information to the tblClubSalesHistory table is a bit more complicated because there's no Club Name information in tblContracts. To build a query to append 1999 sales to club sales history, do the following.

1 Start a new query on the tblClubs table. Add the tblContracts table to the query. You should see Access draw a join line between the ClubID field in tblClubs and the ClubID field in tblContracts.

III

Working with Data

2 Add the ClubID and ClubName fields from tblClubs to the query grid.

3 Add the ContractNo, NumberOfWeeks, ContractPrice, CommissionAgent1, and Status fields from tblContracts.

4 Click in the ClubName field and choose Column from the Insert menu to create a blank field between ClubID and ClubName. In tblClubSalesHistory, the EntertainMonth field is a text field containing the four-digit year, a space, and the two-digit month. To generate this field in your query, enter *EntertainMonth: Format([BeginningDate],"yyyy mm")* in the blank field you just created. On the Criteria row under this column, enter the expression *Between "1999 01" And "1999 12"* to limit the rows selected to the year 1999.

5 You want the information summarized by club and year/month, so click the Totals button on the toolbar or choose Totals from the View menu to see the Totals row in your query. In the Totals row, choose Count under ContractNo, Avg under NumberOfWeeks, and Max under ContractPrice.

6 You need to add a couple of expressions to calculate the average contract price and the total. Click in the CommissionAgent1 field and insert two new columns by choosing Column from the Insert menu twice. Enter *ContractAvg: [ContractPrice]*[NumberOfWeeks]* in the first field and set the Totals row to Avg. Enter the expression *ContractTotal: [ContractPrice]*[NumberOfWeeks]* in the second field and set the Totals row to Sum.

7 Under the CommissionAgent1 field, change the Totals row to Where and enter *"RMP"* on the Criteria row to limit the rows to clubs for whom Ray McCann is the agent.

8 Under the Status field, change the Totals row to Where and enter *"Pd"* on the Criteria line to select only paid contracts.

9 So that all the output fields from this query match columns in the receiving table, rename the ContractNo to NumberOfContracts, the NumberOfWeeks field to ContractAvgWeek, and the ContractPrice field to HighestContractPrice.

10 Change your query to an Append query by choosing Append Query from the Query menu or the Query Type toolbar button. Enter tblClubSalesHistory in the Append To Table Name dialog. If you named all the fields correctly, Access should automatically enter them in the new Append To row on the query grid.

11 Finally, because the append process will run more smoothly if the rows selected by the query are in the same sequence as the Primary Key of the target table, choose Ascending in the Sort row under both the ClubID and EntertainMonth fields.

You can see this query under construction in Figure 9-14. (I clicked the query type button again after finishing the query to show you the Append dialog box.) You can find the completed queries saved as *qryXmplAppendClubSales* and *qryXmplAppendGroupSales* in the Entertainment Scheduling database.

FIGURE 9-14.

A query to calculate and append monthly totals for clubs.

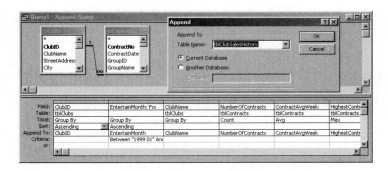

Running an Append Query

As with other action queries, you can run an append query as a select query first to be sure that you'll be copying the right rows. You can either start out by building a select query, running it, and then converting it to an append query, or you can build the append query directly and then switch to Datasheet view from Design view to examine the data that the query will add. Although you can find and delete rows that you append in error, you can save time if you make a backup of the target table first.

After you confirm that the query will append the right rows, you can either run it directly from Design view or save it and run it from the Database window. When you run the qryXmplAppendClubSales query, Access should tell you that 51 rows will be appended, as shown in Figure 9-15 on the next page. If you want to append the rows to the tblClubSalesHistory table, click Yes in the confirmation dialog box. Note that once you click Yes, the only way to undo these changes is to go to the target table and either select and delete the rows manually or build a delete query to do it.

FIGURE 9-15.

The dialog box that asks you to confirm the appending of rows.

Microsoft Access

You are about to append 51 row(s).

Once you click Yes, you can't use the Undo command to reverse the changes. Are you sure you want to append the selected rows?

[Yes]   [No]

> You probably won't want to create or modify a sales summary append query with data for different months and years each time you want to update your summary table. You can substitute parameters in the Between criteria to prompt you for the appropriate date ranges each time you run the query.

Example 1: Using an Append Query to Archive Data

As you've just seen, you can easily convert a total query to an append query to save calculated totals that you think you'll use many times. It's much faster to use calculated data from a stored table than to recalculate the data in a total query.

Another excellent use of append queries is to extract old data from active tables to copy to archive tables. Over time, you might accumulate thousands of rows in your main transaction tables—the contracts, enrollments, or orders you collect in the process of running your business. You probably don't need data that's more than a year old for your day-to-day business. You can improve the performance of the most active parts of your application by periodically moving "old" data to archive tables that you access only infrequently.

To do this, you must first set up some archive tables in which to store the old records. If you need related records in other tables in order to fully understand the data (in this case, the original club and group data for archived contracts), you need to set up archive tables for those records as well. As you'll see in the last section of this chapter, RM Productions uses action queries to purge from the active system any clubs or groups that haven't had any recent activity. If you archive old contracts, you should also archive the related club and group information in case this information ever gets deleted from the active part of the system.

Let's start by building an append query to select certain old contracts from the active tblContracts table. Start a new query on tblContracts, and select all the fields from that table. To make this query easy to use, include a parameter to prompt for the latest date you want to copy to the archive. You can see this query under construction in Figure 9-16. Note that the Criteria row looks for any BeginningDate value that is less than the last date value entered plus one. Remember that date/time values have both a date and a time component. If you look for records containing a value less than or equal to a target last date, you might not get any of the rows for the last date if the date/time field you are checking has a time as well as a date. The date/time value for 8 A.M. on December 31, 1999, is greater than the value for just the date 12/31/99. Adding one to the required date value and looking for any date/time less than that will yield all dates and times on that day.

FIGURE 9-16.

A query to select old contracts using a date parameter.

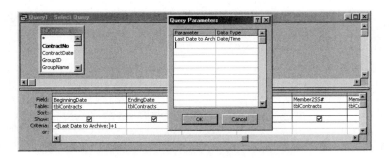

As you did earlier, convert this query to an append query by choosing Append from the Query menu or by selecting Append from the Query Type toolbar button's drop-down list. In the Append dialog box, enter *tblContractHistory* as the target table, as shown in Figure 9-17.

FIGURE 9-17.

Converting the select old contracts query to an append query.

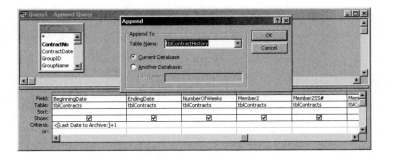

Let's assume that it is now late 2000 and you no longer need any of the contracts from 1999. Save the query (you can find this example saved as *qryXmplArchiveOldContracts* in the Entertainment Scheduling database) and run it. When the Enter Parameter Value dialog box appears, type in the last day of 1999, as shown in Figure 9-18.

FIGURE 9-18.

Entering an archive cutoff date.

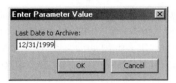

It's very important that you take the time to define the data type of the parameter you included in the query. If you define this parameter as a date/time value, you will not be able to type in an invalid value. If you're running the sample query in the database, try typing in letters to see what happens. Access won't run the query until you type in a valid date. If you enter a date of December 31, 1999, Access will ask you to confirm that the query should append 78 rows to the archive table, as shown in Figure 9-19. Click Yes to copy the old 1999 contracts to the tblContract History table. (You'll learn how to delete them from the active table later.)

FIGURE 9-19.

The dialog box that asks you to confirm the appending of rows.

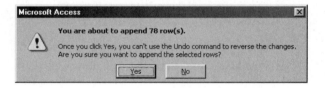

There's also a tblClubHistory table in the database that contains club information for contracts previously archived and a tblGroupHistory table for old group information. You should check the new rows you just copied to see if you also need to copy any missing club or group rows from the active tables. You'll recall from the previous chapter how to build a query to find unmatched data between two tables. That's the starting point for the query you need.

You could use the Find Unmatched Query Wizard to get a jump start on finding rows in tblContractHistory that don't have matching rows in either tblClubHistory or tblGroupHistory, but let's build this query from scratch.

Start a new query on tblContractHistory. Add tblClubHistory to the query—Access will link the two tables using the club ID. Double-click the join line between the two tables, and choose the option to include all records from tblContractHistory and only those records from tblClubHistory where the joined fields are equal. You should see an arrow pointing from tblContractHistory to tblClubHistory. Add tblClubs to the query—again, Access should link tblClubs to tblContractHistory for you, using the club ID. Drag the asterisk (*) field from tblClubs to the design grid. Drag the ClubID field from tblClubHistory to the design grid, clear its Show check box, and add a criterion of Is Null. Click the Properties button on the toolbar, and set Unique Records to Yes. Convert your query into an append query with a destination table set to tblClubHistory. Be sure that nothing appears in the Append To row under the ClubID field from tblClubs. The result should look like that shown in Figure 9-20.

FIGURE 9-20.

A query to select unmatched clubs to add to the archive table.

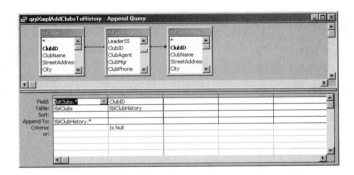

If you switch to Datasheet view, you should see six rows, as shown in Figure 9-21. What's happening? The answer is that the first link (an outer join, remember?) you created between tblContractHistory and tblClubHistory asks for all rows in tblContractHistory regardless of whether there are matching rows in tblClubHistory. When you add the criterion to return only Null values from tblClubHistory, you retrieve only rows in tblContractHistory that don't currently have a matching club yet in tblClubHistory. When you link this result to the main tblClubs table, you can find the data for the six unmatched clubs that you need to insert into tblClubHistory.

FIGURE 9-21.

The six club rows needed to match the archived contracts.

Club ID	Club Name	Street Address	City	State/P	Postal Cod	Mgr Last Na
024259	The Wine Seller	1500 Fairmont Rd.	Burien	Wa	98166	Deane
024269	West Coast Comedy C	14101 Pacific Hwy S.	Union	Wa	98592	Esse
004250	The Candy Bar	6720 Evergreen Way	Union	Wa	98592	Allen
005250	Dirty Dance Club	1616 S. 325th Street	Seattle	Wa	98101	Balquiedra
008500	Lilliput Tavern	3000 Marina Drive	Port Angeles	Wa	98362	Gainer
014400	Mudskipper's	Orchid	Union	Wa	98592	Helvig

Record: 1 of 6

III

Working with Data

> You won't see the six rows in this query unless you have already run the query to archive contracts through the end of 1999, as explained in the previous section.

When you run this query, you insert the club data you need into tblClubHistory. If you run this query again, it won't find any unmatched rows, so there will be nothing to append. This query is saved as *qryXmplAddClubsToHistory* in the Entertainment Scheduling database. There's also a companion *qryXmplAddGroupsToHistory* query.

Troubleshooting Action Queries

Microsoft Access analyzes your action query request and the data you are about to change before it commits changes to your database. When it identifies errors, Access always gives you an opportunity to cancel the operation.

Common Action Query Errors and Problems

Access identifies (traps) four types of errors during the execution of an action query.

- **Duplicate primary keys.** This type of error occurs if you attempt to append a record to a table or update a record in a table when the result is a duplicate primary key or a duplicate of a unique index key value. Access will not update or append any rows that would create duplicate values in primary keys or unique indexes. For example, if the primary key of a contract archive table is ContractID, Access won't append a record that contains a ContractID already in the table. Before attempting to append such rows, you might have to change the primary key values in the source table to avoid the conflict.

- **Data conversion errors.** This type of error occurs when you attempt to append data to an existing table and the data type of the receiving field does not match that of the sending field (and the data in the sending field cannot be converted to the appropriate data type). For example, this error will occur if you attempt to append a text field to an integer field and the text field contains either alphabetic characters or a number string that is too large for the integer field. You might also encounter a conversion error in an update query if you use a formula that attempts a calculation on a field that contains characters. *For information on data conversions and potential limitations, see Table 6-1 in Chapter 6, "Modifying Your Database Design."*

- **Locked records.** This type of error can occur when you run a delete query or an update query on a table that you share with other users on a network. Access cannot update records that are in the process of being updated by some other user. You might want to wait and try again later when no one else is using the affected records to be sure that your update or deletion occurs. Even if you're not sharing the data on a network, you can encounter this error if you have a form or query open on the data you're updating and have started to change some of the data.

- **Validation rule violations.** If any of the rows being inserted or any row being updated violates either a field validation rule or the table validation rule, Access notifies you of an error and does not insert or update any of the rows that fail the validation test.

Another problem that can occur, although it isn't an error, is that Access truncates data that is being appended to text or memo fields if the data does not fit. Access does not warn you when this happens. You must be sure (especially with append queries) that the receiving text and memo fields have been defined as large enough to store the incoming data.

An Error Example

Earlier in this chapter, you learned how to create an append query to copy old contracts to an archive table. What do you suppose would happen if you copied rows through September 30, 1999, forgot to delete them from the main table, and then later asked to copy rows through December 31, 1999? If you try this starting with an empty archive table in the Entertainment Scheduling database, you'll get an error dialog box similar to the one shown in Figure 9-22.

FIGURE 9-22.

The dialog box that alerts you to action query errors.

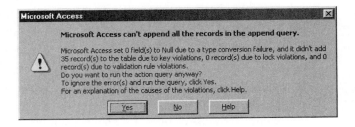

III

Working with Data

The dialog box declares that 35 records won't be inserted because of duplicate primary key values. Access didn't find any data conversion errors. Note that if some fields have conversion problems, Access might still append the row but leave the field set to Null. Because this table isn't shared on a network, there aren't any locking errors. When you see this dialog box, you can click the Yes button to proceed with the changes that Access can make without errors. You might find it difficult later, however, to track down all the records that were not updated successfully. Click the No button to cancel the append query.

Deleting Groups of Rows

You're not likely to keep all the data in your database forever. You'll probably summarize some of your detailed information as time goes by and then delete the data you no longer need. You can remove sets of records from your database using a delete query.

Testing with a Select Query and Parameters

Once you have calculated and saved all the sales data and moved old contracts to the archive table, you should remove the contracts from the active table. This is clearly the kind of query that you will want to save so that you can use it again and again. You can design the query to automatically calculate which records to delete based on the current system date. (If you do this, you should probably change the query qryXmplArchiveOldContracts to work the same way.) The query can also be designed with a parameter so that a user can specify which data to delete when you run the query. Either design makes it unnecessary to change the query at each use.

As with an update query, it's a good idea to test which rows will be affected by a delete query by first building a select query to isolate these records. Start a new query on tblContracts and include the asterisk (*) field. Add the BeginningDate field to the design grid, clear the Show check box, and add either a parameter criterion or something like *<Date( ) – 366* (to see all contracts that are more than a year old). If you use a parameter criterion and convert this select query to a delete query, your result should look like that shown in Figure 9-23.

When you switch to Datasheet view for this query, Access prompts you for a date parameter, as shown in Figure 9-24. In the Enter Parameter Value dialog box, enter *12/31/99* to see all the old contracts from 1999. The result is shown in Figure 9-25.

FIGURE 9-23.
A delete query with a date parameter to remove archived contracts.

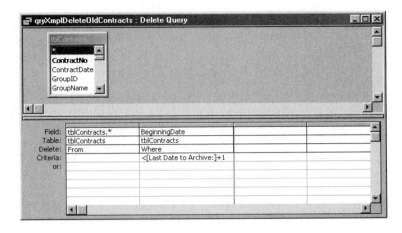

FIGURE 9-24.
Entering the delete query date parameter.

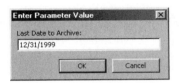

FIGURE 9-25.
Verifying the rows to delete.

Contract Number	Contract Date	Group ID	Group Name	Size	Group
4642	6/26/1999	Apes of Wrath	Apes of Wrath	1	RMP
4643	7/1/1999	the Fullerenes	Bucky and the Fu	5	RMP
4644	7/1/1999	The Belltones	The Belltones	3	RMP
4645	7/3/1999	Blind Logwara	Blind Logwara	2	MKP
4648	7/12/1999	Blind Logwara	Blind Logwara	2	MKP
4650	7/12/1999	e Uncommons	King Tut and the	3	RMP
4651	7/12/1999	's Apprentice	Shaman's Apprer	1	RMP
4652	7/13/1999	he Codpieces	The Codpieces	3	RMP
4655	7/13/1999	The Belltones	The Belltones	3	RMP
4657	7/13/1999	Henry and Otis	Henry and Otis	1	RMP
4661	7/13/1999	The Belltones	The Belltones	3	RMP
4664	7/13/1999	the Fullerenes	Bucky and the Fu	5	RMP
4667	7/13/1999	Urban Runoff	Urban Runoff	4	RMP
4669	7/13/1999	Monk Seal	Monk Seal	2	RMP
4670	7/13/1999	Monk Seal	Monk Seal	2	RMP

Record: 1 of 78

TIP

Access recognizes several different formats for date parameters. For example, for the last day in 1999, you can enter any of the following.

12/31/99   December 31, 1999   31-Dec-1999

The append query you saw earlier that moved these rows to an archive table copied 78 rows, which matches what you see here. After you verify that this is what you want, go back to Design view and run the query to actually delete the rows.

Using a Delete Query

Because you won't be able to retrieve any deleted rows, it's a good idea to first make a backup copy of your table, especially if this is the first time that you've run this delete query. Use the procedure described earlier in the section titled "Running an Update Query" to make a copy of your table.

You can create a delete query from a select query by choosing the Delete command from the Query menu when your query is in Design view. You don't have to make any further changes to select the rows to delete. Simply choose Run from the Query menu or click the Run button on the toolbar to delete the rows you specified. Because you included a parameter in this query, you'll need to respond to the Enter Parameter Value dialog box (shown in Figure 9-24 on the previous page) again. Access selects the rows to be deleted and displays the confirmation dialog box shown in Figure 9-26.

FIGURE 9-26.

The dialog box that asks you to confirm the deletion of rows.

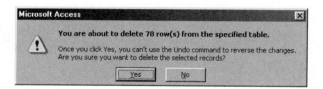

Click the Yes button to proceed with the deletion. Click the No button if you're unsure about the rows that Access will delete.

Deleting Inactive Data

You now know how to copy old contracts to an archive table, how to make sure matching club and group data is also copied to an archive table, and how to delete the old contracts from the main table. Eventually, you should also look at the rows in the active tblClubs and tblGroups tables to purge any rows that aren't active. If you have at least six months' worth of active data, you can create some queries to help you identify clubs or groups that haven't done any business in the last half-year. If you have more than six months' worth of contract data but want to limit your search to only the last six months, you must first create and save a query to filter out this data (similar to the example you saw in the previous chapter in the section titled "Building a Query on a Query"). Start a new query on tblContracts and add criteria, as shown in Figure 9-27. Save the query (or use the qryXmplContractsInLast6Months query in the Entertainment Scheduling database).

FIGURE 9-27.

A query to find active contracts in the last six months.

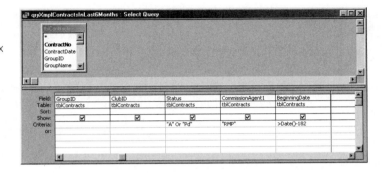

Start a new query on the first query and add the tblClubs table. Change the link to an outer join that retrieves all the rows from tblClubs. Add the asterisk (*) field from tblClubs. Include any field from the query, clear its Show check box, and add a criterion of Is Null. In this particular application, there might be a number of recently added clubs that are new prospects but don't yet have a contract. Since ClubID is an AutoNumber field, all the latest clubs have the highest ClubID values in the table. You know that many of these clubs won't find a match on contracts in the last six months, but you don't want to delete them. To solve this, include a test on ClubID from tblClubs using a parameter. Set the query to exclude from consideration any clubs whose primary key is greater than the value entered. Convert your query to a delete query, and the result should look like that shown in Figure 9-28.

FIGURE 9-28.

A query to delete clubs that had no contracts in the last six months.

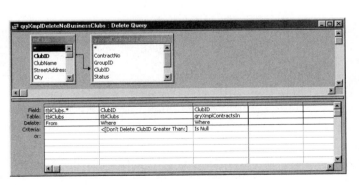

III

Working with Data

You can find this query saved as *qryXmplDeleteNoBusinessClubs* in the Entertainment Scheduling database. As you might expect, there's also a companion qryXmplDeleteNoBusinessGroups query. If you run the qryXmplDeleteNoBusinessClubs query and respond with *99999*, you should find two clubs to delete.

Example 2: Updating/Appending Rows from Imported Data

Earlier in this chapter, you learned how to select rows from one table and insert them into another. Sometimes you might receive data from another source (perhaps a list in a text file or a spreadsheet) that you want to merge into your existing data. In this example, let's suppose that Ray McCann occasionally receives updated club information in a Microsoft Excel workbook file. If he already has the club on file, he wants to be sure that he updates the address, manager name, and phone number information. If the file contains a new club, he wants to add rows to the tblClubs table.

On the companion CD, you can find a file called NewClubs.xls that contains some sample club information. You'll learn how to import this data as a table in the next chapter. For now, you can also find a table called NewClubs in the Entertainment Scheduling database that contains the resulting imported data. If you open this table in Datasheet view, as shown in Figure 9-29, and compare it with the data in tblClubs, you'll find that some rows match on club name and some rows are new.

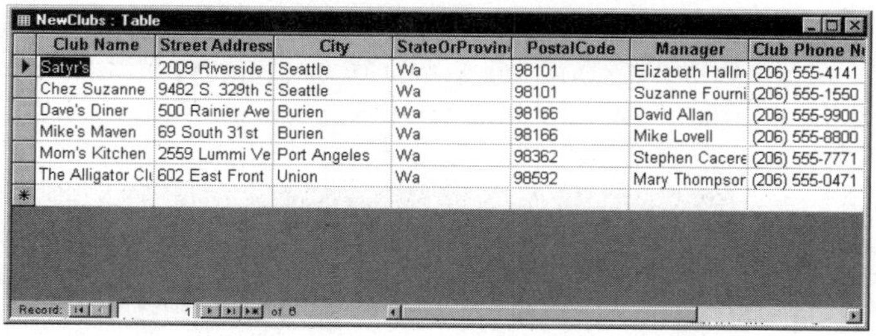
NewClubs : Table

Club Name	Street Address	City	StateOrProvin	PostalCode	Manager	Club Phone N
Satyr's	2009 Riverside I	Seattle	Wa	98101	Elizabeth Hallm	(206) 555-4141
Chez Suzanne	9482 S. 329th S	Seattle	Wa	98101	Suzanne Fourni	(206) 555-1550
Dave's Diner	500 Rainier Ave	Burien	Wa	98166	David Allan	(206) 555-9900
Mike's Maven	69 South 31st	Burien	Wa	98166	Mike Lovell	(206) 555-8800
Mom's Kitchen	2559 Lummi Ve	Port Angeles	Wa	98362	Stephen Cacere	(206) 555-7771
The Alligator Cl	602 East Front	Union	Wa	98592	Mary Thompsor	(206) 555-0471

Record: 1 of 6

FIGURE 9-29.
Imported club information ready to merge into tblClubs.

To complete this example, you need two queries: one to update selected information for matching rows and another to insert the new rows into tblClubs. To create the update query, start a new query using tblClubs. Use the Show Table dialog box to add the NewClubs table to the query. Link the two tables by dragging the ClubName field from tblClubs to the Club Name field in NewClubs (Access won't make this link automatically for you). Next add the following fields from tblClubs to the query grid: StreetAddress, City, StateOrProvince, PostalCode, MgrFirstName, MgrLastName, ClubPhoneNumber, and ClubFaxNumber.

Change the query to an Update Query, and enter the corresponding fields from NewClubs on the Update To row. For example, enter *[NewClub].[Street Address]* under the StreetAddress field in tblClubs. There's a small problem when you get to the MgrFirstName and MgrLastName fields. The name is all one field in the NewClubs table, so you need to use a couple of built-in functions to "parse" out the parts of the name to correctly update first and last names. The incoming Manager field in NewClubs has the first and last names separated by a blank, so you can look for the blank in the middle to extract the names. In the Update To row for the MgrFirstName field, enter the following.

```
Left$([NewClubs].[Manager],
      InStr([NewClubs].[Manager]," ")-1)
```

This uses the InStr function to find the position of the blank and then extracts the characters up to the blank using the Left$ function. (The blank is one position beyond the first name, so we subtract one.) In the Update To row for the MgrLastName field, enter the following.

```
Mid$([NewClubs].[Manager],
     InStr([NewClubs].[Manager]," ")+1)
```

This uses the InStr function again to find the first position beyond the blank. The Mid$ function extracts the characters from that position through the end of the string. The resulting query should look something like Figure 9-30. You can find this query saved as *qryXmplUpdateImportClubData* in the Entertainment Scheduling sample database.

FIGURE 9-30.

A query to update club information from matching imported data.

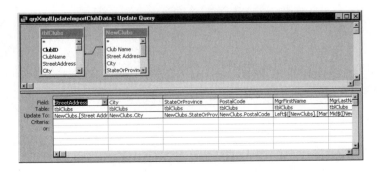

You also want to insert the data from any rows in the NewClubs table that don't match existing data in the tblClubs table. To do so, start a new query on the NewClubs table. Add the tblClubs table to the query, and link the tables again using the Club Name field in NewClubs and the ClubName field in tblClubs. Double-click the join line, and choose the option to include all records from NewClubs and only those records from tblClubs where the joined fields are equal. Include the following fields from the NewClubs table on the query grid: Club Name, Street Address, City, StateOrProvince, PostalCode, Club Phone Number, and Club Fax Number. Create two calculated fields using the functions noted above to extract the first and last names from the Manager field. Your two fields should look like the following.

```
MgrFirstName:Left$([NewClubs].[Manager],
    InStr([NewClubs].[Manager]," ")-1)

MgrLastName:Mid$([NewClubs].[Manager],
    InStr([NewClubs].[Manager]," ")+1)
```

Add the ClubID field from tblClubs, and set a criteria of Is Null. Because of the special join (an outer join) and this test for Null, the query will return only the unmatched rows from the NewClubs table. You can switch to Datasheet view to verify this—you should see three rows.

Finally, change the query to an append query and specify tblClubs as the target table. Access will set the matching field names in the Append To row for City, StateOrProvince, PostalCode, MgrFirstName, and MgrLastName. You'll have to set them yourself for the other fields. Be sure that nothing appears in the Append To row under the ClubID field from tblClubs. Your result should look like Figure 9-31. You can find this query saved as *qryXmplAddNewImportedClubs* in the Entertainment Scheduling database.

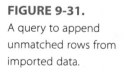

FIGURE 9-31.

A query to append unmatched rows from imported data.

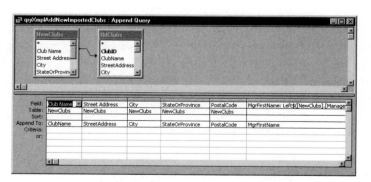

This append query works because the tblClubs table has an AutoNumber field for its primary key, so Access automatically generates new unique numbers for the added rows. If your target table doesn't have an AutoNumber primary key, you must be sure that the source table has unique primary key values that you can append to the target. (You *can* append Long Integer values from incoming rows to an AutoNumber field as long as the new values are unique.)

After you run both queries (the first should update three rows, and the second should append three rows), you can open the tblClubs table to see the result. Figure 9-32 shows the three new club rows.

NOTE

If you have experimented with various action queries to change the data in the Entertainment Scheduling database, you might want to reinstall the database from the companion CD before trying other examples in this book.

FIGURE 9-32.

The result of merging the imported data.

At this point, you should have a reasonable understanding of how action queries can work for you. We'll see some more examples of action queries in Chapter 11, "Advanced Query Design—SQL." In the next chapter, you'll learn how to import data from and export data to outside sources—text files, spreadsheets, other Access databases, and other database management systems.

III

Working with Data

CHAPTER 10

Importing, Linking, and Exporting Data

Although you can use Microsoft Access as a self-contained database and application system, one of its primary strengths is that it allows you to work with many kinds of data in other databases, in spreadsheets, or in text files. In addition to using data in your local Access database, you can *import* (copy in) or *link* (connect to) data that's in text files, spreadsheets, other Access databases, dBASE, Paradox, and any other SQL database that supports the Open Database Connectivity (ODBC) software standard (including Microsoft FoxPro). You can also *export* (copy out) data from Access tables to the databases, spreadsheets, Web pages, or text files of other applications.

A Word About Open Database Connectivity

If you look under the hood of Access, you'll find that it uses a database language called *SQL (Structured Query Language)* to read, insert, update, and delete data. SQL grew out of a relational database research project conducted by IBM in the 1970s. It has been adopted as the official standard for relational databases by organizations such as the American National Standards Institute (ANSI) and the International Standards Organization (ISO). When you're viewing a Query window in Design view, you can see the SQL statements that Access uses by choosing the SQL command from the View menu or by selecting SQL View from the Query View toolbar button's drop-down list.

? SEE ALSO
Chapter 11,"Advanced Query Design—SQL," provides more details about how Access uses SQL.

In an ideal world, any product that "speaks" SQL should be able to "talk" to any other product that understands SQL. You should be able to build an application that can work with the data in several relational database management systems using the same database language. Although standards exist for SQL, most software companies have implemented variations on or extensions to the language to handle specific features of their products. Also, several products evolved before standards were well established, so the companies producing those products invented their own SQL syntax, which differs from the official standard. An SQL statement intended to be executed by Microsoft SQL Server might require modification before it can be executed by other databases that support SQL, such as DB2 or Oracle.

To solve this problem, several years ago a group of influential hardware and software companies—more than 30 of them, including Microsoft Corporation—formed the SQL Access Group. The group's goal was to define a common base SQL implementation that its members' products could all use to "talk" to one another. The companies jointly developed the *Common Language Interface (CLI)* for all the major variants of SQL, and they committed themselves to building CLI support into their products. About a dozen of these companies jointly demonstrated this capability in early 1992.

? SEE ALSO
The appendix to this book provides details about installing and managing ODBC drivers on your computer.

In the meantime, Microsoft formalized the CLI for workstations and announced that Microsoft products—especially those designed for the Microsoft Windows operating system—would use this interface to access SQL databases. Microsoft calls this formalized interface the *Open Database Connectivity (ODBC) standard*. In the spring of 1992, Microsoft announced that more than a dozen database and application software vendors had committed to providing ODBC support in their products by the end of 1992. With Access, Microsoft provides the basic ODBC driver manager and the driver to translate ODBC SQL to Microsoft SQL Server SQL. Microsoft has also worked with several database vendors to develop drivers for other databases. The ODBC architecture is represented in Figure 10-1.

FIGURE 10-1.
The Microsoft ODBC architecture.

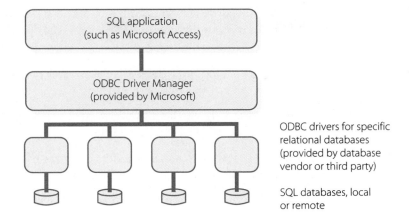

Access was one of Microsoft's first ODBC-compliant products. You have an option to install ODBC when you install Access on your computer. Once you've added the drivers for the other SQL databases that you want to work with, you can use Access to build an application using data from any of these databases.

Microsoft has further refined this architecture with the introduction of ActiveX Data Objects (ADO). You can use ADO as a "universal interface" to both databases that support ODBC as well as those that do not. *See Chapter 22 for details about working with ADO using Visual Basic.*

Importing vs. Linking Database Files

You have the choice of importing or linking data from other databases, but how do you decide which type of access is best? Here are some guidelines.

You should consider *importing* another database file when any one of the following is true.

- The file you need is relatively small and is not changed frequently by users of the other database application.

- You don't need to share the data you create with users of the other database application.

- You're replacing the old database application, and you no longer need the data in the old format.

- You need the best performance while working with the data from the other database (because Access performs best with a local copy of the data in Access's native format).

On the other hand, you should consider *linking* another database file when any one of the following is true.

- The file is larger than the maximum capacity of a local Access database (2 gigabytes).

- The file is changed frequently by users of the other database application.

- You must share the file on a network with users of the other database application.

- You'll be distributing your application to several individual users, and you might offer updates to the application interface you develop. Separating the "application" (queries, forms, reports, macros, and modules) from the "data" (tables) can make it easier to update the application without having to disturb the users' accumulated data.

The samples in this chapter use data you can find in files on the companion CD. You can import the data into or export the data from the Entertainment Scheduling and Microsoft Press Books databases. You might want to work from a copy of these databases to follow along with the examples in this chapter. You can find the result of following many of these examples in the Import Samples database.

Importing Data and Databases

You can copy data from a number of different file formats to create a Microsoft Access table. In addition to copying data from a number of popular database file formats, Access can also create a table from data in a spreadsheet or a text file. When you copy data from another database, Access uses information stored by the source database system to convert or name objects in the target Access table. You can import data not only from other Access databases but also from dBASE, Paradox, and—using ODBC—any SQL database that supports the ODBC standard (including Microsoft FoxPro).

Importing dBASE Files

To import a dBASE file, do the following.

1 Open the Access database that will receive the dBASE file. If that database is already open, switch to the Database window.

2 Choose the Get External Data command from the File menu, and then choose Import from the submenu. Access opens the Import dialog box, as shown below.

Open the Look In list to find the folder that contains your file.

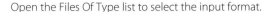

Select the file you want to import from this list.

Click the Import button to start the Import Wizard.

Open the Files Of Type list to select the input format.

3 Select dBASE III, dBASE IV, or dBASE 5, as appropriate, in the Files Of Type drop-down list. Select the source file folder from the Look In drop-down list, and then select or type in the filename in the File Name text box. If you're having difficulty finding the file you want, click the Tools button on the Import window toolbar and choose Find to open a search dialog box.

4 Click the Import button to import the dBASE file you selected. Access displays a message that informs you of the result of the import procedure, as shown below.

III

Working with Data

If the import procedure is successful, the new table will have the name of the dbf file. If Access finds a duplicate table name, it will generate a new name by adding a unique integer to the end of the name. For example, if you import a file named Newstore.dbf and you already have tables named Newstore and Newstore1, Access creates a table named NEWSTORE2.

5   Click the OK button to dismiss the message that confirms the import procedure. Access returns to the Import dialog box. You can select another file to import, or you can click the Close button to dismiss the Import dialog box.

You'll find a dBASE 5 file named Illinois.dbf on the companion CD included with this book. Follow the procedure described above to import this file into the Microsoft Press Books sample database or into a new blank database. When you open the table that Access creates from this dBASE format data, you'll see data for bookstores in Illinois, as shown in Figure 10-2.

FIGURE 10-2.

An imported dBASE file.

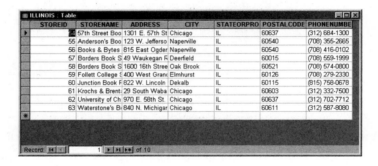

When you look at a table imported from dBASE in Design view, you'll find that Access has converted the data types, as shown in Table 10-1.

TABLE 10-1.   dBASE-to-Access Data Type Conversions

dBASE Data Type	Converts to Access Data Type
Character	Text
Numeric	Number, Field Size property set to Double
Float	Number, Field Size property set to Double
Logical	Yes/No
Date	Date/Time
Memo	Memo

Importing Paradox Files

The procedure for importing Paradox files is similar to the procedure for importing dBASE files. To import a Paradox file, do the following.

1 Open the Access database that will receive the Paradox file. If that database is already open, switch to the Database window.

2 Choose the Get External Data command from the File menu, and then choose Import from the submenu. Access opens the Import dialog box, as shown earlier on page 313.

3 Select Paradox in the Files Of Type drop-down list, and then select the folder and the name of the Paradox file that you want to import.

4 Click the Import button to import the Paradox file you selected.

5 If the Paradox file is encrypted, Access opens a dialog box that asks for the password. Type the correct password and click OK to proceed, or click Cancel to start over.

When you proceed, Access responds with a message that indicates the result of the import procedure. If the import procedure is successful, the new table will have the name of the db file. If Access finds a duplicate table name, it will generate a new name by adding a unique integer to the end of the name. For example, if you import a file named Newstore.db and you already have tables named Newstore and Newstore1, Access creates a table named NEWSTORE2.

6 Click OK to dismiss the message that confirms the import procedure. Access returns to the Import dialog box. You can select another file to import, or you can click Close to dismiss the Import dialog box.

You can try this procedure using the NY pdx.db file that's included on the companion CD.

When you look at a table imported from Paradox in Design view, you'll find that Access has converted the data types, as shown in Table 10-2 on the next page.

III

Working with Data

TABLE 10-2. Paradox-to-Access Data Type Conversions

Paradox Data Type	Converts to Access Data Type
Alphanumeric	Text
Number	Number, Field Size property set to Double
Short Number	Number, Field Size property set to Integer
Currency	Number, Field Size property set to Double
Date	Date/Time
Memo	Memo
OLE	OLE Object (but Access won't be able to activate the object)
Graphic, Binary, Formatted Memo	Not supported

Importing SQL Tables

To import a table from another database system that supports ODBC SQL, you must first have the ODBC driver for that database installed on your computer. *For details, see* Building Applications with Microsoft Access 2000, *online documentation that comes with Access; also see the appendix to this book.*

Your computer must also be linked to the network that connects to the SQL server you want, and you must have an account on that server. Check with your system administrator for information about correctly connecting to the SQL server from which you want to import data.

To import data from an SQL table, do the following.

1 Open the Access database that will receive the SQL data. If that database is already open, switch to the Database window.

2 Choose the Get External Data command from the File menu, and then choose Import from the submenu. Access opens the Import dialog box, as shown earlier on page 313.

3 Select ODBC Databases in the Files Of Type drop-down list. Access opens the Select Data Source dialog box, shown in the following illustration, from which you can select the data source that maps to the SQL server containing the table that you want to import.

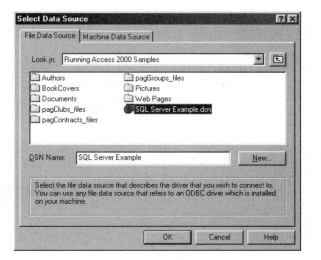

You can point to a data source name (dsn) file that you created previously, or click the Machine Data Source tab, as shown here, to see data sources that are already defined for your computer.

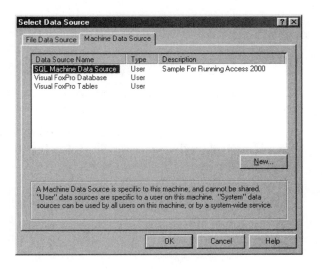

NOTE

Notice that the Machine Data Source tab lists installed sources for both Microsoft FoxPro databases (version 3.0 and later) and individual FoxPro table files. Access 2000 uses ODBC to import and link to Microsoft FoxPro.

III

Working with Data

To create a new data source name file, click the New button and follow the instructions to pick an available ODBC driver and locate the data source. A data source is simply a named set of ODBC driver parameters that provide the information the driver needs to dynamically link to the data. If you're familiar with the parameters required by the driver, you can create a data source name file like the one shown here for SQL Server.

Sample parameters in a data source name (dsn) file for the local SQL Server (Version 7)

Once you select a data source and click OK, the ODBC driver displays the Server Login dialog box for the SQL data source that you selected, as shown below.

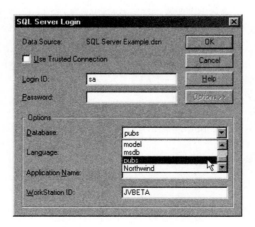

If your source is a FoxPro database or file, the ODBC driver displays the Configure Connection dialog box, as shown below.

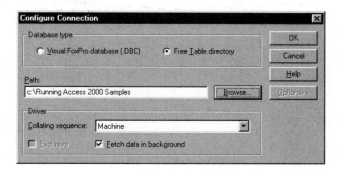

4 For a server database, enter your user ID and your password, and click OK. If you are authorized to connect to more than one database on the server and you want to connect to a database other than your default database, enter your user ID and password and then click the Options button to open the lower part of the dialog box. When you click in the Database text box, Access logs on to the server and returns a list of available database names. Select the one you want, and click OK. If you don't specify a database name and if multiple databases exist on the server, you'll be prompted to select the database you want. When Access connects to the server, you'll see the Import Objects dialog box, which lists the available tables on that server, as shown below.

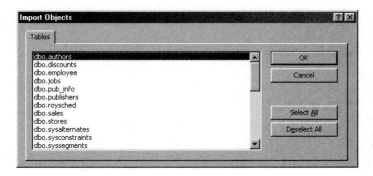

For a Microsoft FoxPro database or table, specify the database name or table folder path in the dialog shown in the last figure under Step 3 above. Click OK to see a list of tables in the database or a list of table files in the folder.

5 From the list of tables, select the ones you want to import. If you select a table name in error, you can click it again to deselect it or you can click the Deselect All button to start over. Click the OK button to import the SQL tables you selected.

6 If the import procedure is successful, the new table will have the name of the SQL table. If Access finds a duplicate table name, it will generate a new name by adding a unique integer to the end of the name. For example, if you import a table named dbo.Newstore and you already have tables named dbo.Newstore and dbo.Newstore1, Access creates a table named dbo.Newstore2.

> **NOTE**

You've no doubt noticed by now that the different databases use different style conventions (dbo.newstore, Newstore, NEWSTORE) for table names.

In general, Access converts SQL and FoxPro data types to Access data types, as shown in Tables 10-3 and 10-4.

TABLE 10-3. SQL-to-Access Data Type Conversions

SQL Data Type	Converts to Access Data Type
CHAR[ACTER]	Text, or Memo if more than 255 characters in length
VARCHAR	Text, or Memo if more than 255 characters in length
TEXT	Memo
TINYINT	Number, Field Size property set to Byte
SMALLINT	Number, Field Size property set to Integer
INT	Number, Field Size property set to Long Integer
REAL	Number, Field Size property set to Double
FLOAT	Number, Field Size property set to Double
DOUBLE	Number, Field Size property set to Double
DATE	Date/Time
TIME	Date/Time
TIMESTAMP	Binary[1]
IMAGE	OLE Object

1. The JET database engine supports a Binary data type (raw hexadecimal), but the Access user interface does not. If you link to a table that has a data type that maps to Binary, you will be able to see the data type in the table definition, but you won't be able to successfully edit this data in a datasheet or form. You can manipulate Binary data in Visual Basic.

TABLE 10-4.   FoxPro-to-Access Data Type Conversions

FoxPro Data Type	Converts to Access Data Type
Character	Text
Numeric	Number, Field Size property set to Integer
Float	Number, Field Size property set to Double
Date	Date/Time
Logical	Yes/No
Memo	Memo
General	OLE Object

Importing Access Objects

When the database from which you want to import data is another Access database, you can import any of the seven major types of Access objects: tables, queries, forms, reports, data access pages, macros, or modules. To achieve the same result, you can also open the source database, select the object you want, choose the Copy command from the Edit menu, open the target database, and then choose the Paste command from the Edit menu. Using the Import command, however, allows you to copy several objects without having to switch back and forth between the two databases.

To import an object from another Access database, take the following steps.

1   Open the Access database that will receive the object. If that database is already open, switch to the Database window.

2   Choose the Get External Data command from the File menu, and then choose Import from the submenu. Access opens the Import dialog box, as shown earlier on page 313.

3   Select Microsoft Access in the Files Of Type drop-down list, and then select the folder and the name of the mdb file containing the object that you want to import.

4   Click the Import button. Access opens the Import Objects dialog box, shown on the next page, which is a representation of the source database's Database window. First click the tab for the object type, and then select the specific object you want to import.

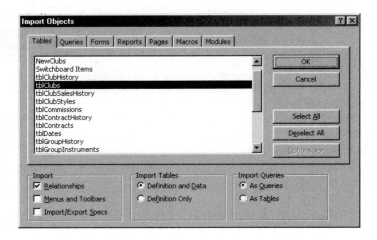

If you select an object in error, you can click the name again to deselect it. If you want to import all objects of a particular type, click the Select All button. You can import multiple objects of different types by clicking each object tab in turn and selecting the objects you want to import.

You can also click the Options button (which has been clicked in the preceding illustration) to select additional options. If you import any tables from the source database, you can select the option to import the table relationships (if any) defined for those tables in the source database. If the object is a table, you can select the option to import the table structure (the table definition) only or to import the structure *and* the stored data. You can also select special options to import all custom menus and toolbars (all command bars) from the source database *(see Chapter 24, "The Finishing Touches")* or all import/export specifications *(see the sidebar titled "Defining An Import Specification" later in this chapter for details)*. You can also choose to import the results of a query rather than import the query definition. Click OK to copy the objects you selected to the current database.

5 If the import procedure is successful, the new object will have the name of the object you selected. If Access finds a duplicate name, it will generate a new name by adding a unique integer to the end of the name. For example, if you import a table named Newstore and you already have tables named Newstore and Newstore1, Access creates Newstore2. Because objects can refer to other objects by name within an Access database, you should carefully check preestablished name references to the new object if the object has to be renamed.

NOTE

> If the source Access database is secured, you must have at least read permission for the database, read data permission for the tables, and read definition permission for all other objects in order to import objects. Once you import the objects into your database, you will own the copies of those objects in the target database. *See Chapter 25, "After Completing Your Application," for an overview of Access security.*

Importing Spreadsheet Data

Access also allows you to import data from spreadsheet files created by Lotus 1-2-3, Lotus 1-2-3 for Windows, and Microsoft Excel versions 2 and later. You can specify a portion of a spreadsheet or the entire spreadsheet file to import into a new table or to append to an existing table. If the first row of cells contains names suitable for field names in the resulting Access table, as shown in the Book Stores.xls spreadsheet in Figure 10-3, you can tell Access to use these names for your fields.

FIGURE 10-3.

The data in the first row of this Excel spreadsheet can be used as field names when you import the spreadsheet into a new Access table.

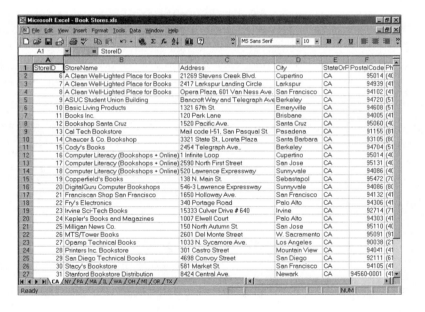

Preparing a Spreadsheet

Access determines the data type for the fields in a new table based on the values it finds in the first few rows of data being imported. When you import a spreadsheet into a new table, Access stores alphanumeric data as the Text data type with an entry length of 255 characters,

III

Working with Data

numeric data as the Number type with the Field Size property set to Double, numeric data with currency formatting as the Currency type, and any date or time data as the Date/Time type. If Access finds a mixture of data in any column in the first few rows, it imports that column as the Text data type.

> If you want to append all or part of a spreadsheet to a target table, you should import or link the entire spreadsheet as a new table and then use an append query to edit the data and move it to the table you want to update.

If the first several rows are not representative of all the data in your spreadsheet, you might want to insert a single "dummy" row at the beginning of your spreadsheet with data values that are representative of the data type you want to use for each column. You can easily delete that row from the table after you import the spreadsheet. For example, if you scroll down in the spreadsheet shown in Figure 10-3 on the previous page, you'll find several entries that have the postal code in ZIP+4 format, one of which is shown in Figure 10-4. Because Access sees only numbers in the first few rows of the PostalCode column, it will use a Number data type for the PostalCode field. However, the entries in ZIP+4 format contain a hyphen, which requires the field to be defined as text. As you'll see a bit later, if you attempt to import this spreadsheet without fixing this problem, Access will generate an error for each row that contains nonnumeric data.

FIGURE 10-4.

PostalCode entry containing data that can't be stored in numeric format.

	A	B	C	D	E	F
24	28	Printers Inc. Bookstore	301 Castro Street	Mountain View	CA	94041
25	29	San Diego Technical Books	4698 Convoy Street	San Diego	CA	92111
26	30	Stacy's Bookstore	581 Market St.	San Francisco	CA	94105
27	31	Stanford Bookstore Distribution	8424 Central Ave.	Newark	CA	94560-0001
28	32	Tower Books	2538 Watt Avenue	Sacramento	CA	95821
29	33	The UCLA BookZone	308 Westwood Plaza	Los Angeles	CA	90024
30	34	University Bookstore	Unviersity of California	Irvine	CA	92717
31	34	University Bookstore Q008	University of California San Diego	La Jolla	CA	92093
32	36	USC Bookstore/Trojan Bookstore	835 W. 36th Place	Los Angeles	CA	90089
33						

Importing a Spreadsheet

To import a spreadsheet into an Access database, do the following.

1 Open the Access database that will receive the spreadsheet. If that database is already open, switch to the Database window.

2 Choose the Get External Data command from the File menu, and then choose Import from the submenu. Access opens the Import dialog box, as shown earlier on page 313.

3 Select the type of spreadsheet you want to import (Excel or Lotus 1-2-3) in the Files Of Type drop-down list. Select the folder and the name of the spreadsheet file that you want to import. If you want to follow along with this example, select the Book Stores.xls file on the companion CD.

4 Click the Import button. If your spreadsheet is from Excel version 5.0 or later, it can contain multiple worksheets. If the spreadsheet contains multiple worksheets or any named ranges, Access shows you the first window of the Import Spreadsheet Wizard, as shown in the following illustration. (If you want to import a range that isn't yet defined, exit the wizard, open your spreadsheet to define a name for the range you want, save the spreadsheet, and then restart the import process in Access.) Select the worksheet or the named range that you want to import, and click Next to continue.

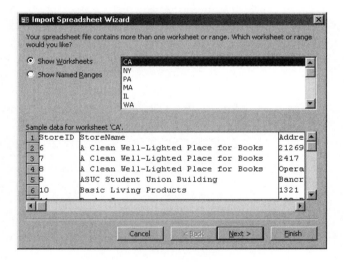

5 After you select a worksheet or a named range, or if your spreadsheet file contains only a single worksheet, the wizard displays the window shown on the next page.

Select the First Row Contains Column Headings check box if you've placed names at the tops of the columns in your spreadsheet. Click Next to go to the next step. In the window that appears, you can specify whether you want to import the data to a new table or append it to an existing one. Click Next to go to the next step.

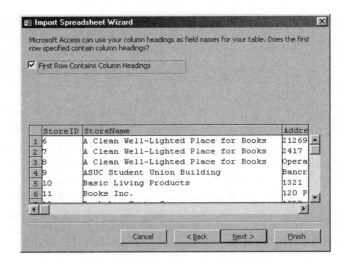

6 If you choose to create a new table, you can scroll left and right to the various fields and tell the wizard which fields should be indexed in the new table. Your indexing choices are identical to the ones you'll find for the Indexed property of a table in Design view. In this case, for the StoreID field, select Yes (No Duplicates) from the Indexed drop-down list box, as shown here, and for the PostalCode field, select Yes (Duplicates OK).

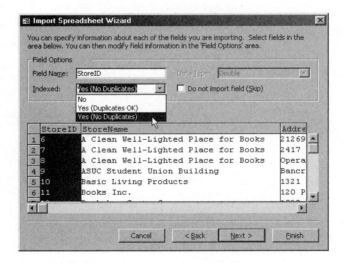

As you move from field to field, the Data Type combo box displays the data type that the wizard picks for each field (based on the data it finds in the first few rows). If what you see here is incorrect, you should exit the wizard and edit your spreadsheet to correct the data in the column. You can also choose to eliminate certain columns that you don't want to appear in the final table. For example, it's quite common to have intervening blank columns to control spacing in a spreadsheet that you print. You can eliminate blank columns by scrolling to them and selecting the Do Not Import Field (Skip) check box. Click Next to go to the next step.

7 In the window shown below, you can designate a field as the primary key of the new table. If you want, you can tell the wizard to build an ID field for you that will use the AutoNumber data type. If multiple fields form a unique value for the primary key, you can tell the wizard not to create a primary key. Later, you can open the resulting table in Design view to set the primary key.

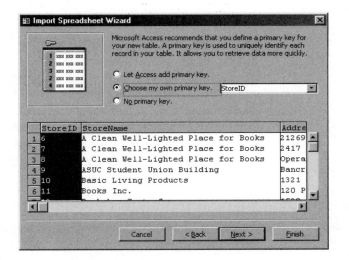

8 Click Next to go to the final window. In the final window, you can type in the name of your new table and select an option to start the Table Analyzer Wizard to analyze your new table. *See Chapter 5, "Building Your Database in Microsoft Access," for details.* If you enter the name of an existing table, Access asks if you want to replace the old table.

9 Click Finish in the last window to import your data. Access opens a message that indicates the result of the import procedure. If the procedure is successful, the new table will have the name of the spreadsheet you selected. If you asked to append the data to an existing table and Access found errors, you can choose to complete the import with errors or go back to the wizard to attempt to fix the problem (such as incorrectly defined columns). You may need to exit the wizard and correct data in the original spreadsheet file as noted in the following section.

Fixing Errors

Earlier in this chapter, in the section titled "Preparing a Spreadsheet," you learned that Access determines data types for the fields in a new table based on the values it finds in the first several rows being imported from a spreadsheet. Figures 10-3 and 10-4, shown earlier, show a spreadsheet whose first few rows would generate a wrong data type for the PostalCode column in a new Access table. The Number data type that Access would generate for that field, based on the first several entries, would not work for all of the remaining entries, some of which have hyphens in them. In addition, one of the rows has a duplicate value in the StoreID column. If you attempt to use this column as the primary key when you import the spreadsheet, you'll get an additional error.

If you were to import that spreadsheet, Access would first display an error message similar to the one shown in Figure 10-5. This indicates that the wizard found a problem with the column that you designated as the primary key. If you have duplicate values, the wizard will also inform you. When the wizard encounters any problems with the primary key column, it imports your data but does not define a primary key. This gives you a chance to correct the data in the table and then define the primary key yourself.

FIGURE 10-5.

Access displays this error message when it encounters a problem with your primary key values.

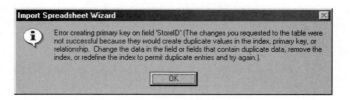

In addition, if the wizard has any problems with data conversion, it displays a message similar to the one shown in Figure 10-6.

FIGURE 10-6.

Access displays this message if it encounters data conversion errors while importing a spreadsheet.

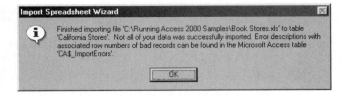

When the wizard has problems with data conversion, it creates an import errors table in your database (with the name of the spreadsheet in the title) that contains a record for each error. Figure 10-7 shows the import errors table that Access creates when you import the spreadsheet shown in Figure 10-3 on page 323. Notice that the table lists not only the type of error but also the field and row in the spreadsheet in which the error occurred. In this case, it lists the one row in the source spreadsheet that contains data in ZIP+4 text format. The row number listed is the relative row number in the source spreadsheet, not the record number in the resulting table.

FIGURE 10-7.

The import errors table that results from importing the spreadsheet shown in Figure 10-3.

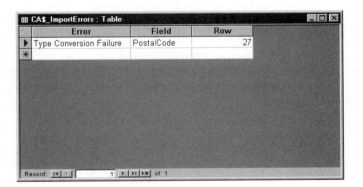

Figure 10-8 on the next page shows the table that results from importing the spreadsheet shown in Figure 10-3. You can find one row that has no entry in the PostalCode column. If you switch to Design view, you can see that the Import Spreadsheet Wizard selected the Number data type for the PostalCode field. If you want to be able to store the values that include hyphens, the PostalCode field must be a text field. Notice that in Design view that there is no primary key defined.

You can correct some of the errors in the Table window in Design view. For example, you can change the data type of the postal field to Text, save the table, and then enter the six missing postal codes. For the row that has a duplicate StoreID (34), you can switch to Datasheet view and then either delete the row or supply a unique value. You can then set StoreID as the primary key in Design view.

FIGURE 10-8.

After importing the spreadsheet shown in Figure 10-3, one row is missing a postal code entry.

Duplicate StoreID values   Missing postal code entry

Importing Text Files

You can import data from a text file into Microsoft Access even though, unlike the data in a spreadsheet, the data in a text file isn't arranged in columns and rows in an orderly way. You make the data in a text file understandable to Access either by creating a *delimited text file,* in which special characters delimit the fields in each record, or by creating a *fixed-width text file,* in which each field occupies the same location in each record.

Preparing a Text File

You might be able to import some text files into Access without changing them, particularly if a text file was created by a program using standard field delimiters. However, in many cases, you'll have to modify the contents of the file, define the file for Access, or do both before you can import it.

Setting Up Delimited Data

Access needs some way to distinguish where a field starts and ends in each incoming text string. Access supports three standard separator characters: a comma, a tab, and a space. When you use a comma as the separator (a very common technique), the comma (or the carriage return at the end of the record) indicates the end of each field, and the next field begins with the first nonblank character. The commas are not part of the data. To include a comma within a text string as data, you must enclose all text strings within single or double quotation marks. If any of your text strings contain double quotation marks, you must enclose the strings within single quotation marks, and vice versa. Access accepts only single or double quotation marks (but not both) as the text delimiter, so all embedded quotes in a file that you want to import into Access must be of the same type. In other words, you can't include a single quotation mark in one field and a double quotation mark in another field within the same file. Figure 10-9 shows a sample comma-separated and double-quote–delimited text file.

FIGURE 10-9.

A comma-separated and double-quote–delimited text file.

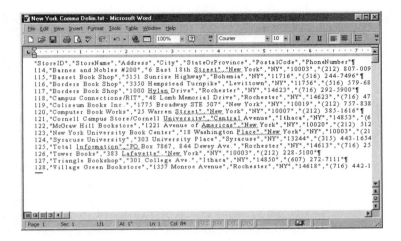

Another common way to separate data is to use the tab character between fields. In fact, when you save a spreadsheet file as text in most spreadsheet programs, the program stores the columns with tab characters between them. Figure 10-10 on the next page shows one of the worksheets from the Book Stores spreadsheet from Microsoft Excel saved as text in Microsoft Word. Notice that Excel added double quotation marks around all of the text strings but did not place quotation marks around the StoreID numeric field. Because this file is tab delimited, Access would accept the text fields without quotation marks as long as the text fields do not contain any quotation marks or commas.

By default, Access assumes that fields in a delimited text file are separated by commas and that text strings are within double quotation marks. As you'll see a bit later, if you want to import a file that is delimited differently, you can specify different delimiters and separators in the Text Import Wizard. The important thing to remember is that your data should have a consistent data type in all the rows for each column—just as it should in spreadsheet files. If your text file is delimited, the delimiters must be consistent throughout the file.

Setting Up Fixed-Width Data

Access can also import text files when the fields appear in fixed locations in each record in the file. You might encounter this type of file if

III

Working with Data

FIGURE 10-10.

A tab-separated text file.

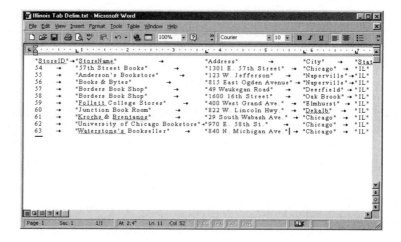

you download a print output file from a host computer. Figure 10-11 shows a sample fixed-width text file. Notice that each field begins in exactly the same location in all the records. (To see this sort of fixed spacing on your screen, you must display the file using a monospaced font such as Courier New.) To prepare this type of file for importing, you must first remove any heading or summary lines from the file. The file must contain only records, with the data you want to import in fixed locations.

FIGURE 10-11.

A fixed-width text file.

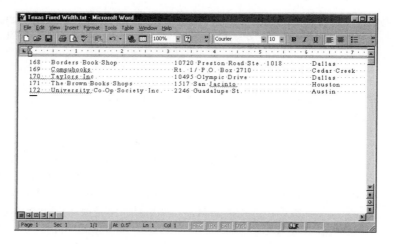

Importing a Text File

Before you can import a text file, you'll probably need to prepare the data or define the file for Access, or both, as discussed earlier in the section titled "Preparing a Text File." After you do that, you can import the text file into an Access database by doing the following.

1   Open the Access database that will receive the text data. If that database is already open, switch to the Database window.

2   Choose the Get External Data command from the File menu, and then choose Import from the submenu. Access opens the Import dialog box, as shown earlier on page 313.

3   Select Text Files in the Files Of Type drop-down list, and then select the folder and the name of the file you want to import. Access starts the Import Text Wizard and displays the first window of the wizard, as shown below.

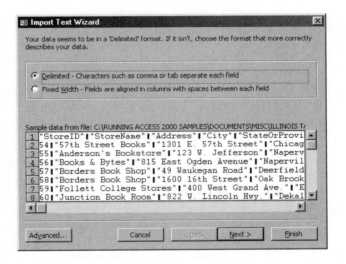

4   In this window, the wizard makes its best guess about whether the data is delimited or fixed-width. It displays the first several rows of data, which you can examine to confirm the wizard's choice. If the wizard has made the wrong choice, your data is probably formatted incorrectly. You should exit the wizard and fix the source file as suggested in the section "Preparing a Text File." If the wizard has made the correct choice, click Next to go to the next step.

5   If your file is delimited, the Import Text Wizard displays the window shown in the illustration on the next page.

III

Working with Data

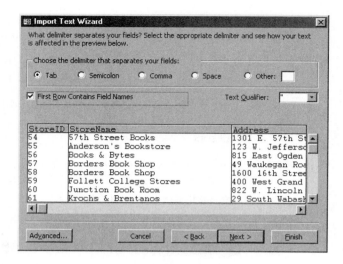

Here you can verify the character that delimits the fields in your text file and the qualifier character that surrounds text strings. Remember that usually when you save a delimited text file from a spreadsheet program, the field delimiter is a tab character and you'll find quotation marks only around strings that contain commas. If the wizard doesn't find a text field with quotation marks in the first line, it might assume that no text is surrounded by quotes. You might need to change the Text Qualifier from {none} to " if this is the case.

If your file is in fixed-width format, the wizard displays the window shown in the following illustration.

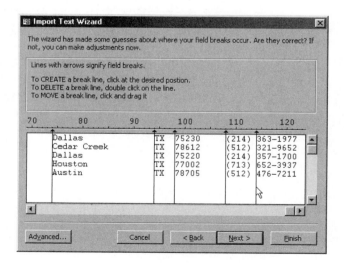

Instead of showing delimiting characters, the wizard offers a graphic representation of where it thinks each field begins. To change the definition of a field, you can drag any line to move it. You can also create an additional field by clicking at the position on the display where fields should be separated. If the wizard creates too many fields, you can double-click any extra delimiting lines to remove them. In the example shown above (using the Texas Fixed Width.txt file on the companion CD), the wizard assumes that the area code is separate from the rest of the phone number. You can double-click the line following the area code to remove it and group all the characters that make up the phone number into a single field.

After you finish in this window, click Next to go to the next step.

6 In the next window, shown below, you specify whether you want to import the text into a new table or append the data to an existing table.

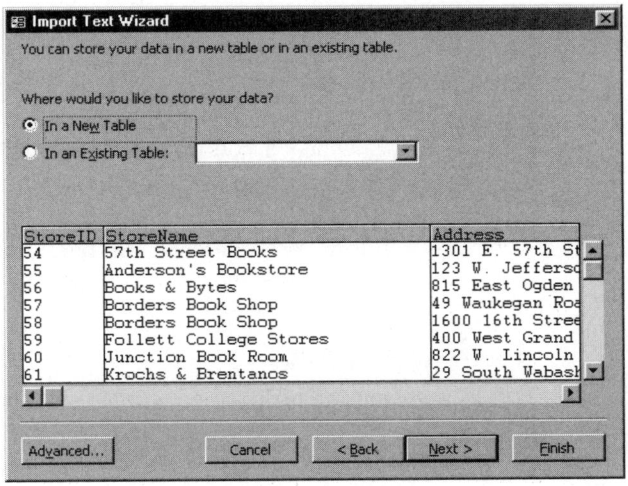

If you decide to create a new table, the wizard displays the window shown on the next page. Here you can specify or confirm field names (you can change field names even if the first row in the text file contains names), select field data types, and set indexed properties. Click Next to go to the next window, where you can select a primary key, much as you did for spreadsheet files.

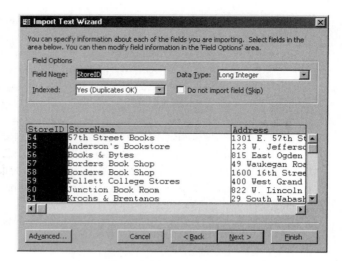

If you decide to append the data to an existing table, either the columns must exactly match the columns in the target table (left to right) or the file must be a delimited file with column names in the first row that match column names in the target table.

7 In the final window of the wizard, you confirm the name of the new table or the target table and click Finish to import your data. Access displays a confirmation message to show you the result of the import procedure. If the wizard encounters an error that prevents any data from being imported, it will reopen the final wizard window. You can click the Back button to return to previous settings to correct them.

Fixing Errors

While importing text files, you might encounter errors that are similar to those described earlier in the section titled "Importing Spreadsheet Data." When you append a text file to an existing table, some rows might be rejected because of duplicate primary keys. Unless the primary key for your table is an AutoNumber field, the rows you append from the text file must contain the primary key fields and the values in those fields must be unique. For delimited text files, Access determines the data type based on the fields in the first several records being imported. If a number appears in a field in the first several records but subsequent records contain text data, you must enclose that field in quotation marks in at least one of the first few rows so that Access will use the Text data type for that field. If a number first appears without decimal places, Access will use the Number data type with the Field

Size property set to Long Integer. This setting will generate errors later if the numbers in other records contain decimal places.

Access displays a message if it encounters any errors. As with errors that are generated when you import a spreadsheet, Access creates an import errors table. The table contains a record for each error. The

---

Defining an Import Specification

If you are likely to import the same fixed-width file often or if you want to be able to use a macro or a Visual Basic procedure to automate importing a text file, you can use the Import Text Wizard to save an import specification for use by your automation procedures. To do so, use the wizard to examine your file, and verify that the wizard identifies the correct fields. Click the Advanced button to see an Import Specification window like the one shown here.

For fixed-width specifications, you can define the field names, data types, start column, width, and indexed properties. You can also specify in the File Origin combo box whether the text file was created using a program running under MS-DOS or under Microsoft Windows. For fixed-width files, you don't need to make a Field Delimiter selection or a Text Qualifier selection; you use these options only to define a specification for delimited files. You can also specify the way Access recognizes date and time values and numeric fractions. Click the Save As button to save your specification, and give it a name. You can also click the Specs button to edit other previously saved specifications.

III

Working with Data

import errors table lists not only the type of error but also the column and row in the text file in which the error occurred.

You can correct some errors in the Table window in Design view. For example, you can change the data type of fields if the content of the fields can be converted to the new data type. *See Table 6-1 in Chapter 6 for data conversion limitations.* With other errors, you must either add missing data in Datasheet view or delete the imported records and import the table again after correcting the values in the text file that originally caused the errors.

Modifying Imported Tables

? SEE ALSO
You can correctly specify most data types, change field names, and add a primary key in the Table window in Design view. For details about modifying your table design, see Chapter 6, "Modifying Your Database Design."

When you import data from an external source, Microsoft Access often has to use default data types or lengths that will accommodate the incoming data. You will then need to correct these default settings for your needs. For example, Access assigns a maximum length of 255 characters to text data imported from a spreadsheet or a text file. Even when the source of the data is another database, Access might choose numeric data types that can accept the data but that might not be correct. For example, numeric data in dBASE might be of the Integer type, but Access stores all numeric data from dBASE with a Field Size setting of Double.

Unless you're importing data from an SQL or Paradox database that has a primary key defined, Access does not define a primary key in the new table, so you must do that yourself. Also, if you did not include field names when importing a text or spreadsheet file, you'll probably want to enter meaningful names in the resulting table.

Linking Files

You can link tables from other Microsoft Access databases—whether the other databases are local or on a network—and work with the data as if these tables were defined in your current Access database. If you want to work with data stored in another database format supported by Access (dBASE, Paradox, or any SQL database that supports ODBC, including Microsoft FoxPro), you can link the data instead of importing it. In most cases, you can read data, insert new records, delete records, or change data just as if the linked file were an Access table. You can also link text and spreadsheet format data so that you can process it with queries, forms, and reports in your Access database. You can update and insert new rows in spreadsheets, but you can't delete rows.

You can only read the data in linked text files. This ability to link data is especially important when you need to access data on a host computer or share data from your application with many other users.

> Microsoft Access 2000 supports linking to Paradox and dBase versions 5.0 and older as read-only files. If you need to update these files or work with later versions, you must install the Borland Database Engine (BDE).

Security Considerations

If you attempt to link a file or a table from a database system that is protected, Access asks you for a password. If the security information you supply is correct and Access successfully links the secured data, Access optionally stores the security information with the linked table entry so that you do not have to enter this information each time you or your application opens the table. Although there is no way to directly access this information in your database from Access, a knowledgeable person might be able to retrieve it by scanning the file with a dump utility. Therefore, if you have linked sensitive information to your Access database and have supplied security information, you should consider encrypting your database. *Consult Chapter 25, "After Completing Your Application," for information about securing and encrypting your Access database.*

If you are linking your database to Microsoft SQL Server tables and are using Microsoft Windows NT domain security, you can set options in SQL Server to accept the Windows NT domain user ID if the user logs on correctly to the network. Therefore, you won't need to store security information with the link. If your server contains particularly sensitive information, you can disable this option to guard against unauthorized access from logged on but unattended network workstations.

Performance Considerations

Access always performs best when working with its own files on your local machine. If you link tables or files from other databases, you might notice slower performance. In particular, you can expect slower performance if you connect over a network to a table or a file in another database, even if the remote table is an Access table.

When sharing data over a network, you should consider how you and other people can use the data in a way that maximizes performance. For example, instead of working directly with the tables, you should work with queries on the shared data whenever possible to limit the amount of data you need at any one time. When inserting new data in a shared table, you should use an Access form that is set only for data entry so that you don't have to access the entire table to add new data. *See Part IV of this book, "Using Forms," for more information.*

You can view and set options for multiple users sharing data by choosing Options from the Tools menu and clicking the Advanced tab of the Options dialog box, as shown in Figure 10-12. The original settings for these options are often appropriate when you share data over a network, so it's a good idea to consult your system administrator before making changes.

FIGURE 10-12.
The Options dialog box with the Advanced tab selected.

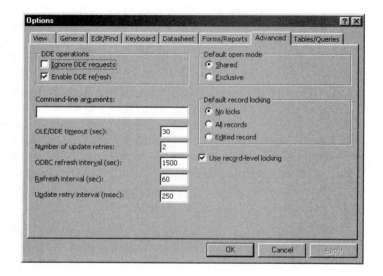

You should set options so that records are not locked if you are simply browsing through data. If you need to update data and you want to ensure that no one else can change a record that you have begun to update, you should set the RecordLocks property to Edited Record. When other users are updating the data you are using, you'll occasionally notice that you cannot update a record. You can set options to limit the number of times Access will retry an update to a locked record on your behalf and how long it will wait between retries. You can also control how often Access reviews updates made by other users to shared data. If this refresh interval is set very low, Access will waste time performing this task repeatedly.

 Prior versions of Microsoft Access lock an entire 2-KB page each time you update, insert, or delete rows. This means that only one user can update any of the rows stored physically within the page. The page size in Access 2000 is now 4 KB, but Access 2000 also supports record-level locking that eliminates locking collisions when two users attempt to update different rows stored on the same data storage page. Unless you are designing an application that frequently needs to update hundreds of rows at a time (for example, with action queries), you should leave the Use Record-Level Locking box checked.

Linking Access Tables

To link a table from another Access database to your database, do the following.

1   Open the Access database to which you want to link the table. If that database is already open, switch to the Database window.

2   Choose the Get External Data command from the File menu, and then choose Link Tables from the submenu. Access opens the Link dialog box, which is similar to the Import dialog box shown earlier on page 313, and which lists the types of databases you can link.

3   Select Microsoft Access in the Files Of Type drop-down list, and then select the folder and the name of the mdb file that contains the table you want to link. If you are connecting over a network, select the logical drive that is assigned to the network server containing the database you want. If you want Access to connect to the network server each time you open the table, type the full network location in the File Name text box instead of selecting a logical drive. For example, on a Microsoft Windows NT network you might enter a network location such as:

\\dbsvr\access\shared\northwind.mdb

After you select the Access database file you want, click the Link button to see the tables in that database.

4   Access opens the Link Tables dialog box, shown on the next page, which lists the tables available in the database you selected. Select one or more tables, and click the OK button to link the tables to the current database. If the link procedure is successful, the new table will have the name of the table you selected.

III

Working with Data

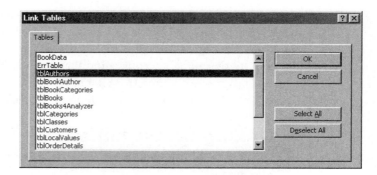

Access marks the icon for linked tables in the Database window with an arrow, as shown in the illustration below. If Access finds a duplicate name, it generates a new name by adding a unique integer to the end of the name. For example, if you link a table named Newstore and you already have tables named Newstore and Newstore1, Access creates a table named Newstore2. Because objects such as forms, reports, macros, and modules might refer to the linked table by its original name, you should carefully check name references if Access has to rename a linked table.

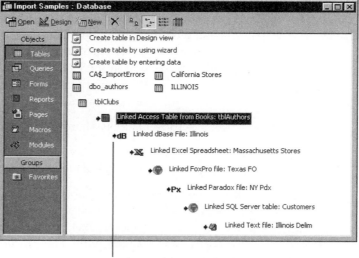

Icons marked with an arrow represent linked tables.

Linking dBASE and Paradox Files

Linking tables from a foreign database is almost as easy as linking an Access table. To link a table from dBASE or Paradox, do the following.

1   Open the Access database to which you want to link the table. If that database is already open, switch to the Database window.

2   Choose the Get External Data command from the File menu, and then choose Link Tables from the submenu. Access opens the Link dialog box, which lists the types of databases you can link.

3   Select dBASE III, dBASE IV, dBASE 5, or Paradox, as appropriate, in the Files Of Type drop-down list, and then select the folder and the name of the database file that you want to link. If you're connecting over a network, select the logical drive that is assigned to the network server that contains the database you want. If you want Access to automatically connect to the network server each time you open the linked file, type the full network location in the File Name text box instead of selecting a logical drive. For example, on a Windows NT network you might enter a network location such as:

\\dbsvr\dbase\shared\newstore.dbf

4   Click the Link button to link the selected dBASE or Paradox file.

5   If you selected a dBASE file and you have the Borland Database Engine (BDE) installed, Access opens the Select Index Files dialog box, shown in the following illustration. If you do not have BDE installed, Access does not prompt you, and your linked file will be read-only.

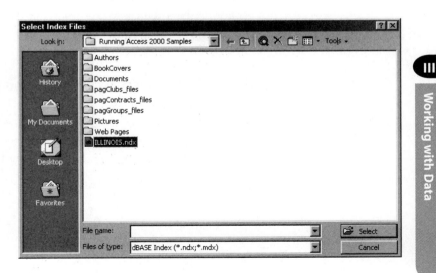

In this dialog box you identify any index files that are associated with the file you want to link. (If there are no index files, simply click the Cancel button.) You must inform Access of all related indexes if you want the indexes updated properly whenever you make a change to the dBASE file using Access. You must not move or delete these index files or the information (inf) file that Access builds when you link the table; if you do, you will not be able to open the dBASE file from Access. You must also be sure that any dBASE application always maintains these indexes. Access can't open a linked dBASE file if its indexes are not current.

Select the index files you need to associate with the dBASE file you're linking. Click the Select button once for each index file you want to add to the information file. Click Close after you select all the appropriate indexes.

6 If the file you selected requires a password to access it (because it's an encrypted Paradox file, for example), Access prompts you for the correct password and then displays a message that indicates the result of the link procedure. If the link procedure is successful, the new table will have the name of the file you selected. If Access finds a duplicate name, it will generate a new name by adding a unique integer to the end of the name. For example, if you link a table named Newstore and you already have tables named Newstore and Newstore1, Access creates a new table named Newstore2.

7 Click the OK button to dismiss the message that confirms the link action. Access returns you to the Link dialog box. You can select another file to link, or you can click the Close button to dismiss the dialog box.

Linking Text and Spreadsheet Files

Linking a text file or an Excel spreadsheet file is almost identical to importing these types of files, as discussed earlier in this chapter. As noted, you can only read linked text files, but you can update and add new rows (but not delete rows) in Excel spreadsheet files.

To link a spreadsheet file or a text file, do the following.

1 Open the Access database to which you want to link the file. If that database is already open, switch to the Database window.

2 Choose the Get External Data command from the File menu, and then choose Link Tables from the submenu. Access opens the Link dialog box, which lists the types of files you can link.

3 Select Microsoft Excel or Text Files, as appropriate, in the Files Of Type drop-down list, and then select the folder and the name of the file that you want to link. If you're connecting over a network, select the logical drive that is assigned to the network server that contains the database you want. If you want Access to automatically connect to the network server each time you open the linked file, type the full network location in the File Name edit box instead of choosing a logical drive. For example, on a Windows NT network you might enter a network location such as:

\\filesvr\excel\shared\book stores.xls

4 Click the Link button to start the Link Spreadsheet Wizard or the Link Text Wizard.

5 Follow the steps in the wizard, which are identical to the steps for importing a spreadsheet or text file, as described earlier in this chapter.

Linking SQL Tables

SEE ALSO

For details about ODBC drivers, see *Building Applications with Microsoft Access 2000*; also see the appendix to this book.

To link a table from another database system that supports ODBC SQL, you must have the ODBC driver for that database installed on your computer. Your computer must also be linked to the network that connects to the SQL server you want, and you must have an account on that server. Check with your system administrator for information about correctly connecting to the SQL server from which you want to link a table.

To link an SQL table, do the following.

1 Open the Access database to which you want to link the SQL table. If that database is already open, switch to the Database window.

2 Choose the Get External Data command from the File menu, and then choose Link Tables from the submenu. Access opens the Link dialog box, which lists the types of files you can link.

3 Select ODBC Databases in the Files Of Type drop-down list. Access opens the Select Data Source dialog box, shown earlier on page 317, in which you can select the data source that maps to the SQL server containing the table you want to link. Select a data source, and click OK. The ODBC driver displays the SQL Server Login dialog box for the SQL data source that you selected. If you are linking to a Microsoft FoxPro database or file, the ODBC driver displays the Configure Connection dialog box.

III

Working with Data

4 Enter your user ID and your password, and click OK. If you are authorized to connect to more than one database on the server and you want to connect to a database other than your default database, enter your user ID and password, and then click the Options button to open the lower part of the dialog box. When you click the Database text box, Access logs on to the server and returns a list of available database names. Select the one you want, and click OK. If you don't specify a database name and if multiple databases exist on the server, Access will prompt you to select the database you want. For Microsoft FoxPro, specify the database name or FoxPro file folder and click OK.

When Access connects to the server or FoxPro database, you'll see the Link Objects dialog box, similar to the Import Objects dialog box shown earlier on page 319, which lists the available tables on that server.

5 From the list of tables, select the ones you want to link. If you select a table name in error, you can click it again to deselect it, or you can click the Deselect All button to start over. Click the OK button to link to the tables you selected.

6 If the link procedure is successful, the new table will have the name of the SQL or FoxPro table. If Access finds a duplicate name, it will generate a new name by adding a unique integer to the end of the name. For example, if you link to a table named Newstore and you already have tables named Newstore and Newstore1, Access creates a table named Newstore2.

Modifying Linked Tables

You can make some changes to the definitions of linked tables to customize them for use in your Access environment. When you attempt to open the Table window in Design view, Access opens a dialog box to warn you that you cannot modify certain properties of a linked table. You can still click OK to open the linked table in Design view.

You can open a linked table in Design view to change the Format, Decimal Places, Caption, Description, and Input Mask property settings for any field. You can set these properties to customize the way you look at and update data in Access forms and reports. You can also give any linked table a new name for use within your Access database (although the table's original name remains unchanged in the source database) to help you better identify the table or to enable you to use the table with the queries, forms, and reports that you've already designed.

Changing a table's design in Access has no effect on the original table in its source database. However, if the design of the table in the source database changes, you must relink the table to Access.

You must also unlink and relink any table if your user ID or your password changes.

Unlinking Linked Tables

It is easy to unlink tables that are linked to your Access database. In the Database window, simply select the table you want to unlink and then press the Del key or choose Delete from the Edit menu. Access displays the confirmation message shown in Figure 10-13. Click the Yes button to unlink the table. Unlinking the table does not delete the table; it simply removes the link from your table list in the Database window.

FIGURE 10-13.

The confirmation message that appears when you unlink a table.

Using the Linked Table Manager

If some or all of your linked tables are moved to a different location, you can easily update the location information by using the Linked Table Manager. To use this handy utility, open the database that contains linked tables that need to be relinked, choose Database Utilities from the Tools menu, and then choose Linked Table Manager from the submenu. The utility opens a dialog box that displays all the linked tables in your database, as shown in Figure 10-14 on the next page. Simply select the ones that you think need to be verified and updated, and then click OK. If any of the linked tables have been moved to a different location, the Linked Table Manager prompts you with a dialog box so that you can specify the new file location. You can also select the Always Prompt For New Location check box to verify the file location for all linked tables.

III

Working with Data

FIGURE 10-14.

The Linked Table Manager dialog box.

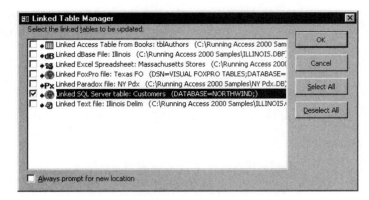

Exporting Data

You can export (copy) any object in a Microsoft Access database to any other Access database. You can also export data from Access tables to spreadsheet files, other databases, text files, Microsoft Word mail merge documents, and SQL tables. Finally, you can export the data in any table or the data selected in any query, form, or report to HTML (Hypertext Markup Language) files that are suitable for display as an Internet or intranet Web page.

Exporting to Another Access Database

Exporting objects from one Access database to another works much like importing Access objects. To export any object from one Access database to another Access database, do the following.

1   Open the Access database from which you want to export an object. If that database is already open, switch to the Database window.

2   Select the object you want to export in the Database window, and then choose the Export command from the File menu. Access opens an Export To dialog box, similar to the one shown in the following illustration, in which you can select the folder and the name of the mdb file to which you want to export the object. After you select these, click Save.

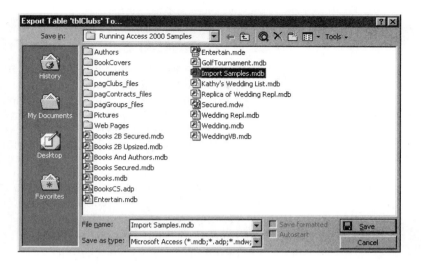

3 Next Access opens the Export dialog box, shown below.

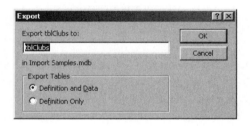

Use the Export dialog box to specify a name for the object in the target database. You can keep the name that Access suggests, or you can change it to make it more appropriate to the target database. Note that if you're exporting a table, you can choose to export both the table definition and the data or the definition only. Click OK to export the object.

4 If the export name you type in already exists in the target database, Access warns you and asks whether you want to replace the existing object. Click Yes to proceed, or click No to stop the export procedure. If the export procedure is successful, you'll find a new object in the target database. Because objects can refer to other objects by name within an Access database, you should carefully check name references in the target database.

III

Working with Data

Exporting to a Spreadsheet or to a dBASE or Paradox File

Use the following procedure to export data from a table, a select query, or a crosstab query to a spreadsheet (Microsoft Excel or Lotus 1-2-3) or to a foreign database (dBASE or Paradox) file.

1 Open the Access database from which you want to export an object. If that database is already open, switch to the Database window.

2 Select the object you want to export in the Database window, and then choose the Export command from the File menu. Access opens the Export To dialog box, shown on the previous page, from which you can select the file type, folder, and name of the file to which you want to export the selected object. After you select these, click Save.

3 If the export procedure is successful, you'll find a new file that you can use with your spreadsheet application or with another database program.

> Access truncates long field names when it exports data to dBASE or Paradox files. If this results in a duplicate field name, Access will not export your data.
>
> To correct this problem, make a temporary copy of your table, edit the field names in the temporary table to avoid duplicates, and try the export procedure again using the temporary table. You should avoid changing the field names in your permanent table because you might cause errors in queries, forms, and reports that use the table.

Quick Export to Microsoft Excel

Access also provides a facility to quickly export the data in any table, select query, or crosstab query to an Excel spreadsheet. In the Database window, select the table or query whose data you want to export. Choose Office Links from the Tools menu, and then choose Analyze It With MS Excel from the submenu (or select Analyze It With MS Excel from the Office Links toolbar button's drop-down list). Access copies the table to an Excel spreadsheet file and opens the file in Excel. If the filename already exists, Access asks whether you want to replace the file. If you click No, Access asks you to provide a different filename. Figure 10-15 shows the tblStores table in the Microsoft Press Books database after it has been exported to Excel.

FIGURE 10-15.

An Access table that has been exported to Excel.

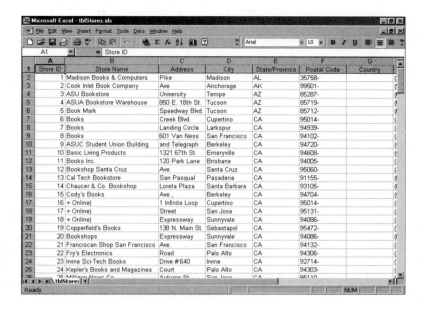

 NOTE

> When you export a table or query to a spreadsheet, Access uses each field's Caption as the column header. If the field does not have a Caption, the field name appears in the column header.

Exporting to a Text File

You can export data from an Access table, a select query, or a crosstab query to a text file in one of two formats: delimited or fixed-width. You might find this procedure particularly useful for copying data from an Access table to an MS-DOS-based word processor or text editor or for uploading the data to a host computer.

To export the data from an Access table, a select query, or a crosstab query to a text file, do the following.

1 Open the Access database from which you want to export the data in a table. If that database is already open, switch to the Database window.

2 Choose the object you want to export and then choose the Export command from the File menu. Access opens the Export To dialog box, in which you can select the text file type, the folder, and the name of the file to which you want to export the data. After you select these, click Save.

3 Access starts the Export Text Wizard, in which you can select a delimited or fixed-width output format.

4 If you're exporting to a delimited text file, you can set the delimiter to separate the exported fields and the qualifier character to surround text strings. You can also tell Access to create an optional first record containing your field names. If you're exporting to a fixed-width format, you can adjust the column widths, as shown in the following illustration. You can also click the Advanced button to edit or select an import/export specification. In the final window of the wizard, you verify the export filename and click Finish to export your data. If the export procedure is successful, you'll find a new file in the text format you selected.

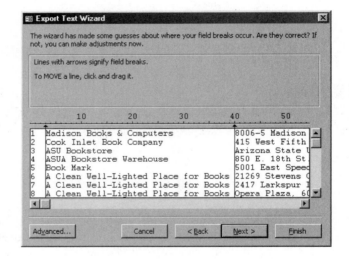

Exporting to a Mail Merge Document in Microsoft Word

Perhaps one of the most useful features of Access is that it enables you to embed data from an Access table or query directly in a Microsoft Word document. This is especially helpful when you have a database of addresses that you want to use with the Word mail merge feature. To embed data from an Access database in a Word document, do the following.

1 Open your database, and select the table or query whose data you want to embed in a Word document.

2 Choose Office Links from the Tools menu, and then choose Merge It With MS Word from the submenu (or select Merge It With MS Word from the Office Links toolbar button's drop-down list). This starts the Microsoft Word Mail Merge Wizard.

3 Select the option to link to an existing Word document or the option to create a new document, as shown in the following illustration. If you want to embed the data in an existing document, the wizard will ask for the document location. When you finish, click OK.

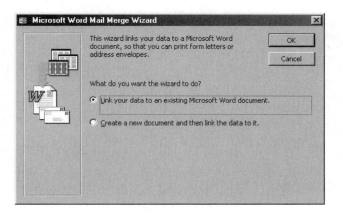

4 The wizard starts Word and activates a mail merge link to your table or query, as shown below.

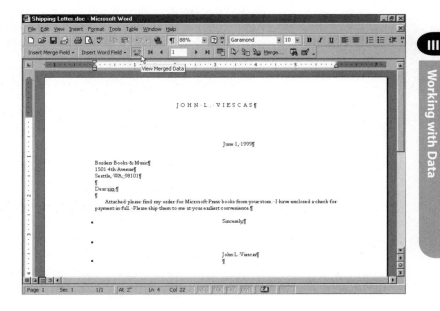

5 The Microsoft Press Books sample database provides the ability to specify a bookstore for an order and to print the order. You might want to attach a cover letter to your order if you plan to mail it. You can find a sample cover letter, Shipping Letter.doc, on the companion CD. The qxmplMailOrdersForJohnV query in the Microsoft Press Books database provides the data for this document. You can use the various features of the Mail Merge toolbar in Word to build your document with fields embedded from Access.

Exporting to an SQL Table

SEE ALSO

For details about ODBC drivers, see *Building Applications with Microsoft Access 2000*; also see the appendix to this book.

You can export data from an Access table or query to define a new table in any SQL database that supports the ODBC standard. To export data in an Access table or query to another database system that supports ODBC SQL, you must have the ODBC driver for that database installed on your computer. Your computer must also be linked to the network that connects to the SQL server you want, and you must have an account on that server. Check with your system administrator for information about correctly connecting to the SQL server to which you want to export data.

To export data to an SQL table, do the following.

1 Open the Access database from which you want to export your data. If that database is already open, switch to the Database window.

2 Choose the Export command from the File menu. Access opens the Export To dialog box, as shown earlier on page 349. Select ODBC Databases in the Save As Type drop-down list.

3 Access then asks for a name for the new table on the server. Type in the name you want, and click OK.

4 Access opens a dialog box in which you can select the data source name of the SQL server that will receive your data. This dialog box is similar to the one shown earlier on page 317. Select the server alias name, and click OK.

5 The ODBC driver displays the SQL Server Login dialog box for the SQL data source that you selected. Enter your user ID and password, and click OK. If you are authorized to create tables in more than one database on the server and you want to connect to a database other than your default database, enter your user ID and password, and then click the Options button to open the lower

part of the dialog box. When you click in the Database text box, Access logs on to the server and returns a list of available database names. Select the one you want, and click OK. If you don't specify a database name and if multiple databases exist on the server, Access will prompt you to select the database you want.

6 For Microsoft FoxPro, choose the FoxPro database name or FoxPro file folder name in the Configure Connection dialog. Click OK to store your Access data in a new SQL table on the server, a new table in a FoxPro database, or a new FoxPro file in the FoxPro file folder. The name of the table on the SQL server will be your user ID, followed by an underscore, followed by the Access table or query name. If the name in Access contains blank spaces, the blank spaces will be replaced by underscores. The name of the new FoxPro table or file will be the Access table or query name.

Now you have all the information you need to import, link, and export data using Access. The next chapter, "Advanced Query Design—SQL," discusses in detail the Access dialect of SQL. The discussion is intended for intermediate and advanced users. If you're not interested in advanced query design, you can skip to Chapter 12, "Form Basics."

III

Working with Data

CHAPTER 11

Advanced Query Design—SQL

U nderlying every query in Microsoft Access is the SQL database command language. Although you can design most queries using the simple Access design grid, Access stores every query you design as an SQL command. For advanced types of queries that use the results of a second query as a comparison condition, you need to know SQL in order to define the second query (called a *subquery*). Also, you cannot use the design grid to construct all the types of queries available in the product; you must use SQL for some of them.

This chapter explores and explains the various syntax elements in the Access variant of SQL, which you can use to build select, total, crosstab, make-table, update, append, and delete queries. With each language element, you'll find examples from the Microsoft Press Books database that illustrate the use of that element. At the end of this chapter are several examples of complex queries that are implemented in the Entertainment Scheduling database. This sample database also uses some of the more complex features of SQL in Access to accomplish tasks described in Part VI of this book. As you become more familiar with SQL, you can learn a lot about the language and how it's implemented in Access by using the design grid to design a query and then switching to SQL view to see how Access translates the query into SQL statements.

This chapter is appropriate for intermediate and advanced users who are interested in using the Access dialect of SQL. If you are a beginning user, or if you prefer not to know the details about SQL, you can skip to the next chapter.

A Brief History of SQL

In the early 1970s, IBM created a language called Structured English Query Language (SEQUEL) for a research project on relational database management systems. This language evolved into SEQUEL/2 and finally into Structured Query Language (SQL). Other companies became interested in the concept of relational databases and the emerging SQL interface. Relational Software, Inc., (now Oracle Corporation) created a relational database product called Oracle in 1979. IBM released its first relational database product, called SQL Data System (SQL/DS), in 1981.

In 1982, the American National Standards Institute (ANSI), realizing the potential significance of the relational model, began work on a Relational Database Language (RDL) standard. By 1984, acceptance in the marketplace of such products as Oracle, SQL/DS, and IBM's DB2 caused the ANSI committee to focus on SQL as the basis for the new RDL standard. The first version of this standard, SQL-86, was adopted by both ANSI and the International Standards Organization (ISO) in October 1986. An update to SQL-86 covering integrity enhancements was adopted in 1989. The current standard, often referred to as "SQL2" or "SQL-92," reflects extensive work by the international standards bodies to both enhance the language and correct many missing, confusing, or ambiguous features in the original 1986 standard.

The standard as it currently exists is both in its core a common subset of the major implementations and in its entirety a superset of almost all implementations. That is, the core of the standard contains features found in virtually every commercial implementation of the language, yet the entire standard includes enhanced features that many vendors have yet to implement.

As mentioned in the previous chapter, the SQL Access Group consortium of database vendors has published what could be regarded as the "commercial standard" for SQL—a variant of the language that can be "spoken" by (or mapped to) every major relational database product. An extended version of this Common Language Interface (CLI) is part of the draft SQL3 standard under consideration in 1998. Microsoft has implemented support for the CLI in the Open Database Connectivity (ODBC) application programming interface (API) for Windows. This allows vendors of applications for Microsoft Windows to connect to each other using the SQL Access Group standard. Microsoft Access connects to many databases via the ODBC standard and also "speaks" a major subset of the SQL Access Group's standard SQL.

SQL Syntax Conventions

Table 11-1 lists the SQL syntax conventions you'll encounter in this chapter.

TABLE 11-1. SQL Syntax Conventions

SQL Convention	Meaning
UPPERCASE	Uppercase letters indicate keywords and reserved words that you must enter exactly as shown. Note that Microsoft Access understands keywords entered in either uppercase or lowercase.
Italic	Italicized words represent variables that you supply.
Angle brackets < >	Angle brackets enclose syntactic elements that you must supply. The words inside the angle brackets describe the element but do not show the actual syntax of the element. Do not enter the angle brackets.
Brackets [ ]	Brackets enclose optional items. If more than one item is listed, the items are separated by a pipe (|) character. Choose one or none of the elements. Do not enter the brackets or the pipe. Note that Access in many cases requires you to enclose names in brackets. In this chapter, when brackets are required as part of the syntax of variables that you must supply, the brackets are italicized, as in *[MyTable].[MyField]*.
Braces { }	Braces enclose one or more options. If more than one option is listed, the options are separated by a pipe (|) character. Choose one option from the list. Do not enter the braces or the pipe.
Ellipses ...	Ellipses indicate that you can repeat an item one or more times. When a comma is shown with an ellipsis, enter the comma between items.

You must enter all other characters, such as parentheses and colons, exactly as they appear in the syntax line.

 TIP

When you build a query in SQL view, you can insert a carriage return between elements to improve readability. In fact, Access inserts carriage returns between major clauses when you save and close your query. The only time you might not include carriage returns in an SQL statement is when you're defining an SQL statement for a string literal in Visual Basic. Visual Basic requires that a literal be defined as a single line in a procedure. (A *literal* is a value that is expressed as itself rather than as a variable's value or as the result of an expression.) In Access version 7.0 (Access for Windows 95) and later, you can create a long literal within Visual Basic by using string concatenation and line continuation characters to make a single SQL statement more readable in code. *See Chapter 22, "Visual Basic Fundamentals," for details.*

NOTE

When you save a query you have written in SQL in your database, Access often examines your SQL command and adds brackets or extra parentheses to make the command easier to parse and compile. In some cases, Access restates complex predicates or changes the ANSI-standard syntax to one it prefers. For this reason, the examples shown in the book may not exactly match what you see in the sample queries when you open them in SQL view. If you enter the SQL exactly as shown in the book, it will return the same result as the sample query you find in the database.

NOTE

This chapter does not document all of the syntax variants accepted by Access, but it does cover all the features of the SELECT statement and of action queries. Wherever possible, ANSI-standard syntax is shown to provide portability across other databases that also support some form of SQL. You might notice that Access modifies the ANSI-standard syntax to a syntax that it prefers after you define and save a query.

SQL SELECT Syntax in Microsoft Access

The SELECT statement forms the core of the SQL database language. You use the SELECT statement to select or retrieve rows and columns from database tables. The SELECT statement syntax contains five major clauses, generally constructed as follows.

```
SELECT <field list>
   FROM <table list>
   [WHERE <row selection specification>]
   [GROUP BY <grouping specification>]
   [HAVING <group selection specification>]
   [ORDER BY <sorting specification>];
```

Microsoft Access implements four significant extensions to the language: TRANSFORM, to allow you to build crosstab queries; IN, to allow you to specify a remote database connection or to specify column names in a crosstab query; DISTINCTROW, to limit the rows returned from the <*table list*> to rows that have different primary key values in the tables that supply columns in the <*field list*>; and WITH OWNERACCESS OPTION, to let you design queries that can be run by users who are authorized to use the query but who have no access rights to the tables referenced in the query.

The following sections in this chapter are a reference guide to the Access implementation of SQL for select, total, and crosstab queries. The language elements are presented in alphabetic order.

NOTE

> You can find many of the examples shown within the following sections in the
> Microsoft Press Books sample database. When an example is in the sample
> database, you'll find the name of the sample query in italics immediately pre-
> ceding the query in the text.

Column-Name

SEE ALSO
FROM Clause, SELECT
Statement, and
Subquery

Specifies the name of a column in an expression.

Syntax

```
[[[]{table-name|select-query-name|
    correlation-name}[]].][[]field-name[]]
```

Notes

You must supply a qualifier to the field name only if the name is ambiguous within the context of the query or subquery (for example, if the same field name appears in more than one table or query listed in the FROM clause).

The *table-name*, *select-query-name*, or *correlation-name* that qualifies the field name must appear in the FROM clause of the query or subquery. If a table or query has a correlation name, you must use the alias, not the actual name of the table or query. (A *correlation name* is an alias you assign to the table or query name in the FROM clause.)

You must supply the enclosing brackets only if the name contains an embedded blank. Embedded blanks and enclosing brackets are not supported in the ANSI standard.

Examples

To specify a field named Customer Last Name in a table named Customer List, use the following.

```
[Customer List].[Customer Last Name]
```

To specify a field named StreetAddress that appears in only one table or query in the FROM clause, enter:

```
StreetAddress
```

Expression

? **SEE ALSO**
Column-name, Predicates, SELECT Statement, Subquery, and UPDATE Statement.

Specifies a value in a predicate or in the select list of a SELECT statement or subquery.

Syntax

```
[+|-] {function | [(]<expression>[)] | literal |
    column-name} [{+|-|*|/|\|^|MOD|&}
    {function | [(]<expression>[)] |literal |
    column-name}]...
```

Notes

function—You can specify one of the SQL total functions: AVG, COUNT, MAX, MIN, STDEV, STDEVP, SUM, VAR, or VARP; however, you cannot use an SQL total function more than once in an expression. You can also use any of the functions built into Access or any function you define using Visual Basic.

[(]<*expression*>[)]—You can construct an expression from multiple expressions separated by operators. Use parentheses around expressions to clarify the evaluation order. (See the examples later in this section.)

literal—You can specify a numeric or an alphanumeric constant. You must enclose an alphanumeric constant in single or double quotation marks. To include an apostrophe in an alphanumeric constant, enter the apostrophe character twice in the literal string or enclose the literal string in double quotation marks. If the expression is numeric, you must use a numeric constant. Enclose a date/time literal within pound (#) signs. A date/time literal you enter in SQL view must follow the U.S. mm/dd/yy (or mm/dd/yyyy) format. This may be different than the format you use on the query design grid, which must follow the format defined for Short Date Style in your Regional Settings in Windows Control Panel.

column-name—You can specify the name of a column in a table or a query. You can use a column name only from a table or query that you've specified in the FROM clause of the statement. If the expression is arithmetic, you must use a column that contains numeric data. If the same column name appears in more than one of the tables or queries included in the query, you must fully qualify the name with the query name, table name, or correlation name, as in *[TableA].[Column1]*. Although in ANSI SQL you can reference an *output-column-name* anywhere within an expression, Microsoft Access supports this only within the *<field-list>* of a SELECT statement. Access does not support references to named expression columns in GROUP BY, HAVING, ORDER BY, or WHERE clauses. You must repeat the expression rather than use the column name. *See "SELECT Statement" later in this chapter for details about output-column-name.*

+ | - | * | / | \ | ^ | MOD—You can combine multiple numeric expressions with arithmetic operators that specify a calculation. If you use arithmetic operators, all expressions within an expression must evaluate as numeric data types.

&—You can concatenate alphanumeric expressions by using the & operator.

Examples

To specify the average of a column named COST, enter the following.

```
AVG(COST)
```

To specify one-half the value of a column named PRICE, enter the following.

```
(PRICE * .5)
```

To specify a literal for 3:00 P.M. on March 1, 1998, enter the following.

```
#3/1/1998 3:00PM#
```

To specify a character string that contains the name *Acme Mail Order Company,* enter the following.

```
"Acme Mail Order Company"
```

To specify a character string that contains a possessive noun (requiring an embedded apostrophe), enter the following.

```
"Andy''s Hardware Store"
```

or

```
'Andy''s Hardware Store'
```

Working with Data

To specify a character string that is the concatenation of fields from a table named Customer List containing a person's first and last name with an intervening blank, enter the following.

```
[Customer List].[First Name] & " " &
    [Customer List].[Last Name]
```

FROM Clause

? SEE ALSO

HAVING Clause, IN Clause, JOIN Operation, SELECT Statement, Subquery, and WHERE Clause.

Specifies the tables or queries that provide the source data for your query.

Syntax

```
FROM {table-name [[AS] correlation-name] |
    select-query-name [[AS] correlation-name] |
    <joined table>},...
    [IN <source specification>]
```

where *<joined table>* is

```
({table-name [[AS] correlation-name] |
    select-query-name [[AS] correlation-name] |
    <joined table>}

{INNER | LEFT | RIGHT} JOIN
    {table-name [[AS] correlation-name] |
    select-query-name [[AS] correlation-name] |
    <joined table>}

ON <join-specification>)
```

Notes

You can supply a correlation name for each table name or query name and use this correlation name as an alias for the full table name when qualifying column names in the *<field-list>*, in the *<join-specification>*, or in the WHERE clause and subclauses. If you're joining a table or a query to itself, you must use correlation names to clarify which copy of the table or query you're referring to in the select list, join criteria, or selection criteria. If a table name or a query name is also an SQL reserved word (for example, "Order"), you must enclose the name in brackets.

If you include multiple tables in the FROM clause with no JOIN specification but do include a predicate that matches fields from the multiple tables in the WHERE clause, Access in most cases optimizes how it solves the query by treating the query as a JOIN. For example,

```
SELECT *
    FROM TableA, TableB
    WHERE TableA.ID = TableB.ID
```

is solved by Access as if you had specified

```
SELECT *
  FROM TableA
    INNER JOIN TableB
    ON TableA.ID = TableB.ID
```

You cannot update fields in a table by using a recordset opened on the query, the query datasheet, or a form bound to a multiple table query where the join is expressed using a table-list and a WHERE clause. In many cases you can update the fields in the underlying tables when you use the JOIN syntax.

When you list more than one table or query without join criteria, the source is the *Cartesian product* of all the tables. For example, *FROM TableA, TableB* instructs Access to search all the rows of TableA matched with all the rows of TableB. Unless you specify other restricting criteria, the number of logical rows that Access processes could equal the number of rows in TableA *times* the number of rows in TableB. Access then returns the rows in which the selection criteria specified in the WHERE and HAVING clauses evaluate to True.

Example

To select information about customers and their purchases of more than $100, enter the following (*qxmplCustomerOrder>100*).

```
SELECT tblCustomers.CustomerID,
       tblCustomers.FirstName,
       tblCustomers.LastName, tblOrders.OrderDate,
       tblOrderDetails.ISBNNumber, tblBooks.Title,
       tblOrderDetails.Quantity,
       tblOrderDetails.Discount,
       tblBooks.SuggPrice,
       Round(CCur(([tblOrderDetails].[Quantity] *
         [tblBooks].[SuggPrice]) *
         (1-[tblOrderDetails].[Discount])), 2)
         AS ExtPrice
  FROM (tblCustomers
       INNER JOIN tblOrders
       ON tblCustomers.CustomerID =
         tblOrders.CustomerID)
       INNER JOIN (tblBooks
         INNER JOIN tblOrderDetails
         ON tblBooks.ISBNNumber =
           tblOrderDetails.ISBNNumber)
       ON tblOrders.OrderID =
         tblOrderDetails.OrderID
 WHERE Round(CCur(([tblOrderDetails].[Quantity] *
   [tblBooks].[SuggPrice]) *
   (1-[tblOrderDetails].[Discount])), 2)>100;
```

III

Working with Data

NOTE

In the ANSI SQL standard, you can also write the WHERE clause as WHERE ExtPrice > 100; Microsoft Access does not support this syntax.

GROUP BY Clause

? SEE ALSO

Total functions—AVG, COUNT, MAX, MIN, STDEV, STDEVP, SUM, VAR, VARP; HAVING Clause; Search-Condition; SELECT Statement; and WHERE Clause.

In a SELECT statement, specifies the columns used to form groups from the rows selected. Each group contains identical values in the specified column(s). In Access, you use the GROUP BY clause to define a total query. You must also include a GROUP BY clause in a crosstab query. *(See the TRANSFORM statement for details.)*

Syntax

```
GROUP BY column-name,...
```

Notes

A column name in the GROUP BY clause can refer to any column from any table in the FROM clause, even if the column is not named in the select list. If the GROUP BY clause is preceded by a WHERE clause, Access creates the groups from the rows selected after it applies the WHERE clause. When you include a GROUP BY clause in a SELECT statement, the select list must be made up of either SQL total functions or column names specified in the GROUP BY clause.

Examples

To find the largest order from any customer within each postal code, create the following two queries. (We'll use the first of these two queries in examples throughout this chapter.)

1 A query to calculate the total for each order (*qxmplOrderTotals*):

```
SELECT tblOrders.OrderID, tblOrders.OrderDate,
       tblCustomers.CustomerID, tblCustomers.City,
       tblCustomers.StateOrProvince,
       tblCustomers.PostalCode,
       Sum(([Quantity]*[SuggPrice])*
       (1-[Discount])) AS OrderTot
FROM (tblCustomers
      INNER JOIN tblOrders
      ON tblCustomers.CustomerID =
         tblOrders.CustomerID)
           INNER JOIN (tblBooks
             INNER JOIN tblOrderDetails
             ON tblBooks.ISBNNumber =
                tblOrderDetails.ISBNNumber)
           ON tblOrders.OrderID =
              tblOrderDetails.OrderID
```

```
GROUP BY tblOrders.OrderID, tblOrders.OrderDate,
         tblCustomers.CustomerID,
         tblCustomers.City,
         tblCustomers.StateOrProvince,
         tblCustomers.PostalCode;
```

2 A query on the first query to find the largest order (*qxmplLargestOrderByPostalCode*):

```
SELECT qxmplOrderTotals.PostalCode,
       Max(qxmplOrderTotals.OrderTot)
          AS MaxOfOrderTot
FROM qxmplOrderTotals
GROUP BY qxmplOrderTotals.PostalCode;
```

To find the average and maximum prices for items in the book catalog by category name, enter the following (*qxmplCategoryAvgMaxPrice*).

```
SELECT tblCategories.Category,
       Avg(tblBooks.SuggPrice) AS AvgOfSuggPrice,
       Max(tblBooks.SuggPrice) AS MaxOfSuggPrice
FROM tblBooks
       INNER JOIN (tblCategories
          INNER JOIN tblBookCategories
          ON tblCategories.CategoryID =
             tblBookCategories.CategoryID)
          ON tblBooks.ISBNNumber =
             tblBookCategories.ISBNNumber
GROUP BY tblCategories.Category;
```

HAVING Clause

SEE ALSO
Total functions—AVG, COUNT, MAX, MIN, STDEV, STDEVP, SUM, VAR, VARP; GROUP BY Clause; Search-Condition; SELECT Statement; and WHERE Clause.

Specifies groups of rows that appear in the logical table (an Access recordset) defined by a SELECT statement. The search condition applies to columns specified in a GROUP BY clause, to columns created by total functions, or to expressions containing total functions. If a group doesn't pass the search condition, it is not included in the logical table.

Syntax

```
HAVING <search-condition>
```

Notes

If you do not include a GROUP BY clause, the select list must be formed by using one or more of the SQL total functions.

The difference between the HAVING clause and the WHERE clause is that WHERE *<search-condition>* applies to single rows before they are grouped, while HAVING *<search-condition>* applies to groups of rows.

III

Working with Data

If you include a GROUP BY clause preceding the HAVING clause, the *<search-condition>* applies to each of the groups formed by equal values in the specified columns. If you do not include a GROUP BY clause, the *<search-condition>* applies to the entire logical table defined by the SELECT statement.

Examples

To find the cities in which customers' average purchase is less than the average of purchases by all customers, create the following two queries.

1 A query to calculate the total for each order (*qxmplOrderTotals*):

```
SELECT tblOrders.OrderID, tblOrders.OrderDate,
       tblCustomers.CustomerID,
       tblCustomers.City,
       tblCustomers.StateOrProvince,
       tblCustomers.PostalCode,
       Sum(([Quantity]*[SuggPrice])*
         (1-[Discount])) AS OrderTot
FROM (tblCustomers
       INNER JOIN tblOrders
       ON tblCustomers.CustomerID =
         tblOrders.CustomerID)
         INNER JOIN (tblBooks
           INNER JOIN tblOrderDetails
           ON tblBooks.ISBNNumber =
             tblOrderDetails.ISBNNumber)
         ON tblOrders.OrderID =
           tblOrderDetails.OrderID
GROUP BY tblOrders.OrderID,
         tblOrders.OrderDate,
         tblCustomers.CustomerID,
         tblCustomers.City,
         tblCustomers.StateOrProvince,
         tblCustomers.PostalCode;
```

2 A query on the first query to find the largest order (*qxmplUnderAvgCities*):

```
SELECT qxmplOrderTotals.City,
       Avg(qxmplOrderTotals.OrderTot)
         AS AvgOfOrderTot
FROM qxmplOrderTotals
GROUP BY qxmplOrderTotals.City
HAVING (((Avg(qxmplOrderTotals.OrderTot))
         <(SELECT Avg([OrderTot])
           FROM qxmplOrderTotals)));
```

To find the average and maximum order amounts for customers in the state of Washington for every month in which the maximum order amount is less than $1,900, create the following two queries.

1 A query to calculate the total for each order (*qxmplOrderTotals*):

```
SELECT tblOrders.OrderID, tblOrders.OrderDate,
       tblCustomers.CustomerID,
       tblCustomers.City,
       tblCustomers.StateOrProvince,
       tblCustomers.PostalCode,
       Sum(([Quantity]*[SuggPrice])*
         (1-[Discount])) AS OrderTot
FROM (tblCustomers
       INNER JOIN tblOrders
       ON tblCustomers.CustomerID =
          tblOrders.CustomerID)
          INNER JOIN (tblBooks
            INNER JOIN tblOrderDetails
            ON tblBooks.ISBNNumber =
               tblOrderDetails.ISBNNumber)
          ON tblOrders.OrderID =
             tblOrderDetails.OrderID
GROUP BY tblOrders.OrderID, tblOrders.OrderDate,
       tblCustomers.CustomerID,
       tblCustomers.City,
       tblCustomers.StateOrProvince,
       tblCustomers.PostalCode;
```

2 A query on the first query to find the largest order
(*qxmplWAOrdersMax<1900*):

```
SELECT Month([OrderDate]) AS Month,
       Avg(qxmplOrderTotals.OrderTot)
         AS AvgOfOrderTot,
       Max(qxmplOrderTotals.OrderTot)
         AS MaxOfOrderTot
FROM qxmplOrderTotals
WHERE (((qxmplOrderTotals.StateOrProvince)="WA"))
GROUP BY Month([OrderDate])
HAVING (((Max(qxmplOrderTotals.OrderTot))<1900));
```

IN Clause

SEE ALSO

SELECT Statement.

Specifies the source for the tables in a query. The source can be another Access database; a dBASE, Microsoft FoxPro, or Paradox file; or any database for which you have an ODBC driver. This is an Access extension to standard SQL.

Syntax

```
IN <"source database name"> <[source connect string]>
```

III

Working with Data

Enter *"source database name"* and *[source connect string]*. (Be sure to include the quotation marks and the brackets.) If your database source is Access, enter only *"source database name"*. Enter these parameters according to the type of database to which you are connecting, as shown in Table 11-2.

TABLE 11-2. IN Parameters for Various Database Types

Database Name	Source Database Name	Source Connect String
Access	*"drive:\path\filename"*	(none)
dBASE III	*"drive:\path"*	[dBASE III;]
dBASE IV	*"drive:\path"*	[dBASE IV;]
dBASE 5	*"drive:\path"*	[dBASE 5.0;]
Paradox 3.*x*	*"drive:\path"*	[Paradox 3.x;]
Paradox 4.*x*	*"drive:\path"*	[Paradox 4.x;]
Paradox 5.*x*	*"drive:\path"*	[Paradox 5.x;]
FoxPro 2.0	*"drive:\path"*	[FoxPro 2.0;]
FoxPro 2.5	*"drive:\path"*	[FoxPro 2.5;]
FoxPro 2.6	*"drive:\path"*	[FoxPro 2.6;]
FoxPro 3.0	*"drive:\path"*	[FoxPro 3.0;]
ODBC	(none)	[ODBC; DATABASE= *defaultdatabase*; UID=*user*; PWD= *password*;DSN= *datasourcename*]

Notes

The IN clause applies to all tables referenced in the FROM clause and any subqueries in your query. You can refer to only one external database within a query. If you need to refer to more than one external file or database, attach those files as tables in Access and use the logical attached table names instead.

For ODBC, if you omit the DSN= or DATABASE= parameters, Access prompts you with a dialog box showing available data sources so that you can select the one you want. If you omit the UID= or PWD= parameters and the server requires a UserID and password, Access prompts you with a login dialog box for each table accessed.

For dBASE, Paradox, and FoxPro databases, you can provide an empty string ("") for *source database name* and provide the path or dictionary filename using the DATABASE= parameter in *source connect string* instead.

 NOTE

> Microsoft Access 2000 supports linking to Paradox and dBase versions 5.0 and older as read-only files. If you need to update these files or work with later versions, you must install the Borland Database Engine (DBE).

Examples

To retrieve the Company Name field in the Northwind Traders sample database without having to attach the Customers table, you could enter the following.

```
SELECT Customers.[CompanyName]
FROM Customers
IN "C:\My Documents\Shortcut to NORTHWIND.MDB";
```

To retrieve data from the CUST and ORDERS sample files distributed with dBASE IV, enter the following.

```
SELECT CUST.CUST_ID, CUST.CUSTOMER,
       ORDERS.DATE_TRANS, ORDERS.PART_ID,
       ORDERS.PART_QTY
FROM CUST
       INNER JOIN ORDERS
       ON CUST.CUST_ID = ORDERS.CUST_ID
IN "" [dBASE IV;DATABASE=C:\DBASE\SAMPLES;];
```

JOIN Operation

 **SEE ALSO**

FROM Clause, HAVING Clause, Predicate: Comparison, Search-Condition, SELECT Statement, and WHERE Clause.

Much of the power of SQL derives from its ability to combine (join) information from several tables or queries and present the result as a single logical recordset. In many cases, Access lets you update the recordset of a joined query as if it were a single base table.

Use a JOIN operation in a FROM clause to specify how you want to link two tables to form a logical recordset from which you can select the information you need. You can ask Access to join only matching rows in both tables (called an *inner join*) or to return all rows from one of the two tables even when a matching row does not exist in the second table (called an *outer join*). You can nest multiple join operations to join, for example, a third table with the result of joining two other tables.

III

Working with Data

Syntax

```
({table-name [[AS] correlation-name] |
    select-query-name [[AS] correlation-name] |
    <joined table>}
{INNER | LEFT | RIGHT} JOIN
    {table-name [[AS] correlation-name] |
    select-query-name [[AS] correlation-name] |
    <joined table>}
ON <join-specification>)
```

where *<joined table>* is the result of another join operation, and where *<join-specification>* is a search condition made up of predicates that compare fields in the first table, query, or joined table with fields in the second table, query, or joined table.

Notes

You can supply a correlation name for each table or query name. You can use this correlation name as an alias for the full table name when qualifying column names in the select list or in the WHERE clause and subclauses. If you're joining a table or a query to itself, you must use correlation names to clarify which copy of the table or the query you're referring to in the select list, join criteria, or selection criteria. If a table name or query name is also an SQL reserved word (for example, "Order"), you must enclose the name in brackets.

Use INNER JOIN to return all the rows that match the join specification in both tables. Use LEFT JOIN to return all the rows from the first logical table (where *logical table* is any table, query, or joined table expression) joined on the join specification with any matching rows from the second logical table. When no row matches in the second logical table, Access returns null values for the columns from that table. Conversely, RIGHT JOIN returns all the rows from the second logical table joined with any matching rows from the first logical table.

> **NOTE**
>
> Both LEFT JOIN and RIGHT JOIN are relational outer joins. Microsoft Access does not support the ANSI-standard FULL OUTER JOIN syntax.

When you use only *equals* comparison predicates in the join specification, the result is called an *equi-join*. The joins that Access displays in the design grid are equi-joins. Access cannot display on the design grid any join specification that uses any comparison operator other than equals (=)—also called a *non-equijoin*. If you want to define a join on a nonequals comparison (<, >, <>, <=, or >=), you must define the query using the SQL view. When you join a table to itself by using an equals comparison predicate, the result is called a *self-join*.

Examples

To select information about books and their authors, sorted by book identifier (ISBN), enter the following (*qxmplBooksAndAuthors*).

```
SELECT tblBooks.*,
       [tblAuthors].[LastName] & ", " &
         [tblAuthors].[FirstName] &
         IIf(IsNull([tblAuthors].[MiddleInit]),Null,
           " " & [tblAuthors].[MiddleInit] & ".")
           AS AuthorName,
       tblAuthors.EmailAddress,
       tblAuthors.Photograph, tblAuthors.Bio
FROM tblBooks
       INNER JOIN (tblAuthors
         INNER JOIN tblBookAuthor
         ON tblAuthors.AuthorID =
           tblBookAuthor.AuthorID)
       ON tblBooks.ISBNNumber =
         tblBookAuthor.ISBNNumber;
```

To find out which customers did not send in order number 25, enter the following (*qxmplNonEquiJoin*).

```
SELECT tblCustomers.CustomerID,
       tblCustomers.LastName,
       tblCustomers.FirstName,
       tblCustomers.MiddleInit

FROM tblCustomers INNER JOIN tblOrders
       ON tblCustomers.CustomerID <>
tblOrders.CustomerID
WHERE (((tblOrders.OrderID)=25));
```

To find out which books haven't been ordered in the last 90 days, create the following two queries.

1 A query to calculate which books have been ordered in the last 90 days (*qxmplBooksInLast90Days*):

```
SELECT DISTINCTROW tblBooks.ISBNNumber
FROM tblBooks
       INNER JOIN (tblOrders
         INNER JOIN tblOrderDetails
         ON tblOrders.OrderID =
           tblOrderDetails.OrderID)
       ON tblBooks.ISBNNumber =
         tblOrderDetails.ISBNNumber
WHERE (((tblOrders.OrderDate) Between Date()
       And Date()-90));
```

III

Working with Data

This query uses DISTINCTROW to see each book only once.

2 A query on the first query to find the unordered books (*qxmplUnorderedBooks*):

```
SELECT tblBooks.ISBNNumber, tblBooks.Title
FROM qxmplBooksInLast90Days
        RIGHT JOIN tblBooks
        ON qxmplBooksInLast90Days.ISBNNumber =
            tblBooks.ISBNNumber
WHERE (((qxmplBooksInLast90Days.ISBNNumber)
        Is Null));
```

To see a list of books and the amounts currently on order, sorted by book category, enter the following (*qxmplOrdersByCategoryAndTitle*).

```
SELECT tblCategories.Category, tblBooks.Title,
        tblOrderDetails.Quantity
FROM tblCategories
        INNER JOIN ((tblBooks
        INNER JOIN tblBookCategories
        ON tblBooks.ISBNNumber =
            tblBookCategories.ISBNNumber)
        INNER JOIN tblOrderDetails
        ON tblBooks.ISBNNumber =
            tblOrderDetails.ISBNNumber)
        ON tblCategories.CategoryID =
            tblBookCategories.CategoryID
ORDER BY tblCategories.Category;
```

ORDER BY Clause

? SEE ALSO

INSERT Statement,
SELECT Statement,
and UNION Query
Operator.

Specifies the sequence of rows to be returned by a SELECT statement or an INSERT statement.

Syntax

```
ORDER BY {column-name | column-number [ASC |
DESC]},...
```

Notes

You use column names or relative output column numbers to specify the columns on whose values the rows returned are ordered. (If you use relative output column numbers, the first output column is 1.) You can specify multiple columns in the ORDER BY clause. The list is ordered primarily by the first column. If rows exist for which the values of that column are equal, they are ordered by the next column in the ORDER BY list. You can specify ascending (ASC) or descending (DESC) order for each column. If you do not specify ASC or DESC,

ASC is assumed. Using an ORDER BY clause in a SELECT statement is the only means of defining the sequence of the returned rows.

Examples

To select customers who first did business in February 1999 or earlier and list them in ascending order by postal code, enter the following (*qxmplCustomersWithOrdersBeforeFeb1999*).

```
SELECT tblCustomers.FirstName,
       tblCustomers.MiddleInit, tblCustomers.LastName,
       tblCustomers.City, tblCustomers.PostalCode
FROM tblCustomers
WHERE ((((#3/1/1999#)>=
       (Select Min([OrderDate]) From tblOrders Where
          tblOrders.CustomerID =
             tblCustomers.CustomerID)))
ORDER BY tblCustomers.PostalCode;
```

> **NOTE**
>
> In this example, the inner subquery makes a reference to the tblCustomers table in the SELECT statement by referring to a column in the outer table (tblCustomers.CustomerID). This forces the subquery to be evaluated for every row in the SELECT statement, which might not be the most efficient way to achieve the desired result. (This type of subquery is also called a *correlated subquery*.) Whenever possible, the Access query plan optimizer solves the query efficiently by reconstructing the query internally as a join between the source specified in the FROM clause and the subquery. In many cases, you can perform this reconstruction yourself, but the purpose of the query may not be as clear as when you state the problem using a subquery.

To find all stores and all customers in the state of Washington and list them in descending order by postal code, enter the following (*qxmplCustomersAndStoresInWA*).

```
SELECT [tblCustomers].[LastName] & ", " &
          [tblCustomers].[FirstName] &
          IIf(IsNull([tblCustomers].[MiddleInit]),
          Null," " & [tblCustomers].[MiddleInit]
          & ".") AS Name,
       tblCustomers.City, tblCustomers.PostalCode
FROM tblCustomers
WHERE tblCustomers.StateOrProvince = "WA"
UNION
SELECT tblStores.StoreName, tblStores.City,
       tblStores.PostalCode
FROM tblStores
WHERE tblStores.StateOrProvince = "WA"
ORDER BY 3 DESC;
```

III

Working with Data

If you decide to use column names in the ORDER BY clause of a UNION query, Access derives the column names from the names returned by the first query. In this example, you would change the ORDER BY clause to read ORDER BY PostalCode.

PARAMETERS Declaration

SEE ALSO
SELECT Statement.

Precedes an SQL statement to define the data types of any parameters you include in the query. You can use parameters to prompt the user for data values or to match data values in controls on an open form.

Syntax

```
PARAMETERS {[parameter-name] data-type},... ;
```

Notes

If your query prompts the user for values, each parameter name should describe the value that the user needs to enter. For example, [Print invoices from orders on date:] is much more descriptive than [Enter date:]. If you want to refer to a control on an open form, use the format

[Forms]![*Myform*]![*Mycontrol*]

To refer to a control on a subform, use the format

[Forms]![*Myform*]![*Mysubformcontrol*].[Form]![*ControlOnSubform*]

Valid data type entries are shown in Table 11-3.

Example

To create a parameter query that summarizes the sales and the cost of goods for all items sold in a given month, enter the following (*qxmplMonthSalesParameter*).

```
PARAMETERS [Year to summarize:] Short,
           [Month to summarize:] Short;
SELECT tblBooks.ISBNNumber, tblBooks.Title,
       Format([OrderDate],"mmmm""", ""yyyy")
          AS OrderMonth,
       Sum(Round(CCur(([Quantity]*[SuggPrice]) *
          (1-[Discount])), 2)) AS OrderTot
FROM tblOrders
     INNER JOIN (tblBooks
       INNER JOIN tblOrderDetails
       ON tblBooks.ISBNNumber =
          tblOrderDetails.ISBNNumber)
     ON tblOrders.OrderID = tblOrderDetails.OrderID
```

```
WHERE (((Year([OrderDate]))=[Year to summarize:]) AND
       ((Month([OrderDate]))=[Month to summarize:]))
GROUP BY tblBooks.ISBNNumber, tblBooks.Title,
        Format([OrderDate],"mmmm""", ""yyyy");
```

TABLE 11-3. **SQL Parameters Data Types**

SQL Parameter Data Types	Equivalent Access Data Type
Char, Text(n)[1], VarChar	Text
Text[1], LongText, LongChar, Memo	Memo
TinyInt, Byte, Integer1	Number, Byte
SmallInt, Short, Integer2	Number, Integer
Integer, Long, Integer4	Number, Long Integer
Real, Single, Float4, IEEESingle	Number, Single
Float, Double, Float8, IEEEDouble	Number, Double
Decimal, Numeric	Number, Decimal
UniqueIdentifier, GUID	Number, Replication ID
DateTime, Date, Time	Date/Time
Money, Currency	Currency
Bit, Boolean, Logical, YesNo	Yes/No
Image, LongBinary, OLEObject	OLE Object
Text, LongText, LongChar, Memo	Hyperlink[2]
Binary, VarBinary	Binary[3]

1. Text with a length descriptor of 255 or less maps to the Access Text data type. Text with no length descriptor is a Memo field.

2. Internally, Access stores a Hyperlink in a Memo field, but sets a custom property to indicate a Hyperlink format.

3. The JET database engine supports a Binary data type (raw hexadecimal), but the Access user interface does not. If you encounter a non-Access table that has a data type that maps to Binary, you will be able to see the data type in the table definition, but you won't be able to successfully edit this data in a datasheet or form. You can manipulate Binary data in Visual Basic.

Predicate: BETWEEN

Compares a value with a range of values.

SEE ALSO
Expression, SELECT Statement, Subquery, and WHERE Clause.

Syntax

```
<expression> [NOT] BETWEEN <expression> AND <expression>
```

III

Working with Data

Notes

The data types of all expressions must be compatible. Comparison of alphanumeric literals (strings) in Access is case-insensitive.

Let a, b, and c be expressions. Then, in terms of other predicates, a BETWEEN b AND c is equivalent to the following.

```
a >= b AND a <= c
```

a NOT BETWEEN b AND c is equivalent to the following.

```
a < b OR a > c
```

The result is undefined if any of the expressions is null.

Example

To determine whether the average of Quantity multiplied by SuggPrice is greater than or equal to $500 and less than or equal to $10,000, enter the following.

```
AVG(Quantity * SuggPrice) BETWEEN 500 AND 10000
```

Predicate: Comparison

? SEE ALSO

Expressions, SELECT Statement, Subquery, and WHERE Clause.

Compares the values of two expressions or the value of an expression and a single value returned by a subquery.

Syntax

```
<expression> {= | <> | > | < | >= | <=}
    {<expression> | <subquery>}
```

Notes

Comparison of strings in Access is case-insensitive. The data type of the first expression must be compatible with the data type of the second expression or with the value returned by the subquery. If the subquery returns no rows or more than one row, an error is returned except when the select list of the subquery is COUNT(*), in which case the return of multiple rows yields one value. If either the first expression, the second expression, or the subquery evaluates to null, the result of the comparison is undefined.

Examples

To determine whether the order date was in 1998, enter the following.

```
Year(OrderDate) = 1998
```

To determine whether the order ID is not equal to 50, enter the following.

```
OrderID <> 50
```

To determine whether an order was placed in the first half of the year, enter the following.

```
Month(OrderDate) < 7
```

To determine whether the maximum value for the total order amount in the group is less than the average total order amount found in the Order Details table, enter the following.

```
MAX([OrderTot]) <
    (SELECT AVG([OrderTot])
        FROM [qxmplOrderTotals])
```

Predicate: EXISTS

SEE ALSO

Expressions, SELECT Statement, Subquery, and WHERE Clause.

Tests the existence of at least one row that satisfies the selection criteria in a subquery.

Syntax

```
EXISTS (<subquery>)
```

Notes

The result cannot be undefined. If the subquery returns at least one row, the result is True; otherwise, the result is False. The subquery need not return values for this predicate; therefore, you can list any columns in the select list that exist in the underlying tables or queries or use an asterisk (*) to denote all columns.

Example

To find all authors that wrote at least one book, enter the following (*qxmplAuthorSomeBook*).

```
SELECT tblAuthors.FirstName, tblAuthors.MiddleInit,
        tblAuthors.LastName
FROM tblAuthors
WHERE Exists
    (SELECT *
      FROM tblBookAuthor
      WHERE tblBookAuthor.AuthorID =
        tblAuthors.AuthorID);
```

Working with Data

III

> **NOTE**

In this example, the inner subquery makes a reference to the tblAuthors table in the SELECT statement by referring to a column in the outer table (tblAuthors.AuthorID). This forces the subquery to be evaluated for every row in the SELECT statement, which might not be the most efficient way to achieve the desired result. (This type of subquery is also called a *correlated subquery*.) Whenever possible, the Access query plan optimizer solves the query efficiently by reconstructing the query internally as a join between the source specified in the FROM clause and the subquery. In many cases, you can perform this reconstruction yourself, but the purpose of the query may not be as clear as when you state the problem using a subquery.

Predicate: IN

SEE ALSO

Expressions, Predicate: Quantified, SELECT Statement, Subquery, and WHERE Clause.

Determines whether a value is equal to any of the values or is unequal to all values in a set returned from a subquery or provided in a list of values.

Syntax

```
<expression> [NOT] IN {(<subquery>) |
    ({literal},...) |<expression>}
```

Notes

Comparison of strings in Access is case-insensitive. The data types of all expressions, literals, and the column returned by the subquery must be compatible. If the expression is null or any value returned by the subquery is null, the result is undefined. In terms of other predicates, *<expression>* IN *<expression>* is equivalent to the following.

```
<expression> = <expression>
```

<expression> IN (*<subquery>*) is equivalent to the following.

```
<expression> = ANY (<subquery>)
```

<expression> IN (*a, b, c,*...), where *a*, *b*, and *c* are literals, is equivalent to the following.

```
(<expression> = a) OR (<expression> = b) OR
    (<expression> = c) ...
```

<expression> NOT IN ... is equivalent to the following.

```
NOT (<expression> IN ...)
```

Examples

To determine whether StateOrProvince is on the West Coast, enter the following.

```
[StateOrProvince] IN ("CA", "OR", "WA")
```

To determine whether CustomerID is the same as any StoreID in Washington state, enter the following.

```
CustomerID IN
  (SELECT StoreID
    FROM tblStores
    WHERE tblStores.[StateOrProvince] = "WA")
```

To list all authors who have not written an "Advanced" book (Category number 13), enter the following (*qxmplAuthorsNotAdvanced*).

```
SELECT tblAuthors.AuthorID, tblAuthors.FirstName,
       tblAuthors.MiddleInit, tblAuthors.LastName
FROM tblAuthors
WHERE tblAuthors.AuthorID NOT IN
       (SELECT tblBookAuthor.AuthorID
         FROM (tblBooks
           INNER JOIN tblBookAuthor
           ON tblBooks.ISBNNumber =
             tblBookAuthor.ISBNNumber)
           INNER JOIN tblBookCategories
           ON tblBooks.ISBNNumber =
             tblBookCategories.ISBNNumber
         WHERE tblBookCategories.CategoryID=13);
```

Predicate: LIKE

? SEE ALSO

Expressions, SELECT Statement, Subquery, and WHERE Clause.

Searches for strings that match a pattern.

Syntax

```
column-name [NOT] LIKE match-string
```

Notes

String comparisons in Access are case-insensitive. If the column specified by *column-name* contains a null, the result is undefined. Comparison of two empty strings or an empty string with the special asterisk (*) character evaluates to True.

You provide a text string as a *match-string value* that defines what characters can exist in which positions for the comparison to be true. Access understands a number of wildcard characters (shown in Table 11-4 on the next page) that you can use to define positions that can contain any single character, zero or more characters, or any single number.

III

Working with Data

TABLE 11-4. Wildcard Characters for String Comparisons

Character	Meaning
?	Any single character
*	Zero or more characters (used to define leading, trailing, or embedded strings that don't have to match any of the pattern characters)
#	Any single number

You can also specify that any particular position in the text or memo field can contain only characters from a list that you provide. To define a list of comparison characters for a particular position, enclose the list in brackets ([ ]). You can specify a range of characters within a list by entering the low-value character, a hyphen, and the high-value character, as in [A-Z] or [3-7]. If you want to test a position for any characters *except* those in a list, start the list with an exclamation point (!). If you want to test for one of the special characters *, ?, #, and [, you must enclose the character in brackets.

Examples

To determine whether a customer's LastName is at least four characters long and begins with *Smi,* enter the following.

```
tblCustomers.LastName LIKE "Smi?*"
```

To test whether PostalCode is a valid Canadian postal code, enter the following.

```
PostalCode LIKE "[A-Z]#[A-Z] #[A-Z]#"
```

Predicate: NULL

? SEE ALSO

Expressions, SELECT Statement, Subquery, and WHERE Clause.

Determines whether the expression evaluates to null. This predicate evaluates only to True or False and will not evaluate to undefined.

Syntax

```
<expression> IS [NOT] NULL
```

Example

To determine whether the customer phone number column has never been filled, enter the following.

```
PhoneNumber IS NULL
```

Predicate: Quantified

? SEE ALSO
Expressions, SELECT Statement, Subquery, and WHERE Clause.

Compares the value of an expression to some, any, or all values of a single column returned by a subquery.

Syntax

```
<expression> {= | <> | > | < | >= | <=}
    [SOME | ANY | ALL] (<subquery>)
```

Notes

String comparisons in Access are case-insensitive. The data type of the expression must be compatible with the data type of the value returned by the subquery.

When ALL is used, the predicate is true if the comparison is true for all the values returned by the subquery. If the expression or any of the values returned by the subquery is null, the result is undefined. When SOME or ANY is used, the predicate is true if the comparison is true for any of the values returned by the subquery. If the expression is a null value, the result is undefined. If the subquery returns no values, the predicate is false.

Examples

To find the books whose cost is greater than all the books about Microsoft Access, enter the following (*qxmplBooksCost>AllAccess*).

```
SELECT tblBooks.ISBNNumber, tblBooks.Title,
       tblBooks.SuggPrice
FROM tblBooks
WHERE tblBooks.SuggPrice > All
       (SELECT tblBooks.SuggPrice
         FROM tblCategories
           INNER JOIN (tblBooks
             INNER JOIN tblBookCategories
             ON tblBooks.ISBNNumber =
               tblBookCategories.ISBNNumber)
           ON tblCategories.CategoryID =
             tblBookCategories.CategoryID
           WHERE tblCategories.Category="Microsoft
               Access");
```

To find the books whose cost is greater than any of the books about Microsoft Access, enter the following (*qxmplBooksCost>AnyAccess*).

```
SELECT tblBooks.ISBNNumber, tblBooks.Title,
       tblBooks.SuggPrice
FROM tblBooks
```

(continued)

III

Working with Data

```
WHERE tblBooks.SuggPrice > Any
      (SELECT tblBooks.SuggPrice
       FROM tblCategories
         INNER JOIN (tblBooks
           INNER JOIN tblBookCategories
           ON tblBooks.ISBNNumber =
              tblBookCategories.ISBNNumber)
         ON tblCategories.CategoryID =
            tblBookCategories.CategoryID
         WHERE tblCategories.Category="Microsoft
            Access");
```

Search-Condition

❓ SEE ALSO

DELETE Statement,
Expressions, HAVING
Clause, Predicates,
SELECT Statement,
Subquery, UPDATE
Statement, and WHERE
Clause.

Describes a simple or compound predicate that is true, false, or undefined for a given row or group. Use a search condition in the WHERE clause of a SELECT statement, a subquery, a DELETE statement, or an UPDATE statement. You can also use it within the HAVING clause in a SELECT statement. The search condition defines the rows that should appear in the resulting logical table or the rows that should be acted upon by the change operation. If the search condition is true when applied to a row, that row is included in the result.

Syntax

```
[NOT] {predicate | (<search-condition>)}
   [{AND | OR | XOR | EQV | IMP}
   [NOT] {predicate | (<search-condition>)}]...
```

Notes

Access effectively applies any subquery in the search condition to each row of the table that is the result of the previous clauses. Access then evaluates the result of the subquery with regard to each candidate row.

If you include a comparison predicate in the form of *<expression> comparison-operator <subquery>*, an error is returned if the subquery returns no rows.

The order of evaluation of the Boolean operators is NOT, AND, OR, XOR (exclusive OR), EQV (equivalence), and IMP (implication). You can include additional parentheses to influence the order in which the Boolean expressions are processed.

You can express AND and OR Boolean operations directly by using the design grid. If you need to use XOR, EQV, or IMP, you must create an expression in the Field row, clear the Show check box, and set the Criteria row to <> False.

When you use the Boolean operator NOT, the following holds: NOT (True) is False, NOT (False) is True, and NOT (undefined) is undefined. The result is undefined whenever a predicate references a null value. If a search condition evaluates to False or undefined when applied to a row, the row is not selected. Access returns True, False, or undefined values as a result of applying Boolean operators (AND, OR, XOR, EQV, IMP) against two predicates or search conditions according to the tables shown in Figure 11-1.

FIGURE 11-1.

Truth tables for SQL Boolean operators.

AND	True	False	Undefined (Null)
True	True	False	Null
False	False	False	False
Undefined (Null)	Null	False	Null

OR	True	False	Undefined (Null)
True	True	True	True
False	True	False	Null
Undefined (Null)	True	Null	Null

XOR	True	False	Undefined (Null)
True	False	True	Null
False	True	False	Null
Undefined (Null)	Null	Null	Null

EQV	True	False	Undefined (Null)
True	True	False	Null
False	False	True	Null
Undefined (Null)	Null	Null	Null

IMP	True	False	Undefined (Null)
True	True	False	Null
False	True	True	True
Undefined (Null)	True	Null	Null

III

Working with Data

Example

To find all books for which the suggested price is greater than $20 and the edition number is equal to 2 or the copyright year is 1995, but not both, enter the following (*qxmplXOR*).

```
SELECT tblBooks.ISBNNumber, tblBooks.Title,
       tblBooks.CopyrightYear, tblBooks.SuggPrice,
       tblBooks.EditionNumber
FROM tblBooks
WHERE tblBooks.SuggPrice>20 And
      (tblBooks.CopyrightYear = 1995 XOR
       tblBooks.EditionNumber = 2);
```

SELECT Statement

(?) SEE ALSO

INSERT Statement, Search-Condition, and UNION Query Operator.

Performs the select, project, and join relational operations to create a logical table (recordset) from other tables or queries. The items in the select list identify the columns or calculated values to project from the source tables to the new recordset. You identify the tables to be joined in the FROM clause, and you identify the rows to be selected in the WHERE clause. Use GROUP BY to specify how to form groups for a total query, and use HAVING to specify which resulting groups should be included in the result.

Syntax

```
SELECT [ALL | DISTINCT | DISTINCTROW | TOP number
       [PERCENT]] <select-list>
    FROM {table-name [[AS] correlation-name] |
      select-query-name [[AS] correlation-name] |
      (<select-statement>) AS correlation-name |
      <joined table>},...
    IN <"source database name"> <[source connect
        string]>
    [WHERE <search-condition>]
    [GROUP BY column-name,...]
    [HAVING <search-condition>]
    [UNION [ALL] <select-statement>]
    [ORDER BY {column-name [ASC | DESC]},...]
    [WITH OWNERACCESS OPTION];
```

where *<select-list>* is

```
{* | {<expression> [AS output-column-name] |
  table-name.* | query-name.* |
  correlation-name.*},...}
```

and where *<joined table>* is

```
({table-name [[AS] correlation-name] |
  select-query-name [[AS] correlation-name] |
  (<select-statement>) AS correlation-name |
  <joined table>}
{INNER | LEFT | RIGHT} JOIN
  {table-name [[AS] correlation-name] |
  select-query-name [[AS] correlation-name] |
  (<select-statement>) AS correlation-name |
  <joined table>}
ON <join-specification>)
```

Notes

You can supply a correlation name for each table or query name. You must supply a correlation name when you embed a *<select-statement>* in a FROM clause. You use this correlation name as an alias for the full table name, query name, or *<select-statement>* expression when qualifying column names in the *<select-list>* or in the WHERE clause and subclauses. If you're joining a table or a query to itself, you must use correlation names to clarify which copy of the table or query you're referring to in the *<select-list>*, join criteria, or selection criteria. If a table name or query name is also an SQL reserved word (for example, "Order"), you must enclose the name in brackets.

When you list more than one table or query without join criteria, the source is the Cartesian product of all the tables. For example, *FROM TableA, TableB* instructs Access to search all the rows of TableA matched with all the rows of TableB. Unless you specify other restricting criteria, the number of logical rows that Access processes could equal the number of rows in TableA *times* the number of rows in TableB. Access then returns the rows in which the selection criteria specified in the WHERE and HAVING clauses are true.

You can further define which rows Access includes in the output recordset by specifying ALL, DISTINCT, DISTINCTROW, TOP *n*, or TOP *n* PERCENT. ALL includes all rows that match the search criteria from the source tables, including potential duplicate rows. DISTINCT requests that Access return only rows that are different from any other row. You cannot update any columns in a query that uses ALL or DISTINCT.

DISTINCTROW (the default in Access version 7.0 and earlier) requests that Access return only rows in which the concatenation of the primary keys from all tables supplying output columns is unique. Depending on the columns you select, you might see rows in the result that contain duplicate values, but each row in the result is derived from a distinct combination of rows in the underlying tables. DISTINCTROW is

III

Working with Data

significant only when you include a join in a query and do not include output columns from all tables. For example, the statement

```
SELECT tblCustomers.StateOrProvince
FROM tblCustomers
  INNER JOIN tblOrders
  ON tblCustomers.CustomerID = tblOrders.CustomerID
WHERE tblOrders.OrderDate > #1/1/1994#;
```

returns 1049 rows in the Microsoft Press Books sample database—one row for each order. On the other hand, the following statement

```
SELECT DISTINCTROW tblCustomers.StateOrProvince
FROM tblCustomers
  INNER JOIN tblOrders
  ON tblCustomers.CustomerID = tblOrders.CustomerID
WHERE tblOrders.OrderDate > #1/1/1994#;
```

returns only 10 rows—one for each *distinct row* in the tblCustomers table, the only table with output columns. The equivalent of the second example in ANSI-standard SQL is as follows.

```
SELECT tblCustomers.StateOrProvince
FROM tblCustomers
WHERE tblCustomers.CustomerID
  IN (Select tblOrders.CustomerID FROM tblOrders
  WHERE tblOrders.OrderDate > '1/1/1994');
```

I suspect Microsoft implemented DISTINCTROW in version 1 because the first release of Access did not support subqueries.

Specify TOP *n* or TOP *n* PERCENT to request that the recordset contain only the first *n* or first *n* percent of rows. In general, you should specify an ORDER BY clause when you use TOP in order to indicate the sequence that defines what rows are first or top. The parameter *n* must be an integer and must be less than or equal to 100 if you include the PERCENT keyword. If you do not include an ORDER BY clause, the sequence of rows returned is undefined. In a TOP query, if the *n*th and any rows immediately following the *n*th row are duplicates, Access returns the duplicates; thus, the recordset may have more than *n* rows. Note that if you specify an order, using TOP does not cause the query to execute any faster; Access must still solve the entire query, order the rows, and return the top rows.

When you include a GROUP BY clause, the select list must be made up of one or more of the SQL total functions or one or more of the column names specified in the GROUP BY clause. A column name in a GROUP BY clause can refer to any column from any table in the FROM clause, even if the column is not named in the select list. If you want to refer to a calculated expression in the GROUP BY clause, you must assign an output column name to the expression in the select list and then refer to that name in the GROUP BY clause. If the GROUP BY clause is preceded by a WHERE clause, Access forms the groups from the rows selected after it applies the WHERE clause.

If you use a HAVING clause but do not include a GROUP BY clause, the select list must be formed using SQL total functions. If you include a GROUP BY clause preceding the HAVING clause, the HAVING search condition applies to each of the groups formed by equal values in the specified columns. If you do not include a GROUP BY clause, the HAVING search condition applies to the entire logical table defined by the SELECT statement.

You use column names or relative output column numbers to specify the columns on whose values the rows returned are ordered. (If you use relative output column numbers, the first output column is 1.) You can specify multiple columns in the ORDER BY clause. The list is ordered primarily by the first column. If rows exist for which the values of that column are equal, they are ordered by the next column on the ORDER BY list. You can specify ascending (ASC) or descending (DESC) order for each column. If you do not specify ASC or DESC, ASC is assumed. Using an ORDER BY clause in a SELECT statement is the only means of defining the sequence of the returned rows.

Normally, the person running the query not only must have rights to the query but also must have the appropriate rights to the tables used in the query. (These rights include reading data to select rows and updating, inserting, and deleting data using the query.) If your application has multiple users, you might want to secure the tables so that no user has direct access to any of the tables and all users can still run queries defined by you. Assuming you're the owner of both the queries and the tables, you can deny access to the tables but allow access to the queries. To make sure that the queries run properly, you must add the WITH OWNERACCESS OPTION clause to allow users the same access rights as the table owner when accessing the data via the query. *See* Building Applications with Microsoft Access 2000, *online documentation that comes with Access, for more details on securing your applications.*

III

Working with Data

Examples

To select information about customers and their purchases of more than $100, enter the following (*qxmplCustomerOrder>100*).

```
SELECT  tblCustomers.CustomerID,
        tblCustomers.FirstName,
        tblCustomers.LastName, tblOrders.OrderDate,
        tblOrderDetails.ISBNNumber, tblBooks.Title,
        tblOrderDetails.Quantity,
        tblOrderDetails.Discount,
        tblBooks.SuggPrice,
        Round(CCur((tblOrderDetails.Quantity*
          tblBooks.SuggPrice) *
          (1-tblOrderDetails.Discount)), 2)
          AS ExtPrice
FROM (tblCustomers
        INNER JOIN tblOrders
        ON tblCustomers.CustomerID =
          tblOrders.CustomerID)
          INNER JOIN (tblBooks
            INNER JOIN tblOrderDetails
            ON tblBooks.ISBNNumber =
              tblOrderDetails.ISBNNumber)
          ON tblOrders.OrderID =
            tblOrderDetails.OrderID
WHERE (((Round(CCur((tblOrderDetails.Quantity*
        tblBooks.SuggPrice) *
        tblOrderDetails.Discount)),2))>100));
```

> **NOTE** In ANSI-standard SQL, you can also write the WHERE clause as WHERE ExtPrice > 100;. Microsoft Access does not support this syntax.

To find the largest order for any customer within each postal code, use the following queries.

1 A query to calculate the total for each order (*qxmplOrderTotals*):

```
SELECT  tblOrders.OrderID, tblOrders.OrderDate,
        tblCustomers.CustomerID,
        tblCustomers.City,
        tblCustomers.StateOrProvince,
        tblCustomers.PostalCode,
        Sum(([Quantity]*[SuggPrice])*
          (1-[Discount])) AS OrderTot
FROM (tblCustomers
        INNER JOIN tblOrders
        ON tblCustomers.CustomerID =
          tblOrders.CustomerID)
```

```
INNER JOIN (tblBooks
   INNER JOIN tblOrderDetails
   ON tblBooks.ISBNNumber =
      tblOrderDetails.ISBNNumber)
   ON tblOrders.OrderID =
      tblOrderDetails.OrderID
GROUP BY tblOrders.OrderID, tblOrders.OrderDate,
      tblCustomers.CustomerID,
      tblCustomers.City,
      tblCustomers.StateOrProvince,
      tblCustomers.PostalCode;
```

2 A query on the first query to find the largest order (*qxmplLargestOrderByPostalCode*):

```
SELECT qxmplOrderTotals.PostalCode,
      Max(qxmplOrderTotals.OrderTot)
         AS MaxOfOrderTot
FROM qxmplOrderTotals
GROUP BY qxmplOrderTotals.PostalCode;
```

To find the average and maximum prices for items in the book catalog by category name, enter the following (*qxmplCategoryAvgMaxPrice*).

```
SELECT tblCategories.Category,
      Avg(tblBooks.SuggPrice) AS AvgOfSuggPrice,
      Max(tblBooks.SuggPrice) AS MaxOfSuggPrice
FROM tblBooks
      INNER JOIN (tblCategories
         INNER JOIN tblBookCategories
         ON tblCategories.CategoryID =
            tblBookCategories.CategoryID)
      ON tblBooks.ISBNNumber =
         tblBookCategories.ISBNNumber
GROUP BY tblCategories.Category;
```

To find the cities where the average of orders for that city is less than the overall average for all cities, create the following queries.

1 A query to calculate the total for each order (*qxmplOrderTotals*):

```
SELECT tblOrders.OrderID, tblOrders.OrderDate,
      tblCustomers.CustomerID,
      tblCustomers.City,
      tblCustomers.StateOrProvince,
      tblCustomers.PostalCode,
      Sum(([Quantity]*[SuggPrice])*
         (1-[Discount])) AS OrderTot
```

(continued)

III

Working with Data

```
FROM (tblCustomers
        INNER JOIN tblOrders
        ON tblCustomers.CustomerID =
          tblOrders.CustomerID)
          INNER JOIN (tblBooks
            INNER JOIN tblOrderDetails
            ON tblBooks.ISBNNumber =
              tblOrderDetails.ISBNNumber)
          ON tblOrders.OrderID =
            tblOrderDetails.OrderID
GROUP BY tblOrders.OrderID, tblOrders.OrderDate,
        tblCustomers.CustomerID,
        tblCustomers.City,
        tblCustomers.StateOrProvince,
        tblCustomers.PostalCode;
```

2 A query on the first query to find the cities where the average of orders in that city is less than the overall average for all cities (*qxmplUnderAvgCities*):

```
SELECT qxmplOrderTotals.City,
        Avg(qxmplOrderTotals.OrderTot)
          AS AvgOfOrderTot
FROM qxmplOrderTotals
GROUP BY qxmplOrderTotals.City
HAVING (((Avg(qxmplOrderTotals.OrderTot))
          <(SELECT Avg([OrderTot])
            FROM qxmplOrderTotals)));
```

To find the average and maximum order amounts for customers in the state of Washington for every month in which the maximum order amount is less than $1,900, create the following queries.

1 A query to calculate the total for each order (*qxmplOrderTotals*):

```
SELECT tblOrders.OrderID, tblOrders.OrderDate,
        tblCustomers.CustomerID,
        tblCustomers.City,
        tblCustomers.StateOrProvince,
        tblCustomers.PostalCode,
        Sum(([Quantity]*[SuggPrice])*
          (1-[Discount])) AS OrderTot
FROM (tblCustomers
        INNER JOIN tblOrders
        ON tblCustomers.CustomerID =
          tblOrders.CustomerID)
          INNER JOIN (tblBooks
            INNER JOIN tblOrderDetails
            ON tblBooks.ISBNNumber =
              tblOrderDetails.ISBNNumber)
          ON tblOrders.OrderID =
            tblOrderDetails.OrderID
```

```
GROUP BY tblOrders.OrderID, tblOrders.OrderDate,
         tblCustomers.CustomerID,
         tblCustomers.City,
         tblCustomers.StateOrProvince,
         tblCustomers.PostalCode;
```

2 A query on the first query to find the largest order (*qxmplWAOrderMax<1900*):

```
SELECT Month([OrderDate]) AS Month,
       Avg(qxmplOrderTotals.OrderTot)
         AS AvgOfOrderTot,
       Max(qxmplOrderTotals.OrderTot)
         AS MaxOfOrderTot
FROM qxmplOrderTotals
WHERE (((qxmplOrderTotals.StateOrProvince)="WA"))
GROUP BY Month([OrderDate])
HAVING (((Max(qxmplOrderTotals.OrderTot))<1900));
```

To find the number of different prices for books currently in print, create the following queries.

1 A query to find each unique price for the books in print (*qxmplDistinctPriceInPrint*):

```
SELECT DISTINCT tblBooks.SuggPrice
FROM tblBooks
WHERE tblBooks.OutOfPrint=False;
```

2 A query on the first query to find the number of different prices (*qxmplCountDistinctPrice*):

```
SELECT COUNT(*)
FROM qxmplDistinctPriceInPrint;
```

To restate the above problem as a single query using an embedded *<select-statement>*, enter the following (*qxmplCountDistinctPriceOneQuery*).

```
SELECT Count(*)
FROM (SELECT DISTINCT tblBooks.SuggPrice
FROM tblBooks
WHERE tblBooks.OutOfPrint=False) AS DistinctPrice;
```

To select information about books and their authors, sorted by book identifier (ISBN), enter the following (*qxmplBooksAndAuthors*).

```
SELECT tblBooks.*,
       [tblAuthors].[LastName] & ", " &
       [tblAuthors].[FirstName] &
       IIf(IsNull([tblAuthors].[MiddleInit]),Null,
         " " & [tblAuthors].[MiddleInit] & ".")
       AS AuthorName,
```

(continued)

Working with Data

```
                tblAuthors.EmailAddress,
                tblAuthors.Photograph,
                tblAuthors.Bio
FROM tblBooks
        INNER JOIN (tblAuthors
          INNER JOIN tblBookAuthor
          ON tblAuthors.AuthorID =
            tblBookAuthor.AuthorID)
        ON tblBooks.ISBNNumber =
          tblBookAuthor.ISBNNumber;
```

To find out which customers did not send in order number 25, enter the following (*qxmplNonEquiJoin*).

```
SELECT  tblCustomers.CustomerID,
        tblCustomers.LastName,
        tblCustomers.FirstName,
        tblCustomers.MiddleInit
FROM tblCustomers INNER JOIN tblOrders ON
    tblCustomers.CustomerID <> tblOrders.CustomerID
WHERE (((tblOrders.OrderID)=25));
```

To find out which books haven't been ordered in the last 90 days, create the following queries.

1 A query to calculate which books have been ordered in the last 90 days; this query uses DISTINCTROW to see each book only once (*qxmplBooksInLast90Days*):

```
SELECT DISTINCTROW tblBooks.ISBNNumber
FROM tblBooks
        INNER JOIN (tblOrders
          INNER JOIN tblOrderDetails
          ON tblOrders.OrderID =
            tblOrderDetails.OrderID)
        ON tblBooks.ISBNNumber =
          tblOrderDetails.ISBNNumber
WHERE (((tblOrders.OrderDate) Between
        Date() And Date()-90));
```

2 A query on the first query to find the unordered books (*qxmplUnorderedBooks*):

```
SELECT tblBooks.ISBNNumber, tblBooks.Title
FROM qxmplBooksInLast90Days
        RIGHT JOIN tblBooks
        ON qxmplBooksInLast90Days.ISBNNumber =
          tblBooks.ISBNNumber
WHERE (((qxmplBooksInLast90Days.ISBNNumber) Is
        Null));
```

To see a list of books and the amounts currently on order, sorted by book category, enter the following (*qxmplOrdersByCategoryAndTitle*).

```
SELECT tblCategories.Category, tblBooks.Title,
       tblOrderDetails.Quantity
FROM tblCategories
       INNER JOIN ((tblBooks
         INNER JOIN tblBookCategories
         ON tblBooks.ISBNNumber =
           tblBookCategories.ISBNNumber)
         INNER JOIN tblOrderDetails
         ON tblBooks.ISBNNumber =
           tblOrderDetails.ISBNNumber)
       ON tblCategories.CategoryID =
         tblBookCategories.CategoryID
ORDER BY tblCategories.Category;
```

To select customers who first did business in February 1999 or earlier and list them in ascending order by postal code, enter the following (*qxmplCustomersWithOrdersBeforeFeb1999*).

```
SELECT tblCustomers.FirstName,
       tblCustomers.MiddleInit,
       tblCustomers.LastName, tblCustomers.City,
       tblCustomers.PostalCode
FROM tblCustomers
WHERE (((#3/1/1999#)>=
       (SELECT Min([OrderDate]) FROM tblOrders WHERE
         tblOrders.CustomerID =
           tblCustomers.CustomerID)))
ORDER BY tblCustomers.PostalCode;
```

> **NOTE**
>
> In this example, the inner subquery makes a reference to the tblCustomers table in the SELECT statement by referring to a column in the outer table (tblCustomers.CustomerID). This forces the subquery to be evaluated for every row in the SELECT statement, which might not be the most efficient way to achieve the desired result. (This type of subquery is also called a *correlated subquery*.) Whenever possible, the Access query plan optimizer solves the query efficiently by reconstructing the query internally as a join between the source specified in the FROM clause and the subquery. In many cases, you can perform this reconstruction yourself, but the purpose of the query may not be as clear as when you state the problem using a subquery.

III

Working with Data

To find all stores and all customers in the state of Washington and list them in descending order by postal code, enter the following (*qxmplCustomersAndStoresInWA*).

```
SELECT [tblCustomers].[LastName] & ", " &
       [tblCustomers].[FirstName] &
       IIf(IsNull([tblCustomers].[MiddleInit]),
         Null, " " & [tblCustomers].[MiddleInit] &
         ".") AS Name,
       tblCustomers.City, tblCustomers.PostalCode
FROM tblCustomers
WHERE tblCustomers.StateOrProvince = "WA"
UNION
SELECT tblStores.StoreName, tblStores.City,
       tblStores.PostalCode
FROM tblStores
WHERE tblStores.StateOrProvince = "WA"
ORDER BY 3 DESC;
```

> **NOTE**
>
> If you decide to use column names in the ORDER BY clause of a UNION query, Access derives the column names from the names returned by the first query. In this example, you would change the ORDER BY clause to read ORDER BY PostalCode.

To find all authors who wrote at least one book, enter the following (*qxmplAuthorSomeBook*).

```
SELECT tblAuthors.FirstName, tblAuthors.MiddleInit,
       tblAuthors.LastName
FROM tblAuthors
WHERE Exists
    (SELECT *
      FROM tblBookAuthor
      WHERE tblBookAuthor.AuthorID =
        tblAuthors.AuthorID);
```

> **NOTE**
>
> In this example, the inner subquery makes a reference to the tblAuthors table in the SELECT statement by referring to a column in the outer table (tblAuthors.AuthorID). This forces the subquery to be evaluated for every row in the SELECT statement, which might not be the most efficient way to achieve the desired result. Whenever possible, the Access query plan optimizer solves the query efficiently by reconstructing the query internally as a join between the source specified in the FROM clause and the subquery. In many cases, you can perform this reconstruction yourself, but the purpose of the query may not be as clear as when you state the problem using a subquery.

To list all authors who have not written an "Advanced" book (Category number 13), enter the following (*qxmplAuthorsNotAdvanced*).

```
SELECT tblAuthors.AuthorID, tblAuthors.FirstName,
       tblAuthors.MiddleInit, tblAuthors.LastName
FROM tblAuthors
WHERE tblAuthors.AuthorID NOT IN
  (SELECT tblBookAuthor.AuthorID
    FROM (tblBooks
            INNER JOIN tblBookAuthor
            ON tblBooks.ISBNNumber =
              tblBookAuthor.ISBNNumber)
            INNER JOIN tblBookCategories
            ON tblBooks.ISBNNumber =
              tblBookCategories.ISBNNumber
        WHERE tblBookCategories.CategoryID=13);
```

To find the books whose cost is greater than all the books about Microsoft Access, enter the following (*qxmplBooksCost>AllAccess*).

```
SELECT tblBooks.ISBNNumber, tblBooks.Title,
       tblBooks.SuggPrice
FROM tblBooks
WHERE tblBooks.SuggPrice > All
  (SELECT tblBooks.SuggPrice
    FROM tblCategories
      INNER JOIN (tblBooks
        INNER JOIN tblBookCategories
        ON tblBooks.ISBNNumber =
          tblBookCategories.ISBNNumber)
      ON tblCategories.CategoryID =
        tblBookCategories.CategoryID
    WHERE tblCategories.Category=
    "Microsoft Access");
```

To find all books for which the suggested price is greater than $20 and the edition number is equal to 2 or the copyright year is 1995, but not both, enter the following (*qxmplXOR*).

```
SELECT tblBooks.ISBNNumber, tblBooks.Title,
       tblBooks.CopyrightYear, tblBooks.SuggPrice,
       tblBooks.EditionNumber
FROM tblBooks
WHERE tblBooks.SuggPrice>20 And
  (tblBooks.CopyrightYear = 1995 XOR
    tblBooks.EditionNumber = 2);
```

To find out the customer name and order summary information for the top 10 orders, enter the following (*qxmplTop10Orders*).

```
SELECT TOP 10 tblCustomers.FirstName,
              tblCustomers.LastName,
              qxmplOrderTotals.OrderID,
              qxmplOrderTotals.OrderDate,
              qxmplOrderTotals.OrderTot
FROM qxmplOrderTotals
     INNER JOIN tblCustomers
     ON qxmplOrderTotals.CustomerID =
        tblCustomers.CustomerID
ORDER BY qxmplOrderTotals.OrderTot DESC;
```

To select from the Customer table and insert into a temporary table the names of customers in the state of Washington, enter the following (*qxmplWACustomerMakeTable*).

```
INSERT INTO TempCust
  SELECT *
    FROM tblCustomers
    WHERE StateOrProvince = "WA";
```

Subquery

? SEE ALSO
Expressions, Predicates, and SELECT Statement.

Selects from a single column any number of values or no values at all for comparison in a predicate.

Syntax

```
(SELECT [ALL | DISTINCT] <select-list>
  FROM {table-name [[AS] correlation-name] |
    select-query-name [[AS] correlation-name] |
    <joined table>},...
  [WHERE <search-condition>]
  [GROUP BY column-name,...]
  [HAVING <search-condition>])
```

where *select-list* is

```
{* | {<expression> | table-name.* |
  query-name.* | correlation-name.*}}
```

and where *<joined table>* is

```
({table-name [[AS] correlation-name] |
  select-query-name [[AS] correlation-name] |
  <joined table>}
{INNER | LEFT | RIGHT} JOIN
  {table-name [[AS] correlation-name] |
  select-query-name [[AS] correlation-name] |
  <joined table>}
ON <join-specification>)
```

Notes

You can use the special asterisk (*) character in the *<select-list>* of a subquery only when the subquery is used in an EXISTS predicate or when the FROM clause within the subquery refers to a single table or query that contains only one column.

You can supply a correlation name for each table or query name. You can use this correlation name as an alias for the full table name when qualifying column names in the select list or in the WHERE clause and subclauses. If you're joining a table or a query to itself, you must use correlation names to clarify which copy of the table or query you're referring to in the *<select-list>*, join criteria, or selection criteria. If a table name or query name is also an SQL reserved word (for example, "Order"), you must enclose the name in brackets.

When you list more than one table or query without join criteria, the source is the Cartesian product of all the tables. For example, *FROM TableA, TableB* asks Access to search all the rows of TableA matched with all the rows of TableB. Unless you specify other restricting criteria, the number of logical rows that Access processes could equal the number of rows in TableA *times* the number of rows in TableB. Access then returns the rows in which the selection criteria specified in the WHERE and HAVING clauses are true.

In the search condition of the WHERE clause of a subquery, you can use an outer reference to refer to the columns of any table or query that is defined in the outer queries. You must qualify the column name if the table or query reference is ambiguous.

A column name in the GROUP BY clause can refer to any column from any table in the FROM clause, even if the column is not named in the *<select-list>*. If the GROUP BY clause is preceded by a WHERE clause, Access creates the groups from the rows selected after the application of the WHERE clause.

When you include a GROUP BY or HAVING clause in a SELECT statement, the *<select-list>* must be made up of either SQL total functions or column names specified in the GROUP BY clause. If a GROUP BY clause precedes a HAVING clause, the HAVING clause's search condition applies to each of the groups formed by equal values in the specified columns. If you do not include a GROUP BY clause, the HAVING clause's search condition applies to the entire logical table defined by the SELECT statement.

Examples

To find all authors who wrote at least one book, enter the following (*qxmplAuthorSomeBook*).

```
SELECT tblAuthors.FirstName, tblAuthors.MiddleInit,
        tblAuthors.LastName
FROM tblAuthors
WHERE Exists
    (SELECT *
        FROM tblBookAuthor
        WHERE tblBookAuthor.AuthorID =
            tblAuthors.AuthorID);
```

 NOTE

> In this example, the inner subquery makes a reference to the tblAuthors table in the SELECT statement by referring to a column in the outer table (tblAuthors.AuthorID). This forces the subquery to be evaluated for every row in the SELECT statement, which might not be the most efficient way to achieve the desired result. (This type of subquery is also called a *correlated subquery*.) Whenever possible, the Access query plan optimizer solves the query efficiently by reconstructing the query internally as a join between the source specified in the FROM clause and the subquery. In many cases, you can perform this reconstruction yourself, but the purpose of the query may not be as clear as when you state the problem using a subquery.

To find the cities in which customers' average purchase is less than the average of purchases by all customers, create the following queries.

1 A query to calculate the total for each order (*qxmplOrderTotals*):

```
SELECT  tblOrders.OrderID,
        tblOrders.OrderDate,
        tblCustomers.CustomerID,
        tblCustomers.City,
        tblCustomers.StateOrProvince,
        tblCustomers.PostalCode,  If
        Sum(([Quantity]*[SuggPrice])*
        (1-[Discount])) AS OrderTot
FROM (tblCustomers
        INNER JOIN tblOrders
        ON tblCustomers.CustomerID =
        tblOrders.CustomerID)
        INNER JOIN (tblBooks
            INNER JOIN tblOrderDetails
            ON tblBooks.ISBNNumber =
            tblOrderDetails.ISBNNumber)
        ON tblOrders.OrderID =
        tblOrderDetails.OrderID
```

```
GROUP BY tblOrders.OrderID,
         tblOrders.OrderDate,
         tblCustomers.CustomerID,
         tblCustomers.City,
         tblCustomers.StateOrProvince,
         tblCustomers.PostalCode;
```

2 A query on the first query to find the largest order (*qxmplUnderAvgCities*):

```
SELECT qxmplOrderTotals.City,
       Avg(qxmplOrderTotals.OrderTot)
         AS AvgOfOrderTot
FROM qxmplOrderTotals
GROUP BY qxmplOrderTotals.City
HAVING (((Avg(qxmplOrderTotals.OrderTot))<
        (SELECT Avg([OrderTot])
           FROM qxmplOrderTotals)));
```

To select customers who first did business in February 1999 or earlier and list them in ascending order by postal code, enter the following (*qxmplCustomersWithOrdersBeforeFeb1999*).

```
SELECT tblCustomers.FirstName,
       tblCustomers.MiddleInit,
       tblCustomers.LastName,
       tblCustomers.City,
       tblCustomers.PostalCode
FROM tblCustomers
WHERE (((#3/1/1999#)>=
        (SELECT Min([OrderDate]) FROM tblOrders
           WHERE tblOrders.CustomerID =
             tblCustomers.CustomerID)))
ORDER BY tblCustomers.PostalCode;
```

> **NOTE**
>
> In this example, the inner subquery makes a reference to the tblCustomers table in the SELECT statement by referring to a column in the outer table (tblCustomers.CustomerID). This forces the subquery to be evaluated for every row in the SELECT statement, which might not be the most efficient way to achieve the desired result. Whenever possible, the Access query plan optimizer solves the query efficiently by reconstructing the query internally as a join between the source specified in the FROM clause and the subquery. In many cases, you can perform this reconstruction yourself, but the purpose of the query may not be as clear as when you state the problem using a subquery.

III

Working with Data

To find the books whose cost is greater than any of the books about Microsoft Access, enter the following (*qxmplBooksCost>AnyAccess*).

```
SELECT tblBooks.ISBNNumber, tblBooks.Title,
       tblBooks.SuggPrice
FROM tblBooks
WHERE tblBooks.SuggPrice > Any
      (SELECT tblBooks.SuggPrice
        FROM tblCategories
          INNER JOIN (tblBooks
            INNER JOIN tblBookCategories
            ON tblBooks.ISBNNumber =
              tblBookCategoriesISBNNumber)
          ON tblCategories.CategoryID =
            tblBookCategories.CategoryID
        WHERE tblCategories.Category="Microsoft
          Access");
```

Total Function: AVG

? SEE ALSO

Expressions, GROUP BY Clause, HAVING Clause, SELECT Statement, Subquery, and TRANSFORM Statement.

In a logical table defined by a SELECT statement or a subquery, creates a column value that is the numeric average of the values in the expression or column name specified. You can use the GROUP BY clause to create an average for each group of rows selected from the underlying tables or queries.

Syntax

```
AVG(<expression>)
```

Notes

You cannot use another total function reference within the expression. If you use an SQL total function in the select list of a SELECT statement, any other columns in the select list must be derived using a total function, or the column name must appear in a GROUP BY clause. An expression must contain a reference to at least one column name, and the expression or column name must be a numeric data type.

Null values are not included in the calculation of the result. The data type of the result is generally the same as that of the expression or column name. If the expression or column name is an integer, the resulting average is truncated. For example, AVG(n)—where n is an integer and the values of n in the selected rows are equal to 0, 1, and 1—returns the value 0.

Examples

To find the average and maximum prices for items in the book catalog by category name, enter the following (*qxmplCategoryAvgMaxPrice*).

```
SELECT tblCategories.Category,
       Avg(tblBooks.SuggPrice) AS AvgOfSuggPrice,
       Max(tblBooks.SuggPrice) AS MaxOfSuggPrice
FROM tblBooks
       INNER JOIN (tblCategories
         INNER JOIN tblBookCategories
         ON tblCategories.CategoryID =
           tblBookCategories.CategoryID)
       ON tblBooks.ISBNNumber =
         tblBookCategories.ISBNNumber
       GROUP BY tblCategories.Category;
```

To find the average price of books currently in print, enter the following (*qxmplAvgBookPrice*).

```
SELECT Avg(tblBooks.SuggPrice)
FROM tblBooks
WHERE Not tblBooks.[OutOfPrint];
```

Total Function: COUNT

? SEE ALSO

Expressions, GROUP BY
Clause, HAVING Clause,
SELECT Statement,
Subquery, and
TRANSFORM State-
ment.

In a logical table defined by a SELECT statement or a subquery, creates a column value that is equal to the number of rows in the result table. You can use the GROUP BY clause to create a count for each group of rows selected from the underlying tables or queries.

Syntax

```
COUNT({* | <expression>})
```

Notes

You cannot use another total function reference within the expression. If you use an SQL total function in the select list of a SELECT statement, any other columns in the select list must be derived using a total function, or the column name must appear in a GROUP BY clause. An expression must contain a reference to at least one column name.

Null values are not included in the calculation of the result. The data type of the result is a long integer. Access does not support the ANSI-standard COUNT(DISTINCT *expression*).

Examples

To count customers who first did business in February 1999 or earlier in groups by postal code, enter the following (*qxmplCountCustOrdersBeforeFeb1999*).

```
SELECT tblCustomers.PostalCode, Count(*)
FROM tblCustomers
WHERE (((#3/1/1999#)>=
        (SELECT Min([OrderDate]) FROM tblOrders
          WHERE tblOrders.CustomerID =
            tblCustomers.CustomerID)))
GROUP BY tblCustomers.PostalCode;
```

> **NOTE**
>
> In this example, the inner subquery makes a reference to the tblCustomers table in the SELECT statement by referring to a column in the outer table (tblCustomers.CustomerID). This forces the subquery to be evaluated for every row in the SELECT statement, which might not be the most efficient way to achieve the desired result. (This type of subquery is also called a *correlated subquery.*) Whenever possible, the Access query plan optimizer solves the query efficiently by reconstructing the query internally as a join between the source specified in the FROM clause and the subquery. In many cases, you can perform this reconstruction yourself, but the purpose of the query may not be as clear as when you state the problem using a subquery.

To find the number of different prices for books currently in print, create the following queries.

1 A query to find each unique price for the books in print (*qxmplDistinctPriceInPrint*):

```
SELECT DISTINCT tblBooks.SuggPrice
FROM tblBooks
WHERE tblBooks.OutOfPrint=False;
```

2 A query to find the number of rows in the first query (*qxmplCountDistinctPrice*):

```
SELECT COUNT(*)
   FROM qxmplDistinctPriceInPrint;
```

Total Function: MAX

 SEE ALSO

Expressions, GROUP BY Clause, HAVING Clause, SELECT Statement, Subquery, and TRANSFORM Statement.

In a logical table defined by a SELECT statement or a subquery, creates a column value that is the maximum value in the expression or column name specified. You can use the GROUP BY clause to create a maximum value for each group of rows selected from the underlying tables or queries.

Syntax

```
MAX(<expression>)
```

Notes

You cannot use another total function reference within the expression. If you use an SQL total function in the select list of a SELECT statement, any other columns in the select list must be derived using a total function, or the column name must appear in a GROUP BY clause. An expression must contain a reference to at least one column name.

Null values are not included in the calculation of the result. The data type of the result is the same as the data type of the expression or the column name.

Examples

To find the largest order from any customer within each postal code, create the following queries.

1 A query to calculate the total for each order (*qxmplOrderTotals*):

```
SELECT  tblOrders.OrderID, tblOrders.OrderDate,
        tblCustomers.CustomerID,
        tblCustomers.City,
        tblCustomers.StateOrProvince,
        tblCustomers.PostalCode,
        Sum(([Quantity]*[SuggPrice])*
        (1-[Discount])) AS OrderTot

FROM (tblCustomers
        INNER JOIN tblOrders
        ON tblCustomers.CustomerID =
           tblOrders.CustomerID)
           INNER JOIN (tblBooks
             INNER JOIN tblOrderDetails
             ON tblBooks.ISBNNumber =
                tblOrderDetails.ISBNNumber)
           ON tblOrders.OrderID =
              tblOrderDetails.OrderID
GROUP BY tblOrders.OrderID, tblOrders.OrderDate,
        tblCustomers.CustomerID,
        tblCustomers.City,
        tblCustomers.StateOrProvince,
        tblCustomers.PostalCode;
```

III

Working with Data

2 A query on the first query to find the largest order (*qxmplLargestOrderByPostalCode*):

```
SELECT qxmplOrderTotals.PostalCode,
       Max(qxmplOrderTotals.OrderTot)
           AS MaxOfOrderTot
FROM qxmplOrderTotals
GROUP BY qxmplOrderTotals.PostalCode;
```

To find the book currently in print with the largest sales, create the following two queries.

1 A query to calculate the total sales for each book (*qxmplTotalSalesByBook*):

```
SELECT tblBooks.ISBNNumber, tblBooks.Title,
       Sum(Round(CCur(([Quantity]*[SuggPrice]) *
       (1-[Discount])), 2)) AS TotSales
FROM tblBooks
       INNER JOIN tblOrderDetails
       ON tblBooks.ISBNNumber =
       tblOrderDetails.ISBNNumber
WHERE Not tblBooks.OutOfPrint
GROUP BY tblBooks.ISBNNumber, tblBooks.Title;
```

2 A query on the first query to find the book with the largest sales (*qxmplHighestSellingBook*):

```
SELECT tblBooks.ISBNNumber, tblBooks.Title,
       qxmplTotalSalesByBook.TotSales
FROM qxmplTotalSalesByBook
       INNER JOIN tblBooks
       ON qxmplTotalSalesByBook.ISBNNumber =
       tblBooks.ISBNNumber
WHERE qxmplTotalSalesByBook.TotSales=
       (SELECT Max(TotSales)
           FROM qxmplTotalSalesByBook);
```

Total Function: MIN

? SEE ALSO
Expressions, GROUP BY Clause, HAVING Clause, SELECT Statement, Subquery, and TRANSFORM Statement.

In a logical table defined by a SELECT statement or a subquery, creates a column value that is the minimum value in the expression or column name specified. You can use the GROUP BY clause to create a minimum value for each group of rows selected from the underlying tables or queries.

Syntax

```
MIN(<expression>)
```

Notes

You cannot use another total function reference within the expression. If you use an SQL total function in the select list of a SELECT statement, any other columns in the select list must be derived using a total function, or the column name must appear in a GROUP BY clause. An expression must contain a reference to at least one column name.

Null values are not included in the calculation of the result. The data type of the result is the same as the data type of the expression or the column name.

Examples

To find the smallest order from any customer within each postal code, create the following queries.

1 A query to calculate the total for each order (*qxmplOrderTotals*):

```
SELECT tblOrders.OrderID, tblOrders.OrderDate,
       tblCustomers.CustomerID,
       tblCustomers.City,
       tblCustomers.StateOrProvince,
       tblCustomers.PostalCode,
       Sum(([Quantity]*[SuggPrice])*
       (1-[Discount])) AS OrderTot
FROM (tblCustomers
       INNER JOIN tblOrders
       ON tblCustomers.CustomerID =
         tblOrders.CustomerID)
         INNER JOIN (tblBooks
           INNER JOIN tblOrderDetails
           ON tblBooks.ISBNNumber =
             tblOrderDetails.ISBNNumber)
         ON tblOrders.OrderID =
           tblOrderDetails.OrderID
GROUP BY tblOrders.OrderID, tblOrders.OrderDate,
       tblCustomers.CustomerID,
       tblCustomers.City,
       tblCustomers.StateOrProvince,
       tblCustomers.PostalCode;
```

2 A query on the first query to find the smallest order (*qxmplSmallestOrderByPostalCode*):

```
SELECT qxmplOrderTotals.PostalCode,
       Min(qxmplOrderTotals.OrderTot)
           AS MinOfOrderTot
FROM qxmplOrderTotals
GROUP BY qxmplOrderTotals.PostalCode;
```

III

Working with Data

To find the book currently in print with the smallest sales, create the following two queries.

1 A query to calculate the total sales for each book (*qxmplTotalSalesByBook*):

```
SELECT tblBooks.ISBNNumber, tblBooks.Title,
        Sum(Round(CCur(([Quantity]*[SuggPrice]) *
        (1-[Discount])), 2)) AS TotSales
FROM tblBooks
        INNER JOIN tblOrderDetails
        ON tblBooks.ISBNNumber =
        tblOrderDetails.ISBNNumber
WHERE Not tblBooks.OutOfPrint
GROUP BY tblBooks.ISBNNumber, tblBooks.Title;
```

2 A query on the first query to find the book with the smallest sales (*qxmplLowestSellingBook*):

```
SELECT tblBooks.ISBNNumber, tblBooks.Title,
        qxmplTotalSalesByBook.TotSales
FROM qxmplTotalSalesByBook
        INNER JOIN tblBooks
        ON qxmplTotalSalesByBook.ISBNNumber =
        tblBooks.ISBNNumber
WHERE qxmplTotalSalesByBook.TotSales=
        (SELECT Min(TotSales)
        FROM qxmplTotalSalesByBook);
```

Total Functions: STDEV, STDEVP

SEE ALSO

Expressions, GROUP BY Clause, HAVING Clause, SELECT Statement, Subquery, and TRANSFORM Statement.

In a logical table defined by a SELECT statement or a subquery, creates a column value that is the standard deviation (square root of the variance) of the values in the expression or column name specified. You can use the GROUP BY clause to create a standard deviation for each group of rows selected from the underlying tables or queries. STDEVP produces an estimate of the standard deviation for the entire population on the basis of the sample provided in each group.

Syntax

```
{STDEV | STDEVP} (<expression>)
```

Notes

You cannot use another total function reference within the expression. If you use an SQL total function in the select list of a SELECT statement, any other columns in the select list must be derived using a total function, or the column name must appear in a GROUP BY clause. An expression must contain a reference to at least one column name, and the expression or column name must be a numeric data type.

Null values are not included in the calculation of the result. The data type of the result is a double-precision floating point number. If there are not at least two members in a group, STDEV returns a null value. STDEVP returns an estimate if there is at least one non-null value in the group.

Example

To find the standard deviation and the population standard deviation of the price of books, grouped by copyright year, enter the following (*qxmplStdDev*).

```
SELECT  tblBooks.CopyrightYear,
        Count(tblBooks.ISBNNumber)
          AS CountOfISBNNumber,
        StDev(tblBooks.SuggPrice) AS StDevOfSuggPrice,
        StDevP(tblBooks.SuggPrice)
          AS StDevPOfSuggPrice
FROM tblBooks
GROUP BY tblBooks.CopyrightYear;
```

Total Function: SUM

? SEE ALSO

Expressions, GROUP BY Clause, HAVING Clause, SELECT Statement, Subquery, and TRANSFORM Statement.

In a logical table defined by a SELECT statement or a subquery, creates a column value that is the numeric sum of the values in the expression or column name specified. You can use the GROUP BY clause to create a sum for each group of rows selected from the underlying tables or queries.

Syntax

```
SUM(<expression>)
```

Notes

You cannot use another function reference within the expression. Also, a column name must not refer to a column in a query derived from a function. If you use an SQL total function in the select list of a SELECT statement, any other columns in the select list must be derived using a total function, or the column name must appear in a GROUP BY clause. An expression must contain a reference to at least one column name, and the expression or column name must be a numeric data type.

Null values are not included in the calculation of the result. The data type of the result is generally the same as that of the expression or the column name.

Examples

To create a parameter query that summarizes the sales and the cost of goods for all items sold in a given month, enter the following (*qxmplMonthSalesParameter*).

```
PARAMETERS [Year to summarize:] Short,
           [Month to summarize:] Short;
SELECT tblBooks.ISBNNumber, tblBooks.Title,
       Format([OrderDate],"mmmm""", """yyyy")
         AS OrderMonth,
       Sum(Round(CCur(([Quantity]*[SuggPrice]) *
       (1-[Discount])), 2)) AS OrderTot
FROM tblOrders
       INNER JOIN (tblBooks
       INNER JOIN tblOrderDetails
       ON tblBooks.ISBNNumber =
         tblOrderDetails.ISBNNumber)
       ON tblOrders.OrderID = tblOrderDetails.OrderID
WHERE (((Year([OrderDate]))=[Year to summarize:]) AND
       ((Month([OrderDate]))=[Month to summarize:]))
GROUP BY tblBooks.ISBNNumber, tblBooks.Title,
         Format([OrderDate],"mmmm""", """yyyy");
```

To find the total sales for each book, enter the following (*qxmplTotalSalesByBook*).

```
SELECT tblBooks.ISBNNumber, tblBooks.Title,
       Sum(Round(CCur(([Quantity]*[SuggPrice]) *
       (1-[Discount])), 2)) AS TotSales
FROM tblBooks
     INNER JOIN tblOrderDetails
     ON tblBooks.ISBNNumber =
tblOrderDetails.ISBNNumber
WHERE Not tblBooks.OutOfPrint
GROUP BY tblBooks.ISBNNumber, tblBooks.Title;
```

Total Functions: VAR, VARP

? SEE ALSO
Expressions, GROUP BY Clause, HAVING Clause, SELECT Statement, Subquery, and TRANSFORM Statement.

In a logical table defined by a SELECT statement or a subquery, creates a column value that is the variance (average of the square of the difference from the mean) of the values in the expression or column name specified. You can use the GROUP BY clause to create a variance for each group of rows selected from the underlying tables or queries. VARP produces an estimate of the variance for the entire population on the basis of the sample provided in each group.

Syntax

```
{VAR | VARP} (<expression>)
```

Notes

You cannot use another total function reference within the expression. If you use an SQL total function in the select list of a SELECT statement, any other columns in the select list must be derived using a total function, or the column name must appear in a GROUP BY clause. An expression must contain a reference to at least one column name, and the expression or column name must be a numeric data type.

Null values are not included in the calculation of the result. The data type of the result is a double-precision floating point number. If there are not at least two members in a group, VAR returns a null value. VARP returns an estimate if there is at least one non-null value in the group.

Example

To find the variance and the population variance of the price of books, grouped by copyright year, enter the following (*qxmplVariance*).

```
SELECT  tblBooks.CopyrightYear,
        Count(tblBooks.ISBNNumber)
          AS CountOfISBNNumber,
        Var(tblBooks.SuggPrice) AS VarOfSuggPrice,
        VarP(tblBooks.SuggPrice) AS VarPOfSuggPrice
FROM tblBooks
GROUP BY tblBooks.CopyrightYear;
```

TRANSFORM Statement

SEE ALSO

GROUP BY Clause, HAVING Clause, SELECT Statement, and Total Functions.

Produces a crosstab query that lets you summarize a single value by using the values found in a specified column or in an expression as the column headers and using other columns or expressions to define the grouping criteria to form rows. The result looks similar to a spreadsheet and is most useful as input to a graph object.

Syntax

```
TRANSFORM <total-function-expression>
  <select-statement>
PIVOT <expression>
[IN (<column-value-list>)]
```

where *<total-function-expression>* is an expression created with one of the total functions, *<select-statement>* contains a GROUP BY clause, and *<column-value-list>* is a list of required values expected to be returned by the PIVOT expression, enclosed in quotes and separated by commas. (You can use the IN clause to force the output sequence of the columns.)

III

Working with Data

Notes

The *<total-function-expression>* parameter is the value that you want to appear in the "cells" of the crosstab datasheet. PIVOT *<expression>* defines the column or expression that provides the column headings in the crosstab result. You might use this value to provide a list of months with total rows defined by product categories in the *<select-statement>* GROUP BY clause. You can use more than one column or expression in the SELECT statement to define the grouping criteria for rows.

Example

To produce a total sales amount for each month in the year 1999, categorized by book, enter the following (*qxmpl1999SalesByBookXtab*).

```
TRANSFORM  Sum(Round(CCur(([Quantity]*[SuggPrice])*
   (1-[Discount])), 2)) AS Expr1
SELECT tblBooks.ISBNNumber, tblBooks.Title,
      Sum(Round(CCur(([Quantity]*[SuggPrice])*
         (1-[Discount])), 2)) AS TotSales
FROM tblOrders
      INNER JOIN (tblBooks
         INNER JOIN tblOrderDetails
         ON tblBooks.ISBNNumber =
            tblOrderDetails.ISBNNumber)
         ON tblOrders.OrderID = tblOrderDetails.OrderID
WHERE (((tblBooks.OutOfPrint)=False))
GROUP BY tblBooks.ISBNNumber,
         tblBooks.Title
PIVOT Format([OrderDate],"mmm yyyy")
   IN ("Jan 1999","Feb 1999","Mar 1999",
         "Apr 1999","May 1999","Jun 1999",
         "Jul 1999","Aug 1999","Sep 1999",
         "Oct 1999","Nov 1999","Dec 1999");
```

> **NOTE**
>
> This example shows a special use of the IN predicate to define not only which months should be selected but also the sequence in which Access displays the months in the resulting recordset.

UNION Query Operator

SEE ALSO

ORDER BY Clause and SELECT Statement.

Produces a result table that contains the rows returned by both the first select statement and the second select statement. You must use SQL view to define a UNION query.

Syntax

```
<select-statement>
UNION [ALL]
  <select-statement>
[ORDER BY {column-name | column-number
[ASC | DESC]},...]
```

Notes

If you specify ALL, Access returns all rows in both logical tables. If you do not specify ALL, Access eliminates duplicate rows. The tables returned by each *<select-statement>* must contain an equal number of columns, and each column must have identical attributes.

You must not use the ORDER BY clause in the *<select-statements>* that are joined by query operators; however, you can include a single ORDER BY clause at the end of a statement that uses one or more query operators. This action will apply the specified order to the result of the entire statement. Access derives the column names of the output from the column names returned by the first *<select-statement>*. If you want to use column names in the ORDER BY clause, be sure to use names from the first query. You can also use the output column numbers to define ORDER BY criteria.

You can combine multiple select statements using UNION to obtain complex results. You can also use parentheses to influence the sequence in which Access applies the operators, as shown here:

```
SELECT...UNION (SELECT...UNION SELECT...)
```

Example

To find the names of all stores and current customers in the state of Washington, to eliminate duplicates, and to sort the names by postal code, enter the following (*qxmplCustomersAndStoresInWA*).

```
SELECT [tblCustomers].[LastName] & ", " &
       [tblCustomers].[FirstName] &
       IIf(IsNull([tblCustomers].[MiddleInit]),
       Null,
         " " & [tblCustomers].[MiddleInit] & ".")
       AS Name,
     tblCustomers.City, tblCustomers.PostalCode
FROM tblCustomers
WHERE tblCustomers.StateOrProvince = "WA"
UNION
SELECT tblStores.StoreName, tblStores.City,
     tblStores.PostalCode
FROM tblStores
WHERE tblStores.StateOrProvince = "WA"
ORDER BY PostalCode DESC;
```

III

Working with Data

WHERE Clause

? SEE ALSO

DELETE Statement,
Expressions, Predicates,
Search-Condition,
SELECT Statement,
Subquery, and UPDATE
Statement.

Specifies a search condition in an SQL statement or an SQL clause. The DELETE, SELECT, and UPDATE statements and the subquery containing the WHERE clause operate only on those rows that satisfy the condition.

Syntax

```
WHERE <search-condition>
```

Notes

Access applies the *<search-condition>* to each row of the logical table assembled as a result of executing the previous clauses, and it rejects those rows for which the *<search-condition>* does not evaluate to True. If you use a subquery within a predicate in the *<search-condition>* (often called an *inner query*), Access must first execute the subquery before it evaluates the predicate.

In a subquery, if you refer to a table or a query that you also use in an outer FROM clause (often called a *correlated subquery*), Access must execute the subquery for each row being evaluated in the outer table. If you do not use a reference to an outer table in a subquery, Access must execute the subquery only once. A correlated subquery can also be expressed as a join, which generally executes more efficiently. If you include a predicate in the *<search-condition>* in the form

```
expression comparison-operator subquery
```

an error is returned if the subquery returns no rows.

The order of evaluation of the Boolean operators used in the *<search-condition>* is NOT, AND, OR, XOR (exclusive OR), EQV (equivalence), and then IMP (implication). You can include additional parentheses to influence the order in which Access processes Boolean expressions.

Example

To find all books that have a suggested price greater than $20 and an edition number equal to 2 or a copyright year of 1995, but not both, enter the following (*qxmplXOR*).

```
SELECT tblBooks.ISBNNumber, tblBooks.Title,
        tblBooks.CopyrightYear, tblBooks.SuggPrice,
        tblBooks.EditionNumber
FROM tblBooks
WHERE tblBooks.SuggPrice>20 And
        (tblBooks.CopyrightYear = 1995
        XOR tblBooks.EditionNumber = 2);
```

SQL Action Queries

Use SQL action queries to delete, insert, or update data or to create a new table from existing data. Action queries are particularly powerful because they allow you to operate on sets of data, not single rows. For example, an UPDATE statement or a DELETE statement affects all rows in the underlying tables that meet the selection criteria you specify.

DELETE Statement

? SEE ALSO

IN Clause, INSERT Statement, Predicates, Search-Condition, and Subquery.

Deletes one or more rows from a table or a query. The WHERE clause is optional. If you do not specify a WHERE clause, all rows are deleted from the table or the query that you specify in the FROM clause. If you specify a WHERE clause, the search condition is applied to each row in the table or the query, and only those rows that evaluate to True are deleted.

Syntax

```
DELETE [<select-list>]
  FROM {table-name [[AS] correlation-name] |
    select-query-name [[AS] correlation-name] |
    <joined table>},...
  [IN <source specification>]
  [WHERE <search-condition>];
```

where *<select-list>* is

```
[* | table-name.*]
```

and where *<joined table>* is

```
({table-name [[AS] correlation-name] |
    select-query-name [[AS] correlation-name] |
    <joined table>}
{INNER | LEFT | RIGHT} JOIN
    {table-name [[AS] correlation-name] |
    select-query-name [[AS] correlation-name] |
    <joined table>}
ON <join-specification>)
```

Notes

If you specify a query name in a DELETE statement, the query must not be constructed using the UNION query operator. The query also must not contain an SQL total function, the DISTINCT keyword, a GROUP BY or HAVING clause, or a subquery that references the same base table as the DELETE statement.

III

Working with Data

If you join two or more tables in the FROM clause, you can delete rows only from the "many" side of the relationship if the tables are related one-to-many; if the tables are related one-to-one, you can delete rows from either side. When you include more than one table in the FROM clause, you must also specify from which table the rows are to be deleted by using *table-name.** in the *<select-list>*. When you specify only one table in the FROM clause, you do not need to provide a *<select-list>*.

You can supply a correlation name for each table or query name. You can use this correlation name as an alias for the full table name when qualifying column names in the WHERE clause and in subclauses. You must use a correlation name when referring to a column name that occurs in more than one table in the FROM clause.

If you use a subquery in the *<search-condition>*, you must not reference the target table or the query or any underlying table of the query in the subquery.

Examples

To delete all rows in the tblOrderDetails table, enter the following.

```
DELETE FROM tblOrderDetails;
```

To delete all rows in the tblBooks table that are books about MS-DOS, enter the following (*qxmplDeleteMS-DOSBooks*).

```
DELETE tblBooks.*
FROM tblBooks
WHERE tblBooks.ISBNNumber In
    (SELECT tblBookCategories.ISBNNumber
     FROM tblCategories
       INNER JOIN tblBookCategories
       ON tblCategories.CategoryID =
            tblBookCategories.CategoryID
     WHERE tblCategories.Category="MS-DOS");
```

INSERT Statement (Append Query)

(?) SEE ALSO
DELETE Statement, IN Clause, SELECT Statement, and Subquery.

Inserts one or more new rows into the specified table or query. When you use the VALUES clause, only a single row is inserted. If you use a select statement, the number of rows inserted equals the number of rows returned by the select statement.

Syntax

```
INSERT INTO table-name [({column-name},...)]
[IN <source specification>]
{VALUES({literal},...) | select-statement}
```

Notes

If you do not include a column-name list, you must supply values for all columns defined in the table in the order in which they were declared in the table definition. If you include a column-name list, you must supply values for all columns in the list, and the values must be compatible with the receiving column attributes. You must include in the list all columns in the underlying table whose Required attribute is Yes and that do not have a default value.

If you include an IN clause in both the INSERT INTO and the FROM clause of the select statement, both must refer to the same source database.

If you supply values by using a select statement, the statement's FROM clause cannot have the target table of the insert as its table name or as an underlying table. The target table also cannot be used in any subquery.

Because Access allows you to define column-value constraints, a table validation rule, and referential integrity checks, any values that you insert must pass these validations before Access will allow you to run the query.

Examples

To insert a new row in the tblStores table, enter the following.

```
INSERT INTO tblStores (StoreName,
        Address, City, StateOrProvince, PostalCode,
        Country, PhoneNumber, FaxNumber, Email)
VALUES ("Books Unlimited", "12345 Camino Real",
        "San Jose", "CA", "95000", "USA",
        "(408) 881-2051", "(408) 881-2055",
        "BooksUn@msn.com");
```

To calculate the sales totals for a given month and insert them into a summary working table, enter the following.

```
PARAMETERS [Year to summarize:] Short,
        [Month to summarize:] Short;
INSERT INTO zSumSalesWork (ISBNNumber, Title,
        SaleMonth, SalesTotal)
SELECT tblBooks.ISBNNumber, tblBooks.Title,
        Format([OrderDate],"mmmm"", ""yyyy")
        AS OrderMonth,
        Sum(Round(CCur(([Quantity]*[SuggPrice])*
        (1-[Discount])), 2)) AS OrderTot
```

(continued)

```
FROM tblOrders
        INNER JOIN (tblBooks
          INNER JOIN tblOrderDetails
          ON tblBooks.ISBNNumber =
            tblOrderDetails.ISBNNumber)
        ON tblOrders.OrderID =
          tblOrderDetails.OrderID
    WHERE (((Year([OrderDate]))=[Year to summarize:])
          AND
          ((Month([OrderDate]))=[Month to summarize:]))
    GROUP BY tblBooks.ISBNNumber, tblBooks.Title,
            Format([OrderDate],"mmmm""", ""yyyy");
```

Although Access accepts the ANSI-standard VALUES clause, you will discover that Access converts a statement such as

```
INSERT INTO MyTable (ColumnA, ColumnB)
VALUES (123, "Jane Doe");
```

to

```
INSERT INTO MyTable (ColumnA, ColumnB)
SELECT 123 As Expr1, "Jane Doe" as Expr2;
```

SELECT . . . INTO Statement (Make-Table Query)

? SEE ALSO

IN Clause, JOIN Operation, Search-Condition, and SELECT Statement.

Creates a new table from values selected from one or more other tables. Make-table queries are most useful for providing backup snapshots or for creating tables with rolled-up totals at the end of an accounting period.

Syntax

```
SELECT [ALL | DISTINCT | DISTINCTROW |
        TOP number PERCENT]] <select-list>
INTO new-table-name
  [IN <source specification>]
  FROM {table-name [[AS] correlation-name] |
    select-query-name [[AS] correlation-name] |
    <joined table>},...
  [IN <source specification>]
  [WHERE <search-condition>]
  [GROUP BY column-name,...]
  [HAVING <search-condition>]
[UNION [ALL] <select-statement>]
  [[ORDER BY {column-name [ASC | DESC]},...] |
  IN <"source database name"> <[source connect
      string]>
  [WITH OWNERACCESS OPTION];
```

where *<select-list>* is

```
{* | {<expression> [AS output-column-name] |
   table-name.* | query-name.* |
   correlation-name.*},...}
```

and where *<joined table>* is

```
({table-name [[AS] correlation-name] |
   select-query-name [[AS] correlation-name] |
   <joined table>}
{INNER | LEFT | RIGHT} JOIN
   {table-name [[AS] correlation-name] |
   select-query-name [[AS] correlation-name] |
   <joined table>}
ON <join-specification>)
```

Notes

A SELECT...INTO query creates a new table with the name specified in *new-table-name*. If the table already exists, Access displays a dialog box that asks you to confirm the deletion of the table before it creates a new one in its place. The columns in the new table inherit the data type attributes of the columns produced by the *<select-list>*.

You can supply a correlation name for each table or query name. You can use this correlation name as an alias for the full table name when qualifying column names in the *<select-list>* or in the WHERE clause and subclauses. If you're joining a table or a query to itself, you must use correlation names to clarify which copy of the table or query you're referring to in the *<select-list>*, join criteria, or selection criteria. If a table name or a query name is also an SQL reserved word (for example, "Order"), you must enclose the name in brackets.

When you list more than one table or query without join criteria, the source is the Cartesian product of all the tables. For example, *FROM TableA, TableB* asks Access to search all the rows of TableA matched with all the rows of TableB. Unless you specify other restricting criteria, the number of logical rows that Access processes could equal the number of rows in TableA *times* the number of rows in TableB. Access then returns the rows in which the selection criteria specified in the WHERE and HAVING clauses are true.

You can further define which rows Access includes in the output recordset by specifying ALL, DISTINCT, DISTINCTROW, TOP *n*, or TOP *n* PERCENT. ALL includes all rows that match the search criteria from the source tables, including potential duplicate rows. DISTINCT requests that Access return only rows that are different from any other row. You cannot update any columns in a query that uses ALL or DISTINCT.

DISTINCTROW requests that Access return only rows in which the concatenation of the primary keys from all tables supplying output columns is unique. Depending on the columns you select, you might see rows in the result that contain duplicate values, but each row in the result is derived from a distinct combination of rows in the underlying tables. Specify TOP *n* or TOP *n* PERCENT to request that the recordset contain only the first *n* or first *n* percent of rows. The parameter *n* must be an integer and must be less than or equal to 100 if you include the PERCENT keyword. Note that if you do not include an ORDER BY clause, the sequence of rows returned is undefined.

If you include an IN clause for both the INTO and the FROM clauses, both must refer to the same source database.

When you include a GROUP BY clause, the *<select-list>* must be made up of either SQL total functions or column names specified in the GROUP BY clause. A column name in a GROUP BY clause can refer to any column from any table in the FROM clause, even if the column is not named in the *<select-list>*. If you want to refer to a calculated expression in the GROUP BY clause, you must assign an *output-column-name* to the expression in *<select-list>* and then refer to that name in the GROUP BY clause. If the GROUP BY clause is preceded by a WHERE clause, Access forms the groups from the rows selected after it applies the WHERE clause.

If you use a HAVING clause but do not include a GROUP BY clause, the *<select-list>* must be formed using SQL total functions. If you include a GROUP BY clause preceding the HAVING clause, the HAVING *<search-condition>* applies to each of the groups formed by equal values in the specified columns. If you do not include a GROUP BY clause, the HAVING *<search-condition>* applies to the entire logical table defined by the SELECT statement.

You use column names or relative output column numbers to specify the columns on whose values the rows returned are ordered. (If you use relative output column numbers, the first output column is 1.) You can specify multiple columns in the ORDER BY clause. The list is ordered primarily by the first column. If rows exist for which the values of that column are equal, they are ordered by the next column on the

ORDER BY list. You can specify ascending (ASC) or descending (DESC) order for each column. If you do not specify ASC or DESC, ASC is assumed. Using an ORDER BY clause in a SELECT statement is the only means of defining the sequence of the returned rows.

Normally, the person running the query not only must have rights to the query but also must have the appropriate rights to the tables used in the query. (These rights include reading data to select rows, updating, inserting, and deleting data using the query.) If your application has multiple users, you might want to secure the tables so that no user has direct access to any of the tables and all users can still run queries defined by you. Assuming you are the owner of both the queries and the tables, you can deny access to the tables but allow access to the queries. To make sure that the queries run properly, you must add the WITH OWNERACCESS OPTION clause to allow the users to have the same access rights as the table owner when accessing the data via the query. *See* Building Applications with Microsoft Access 2000, *online documentation that comes with Access, for more details on securing your applications.*

Example

To create a new table that summarizes all sales by book and by month, enter the following (*qxmplTotalBookSalesMakeTable*).

```
SELECT  tblBooks.ISBNNumber, tblBooks.Title,
        Format([OrderDate],"yyyy mmm") AS SaleMonth,
        Sum(Round(CCur(([Quantity]*[SuggPrice])*
        (1-[Discount]))), 2))
        AS TotSales INTO ztblMonthlySales
  FROM tblOrders
        INNER JOIN (tblBooks
          INNER JOIN tblOrderDetails
          ON tblBooks.ISBNNumber =
            tblOrderDetails.ISBNNumber)
        ON tblOrders.OrderID =
          tblOrderDetails.OrderID
  WHERE (((tblBooks.OutOfPrint)=False))
  GROUP BY tblBooks.ISBNNumber, tblBooks.Title,
        Format([OrderDate],"yyyy mmm");
```

III

Working with Data

UPDATE Statement

Expressions, IN Clause, Predicates, Search-Condition, and WHERE Clause.

In the specified table or query, updates the selected columns (either to the value of the given expression or to null) in all rows that satisfy the search condition. If you do not enter a WHERE clause, all rows in the specified table or query are affected.

Syntax

```
UPDATE {table-name [[AS] correlation-name] |
    select-query-name [[AS] correlation-name] |
    <joined table>},...
[IN <source specification>]
SET {column-name = {<expression> | NULL}},...
[WHERE <search-condition>]
```

where *<joined table>* is

```
({table-name [[AS] correlation-name] |
    select-query-name [[AS] correlation-name] |
    <joined table>}
{INNER | LEFT | RIGHT} JOIN
    {table-name [[AS] correlation-name] |
    select-query-name [[AS] correlation-name] |
    <joined table>}
ON <join-specification>)
```

Notes

If you provide more than one table name, you can update columns only in the table on the "many" side of a one-to-many relationship. If the tables are related one-to-one, you can update columns in either table. Access must be able to determine the relationship between queries in order to update columns in a query. In general, if a table is joined by its primary key to a query, you can update columns in the query (because the primary key indicates that the table is on the "one" side of the join). You cannot update a table joined to a query. If you want to update a table with the results of a query, you must insert the query results into a temporary table that can be defined with a one-to-many or one-to-one relationship with the target table and then use the temporary table to update the target.

If you specify a *<search-condition>*, you can reference only columns found in the target table or query. If you use a subquery in the *<search-condition>*, you must not reference the target table or the query or any underlying table of the query in the subquery.

In the SET clause, you cannot specify a column name more than once. Values assigned to columns must be compatible with the column attributes. If you assign the null value, the column cannot have the Required property set to Yes.

Access lets you define column-value constraints, a table validation rule, or referential integrity checks, so any values that you update must pass these validations or Access will not let you run the query.

Examples

To raise the price of all books about Visual Basic by 10 percent, enter the following (*qxmplUpdateVisualBasicPrices*).

```
UPDATE tblBooks
  SET tblBooks.SuggPrice =
    Round(CCur([SuggPrice]*1.10), 2)
  WHERE (((tblBooks.ISBNNumber)
    IN (SELECT tblBookCategories.ISBNNumber
        FROM tblCategories
          INNER JOIN tblBookCategories
          ON tblCategories.CategoryID =
            tblBookCategories.CategoryID
          WHERE tblCategories.Category="Visual
            Basic")));
```

To discount the price of all books by 5 percent, enter the following.

```
UPDATE tblBooks
  SET tblBooks.SuggPrice =
      Round(CCur([SuggPrice] * .95), 2);
```

Complex Query Examples

Although the preceding sections provide many examples, it's useful for you to examine how complex queries are constructed for the Entertainment Scheduling sample application. The first example in this section shows you how to create a query that returns the date of every Monday between January 1, 1995, and January 1, 2001. The second example uses the first query to generate a week-by-week booking list for all clubs and groups. It then shows you how to revise an SQL SELECT statement produced by the Access design grid to handle a special JOIN criteria expression. The third example expands the week-by-week booking list to show weeks in which there are no bookings for clubs and groups.

> You can find these complex query examples in the Entertainment Scheduling sample database.

Example 1: Returning the Date of Every Monday

To produce reports that show weekly bookings for clubs and groups, the Entertainment Scheduling sample database uses several scheduling queries. Because you want the reports to show bookings for clubs and groups by week, beginning on each Monday, you need some way to return the date of Monday for every week in which there is a booking. You can accomplish this by creating a query that returns the date of every Monday and then basing the scheduling queries on a combination of this query and the tables in which the booking information is stored.

To create the Monday dates query, called qryMondays, you start with a table, tblDates, that stores all dates between January 1, 1992, and December 31, 2035. Each date record has a corresponding DayOfWeek field that stores an integer value indicating the day of the week that the date falls on—1 for Monday, 2 for Tuesday, and so on. Add the tblDates table to the upper part of the Query window in Design view, and then drag the SchedDate and DayOfWeek fields to the design grid. To create a query that returns Monday dates since January 1, 1997, set the criterion for the SchedDate field to ">=#1/1/97#", and then set the criterion for the DayOfWeek field to 1.

Your query should look like the one shown in Figure 11-2.

FIGURE 11-2.

A query that returns a list of Monday dates.

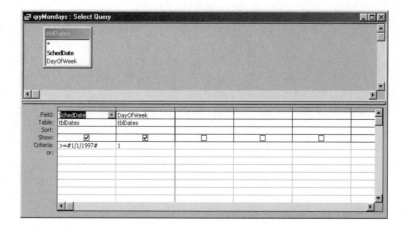

To see the underlying SQL code for the query, select SQL View from the Query View toolbar button's drop-down list. In SQL view, the query should look like this:

```
SELECT tblDates.SchedDate, tblDates.DayOfWeek
  FROM tblDates
  WHERE (((tblDates.SchedDate)>=#1/1/97#)
    AND ((tblDates.DayOfWeek)=1));
```

Mapping SQL Keywords to the Query Design Grid

You might find it useful to understand where Access displays elements of major clauses on its graphical query design grid. The following lists major clauses and the location of each on the design grid.

Clause or Keyword	Location
SELECT *<select-list>*	The *<select-list>* appears on the Field line in the lower part of the grid. Adding a field name followed by a colon at the beginning of a field expression generates an AS clause.
AVG, MIN, MAX, SUM, COUNT, STDEV, VAR (total functions)	Appears on the Total line in a totals query.
ALL	Specifying No for both Unique Values and Unique Records on the query property sheet is the same as using the ALL keyword. Access does not generate this keyword, but accepts it in SQL for compatibility with the ANSI standard.
DISTINCT	The value Yes specified for Unique Values on the query property sheet.
DISTINCTROW	The value Yes specified for Unique Records on the query property sheet.
TOP, PERCENT	A value entered in the Top Values property on the query property sheet.
FROM	The graphical display of field lists in the top part of the query design grid.
IN	Values entered in the Source Database and Source Connect Str properties on the query property sheet.
WHERE	Expressions entered on the Criteria and Or lines unless the Total line specifies Group By or a total function. See HAVING.

(continued)

III

Working with Data

Mapping SQL Keywords to the Query Design Grid *continued*	

Clause or Keyword	Location
GROUP BY	In a totals query, fields or expressions that have Group By specified on the Total line.
HAVING	In a totals query, expressions entered on the Criteria or Or lines under fields where the Total line specifies Group By or one of the total functions.
UNION	Access cannot display a UNION query on the design grid.
ORDER BY	Specifications on the Sort line.
WITH OWNERACCESS OPTION	Specifying Owner's in the Run Permissions property on the query property sheet.
TRANSFORM *expression*	In a crosstab query, *expression* is the field or expression for which you have specified Value on the Crosstab row.
PIVOT *expression* [IN *column-value list*]	In a crosstab query, *expression* is the field or expression for which you have specified Column Heading on the Crosstab row. The IN clause here is values specified in the Column Headings property on the query property sheet.

Example 2: Generating a Week-by-Week Booking List

To see all the weekly bookings for clubs and groups, you need to create a query that combines information about each group's bookings with information about clubs. You can get information about each booking from a group's contract, which is stored in the master contracts table. Information about clubs is stored in the master clubs table. Creating a query that uses these two tables alone won't give you a week-by-week list of bookings, however. That's where the Monday dates query you created in the previous example comes in.

To create the master clubs and groups schedule query, called qrySchedClubsAndGroups, you'll combine information from the master contracts table (tblContracts), the master clubs table (tblClubs), and the Monday dates query (qryMondays). You can start by adding the two tables and the query to the upper part of the Query window in Design view. Because a relationship has already been defined for the contracts and clubs tables, a one-to-many join is already established between the ClubID fields of the two tables. You can then relate the Monday dates query to the contracts table by establishing an equi-join between the SchedDate field in qryMondays and the BeginningDate field in tblContracts. Then drag the following fields to the design grid.

Field	Table/Query
SchedDate	qryMondays
ContractNo	tblContracts
GroupID	tblContracts
GroupName	tblContracts
ClubID	tblContracts
Status	tblContracts
BeginningDate	tblContracts
EndingDate	tblContracts
ClubName	tblClubs

Because you don't want to include bookings for contracts that have been cancelled, set the criterion for the Status field to <>"D".

Your query should look like the one shown in Figure 11-3.

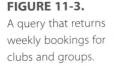

FIGURE 11-3.

A query that returns weekly bookings for clubs and groups.

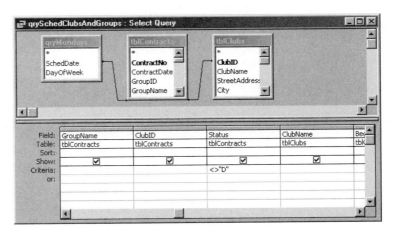

So far, creating the master clubs and groups schedule query is like creating any other simple query. However, if you run the query you'll see that it doesn't yet produce the results you want: It returns only the bookings whose beginning date is a Monday, but most bookings begin on a Friday, a Saturday, or another day of the week. To return a Monday schedule date for a booking that begins on another day, you need to revise the query to include bookings whose beginning date is within seven days of each Monday date. In addition, you need to include bookings whose ending date occurs in the week following the Monday schedule date. When a contract spans multiple weeks, you'll see that this technique generates one output row for each week of the contract's term.

You can accomplish this by adding criteria to the BeginningDate and EndingDate fields in the master clubs and groups schedule query. Translating what you want into SQL expressions gives you the following criteria.

Field	Criteria
BeginningDate	qryMondays.SchedDate > tblContracts.BeginningDate -7
EndingDate	qryMondays.SchedDate <= tblContracts.EndingDate

Because greater than (>) and less than or equal to (<=) operators can't be represented in the design grid, you need to specify the criteria in a custom join expression in the query's underlying SQL code. Open the query in SQL view and replace the SELECT statement's FROM clause with the following.

```
FROM qryMondays
  INNER JOIN (tblContracts
    INNER JOIN tblClubs
    ON tblClubs.ClubId = tblContracts.ClubID)
    ON (qryMondays.SchedDate >
      tblContracts.BeginningDate -7)
      AND (qryMondays.SchedDate <=
        tblContracts.EndingDate)
```

In SQL view, the completed query should look like this:

```
SELECT qryMondays.SchedDate,
        tblContracts.ContractNo, tblContracts.GroupID,
        tblContracts.GroupName, tblContracts.ClubID,
        tblContracts.Status,
        tblContracts.BeginningDate,
        tblContracts.EndingDate, tblClubs.ClubName
FROM qryMondays
        INNER JOIN (tblContracts
          INNER JOIN tblClubs
          ON tblClubs.ClubId = tblContracts.ClubID)
          ON (qryMondays.SchedDate >
            tblContracts.BeginningDate -7)
            AND (qryMondays.SchedDate <=
              tblContracts.EndingDate)
WHERE tblContracts.Status <> "D";
```

Example 3: Showing Weeks in Which There Are No Bookings

Now that you've created a master clubs and groups schedule query, you can use it as the basis for other queries. For example, you can create a master schedules query that shows all weeks—those with bookings as well as those without.

To build the master schedules query, called qrySchedules, create a new query and add the qrySchedClubsAndGroups and qryMondays queries to the upper part of the Query window in Design view. Drag the SchedDate field from the qryMondays field list to the SchedDate field in the qrySchedClubsAndGroups field list. Double-click the resulting join line, and then select option 2 in the Join Properties dialog box. Then drag the following fields to the design grid.

Field	Table/Query
SchedDate	qryMondays
ContractNo	qrySchedClubsAndGroups
Status	qrySchedClubsAndGroups
GroupID	qrySchedClubsAndGroups
GroupName	qrySchedClubsAndGroups
ClubID	qrySchedClubsAndGroups
ClubName	qrySchedClubsAndGroups
BeginningDate	qrySchedClubsAndGroups
EndingDate	qrySchedClubsAndGroups

Sort the SchedDate field in ascending order. Your query should look like the one shown in Figure 11-4.

FIGURE 11-4.

A master schedules query.

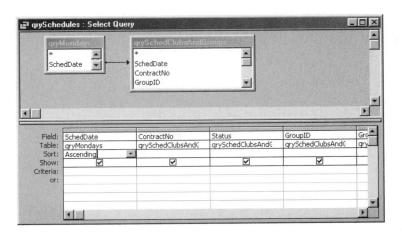

In SQL view, the query should look like this:

```
SELECT qryMondays.SchedDate,
       qrySchedClubsAndGroups.ContractNo,
       qrySchedClubsAndGroups.Status,
       qrySchedClubsAndGroups.GroupID,
       qrySchedClubsAndGroups.GroupName,
       qrySchedClubsAndGroups.ClubID,
       qrySchedClubsAndGroups.ClubName,
       qrySchedClubsAndGroups.BeginningDate,
       qrySchedClubsAndGroups.EndingDate
FROM qryMondays LEFT JOIN qrySchedClubsAndGroups
     ON qryMondays.SchedDate =
        qrySchedClubsAndGroups.SchedDate
ORDER BY qryMondays.SchedDate;
```

At this point, you should have a good working understanding of how to build complex queries using the SQL syntax understood by Access. In Parts IV and V of this book, you'll learn how to build forms and reports that use queries. In Part VI, you'll learn how to use macros and Visual Basic to tie it all together.

PART IV

Using Forms

Form Basics

I f you've worked through this book to this point, you should understand all the mechanics of designing and building databases (and connecting to external ones), entering and viewing data in tables, and building queries. You need to understand tables and queries before you jump into forms because most of the forms you design will be bound to an underlying table or a query.

This chapter focuses on the external aspects of forms—why forms are useful, what they look like, and how to use them. You'll look at examples of forms from the Microsoft Press Books sample database. In Chapters 13 and 14, you'll learn how to design and build your own forms by creating portions of the database application for the Microsoft Press Books and Entertainment Scheduling databases.

Uses of Forms

Forms are the primary interface between users and your Microsoft Access application. You can design forms for many different purposes.

- **Displaying and editing data.** This is the most common use of forms. Forms provide a way to customize the presentation of data in your database. You can also use forms to change or delete data in your database or add data to it. You can set options in a form to make all or part of your data read-only, to fill in related information from other tables automatically, to calculate the values to be displayed, or to show or hide data on the basis of either the values of other data in the record or the options selected by the user of the form.

- **Controlling application flow.** You can design forms that work with macros or with Microsoft Visual Basic procedures to automate the display of certain data or the sequence of certain actions. You can create special controls on your form, called *command buttons,* that run a macro or a Visual Basic procedure when you click them. With macros and Visual Basic procedures, you can open other forms, run queries, restrict the data that is displayed, execute a menu command, set values in records and forms, display menus, print reports, and perform a host of other actions. You can also design a form so that macros or Visual Basic procedures run when specific events occur—for example, when someone opens the form, tabs to a specific control, clicks an option on the form, or changes data in the form. *See Part VI of this book for details about using macros and Visual Basic with forms to automate your application.*

- **Accepting input.** You can design forms that are used only for entering new data in your database or for providing data values to help automate your application.

- **Displaying messages.** Forms can provide information about how to use your application or about upcoming actions. Access also provides a MsgBox macro action and a *MsgBox* Visual Basic function that you can use to display information, warnings, or error messages. *See Chapter 20, "Adding Power with Macros," for more detail.*

- **Printing information.** Although you should design reports to print most information, you can also print the information in a form. Because you can specify one set of options when Access displays a form and another set of options when Access prints a form, a form can serve a dual role. For example, you might design a form with two sets of display headers and footers, one set for entering an order and another set for printing a customer invoice from the order.

A Tour of Forms

The Microsoft Press Books sample database is full of interesting examples of forms. The rest of this chapter takes you on a tour of some of the major features of those forms. In the next chapter, you'll learn how to design and build forms for this database.

Begin by opening the Microsoft Press Books database and clicking the Forms button in the Database window to see the list of available forms. (If you started the application, click Exit on the sign-on form or the main switchboard form to return to the Database window.)

Headers, Detail Sections, and Footers

You'll normally place the information that you want to display from the underlying table or query in the detail section in the center of the Form window. You can add a header at the top of the window or a footer at the bottom of the window to display information or controls that don't need to change with each different record.

An interesting form in the Microsoft Press Books database that includes both a header and a footer is frmBookSummary. The application uses this form to display the summary results of a book search whenever the search finds more than 10 matching books. You can also open this form directly from the Database window—if you do so, it will show you all the books in the database. Find the frmBookSummary form in the forms list in the Database window, select the form, and then click the Open button to see a window similar to the one shown in Figure 12-1.

FIGURE 12-1.

The frmBookSummary form, which has a header, a detail section, and a footer.

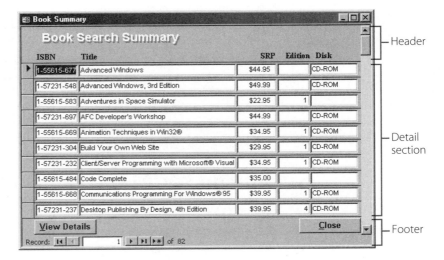

The area at the top of the window containing the title *Book Search Summary* is the header for the form. The header also includes the column names. The area at the bottom of the window is the footer for the form. You can click the View Details button to see all details for the currently selected book (the book with the arrow on the row selector), or you can click Close to close the form. At the bottom left corner of the form is the record number box that you saw in tables and queries in Datasheet view. Click the arrow button immediately to the right of the record number, and the row selector arrow will move to the next book record in the detail section of the form; notice that the header and footer don't change when you do this. If you move down several records, you can see the records scroll up in the detail section of the form.

If you click the View Details button in the footer, this form closes and the frmBooks form opens, showing details of the book record that was selected when you clicked the button. The way the form is designed, the View Details button opens the frmBooks form using a filter to show you the currently selected book. If you decide that you don't want to see details, you can click the Close button to dismiss the form.

Multiple-Page Forms

When you have a lot of information from each record to display in a form, you can design a *multiple-page form*. Open the frmAuthors form in the Microsoft Press Books database to see an example. When you open the form, you'll see the first page of author data for the first author. You can use the record number box and the buttons in the lower left corner of the form to move through the records, viewing the first page of information for each author. Figure 12-2 shows the first page of the 40th author record. (For those of you who want to drop me a line, that's my real e-mail address in the form!) To see the second page of information for any author, press the Page Down key. Figure 12-3 shows the second page of my author record. (Notice that this form has a header but no footer.) As you view different pages of a multiple-page form, the header at the top of the form (with the form title and some command buttons) doesn't change.

Continuous Forms

You can create another type of form that is useful for browsing through a list of records when each record has only a few data fields. This type of form is called a *continuous form*. Rather than showing

FIGURE 12-2.

The first page of a record in the multiple-page frmAuthors form.

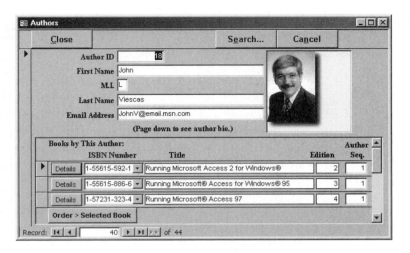

FIGURE 12-3.

The second page of a record in the frmAuthors form.

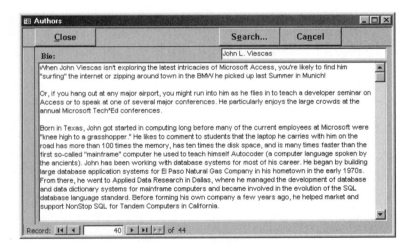

you only a single record at a time, a continuous form displays formatted records back to back, in the manner of a datasheet.

The frmBookSummary form shown earlier in Figure 12-1 is a continuous form. The frmAuthorSummary form, shown in Figure 12-4 on the next page, is also a continuous form. You can use the vertical scroll bar to move through the record display, or you can click the record number box and the buttons in the lower left corner of the form to move from record to record. As you might guess, the application uses this form to display the results of an author search that returns more than 10 rows.

FIGURE 12-4.

frmAuthorSummary is a continuous form.

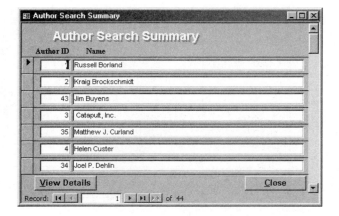

Subforms

Subforms are a good way to show related data from the "many" side of a one-to-many relationship. For example, the frmAuthors form shown earlier in Figure 12-2 shows one author and the many books that the author has written for Microsoft Press. Another good example of a subform is the frmOrders form, shown in Figure 12-5. Although both of these forms look much like a single display panel, each has a subform (which looks more like a datasheet than a form) embedded in the main form. The main part of the frmOrders form displays information from the tblOrders table, while the subform in the lower part of the window shows information from the tblOrderDetails table about the books that were requested in the current order.

FIGURE 12-5.

The frmOrders form with an embedded subform that shows the books requested in the order.

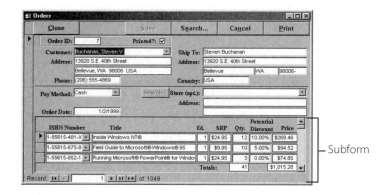

This form looks pretty complicated, but it really isn't difficult to build. Because the Microsoft Press Books database is well designed, it doesn't take much effort to build the queries that allow the form to display information from five different tables. Most of the work of creating the form goes into selecting and placing the controls that display the data. To link a subform to a main form, you have to set only two properties that tell Access which linking fields to use. In Chapter 15, "Advanced Form Design," you'll build a subform and link it to a form.

Pop-Up Forms

Sometimes it's useful to provide information in a window that stays on top regardless of where you move the focus in your application. You've probably noticed that the default behavior for windows in Microsoft Windows is for the active window to move to the front and for all other windows to move behind the active one. One exception is the Office toolbars. If you grab a toolbar and undock it, it stays floating on top so that you can still access its commands regardless of what you are doing behind it. This sort of floating window is called a *pop-up window*.

You can create forms in Access that open in pop-up windows (called pop-up forms in Access). If you open any form in the Microsoft Press Books application and then choose About Microsoft Press Books from the Help menu, this opens the frmAbout form shown in Figure 12-6, which is designed as a pop-up form. *See Chapter 24, "The Finishing Touches," for more details about how to create custom menus for forms.* Switch to the Database window and open the frmAbout form to see how it behaves. Notice that if you click in the Database window behind it, the frmAbout form stays on top. Click the OK button on the form to close it.

FIGURE 12-6.

The frmAbout pop-up form "floats" on top of the Database window, which has the focus.

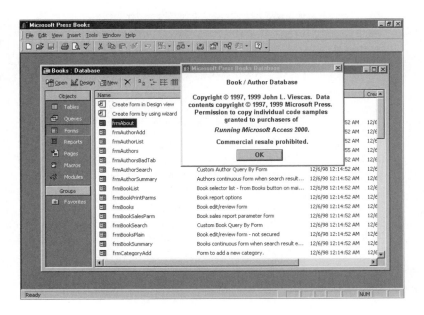

Modal Forms

As you add functionality to your application, you'll encounter situations in which you need to obtain some input from the user or convey some important information to the user before Access can proceed. Access provides a special type of form, called a *modal form,* that requires a response before the user can continue working in the application. The frmBookSearch dialog box in the Microsoft Press Books database, shown in Figure 12-7, is a modal form. This dialog box normally opens when you click the Books button on the main switchboard form and then click the Search button on the resulting Select Books (frmBookList) form, but you can also open the form on which the dialog box is based directly from the Database window. You'll notice that as long as this dialog box is open, you can't select any other window or menu in the application. To proceed, you must either enter some search criteria and click the Search button or click the Cancel button to dismiss the form.

FIGURE 12-7.

The frmBookSearch dialog box is a modal form.

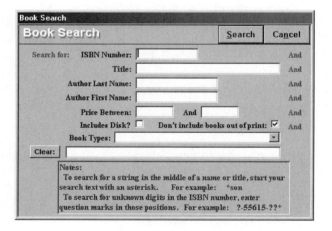

Special Controls

The information in a form is contained in *controls.* The most common control you'll use on a form is a simple text box. A text box can display data from an underlying table or query, or it can display data calculated in the form itself. You've probably noticed that many controls allow you to choose from among several values or to see additional content. You can also use controls to trigger a macro or a Visual Basic procedure. These controls are discussed in the next five sections.

Option Buttons, Check Boxes, Toggle Buttons, and Option Groups

Whenever the data you're displaying can have only two or three valid values, you can use option buttons, check boxes, or toggle buttons to see or set the value you want in the field. For example, when there are two values, as in the case of a simple Yes/No field, you can use a check box to graphically display the value in the field. A check box that's selected means the value is "Yes," and a check box that's clear means the value is "No." The Printed? control on the frmOrders form (see Figure 12-5) is a good example of the use of a check box.

To provide a graphical choice among more than two values, you can place controls in a group. Only one of the controls in a group can have a Yes value. For example, the frmBookPrintParms form (shown in Figure 12-8) that opens when you click the Reports button on the frmBooks form lists the various book reporting options. If you open this form and click the available option buttons, you can see that when you click one button, the previously selected one resets. When you click one of the sales reports buttons on this form, the form expands to let you enter a date range for your sales report. As you'll read about in more detail later, Access uses the relative numeric value of the control to determine the value in the underlying field. A Visual Basic procedure tests the value when you click one of the controls and expands the form to reveal the date text boxes when appropriate.

FIGURE 12-8.

An option group on the frmBookPrint-Parms form.

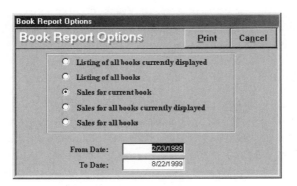

List Boxes and Combo Boxes

When you want to display a list of data values that remains visible, a list box is a good choice. When you view objects in the Database window in detail list mode, you're looking at the tables, queries, forms, reports, macros, or modules in a list box. A list box can show a list of values you entered when you designed the control, a list of values returned by an SQL statement, the value of a field in a table or in a query, or a list of field names from a table or a query. In the example shown in Figure 12-9 (the frmAuthorList form), the list includes the set of names from the tblAuthors table.

FIGURE 12-9.

A list box can show a list of values or a list of field names.

When you select a value from the list, you set the value of the control. If the control represents a field in the underlying table or query, you update that field. A list box like this one can use data from more than one field. You can, for example, display the more meaningful author name (from the FirstName, MiddleInit, and LastName fields in the tblAuthors table) in the list but set the control to the value of the related AuthorID field when the name is selected. In the Microsoft Press Books database, this sample list box lets you select multiple entries by holding down the Shift key to select a contiguous range or by holding down the Ctrl key to select several noncontiguous entries. When you click the View button, a Visual Basic procedure evaluates your choices and opens the frmAuthors form to display the selected authors.

Combo boxes are similar to list boxes. The major difference is that a combo box has both a text box *and* a drop-down list. One advantage of a combo box is that it requires space on the form for only one of the values in the underlying list. The Store field in the frmOrders form is set using a combo box, as shown in Figure 12-10. The combo box uses three fields from the underlying query—the StoreName field, a

FIGURE 12-10.

An open combo box.

calculated field (which combines the City and StateOrProvince fields), and the StoreID field (which you can't see). When you select a store, the combo box sets the StoreID field in the underlying record—a very useful feature.

> **NOTE**

Unless you start the application and "sign on" with a valid user name, you won't be able to select a new value in the StoreID field. If you already have the database open, open frmCopyright to start the application. Click the Orders button on the main switchboard form, and then click the option (number 2) to Edit Open Orders For The Current Customer.

Tab Controls

Earlier in this chapter, you saw that one way to deal with the need to display lots of information on one form is to use a multiple-page form (frmAuthors, shown in Figure 12-2 and Figure 12-3). Another way to organize the information on a single form is to use the tab control to provide what look like multiple folder tabs that reveal different information depending on the tab chosen—much like the Options dialog box in Microsoft Access (choose Options from the Tools menu) provides View, General, Edit/Find, Keyboard, Datasheet, Forms/Reports, Advanced, and Tables/Queries tabs. In the Microsoft Press Books database, a book has categories, authors, and the liner notes that provide a summary of the book's contents. Open the frmBooks form to see how the tab control displays only one of these pieces of information at a time, as shown in Figure 12-11.

FIGURE 12-11.

Information on the Categories tab in the frmBooks form.

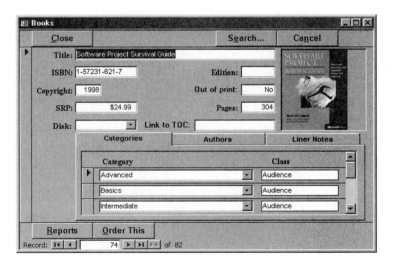

You can click the Authors tab (as shown in Figure 12-12) or the Liner Notes tab to see other information. Note that there's no programming required to implement tab selection and data display. *See Chapter 15, "Advanced Form Design," for details about how to use the tab control.*

FIGURE 12-12.

Another tab displays different data in a complex form.

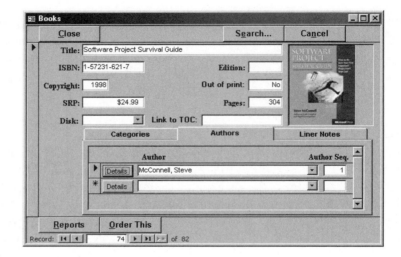

ActiveX Objects

You saw the author picture in the frmAuthors form earlier. This picture is stored in a field in the tblAuthors table using Microsoft's ActiveX technology. The logo in the top part of the main switchboard form in the Microsoft Press Books database, on the other hand, is a picture that Access has stored as part of the form. The control that you use to display a picture or any other ActiveX object is called an *object frame*. A bound object frame control is used to display an ActiveX object that is stored in a field in a table. An unbound object frame control is used to display an object that is not stored in a table.

When you include an object frame control on a form and bind the control to an ActiveX object in the database, you can edit that object by selecting it and then choosing the command at the bottom of the Edit menu that starts the object's application, as shown in Figure 12-13.

If the object is a picture, a graph, or a spreadsheet, you can see the object in the object frame control and you can activate its application by double-clicking the object. If the object is a sound file, you can hear it by double-clicking the object frame control.

FIGURE 12-13.

You can select a picture and then edit it by choosing the Bitmap Image Object command from the Edit menu and then choosing Edit from the submenu.

Figure 12-13 shows one of the photographs stored in the tblAuthors table that is bound in an object frame control on the frmAuthors form. When you double-click the picture or select the picture and choose Bitmap Image Object from the Edit menu and then choose Edit from the submenu, Access starts the Microsoft Paint application, in which the picture was created. In Windows, Paint is an ActiveX application that can "activate in place," as shown in Figure 12-14 on the next page. You can still see the Access form, menus, and toolbars, but Paint has added its own toolbars and menu commands. You can update the picture by using any of the Paint tools. You can paste in a different picture by copying a picture to the Clipboard and choosing the Paste command from Paint's Edit menu. After you make your changes, simply click in another area on the Access form to deactivate Paint and store the result of your edits in the object frame control. If you save the record, Access saves the changed data in your ActiveX object.

> **NOTE**
>
> If you have registered an application other than Microsoft Paint to handle bitmap objects, that application will be activated when you select Edit from the submenu.

Command Buttons

Another useful control is the command button, which you can use to link many forms to create a complete database application. In the

FIGURE 12-14.

The ActiveX object from Figure 12-13 being edited "in place" with its host application.

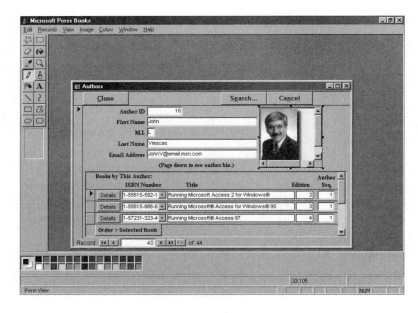

Microsoft Press Books database, for example, most of the forms are linked to the main switchboard form (frmMain), shown in Figure 12-15, in which the user can click command buttons to launch various functions in the application. The advantage of command buttons is really quite simple—they offer an easy way to trigger a macro or a Visual Basic procedure. The procedure might do nothing more than open another form, print a report, or run an action query to update many records in your database. As you'll see when you get to the end of this book, you can build a fairly complex application using forms, reports, macros, and some simple Visual Basic procedures.

NOTE

If you open frmMain directly from the Database window, the application displays a warning message indicating that you are not "signed on" to the application. You can ignore the warning and click OK to see the main switchboard form. If you aren't signed on, you won't be able to edit any of the data in the forms or to order books. You can see the main switchboard form by allowing the application to start when you open it (don't hold down the Shift key). If you want to start the Microsoft Press Books sample application from the Database window so that you can sign on, open the frmCopyright form. The sign-on form includes information on the correct password to use to sign on.

FIGURE 12-15.
The command buttons on the frmMain switchboard form.

Moving Around on Forms and Working with Data

The rest of this chapter shows you how to move around on and work with data in the various types of forms discussed earlier in the chapter.

Viewing Data

If you've read Chapter 7, "Using Datasheets," and you have tried using the form examples in this chapter, you should have a pretty good idea of how to move around on forms and view data in forms. Moving around on a form is similar to moving around in a datasheet, but there are a few subtle differences between forms and datasheets (usually having to do with how a form was designed) that determine how a form works with data. You can use the frmBooksPlain form (a copy of the frmBooks form that doesn't require you to start the application to use it) in the Microsoft Press Books database to explore the ways in which forms work.

First, open the Microsoft Press Books database. (If you started the application, click Exit on the main switchboard form to return to the Database window.) Next, click the Forms button in the Database window. Select the frmBooksPlain form, and click the Open button to see the form shown in Figure 12-16 on the next page.

FIGURE 12-16.

The frmBooksPlain form in the Microsoft Press Books database.

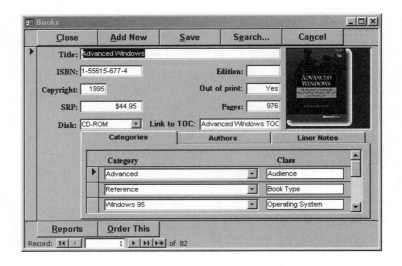

Moving Around

The way you move around on a form depends in part on the form's design. For example, the frmBooksPlain form contains two subforms—one for book categories and another for authors—embedded within the tab control. Note that once you tab into a displayed subform, using Tab or Shift+Tab moves only within the fields on the subform. If you want to tab out of the subform, use Ctrl+Tab to tab forward to the next field or object in the tab order following the subform, and use Ctrl+Shift+Tab to move backwards out of the subform.

The fsubBookCategories2 subform on the first tab is a continuous form. You move around in it in ways similar to how you move around in a datasheet. On this subform you can use the vertical scroll bar on the right side to move the display up or down. The subform can be toggled between two different views—Form view (its current state) and Datasheet view. If you want to see the Datasheet view of the fsubBookCategories2 subform, click in any of the fields on the subform (to ensure that the focus is on the subform) and then open the View menu. You'll notice that the Subform Datasheet command is not checked. This command is a toggle. If you choose the Subform Datasheet command, the fsubBookCategories2 subform will now look like Figure 12-17. You can choose the Subform Datasheet command (which is now checked) from the View menu again to restore the continuous form display.

In the frmBooksPlain form, you view different book records by using the record number box at the bottom of the form. To see the next book, use the main form's record number box; to see different categories

FIGURE 12-17.

The subform fsubBookCategories2 in Datasheet view.

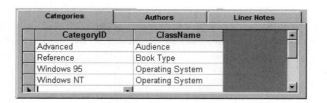

for a particular book, use the vertical scrollbar within the subform. Note that you can also design a subform with its own record number box as an additional tool for moving among records. However, I often avoid using the second record number box because it can be confusing.

You can also choose the Go To command from the Edit menu to move to the first, last, next, or previous record in the main form or in the subform. You can select any field in the form by clicking anywhere in that field. To use the Go To command you must first move to the form or the subform, depending on which set of records you want to view.

Keyboard Shortcuts

If you're typing in new data, you might find it easier to use the keyboard rather than the mouse to move around on a form. Some of the keyboard shortcuts you can use with forms are listed in Table 12-1 (for moving around in fields and records) and in Table 12-2 on the next page (for actions in a list box or in a combo box). Note that a form that edits data can be in one of two modes: Edit mode or Navigation mode. You're in Edit mode on a form when you can see a flashing cursor in the current field. To enter Navigation mode, tab to the next field or press the F2 key to select the current field.

TABLE 12-1.   Keyboard Shortcuts for Fields and Records

Key(s)	Movement in Fields and Records
Tab	Moves to the next field.
Shift+Tab	Moves to the previous field.
Home	In Navigation mode, moves to the first field of the current record. In Edit mode, moves to the beginning of the current field.
End	In Navigation mode, moves to the last field of the current record. In Edit mode, moves to the end of the current field.
Ctrl+Page Up	Moves to the current field of the previous record.

(continued)

TABLE 12-1. *continued*

Key(s)	Movement in Fields and Records
Ctrl+Page Down	Moves to the current field of the next record.
Ctrl+Up arrow	In Navigation mode, moves to the current field of the first record.
Ctrl+Down arrow	In Navigation mode, moves to the current field of the last record.
Ctrl+Home	In Navigation mode, moves to the first field of the first record.
Ctrl+End	In Navigation mode, moves to the last field of the last record.
Ctrl+Tab	If on a subform and a field is selected, moves to the next field in the main form. If the subform is the last field in tab sequence in the main form, moves to the first field in the next main record. If on a subform and a tab control is selected, cycles among the tabs. If not on a subform, moves to the next field.
Ctrl+Shift+Tab	If on a subform with a tab control, cycles among the tabs. If on a subform with no tab control, moves to the previous field in the main form. If the subform is the first field in tab sequence in the main form, moves to the last field in the previous main record. If not on a subform, moves to the previous field.
Ctrl+Shift+Home	In Navigation mode, moves to the first field in the main form.
F5	Moves to the record number box.

TABLE 12-2.   Keyboard Shortcuts for a List Box or a Combo Box

Key(s)	Action in a list box or a combo box
F4 or Alt+Down arrow	Opens a combo box or a drop-down list box.
Down arrow	Moves down one line.
Up arrow	Moves up one line.
Page Down	Moves down to next group of lines.
Page Up	Moves up to next group of lines.
Tab	Exits the box.

Adding Records and Changing Data

You'll probably design most forms so that you can insert new records, change field values, or delete records in Form view or in Datasheet view. The following sections explain procedures for adding new records and changing data.

Adding a New Record

The procedure for entering a new record varies depending on the design of the form. With a form that's been designed for data entry only, you open the form and enter data in the (usually empty) data fields. Sometimes forms of this type open with default values in the fields or with data entered by a macro or Visual Basic procedure. Another type of form displays data and also allows you to add new records. You can open the frmBooksPlain form and then choose the Data Entry command from the Records menu or click the New Record button on the toolbar to shift the form into data-entry mode, as shown in Figure 12-18. Notice that the form also provides its own Add New button that changes the form to data-entry mode when you click it.

FIGURE 12-18.

The frmBooksPlain form in data-entry mode.

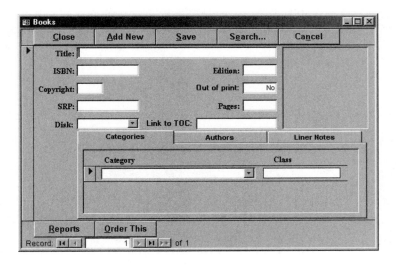

After you finish entering new records, you can choose Remove Filter/Sort from the Records menu or click the Show All button on the form (which is displayed if you used the Add New button) to return to normal data display.

There's also a "blank" row at the end of the normal data display that you can use to enter new rows. You can jump to the blank row to begin adding a new record by choosing the Go To command from the

Edit menu and then choosing New Record from the submenu, or by pressing Ctrl+plus sign. Access places the cursor in the first field when you start a new record. As soon as you begin typing, Access changes the indicator on the row selector (if your form shows the row selector) to a pencil icon to indicate that updates are in progress. Press the Tab key to move to the next field.

If you violate a field's validation rule, Access notifies you as soon as you attempt to leave the field. You must provide a correct value before you can move to another field. Press Shift+Enter in any field in the record or press the Tab key in the last field in the record to save your new record in the database. If the data you enter violates a table validation rule, Access displays an error message and does not save the record. If you want to cancel a new record, press the Esc key twice.

If you're adding a new record to a form such as frmBooksPlain, you'll encounter a special situation. You'll notice when you tab to the picture object frame control that you can't type anything in it. This is because the field in the underlying table is an ActiveX object. To enter data in this type of field in a new record, you must create the object in an application that supports ActiveX before you can store the data in Access. To do this, select the object frame control and choose the Object command from the Insert menu. Access displays the Insert Object dialog box, shown in Figure 12-19. Select the object type you want (in this case, Bitmap Image), and click OK. Access starts the application that's defined in the Windows registry as the default application for this type of data (for bitmaps, usually the Paint application).

FIGURE 12-19.

The Insert Object dialog box.

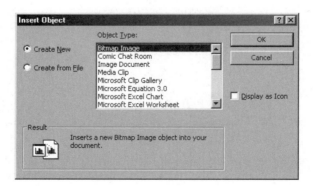

If you have an appropriate file available to copy into the ActiveX object field in Access, select the Create From File option button in the dialog box. Access changes the option list to let you enter the pathname and filename, as shown in Figure 12-20. You can click the Browse button to open the Browse dialog box, which lets you search for the file you want. After you select a file, you can select the Link check box to create an active link between the copy of the object in Access and the actual file. If you do so, whenever you change the file the linked object in Access will also change. Select the Display As Icon check box to display the Paint application icon instead of the picture in Access. (You can find an assortment of author and book cover bitmap files on the companion CD that you can use for practice.)

FIGURE 12-20.

Inserting an object from a file.

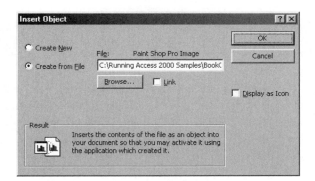

The frmBooksPlain form also includes a text box that lets you edit the hyperlink that refers to a related table of contents document. To edit the hyperlink, you can tab to or click in the empty hyperlink field (remember that if the link field contains a valid link, clicking in it activates the link!) and then choose Hyperlink from the Insert menu. (You can also right-click the link field, choose Hyperlink from the shortcut menu, and then choose Edit Hyperlink from the submenu.) Access displays the dialog box shown in Figure 12-21 on the next page, which lets you edit the link.

You can enter the descriptor in the Text To Display box at the top. I clicked the ScreenTip button to open the Set Hyperlink ScreenTip dialog you see in Figure 12-21. The ScreenTip displays when you hover over the hyperlink with your mouse pointer. You can type the document address directly into the Type The File Or Web Page Name box. If the document is in a folder relative to the current database location, you can type in just the subfolder name and filename. You can also enter a specific drive, folder, and filename; network pathname; or Internet or intranet address.

FIGURE 12-21.

The Insert Hyperlink dialog box showing a link to the table of contents document for *Build Your Own Web Site*.

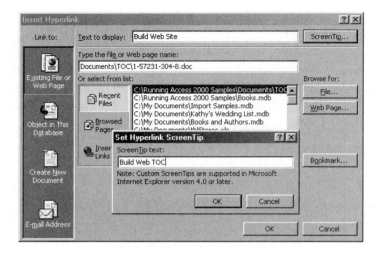

Click the Recent Files, Browsed Pages, or Inserted Links button to choose from a list of files or Internet addresses you have recently visited. Click the File or Web Page button to locate any file or Web page on your local computer or on any network computer to which you're connected.

Whether you are creating a link to an Internet site or to a file, after you have chosen a link address, you can use the Bookmark button (see Figure 12-21) to specify a location within the file or Internet site document. After you click the Bookmark button, you can click the Browse button to start the target application of the link address to search for named locations. For example, in a Microsoft Word document, Bookmarks are named locations within the document. Click OK to save your link. *See the section titled "Working with Hyperlinks" in Chapter 7, "Using Datasheets," for more details about hyperlinks.*

Try adding a new record by using the frmBooksPlain form. Open the form, choose the Go To command from the Edit menu, and choose New Record from the submenu. You should see a screen similar to the one shown earlier in Figure 12-18. You can start adding information for a book that was published in 1997. Note that the ISBN field provides an input mask to help you enter the book number in the right format. Tab to the book cover picture field, and follow the procedure discussed above to create a new picture. You can find several appropriately sized bitmap pictures of book covers on the companion CD.

> **NOTE**

As soon as you begin to enter new data in a table that has an AutoNumber field as its primary key, Access assigns a new number to that field. If you decide to cancel the new record before saving it, Access won't reuse this AutoNumber value. Access does this to ensure that multiple users sharing a database don't get the same value for a new table row. In the Microsoft Press Books database, the primary key is a text field (ISBNNumber), so it is not affected by this rule. However, both tblAuthors and tblOrders use an AutoNumber field for the primary key.

To begin adding some categories for your new book, click the Categories tab to reveal the appropriate subform. Select a category, as shown in Figure 12-22, or type a new one. Note that when you click in the subform, Access saves the book data in the main form. Access does this to ensure that it can create a link between the new row in the main form and any row you might create in the subform. (The new book number has to be saved in the main form before you can create related book category records in the subform.) When you press Tab in the last field or press Shift+Enter, Access adds the new category for you. Access also inserts the information required to link the record in the main form and the new record in the subform. Here, Access adds the book ISBN you entered to the new record in the tblBookCategories table. You can click the Authors tab to specify one or more authors for this book. If the category or author you specify in the subform isn't

FIGURE 12-22.
Adding a new record in the frmBooksPlain form.

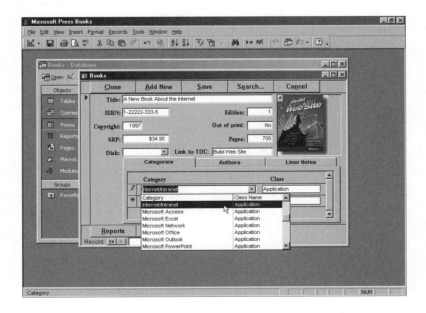

already listed in the database, you will be prompted to create a new record for the item in the appropriate table.

Changing and Deleting Data

If your form permits updates, you can easily change or delete existing data in the underlying table or query. If the form is designed to be used in Datasheet view, you can use the same techniques you learned in Chapter 7, "Using Datasheets," to work with your data.

In Form view, your data might appear in one of several formats. If the form is designed to be a single form, you can see the data for only one record at a time. If the form is designed as a continuous form, you might be able to see data for more than one record at a time.

As with datasheets, you must select a field in the form in order to change the data in the field. To select a field, either tab to the field or click in the field with the mouse. (Remember, if the field contains a hyperlink, clicking in it will activate the link. To edit a hyperlink, either tab to the field or right-click the field to open the shortcut menu from which you can choose commands to edit the hyperlink.) After you select a field, you can change the data in it by using the same techniques you used for working with data in a datasheet. You can type over individual characters, replace a sequence of characters, or copy and paste data from one field to another.

You might find that you can't tab to or select some fields in a form. When you design a form, you can set the properties of the controls on the form so that a user can't select the control. These properties prevent users from changing fields that you don't want updated, such as calculated values or fields from the "one" side of a query. You can also set the tab order to control the sequence of field selection when you use Tab or Shift+Tab to move around on the form. *See Chapter 14, "Customizing Forms," for details.*

Deleting a record in a single form or in a continuous form is different from deleting a record in a datasheet. First, you must select the record as you would select a record in a datasheet. If the form is designed with row selectors, simply click the row selector to select the record. If the form does not have row selectors, choose the Select Record command from the Edit menu. To delete a selected record, press the Delete key or choose the Delete command from the Edit menu. You can also choose the Delete Record command from the Edit menu to delete the current record without first having to select it.

Searching for and Sorting Data

When you use forms to display and edit your data, you can search for data or sort it in a new order in much the same way that you search for and sort data in datasheets. *See Chapter 7, "Using Datasheets."* The following sections show you how to use some of the form filter features to search for data in a form or use the Quick Sort commands to reorder your data.

Performing a Simple Search

You can use Microsoft Access's Find feature in a form just as you would in a datasheet. First select the field, and then choose the Find command from the Edit menu or click the Find button on the toolbar to open the Find dialog box that you saw in Figure 7-28 in Chapter 7. You can enter search criteria exactly as you would for a datasheet. Note that in a form you can also perform a search on any control that you can select, including controls that display calculated values.

Performing a Quick Sort on a Form Field

As you can with a datasheet, you can select just about any control that contains data from the underlying recordset and click the Sort Ascending or Sort Descending button on the toolbar to reorder the records you see, based on the selected field. You can't quick-sort fields in a subform. If you want to perform a quick sort, open the frmBooksPlain form, click in the SRP (Suggested Retail Price) field in the form, and then click the Sort Descending button on the toolbar. The book with the highest price (the largest number) is displayed first.

Adding a Filter to a Form

One of Access's most powerful features is its ability to further restrict or sort the information displayed in the form without you having to create a new query. This restriction is accomplished with a filter that you define while you're using the form. When you apply the filter, you see only the data that matches the criteria you entered.

As with datasheets, you can define a filter using Filter By Selection, Filter By Form, or the Advanced Filter definition facility. Open the frmBooksPlain form and click the Filter By Form button on the toolbar. Access adds features to the form to let you enter filter criteria, as shown in Figure 12-23 on the next page. In this example, we're looking for all books that cost less than $40, come with a companion CD-ROM, and are not out of print. You'll see that for each field Access provides a drop-down list that contains all the values for that field currently in the database. If your database contains many thousands of rows, Access might not show the list if the field has more than several hundred unique values—it would take an unacceptably long time to retrieve all the lists. You can also type in your own criteria, as shown in the SRP field in Figure 12-23.

FIGURE 12-23.

The Filter window for the frmBooksPlain form.

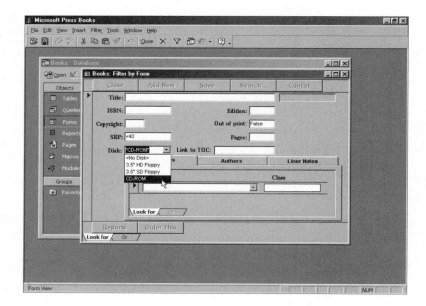

As you can with datasheets, you can enter one set of criteria and then click an "Or" tab to enter additional criteria. If you don't like some of the criteria you've entered, click the Clear Grid button on the toolbar to start over. Click the Apply Filter button on the toolbar to filter your records. Click the Close button on the toolbar to exit the Filter window without applying the new filter. Note that if you specify criteria on a subform, Access applies the filter only for records related to the record currently displayed on the main form. For example, you can't create a filter in Categories for books about the Internet and then expect to see only books about the Internet—you'll see only categories for the current book that match the value "Internet".

To turn off the filter, click the Remove Filter button on the toolbar or choose the Remove Filter/Sort command from the Records menu. To see the filter definition, choose Filter from the Records menu and then choose Advanced Filter/Sort from the submenu. After you apply the filter shown in Figure 12-23 and do an ascending quick sort on the

ISBNNumber field, the Advanced Filter window should look something like that shown in Figure 12-24.

FIGURE 12-24.

The Advanced Filter window for the frmBooksPlain form with criteria previously entered using Filter By Form.

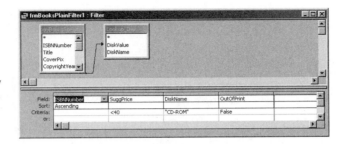

> **NOTE**
>
> If you use one of the Quick Sort buttons, you'll discover that quick sort uses the form's filter definition to create the sorting criteria. For example, if you do a quick sort to arrange book titles in descending order, you'll find the Title field in the form filter with the Sort row set to Descending when you choose Advanced Filter/Sort from the submenu of the Filter command on the Records menu.

If you often use the same filter with your form, you can save the filter as a query and give it a name. Open the Advanced Filter/Sort window and create the filter. Choose the Save As Query command from the File menu and type in a name for the query when Access prompts you. You can also load an existing query definition to use as a filter. Open the Advanced Filter/Sort window, and choose the Load From Query command from the File menu. Access presents a list of valid select queries (those that are based on the same table or tables as the form you're using).

Printing Forms

You can use a form to print information from a table. When you design the form, you can specify different header and footer information for the printed version. You can also specify which controls are visible. For example, you might define some gridlines that are visible on the printed form but are not displayed on the screen.

An interesting form to print in the Microsoft Press Books database is the frmAuthorSummary form. Open the form, and then click the Print Preview button on the toolbar or choose the Print Preview command from the File menu. You probably won't be able to read any of the data unless you have a large screen. Click the Zoom button and scroll to the top of the first page. You should see a screen that looks like the one shown in Figure 12-25. Notice that the form footer that you saw earlier in Figure 12-4 does not appear in the printed version. In fact, this form has one set of headers and footers designed for printing and another set for viewing the form on the screen.

FIGURE 12-25.

The window for the frmAuthorSummary form in Print Preview.

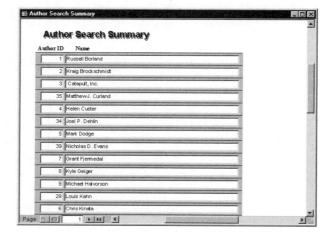

You can use the scroll bars to move around on the page. Use the page number box in the lower left corner of the form in the same way that you use the record number box on a form or in a datasheet. Click the Zoom button again to see the entire page on the screen.

Choose Page Setup from the File menu. Access displays the Page Setup dialog box, which you can use to customize the way the form prints. Click the Margins tab to set top, bottom, left, and right margins. Click the Page tab (shown in Figure 12-26) to select Portrait or Landscape print mode, the paper size and source, and the printer. Access will store these specifications with the definition of your form.

Click the Columns tab of the Page Setup dialog box to see additional options, as shown in Figure 12-27. If the data in your form appears in a fairly narrow width, you can ask Access to stack the data from the form either horizontally or vertically across the page.

You should now have a good understanding of how forms work and of many design elements that you can include when you build forms. Now, on to the fun part—building your first form in the next chapter.

FIGURE 12-26.

The Page tab of the Page Setup dialog box for forms.

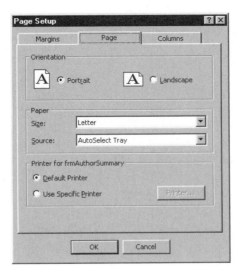

FIGURE 12-27.

The Columns tab of the Page Setup dialog box for forms.

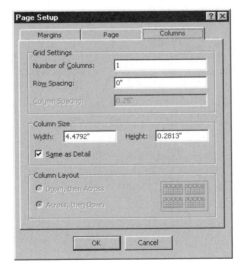

Building Forms

From the perspective of daily use, forms are the most important objects you'll build in your Microsoft Access application. Forms are what users see and work with every time they run the application. This chapter shows you how to design and build forms in Access. You'll learn how to work with a Form window in Design view to build a basic form based on a single table, and you'll learn how to use an Access Form Wizard to simplify the form-creation process. The last section of this chapter, "Simplifying Data Input with a Form," shows you how to use some of the special form controls to simplify data entry on your forms.

Forms and Object-Oriented Programming

Microsoft Access was not designed to be a full object-oriented programming environment, yet it has many characteristics found in object-oriented application development systems. Before you dive into building forms, it's useful to examine how Access implements objects and actions, particularly if you come from the world of procedural application development.

In classic procedural application development, the data you need for the application is distinct from the programs you write to work with the data and from the results produced by your programs. Each program works with the data independently and generally has little structural connection with other programs in the system. For example, an order-entry program accepts input from a clerk and then writes the order to data files. Later, a billing program processes the orders and prints invoices. Another characteristic of procedural systems is that events must occur in a specific order and cannot be executed out of sequence. A procedural system has difficulty looking up supplier or price information while in the middle of processing an order.

In an object-oriented system, however, all objects are defined in terms of a subject and an action performed on that subject. Objects can contain other objects as subjects. When an object defines a new action on another object, it inherits the attributes and properties of the other object and expands on the object's definition. In Access, queries define actions on tables, and the queries then become new logical tables known as *recordsets*. You can base a query on another query with the same effect. Queries inherit the integrity and formatting rules defined for the tables. Forms further define actions on tables or queries, and the fields you include in forms initially inherit the underlying properties, such as formatting and validation rules, of the fields in the source tables or queries. You can define different formatting or more restrictive rules, but you cannot override the rules defined for the tables.

Within an Access database, you can interrelate application objects and data. For example, you can set startup properties or define an initial macro (called *Autoexec*) that prepares your application to run. As part of the application startup, you will usually open a switchboard form. The switchboard form might act on some of the data in the database, or it might offer controls that open other forms, print reports, or close the application.

? SEE ALSO

For more information about startup properties and the *Autoexec* macro, see Chapter 24, "The Finishing Touches."

Figure 13-1 shows the conceptual architecture of an Access form. In addition to operating on tables or queries in a database, forms can contain other forms, called *subforms*. These subforms can, in turn, define actions on other tables, queries, or forms, and they can trigger additional macro actions or Visual Basic procedures. As you'll learn when you read about advanced form design, macro actions and Visual Basic procedures can be triggered in many ways. The most obvious way to trigger an action is by clicking a command button on a form. But you can also define macros or Visual Basic procedures that execute when an event occurs, such as clicking in a field, changing the data in a field, pressing a key, adding or deleting a row, or simply moving to a new row in the underlying table or query.

FIGURE 13-1.

The conceptual architecture of an Access form.

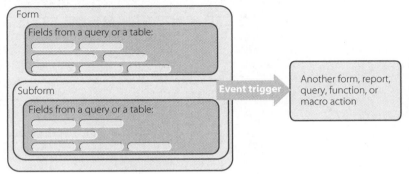

In Chapter 23, "Automating Your Application with Visual Basic," you'll learn how several of the more complex forms in the Microsoft Press Books and Entertainment Scheduling sample databases are automated with Visual Basic. Figure 13-2 on the next page shows a few of the automated processes for the frmContracts form in the Entertainment Scheduling database. For example, printing the contract currently displayed in the form is triggered by using a command button.

When you print the contract, a Visual Basic procedure marks the contract "Active." If the contract is issued by RM Productions (the first agent code is RMP), another Visual Basic procedure generates one payment record in the tblCommissions table for each week of the contract with the appropriate commission due. Clicking the Payments button opens a form for recording payments for the current contract. If you change the group name in the contract, other procedures copy the group member information. (This application copies the group member information because the group membership can change over time; each contract records the band members at the time the contract is issued.) When you change the start or end date of a contract, a Visual Basic procedure automatically calculates the contract's length, in weeks.

Object-oriented systems are not restricted to a specific sequence of events. So a user entering a contract in Access can minimize the contract form and start a search in a groups table for musical style or start a search in a clubs table without first having to finalize the contract. You could provide a simpler way for the user to do this in your application by means of a command button on the contract form.

FIGURE 13-2.

Some of the automated processes for the frmContracts form.

Changing the group ID copies the new group data to the contract.

Clicking the Print button prints the contract.

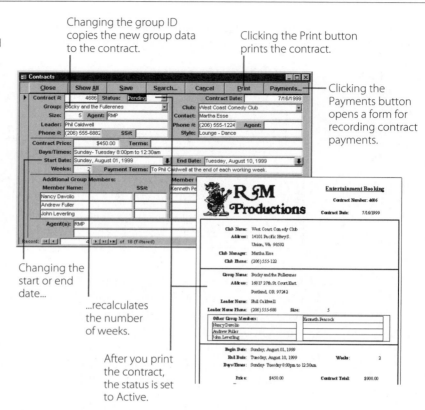

Clicking the Payments button opens a form for recording contract payments.

Changing the start or end date...

...recalculates the number of weeks.

After you print the contract, the status is set to Active.

Starting from Scratch—A Simple Input Form

To start, you'll create a simple form that accepts and displays data in the tblClubs table in the Entertainment Scheduling database. Later, you'll create a form for the Microsoft Press Books database by using an Access Form Wizard.

Building a New Form with Design Tools

To begin building a new form, open your database. In the Database window, select the table or query that you want to use for the form. (To follow this example, select the tblClubs table in the Entertainment Scheduling database.) Select New Form from the New Object toolbar button's drop-down list, or choose Form from the Insert menu. Access opens the New Form dialog box, shown in Figure 13-3.

FIGURE 13-3.

The New Form dialog box.

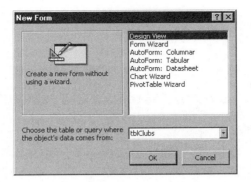

In the combo box in the lower part of the dialog box, Access displays the name of the table or query that you selected in the Database window. If you want to select a different table or query, you can open the combo box's drop-down list to see all the tables and queries in your database. You'll build this first form without the aid of a Form Wizard so that you'll understand the variety of components that go into form design.

Select Design View in the dialog box, and then click OK. Access opens the Form window in Design view and with it a toolbox that contains several design tools, as shown in Figure 13-4 on the next page. (You might not see all the windows shown in Figure 13-4.) If you've already experimented with forms in Design view and have moved some of the windows around, Access opens them where you last placed them on the screen.

Access starts with a form that has only a Detail section (a gray grid). You can click the edge of the Detail section and then drag the edge to make the section larger or smaller. You can remove the grid dots from the Detail section by choosing the Grid command from the View menu. If you want to add headers or footers to the form, choose the Form Header/Footer command from the View menu.

The Detail section starts out at 5 inches (12.7 centimeters) wide by 2 inches (5.08 centimeters) high. The measurement gradations on the rulers are relative to the size and resolution of your screen. On a standard (640×480) VGA screen, a pop-up form measuring approximately 6.5 inches wide by 5 inches high will fill the full screen. By default, Access sets the grid at 24 dots per inch horizontally and 24 dots per inch vertically. You can change the density of the grid dots by altering the Grid X and Grid Y properties on the form's property sheet.

FIGURE 13-4.

A Form window in Design view with its design tools.

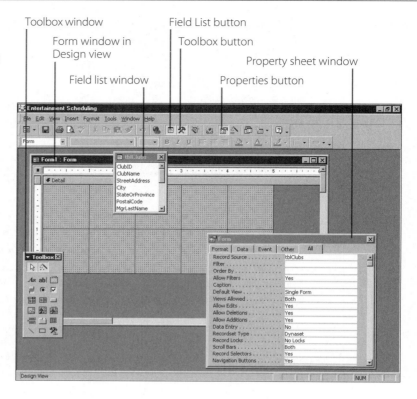

Toolbox window

Form window in Design view

Field list window

Field List button

Toolbox button

Properties button

Property sheet window

The Grid X and Grid Y property settings determine the intervals per unit of measurement in the grid. You can enter a number from 1 (coarsest) through 64 (finest). You set the unit of measure (U.S. or metric) by default when you select a country from the drop-down list on the Regional Settings tab of the Regional Settings Properties dialog box. (You open this dialog box by double-clicking the Regional Settings icon in the Windows Control Panel.)

For example, if your unit of measurement is inches and you specify a Grid X setting of 10, Access divides the grid horizontally into 0.1-inch increments. When your measurement is in inches and you set the Grid X and Grid Y values to 24 or less, Access displays the grid dots on the grid. In centimeters, you can see the grid dots when you specify a setting of 9 or less. If you set a finer grid, Access won't display the grid dots but you can still use the grid to line up controls. Access always displays grid lines at 1-inch intervals (U.S.) or 1-centimeter intervals (metric), even when you set fine Grid X or Grid Y values.

The following sections describe some of the tools you can use to design a form.

The Toolbox

The toolbox, shown in Figure 13-5, is the "command center" of form design. You can move the toolbox by dragging its title bar, and you can change the shape of the toolbox by dragging its sides or corners. You can even move the toolbox to the top of the workspace and "dock" it as a toolbar. You can close the toolbox by clicking the Close button in the upper right corner of the toolbox, by choosing the Toolbox command from the View menu, or by clicking the Toolbox button on the toolbar.

 TIP

If you don't see the toolbox displayed with the Form window in Design view, choose the Toolbox command from the View menu or click the Toolbox button on the toolbar.

FIGURE 13-5.

The toolbox.

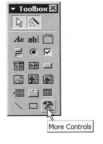

The toolbox contains buttons for all the controls you can use on a form. It also contains a button (named More Controls) that gives you access to all the ActiveX controls (for example, the calendar control that comes with Access) that you have installed on your system. To place a particular control on a form, you click the control's button in the toolbox. When you move the mouse pointer over the form, the mouse pointer turns into an icon that represents the tool you selected. Position the mouse pointer where you want to place the control, and press the left mouse button to place the control on the form. If you want to size the control as you place it, drag the mouse pointer to make the control the size you want. (You can also size a control after it's placed by dragging the sizing handles at its sides or corners.)

Left to right, top to bottom, the tools in the toolbox are described in Table 13-1 on the next page.

TABLE 13-1. Toolbox Tools

Tool	Description
	Select Objects tool. This is the default tool. Use this tool to select, size, move, and edit existing controls.
	Control Wizards button. Click this button to activate the Control Wizards. When this button appears pressed, a Control Wizard will help you enter control properties whenever you create a new option group, combo box, list box, or command button.
	Label tool. Use this tool to create label controls that contain fixed text. By default, most controls have a label control attached. You can use this tool to create stand-alone labels for headings and for instructions on your form.
	Text Box tool. Use this tool to create text box controls for displaying text, numbers, dates, times, and memo fields. You can bind a text box to one of the fields in an underlying table or query. If you allow a text box that is bound to a field to be updated, you can change the value in the field in the underlying table or query by entering a new value in the text box. You can also use a text box to display calculated values.
	Option Group tool. Use this tool to create option group controls that contain one or more toggle buttons, option buttons, or check boxes. *(See the description of these controls below.)* You can assign a separate numeric value to each button or check box that you include in the group. When you have more than one button or check box in a group, you can select only one button or check box at a time, and the value assigned to that button or check box becomes the value for the option group. You can select one of the buttons or check boxes in the group as the default value for the group. If you bind the option group to a field in the underlying query or table, you can set a new value in the field by selecting a button or a check box in the group.
	Toggle Button tool. Use this tool to create a toggle button control that holds an on/off, true/false, or yes/no value. When you click a toggle button, its value becomes –1 (to represent on, true, or yes) and the button appears pressed. Click the button again, and its value becomes 0 (to represent off, false, or no). You can include a toggle button in an option group and assign the button a unique numeric value. If you create a group with multiple controls, selecting a new toggle button clears any previously selected toggle button, option button, or check box in that group. If you bind the toggle button to a field in the underlying table or query, you can toggle the field's value by clicking the toggle button.

TABLE 13-1. *continued*

Tool	Description
	Option Button tool. Use this tool to create an option button control (sometimes called a *radio button control*) that holds an on/off, true/false, or yes/no value. When you click an option button, its value becomes –1 (to represent on, true, or yes) and a filled circle appears in the center of the button. Click the button again, and its value becomes 0 (to represent off, false, or no). You can include an option button in an option group and assign the button a unique numeric value. If you create a group with multiple controls, selecting a new option button clears any previously selected toggle button, option button, or check box in that group. If you bind the option button to a field in the underlying table or query, you can toggle the field's value by clicking the option button.
	Check Box tool. Use this tool to create a check box control that holds an on/off, true/false, or yes/no value. When you click a check box, its value becomes –1 (to represent on, true, or yes) and a check mark appears in the box. Click the check box again, and its value becomes 0 (to represent off, false, or no) and the check mark disappears from the box. You can include a check box in an option group and assign the check box a unique numeric value. If you create a group with multiple controls, selecting a new check box clears any previously selected toggle button, option button, or check box in that group. If you bind the check box to a field in the underlying table or query, you can toggle the field's value by clicking the check box.
	Combo Box tool. Use this tool to create a combo box control that contains a list of potential values for the control and an editable text box. To create the list, you can enter values for the Row Source property of the combo box. You can also specify a table or a query as the source of the values in the list. Access displays the currently selected value in the text box. When you click the down arrow to the right of the combo box, Access displays the values in the list. Select a new value in the list to reset the value in the control. If the combo box is bound to a field in the underlying table or query, you can change the value in the field by selecting a new value in the list. You can bind multiple columns to the list, and you can hide one or more of the columns in the list by setting a column's list width to 0. You can bind the actual value in the control to a hidden column. When a multiple-column list is closed, Access displays the value in the first column whose width is greater than 0. Access displays all nonzero-width columns when you open the list.

(continued)

TABLE 13-1. *continued*

Tool	Description
	List Box tool. Use this tool to create a list box control that contains a list of potential values for the control. To create the list, you can enter the values in the Row Source property of the list box. You can also specify a table or a query as the source of the values in the list. List boxes are always open, and Access highlights the currently selected value in the list box. You select a new value in the list to reset the value in the control. If the list box is bound to a field in the underlying table or query, you can change the value in the field by selecting a new value in the list. You can bind multiple columns to the list, and you can hide one or more of the columns in the list by setting a column's list width to 0. You can bind the actual value in the control to a hidden column. Access displays all nonzero-width columns that fit within the defined width of the control.
	Command Button tool. Use this tool to create a command button control that can activate a macro or a Visual Basic procedure.
	Image tool. Use this tool to place a static picture on your form. You cannot edit the picture on the form, but Access stores it in a format that is very efficient for application speed and size. If you want to use a picture as the entire background of your form, you can set the form's Picture property.
	Unbound Object Frame tool. Use this tool to add an object from another application that supports object linking and embedding. The object becomes part of your form, not part of the data from the underlying table or query. You can add pictures, sounds, graphs, or slides to enhance your form.
	Bound Object Frame tool. Use this tool to make available on your form an ActiveX object (OLE Object data type) from the underlying data. Access can display most pictures and graphs directly on a form. For other objects, Access displays the icon for the application in which the object was created. For example, if the object is a sound object created in Sound Recorder, you'll see a speaker icon on your form.
	Page Break tool. Use this tool to add a page break between the pages of a multiple-page form.
	Tab Control tool. Use this tool to create a series of tab pages on your form. Each page can contain a number of other controls to display information. The Tab Control works much like

TABLE 13-1. *continued*

Tool	Description
	many of the option dialog or property sheet windows in Access—when a user clicks a different tab, Access displays the controls contained on that tab. *See Chapter 15, "Advanced Form Design," for details about using the Tab Control tool.*
	Subform/Subreport tool. Use this tool to embed another form in the current form. You can use the subform to show data from a table or a query that is related to the data in the main form. Access maintains the link between the two forms for you.
	Line tool. Use this tool to add lines to a form to enhance its appearance.
	Rectangle tool. Use this tool to add filled or empty rectangles to a form to enhance its appearance.
	More Controls button. Click this button to open a dialog box showing all the ActiveX controls you have installed on your system. Not all ActiveX controls work with Microsoft Access.

TIP

When you select a tool other than the Select Objects tool, that tool becomes deselected after you use it to place a control on your form. If you plan to create several controls using the same tool—for example, a series of check boxes in an option group—double-click the control button in the toolbox to "lock" it. You can unlock it by clicking any other tool button (including the Select Objects tool).

The Field List

SEE ALSO

For more information about using controls on forms, see Chapter 14, "Customizing Forms," and Chapter 15, "Advanced Form Design."

Use the field list in conjunction with the toolbox to place bound controls (controls linked to fields in a table or a query) on your form. You can open the field list by clicking the Field List button on the toolbar or by choosing the Field List command from the View menu. Access displays the name of the underlying table or query in the field list title bar, as shown in Figure 13-6 on the next page. You can drag the edges of the window to resize the field list so that you can see any long field names. You can drag the title bar to move the window out of the way. Use the scroll bar along the right side of the window to move through the list of available field names.

FIGURE 13-6.

A field list showing the
names of the fields in
the underlying table
or query.

To use the field list to place a bound control on a form, first select the
type of control you want in the toolbox. (If no control tool is selected,
the default type is the text box control.) Then drag the field you want
from the field list and drop it into position on the form. If you select a
control that's inappropriate for the data type of the field, Access selects
the default control for the data type. For example, if you select anything
but the Bound Object Frame tool when placing an ActiveX object field
(OLE Object data type) on a form, Access creates a bound object frame
control for you anyway. If you try to drag any field using the subform/
subreport, unbound object frame, line, rectangle, or page break control,
Access creates a text box control or bound object frame control instead.
If you drag a field from the field list without choosing a control, Access
uses either the display control you defined for the field in the table definition or a control appropriate for the field data type.

The Property Sheet

The form, each section of the form (header, detail, footer), and each
control on the form has a list of properties associated with it, and you
set these properties using a property sheet. The kinds of properties you
can specify vary depending on the object. To open the property sheet
for an object, select the object and then click the Properties button on
the toolbar or choose the Properties command from the View menu.
Access opens a window similar to the one shown in Figure 13-7.

You can drag the title bar to move the property sheet window around
on your screen. You can also drag the edges of the window to resize it
so that you can see more of the property settings. Because a form has
more than 70 properties that you can set and because many controls
have more than 30 properties, Access provides tabs at the top of the
property sheet so that you can choose to display all properties (the
default) or to display only format properties, data properties, event
properties, or other properties. A form property sheet displaying only
the data properties is shown in Figure 13-8.

FIGURE 13-7.

The property sheet for a form.

FIGURE 13-8.

A form property sheet displaying only the data properties.

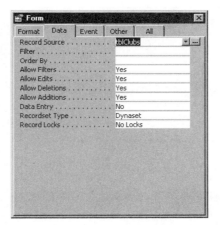

When you click in a property box that provides a list of valid values, a down arrow button appears on the right side of the property box. Click this button to see a drop-down list of the values. For properties that can have a very long value setting, you can press Shift+F2 to open a Zoom window. The Zoom window provides an expanded text box for entering or viewing an entry.

Even better than the Zoom window are the builders that help you create property settings for properties that can accept a complex expression, a query definition, or code (a macro or a Visual Basic procedure) to respond to an event. When a builder is available for a property setting, Access displays a small button with an ellipsis (…) next to the property box when you select the property; this is the Build button. If you click the Build button, Access responds with the appropriate builder dialog boxes. For example, display the property sheet for the form, click the Data tab to display the form's data properties, select the Record Source property, and then click the Build button next to Record Source to start the Query Builder. Access asks whether you want to build a new query based on the table that is currently the source for this form. If you click Yes, Access opens a new Query window in Design view with the tblClubs field list displayed in the upper part of the window, as shown in Figure 13-9.

FIGURE 13-9.

Using the Query Builder to create a query for the form's Record Source property.

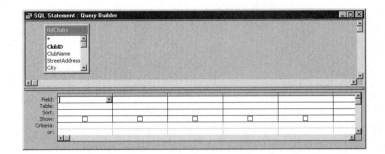

Suppose that you want to base this form on a query that sorts the clubs in ascending order by club name. You'll need all the fields in the tblClubs table for this form, so select them and drag them to the design grid. For ClubName, specify Ascending as the sorting order.

Your result should look like the window shown in Figure 13-10.

FIGURE 13-10.

Building a query for the Record Source property of the form.

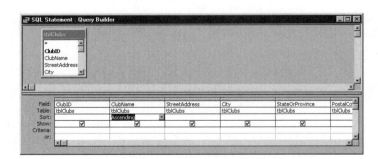

TIP

To easily select all the fields from a field list displayed in the upper part of the Query window, double-click the title bar of the field list. Access highlights all the fields for you. Then simply click any of them and drag the fields as a group to the design grid.

If you close the Query window at this point, Access asks whether you want to update the property. If you click Yes, Access stores the SQL text for the query in the Record Source property box. A better approach is to save the query and give it a name, such as *qryClubsSortedByName,* so do that now. Then, when you close the query, Access asks whether you want to save the query and update the property. If you click Yes, Access places the name of the query (rather than the SQL text) in the property sheet.

Building a Simple Input Form for the tblClubs Table

Now let's create a simple input form for the tblClubs table in the Entertainment Scheduling database. If you've followed along to this point, you should have a blank form based on the qryClubsSortedByName query that you created using the Query Builder. If you haven't followed along, switch to the Database window, open the Tables list, select the tblClubs table, and select New Form from the New Object toolbar button's drop-down list (or choose Form from the Insert menu).

Select the Design View option in the New Form dialog box. You'll see the Form window in Design view and a set of design tools, as shown earlier in Figure 13-4. If necessary, open the toolbox, field list, and property sheet by clicking the appropriate buttons on the toolbar. Select the Record Source property, and then click the Build button and follow the procedures discussed in the previous sections, whose results are shown in Figures 13-9 and 13-10; this will create the query you need and make it the source for the form.

In the blank form for the qryClubsSortedByName query, drag the bottom of the Detail section downward to make some room to work. Because you'll be using default text boxes, you don't need to select a tool from the toolbox. If you'd like to practice, though, double-click the Text Box tool in the toolbox before dragging fields from the field list. In this way, you can drag fields one at a time to the Detail section of the form. Follow this procedure to drag each of the fields between the ClubID field and the ClubFaxNumber field from the field list to the Detail section. Your form should now look something like the one shown in Figure 13-11 on the next page.

FIGURE 13-11.

The text box controls that are created on a form when you drag fields from the qryClubsSortedByName field list.

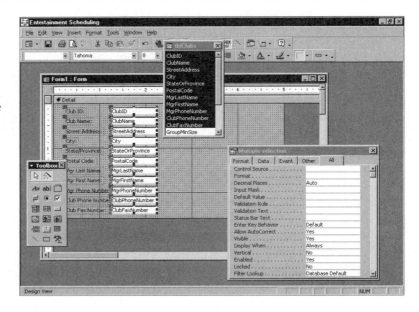

 TIP

A quick way to place several successive fields on a form is to click the first field you want in the field list, scroll down until you see the last field you want, and then hold down the Shift key while you click the last field. This procedure selects all the fields between the first and last fields you selected. You can also double-click the title bar of the field list to select all the fields in the field list. Holding down the Ctrl key and clicking several noncontiguous fields works too. Click any of the highlighted fields and drag the fields as a group to the Detail section of the form.

When you position the field icon that you've dragged from the field list, the upper left corner of the new text box will be at the position of the mouse pointer when you release the mouse button. For default text boxes, Access attaches a label that displays the field's Caption property (or its field name, if you didn't specify a Caption property when you designed the field), 1 inch to the left of the text box. You should drop each text box about 1.25 inches (3 centimeters) from the left edge of the Detail section to leave room to the left of the text box for Access to place the control labels. If you don't leave room, the text boxes will overlap the labels. Even if you do leave room, if a caption is too long to fit in the 1-inch space between the default label and the default text box (for example, *Club Phone Number* in Figure 13-11), the text box will overlap the label.

IV

Using Forms

In the example shown in Figure 13-11, the property sheet indicates that you have selected multiple controls. (In this case, I dragged all the selected fields to the Detail section at one time.) Whenever you select multiple controls on a form in Design view, Access displays the properties that are common to all the controls you selected. If you change a property in the property sheet while multiple controls are selected, Access makes the change to all of the selected controls.

Moving and Sizing Controls

By default, Access creates text boxes that are 1 inch wide. For some of the fields, 1 inch is larger than necessary to display the field value—especially if you are using the default 8-point font size. For other fields, the text box isn't large enough. You probably also want to adjust the location of some of the controls.

To change a control's size or location, you usually have to select the control first. Be sure that the Select Objects tool is selected in the toolbox. Click the control you want to resize or move, and moving and sizing handles appear around the control. The handles are small boxes that appear at each corner of the control—except at the upper left corner, where the larger handle indicates that it cannot be used for sizing. In Figure 13-11, handles appear around all the text boxes because they are all selected. To select just one control, click anywhere in the blank area of the form; this changes the selection to the Detail section. Then click the control you want. If the control is wide enough or high enough, Access provides additional handles at the midpoints of the edges of the control.

To change the size of a control, you can use the sizing handles on the edges, in either of the lower corners, or in the upper right corner of the control. When you place the mouse pointer over one of these sizing handles, the pointer turns into a double arrow, as shown in Figure 13-12. With the double-arrow pointer, drag the handle to resize the control. You can practice on the form by shortening the ClubID text box so that it's 0.5 inch long. The name and address fields need to be stretched until they are each about 1.75 inches long. You might also want to adjust the state or province, postal code, and phone number fields.

FIGURE 13-12.
You can drag a corner handle of a selected control to change the control's width or height or both.

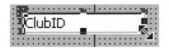

To move a control that is not currently selected, click the control and drag it to a new location. After you select a control, you can move it by placing your mouse pointer anywhere between the handles along the edge of the control. When you do this, the mouse pointer turns into an open hand, as shown in Figure 13-13, and you can then drag the control to a new location. Access displays an outline of the control as you move the control to help you position it correctly. When a control has an attached label, moving either the control or the label in this way moves both of them.

FIGURE 13-13.

You can drag the edge of a selected control to move the control.

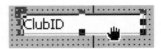

You can position a control and its attached label independently by dragging the larger handle in the upper left corner of the control or label. When you position the mouse pointer over this handle, the pointer turns into a hand with a pointing finger, as shown in Figure 13-14. Drag the control to a new location relative to its label.

FIGURE 13-14.

You can drag the large handle of a selected control to move the control independently of its label.

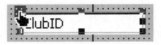

You can delete a label from a control by selecting the label and pressing the Delete key. If you want to create a label that is independent of a control, you can use the Label tool. If you inadvertently delete a label from a control and you've made other changes so that you can no longer undo the deletion, you can attach a new label by doing the following.

1 Use the Label tool to create a new unattached label.

2 Select the label, and then choose Cut from the Edit menu to move the label to the Clipboard.

3 Select the control to which you want to attach the label, and then choose Paste from the Edit menu.

The Formatting Toolbar

The Formatting toolbar, shown in Figure 13-15, provides a quick and easy way to alter the appearance of a control by allowing you to click buttons rather than set properties. This toolbar is also handy for setting background colors for sections of the form. Table 13-2 describes each of the toolbar buttons.

FIGURE 13-15.

The Formatting toolbar.

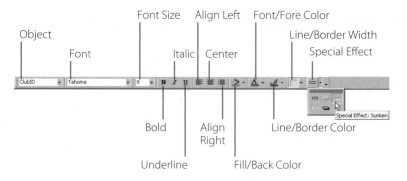

TABLE 13-2. **Formatting Toolbar**

Button	Description
Object	Use to select a specific object on your form. This is particularly handy if you stack multiple controls on top of each other.
Font	Use to set the font for labels, text boxes, command buttons, toggle buttons, combo boxes, and list boxes.
Font Size	Use to set font size.
Bold	Click to set font style to bold.
Italic	Click to set font style to italic.
Underline	Click to underline text.
Align Left	Click to left-align text.
Center	Click to center text.
Align Right	Click to right-align text.
Fill/Back Color	Use to set the background color of the control or form area. You can also set the background color to transparent.
Font/Fore Color	Use to set the foreground color of the control.
Line/Border Color	Use to set the border color of the control. You can also set the border color to transparent.
Line/Border Width	Use to set the border width from hairline to 6 points wide.
Special Effect	(Shown with options opened.) Use to set the look of the control to flat, raised, sunken, etched, shadowed, or chiseled.

IV

Using Forms

> NOTE

You can select only one of the alignment buttons—Align Left, Align Right, or Center—at a time. If you do not click a button, alignment is set to General— text data aligns left and numeric data aligns right. If you are working on a low- resolution screen and the Align Right button is not available, you can right-align text by setting the Text Align property in the property sheet. On higher resolution screens or when you undock the Formatting toolbar, Access makes the Align Right toolbar button available.

Depending on the object you select, some of the Formatting toolbar options might not be available. For example, you can't set text color on a bound object frame control, nor can you set fill or border colors on a toggle button because these areas are always set to gray for this kind of control. If you have the property sheet open and you scroll through it so that you can see the properties the Formatting toolbar sets, you can watch the settings in the property sheet change as you click different options on the toolbar.

Setting Text Box Properties

The next thing you might want to do is change some of the text box properties. Figure 13-16 shows the first 53 properties for the ClubID control. (The remaining properties are all Event properties. *See Chapter 18, "Advanced Report Design," for details.*) Because the ClubID field in the Entertainment Scheduling database is an AutoNumber field, which a user cannot change, you should change the properties of this control to prevent it from being selected on the form. To prevent the selection of a control, set the control's Enabled property to No. Because Access shades a control if it isn't enabled and isn't locked, you should set the Locked property to Yes to indicate that you won't be updating this control. The control will not be shaded, and you will not be able to tab to it or select it on the form in Form view.

If you specify a Format, Decimal Places, or Input Mask property set- ting when you define a field in a table, Access copies these settings to any text box that is bound to the field. Any data you enter using the form must conform to the field validation rule defined in the table; however, you can define a more restrictive rule for this form. New rows inherit default values from the table unless you provide a differ- ent default value in the property sheet. The Status Bar Text property derives its value from the Description property setting you entered for the field in the table.

FIGURE 13-16.

The first 53 properties for the ClubID text box control.

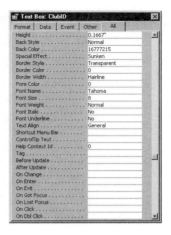

Toward the end of the list in Figure 13-16, you can see properties labeled Before Update and After Update and several properties beginning with the word On. If you scroll beyond this point or click the Event tab, you'll see all of the properties you can set to respond to events in this text box. By entering macro names as values here, you can make certain events trigger certain actions. *See Chapter 20, "Adding Power with Macros."* You can also reference Visual Basic procedures that are stored separately in modules or locally with this form. *See Chapter 22, "Visual Basic Fundamentals," and Chapter 23, "Automating Your Application with Visual Basic."* Other properties in this property sheet can be set to customize a form. *See Chapter 14, "Customizing Forms."*

Setting Label Properties

You can also set separate properties for the labels attached to controls. Click the label for ClubID to see the property sheet shown in Figure 13-17 on the next page. Access copies the Caption property from the field in the underlying table to the Caption property in the associated control label. Notice that in Figure 13-17, the caption has been changed from *ClubID* (the field name) to *Club ID:* (which includes a space and a colon for readability).

You also can correct the caption inside a label by selecting the label, moving the mouse pointer inside the label until the pointer changes into an I-beam shape, and then clicking to set the insertion point inside the label text. You can delete unwanted characters, and you can type in new characters. When you finish correcting a label caption, you might find that the control is either too large or too small to adequately display the new name. You can change settings using the

FIGURE 13-17.

The property sheet for the ClubID label control.

property sheet to adjust the size of a label, or you can select the control and drag the control's handles to adjust the size and alignment of the control.

 TIP

To quickly adjust the size of a label, select the label, choose the Size command from the Format menu, and then choose To Fit from the submenu.

Setting Form Properties

You can display the form's properties in the property sheet (as shown in Figure 13-18) by clicking anywhere outside the Detail section of the form or by choosing the Select Form command from the Edit menu. In Figure 13-18, the caption has been set to *Club Names And Addresses*. This value will appear on the Form window's title bar in Form view or in Datasheet view.

The properties beginning with On Current in the property sheet can be set to run macros or Visual Basic procedures. The events associated with these properties can trigger macro actions.

In the second part of the list of properties in Figure 13-18 are the Grid X and Grid Y properties that control the density of dots on the grid. The defaults are 24 dots per inch across (Grid X) and 24 dots per inch down (Grid Y), if your measurements are in U.S. units. For metric measurements, the defaults are 5 dots per centimeter in both directions. Access also draws a shaded line on the grid every inch or centimeter to help you line up controls. If you decide to turn on the Snap To Grid command on the Format menu to help you line up controls

FIGURE 13-18.

The first 52 properties for the tblClubs form.

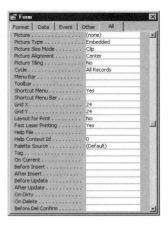

on your form, you might want to change the density of the grid dots to give you greater control over where you place objects on the form.

> You won't see the grid dots if you set either the Grid X or Grid Y property to more than 24 in U.S. measurements or more than 9 in metric measurements.

Checking Your Design Results

When you finish working on this form in Design view, it might look something like the one shown in Figure 13-19 on the next page.

To make the fields on the form stand out, you can click in the Detail section and then set the background to dark gray using the Back Color button on the Formatting toolbar. To make the labels stand out against this dark background, drag the mouse pointer around all the label controls or click the horizontal ruler directly above all the label controls, and then set the Back Color to white. If you also want to make the Detail section fit snugly around the controls on your form, drag the edges of the Detail section inward.

> To select all controls in a vertical area, click the horizontal ruler above the area containing the controls you want to select. Likewise, to select all controls in a horizontal area, click the vertical ruler.

Click the Form View button on the toolbar to see your form. It will look similar to the form shown in Figure 13-20 on the next page. (You can find this form saved as *frmXmplClub1* in the sample database.) To size the Form window to exactly fit the boundaries of your form

FIGURE 13-19.
Adding contrast to the
Club Names and
Addresses form.

First click here to
select all labels...

...and then choose white
as the background color.

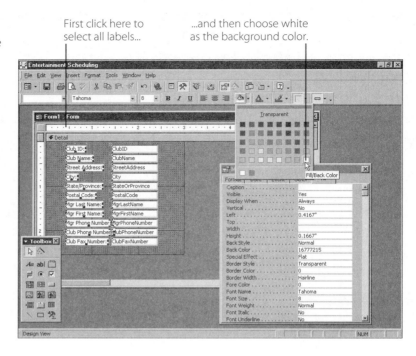

design, choose Size To Fit Form from the Window menu, as shown in
the figure. Click the Save button on the toolbar or choose Save from
the File menu to save your new form design.

FIGURE 13-20.
The finished Club
Names and Addresses
form in Form view.

NOTE

Microsoft Access 2000 introduces a new feature to allow you to further modify the design of your forms even while you are in Form view. You can set the Allow Design Changes property of the form to All Views. This lets you open the property sheet while in Form view to make additional design changes, as shown in Figure 13-20. All new forms in Access have Allow Design Changes set to All Views by default. You should be sure to set this property to Design View Only before using any form in a finished application.

Working with Form Wizards

Now that you understand the basic mechanics of form design, you could continue to build all your forms from scratch in Design view. However, even the most experienced developers take advantage of the many wizards built into Microsoft Access to get a jump start on design tasks. This section shows you how to use a Form Wizard to quickly build a custom form.

 NOTE

The remaining examples in this chapter are based on the Microsoft Press Books sample database on the companion CD.

Creating the Basic Orders Form with a Form Wizard

Begin by opening the Microsoft Press Books database in Design view, and then switch to the Database window and select the tblOrders table. Next select Form from the New Object toolbar button's drop-down list or choose Form from the Insert menu. Access opens the New Form dialog box, as shown in Figure 13-21.

FIGURE 13-21.
The New Form dialog box, in which you select a Form Wizard.

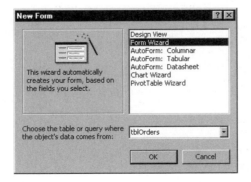

As you can see, you have seven choices in this dialog box: Design View (which you used in the previous section), Form Wizard, AutoForm: Columnar, AutoForm: Tabular, AutoForm: Datasheet, Chart Wizard, and PivotTable Wizard. The AutoForm Wizards quickly build a form, selecting all the defaults along the way. The Chart Wizard builds a form containing a graph object and walks you through all the steps to define the data for the graph and customize the way the graph works. The PivotTable Wizard creates a form with an embedded Microsoft Excel object and then shows you how to use Excel's pivot table capabilities to create a data summary for display in your Access application. Note that in the New Form dialog box you can change the data source for your form by changing the table or query name displayed in the combo box.

For this example, select Form Wizard and click OK. Access opens the window shown in Figure 13-22. You can select any field in the Available Fields list and click the single-right-arrow button to copy that field to the Selected Fields list. You can also click the double-right-arrow button to copy all available fields to the Selected Fields list. If you copy a field in error, you can select the field in the Selected Fields list and click the single-left-arrow button to remove the field from the list. You can remove all fields and start over by clicking the double-left-arrow button. For this example, click the double-right-arrow button to use all the tblOrders table's fields in the new form.

FIGURE 13-22.

The Form Wizard window for selecting fields.

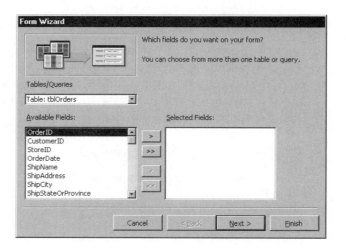

As you'll learn in Chapter 15, "Advanced Form Design," you can select fields from one table or query and then change the data source name in the Tables/Queries combo box to select a different but related table or query. If you have defined the relationships between tables in your database, the Form Wizard can determine how the data from multiple sources is related and can offer to build either a simple form to display all the data or a more complex one that shows some of the data in the main part of the form with related data displayed in an embedded subform. You'll use this technique to build a more complex form in Chapter 15.

At any time, you can click the Finish button to go directly to the last step of the wizard. You can also click the Cancel button at any time to stop creating the form.

After you select all the fields from the tblOrders table, click Next. In the window that appears, the wizard gives you choices for the layout of your form. You can choose to display the controls on your form in columns, arrange the controls across the form in a tabular format (this also creates a continuous form), place the columns back-to-back in a "justified" view, or create a form in Datasheet view. For this example, select Columnar, and then click Next.

The wizard next displays a window in which you can select a style for your form, as shown in Figure 13-23. Note that if you choose to display the form in a Datasheet view, the style won't apply to the datasheet but will appear if you shift from Datasheet view to Form view. The nice thing about this window is that the wizard shows you a sample of each selection on the left side of the window. You can look at each one and decide which you like best. In this example, the Stone style is selected. In Chapter 14, "Customizing Forms," you'll learn how to use the AutoFormat facility to create a custom look for your forms.

FIGURE 13-23.

The Form Wizard window for selecting the style for your form.

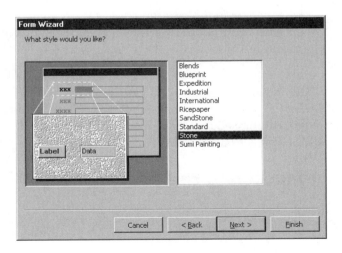

CAUTION

When you select a style in the Form Wizard, the new style becomes the default for new forms you create until you change the style setting again, either in the Form Wizard or in the AutoFormat facility. *See Chapter 14.*

Click Next to display the final window, where the Form Wizard asks for a title for your form. Type an appropriate title, such as *Orders*. The wizard places this title in the Caption property of the form and also saves the form with this name. (If you already have a form named Orders, Access appends a number to the end of the name to create a unique name.) Select the Open The Form To View Or Enter Information option, and then click the Finish button to go directly to Form view. Or you can select the Modify The Form's Design option, and then click Finish to open the new form in Design view. The finished form is shown in Form view in Figure 13-24.

FIGURE 13-24.

The Orders form in a columnar format.

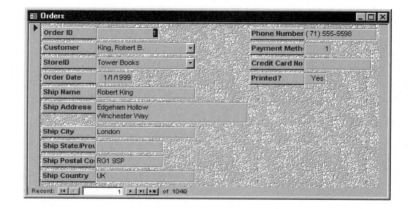

If you're curious to see the Tabular format, you can start a new form on the tblOrders table and use the Form Wizard again. Select all the fields except the StoreID field. Select Tabular for the layout and set the style back to Standard. For a title, type *Orders - Tabular*, and open the new form in Form view. It should look something like the form shown in Figure 13-25. Close this form when you finish looking at it.

If you're curious about what the Justified form looks like, you can go through the exercise again and select Justified for the layout on the second window in the Form Wizard. If you choose the Industrial style, your result should look something like the one shown in Figure 13-26. Close this form when you finish looking at it.

Modifying the Orders Form

The Form Wizard took care of some of the work, but there's still a lot you can do to improve the appearance and usability of this form. And even though the Form Wizard adjusted the display control widths, they're still not perfect. For example, the display control for Ship Name could be larger. Several other controls could be narrower. Also, you

FIGURE 13-25.

The Orders form in a tabular format.

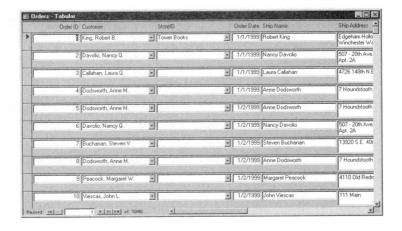

FIGURE 13-26.

The Orders form in a justified format.

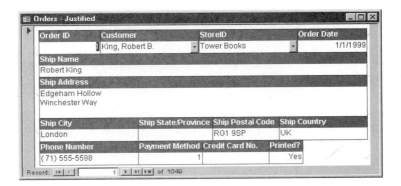

could make better use of the space on the form if you rearranged the field columns.

You can either start with the columnar format form (shown in Figure 13-24) or start a new form with the Standard style. (I decided to start over in Standard style for the following examples.) Open the form in Design view. To help align controls, click outside the Detail section so that the form is selected (or choose the Select Form command from the Edit menu), and make sure that the Grid X and Grid Y properties on the form's property sheet are set to 24. (Leave the settings at Grid X = 5 and Grid Y = 5 if you're working in metric measurements.) Be sure the Grid command is checked on the View menu. Move controls around until the form looks similar to the one shown in Figure 13-27 on the next page. Change the alignment of all the labels to right align. Modify the labels for the ship name, ship city, ship state or province, ship postal code, and ship country controls and place these controls in a column. Add the descriptive label *Shipping Information:* in a bold font.

FIGURE 13-27.
The modified Orders form in Design view.

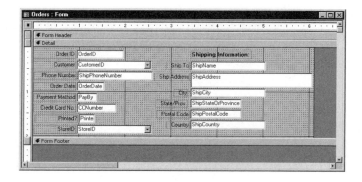

Now switch to Form view. Your form should look something like the one shown in Figure 13-28. The form now looks a bit more custom-ized—and somewhat more like the top part of the frmOrders form in the Microsoft Press Books application. You can find this form saved as *fxmplOrders1* in the sample database.

FIGURE 13-28.
The modified Orders form in Form view.

Simplifying Data Input with a Form

One drawback to working with a relational database is that often you have to deal with information stored in multiple tables. That's not a problem if you're using a query to link data, but working with multiple tables can be confusing if you're entering new data. Microsoft Access provides some great ways to show information from related tables, thus making data input much simpler.

Combo Boxes and List Boxes

In Chapter 12, "Form Basics," you saw how you can use a combo box or a list box to present a list of potential values for a control. To create the list, you can type the values in the Row Source property box of the control. You can also specify a table or a query as the source of the val-ues in the list. Access displays the currently selected value in the text box portion of the combo box or as a highlighted selection in the list.

IV

Using Forms

Creating a Combo Box to Display the Payment Method

Codes don't mean much to the people who read a form, but for efficiency's sake you need a code, not a description, to identify the payment method in the tblOrders table. If you really plan ahead, you can use the Display Control property of the PayBy field in the table to define a combo box in advance for all your queries and forms. In this example, the Display Control property is set to Text Box so that you can learn how to create a combo box for the PayBy field. You can build a combo box that shows the user the related payment method description fields but stores the corresponding code in the tblOrders table when the user chooses a description.

To see how a combo box works, you can replace the PayBy text box control with a combo box on the Orders form. In Design view, select the PayBy text box control and then press the Delete key to remove the text box control from the form (this also removes the related label control). Be sure the Control Wizards button is selected in the toolbox, and then click the Combo Box button in the toolbox and drag the PayBy field from the field list to the form. The new control appears on the form, and Access starts the Combo Box Wizard, as shown in Figure 13-29, to help you out.

FIGURE 13-29.
The first window of the Combo Box Wizard.

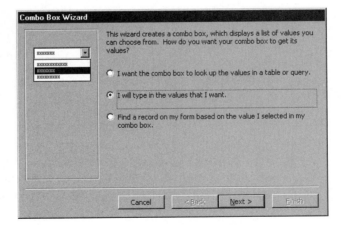

TIP

To change a text box to a different type of control, select the text box, choose Change To from the Format menu, and then choose the new type of control from the submenu. To change a text box to a combo box, however, you have to set the properties for the display list yourself.

Follow this procedure to build your combo box.

1 You want the combo box to display values from a short list that you enter, so select the second option, and then click the Next button to go to the next window.

2 In the second window, the wizard displays a box where you can enter the number of columns you need. Type the number *2* in this box, and tab out of the box to see two blank columns in the area below the box. You need one column to hold the code for the PayBy field and a second column to display the description of the code.

3 Next enter the value *1* in the first column and the description *Cash* in the second column. When you leave the first row, Access makes another row available to enter more data. Continue entering codes and descriptions until you have all six sets of values that you need, as shown here.

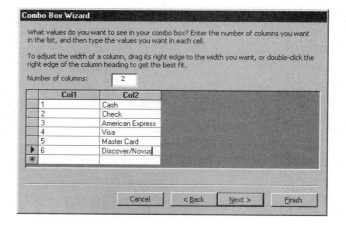

4 After entering the code and description data, you can set the width of any columns you want displayed when you open the combo box on the form. To size a column, place your mouse on the dividing line between columns at the top, click, and drag the line. This works just like adjusting column widths in a datasheet, as you learned in Chapter 7. You probably want to shrink the first column to zero width (the column containing the code) so that it isn't displayed when the combo box is dropped down. You can adjust the size of the second column to be sure it displays all of the available descriptions properly. Also, you can use this window to change the order of the fields. This is important because Access displays only the data in the first unhidden field when the combo box is closed. Click Next to go on.

5 The wizard next asks you which of the columns will supply the value that will be saved in the underlying field when you choose a row in the combo box. Since the first column contains the code number you need to store in the table, choose Col1. Click Next to go on.

6 In the next window, the wizard asks whether you want to store the value from the combo box in a field from the table or query that you're updating with this form or simply save the value selected in an unbound control "for later use." You'll see in Part VI of this book that unbound controls are useful for storing calculated values or for providing a way for the user to enter parameter data for use by your macros or Visual Basic procedures. In this case, you want to update the PayBy field, so be sure to select the Store That Value In This Field option and select PayBy from the drop-down list. Click Next to go to the last window of the wizard.

7 In the final window, shown below, notice that the wizard has chosen the caption from the bound field as the label for the combo box. Because you'll be showing descriptions and not codes in the combo box, change the caption as shown. Click Finish, and you're all done.

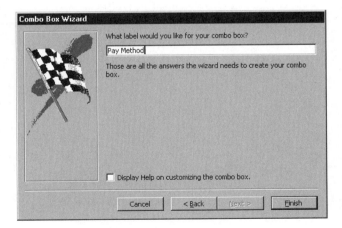

If you have the property sheet open, you can study the properties set by the Combo Box Wizard, as shown in Figure 13-30 on the next page. The Control Source property shows that the combo box is bound to the PayBy field. The Row Source Type property indicates that the data filling the combo box comes from a list that's typed in the Row Source property box. You can also specify a query or table as the Row Source, or you can ask Access to create a list from the names of fields in the query or table specified in the Row Source property.

FIGURE 13-30.

The properties set by the Combo Box Wizard.

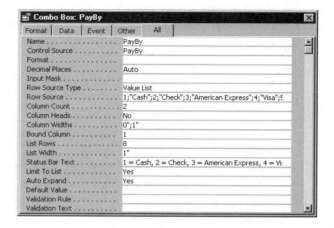

The Row Source property shows the list of values that you typed in the second window in the wizard. The Column Count property is set to 2 to indicate that two columns should be created from the list. Note that the list has pairs of code numbers and descriptions. Since the Column Count property is set to 2, Access pulls two values from the list to form each row in the final list. You have the option of asking Access to display column headings when the combo box is open, but you don't need that for this example, so leave the Column Heads property set to No. Notice that the first entry in the Column Widths property is 0 inches. This is how you "hide" a column in a combo box. Remember, you don't want to show the PayBy code, but you do want to save it in the table when you select a description from the combo box. The next property, Bound Column, indicates that the "hidden" first column (the code number in each pair of values in the list) is the one that sets the value of the combo box and, therefore, the value of the bound field in the table.

When you open the form in Form view, it should look like the one shown in Figure 13-31. Notice that the PayBy combo box now shows meaningful descriptions instead of numbers; the description you select will set the correct payment code in the record. (You can find this form saved as *fxmplOrders2* in the sample database.)

If you want Access to select the closest matching entry when you type a few leading characters in a combo box, set the Auto Expand property to Yes.

FIGURE 13-31.
The finished PayBy combo box in operation.

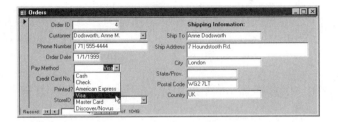

Toggle Buttons, Check Boxes, and Option Buttons

If your table contains a field that has a yes/no, true/false, or on/off value, you can choose from three types of controls that graphically display and set the status of this type of field: toggle buttons, check boxes, and option buttons.

The tblOrders table has a Printed field that indicates whether the particular order has been finalized and a purchase order printed. As you can see in the original text box control created by the Form Wizard (see Figure 13-24), the word Yes or No appears depending on the value in the underlying field. This field might be more appealing and understandable if it were displayed in a check box control.

To change the Printed control on the Orders form, first delete the Printed text box control. Next select the Check Box tool, and then drag the Printed field from the field list onto the form in the open space you left in the form. Your form in Design view should now look like the one shown in Figure 13-32.

FIGURE 13-32.
The Orders form with a check box control to display the Printed field.

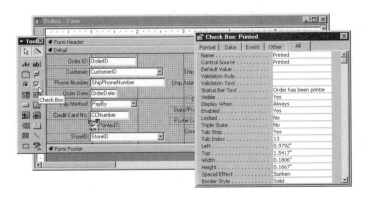

Click the Form View button to see the result. Your form should look like the one shown in Figure 13-33. One of the interesting side effects of using a special control to display data in a form is that the control properties carry over to Datasheet view. Switch to the Datasheet view of this form. The PayBy field is displayed as a drop-down list on the datasheet and the Printed field still looks like a check box. You might decide to design some forms to be used in Datasheet view, but you can customize the look of the datasheet by using controls other than text boxes while in Design view. By the way, this design sample is saved as *fxmplOrders3* in the Microsoft Press Books database.

FIGURE 13-33.

The final Orders form in Form view.

By now, you should be getting a feel for the process of designing and building forms. In the next chapter, you'll learn how to customize the appearance of your forms.

CHAPTER 14

Customizing Forms

I n the previous chapter, you learned how to create a basic form by building it from scratch or by using a Form Wizard. In this chapter, you'll look at ways that you can refine your form's appearance.

Aligning and Sizing Controls

In Chapter 13, "Building Forms," you built a form based on the Orders table in the Microsoft Press Books sample database, as shown in Figure 14-1 on the next page. This form looks pretty good, but the labels and fields are different sizes and are out of alignment. If you threw the form together quickly to help you enter some data (as you did in the previous chapter to create a simple Clubs input form in the Entertainment Scheduling database), it probably doesn't matter if the form doesn't look perfect. But if you're designing the form to be used continuously in an application, it's worth the extra effort to fine-tune the design. Otherwise, your database will look less than professional, and users might suffer eyestrain and fatigue.

FIGURE 14-1.

The Orders form you created in Chapter 13 with the help of a wizard (fxmplOrders3).

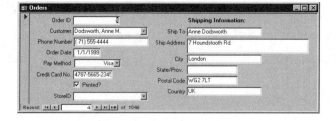

NOTE

Even if you follow along precisely with the steps described in this chapter, your results might vary slightly. All of the alignment commands are sensitive to your current screen resolution. When your screen driver is set to a high resolution (for example, 1024×768), the distance between grid points might be smaller than it is when the screen driver is set to a low resolution (such as 640×480). You should design your forms at the same resolution as the computers that will run your application.

To examine the alignment and relative size of controls on your form, you can open the property sheet in Design view and click various controls. For example, Figure 14-2 shows the property sheets for the PayBy and CCNumber controls. You can see by looking at the values for the Left property (the distance from the left edge of the form) that the CCNumber control is a bit closer to the left margin than the PayBy control is.

FIGURE 14-2.

The properties that define the placement and size of the PayBy and CCNumber controls.

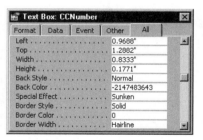

You could move around the form and adjust controls so that they fit your data. You could painstakingly enter values for each control's Left property to get all controls in a column to line up exactly and then set the Top property (defining the distance from the top of the Detail section) for controls that you want to appear in a row. You could also adjust the values for the Width and Height properties so that controls and labels are the same width and height where appropriate. Fortunately, there are easier ways to make all of these adjustments.

IV

Using Forms

Sizing Controls to Fit Content

One of the first things you can do with the Orders form is to ensure that all the controls are the right size for displaying your data. Access has a command called Size/To Fit that sizes label controls to fit around the label text. This command also ensures that text boxes, combo boxes, and list boxes are tall enough to display your data using the font size you've selected. For example, the wizard built the ShipAddress control two lines high. You can shrink the control to approximately one line high and then use Size/To Fit to make sure the control has the correct height.

> **TIP**
>
> You can "size to fit" any individual control or label by double-clicking any of its sizing handles.

Because you created all of the controls and labels on this form using the same font, it makes sense to resize them all at once. First choose Select All from the Edit menu to highlight all the controls on your form. (To select a specific group of labels or controls, click the first one and then hold down the Shift key as you click each additional control or label that you want to select. You can also drag the mouse pointer across the form—as long as you don't start dragging while you are over a control—and the mouse pointer will delineate a selection box. Any controls that are inside the selection box when you release the mouse button will be selected.) After you select the controls you want, choose the Size command from the Format menu, and then select To Fit from the submenu. The Detail section should now look something like that shown in Figure 14-3.

FIGURE 14-3.

The Orders form after you shrink the height of the ShipAddress control, select all controls, and size the controls to fit.

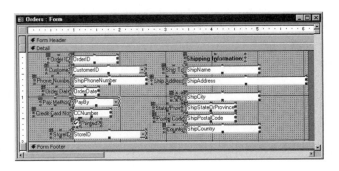

TIP

If you think you'll select multiple controls often, you might want to experiment with an option setting that governs how you can select controls with your mouse pointer. From the Tools menu, choose Options, and then click the Forms/Reports tab of the Options dialog box. When you select the Partially Enclosed option, the selection box you draw with your mouse needs only to touch any part of a control to select it. If you select the Fully Enclosed option, the selection box must contain the entire control in order for the control to be selected. Fully Enclosed is most useful for complex forms with many controls that are close to each other; that way you don't have to worry about inadvertently selecting controls that you touch but don't fully enclose with the selection box.

You can also select all controls in a vertical or a horizontal band by making the rulers visible (choose the Ruler command from the View menu) and then dragging the mouse along the top or side ruler.

Adjusting Control Layout

When the Form Wizard lays out controls in a columnar format, it stacks the controls that are bound to data fields one on top of another, without any regard to "clusters" of fields that might work well lined up side by side. For example, you really don't need separate controls with labels to edit the shipping city, state or province, and postal code. If you're writing an address, you tend to place all three of these items on one line, so it makes sense to do the same thing on this form. Arranging these controls also saves vertical space on the form and ultimately makes it easier to line up the controls.

To adjust your sample Orders form in this way, follow these steps.

1 Click the label for ShipCity, and press the Delete key to remove the label. Likewise, delete the labels for ShipStateOrProvince and ShipPostalCode. (Do not delete the text box controls that display this data.)

2 ShipAddress doesn't need to be quite so wide, so select the control and then drag the right border in until the control is a bit more than two inches wide.

3 Shrink the ShipCity control so that it's about half the size of the ShipAddress control.

4 Shrink the ShipPostalCode control to about a half-inch and make the ShipStateOrProvince control just a bit narrower than that. Drag these two controls so that they line up next to the ShipCity

control, under the ShipAddress control. Don't worry for now about aligning these controls precisely.

5 Move up the ShipCountry control to where ShipStateOrProvince was before you moved it. Select all of the controls from the Shipping Information label down to ShipCountry by drawing a selection box with your mouse, and then move the cluster of controls down so that the Shipping Information label is about level with the Phone Number label in the left column.

6 Grab the Printed check box, and move it to the open area in the upper right corner of the form.

7 Move the StoreID control up into the space vacated by the Printed check box.

When you're done, you should have a form design that looks something like the one shown in Figure 14-4. Now you're ready to fine-tune your form using alignment and control-size adjustments.

FIGURE 14-4.
The Orders form after you shrink the size of the ShipStateOrProvince and ShipPostalCode controls and arrange the controls into clusters that make more sense.

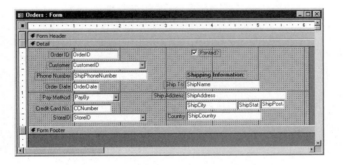

"Snapping" Controls to the Grid

It's a good idea to verify that all the controls are spaced evenly down the form. One way to do this is to take advantage of the grid. You can adjust the density of the grid by changing the Grid X and Grid Y properties in the property sheet of the form. Be sure that the property sheet is open, and then choose Select Form from the Edit menu. Also, be sure that the Grid command on the View menu has a check mark in front of it.

For this example, set the Grid X and Grid Y properties to 16 (0.0625 inch between grid points). This works well for the default 8-point MS Sans Serif font because the "sized to fit" text boxes will be 0.17 inch high. You can place these text boxes every 0.25 inch (four grid points) down the form, which leaves adequate space between the controls.

You can "snap" the controls to the grid in one of two ways. If you want to handle each control individually, choose the Snap To Grid command from the Format menu. (You'll see a check mark in front of this command when it is active.) Now click each control and drag it vertically to positions every 0.25 inch (every fourth grid point) down the grid. When you release the mouse button, you'll see the upper left corner of the control "snap" to the nearest grid point. As you saw in the previous chapter, Access moves a control and its label as a unit. So if you previously moved the label up or down independently of the attached control, you might need to use the positioning handle in the upper left corner of the control or the label to align them horizontally.

A faster way to snap all controls to the grid is to choose Select All from the Edit menu, choose Align from the Format menu, and then choose To Grid from the submenu. The result might look something like that shown in Figure 14-5—and it might look like you made it worse instead of better! Snapping to the grid helps spread the controls apart to make them easier to work with. You'll see in the next few steps that it's easy to line them all up properly.

FIGURE 14-5.

The Orders form after you "snap" the controls to the grid.

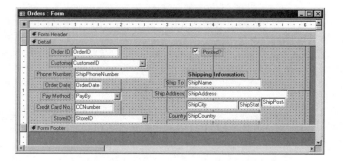

TIP

Another way to create even vertical or horizontal spacing between controls is to use other options available on the Format menu. For example, to evenly space a series of controls in a column, select all of the controls, choose Vertical Spacing from the Format menu, and then select Make Equal from the submenu. Likewise, to create even horizontal spacing between controls, select the controls, choose Horizontal Spacing from the Format menu, and then select Make Equal from the submenu. You should notice that these submenus also have options to increase or decrease horizontal or vertical spacing across a group of selected controls.

Lining Up Controls

You now have your controls spaced evenly down the form, but they probably aren't aligned vertically. That's easy to fix. To get started, select all the labels in the far left column. You can do this by clicking the first label (not its associated control) and then holding down the Shift key as you click each of the remaining labels in the column. Or you can click in the ruler above the labels. When you have selected them all, your form should look something like the one shown in Figure 14-6. Notice that Access also shows the large handles in the upper left corner of all the related controls but no sizing handles on the controls.

FIGURE 14-6.

The Orders form with a column of labels selected.

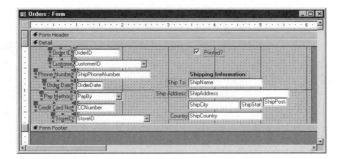

The labels will look best if their right edges align. You have two choices at this point. If you turn off the Snap To Grid command, you can have Access align all the labels with the label whose right edge is farthest to the right, even if that edge is between dots on the grid. If you leave Snap To Grid on, you can have Access align the labels with the label farthest to the right and then snap the entire group to the nearest grid point.

When you're ready to align the selected controls on your form, choose the Align command from the Format menu. Select the Right command from the submenu, as shown in Figure 14-7 on the next page, and then click inside the grid to deselect the labels. Your form should look similar to the one shown in Figure 14-8 on the next page.

To further improve the alignment of the controls on the Orders form, do the following.

1 To fix any overlap of the ShipCity, ShipStateOrProvince, and ShipPostalCode controls, and to evenly space them, select all three controls, choose Align from the Format menu, and then select Left from the submenu.

FIGURE 14-7.

The Align command and its submenu.

FIGURE 14-8.

The labels from Figure 14-6 are right aligned.

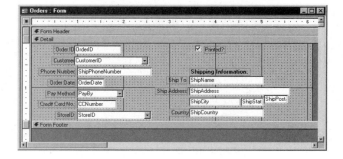

2 Select the OrderID, CustomerID, ShipPhoneNumber, OrderDate, PayBy, CCNumber, and StoreID controls. Choose Align from the Format menu, and then select Left from the submenu. (If any of these controls overlaps the labels you aligned earlier, first select the offending control and drag it to the right using the large handle in the control's upper left corner; this moves the control independently of its label.)

3 Select the Ship To, Ship Address, and Country labels, and right align them.

4 Select the Shipping Information label and the ShipName, ShipAddress, ShipCity, and ShipCountry text box controls, and left align them. (Again, if any of these controls overlaps the labels you aligned in step 3, first select the offending control and drag it to the right using the large handle in the control's upper left corner.)

5 Line up ShipCountry and its label with StoreID and its label by selecting all four controls, choosing the Align command from the Format menu, and then choosing either Top or Bottom from the submenu, whichever will work out better.

6 Similarly, line up CCNumber and its label horizontally together with the ShipCity, ShipStateOrProvince, and ShipPostalCode controls.

7 Line up PayBy and its label with ShipAddress and its label. Continue up the column, aligning ShipName with OrderDate and the Shipping Information label with ShipPhoneNumber.

8 Move the Printed check box over near the OrderID text box and slightly below it. Select the Order ID label, the OrderID text box, the Printed check box, and its label. Then align all four controls at the top by choosing Align from the Format menu, and then choosing Top from the submenu.

After you complete these steps, your form should look something like the one shown in Figure 14-9.

FIGURE 14-9.
The controls and labels are aligned horizontally and vertically.

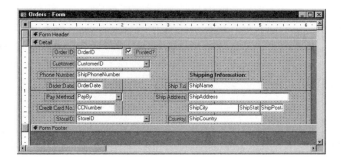

TIP

If you want to move one or more controls only horizontally or only vertically, hold down the Shift key as you select the control (or the last control in a group) that you want to move, and then drag either horizontally or vertically. When Access detects movement either horizontally or vertically, it "locks" the movement and won't let the objects stray in the other axis. If you inadvertently start to drag horizontally when you mean to move vertically (or vice versa), click the Undo button and try again.

Adjusting Control Width

Two long controls—ShipName and ShipAddress—stretch across a large portion of the form in the right column. You aligned their left edges, but it would be nice if their right edges also aligned with the ShipPostalCode control. You can do this by adjusting the Width property of both the ShipName and the ShipAddress controls. First select both the ShipName and ShipAddress controls, choose Size from the Format menu, and then select To Widest from the submenu.

Next it would be nice to set the width and placement of the ShipCity, ShipStateOrProvince, and ShipPostalCode text boxes so that the left edge of ShipCity lines up with the left edge of ShipAddress and the right edge of ShipPostalCode lines up with the right edge of ShipAddress. You can do this in one of two ways.

- If the ShipPostalCode text box should be wider to fully display all the data, you can stretch it from its current position so that its right edge lines up with the right edge of ShipAddress. To determine what adjustment you need (if any), first take a look at the Left and Width properties of the ShipAddress control's property sheet, as shown in Figure 14-10. In this example, the ShipAddress text box starts 3.4375 inches from the left edge of the form and is 2.3 inches wide. This means that the right edge is 5.7375 inches from the left edge of the form. Next take a look at the Left and Width properties of the ShipPostalCode control, whose property sheet is also shown in Figure 14-10. You don't want to move this control from its location 5.0931 inches from the left edge, because it's left aligned with the other controls in that row. The sum of the Left and Width properties of the ShipPostalCode control should equal 5.7375 inches in order to align the right edge of the ShipPostalCode control with the right edge of the ShipAddress control. So you need to change the ShipPostalCode control's Width property from 0.6 inch to 0.6444 inch (5.7375 minus 5.0931) to achieve the desired result. (Access might adjust this length slightly to align with the nearest display pixel.)

FIGURE 14-10.

The values for the Left and Width properties can be compared and adjusted to align the right edges of two controls.

- If the ShipPostalCode is already wide enough, you can avoid the complicated calculation. Provided your design looks something like Figure 14-9 on the previous page (the right edge of ShipPostalCode is to the left of the right edge of ShipAddress), select the ShipPostalCode and ShipAddress text boxes and right align them. Next select the ShipCity, ShipStateOrProvince, and ShipPostalCode text boxes, choose Horizontal Spacing from the Format menu, and choose Make Equal on the submenu.

Likewise, it might be a good idea to align the right edge of ShipCountry with the right edge of ShipStateOrProvince. The only way to do this is to use a similar mathematical calculation as noted in the first option above (add the Left and Width properties for

ShipStateOrProvince, and subtract the Left property for ShipCountry) to obtain a new Width setting for ShipCountry.

When you finish, switch to Form view and choose Size To Fit Form from the Window menu. Your form should look something like the one shown in Figure 14-11. You can find this form saved as *fxmplOrders4* in the Microsoft Press Books sample database.

 TIP

Forms have an Auto Resize property. If you set this property to Yes, Access sizes the Form window to exactly fit the form. Note that Access won't automatically resize a form if you've switched from Design view to Form view. You can set the Auto Center property to Yes to center the Form window in the current Access workspace.

FIGURE 14-11.
The Orders form with controls aligned and sized.

	Orders		
Order ID		☑ Printed?	
Customer	King, Robert B.		
Phone Number	(71) 555-5598	**Shipping Information:**	
Order Date	1/1/1999	Ship To	Robert King
Pay Method	Cash	Ship Address	Edgeham Hollow
Credit Card No.			London RG1 9SP
StoreID	Tower Books	Country	UK

Record: |◄ ◄| 1 |► ►| ►*| of 1049

Enhancing the Look of a Form

When you first built the Orders form using a Form Wizard and specified the Standard format, the wizard automatically added one enhancement—a gray background color. In this section, you'll learn about additional enhancements you can make to your form's design.

Lines and Rectangles

Microsoft Access comes with two drawing tools, the Line tool and the Rectangle tool, that you can use to enhance the appearance of your forms. You can add lines to separate parts of your form visually. Rectangles are useful for surrounding and setting off a group of controls on a form.

On the Orders form, it might be helpful to add a line to separate the primary information about the order in the first column from shipping information in the second column. To make room for the line, you need to move the controls in the second column about a quarter inch to the right. The easiest way to do this is to switch to Design view, select all the affected controls and labels, and then move them as a group. Start by clicking the top ruler (if you can't see the rulers, be sure that Ruler command is checked on the View menu) just above the right edge of the controls, and then drag in the ruler toward the left until the selection indicators touch all the labels in the right column. Release the mouse button, and all the controls and labels in the right column will be selected. To be sure you move all of these controls as a group, choose Group from the Format menu. Access shows you that the controls are now grouped by placing a rectangular line around all of the controls. Place the mouse pointer over the edge of the group so that the pointer changes to a hand shape (see Figure 14-12), and slide the entire group right a bit. (You might have to first drag the right margin of the Detail section to make room.)

FIGURE 14-12.
Moving a set of grouped controls.

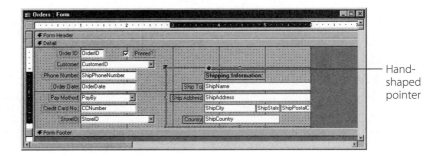

Hand-shaped pointer

Next select the Line tool from the toolbox. To draw your line, click near the top of the form between the two columns, about two grid rows below the top edge, and drag toward the form's bottom edge. If the line isn't exactly vertical, you can drag the bottom end left or right to adjust it. You can also set its Width property to 0 in the property sheet to make it perfectly vertical. Use the Border Width button on the toolbar to make the line a little thicker if you want. Your form should now look similar to the one shown in Figure 14-13.

 **TIP**

> When drawing a line on your form, you can make your line exactly horizontal or exactly vertical if you first hold down the Shift key as you click and draw the line.

You can add emphasis to the form by drawing a rectangle around all the controls. To do this, you might first need to move all the controls down and to the right a bit and make the Detail section slightly wider and taller. First expand your form by about 0.5 inch across and down. Choose Select All from the Edit menu, and then drag all the controls so that you have about 0.25 inch of space around all the edges. (This might seem like too much space, but we'll use the extra space to have

FIGURE 14-13.

Use the Line tool to draw a line on a form; use the Border Width button to adjust the line width.

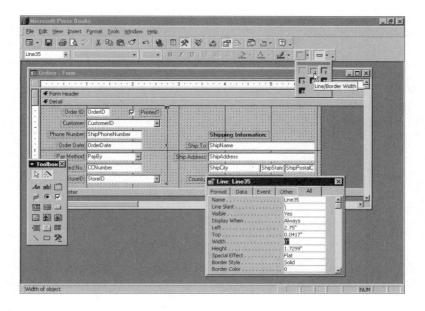

some fun a bit later.) Select the Rectangle tool, click where you want to place one corner of the rectangle, and drag to the intended location of the opposite corner. When you draw a rectangle around all the controls, your form will look similar to the one shown in Figure 14-14.

FIGURE 14-14.

The Orders form after a rectangle with a default etched look is added.

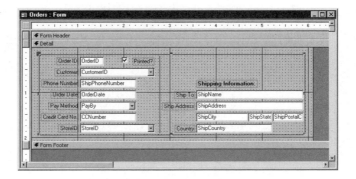

Note that the default rectangle is transparent with an etched special effect. If you ever want to create a solid rectangle, you can select the Rectangle tool and then use the Fill/Back Color button on the toolbar to select the color you want. When you add a solid control like this after you've created other controls, the solid control will cover the previous controls. You can choose Send To Back from the Format menu to reveal the covered controls and keep the solid control in the background.

Now switch to Form view, and choose Size To Fit Form from the Window menu. Your Orders form should look similar to the one shown in Figure 14-15.

FIGURE 14-15.

The Orders form in Form view with a line and a rectangle added.

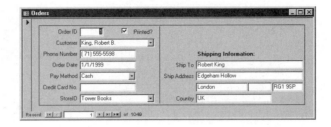

Colors and Special Effects

The Form Wizard added a light gray color to the background of the Orders form when you first created it. You can also use color and special effects to highlight objects on your form. For example, you can make all the controls appear to "float" on a raised surface on the form. To do so, switch to Design view and select the rectangle you just created. Use the Back Color button on the toolbar to set the background color to light gray. Use the Special Effect button to change the rectangle from Etched to Raised. Choose Send To Back from the Format menu to ensure that all the other controls appear on top of the colored background. Your form will look similar to the one shown in Figure 14-16.

FIGURE 14-16.

The rectangle behind the controls is now "raised" and light gray in color.

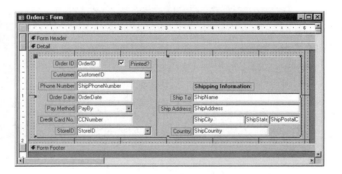

Next select the Rectangle tool again, and set Back Color to dark gray and Special Effect to Sunken using the buttons on the toolbar. Draw a second rectangle so that it forms a border about halfway between the edge of the first rectangle and the edge of the grid. Choose Send To Back from the Format menu to send this latest rectangle to the background. Switch to Form view to see the result. The controls now appear to float on the light gray rectangle on the form, surrounded by a "moat" of dark gray, as shown in Figure 14-17.

IV

Using Forms

FIGURE 14-17.
Controls appear to float on the form using special effects.

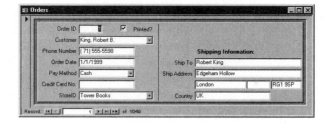

Fonts

Another way you can enhance the appearance of your forms is by varying the fonts and font sizes you use. When you select any control or label that can display text or data, Access makes font, font size, and font attribute controls available on the Formatting toolbar so that you can easily change how that control or label looks. Simply click the down arrow next to the Font Name combo box to open a list of all the available fonts, as shown in Figure 14-18. Select the font you want for the control or label.

FIGURE 14-18.
The list of fonts in the Font Name combo box.

The font list shows all fonts currently installed on your computer. Use the Fonts folder in the Windows Control Panel to add or remove fonts. A double-T icon next to the font name in the list indicates a TrueType font that is suitable for both screen display and printing. A printer icon next to the font name indicates a font designed for your printer but which might not look exactly the same when displayed on your screen. A font with no icon indicates a font designed for your screen; a screen font might look different when you print it.

If you want to add some variety, you can use bold or italic type in a few key places. In this case, you might select all the labels on the form and select a serif font such as Times New Roman. You can add a label to the header of the form to display a title such as *Orders*. (This is probably overkill since the form caption already tells us the subject of this form.) Set the label in the header to the Arial font (a sans serif font), bold, italic, and 18 points in size. You can see a portion of this work under way in Figure 14-19.

FIGURE 14-19.

Using special font settings in a form header label.

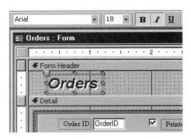

You can create the special "shadowed" effect you see in this label by first creating the label with a black foreground color.

1 Copy the label to the Clipboard, and paste it in the header.

2 Change its foreground color to white, and then choose Send To Back from the Format menu.

3 Turn off the Snap To Grid command on the Format menu, and drag the white label so that it is slightly lower and to the right of the first label.

When you finish, the form should look similar to the one shown in Figure 14-20. (You can find this form saved in the Microsoft Press Books database as *fxmplOrders6.*)

FIGURE 14-20.

The Orders form using some different fonts for variety.

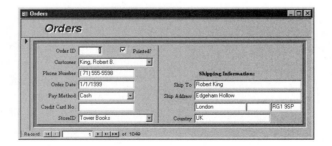

You should note that a form with too many fonts or font sizes will look busy and jumbled. In general, you should use only two or three fonts per form. Use one font and font size for most data in controls and labels. Make the label text bold or colored for emphasis. Select a second font for controls in the headers and perhaps a third (at most) for information in the footers.

Setting Control Properties

Microsoft Access gives you several additional properties for each control to allow you to customize the way your form works. These properties affect formatting, the presence or absence of scroll bars, and the enabling or locking of records.

Formatting Properties

In the property sheet for each text box, combo box, and list box are three properties that you can set to determine how Access displays the data in the form. These properties are Format, Decimal Places, and Input Mask, as shown in Figure 14-21.

FIGURE 14-21.

The list of format settings for the OrderDate control, which uses the Date/Time data type.

I recommended earlier that you change the date display in your Regional Settings in Control Panel to display a four-digit year. Although Access adjusts the century digits automatically when you enter two-digit years, you will avoid confusion about the actual value stored after the year 1999 if you always display the full year. All samples you see in this book using the Short Date format show four-digit years because I changed the settings on my machine. If your machine is set to display a two-digit year, you will see a different result everywhere I used the Short Date format.

SEE ALSO

For details on the Input Mask property, see Chapter 5, "Building Your Database in Microsoft Access." For details on defining conditional formatting of controls based on the value currently displayed, see Chapter 15, "Advanced Form Design."

Access copies these properties from the definition of the fields in the underlying table. If you haven't specified a Format property in the field definition, Access sets a default Format property for the control, depending on the data type of the field bound to the control. In the control's property sheet, you can customize the appearance of your data by selecting a format setting from the Format property's drop-down list or by entering a custom set of formatting characters. The following sections present the format settings and formatting characters available for each data type.

Numbers and Currency

If you don't specify a Format property setting for a control that displays a number or a currency value, Access displays numbers in the General Number format and currency in the Currency format. You can choose from among six Format property settings, as shown in Table 14-1.

TABLE 14-1.   Format Property Settings for Number and Currency Data Types

Format	Description
General Number	Displays numbers as entered with up to 11 significant digits. If a number contains more than 11 significant digits or the control you are using to display the value is not wide enough to show all digits, Access first rounds the number and then uses scientific (exponential) notation for very large or very small numbers (more than 10 digits to the right or to the left of the decimal point).
Currency	Displays numeric data according to the Currency setting in the Regional Settings section of the Windows Control Panel. In the U.S. layout, Access uses a leading dollar sign, maintains two decimal places (rounded), and encloses negative numbers in parentheses.
Fixed	Displays numbers without thousands separators and with two decimal places.
Standard	Displays numbers with thousands separators and with two decimal places.
Percent	Multiplies the value by 100, displays two decimal places, and adds a trailing percent sign.
Scientific	Displays numbers in scientific (exponential) notation.

You can also create a custom format. You can specify a different display format for Access to use (depending on whether the numeric value is positive, negative, 0, or Null) by providing up to four format specifications in the Format property. The specifications must be separated by semicolons. When you enter two specifications, Access uses the first for all nonnegative numbers and the second for negative numbers. When you provide three specifications, Access uses the third specification to display numbers with a value of 0. Use the fourth specification to indicate how you want Null values handled.

To create a custom number format, use the formatting characters shown in Table 14-2. Notice that you can include text strings in the format and specify a color to use.

TABLE 14-2. Formatting Characters for Number and Currency Data Types

Character	Usage
Decimal separator	Use to indicate where you want Access to place the decimal point. Use the decimal separator defined in the Regional Settings section of the Windows Control Panel. In the English (United States) layout, the separator is a period (.).
Thousands separator	Use to indicate placement of the thousands separator character that is defined in the Regional Settings section of the Windows Control Panel. In the English (United States) layout, the separator is a comma (,).
0	Use to indicate digit display. If no digit exists in the number in this position, Access displays 0.
#	Use to indicate digit display. If no digit exists in the number in this position, Access displays a blank space.
- + $ ( ) or a blank space	Use these characters anywhere you want in your format string.
"text"	Use double quotation marks to embed any text you want displayed.
\	Use to always display the character immediately following (the same as including a single character in double quotation marks).
!	Use to force left alignment.

(continued)

TABLE 14-2. *continued*

Character	Usage
*	Use to designate the immediately following character as the fill character. Access normally displays formatted data right aligned and filled with blank spaces to the left.
%	Use to multiply the value by 100 and include a trailing percent sign.
E- or e-	Use to generate scientific (exponential) notation and to display a minus sign preceding negative exponents. It must be used with other characters, as in *0.00E-00*.
E+ or e+	Use to generate scientific (exponential) notation and to display a minus sign preceding negative exponents and a plus sign preceding positive exponents. It must be used with other characters, as in *0.00E+00*.
[*color*]	Use brackets to display the text in the color specified. Valid color names are Black, Blue, Green, Cyan, Red, Magenta, Yellow, and White. A color name must be used with other characters, as in *0.00[Red]*.

For example, to display a number with two decimal places and comma separators when positive, enclosed in parentheses and shown in red when negative, *Zero* when *0*, and *Not Entered* when Null, you would specify the following.

    #,##0.00;(#,##0.00)[Red];"Zero";"Not Entered"

To format a U.S. phone number and area code from a numeric field, you would specify the following.

    (000) 000-0000

Text

If you don't specify a Format property setting for a control that displays a text value, Access left aligns the data in the control. You can also specify a custom format with one or two entries separated by semicolons. If you include a second format specification, Access uses that specification to show empty values. (If you want to test for Null, you must use the Immediate If (IIf) and IsNull built-in functions.) Notice that when you specify formatting for text, Access right aligns the data in the control unless you include the ! formatting character.

If a text field contains more characters than the number of formatting characters you provide, Access uses up the formatting characters and then appends the extra characters at the end with the fill character (if any) in between. Table 14-3 lists the formatting characters that are applicable to the Text data type.

TABLE 14-3. Formatting Characters for the Text Data Type

Character	Usage
@	Use to display any available character or a space in this position.
&	Use to display any available character in this position. If no characters are available to display, Access displays nothing.
<	Use to display all characters in lowercase.
>	Use to display all characters in uppercase.
- + $ ( ) or a blank space	Use these characters anywhere you want in your format string.
"text"	Use double quotation marks to embed any text you want displayed.
\	Use to always display the character immediately following (the same as including a single character in double quotation marks).
!	Use to force left alignment. This also forces placeholders to fill left to right instead of right to left.
*	Use to designate the immediately following character as the fill character. Access normally displays formatted data right aligned and filled with blank spaces to the left. The asterisk must be used with other characters, as in >*@-@@@.
[color]	Use brackets to display the text in the color specified. Valid color names are Black, Blue, Green, Cyan, Red, Magenta, Yellow, and White. A color name must be used with other characters, as in >[Red].

For example, if you want to display a six-character part number with a hyphen between the second character and the third character, left aligned, specify the following.

    !@@-@@@@

To format a check amount string in the form of *Fourteen Dollars and 59 Cents* so that Access displays an asterisk (*) to fill any available space between the word *and* and the cents amount, specify the following.

    **@@@@@@@@

Showing the Null Value in Text Fields

As you may have noticed, there is no third optional format specification you can supply for a Null value in a Text field as there is with Number, Currency, and Date/Time data types. If the field is Null, Access displays it as though it is empty. If the field can contain an empty string or a Null, you can distinguish it visibly by using the second optional format specification. Assuming your text field is five characters long, your Format specification could look like:

> @@@@@;"<empty string>"

If the field has a value, Access displays the value. If the field is an empty string, you will see "<empty string>" (without the quotation marks) in the text box until you click in it. If the field is Null, the text box will be blank.

An alternative is to use the IIf and IsNull built-in functions in the Control Source of the text box. Your control source could look like:

> =IIf(IsNull([FieldToDisplay]), "*Null Value*",[FieldToDisplay])

If you do this, however, you won't be able to update the field because the source will be an expression.

Using the format from the previous page in a text box wide enough to display 62 characters, Access displays *Fourteen Dollars and 59 Cents* as

> Fourteen Dollars and ********************************59 Cents

and *One Thousand Two Hundred Dollars and 00 Cents* as

> One Thousand Two Hundred Dollars and *****************00 Cents

Date/Time

If you don't specify a Format property setting for a control that displays a Date/Time value, Access displays the date/time in the General Date format. You can also select one of the six other Format property settings shown in Table 14-4.

You can also specify a custom format with one or two entries separated by semicolons. If you include a second format specification, Access uses that specification to show Null values. Table 14-5 lists the formatting characters that are applicable to the Date/Time data type.

For example, to display a date as full month name, day, and year (say, *December 20, 1997*) with a color of cyan, you would specify the following.

> mmmm dd, yyyy[Cyan]

TABLE 14-4. Format Property Settings for the Date/Time Data Type

Format	Description
General Date	Displays the date as numbers separated by the date separator character. Displays the time as hours and minutes separated by the time separator character and followed by an AM/PM indicator. If the value has no time component, Access displays the date only. If the value has no date component, Access displays the time only. Example: 3/17/99 06:17 PM.
Long Date	Displays the date according to the Long Date setting in the Regional Settings section of the Windows Control Panel. Example: Wednesday, March 17, 1999.
Medium Date	Displays the date as dd-mmm-yy. Example: 17-Mar-99.
Short Date	Displays the date according to the Short Date setting in the Regional Settings section of the Windows Control Panel. Example: 3/17/1999. To avoid confusion for dates in the twenty-first century, I strongly recommend you take advantage of the new Use Four-Digit Year formatting options. Choose Options from the Tools menu to set these options.
Long Time	Displays the time according to the Time setting in the Regional Settings section of the Windows Control Panel. Example: 6:17:12 PM.
Medium Time	Displays the time as hours and minutes separated by the time separator character and followed by an AM/PM indicator. Example: 06:17 PM.
Short Time	Displays the time as hours and minutes separated by the time separator character, using a 24-hour clock. Example: 18:17.

TABLE 14-5. Formatting Characters for the Date/Time Data Type

Character	Usage
Time separator	Use to show Access where to separate hours, minutes, and seconds. Use the time separator defined in the Regional Settings section of the Windows Control Panel. In the English (United States) layout, the separator is a colon (:).
Date separator	Use to show Access where to separate days, months, and years. Use the date separator defined in the Regional Settings section of the Windows Control Panel. In the English (United States) layout, the separator is a forward slash (/).

(continued)

TABLE 14-5. *continued*

Character	Usage
c	Use to display the General Date format.
d	Use to display the day of the month as one or two digits, as needed.
dd	Use to display the day of the month as two digits.
ddd	Use to display the day of the week as a three-letter abbreviation. Example: Saturday = Sat.
dddd	Use to display the day of the week fully spelled out.
ddddd	Use to display the Short Date format.
dddddd	Use to display the Long Date format.
w	Use to display a number for the day of the week. Example: Sunday = 1.
m	Use to display the month as a one-digit or two-digit number, as needed.
mm	Use to display the month as a two-digit number.
mmm	Use to display the name of the month as a three-letter abbreviation. Example: March = Mar.
mmmm	Use to display the name of the month fully spelled out.
q	Use to display the calendar quarter number (1–4).
y	Use to display the day of the year (1–366).
yy	Use to display the last two digits of the year.
yyyy	Use to display the full year value (within the range 0100–9999).
h	Use to display the hour as one or two digits, as needed.
hh	Use to display the hour as two digits.
n	Use to display the minutes as one or two digits, as needed.
nn	Use to display the minutes as two digits.
s	Use to display the seconds as one or two digits, as needed.
ss	Use to display the seconds as two digits.
ttttt	Use to display the Long Time format.
AM/PM	Use to display 12-hour clock values with trailing AM or PM, as appropriate.

TABLE 14-5. *continued*

Character	Usage
A/P or a/p	Use to display 12-hour clock values with trailing A or P, as appropriate.
AMPM	Use to display 12-hour clock values using forenoon/afternoon indicators as specified in the Regional Settings section of the Windows Control Panel.
- + $ ( ) or a blank space	Use these characters anywhere you want in your format string.
"*text*"	Use quotation marks to embed any text you want displayed.
\	Use to always display the character immediately following (the same as including a single character in double quotation marks).
!	Use to force left alignment.
*	Use to designate the immediately following character as the fill character. Access normally displays formatted data right aligned and filled with blank spaces to the left. The asterisk must be used with other characters, as in *A/P*#*.
[*color*]	Use brackets to display the text in the color specified. Valid color names are Black, Blue, Green, Cyan, Red, Magenta, Yellow, and White. A color name must be used with other characters, as in *ddddd[Red]*.

Yes/No

You can choose from among three standard formats—Yes/No, True/False, or On/Off—to display Yes/No data type values, as shown in Table 14-6. The Yes/No format is the default. As you saw earlier, it's often more useful to display Yes/No values using a check box or an option button rather than a text box.

TABLE 14-6. Format Property Settings for the Yes/No Data Type

Format	Description
Yes/No (the default)	Displays 0 as No and any nonzero value as Yes.
True/False	Displays 0 as False and any nonzero value as True.
On/Off	Displays 0 as Off and any nonzero value as On.

You can also specify your own custom word or phrase for Yes and No values. To do that, specify a format string containing three parts separated by semicolons. Leave the first part empty, specify a string enclosed in double quotation marks (and with an optional color modifier) in the second part for Yes values, and specify another string (also with an optional color modifier) in the third part for No values.

To display *Invoice Sent* in red for Yes and *Not Invoiced* in blue for No, you would specify the following.

;"Invoice Sent"[Red];"Not Invoiced"[Blue]

> **NOTE**

If you specify both an Input Mask setting (see Chapter 5, "Building Your Database in Microsoft Access") and a Format setting, Access uses the Input Mask setting to display data when you move the focus to the control and uses the Format setting at all other times. If you don't include a Format setting but do include an Input Mask setting, Access formats the data using the Input Mask setting. Be careful not to define a Format setting that conflicts with the Input Mask. For example, if you define an Input Mask setting for a phone number that looks like

!\(###") "000\-0000;0;_

(this stores the parentheses and hyphen with the data) and a Format setting that looks like

(&&&) @@@-@@@@

your data will display as

(206() 5) 55--1212

Adding a Scroll Bar

When you have a field that can contain a long data string (for example, the Bio field in the Authors table), it's a good idea to provide a scroll bar in the control to make it easy to scan through all the data. This scroll bar appears whenever you select the control. If you don't add a scroll bar, you must use the arrow keys to move up and down through the data.

To add a scroll bar, first open the form in Design view. Select the control, and open its property sheet. Then set the Scroll Bars property to Vertical. For example, if you open the frmAuthors form in Form view and tab to (or click in) the Bio text box on the second page, the vertical scroll bar appears, as shown in Figure 14-22.

FIGURE 14-22.
The Bio text box with
a scroll bar added.

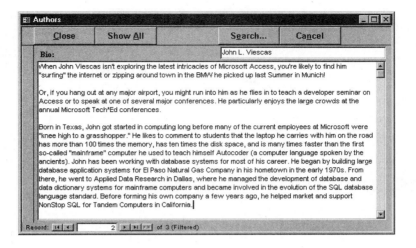

Enabling and Locking Controls

You might not want users of your form to select or update certain controls. You can set these conditions with the control's Enabled and Locked properties. For example, if you use a control to display an AutoNumber field, you can be certain that Access will provide the field's value. So it's a good idea to set the control's Enabled property to No (so that the user can't select it) and the control's Locked property to Yes (so that the user can't update it). Table 14-7 shows the effects of the Enabled and Locked property settings. Note, however, that if you want the user to be able to use the Access built-in Find facility to search for a particular AutoNumber value (such as AuthorID in the frmAuthors form), you should leave Enabled set to Yes to allow the user to select the field and find values in it.

TABLE 14-7. Settings for the Enabled and Locked Properties

Enabled	Locked	Description
Yes	Yes	Control can have the focus. Data is displayed normally and can be copied but not changed.
No	No	Control can't have the focus. Control and data appear dimmed.
Yes	No	Control can have the focus. Data is displayed normally and can be copied and changed.
No	Yes	Control can't have the focus. Data is displayed normally but can't be copied or changed.

In some cases, you might want to allow a control to be selected with the mouse but to be skipped over as the user tabs through the controls on the form. You can set the control's Tab Stop property to No while leaving its Enabled property set to Yes. This might be useful for controls for which you also set the Locked property to Yes. Setting the Tab Stop property to No keeps the user from tabbing into the control, but the user can select the control with the mouse to use the Find command or to copy the data in the control to the Clipboard.

Setting Form Properties

In addition to the controls on a form, the form itself has a number of properties that you can use to control its appearance and how it works.

The Default View and Views Allowed Properties

When the Form Wizard built the original Orders form for you, it set the Default View property of the form to Single Form. This is the view you'll see first when you open the form. With the Single Form setting, you can see only one record at a time and you have to use the record number box, the arrows to the left and right of the record number box, or the Go To command on the Records menu to move to another record. If you set the Default View property of the form to Continuous Forms, you can see multiple records on a short form and you can use the scroll bar on the right side of the form to scroll through the records. Because one record's data in the Orders table fills the form, the Single Form setting is probably the best choice.

Another property, Views Allowed, lets you control whether a user can change to the Datasheet view of the form. The default setting is Both, meaning that a user can use the toolbar or the View menu to switch between views. If you're designing a form to be used in an application, you will usually want to eliminate either Form or Datasheet view. For the Orders form, set the Views Allowed property to Form; the Datasheet View option on the Form View toolbar button's drop-down list should become unavailable (appear dimmed).

Setting the Tab Order

After the Form Wizard built the Orders form, you moved several controls around and changed the PayBy control to a combo box and the Printed control to a check box. As you design a form, Access sets the tab order for the controls in the order in which the controls are defined. When you delete a control and replace it with another, Access places the new control at the end of the tab order. If you want to change the tab order that Access created, you can set a different tab order. Choose the Tab Order command from the View menu to open the Tab Order dialog box, as shown in Figure 14-23.

FIGURE 14-23.

The Tab Order dialog box.

As you can see, the PayBy and Printed controls don't appear where they should in the Custom Order list. Click the Auto Order button to reorder the controls so that the tab order corresponds to the arrangement of the controls on the form, from left to right and from top to bottom. You can make additional adjustments to the list by clicking the row selector for a control to highlight it and then clicking the row selector again and dragging the control to its new location in the list. Since this form has two columns, you might want to rearrange the tab order to first move down one column and then the other. Click OK to save your changes to the Custom Order list.

You can also change an individual control's place in the tab order by setting the control's Tab Index property. The Tab Index property of the first control on the form is 0, the second is 1, and so on. If you use this method to assign a new Tab Index setting to a control and some other control already has that Tab Index setting, Access resequences the Tab Index settings. The result is the same as if you had dragged the control to that relative position (as indicated by the new Tab Index setting) in the Tab Order dialog box.

The Record Selectors, Scroll Bars, and Navigation Buttons Properties

Because the Orders form you've been designing displays one record at a time, it might not be useful to display the row selector on the left side of the form. You've also designed the form to show all the data in a single window, so a scroll bar along the right side of the window isn't necessary. You also don't need a horizontal scroll bar. You probably should keep the record number box at the bottom of the form, however. To make these changes, set the form's Record Selectors property on the property sheet to No, the Scroll Bars property to Neither, and the Navigation Buttons property to Yes. Your form should look something like the one shown in Figure 14-24 on the next page.

FIGURE 14-24.
The Orders form without a record selector.

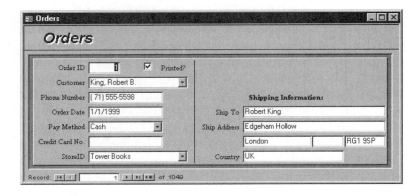

The Pop Up and Modal Properties

You might occasionally want to design a form that stays on top of all other forms even when it doesn't have the focus. Notice that the toolbox, property sheet, and field list in Design view all have this characteristic. These are called *pop-up forms*. You can make the Orders form a pop-up form by setting the form's Pop Up property to Yes. Figure 14-25 shows the Orders form as a pop-up form on top of the Database window, which has the focus. Note that the form can "float" on top of other forms or windows, and it can also be moved over the toolbars and menu bars. A form that isn't a pop-up form cannot leave the Access workspace below the toolbars.

As you'll learn in Part VI of this book, it's sometimes useful to create forms that ask the user for information that's needed in order to perform the next task. Forms have a Modal property that you can set to Yes to "lock" the user into the form when it's open. The user must make a choice in the form or close the form in order to go on to other tasks. When a modal form is open, you can switch to another application but you can't select any other form, menu, or toolbar button in Access until you dismiss the modal form. You've probably noticed that most dialog boxes are modal forms. Modal isn't a good choice for the

FIGURE 14-25.

The Orders form as a pop-up form on top of the Database window.

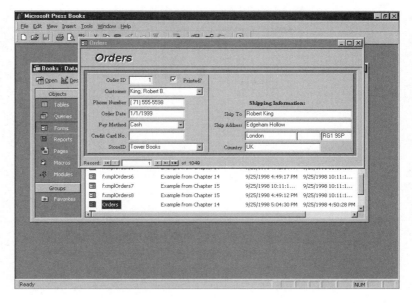

Orders form, but you'll use the Modal property later to help control application flow.

> **NOTE**
>
> As you'll see later, you can set a form's Control Box property to No to remove all control features from the form's title bar. This means that both the Control-menu box (which contains the Close command) and the form's Close button (at the right end of the title bar) will not appear. If you also set the form's Modal property to Yes, you should always provide an alternative way to close a modal form, such as a command button that runs a Close macro action. Otherwise, the only way to close the form is to use the Windows Ctrl+F4 key combination. *See Chapter 18, "Advanced Report Design," for details about adding a command button to close a form.*

Controlling Editing and Filtering

You can set several properties on forms to control whether data in the form can be updated or whether data in the underlying tables can change. You can also prevent or allow user-applied filters on the form. These properties and their settings are shown in Table 14-8 on the next page.

TABLE 14-8. **Properties for Controlling Editing and Filtering**

Property	Description
Filter	Contains the latest criteria applied as a filter on this form. Forms also have a FilterOn property that you can't see in the Form window in Design view. When FilterOn is True, the data displayed in the form is filtered by the criteria string found in the Filter property.
Order By	Contains the latest sorting criteria applied to this form. Forms also have an OrderByOn property that you can't see in the Form window in Design view. When OrderByOn is True, the data displayed in the form is sorted by the criteria string found in the Order By property.
Allow Filters	Determines whether a user can see selected records by applying filtering and sorting criteria and whether the user can see all records by choosing the Show All Records command from the Records menu. If you set the Data Entry property to Yes and set the Allow Filters property to No, the user can enter only new data and cannot change the form to view other existing records. The valid settings for the Allow Filters property are Yes and No.
Allow Edits	Determines whether a user can change records in this form. The valid settings are Yes and No.
Allow Deletions	Determines whether a user can delete records in this form. The valid settings are Yes and No.
Allow Additions	Determines whether a user can add records using this form. The valid settings are Yes and No.
Data Entry	Determines whether the form opens a blank record in which you can insert new data. Access won't retrieve rows from the form's recordset. Setting Data Entry to Yes is effective only when Allow Additions is set to Yes.

The Control Box and Min Max Buttons Properties

In some cases, you might want to prevent the user from opening the form's Control menu (the Control menu contains the Restore, Move, Size, Minimize, Maximize, Close, and Next commands) or from using the Minimize and Maximize buttons. If you want to perform special processing before a form closes, you might want to provide a command button to do the processing and then close the form. You can set the form's Control Box property to No to remove the Control-menu box from the upper left corner of the form window and the Close button from the upper right corner. This also removes the Minimize and Maximize buttons.

You can set the form's Close Button property to No to remove the Close button but leave the Control-menu box (with Close disabled on the Control menu). You can set the form's Min Max Buttons property to Both Enabled, None, Min Enabled, or Max Enabled. If you disable a Minimize or Maximize button, the related command on the form's Control menu becomes grayed out. Finally, you can set the Whats This Button property to Yes to display the Help button, but to do this you must set the Min Max Buttons property to No.

> If you remove the form's Control-menu box and don't provide an alternative way to close the form, the only way you can close the form is to use the Ctrl+F4 key combination. If you create an AutoKeys macro that intercepts the Ctrl+F4 key combination, you must provide an alternative way to close the form—most likely with a command button. *See Chapter 18, "Advanced Report Design," for details about adding a command button to close a form. See Chapter 23, "Automating Your Application with Visual Basic," for details on creating an AutoKeys macro.*

Setting the Border Style

In most cases, you'll want to create forms with a normal border that allows you to size the window and move it around. Forms have a Border Style property that lets you define the look of the border and whether the window can be sized or moved. The Border Style property settings are shown in Table 14-9.

TABLE 14-9. Settings for the Border Style Property

Setting	Description
None	The form has no borders, Control-menu box, title bar, or Minimize and Maximize buttons. You cannot resize or move the form when it is open. You can select the form and press Ctrl+F4 to close it unless the form's Pop Up property is set to Yes. You should provide an alternative way to close this type of form.
Thin	The form has a thin border, signifying that the form cannot be resized.

(continued)

TABLE 14-9. *continued*

Setting	Description
Sizeable	This is the default setting. The form can be resized.
Dialog	If the Pop Up property is set to Yes, the form's border is a thick double line (like that of a true Windows dialog box), signifying that the form cannot be resized. If the Pop Up property is set to No, the Dialog setting is the same as the Thin setting.

Setting Form and Control Defaults

You can use the Set Control Defaults command on the Format menu to change the defaults for the various controls on your form. If you want to change the default property settings for all new controls of a particular type, select a control of that type, set the control's properties to the desired default values, and then choose the Set Control Defaults command from the Format menu. The settings of the currently selected control will become the default settings for any subsequent definitions of that type of control on your form.

For example, you might want all new labels to show blue text on a white background. To make this change, place a label on your form and set the label's Fore Color property to blue and its Back Color property to white using the Fore Color and Back Color toolbar buttons. Choose the Set Control Defaults command from the Format menu while this label is selected. Any new labels you place on the form will have the new default settings.

You can also create a special form to define new default properties for all your controls. To do this, open a new blank form and place on it one of each type of control for which you want to define default properties. Modify the properties of the controls to your liking, use these controls to reset the control defaults for the form (by choosing Set Control Defaults from the Format menu for each control), and save the form with the name *Normal*. The Normal form becomes your *form template*. Any new control that you place on a form created after you define a template (except forms for which you've already changed the default for one or more controls) will use the default property settings you defined for that control type on the Normal form. To define a name other than *Normal* for your default form and report templates, choose Options from the Tools menu, and then click the Forms/

Reports tab. Enter the new name in the Form Template text box. Then save your template under the new name you specified on the Form/Reports tab.

Working with AutoFormat

After you define control defaults that give you the "look" you want for your application, you can also set these defaults as an *AutoFormat* that you can use in the Form Wizards. To create an AutoFormat definition, open the form that has the defaults set the way you want them and then click the AutoFormat button on the toolbar or choose AutoFormat from the Format menu. Click the Customize button to open the dialog box shown in Figure 14-26. Select the Create A New AutoFormat option to save a format that matches the form you currently have open, and then click OK. In the next dialog box, type a name for your new format and then click OK. Your new format will now appear in the list of form AutoFormats. As you saw in Chapter 13, "Building Forms," you can select any of the form AutoFormats to dictate the look of a form created by the wizards.

FIGURE 14-26.

Creating a new Auto-Format definition.

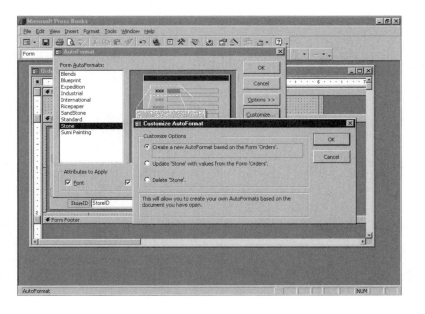

If you have previously defined an AutoFormat, you can update it or delete it using the AutoFormat dialog box. You cannot update or delete any of the built-in formats, however.

Now you should be comfortable with designing forms and adding special touches to make your forms more attractive and usable. In the next chapter, you'll learn advanced form design techniques: using multiple-table queries in forms, building forms within forms, and performing simple form linking using command buttons.

CHAPTER 15

Advanced Form Design

I n Chapters 13 and 14, you learned how to design a form that works with data in a table and you saw how to display data from another table by using a combo box or a list box. In this chapter, you'll learn how to design a form that consolidates information from multiple tables. You'll find out how to:

- Create a form based on a query that joins multiple tables

- Embed a subform in a main form so that you can work with related data from two tables or queries at the same time

- Define conditional formatting of a control based on the data values in the form

- Use the ActiveX tab control to handle multiple subforms within one area on a form

- Create a form that spreads many data fields across multiple pages

- Link two related forms using a simple command button built with a wizard

Basing a Form on a Multiple-Table Query

In Chapter 8, "Adding Power with Select Queries," you learned how to bring together data from multiple tables using select queries. The result of a select query is called a *recordset*. A recordset contains all the information you need, but it's in the unadorned Datasheet view format. Forms enable you to present this data in a more attractive and meaningful way. And in the same way that you can update data in queries, you can also update data using a form that is based on a query.

A Many-to-One Form

As you discovered in the previous two chapters, it's easy to design a form that allows you to view and update the data from a single table. You also learned how to include selected fields from related tables using a list box or a combo box. But what if you want to see more information from the related tables? The best way to do this is to design a query based on the two (or more) related tables and use that query as the basis of your form.

When you create a query with two or more tables, you're usually working with one-to-many relationships among the tables. As you learned earlier, Microsoft Access lets you update any data in the table that is on the "many" side of the relationship and any nonkey fields on the "one" side of the relationship. This means that when you base a form on a query, you can update all of the fields in the form that come from the "many" table and most of the fields from the "one" side. Because the primary purpose of the form is to search and update records on the "many" side of the relationship while reviewing information on the "one" side, this is called a *many-to-one form*.

In Chapter 8, "Adding Power with Select Queries," you learned how to build a multiple-table query that displays both Club and Contract information in the Entertainment Scheduling sample database. In Chapter 13, "Building Forms," you explored the fundamentals of form construction by creating a simple form to display club data. The key task in the Entertainment Scheduling database is the creation of contracts that define which groups have agreed to play in which clubs on specific dates and for a specific fee. You clearly need a form to edit the tblContracts table to do this. While the tblContracts table does carry forward some of the details about the group (such as the names of the current group members), it has only the ClubID field to link you back to the club information. When you look at contract data in a form, you probably want to see more than just the club ID.

You learned near the end of Chapter 13 how to create a combo box control to display more meaningful data from the "one" side of a many-to-one relationship. You could use a combo box to display a club name instead of a number in the contract form. But what if you want to see the club address and manager name or phone number when you select a new club? And how can you make the current data from the tblGroups table available to procedures that you might create to use with the form to automatically copy the current group information to a new contract? To perform these tasks, you need to base your contract form on a query that joins multiple tables.

Designing a Many-to-One Query

Open the Entertainment Scheduling sample database, and then open a new Query window in Design view. Add the tblClubs, tblContracts, and tblGroups field lists using the Show Table dialog box that appears. You should see a relationship line from the ClubID field in the tblClubs field list to the ClubID field in the tblContracts field list. Similarly, you should see a relationship line linking the GroupID field in the tblGroups field list to the GroupID field in the tblContracts list. If you don't see these lines, you should close the Query window and switch back to the Database window, choose the Relationships command from the Tools menu, add the appropriate one-to-many relationships between the tblClubs and tblContracts tables and the tblGroups and tblContracts tables, and then open a new Query window and add the three field lists.

You want to be able to update all fields in the tblContracts table, so drag the special "all fields" indicator (*) from the tblContracts field list to the design grid. From the tblGroups table, you need most of the detail fields, such as group leader name (first and last name fields), address, phone numbers, and group size. Do not include the GroupID field from tblGroups; you want to be able to update the GroupID field, but only in the tblContracts table. If you include the GroupID field from the tblGroups table, it might confuse you later as you design the form. From the tblClubs table, you need fields such as manager name, address, days and times the club is open, and so forth.

You can find a query already built for this purpose (named *qryXmplContracts*) in the Entertainment Scheduling database, as shown in Figure 15-1 on the next page. If you explore the database and look up the Record Source property for the frmContracts form, you'll discover that it uses the qryContracts query. In this query, many of the fields from the tblGroups table have been given aliases to make them easy to distinguish from fields of the same name in the tblContracts table. Also, the group leader name and the club manager name are each a single field in the tblContracts table but are separate first and last names in the original tables. This query uses expressions to concatenate these names into a single field. Finally, the query eliminates any contracts that have a deleted ("D") status code. There's no point in editing or cluttering up the display with contracts that have been deleted. For this example, the simpler query, qryXmplContracts, with only the names and addresses from the two tables related to contracts, will do quite nicely.

FIGURE 15-1.

The qryXmplContracts query in Design view.

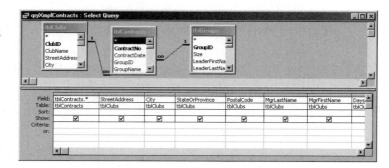

Designing a Many-to-One Form

Now that you have the query you need, find the query definition in the Database window and open a new form based on the query. You can use the Form Wizard if you like. From the tblContracts table, include the ContractNo, ContractDate, GroupID, ClubID, ContractPrice, ContractTerms, BeginningDate, EndingDate, and NumberOfWeeks fields. From tblClubs, include the StreetAddress, City, StateOrProvince, PostalCode, MgrLastName, MgrFirstName, and DaysTimes fields. From tblGroups, select the Size, LeaderFirstName, LeaderLastName, StreetAddress, City, StateOrProvince, and PostalCode fields. If you're using the Form Wizard, your field selections should include those shown in Figure 15-2. Click Next to go to the second window of the wizard.

When you start with a query containing multiple tables, or if you select fields from multiple tables in the first window of the Form Wizard, the wizard gives you some interesting choices if it can determine which tables are on the "one" side and which are on the "many." As you can see in Figure 15-3, the wizard assumes that you want to see all the fields as a single view from the "many" (tblContracts) side of this relationship. If you select either "by tblClubs" or "by tblGroups" from the list on the left, the wizard changes the display on the right to offer either a main form and subform or linked forms. (You'll learn about building subforms in the next section.) If you select linked forms, the

FIGURE 15-2.
Selecting fields from a
multiple-table query
in the Form Wizard.

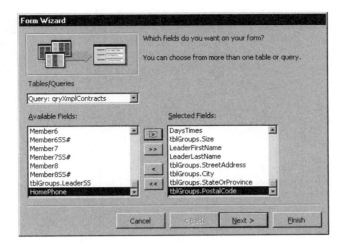

FIGURE 15-3.
Selecting a single form
for fields from multiple
tables.

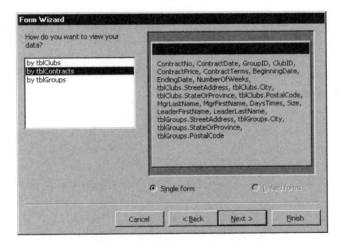

wizard creates two forms for you. The first form displays only the information from the "one" side (either tblGroups or tblClubs). A command button on the first form opens the second form, which displays the information from the "many" side (tblContracts).

For now, select "by tblContracts" to see all the fields on one form. Select a columnar layout in the next window, and select the style you want in the window that follows. Give your form a title of *Contracts* in the last step. When the wizard finishes, you should see a form similar to that shown in Figure 15-4 on the next page.

This form could use some polishing, but the wizard has very nicely placed everything on the form for us. Note the combo boxes for

FIGURE 15-4.

A "many-to-one" form to display data from multiple tables.

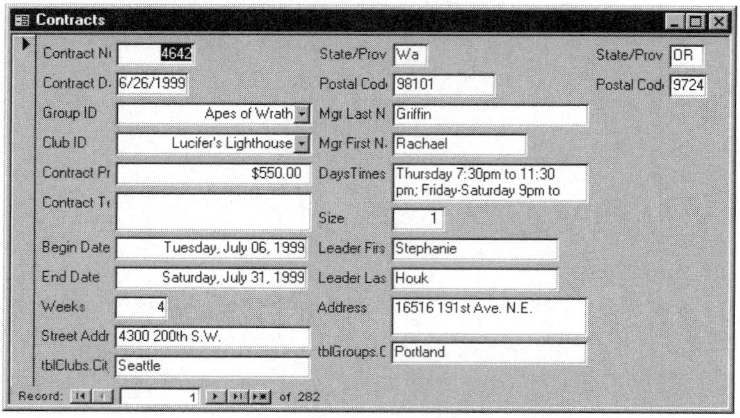

Group ID and Club ID. The wizard placed these on the form because the tblContracts table had Lookup properties set for both of these fields to display a more meaningful group or club name. Perhaps you can begin to appreciate how important it is to pay attention to these sorts of details when you design your table. Doing so will save you a lot of work as you build your application.

Try changing the club ID on the first contract to something else and watch what happens. You should see the corresponding manager name and club address information pop into view, as shown in Figure 15-5. Because you haven't done anything to set the Locked property for any of the fields, you can also update the address and city information for the displayed club. If you do this, the new club information appears for all contracts created for that club.

FIGURE 15-5.

Changing the Club ID displays new related club information automatically.

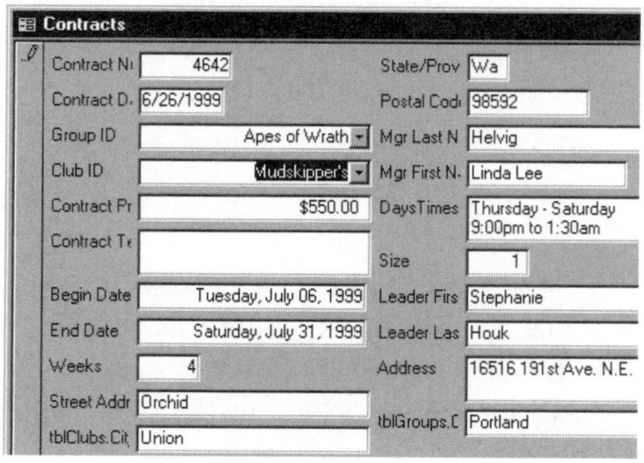

You'll discover later when you explore the actual frmContracts form that the query automatically pulls in the related information from the "one" side if you change the foreign key on the "many" side. In the Entertainment Scheduling application, a Visual Basic procedure runs whenever you change either the club ID or the group ID in the contracts form. This code copies the new data to the appropriate fields in the underlying contracts table. Because this sample form isn't yet designed to update the underlying contracts table, you shouldn't change the club ID or the group ID in too many contracts using this form.

Creating and Embedding Subforms

If you want to show data from several tables and be able to update the data in more than one of the tables, you probably need to use something more complex than a standard form. In the Microsoft Press Books database, the main order information is in the tblOrders table. Of course, an order is pretty meaningless without some books associated with the order. The tblBooks table lists all the books in this database available for sale.

Because any one order might have many different books and any one book might appear in many orders, the tblOrders table is related to the tblBooks table in a many-to-many relationship. *See Chapter 5, "Building Your Database in Microsoft Access," for a review of relationship types.* The tblOrderDetails table establishes the necessary link between the orders and the books in each order.

When you are viewing information about a particular order, you surely also want to see and edit the order detail information. You could create a single form that displays tblOrders joined with tblOrderDetails, similar to the frmContracts form you built in the previous section. However, the focus would be on the order details, so you would be able to see in a single form row only one book per row. You could perhaps design a Continuous View form, but you would see the information from tblOrders repeated over and over.

Subforms can help solve this problem. You can create a main form that displays the order information (you already did this in the two previous chapters) and embed in it a subform that displays all the related rows from the linking table. If you use a combo box on the subform, you can display the names of the books that match the ISBN numbers in the tblOrderDetails table.

Specifying the Subform Source

You can embed up to two layers of subforms within another form. It's often easier to start by designing the innermost form and working outward. Begin by deciding on the data source for the subform.

In the example described above, you want to create or update rows in the tblOrderDetails table to create, modify, or delete links between orders in the tblOrders table and books in the tblBooks table. You also want to modify the display because the tblOrderDetails table contains only the linking fields for OrderID and ISBNNumber—not very useful information to display on a form. You need to make sure that the Lookup properties for the ISBNNumber field are set to display the book titles (and, perhaps, edition numbers) from the tblBooks table. (They are.) Since it makes sense to see the ISBN number, book title, and edition number after setting an ISBN number in the linking field, you need to include the tblBooks table in the subform data source so that you can pull the book title and edition number from this table for display. You'll also need this table if you want to calculate the amount owed, because you can find the book's suggested retail price only in tblBooks, not in tblOrderDetails. Of course, you'll also need the Quantity and Discount fields from tblOrderDetails.

Start by opening a new query in Design view. In the Show Table dialog box, add the field lists for the tblOrderDetails and tblBooks tables to the Query window. You want to be able to update all the fields in the tblOrderDetails table, so copy them to the design grid. You can do so by using the all fields indicator (*). Add the Title, EditionNumber, and SuggPrice fields from the tblBooks table. Add a calculated field called ExtPrice to display the extended price.

Figure 15-6 shows the formula for calculating the extended price. As you learned in Chapter 8, "Adding Power with Select Queries," you can use the Round and CCur functions to round to the nearest penny. The formula shown here also includes the NZ (null to zero) built-in function to display a zero value if any argument is Null. The reason you need to use the NZ function is that no price will be available until you set an ISBN number in a new tblOrderDetails row when adding a book to an order. If you don't include NZ, the form will display #Error in the extended price control if you enter an order quantity before setting the ISBN number. Users aren't likely to enter a quantity before choosing a book, but if they do, you can be sure they'll come ask you about the #Error display if you don't take care of this little detail!

FIGURE 15-6.

The formula to calculate the extended price in the qryOrderDetails query.

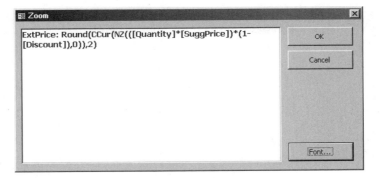

Your query should look similar to the one shown in Figure 15-7. (This query is saved as *qryOrderBooks* in the Microsoft Press Books sample database.) Notice that the tblBooks table has a one-to-many relationship with the tblOrderDetails table. This means that you can update any field in the tblOrderDetails table (including both primary key fields, as long as you don't create a duplicate row) because the tblOrderDetails table is on the "many" side of the relationship. Save the query so that you can use it as you design the subform. You can save your query as qryOrderDetails, as shown in Figure 15-7, or use the sample query.

FIGURE 15-7.

A query for updating the tblOrderDetails table from a subform while displaying related information from the tblBooks table.

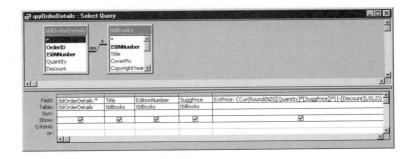

Designing the Subform

You'll end up displaying the single ISBNNumber field bound to a combo box that shows the book title and edition number. After you choose an ISBN number, you probably still want to see the title and edition—but in controls that can't be updated. (You don't want a user to be able to accidentally change book titles via this form!) Of course, you need the Quantity and Discount fields from tblOrderDetails so that you can update these fields. You should also display the price (the SuggPrice field) and the extended price calculation (the ExtPrice field).

For this purpose, you could use a form in either Datasheet or Continuous Forms view. It's simple to build a subform designed to be used in Datasheet view because you only need to include the fields you want to display in the detail section of the form, without any regard to alignment or placement. Access takes care of ordering, sizing, and providing column headers in the datasheet. However, I like to use Continuous Forms view because that view lets you control the size of the columns—in Datasheet view, a user can resize the columns, including shrinking a column so that it's no longer visible. Furthermore, if the subform is in Single Form view or Continuous Form view, the Size/To Fit command will make the subform control the right size. If the subform is in Datasheet view, however, the Size/To Fit command will size the control to the size of the subform in Form view, not to an even number of datasheet rows wide or high. Also, the user is free to resize the row height and column width in Datasheet view, so how you size the subform control in Design view is only a guess.

Start by opening a new form based on the query you just created (or use the qryOrderBooks query that's already defined in the Microsoft Press Books sample database). Try creating the form without using the Form Wizard.

Once you're in Design view for the subform, click the text box control in the toolbox and then open the property sheet window and set the Auto Label property to No. Do the same for the combo box control. This lets you create these controls in the Detail section without a label attached. Also, be sure you turn off the Control Wizard in the toolbox, because the combo box you need to build already has Lookup properties set from the table design. To build the form, follow these steps.

1 Click the combo box control, and drag the ISBNNumber field to the Detail section of the subform. Because the Lookup properties are defined properly in the source table, the combo box is already the way you want it. Size the box to be about one inch wide.

2 Drag the Title field to the form, and position it next to the ISBNNumber combo box. Size the resulting text box to be about 2.25 inches wide.

3 Add text boxes for the EditionNumber, SuggPrice, Quantity, Discount, and ExtPrice fields next to the other two fields. The text box for Edition can be quite narrow; it normally will display a single digit. Size the other text boxes to be about 0.4 inch wide.

4 Choose Align from the Format menu, and then choose Top from the submenu to line up all the controls in the Detail section. You

might also want to use the Horizontal Spacing/Make Equal command on the Format menu to make the spacing uniform across the form. Move all the controls near the top of the Detail section, and size the Detail section to be about 0.25 inch high. (You can size the Detail section precisely by clicking the Detail section bar and then setting the Height property on the property sheet.) This gives you a small amount of space above and below the controls.

5 Be sure that Form Header/Footer is checked on the View menu. Size the header to be about 0.35 inch high, and the footer to about 0.2 inch high.

6 Use the Label tool to create labels in the Form Header section above each field in the Detail section. To create a multiline label, hold down the Ctrl key and press Enter to store a carriage return while typing in the Caption property of the label.

7 Add two unbound text boxes to the Form Footer section, one under the Quantity field and the other under the ExtPrice field. In the first text box, set the Control Source property to *=Sum([Quantity])*. Set the Control Source in the second text box to *=Sum([ExtPrice])*, and set the Format property to Currency. These two controls will display the totals for the order. Add a descriptive label with a Caption property set to *Totals:*.

All you have left to do is to set the subform's Default View property to Continuous Forms, set the Scroll Bars property to Vertical Only (your design should fit all the fields within the subform control on the main form so that the user won't need to scroll left and right), and set the Navigation Buttons property to No (you can use the vertical scrollbar to move through the multiple rows). The result of your work should look something like Figure 15-8.

FIGURE 15-8.

The subform to edit order details in Design view.

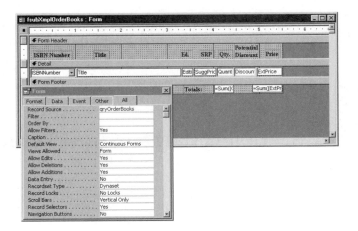

You can switch to the subform's Form view to check your work. You can see the Continuous Form view in Figure 15-9. Because this form isn't linked in as a subform yet (which will limit the display to the current order), the totals displayed in the form footer are the totals for all orders. You can find this form saved as *fsubXmplOrderBooks* in the Microsoft Press Books sample database.

FIGURE 15-9.

The order details subform in Continuous Form view.

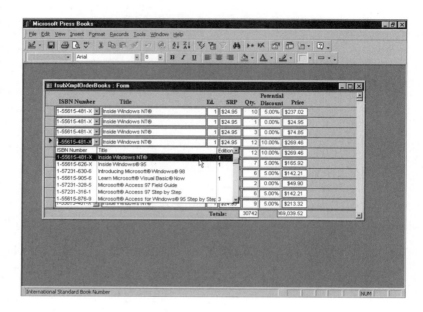

 NOTE

> If you'll be using a subform in Datasheet view when it's embedded in another form, you have to switch to Datasheet view to adjust how the datasheet looks and then save the subform from Datasheet view to preserve the look you want. Also, in Datasheet view, all columns inherit their captions from the label attached to the control in Design view. The label must be attached to the control for this to work. If the label isn't attached, you'll see the field's name displayed—it won't even inherit the Caption property from the field. You must also use the Datasheet view of the form to make adjustments to fonts and row height. The font in Datasheet view is independent of any font defined for the controls in Form view.

Specifying the Main Form Source

Now it's time to move on to the main form. You need a table or a query as the source of the form. You want to be able to view, update, add, and delete orders, so your row source should include the tblOrders table. You can also apply the techniques you just learned for building a "many-to-one" form that allows you to insert and update data in tblOrders while viewing information from tables related on the "one" side—tblCustomers and tblStores. You can build the query you need by performing the following steps.

1   Start a new query on the tblOrders table and include all the fields in the design grid by using the special "*" field.

2   Add the tblCustomers field list to the query, and then drag the LastName, FirstName, MiddleInit, Address, City, StateOrProvince, PostalCode, and Country fields to the query design grid.

3   Add criteria to sort in ascending order under LastName and FirstName. (You'll recall from Chapter 8, "Adding Power with Select Queries," that the sequence of fields in the design grid is important for sorting—so be sure that LastName is before FirstName on the query design grid.)

4   Add the tblStores field list to your design grid.

5   Double-click the join line Access creates, and select the option to include all records from tblOrders and only those records from tblStores where the joined fields are equal. In this application, specifying a store in an order is optional, so many orders might not have a store specified. If you don't create an outer join in your query, you'll see only orders that have stores specified in the resulting recordset.

6   Include the StoreName, Address, City, StateOrProvince, PostalCode, and Country fields from tblStores.

7   Because you also have Address, City, StateOrProvince, PostalCode, and Country fields from tblCustomers in this query, it might be a good idea to "rename" the store fields to make them easier to use in the final form. In the sample query in the Microsoft Press Books database (*qxmplOrdersSorted*), I added "St" in front of the field names so that the Address field from tblStores is named StAddress, the City field is named StCity, and so on.

8   Finally, add the OrderID and OrderDate fields from tblOrders to the query, clear the Show box (these fields are already included in tblOrders.*), and add criteria to sort in Ascending order.

Your query should look something like that shown in Figure 15-10 on the next page. (I moved the fields lists in the top of the query window to make the relationships easier to see.) You can find this query saved as *qxmplOrdersSorted* in the sample database.

FIGURE 15-10.
A query for updating the tblOrders table from a main form while displaying related customer and store information.

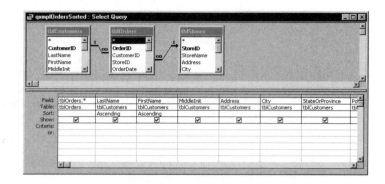

Creating the Main Form

Building the form for the tblOrders table is fairly straightforward. In fact, you can select the query you just created and use a Form Wizard to build the basic form in columnar format. I actually started with the fxmplOrders6 form (which we built in Chapter 13, "Building Forms"), changed the Record Source to point to the sorted query, and moved a few things around. The sample design shown in Figure 15-11 has a space at the bottom of the Detail section where you can place the subform to display order detail data. You can find this form saved as *fxmplOrders7* in the sample database.

FIGURE 15-11.
A main form to display order data, with space for a subform.

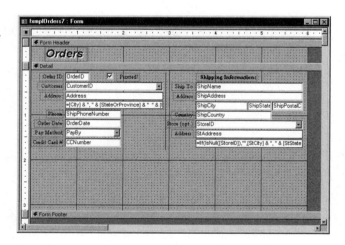

Embedding a Subform

You can use a couple of techniques to embed a subform in your main form. First, you can deselect the Control Wizards button in the toolbox, select the Subform/Subreport tool in the toolbox, and then click the upper left corner of the main form's empty area and drag the mouse pointer to create a subform control. If you leave the Control Wizards active, Access starts a wizard to help you build the subform when you place a subform control on your main form. Because you already built the subform, you don't need the wizard's help. Once the control is in place, set its Source Object property to point to the subform you built (or use the sample fsubXmplOrderBooks).

Another way to embed the subform (if you have a large enough screen to do this) is to place the Form window and the Database window side by side, find the form you want to embed as a subform, and then drag it from the Database window and drop it onto your form. In any case, your result should look something like Figure 15-12. You can find this form saved as *fxmplOrders8* in the Microsoft Press Books sample database.

FIGURE 15-12.

The new subform embedded in the form to edit orders.

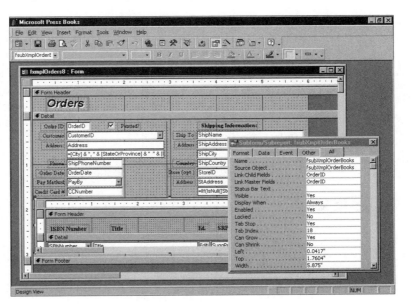

Access provides two key properties in the subform control that define the link between the outer form and the subform: Link Master Fields and Link Child Fields. The Link Master Fields property defines the field or fields in the Record Source of the outer form that Access uses to filter what you see on the subform. The Link Child Fields property defines the names of the related field(s) in the Record Source of the form that's inside the subform control. As you move from row to row in the outer form, Access uses the values it finds in the field(s) defined in Link

Master Fields as a filter against the fields in the subform defined in Link Child Fields. When you need to define multiple fields that provide the link, separate the field names in the property with a semicolon.

In this case, the OrderID field from tblOrders on the outer form is the link to the related rows on the subform. Likewise, the same OrderID field in tblOrderDetails is the field you want Access to filter to show related rows in the subform. Set both the Link Master Fields and Link Child Fields properties in the subform control to *OrderID*.

> If the Record Source of the outer form is a single table, Access automatically sets the Link Master Fields and Link Child Fields properties for you when it can find a related field in the table or query that you define as the Record Source of the form within the subform control. It does this when you either drag the subform to the main form or set the Source Object property of the subform control.

Sizing a subform that you display in Form view is quite simple. Choose the subform control, choose Size from the Format menu, and then choose To Fit from the submenu. In this case, you're using a subform in Continuous Form view, so Access will size the subform control to the correct width and to the nearest vertical height to fully display rows in the detail section. Note that if your subform default view is Datasheet view, using the Size/To Fit command won't work unless the form's Design view is exactly the same size as the datasheet. You have to switch in and out of Form view and manually adjust the size of the subform control.

> Access 2000 introduces a feature that allows you to directly edit your subform once you have defined it as the source for your subform control. As you can see in Figure 15-12 on the previous page, the design of form fsubXmplOrderBooks is visible in the subform control on the fxmplOrders8 form. You can click any control in the inner form and change its size or adjust its properties using the property sheet or the Formatting toolbar. You might need to temporarily expand the size of the subform control in order to work with the inner form easily. Note, however, that you cannot open the inner form in Design view separately from the Database window as long as you have the outer form open. You also cannot use File / Save As to save your changes to a different form definition.

When you finish, click the Form View button on the toolbar to see the completed form, as shown in Figure 15-13. Because you designed the main form using a "many-to-one" query, you can see that the customer name and address are updated by Access automatically each time you set a different CustomerID for the order. Likewise, Access shows you the related store information when you choose a StoreID for the order by using the combo box. Because you properly set the linking field information for the subform control, you can see the books for each order in the subform as you move from one order to another.

By the way, you can also use a Form Wizard to create a form with a subform. The wizard creates a single-column form for the main form and either a Tabular view or a Datasheet view of the subform.

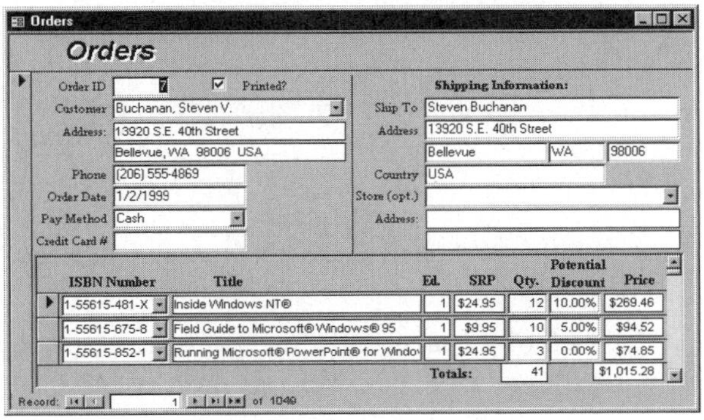

FIGURE 15-13.
A form to edit orders in a main form and order details in a subform.

⟨2000⟩ Using Conditional Formatting

Access 2000 includes a new feature that allows you to define dynamic modification of the formatting of text boxes and combo boxes. You can define an expression that tests the value in the text box or combo box or any other field available in the form. If the expression is true, Access will modify the Bold, Italic, Underline, Back Color, Fore Color, and Enabled properties for you based on the custom settings you associate with the expression.

This feature can be particularly useful for controlling field display in a subform in Continuous Form view. In previous releases, you had to write a macro or Visual Basic code to test values each time the user moved to a new row and then change the settings accordingly. This didn't work well in a subform because there's really only one copy of each control. For example, if you wanted to set the background color of the Discount field in the subform shown in Figure 15-13 when the value exceeded a certain percentage, you couldn't do it. You could detect when the user moved to a row with a high percentage discount, but setting the background of the Discount field would change the background for all rows the user could see.

To define conditional formatting, first open the form you need to modify in Design view. In this example, you can use the subform you find defined on fxmplOrders8 that you saw earlier in Figure 15-12. Click the Discount field in the subform, and then choose Conditional Formatting from the Format menu to see the dialog box shown in Figure 15-14.

FIGURE 15-14.

Defining conditional formatting for the Discount field.

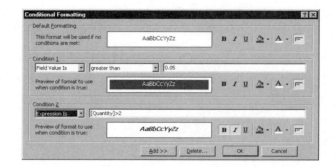

In the Default Formatting box, you can see the currently defined format for the control. You can use the Bold, Italic, Underline, Back Color, Fore Color, and Enabled buttons to modify the default. When you first open this dialog box, Access displays a single blank Condition 1. In the leftmost combo box, you can choose Field Value Is to test for a value in the field, Expression Is to create a logical expression that can test other fields on the form or compare another field to this one, and Field Has Focus to define settings the control will inherit when the user clicks in the control.

When you choose Field Value Is as shown in the first condition in Figure 15-14, the second combo box provides logical comparison options such as Less Than, Equal To, or Greater Than. Choose the logical comparison you want, and then enter the value to compare the field to in the text box on the right. Set the formatting properties you want the control to have if the test is true in the buttons to the right. In the example shown, I entered a test for Discount greater than 5 percent. When the discount exceeds this amount, I have asked Access to set the background to a dark color with white text.

To define additional tests, click the Add button at the bottom of the dialog box. Each time you click this button, Access displays an additional Condition definition row. In the second and subsequent rows, you can choose from Field Value Is or Expression Is in the leftmost combo box. In the example shown, I entered an expression to test for a value in Quantity greater than 2. When this is true, I have asked Access to display the value in Bold and Italic. Note that Access tests the conditions beginning with the first one and stops when it finds a condition is true. Therefore using the example shown, Access will display the Discount with white characters on a dark background whenever the value exceeds 5 percent, even if the Quantity is also greater than 2.

If you switch to Form View after entering this conditional formatting criteria, you should see a result similar to the one shown in Figure 15-15. You can find this form and subform, saved as *fxmplOrders9* and *fsubXmplOrderBooks2*, respectively, in the sample Microsoft Press Books database.

FIGURE 15-15.
Access displays the Discount as white on a dark background when the discount exceeds 5 percent and in bold italics when more than two copies are ordered (but the discount does not exceed 5 percent).

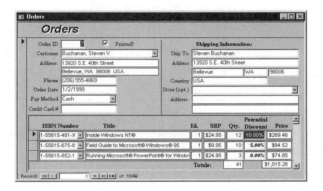

Introducing ActiveX Controls—The Tab Control

As you have just seen, a subform is an excellent way to create a form that lets you edit information from the "one" side of a relationship in the main form (Orders) while editing data from the "many" side of a relationship (Order Details) in the subform window. Building a subform is very simple for a single one-to-many relationship, but what can you do when you have either multiple relationships or lots of data you want to deal with on a form that must fit within a single "page" on the screen? As you saw in Chapter 12, "Form Basics," when working with the form to edit book data (see Figure 12-11), Access provides an ActiveX tab control that lets you place multiple controls on individual tabs within a form. The controls on a tab can be as complex as subforms (in the case of the Microsoft Press Books database, to display author and category information) or as simple as text boxes (which can display the potentially lengthy Liner Notes information). You can see the frmBooksPlain form (the copy of the form that doesn't require

you to start the application to see all the form's features) with the tab
that shows book categories selected in Figure 15-16.

FIGURE 15-16.

A form to edit books
using the ActiveX tab
control.

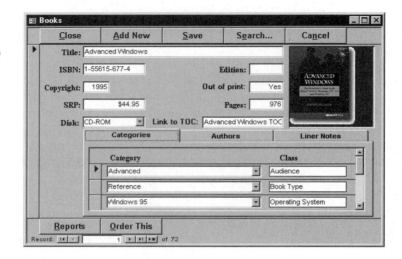

Working with the tab control is quite simple. If you like, you can start
with a simple columnar form built by the Form Wizard. Use
qryBooksSorted as the Record Source (don't include the LinerNotes
field), and leave a space at the bottom of the form to add a tab control. You can also start with fxmplBooks1, which you can find in the
Microsoft Press Books sample database. To build a control that lets
you alternately see category, author, or liner notes information for the
current book, perform the following steps.

1 Click the Tab Control tool in the toolbox, and drag an area on
the form about 1.5 inches from the top and approximately 4.75
inches wide and 1.5 inches high. Access shows you a basic tab
control with two tabs defined. Open the property sheet window,
and set the Tab Fixed Width property to 1.5 inches (after we add
a third tab, the tabs will stretch across nearly the entire width of
the control).

2 While the tab control has the focus, choose Tab Control Page
from the Insert menu, as shown here. Access will add a third tab
to the control.

3 Access always inserts new tabs in front of the currently selected tab. If you want to place the new tab at the end of the tab order, you can select the tab and set its Page Index property. Another way to set the tab sequence is to right-click the control, and then choose Page Order from the shortcut menu to see the dialog box shown here. Select a tab, and move it up or down to get the sequence you want.

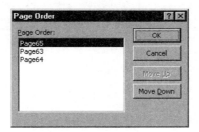

4 Click the first tab, and set the Caption property in the property sheet to Categories.

5 Click the second tab, and set the Caption property to Authors.

6 Click the third tab, and set the Caption property to Liner Notes.

7 Click the Categories tab to bring it to the front. Click the subform control in the Toolbox, and set the Auto Label property to No. Add a subform control to the Categories tab, set its Source Object property to fsubXmplBookCategories (the Microsoft Press Books database contains built-in subforms to make this exercise easy), and set the Link Child Fields and Link Master Fields properties to ISBNNumber. You can also drag the subform from the Database window and drop it onto the tab if you like.

8 Click the Authors tab, and add the fsubXmplBookAuthors form to that tab as a subform. Be sure to set the link properties of the subform control to ISBNNumber.

9 Click the Liner Notes tab to bring it to the front. Drag the LinerNotes field from the qryBooksSorted field list, drop it onto this tab, and remove the attached label.

10 Adjust the positioning and size of the controls on each tab. Set each Left property to approximately 0.75 inch, Top to 1.75 inches, Width to 4.5 inches, and Height to 1 inch. Select each control, choose Size from the Format menu, and then choose To Fit from the submenu.

Your result should look something like Figure 15-17. You can find this form saved as *fxmplBooks2* in the Microsoft Press Books sample database.

FIGURE 15-17.

The completed tab control in Design view.

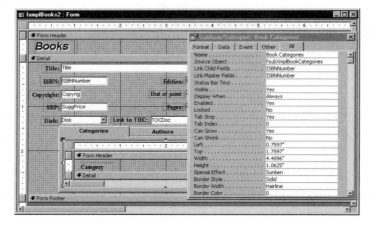

Note that clicking each tab in Design view reveals the controls you stored on that tab. Switch to Form view to see the form in action, as shown earlier in Figure 15-16. As you'll see in Chapter 23, "Automating Your Application with Visual Basic," some ActiveX controls require Visual Basic code to make them work well. The tab control works without doing any programming! Table 15-1 lists other useful tab control property settings.

TABLE 15-1. Useful Tab Control Formatting Properties

Property	Settings	Usage
Multi Row	No (default)	If the control has more tabs than will fit on a single row, the control displays horizontal scroll arrows to move through all the tabs.
	Yes	If the control has more tabs than will fit on a single row, the control displays multiple rows of tabs.
Style	Tabs (default)	The control displays tabs to select the various pages.
	Buttons	The control displays buttons (which look like command buttons but work like the buttons in an option group) to select the various pages.
	None	The control displays neither tabs nor buttons. Different pages can be displayed from a Visual Basic procedure or a macro by setting relative tab numbers in the tab control's Value property.
Tab Fixed Height	0 (default)	The tab height is based on the font of the caption or size of the tab bitmap.
	[size in inches]	The tab height is fixed at the value entered.
Tab Fixed Width	0 (default)	The tab width is based on the font of the caption or size of the tab bitmap.
	[size in inches]	The tab width is fixed at the value entered.

Creating Multiple-Page Forms

As you've seen, Microsoft Access makes it easy to display a lot of related information about one subject in a single form, either by using a query as the source of the form or by displaying the related information in a subform. As described in the previous section, if you have too much information to fit in a single, screen-sized form you can use the ActiveX tab control. Another way to handle the problem is to split the form into multiple "pages."

You can create a form that's up to 22 logical inches high. If you're working on a basic 640-by-480-pixel screen, you cannot see more than about 3 logical inches vertically at one time (if toolbars are displayed). If the information you need to make available in the form won't fit in that height, you can split the form into multiple pages by using a page break control. When you view the form, you can use the Page Up and Page Down keys to move easily through the pages.

Creating a smoothly working multiple-page form takes a bit of planning. First, you should plan to make all pages the same height. You should also design the form so that the page break control is in a horizontal area by itself. If the page break control overlaps other controls, your data might be displayed across the page boundary. You also need to be aware that when you set the form's Auto Resize property to Yes, Access sizes the form to the largest page. If the pages aren't all the same size, you'll get choppy movement using the Page Up and Page Down keys.

The fxmplAuthors form in the Microsoft Press Books database is a good example of a multiple-page form. If you open the form in Design view and select the Detail section of the form, you can see that the height of this area is exactly 6 inches, as shown in Figure 15-18. If you click the page break control, shown at the left edge of the Detail section in Figure 15-18, you'll find that it's set at exactly 3 inches from the top of the page.

When you look at this form in Form view (as shown in Figures 15-19 and 15-20) and use the Page Up and Page Down keys, you'll see that the form moves smoothly from page to page. (You need to open this form from the Database window, not from Design view, to get it to

FIGURE 15-18.

The fxmplAuthors form with a page break control added.

Page break control

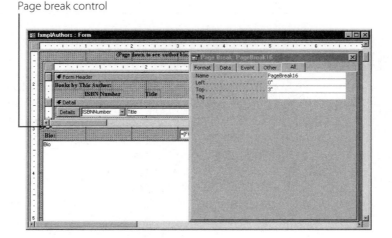

IV

Using Forms

size properly.) In fact, if you're at the bottom of the Bio control on the second page of the form and you press Page Down again, you'll move smoothly to the second page of the next record. Note that certain key information (such as the author name) is duplicated on the second page so that it's always clear which record you're editing.

FIGURE 15-19.

The first page of the fxmplAuthors form.

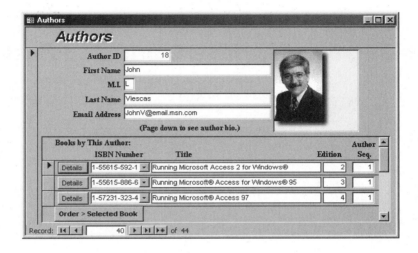

FIGURE 15-20.

The second page of the fxmplAuthors form.

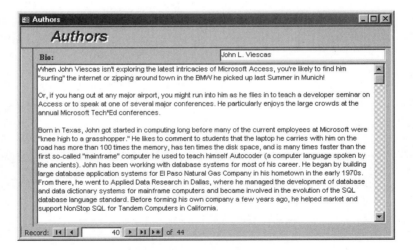

A key form property that makes multiple-page forms work is the Cycle property. On this sample form, the Cycle property is set to Current Page. Other options are All Records (the default) and Current Record. If you don't set the Cycle property to Current Page, you must place the first and last controls on a page that can receive the focus exactly on the page boundary. If you don't do this, you'll find that the form scrolls only partially down a page as you tab from the last control on one page to the first control on the next page. Because it's not likely that you'll design your form with controls exactly aligned on the page boundary, you must use some special techniques to properly align form pages if you want to allow tabbing between pages or records. *See "Controlling Tabbing on a Multiple-Page Form" in Chapter 23 for details.*

Linking Forms with a Command Button

One of the most useful features of Access is its ability to trigger macros or Visual Basic procedures when events occur on forms. Let's go back to the Entertainment Scheduling database for this example. Suppose you're browsing through the club records. Once you find a club that interests you, wouldn't it be nice to have an easy way to see all the contracts for the current club? Although later you'll learn how to do this with Visual Basic, it's easy to accomplish the same thing by using the Control Wizards to create a command button.

Adding a Command Button

For this example, you can start with the form frmXmplClub1, which you built in Chapter 13, "Building Forms," to edit clubs. Open the frmXmplClub1 form in Design view. Choose Form Header/Footer from the View menu and add a label, such as *Clubs*, leaving some room on the right end of the header. Make sure the Control Wizards button is selected in the toolbox. Select the Command Button control, and place it in the newly created header of your form. After a short pause, the Command Button Wizard starts and shows you the first window, as shown in Figure 15-21.

FIGURE 15-21.
The first window in the Command Button Wizard.

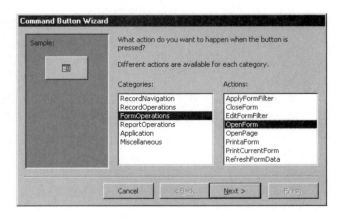

Because you want to open a related form, choose Form Operations from the Categories list, and choose Open Form from the Actions list. Click Next to go to the next step. In the second window, select frmContracts from the list of available forms. Click Next to go on. In the third window, select the Open The Form And Find Specific Data To Display option. Click Next to see the wizard's fourth window, as shown in Figure 15-22.

FIGURE 15-22.

Choosing the related fields in the two forms.

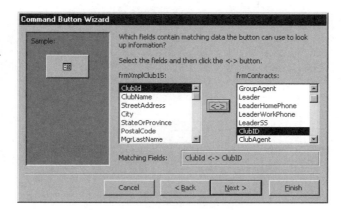

Select the ClubID field in the two field lists, and then click the two-headed arrow button between the lists to set the relationship. Note that the wizard is limited to opening a related form at a specific record based on the value in only one related field. Click Next to go to the fifth window. Here you can either enter a caption for the command button or specify a bitmap picture file. Click Next. On the sixth window, specify a name for the command button control, and click Finish to have the wizard add the button and the necessary Visual Basic code to your form to create the link. You can see the result in Figure 15-23 on the next page. I added a ControlTip Text property setting to give a clue about what the button does when you hover the mouse pointer over the button.

Switch to Form view to see the result shown in Figure 15-24 on the next page. You can find this form saved as *frmXmplClub15* in the Entertainment Scheduling sample database. You can see that the ScreenTip is displayed when you place the mouse pointer over the command button for a second.

Click the command button and the frmContracts form opens, showing the contracts for the club currently displayed in the first form, as shown in Figure 15-25 on the next page.

FIGURE 15-23.

The command button built by the wizard.

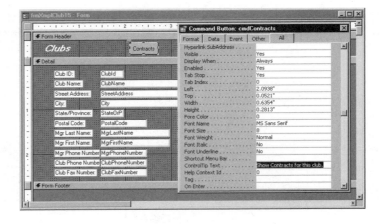

FIGURE 15-24.

The Clubs form command button shows a ScreenTip.

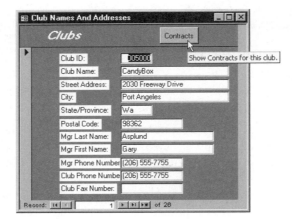

FIGURE 15-25.

The Contracts form opened from clicking the command button on your Clubs form.

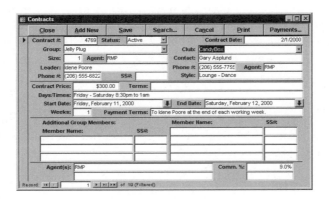

The frmContracts form opens when you click the new command button on the Clubs form.

If you're curious, you can return to Design view for the club edit form, click the new command button, and then click the On Click property in the property sheet. (The property should be set to [Event Procedure].) Click the Build button next to the property (the button with three dots on it) to see the Visual Basic code built by the Command Button Wizard.

This is the last chapter about designing forms. You'll learn a few more design tricks when you start to build an application using macros and Visual Basic in Part VI of this book. Now it's time to learn about reports in Part V.

PART V

Publishing Information

Report Basics

In previous chapters, you learned that you can format and print tables and queries in Datasheet view and that this technique is useful for producing printed copies of simple lists of information. You also learned that you can use forms not only to view and modify data but also to print data—including data from several tables. However, because the primary function of forms is to allow you to view single records or small groups of related records displayed on the screen in an attractive way, forms aren't the best way to print and summarize large sets of data in your database.

This chapter explains why and when you should use a report instead of another method of printing data, and it describes the features that reports offer. The examples in this chapter are based on the Microsoft Press Books sample database. After you learn what you can do with reports, you'll look at the process of building reports in the following two chapters.

Uses of Reports

Reports are the best way to create a printed copy of information that is extracted or calculated from data in your database. Reports have two principal advantages over other methods of printing data.

- Reports can compare, summarize, and subtotal large sets of data.

- Reports can be created to produce attractive invoices, purchase orders, mailing labels, presentation materials, and other output you might need in order to efficiently conduct business.

Reports are designed to group data, to present each grouping separately, and to perform calculations. They work as follows.

- You can define up to 10 grouping criteria to separate the levels of detail.

- You can define separate headers and footers for each group.

- You can perform complex calculations not only within a group or a set of rows but also across groups.

- In addition to page headers and footers, you can define a header and a footer for the entire report.

As with forms, you can embed pictures or graphs in any section of a report. You can also embed subreports or subforms within report sections.

A Tour of Reports

You can explore reports by examining the features of the sample reports in the Microsoft Press Books database. A good place to start is the rptOrders report. Open the database, and go to the Database window. (If you let the application start, click the Exit button on the main switchboard form.) Click the Reports button, and scroll down the list of reports until you see the rptOrders report, as shown in Figure 16-1. Double-click the report name (or select it and click the Preview button) to see the report in Print Preview—a view of how the report will look when it's printed.

 NOTE

All of the reports in the sample databases are set to print to the system default printer. The default printer on your system is probably not the same printer that I used as a default when I designed the report. Some of the sample reports are designed with margins other than the default of one inch on all sides. If your default printer cannot print as close to the edge of the paper as the report is designed, Access will adjust the margins to the minimums for your printer. This means that some reports may not appear exactly as you see them in the book, and some data may appear on different pages.

FIGURE 16-1.

The Reports list in the Database window.

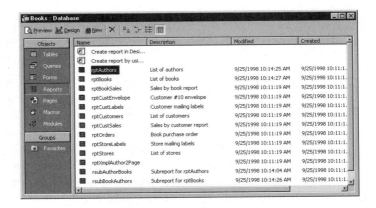

Print Preview—A First Look

The rptOrders report is based on the qryOrderReport query, which brings together information from the tblCustomers, tblOrders, tblStores, tblOrderDetails, and tblBooks tables. When the report opens in Print Preview, you'll see a view of the report in the Orders window, as shown in Figure 16-2. When you open the report from the Database window, the report shows information for all orders. If you start the application (by opening frmCopyright), click the Orders button on the main switchboard form, choose option 4 to review all orders for a specific customer on the Order Options form, and then click the Print

FIGURE 16-2.

The rptOrders report in Print Preview.

Zoom box

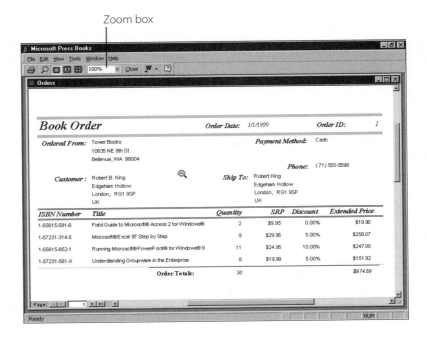

button on the Orders form, you'll see a dialog box form that offers to either print the order or print a mailing label. If you print the order, you'll see the Print Preview of the order you were editing.

You can expand the window in Print Preview to see a large portion of the rptOrders report at one time. Use the vertical and horizontal scroll bars to position the report so that you can see most of the upper half of the first page, as shown in Figure 16-2 on the previous page. You can also turn off Num Lock and use the arrow keys to move up, down, left, and right. If you are using a standard VGA screen (640×480 pixels), select 75% in the Zoom Control box on the toolbar to see a bit more of the report. If your screen resolution is 800×600 or higher, you should be able to easily view the report at 100%.

To view other pages of the report, use the page number box at the bottom left of the window, as shown here.

To move forward one page at a time, click the arrow button immediately to the right of the page number box. You can also click the page number (or press F5 to select the page number), change the number, and press Enter to move to the page you want. As you might guess, the arrow button immediately to the left of the page number box moves you back one page, and the two outer arrows (each pointing to a vertical bar) on either end of the page number box move you to the first or the last page of the report. You can also move to the top of the page by pressing Ctrl+Up arrow, move to the bottom of the page by pressing Ctrl+Down arrow, move to the left edge of the page by pressing Home or Ctrl+Left arrow, and move to the right edge of the page by pressing End or Ctrl+Right arrow. Pressing Ctrl+Home moves you to the upper left corner of the page, and pressing Ctrl+End moves you to the lower right corner of the page.

Headers, Detail Sections, Footers, and Groups

Although the rptOrders report shown in Figure 16-2 looks simple at first glance, it actually contains a lot of information. On the first page you can see a page header that appears at the top of every page. As you'll see later when you learn to design reports, you can also define a header for the entire report and choose whether to print this report header on a page by itself or with the first page header.

The data in this report is grouped by Order ID, and the detail lines are sorted by book title. You could, if you wanted, print a heading for each group in your report. This report could easily be designed, for example, to display the book price in a header line (to group the books by price), the book name in another header line, and then the related detail lines.

Next Access prints the detail information, one line for each row in the recordset formed by the query. In the Detail section of a report, you can add unbound controls to calculate a result using any of the columns in the record source. You can also calculate percentages for a group or for the entire report by including a control that provides a summary in the group or report footers and then referencing that control name in a calculation in the Detail section. Access can do this because its report writer can look at the detail data twice—once to calculate any group or grand totals, and a second time to calculate expressions that reference those totals.

On the first or second page of the report, you can see the group footer for the entire order, as shown in Figure 16-3. If you scroll down to the bottom of the page, you'll see a page number, which is in the page footer.

> **NOTE**
>
> If you're working with a report that has many pages, it might take a long time to move to the first or last page or to move back one page. You can press Esc to cancel your movement request. Microsoft Access then closes the report.

V

Publishing Information

FIGURE 16-3.

The rptOrders report has a subtotal for each order.

Page header

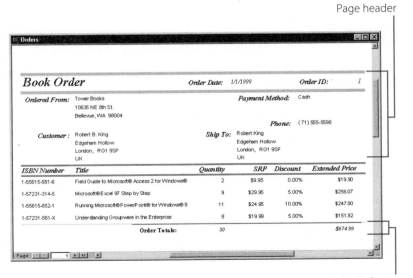

Order ID footer

Another slightly more complex report is rptBookSales. Open that report, and skip to the last page of the report (about page 261—the page number might vary slightly depending on the default printer defined for your computer). As shown in Figure 16-4, at the end of this report you can see the quantity and price totals for the most recent month, for the last book in the report, and for all orders in the database (the grand totals). The grand totals are part of the report footer.

FIGURE 16-4.

The rptBookSales report's grand total calculations are in the report footer.

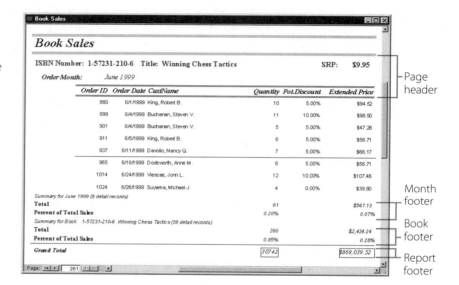

Subreports

Just as you can embed subforms within forms, you can embed subreports (or subforms) within reports. Subreports are particularly useful for showing related details or totals for the records that make up the source rows of your report. For example, you can create a report to calculate grand totals by quarter and then embed that report as a subreport in one of the headers of your main report. In the Microsoft Press Books database, the author information includes related books written by that author. Book information includes related authors and book category information. You can place detailed data about authors or book categories in a subreport and then embed that subreport in the detail section of a report that displays book data—much as you did for the fxmplBooks2 form exercise in the previous chapter.

You can see an example of this use of a subreport in the rptBooks report and in the rsubBookAuthors and rsubBookCategories subreports in the Microsoft Press Books database. If the Books database is not already open, open it and switch to the Database window. (If you let the application start, click the Exit button on the main switchboard form to return to the Database window.) Open the rsubBookAuthors (not rsubAuthorsBooks) subreport in Design view by selecting the subreport in the Database window and then clicking the Design button, as shown in Figure 16-5. The Report window in Design view is shown in Figure 16-6.

FIGURE 16-5.

The rsubBookAuthors subreport about to be opened in Design view.

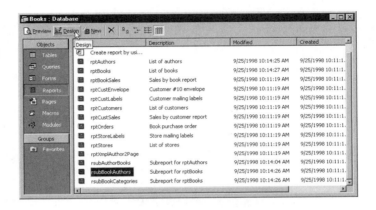

FIGURE 16-6.

The Report window for the rsubBookAuthors subreport in Design view.

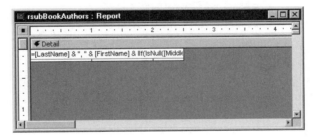

You can see that this subreport is very simple; it has only a Detail section. If you look at the Record Source property for the subreport, you'll find that it uses the qryBookAuthors query, which contains information from the tblBookAuthor table and from related tblAuthors rows. In fact, this subreport doesn't display any book information at all. Open the subreport in Print Preview. You'll see a simple list of various authors, as shown in Figure 16-7 on the next page.

Close the subreport and run the rptBooks report, shown in Figure 16-8 on the next page. Notice as you move from page to page that the data displayed in the two subreports changes to match the book currently displayed. The data from the rsubBookAuthors subreport now makes sense within the context of a particular book. Access links the data from each subreport in this example using the Link Master Fields and Link Child Fields properties of the subreport (which are set to the

FIGURE 16-7.

The rsubBookAuthors subreport in Print Preview.

FIGURE 16-8.

The rptBooks report with two embedded subreports.

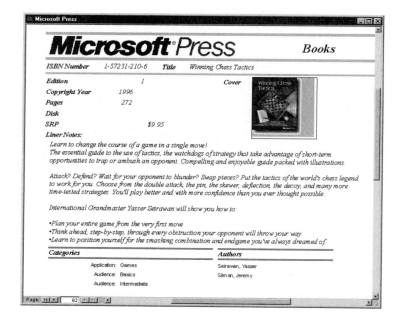

linking ISBNNumber field)—just as with the subforms you created in Chapter 15, "Advanced Form Design."

As you'll see in the next section, when we examine some features of the rptAuthors report, that report also uses subreports to link information from three related tables to each row displayed from the tblAuthors table.

Objects in Reports

As with forms, you can embed ActiveX objects in reports. The objects embedded in or linked to reports are usually pictures or charts. You can embed a picture or a chart as an unbound object in the report itself, or you can link a picture or a chart as a bound object from data in your database.

The rptAuthors report in the Microsoft Press Books database has both unbound and bound objects. When you open the rptAuthors report in Print Preview, you can see the Microsoft Press logo (a stylized font graphic) embedded in the report title as an unbound bitmap image object, as shown in Figure 16-9. This object is actually a part of the report design.

FIGURE 16-9.

An unbound bitmap image object (the Microsoft Press logo) embedded in the rptAuthors report.

If you scroll down the first page of the report, you can see a picture displayed on the form, as shown in Figure 16-10. This picture is a bound bitmap image object from the tblAuthors table (a picture of the author). Scroll down further on the report page, and you can see the list of books for each author, generated by an embedded subreport.

FIGURE 16-10.

A bound bitmap image object displayed in the rptAuthors report.

Printing Reports

Earlier in this chapter you learned the basics of viewing a report in Print Preview. Here are a few more tips and details about setting up reports for printing.

Print Setup

Before you print a report, you might first want to check its appearance and then change the printer setup. Select the rptAuthors report (which you looked at earlier) in the Database window, and click the Preview button to run the report. After Microsoft Access shows you the report, click the Zoom button, and then size the window to see the full-page view. Click the Two Pages button to see two pages side-by-side, as shown in Figure 16-11 on the next page.

V

Publishing Information

FIGURE 16-11.

The two-page view of the rptAuthors report in Print Preview.

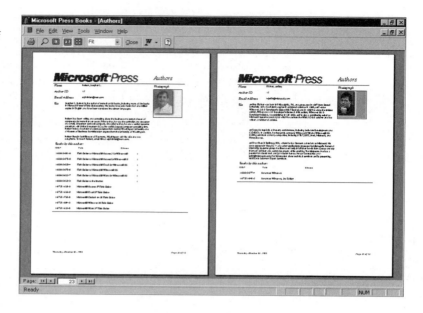

This report is narrow enough to print two pages side-by-side in land-scape mode on 14-inch-long paper. To print it that way, you need to modify some parameters in the Page Setup dialog box.

Open the Page Setup dialog box by choosing Page Setup from the File menu. (You can also define the page setup for any report without opening the report: select the report in the Database window, and choose Page Setup from the File menu.) Access displays a dialog box similar to the one shown in Figure 16-12.

FIGURE 16-12.

The Page Setup dialog box.

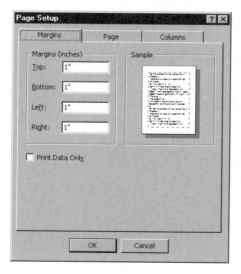

To print the rptAuthors report with two logical pages per physical page, you first need to adjust the margins. You haven't changed the page orientation yet, so the settings that are currently the "top" and "bottom" will become the "left" and "right" margins after you rotate the page. The pages need to print very close to the edge of the paper, so set the top margin to 0.25 inch, set the bottom margin to about 0.7 inch, and set the left and right margins to 1 inch. Click the Page tab to display the next set of available properties, as shown in Figure 16-13.

FIGURE 16-13.

The Page tab of the Page Setup dialog box.

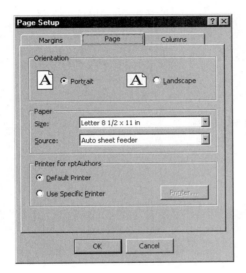

On the Page tab, you can select the orientation of the printed page— Portrait to print vertically down the length of the page, or Landscape to print horizontally across the width of the page. Since we're trying to print two pages across a single sheet of paper, select the Landscape option. The report is also about 6½ inches wide, so you'll need wider paper to fit two logical pages to a printed page. Select 8½-by-14-inch (Legal) paper from the paper size list.

In general, it's best to leave the printer set to the default printer that you specified in your Windows settings. If you move your application to a computer that's attached to a different type of printer, you won't have to change the settings. You can print any report you design in Access to any printer supported by Windows with good results. However, if you've designed your report to print on a specific printer, you can save those settings by using the Page Setup dialog box. On the Page tab, select the Use Specific Printer option and then click the Printer button to open a dialog box in which you can select any printer installed on your system. Click the Properties button to adjust settings for that printer in the Properties dialog box, shown in Figure 16-14. The Properties dialog box you see might look different, depending on the capabilities of the printer you selected and how Windows supports that printer.

FIGURE 16-14.

Setting properties for a specific printer.

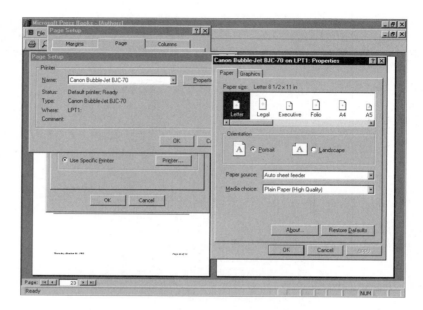

After you set the page orientation to Landscape, click the Columns tab, as shown in Figure 16-15, to set up a multiple-column report. In this case, you want to print two "columns" of information. After you set the Items Across property to a value greater than 1 (in this case, 2), you can set spacing between rows and spacing between columns. You can also set a custom width and height that are larger or smaller than the underlying report design size. Note that if you specify a smaller size, Access crops the report. When you have detail data that fits in more than one column or row, you can also tell Access whether you want the detail produced down and then across the page or vice versa.

 NOTE

> If you created the report or have permission to modify the design of the report, you can change the page layout settings and save them with the report. The next time you print or view the report, Access will use the last page layout settings you specified. All of the reports in the sample databases were created using the default Admin user ID. If you start Access without security or sign on with the default ID, you will have full ownership of all objects in the sample databases.

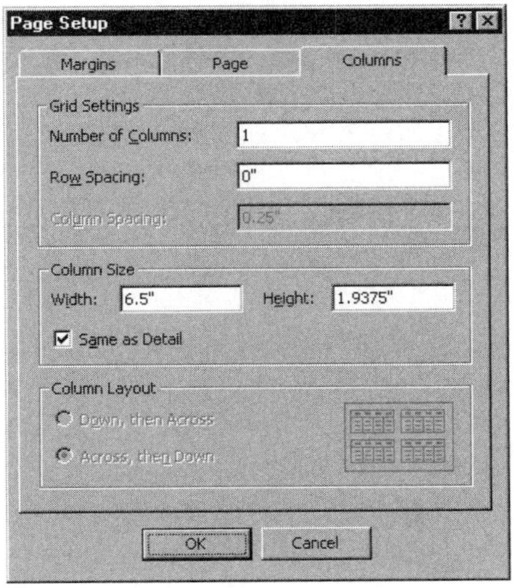

FIGURE 16-15.

Setting report column properties.

FIGURE 16-16.

The rptAuthors report in Print Preview, displayed in landscape orientation and in two columns.

After you enter the appropriate settings in the Page Setup dialog box, your report in Print Preview should look like the one shown in Figure 16-16. (You'll need to set the Force New Page property on the report's Detail section to None to allow two records to be printed on a single page.) You can find this modified version of the Authors report saved in the sample database as *rptXmplAuthor2Page*.

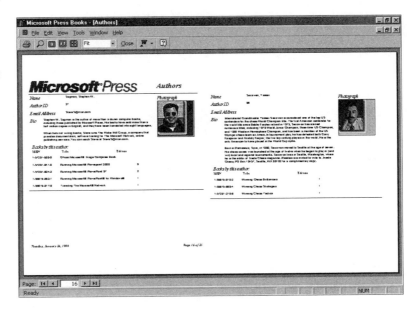

V

Publishing Information

That covers the fundamentals of reports and how to view them and set them up for printing. The next two chapters will show you how to design and build reports for your application.

Constructing a Report

Constructing a report is very similar to building a form. In this chapter, you'll apply many of the techniques that you used in working with forms, and you'll learn about some of the unique features of reports. After a quick tour of the report design facilities, you'll build a simple report for the Entertainment Scheduling database, and then you'll use a Report Wizard to create the same report.

Starting from Scratch— A Simple Report

You're most likely to use a report to look at the "big picture," so you'll usually design a query that brings together data from several related tables as the basis for the report. In this section, you'll build a relatively simple report as you tour the report design facilities. The report you'll build uses the tblClubs and tblContracts tables in the Entertainment Scheduling sample database. The report groups contract data by club, prints a single summary line for each contract, and calculates the number of contracts, the total number of booked weeks, and the total contract amount for each club.

Building the Report Query

To construct the underlying query for the report, you need the ContractNo, GroupName, BeginningDate, and NumberOfWeeks fields from the tblContracts table. Create a new query based on the tblContracts table, and then add these fields to the design grid. You need to create one calculated field in your query that multiplies NumberOfWeeks by ContractPrice to determine the total value of the contract. Call that field ContractAmount, and be sure to set its Format property to Currency. You also need the Status field from tblContracts to be able to select only Active ("A") and Paid ("Pd") contracts. Add the Status field to the design grid, and then type in the criterion *"A" Or "Pd"* in the Status fields Criteria row. You could include a list box on the report to extract the matching ClubName field from the tblClubs table, but it's more efficient to include that information in a query that provides the data for the report than to include the information in the report itself. So, add the tblClubs table to the query, and then add the ClubID and ClubName fields to the design grid. Figure 17-1 shows the query you need for this first report. (You can find this query saved as *qryXmplClubContractReport* in the Entertainment Scheduling database.)

FIGURE 17-1.

A query that selects contract data for a report.

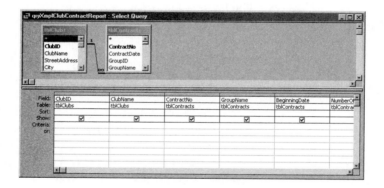

Note that although you're designing a report that will summarize the data, you are not building a Totals query. If you used a Totals query as the record source for the report, you would see only the summary in the report. One of the beauties of reports is that you can see the detail information and also ask the report to produce summaries.

Designing the Report

Now you're ready to start designing the report. In the Database window, select the query you just built and then select Report from the New Object toolbar button's drop-down list (or choose Report from the Insert menu). Microsoft Access displays the New Report dialog box, as shown in Figure 17-2.

FIGURE 17-2.

The New Report dialog box.

SEE ALSO

The field list, the property sheet, the toolbox, and the Formatting toolbar are similar to the features you used in building forms. See Chapter 13, "Building Forms," for detailed descriptions of their uses.

The name of the query you selected appears in the combo box in the lower part of the dialog box. (If you want to select a different table or query, open the drop-down list to see a list of all the tables and queries in your database and select another.) Later in this chapter, you'll use a Report Wizard to create a report. But for now, select Design View and click OK to open a new Report window in Design view, as shown in Figure 17-3 on the next page. You can see both the Report Design toolbar and the Formatting toolbar at the top of the Access window. The Report window is in the background (but on top of the Database window), and the field list, property sheet, and toolbox are open to assist you in building your report. (If necessary, you can use the Field List, Properties, and Toolbox commands on the View menu to open these windows.)

The blank report has Page Header and Page Footer sections and a Detail section between them, which is 2 inches high and 5 inches wide. The rulers along the top and left edges of the Report window help you plan space on the printed page. If you want standard 1-inch side margins, the body of the report can be up to 6½ inches wide on an 8½-by-11-inch page. The available vertical space depends on how you design your headers and footers and how you define the top and bottom margins. As with forms, you can drag the edge of any report section to make the section larger or smaller. Note that the width of all sections must be the same, so if you change the width of one section, Access changes the width of all other sections to match.

Within each section you can see a grid that has 24 dots per inch horizontally and 24 dots per inch vertically, with a solid gray line displayed at 1-inch intervals. If you're working in centimeters, Access divides the

V

Publishing Information

FIGURE 17-3.

The Report window in Design view.

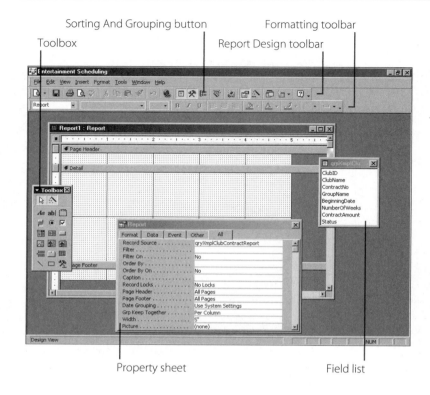

Sorting And Grouping button

Formatting toolbar

Toolbox

Report Design toolbar

Property sheet

Field list

grid into 5 dots per centimeter both vertically and horizontally. You can change these settings using the Grid X and Grid Y properties in the report's property sheet. (If the dots are not visible in your Report window, choose the Grid command from the View menu; if the Grid command is checked and you still can't see the dots, try resetting the Grid X and Grid Y properties to lower numbers in the property sheet.)

The page header and page footer will print in your report at the top and bottom of each page. You can choose the Page Header/Footer command from the View menu to add or remove the page header and page footer. You can also add a report header that prints once at the beginning of the report and a report footer that prints once at the end of the report. To add these sections to a report, choose the Report Header/Footer command from the View menu. You'll learn how to add group headers and group footers later in this chapter.

Sorting and Grouping Information

A key way in which reports differ from forms is that on reports you can group information for display using the Sorting And Grouping window. Click the Sorting And Grouping button on the toolbar (shown in Figure 17-3) to open the Sorting And Grouping window, as shown in Figure 17-4. In this window you can define up to 10 fields or expressions that you will use to form groups in the report. The first item in the list determines the main group, and subsequent items define groups within groups. (You saw the nesting of groups in the previous chapter in the rptOrders report; each order had a main group, and within that main group was a subgroup for each title.)

FIGURE 17-4.

The Sorting And Grouping window.

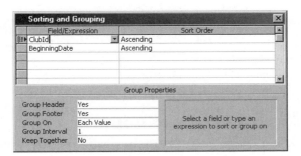

In the simple report you're creating for contracts, you need to group data by club ID so that you can total the number of contracts, the number of weeks, and the contract amounts for each club. If you click in the first row of the Field/Expression column, a down arrow button appears on the right side of the field. Click this arrow (or press Alt+Down arrow) to open the list of fields from the underlying query or table. Select the ClubID field to place it in the Field/Expression column. You can also use the Field/Expression column to enter an expression based on any field in the underlying table or query. You let Access know you're entering an expression by first typing an equal sign (=) followed by your expression.

By default, Access sorts each grouping value in ascending order. You can change the sorting order by selecting Descending from the drop-down list that appears when you click in the Sort Order column. In this case, you're asking the report to sort the rows in ascending numerical order by club ID. If you want to see the clubs in alphabetical order by name, you can group and sort on the ClubName field.

You need a place to put a header for each group (at least for the ClubID field) and a footer for two calculated total fields (the counted and summed values). To add these sections, change the settings for the Group Header and the Group Footer properties to Yes, as shown in Figure 17-4. When you do that, Access adds those sections to the Report window for you. You'll learn how to use the Group On, Group Interval, and Keep Together properties in the next chapter. For now, leave them set to their default values. It would also be nice to see the contracts in ascending date order for each club. Add the BeginningDate field below ClubID, but don't set Group Header or Group Footer to Yes. Close the Sorting And Grouping window by clicking the Close button on its title bar or by clicking the Sorting And Grouping button on the toolbar.

> **TIP**
>
> You can specify sorting criteria in the query for a report, but after you set any criteria in the Sorting And Grouping window, the report ignores any sorting in the query. The best way to ensure that your report data sorts in the order you want is to always specify sorting criteria in the Sorting And Grouping window and not in the underlying query.

Completing the Report

Now you're ready to finish building a summary report based on the tblContracts table. Take the following steps to construct a report similar to the one shown in Figure 17-5. (You can find this report saved as *rptXmplClubContractSummary1* in the Entertainment Scheduling database.)

FIGURE 17-5.

The Club Contract Summary report in the Report window in Design view.

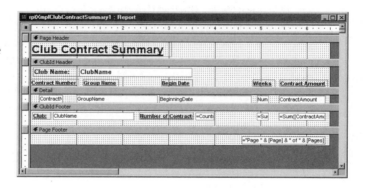

1 Place a label control on the Page Header section, and type *Club Contract Summary* as the label's caption. Select the label control, and then, using the Formatting toolbar, select the Arial font in 18-point bold and underlined. Choose Size from the Format menu, and then choose To Fit from the submenu to set the control size to accommodate the new font size.

2 Drag the ClubName field from the field list onto the ClubID Header section. Use Arial 10-point bold for the label and the control.

3 You'll need some column labels in the ClubID Header section. The easiest way to create them is to set up the text box control so that it has an attached label with no colon, set the defaults for the label control to the font you want, and then drag the fields you need onto the Detail section. First, make sure the property sheet is open, and then click the Text Box tool in the toolbox. Scroll down the property sheet, and check that the Auto Label property is set to Yes and that the Add Colon property is set to No. Click the Label tool, and set its font to Arial 8-point bold and underlined. Now lengthen the Detail section to give yourself some room, and then drag the ContractNo, GroupName, BeginningDate, NumberOfWeeks, and ContractAmount fields from the field list onto the Detail section. Select the label for ContractNo, and then choose the Cut command from the Edit menu (or press Ctrl+X) to separate the label from the control and place the label on the Clipboard. Click the ClubID Header bar, and then choose the Paste command from the Edit menu (or press Ctrl+V) to paste the label into the upper left corner of the header section. You can now place the label independently in the ClubID Header section. (If you try to move the label before you separate it from the control to which it's attached, the control moves with it.) Separate the labels from the GroupName, BeginningDate, NumberOfWeeks, and ContractAmount controls one at a time, and move the labels to the ClubID Header section of the report.

4 Line up the column labels in the ClubID Header section, placing the Contract Number label near the left margin, the Group Name label about 1.1 inches from the left margin, the Begin Date label about 2.8 inches from the left margin, the Weeks label about 4.8 inches from the left margin, and the ContractAmount label about 5.4 inches from the left margin. (You might also want to edit the ContractAmount label to add a space between the two words.) You can set these distances in the Left property of each label's property sheet. Line up the tops of the labels by dragging a selection box around all five labels using the Select Object tool and then choosing the Align command from the Format menu and then Top from the submenu.

5 You can enhance the appearance of the report by placing a line control across the top of the ClubID Header section. Click the Line tool in the toolbox, and place a line in the ClubID Header section. Select the line control, open its property sheet, and set the following properties: Left 0, Top 0, Width 6.5, and Height 0.

6 Align the controls for ContractNo, GroupName, BeginningDate, NumberOfWeeks, and ContractAmount under their respective labels. The controls for ContractNo and NumberOfWeeks can be made smaller. You'll need to make the GroupName control about 1.75 inches wide and the BeginningDate control about 2 inches wide. Set the Text Align property for the BeginningDate control to Left.

7 The height of the Detail section determines the spacing between lines in the report. You don't need much space between report lines, so make the Detail section smaller, until it's only slightly higher than the row of controls for displaying your data.

8 Now add two lines at the top edge of the ClubID Footer section, one about 0.3 inch wide and aligned under NumberOfWeeks, and a second about 0.75 inch wide aligned under ContractAmount. (You can use a single line if you prefer.) It's a good idea to repeat the grouping information in the footer in case the detail lines span a page boundary, so drag the ClubName field again onto the left end of the ClubID Footer section. Add three more unbound text boxes to the ClubID Footer section.

9 Change the caption label of the first unbound text box to read *Number of Contracts:*, and then size it to display the entire label. In the Control Source property of the text box, enter the formula *=Count([ClubID])*. This formula counts the number of rows in the group.

10 Delete the label of the second unbound text box. Enter the formula *=Sum([NumberOfWeeks])* in the Control Source property of the text box. This formula calculates the total number of booked weeks of all the contracts within the report group. Align this control under the NumberOfWeeks control in the Detail section.

11 Delete the label of the third unbound text box. Enter the formula *=Sum([ContractAmount])* in the Control Source property of the text box. This formula calculates the total of all the contracts within the report group. Align this control under the ContractAmount column, and set its Format property to Currency.

12 Finally, create an unbound text box in the lower right corner of the Page Footer section and delete its label. Enter the formula *="Page " & [Page] & "of " & [Pages]* in the Control Source property of the text box. *[Page]* is a report property that displays the current page number. *[Pages]* is a report property that displays the total number of pages in the report.

After you finish, click the Print Preview button on the toolbar to see the result, shown in Figure 17-6. (I moved to page 3 of the report to show some smaller groups so that you could see the effect of the page header, group header, and group footer in a single example.) Notice that in this figure, the detail lines are sorted in ascending order by Begin Date. You'll recall from Figure 17-4 that the sorting and grouping specifications include a request to sort within group on BeginningDate.

FIGURE 17-6.

The Club Contract Summary report in Print Preview.

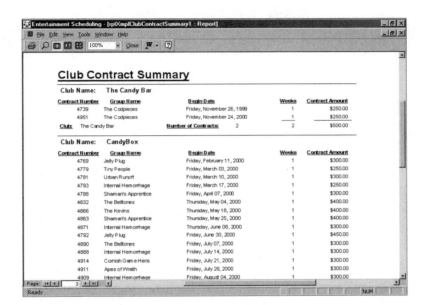

Publishing Information

Using a Report Wizard

The Report Wizards that Microsoft Access provides to assist you in constructing reports are similar to the Form Wizards you used earlier to create forms. To practice using a Report Wizard, build the Club Contract Summary report again. Open the Database window, click the Queries button, and select the qryXmplClubContractReport query. Select Report from the New Object toolbar button's drop-down list or choose Report from the Insert menu to open the New Report dialog box.

Selecting a Report Type

The New Report dialog box offers the following six options, as shown in Figure 17-7 on the next page.

FIGURE 17-7.

The Report Wizard options in the New Report dialog box.

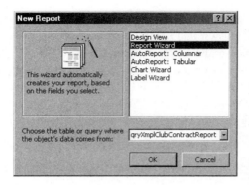

Design View	You selected this option in the first example in this chapter to create a report from scratch.
Report Wizard	This option opens the main Report Wizard, where you can select the fields you want to include and select formatting options, grouping options, and summary options. (You'll use this wizard in this exercise to create the Club Contract Summary report again.)
AutoReport: Columnar	Using this Report Wizard is the same as selecting AutoReport from the New Object toolbar button's drop-down list. This option creates a very simple columnar report that lists the fields from a table or a query in a single column down the page.
AutoReport: Tabular	This Report Wizard displays the data from fields in a query or a table in a single row across the report. If the wizard detects a one-to-many relationship in a query, it automatically creates a group for the data from the "one" side, but it does not generate any totals. It generates a report using the last style you selected either in a wizard or via AutoFormat in a Report window in Design view.
Chart Wizard	This Report Wizard helps you create an unbound OLE object containing a Microsoft Graph application object to chart data from your database.
Label Wizard	This Report Wizard lets you select name and address fields and format them to print mailing labels. You can select from a number of popular label types. The Label Wizard will size the labels correctly.

Because you want to control all options, including setting a group and subtotals, select the Report Wizard option, and click OK.

Specifying Wizard Options

In the first window of the wizard, shown in Figure 17-8, select the fields you want in your report. You can select all available fields in the order in which they appear in the underlying query or report by clicking the double right arrow (>>) button. If you want to select only some of the fields or if you want to specify the order in which the fields appear in the report, select one field at a time in the list box on the left and click the single right arrow (>) button to move the field to the list box on the right. If you make a mistake, you can select the field in the list box on the right and then click the single left arrow (<) button to move the field to the list box on the left. Click the double left arrow (<<) button to remove all selected fields from the list box on the right and start over.

FIGURE 17-8.

Selecting fields in the Report Wizard.

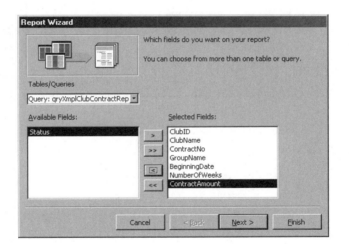

To create the Club Contract Summary report, you should select all of the fields except Status. When you finish selecting fields, click the Next button to go to the next window.

You can also select fields from one table or query and then change the table or query selection in the Tables/Queries combo box. The Report Wizard uses the relationships you defined in your database to build a new query that correctly links the tables or queries you specify. If the wizard can't determine the links between the data you select, it warns you and won't let you proceed unless you include data only from related tables.

The wizard examines your data and tries to determine whether there are any "natural" groups in the data. Since this query includes information from tblClubs that is related one-to-many to information from tblContracts, the wizard assumes that you might want to group the information by clubs (ClubID and ClubName), as shown in Figure 17-9. If you don't want any report groups or you want to set the grouping criteria yourself, select By tblContracts. In this case, the wizard has guessed correctly, so click Next to go to the next step.

FIGURE 17-9.

Verifying primary grouping criteria in the Report Wizard.

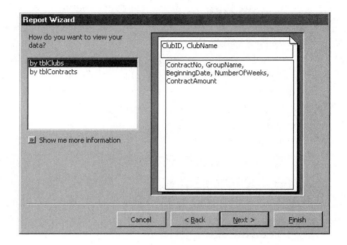

In the next window (shown in the background in Figure 17-10), the wizard asks which additional fields you want to use for grouping records. If you chose to set the criteria yourself, you will see a similar window with no first group selected. You can select up to four grouping levels. The wizard doesn't allow you to enter an expression as a grouping value—something you can do when you build a report from scratch. If you want to use an expression as a grouping value in a Report Wizard, you have to include that expression in the underlying query. For this report, you could also group within each club by the group name.

If you select an additional field (by double-clicking its name), the wizard makes the Grouping Options button available. You can click this button to see the Grouping Intervals dialog box, shown in Figure 17-10. For a text field, you can group by the entire field or by one to five of the leading characters in the field. For a date/time field, you can group by individual values or by year, quarter, month, week, day, hour, or minute. For a numeric field, you can group by individual values or in increments of 10, 50, 100, 500, 1,000, and so on, up to

500,000. If you want to closely duplicate the report you built earlier, *don't select* any additional grouping fields, and click Next to go to the next step.

FIGURE 17-10.

Setting the grouping interval on an additional grouping field in the Report Wizard.

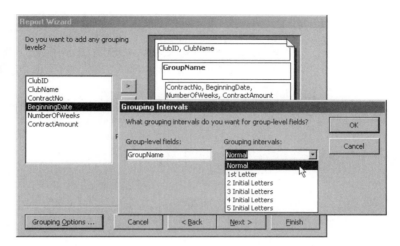

In the next window, shown in Figure 17-11, the wizard asks you to specify any additional sorting criteria for the rows in the detail section. You can select up to four fields from your table or query by which to sort the data. By default, the sorting order is ascending. Click the control button to the right of the field selection combo box to change the order to descending. Again, you can sort only on fields in your query. You can't enter expressions as you can in the Sorting And Grouping window. In this report, you need to sort in ascending order on the BeginningDate field, as shown in the figure.

FIGURE 17-11.

Specifying sorting criteria in the Report Wizard.

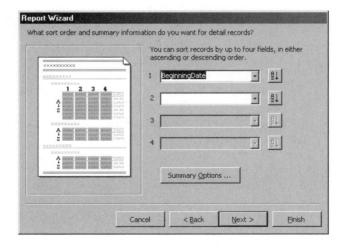

Click the Summary Options button to open the dialog box shown in Figure 17-12. Here you can ask the wizard to display summary values for certain fields in the group footers. The wizard shows you any numeric fields that would be appropriate for summary calculations. In this case, you want to select Sum for both the NumberOfWeeks and ContractAmount fields. Note that you also have choices to calculate the average (Avg) of values over the group or to display the smallest (Min) or largest (Max) value. You can select multiple options. You can also indicate that you don't want to see any of the detail lines by selecting the Summary Only option. (Sometimes you're interested in only the totals for the groups in a report, not all of the detail.) If you select the Calculate Percent Of Total For Sums option, the wizard will also display, for any field for which you have selected the Sum option, an additional field that shows what percent of the grand total this sum represents. When you have the settings the way you want them, click OK to close the dialog box. Click Next in the Report Wizard window to go on.

FIGURE 17-12.

Selecting summary options in the Report Wizard.

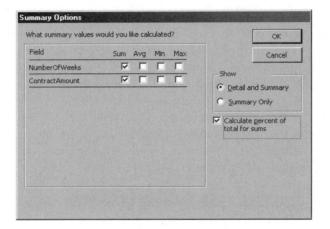

In the next window, shown in Figure 17-13, you can select a layout style and a page orientation for your report. When you select a layout option, the wizard displays a preview on the left side of the window. In this case, the Stepped layout option in Portrait orientation will come closest to the "hand-built" report you created earlier in this chapter. You should also select the check box for adjusting the field widths so that all of the fields fit on one page.

FIGURE 17-13.

Selecting a layout style and page orientation in the Report Wizard.

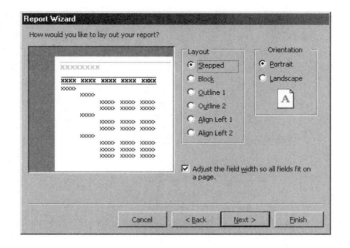

Click Next to go to the next-to-last window of the wizard. In this window you can select from several built-in report styles. If you defined your own custom report style using AutoFormat in a Report window in Design view (similar to the way you defined a format for a form in Chapter 14, "Customizing Forms"), you can also select your custom style. The built-in styles include Bold, Casual, Compact, Corporate, Formal, and Soft Gray. The Bold and Casual styles are probably best suited for informal reports in a personal database. The other formats look more professional. For this example, select the Corporate style. Click Next to go to the last window of the wizard.

In the final window, shown in Figure 17-14, you can type a report title. Note that the wizard uses this title to create the report caption,

FIGURE 17-14.

The Report Wizard window for specifying a report title.

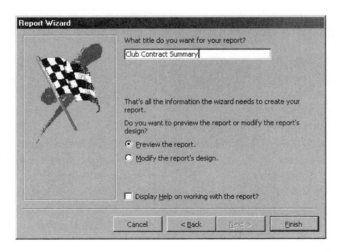

the label in the report header, and the report name. It's probably best to type in a title that's appropriate for the caption and label and to not worry about the title being a suitable report name. If you're using a naming convention (such as prefixing all reports with *rpt* as I've done in the Entertainment Scheduling sample database), it's easy to switch to the Database window after the wizard is done to rename your report.

Viewing the Result

Select the Preview The Report option in the final window, and then click the Finish button to create the report and display the result in Print Preview, as shown in Figures 17-15 and 17-16.

FIGURE 17-15.

The first page of the Club Contract Summary report created using the Report Wizard.

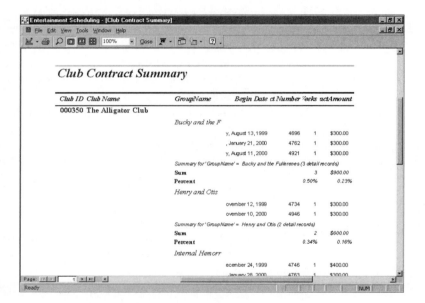

You can press Esc at any time to return to Design view for the report. It's easy to use Design view to modify minor items (such as adjusting the width and alignment of the BeginningDate and GroupName fields and resizing the labels) to obtain a result nearly identical to the report you constructed earlier. You can find the wizard's report saved as *rptXmplClubContract-Summary2* in the Entertainment Scheduling database. As you might imagine, Report Wizards can help you to get a head start on more complex report designs.

FIGURE 17-16.

A later page in the Club Contract Summary report showing club summary data.

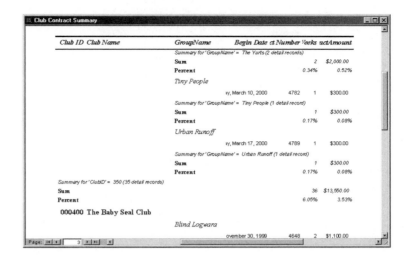

You should now feel comfortable with constructing reports. In the next chapter, you'll learn how to build more complex reports that contain subreports and calculated values.

V

Publishing Information

Advanced Report Design

In the previous chapter, you learned how to create a relatively simple report with a single subtotal level. You also saw how a Report Wizard can help you construct a new report. This chapter shows you how to:

- Design a report with multiple subtotal groups

- Add complex calculations to a report

- Embed a report within another report

- Create a complex "spreadsheet" report

To learn how to work with these features, you'll create a Group Contract Status report for the Entertainment Scheduling database. In a second example, you'll learn how to use the results from two advanced queries in embedded subreports to produce an easy-to-use report that displays openings in club and group schedules. In the final example in this chapter, you'll learn a creative way to design a report similar to a spreadsheet, using a total query to display multiple categories of totals across by month and down by group.

Building a Query for a Complex Report

As noted in the previous chapter, reports tend to bring together information from many tables, so you are likely to begin constructing a report by designing a query to retrieve the data you need for the report. For this example, you need information from the tblClubs, tblContracts, and tblCommissions tables in the Entertainment Scheduling database. Open a new Query window in Design view, and add these tables to the query.

The Group Contract Status report needs to include not only contracts marked Active and Paid but also those marked Pending (contracts that have been booked but not confirmed). As you'll learn in Chapter 23, "Automating Your Application with Visual Basic," when you study the main frmContracts form, code behind the form creates appropriate matching tblCommissions rows (one row per contract week—a contract might span several weeks, but commission payments are due weekly from the group) whenever a contract is marked Active or Paid. However, contracts marked Pending don't have any matching tblCommissions rows. You'll recall from Chapter 8, "Adding Power with Select Queries," that you get only rows that match on both sides of a join unless you change the join criteria. Double-click the join line between tblContracts and tblCommissions to open the Join Properties dialog box. Select the option to return all records from tblContracts and matching records from tblCommissions. The upper part of the Query window should look similar to the one shown in Figure 18-1.

FIGURE 18-1.

The qryActivePaid-Contracts query for the Group Contract Status report.

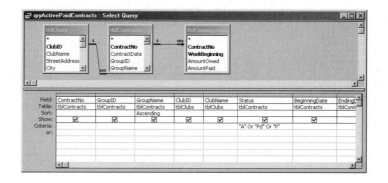

To continue, add the fields listed in Table 18-1 to the design grid. (You can find this query saved as *qryActivePaidContracts* in the sample database.)

TABLE 18-1. Fields in the qryActivePaidContracts Query

Field/Expression	Source Table	Criterion
ContractNo	tblContracts	
GroupID	tblContracts	
GroupName	tblContracts	Sort: Ascending
ClubID	tblClubs	
ClubName	tblClubs	
Status	tblContracts	"A" Or "Pd" Or "P"
BeginningDate	tblContracts	
EndingDate	tblContracts	
WeekBegin: IIf(IsNull([WeekBeginning]), [BeginningDate]–Weekday ([BeginningDate],2)+1, [WeekBeginning])		
WeekBeginning	tblCommissions	
AmountOwed	tblCommissions	
AmountPaid	tblCommissions	
CommissionAgent1	tblContracts	"RMP"

When there are matching rows in the tblCommissions table, this query generates one output row per week of the contract. Remember that some contracts won't have any weekly commissions rows yet. However, the report that uses this query is designed to subtotal by week and by month. If every row had commissions, the WeekBeginning date would work to produce the subtotal breaks. The WeekBegin calculated field tests for rows that don't have commissions. (The WeekBeginning field will be Null.) When no WeekBeginning date is available, WeekBegin calculates the date of the Monday preceding the BeginningDate field in the tblContracts table by subtracting an offset using the Weekday built-in function. This results in a field in the query that you can use in the report to create the necessary subtotals. You should click the WeekBegin field, open its property sheet, and set the Format property to Short Date and the Caption property to Week Beginning Date.

Either save your query and select it in the Database window, or select the qryActivePaidContracts query in the Database window and then select Report from the New Object toolbar button's drop-down list. Select Design View in the New Report dialog box to open the Report window in Design view. (Because there are so many fields in this report, it is easier to build the report without a Report Wizard.)

Defining Sorting and Grouping Criteria

The first thing you need to do is define the sorting and grouping criteria for the report. Click the Sorting And Grouping button on the toolbar to open the Sorting And Grouping window. This report should display the contract and commission data by group and then by month, with the detail showing the weekly contract and commission data from the query. Select the GroupName field in the first line of the Sorting And Grouping window, and then set the Group Footer property to Yes. Notice that when you set the Group Header or Group Footer property to Yes for any field or expression in the Sorting And Grouping window, Microsoft Access shows you a grouping symbol on the row selector for that row. Access also adds an appropriate section to your report. You want to make sure that a group header doesn't get "orphaned" at the bottom of a page, so set the Keep Together property to With First Detail. Note that you can also ask Access to attempt to keep all the detail for this level of grouping on one page by setting the Keep Together property to Whole Group. When you do this, Access will produce a new page if all the detail for the next group won't fit on the current page. Because we know that many of the groups have too many contract rows to fit on a single page, you can set the Keep Together property to Whole Group. As you'll see a bit later, the report sections also have properties that you can set to force a new page with the start of each group.

The WeekBegin field from the query returns the date of Monday for each week over the life span of each contract. However, commission payments are due at the end of the week. We want this report to also provide subtotals by month, but the months should be grouped on dates when the payments are due. You can ensure the correct grouping by specifying an expression in the Sorting And Grouping window. If WeekBegin is always a Monday, [WeekBegin]+6 must be the Sunday at the end of the week. Type this expression in the Field/Expression column preceded by an equal sign (=), and set the Group Footer property to Yes and the Group On property to Month. (The following section discusses other grouping options that depend on data type.) Finally, you should sort the detail rows by the week ending date by typing *=[WeekBegin]+6* again in the Field/Expression column (but without changing any of the group properties). Even though the qryActivePaidContracts query has sorting criteria, you must also define the sorting criteria you want in the report. Reports ignore any sorting specification from the source query if you define any criteria in the Sorting And Grouping window. Your result should look something like that shown in Figure 18-2.

FIGURE 18-2.

The sorting and grouping criteria for the Group Contract Status report.

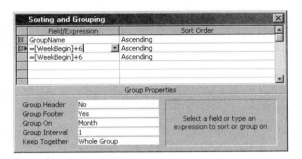

Setting Group Ranges by Data Type

For each field or expression in the upper part of the Sorting And Grouping window, you can set Group On and Group Interval properties. Normally, you'll want to start a new grouping of data whenever the value of your field or expression changes. You can, however, specify that a new grouping start whenever a field or an expression changes from one range of values to another. The kind of range you can specify varies depending on the data type of the field or the expression.

For text grouping fields, you can tell Microsoft Access to start a new group based on a change in value of one or more leading characters in the string. For example, you can create a new group based on a change in the first letter of the field (rather than on a change anywhere in the field) to create one group per letter of the alphabet—a group of items beginning with *A,* a group of items beginning with *B,* and so on. To group on such a prefix, set the Group On property to Prefix Characters and the Group Interval property to the number of leading characters that will differentiate each group.

For numbers, you can set the Group On property to Interval. When you specify this setting, you can enter a setting for the Group Interval property that will cluster multiple values within a range. Access calculates ranges from 0. For example, if you specify 10 as the interval value, you'll see groups for the values −20 through −11, −10 through −1, 0 through 9, 10 through 19, 20 through 29, and so on.

For date/time fields, you can set the Group On property to calendar or time subdivisions and multiples of those subdivisions, such as Year, Qtr, Month, Week, Day, Hour, or Minute. Include a setting for the Group Interval property if you want to group on a multiple of the subdivision—for example, set Group On to Year and Group Interval to 2 if you want groupings for every two years.

 NOTE

> When you create groupings in which the Group Interval property is set to something other than Each Value, Access sorts only the grouping value, not the individual values within each group. If you want Access to sort the detail items within the group, you must include a separate sort specification for those items. For example, if you group on the first two letters of a Name field and also want the names within each group sorted, you must enter *Name* as the field in the Sorting And Grouping window with Group Header (and possibly Group Footer) set to Yes, Sort Order set to Ascending, Group On set to Prefix Characters, and Group Interval set to 2. You must then enter *Name* again as an additional sorting and grouping field with Sort Order set to Ascending and Group On set to Each Value.

Creating the Basic Group Contract Status Report

Now that you've defined the groups, you're ready to start building the report. Before you go any further, choose the Save As command from the File menu, and save the report as *rptMyGroupContractStatus*. (A version of the completed report used by the application is saved as *rptContractStatusByGroup* in the Entertainment Scheduling database.) You can create the basic report by taking the following steps.

1 Choose Page Setup from the File menu to open the Page Setup dialog box. Click the Page tab, and set the page orientation to Landscape. Click the Margins tab, and set the top and bottom margins to 1 inch and the left and right margins to 0.5 inch. Click OK to close the Page Setup dialog box. In the Report window, drag the right border of the Detail section to widen the report to exactly 10 inches.

Some printers have physical limitations that won't allow you to print as close as one-half inch from some edges. I designed many of the sample reports using a laser printer as my default system printer, which allowed me to design a few of the samples with margins as narrow as one-quarter inch. If your default printer won't let you print this close to an edge, you might have adjust some of the margins to see the reports correctly.

2 Place a label in the page header, and type *Contract Status By Group*. Select the label, and use the toolbar to set the font to Times New Roman and the font size to 14 points. Click the Bold button to make the title stand out. Choose the Size command from the Format menu, and then choose To Fit from the submenu to expand the label to fit your text. Set the Top property to approximately 0.1 inch. Add a line control to the Page Header section. Set its Top property to 0.05 inch, Left property to 0 inch, Height property to 0 inch, and Width property to 10 inches. Choose Duplicate from the Edit menu five times to create six copies of the line that stretch all the way across the Page Header section. Drag the bottom edge of the Page Header section to make it just under 1 inch tall. Move the lines so that two of them are above the label you just created. Move the remaining four lines two at a time to create a band for your column heading labels. Leave approximately 0.25 inch between the two bands of lines for the labels.

3 Click the Label tool in the toolbox, open the property sheet if necessary, and check that the default Font is Times New Roman, Font Size is 10, and Font Weight is Bold. Click the Text Box tool in the toolbox, and check that its default properties are: Font Times New Roman, Font Size 10, Font Weight Normal, Auto Label Yes, and Add Colon No.

4 Open the field list, and drag the following fields onto the Detail section: GroupName, ContractNo, ClubName, WeekBegin, Status, AmountOwed, and AmountPaid.

5 Select all the labels on the controls you just added to the Detail section, and then use the Cut command on the Edit menu to place them on the Clipboard. Click in the Page Header section, and use the Paste command on the Edit menu to paste the labels there. Move the Group Name label to the left edge between the two rows of line controls. Place the Contract Number label approximately 1.5 inches from the left edge. Place Club Name at 2.7

inches, Week Beginning Date at 4.6 inches, Status at 5.8 inches, Amount Owed at 6.7 inches, and Amount Paid at 8.5 inches. Select all of these column heading labels, choose the Align command from the Format menu, and then choose Top from the submenu to align the tops of the controls. Adjust the entire group vertically so that the text box controls are evenly spaced between the two rows of line controls.

6 In the Detail section, move all of the text box controls so that they line up under their respective labels along the top edge of the section. Make the GroupName and ClubName controls about 1.85 inches wide. Set ContractNo and Status to 0.75 inch wide. Make WeekBegin about 1 inch wide, and set AmountOwed and AmountPaid to 1.5 inches wide. Make sure that your report is still 10 inches wide. Drag the bottom of the Detail section upward so that it is the same height as the text box row.

7 Change the Amount Owed label's caption to *Commission Owed,* and change the Amount Paid label's caption to *Commission Paid.*

Your report design should now look something like that shown in Figures 18-3 and 18-4.

When you click the Print Preview button on the toolbar and maximize the Report window, the result should look something like that shown in Figure 18-5. You can find this stage of the report design saved as *rptXmplContractStatusByGroupStep1* in the sample database.

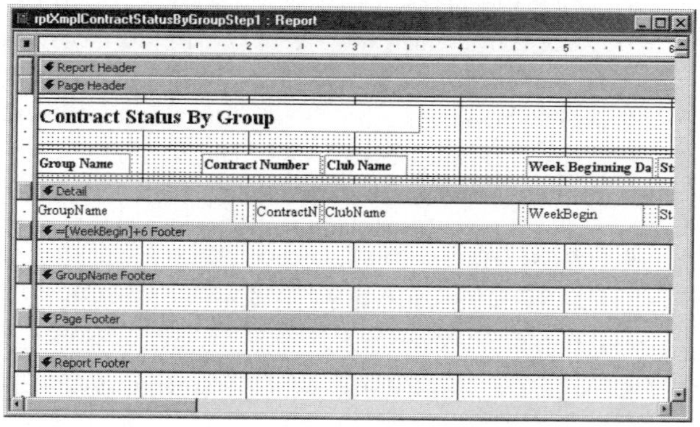

FIGURE 18-3.

The upper left section of the Group Contract Status report in Design view.

FIGURE 18-4.

The right side of the Group Contract Status report in Design view.

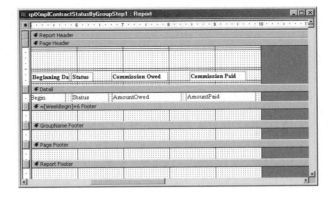

FIGURE 18-5.

The Group Contract Status report in Print Preview.

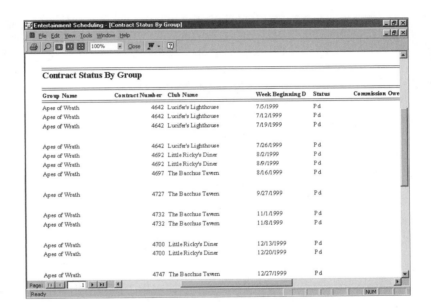

 NOTE

Keep in mind that we're displaying the WeekBegin field from the contract on the report, but a contract commission isn't payable until the end of a week. When grouping commissions due by month, a week that begins within six days of the end of a month won't be payable until the following month. This is why a performance contract that begins on July 26, 1999, groups with other contracts due in August on the sample report.

Setting Section and Report Properties

You've probably noticed that Microsoft Access has a property sheet for each section in the Report window in Design view. You can set section properties not only to control how the section looks but also to control whether Access should attempt to keep a group together or start a new page before or after the group. There's also a property sheet for the report as a whole. You don't need to change any of these properties at this point, but the following sections explain the available property settings.

Section Properties

When you click in the blank area of any group section or Detail section of a report and then click the Properties button, Access displays a property sheet, such as the one shown in Figure 18-6.

FIGURE 18-6.

A property sheet for a report section.

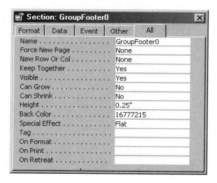

Some of the available properties and their uses are described in Table 18-2 below.

TABLE 18-2.   Properties for a Section

Property	Description
Name	Access automatically generates a unique section name for you.
Force New Page	Set this property to Before Section to force the section to print at the top of a new page. Set this property to After Section to force the next section to print at the top of a new page.

TABLE 18-2. *continued*

Property	Description
New Row Or Col	When you use the Page Setup dialog box to format your report with more than one column (vertical) or more than one row (horizontal) of sections, you can set this property to Before Section, After Section, or Before & After to produce the section again at the top, bottom, or both top and bottom of a new column or row. This property is useful for forcing headers to print at the top of each column in a multiple-column report.
Keep Together	Set this property to No to allow a section to flow across page boundaries. The default Yes setting tells Access to attempt to keep all lines within a section together on a page. You can tell Access to attempt to keep detail lines together with group headers and footers by setting the Keep Together property to Yes for the grouping specification in the Sorting And Grouping window.
Visible	Set this property to Yes to make the section visible or to No to make the section invisible. This is a handy property to set from a macro or from a Visual Basic procedure while Access formats and prints your report. You can make sections disappear depending on data values in the report. *See Chapter 20, "Adding Power with Macros," for details.*
Can Grow	Access sets this value to Yes when you include any control in the section that also has its Can Grow property set to Yes. This allows the section to expand to accommodate controls that might expand because they display memo fields or long text strings. You can design a control to display only one line of text, but you should allow the control to expand to display more lines of text as needed.
Can Shrink	This property is similar to Can Grow. You can set it to Yes to allow the section to become smaller if controls in the section become smaller to accommodate less text. You'll use the Can Shrink property later in this chapter to make a control disappear when the control contains no data.
Height	This property defines the height of the section. You normally change this property by dragging the bottom edge of the section. If you want a specific height, you can enter it here, and Access changes the display to match as long as all controls fit within the defined height.

V

Publishing Information

(continued)

TABLE 18-2. *continued*

Property	Description
Back Color	For most reports, the back color of a section will be the RGB color value for white (16,777,215). It's best to set this value to a standard color other than white by using the Formatting toolbar. You can also choose a custom color value by clicking in the property and then clicking the build button (...) next to the property box to open the Color setting dialog box.
Special Effect	For most reports, you should use a flat effect. You can also set a raised or sunken effect for a section on the Formatting toolbar or by choosing this effect from the drop-down list for the property.
Tag	Use this property to store additional identifying information about the section. You can use this property in macros and in Visual Basic procedures to temporarily store information that you want to pass to another routine.
On Format	Enter the name of a macro or a Visual Basic procedure that you want Access to execute when it begins formatting this section. *See Chapter 20, "Adding Power with Macros," and Chapter 22, "Visual Basic Fundamentals," for details.*
On Print	Enter the name of a macro or a Visual Basic procedure that you want Access to execute when it begins printing this section or when it displays the section in Print Preview. *See Chapter 20, "Adding Power with Macros," for details.*
On Retreat	Enter the name of a macro or a Visual Basic procedure that you want Access to execute when it has to "back up" over a section after it finds that the section won't fit on the current page and you've set the Keep Together Property to Yes. This event happens after On Format but before On Print, so you can use it to undo settings you might have changed in your On Format routine. Access calls On Format again when it formats the section on a new page.

For page headers and footers, only the Name, Visible, Height, Back Color, Special Effect, Tag, On Format, and On Print properties are available.

Report Properties

If you choose the Select Report command from the Edit menu (or click in the Report window beyond the right edge of the Detail section) and then click the Properties button, Access displays the report's properties in the property sheet, as shown in Figure 18-7.

FIGURE 18-7.

The property sheet for a report.

The available properties and their uses are described in Table 18-3.

TABLE 18-3. Properties for a Report

Property	Description
Record Source	This property displays the name of the table or query that provides the data for your report.
Filter	This property shows any filter inherited from the Record Source property or applied by a macro or Visual Basic procedure the last time the report was opened.
Filter On	Set this property to Yes if you want the filter defined for the report to be applied automatically each time the report opens. Note that you can set the Filter and Filter On properties from a macro or a Visual Basic procedure.
Order By	This property shows any ordering criteria inherited from the Record Source property or applied by a macro or a Visual Basic procedure the last time the report was opened.
Order By On	Set this property to Yes if you want the Order By property defined for the report to be applied automatically each time the report opens. Note that you can set the Order By and Order By On properties from a macro or a Visual Basic procedure. Remember that Order By and Order By On have no effect if you have specified any settings in the Sorting And Grouping window.
Caption	Use this property to set the text that appears in the title bar when you open the report in Print Preview.

(continued)

V

Publishing Information

TABLE 18-3. *continued*

Property	Description
Record Locks	Set this property to All Records if the data for your report is on a network shared by others and you want to be sure that no one can update the records in the report until Access creates every page in the report. You should not set this property to All Records for a report that you plan to view in Print Preview because you'll lock out other users for the entire time that you're viewing the report on your screen.
Page Header	This property controls whether the page header appears on all pages. You might choose not to print the page header on the first and last pages if these pages contain a report header or a report footer.
Page Footer	This property controls whether the page footer appears on all pages. You might choose not to print the page footer on the first and last pages if these pages contain a report header or a report footer.
Date Grouping	Use this property to determine how Access groups date and time values that you've specified in the Sorting And Grouping window. You can set this property to US Defaults or Use System Settings. For US Defaults, the first day of the week is Sunday and the first week of the year starts on January 1. If you specify Use System Settings, the first day of the week and first week of the year are determined by the Regional Settings section in the Windows Control Panel.
Grp Keep Together	Set this property to Per Page if you want Access to honor the Sorting And Grouping Keep Together property by page. Set it to Per Column for a multiple-column report if you want Access to attempt to keep a group together within a column.
Width	Access sets this property when you increase the width of the report in the design grid.
Picture, Picture Type	For these properties, you enter the full pathname and filename of a bitmap that you want to use as the background of the report. If you set the Picture Type property to Embedded, Access copies the bitmap to the Report object and sets the Picture property to (bitmap). If you set the Picture Type property to Linked, Access uses the pathname stored in the Picture property to load the bitmap each time you open the report. The Picture and Picture Type properties are also available on forms.

TABLE 18-3. *continued*

Property	Description
Picture Size Mode	When your background picture is not the same size as your page, you can set the Picture Size Mode property so that Access adjusts the size. The Clip setting displays the picture in its original size, and if the page is smaller than the picture, Access clips the right and bottom edges of the picture. The Zoom setting maintains the aspect ratio and shrinks or enlarges the picture to fit the page. If your picture doesn't have the same horizontal-to-vertical dimension ratio as your page, Access might show some blank space at the right or bottom edge of the page. The Stretch setting expands the picture to fit the page size and might distort the image if the aspect ratio of the picture does not match the aspect ratio of the page.
Picture Alignment	When you set the Picture Size Mode property to Clip, you can use Picture Alignment to place the picture in the center of the page or in one of the corners before the picture is clipped.
Picture Tiling	When you set the Picture Size Mode property to Clip and your picture is smaller than the page size, you can set the Picture Tiling property to Yes so that Access will place multiple copies of the picture across and down the page.
Picture Pages	You can set this property to show the picture on All Pages, First Page, or No Pages.
Menu Bar	Enter the name of a custom menu bar or the name of the macro that defines a custom menu bar. Access displays the menu bar when you open the report in Print Preview. *See Chapter 24, "The Finishing Touches," for details on creating custom menu bars and custom toolbars.*
Toolbar	Enter the name of a custom toolbar. Access displays the toolbar when you open the report in Print Preview. *See Chapter 24 for details.*
Shortcut Menu Bar	Enter the name of a custom shortcut menu or the name of the macro that defines a custom shortcut menu. Access displays the shortcut menu when you open the report in Print Preview and right-click in the Report window.
Grid X, Grid Y	Specify the number of horizontal (X) or vertical (Y) divisions per inch or per centimeter for the dots in the grid. When you use inches (when Measurement is set to U.S. in the Regional Settings section of the Windows Control Panel), you can see the dots whenever you specify a value of 24 or less for both X and Y. When you use centimeters (when Measurement is set to Metric), you can see the dots when you specify values of 9 or less.

Publishing Information

TABLE 18-3. *continued*

Property	Description
Layout For Print	When this property is set to Yes, you can select from among several TrueType and printer fonts for your design. When this property is set to No, only screen fonts are available.
Fast Laser Printing	Some laser printers support the drawing of lines (such as the edges of rectangles, the line control, or the edges of text boxes) with rules. If you set the Fast Laser Printing property to Yes, Access sends rule commands instead of graphics to your printer to print rules. Rules print faster than graphics.
Help File, Help Context Id	You can set the Help File property to point to any Help file format supported by Windows and Office 2000, including the new HTML help format. Use the Help Context ID property to point to a specific help topic within the file.
Palette Source	With this property, if you have a color printer, you can specify a device-independent bitmap (dib) file, a Microsoft Windows Palette (pal) file, a Windows icon (ico) file, or a Windows bitmap (bmp) file to provide a palette of colors different from those in the Access default palette.
Tag	Use this property to store additional identifying information about the report. You can use this property in macros and in Visual Basic procedures to temporarily store information that you want to pass to another routine.
On Open	Enter the name of a macro or a Visual Basic procedure that you want Access to execute when it begins printing your report or when it displays the report in Print Preview.
On Close	Enter the name of a macro or a Visual Basic procedure that you want Access to execute when you close Print Preview or when Access has finished sending the report to your printer.
On Activate	Enter the name of a macro or a Visual Basic procedure that you want Access to execute when the Report window gains the focus in Print Preview. This property provides a convenient method of opening a custom menu bar or toolbar.
On Deactivate	Enter the name of a macro or a Visual Basic procedure that you want Access to execute when the Report window loses the focus in Print Preview. This property provides a convenient method of closing a custom menu bar or toolbar.

? SEE ALSO

See Chapter 20, "Adding Power with Macros," for details about the "On..." properties.

TABLE 18-3. *continued*

Property	Description
On No Data	Enter the name of a macro or a Visual Basic procedure that you want Access to execute when the report opens but the record source contains no data.
On Page	Enter the name of a macro or a Visual Basic procedure that you want Access to execute when all the sections of a page have been formatted but have not yet been printed. In Visual Basic, you can use special methods to draw custom graphics on the page.
On Error	Enter the name of a macro or a Visual Basic procedure that you want Access to execute when any errors occur in the report.
Has Module	This property indicates whether the report has an associated Visual Basic class module. A class module is a Visual Basic module that is specific to a single form or report.

Using Calculated Values

Much of the power of Microsoft Access reports comes from their ability to perform both simple and complex calculations on the data from the underlying tables or queries. Access also provides dozens of built-in functions that you can use to work with your data or to add information to a report. The following sections provide examples of the types of calculations you can perform.

Adding the Print Date and Page Numbers

One of the pieces of information you might frequently add to a report is the date on which you prepared the report. You'll probably also want to add page numbers. Access provides two built-in functions that you can use to add the current date and time to your report. The Date function returns the current system date as a Date/Time value with no time component. The Now function returns the current system date and time as a Date/Time value.

To add the current date to your report, create an unbound text box control on the Page Header section and set its Control Source property to =*Now( )*. Then, in the Format property box, specify a Date/Time setting. Go back to the report, and type in a meaningful caption for the label, or delete the label if you don't want a caption. You can see an example of using the Now function in Figure 18-8 on the next page. The result in Print Preview is shown in Figure 18-9, also on the next page.

FIGURE 18-8.

Using the Now function to add the date to a report.

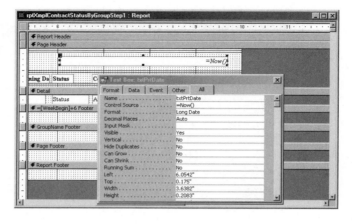

FIGURE 18-9.

The current date displayed in the report in Print Preview.

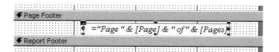

To add a page number, use the Page property for the report. You can't see this property in any of the property sheets because it is maintained by Access. Access also provides the Pages property, which contains a count of the total number of pages in the report. To add the current page number to a report (in this example, in the Page Footer section), create an unbound text box control and set its Control Source property to *="Page " & [Page] & " of " & [Pages]*, as shown in Figure 18-10.

 TIP

> You can reset the value of the Page property in a macro or a Visual Basic procedure that you activate from an appropriate report property. For example, if you're printing several multiple-page invoices for different customers in one pass, you might want to reset the page number to 1 when you start to format the page for a different customer. You can include a Group Header section for each customer and then use a macro or a Visual Basic procedure to set the Page property to 1 each time Access formats that section (indicating that you're on the first page of a new customer invoice).

FIGURE 18-10.

Using the Page and Pages properties to add page numbers to a report.

Performing Calculations

Another task you might perform frequently is calculating extended values from detail values in your tables. You'll recall from Chapter 4, "Designing Your Database Application," that it's usually redundant and wasteful of storage space to define in your tables a field that you can calculate from other fields. (The only situation in which this is acceptable is when saving the calculated value will greatly improve performance in parts of your application.)

Performing a Calculation on a Detail Line

You can use arithmetic operators to create complex calculations in the Control Source property of any control that can display data. You can also use any of the many built-in functions or any of the functions you define yourself in a module. If you want, you can use the Expression Builder that you learned about in Chapter 8, "Adding Power with Select Queries," to build the expression for any control. You let Access know that you are using an expression in a Control Source property by starting the expression with an equal sign (=).

In the Detail section of the Group Contract Status report, you can make a couple of enhancements to the way data is displayed. First, even though the contracts are listed in the query by week beginning date, the report summarizes by week ending date and by month. So the report might display a detail line with a week beginning date of Monday, June 28, 1999, but total that detail line in July because the payment isn't due until Sunday, July 4. This might be confusing, so it makes more sense to display a week ending date for each detail line. Change the label for Week Beginning Date to Week Ending Date. Set the Control Source property of the text box in the Detail section to =[WeekBegin]+6, and change the name of the text box to something other than WeekBegin. If you don't change the control name, you will create a circular reference in the control source because the reference to [WeekBegin] in the Control Source property first looks for a control by that name. If no control has a matching name, Access looks for a field in the record source by that name—which is what you want to have happen in this case. If you've ever seen a report control display #ERROR in Print Preview, it's probably because of a circular reference—the control references itself.

The second calculation you will want to perform on the detail line replaces the status code with a word that matches the code. Before you built this query and report, you could have gone to the tblContracts table and set the Lookup property of the Status field to a list box that displays a matching value from a list (as you learned to do in Chapter 6, "Modifying Your Database Design"). Because this query returns only three status codes, you can get the same effect by using a built-in function called Switch to replace the codes with names. The Switch function lets you enter up to seven pairs of expressions. If the first expression in a pair evaluates to True, Switch returns whatever is in the second expression. Once it finds a true expression, it stops, so putting the most common test first is a good idea.

Change the name of the Status text box to txtStatus, and then enter an expression using the Switch function in the Control Source property box, as shown in Figure 18-11. The function is shown below.

=Switch([Status]="A","Active",[Status]="Pd","Paid",[Status]="P","Pending")

As you can see, this expression asks Switch to first test Status for "A" and return "Active" if true, and then test for "Pd" and return "Paid", and finally test for "P" and return "Pending".

FIGURE 18-11.

A calculated expression using the Switch function.

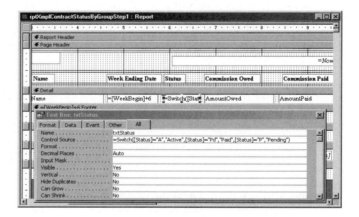

Figure 18-12 shows the result in Print Preview. You can see that Access has performed the required calculations on each status value and displayed a more meaningful result for each.

FIGURE 18-12.

The calculated detail line values within a group in Print Preview.

umber	Club Name	Week Ending Date	Status	Commission Owed	Commission Paid
4642	Lucifer's Lighthouse	7/11/1999	Paid	$55.00	$55.00
4642	Lucifer's Lighthouse	7/18/1999	Paid	$55.00	$55.00
4642	Lucifer's Lighthouse	7/25/1999	Paid	$55.00	$55.00
4642	Lucifer's Lighthouse	8/1/1999	Paid	$55.00	$55.00
4692	Little Ricky's Diner	8/8/1999	Paid	$82.50	$82.50
4692	Little Ricky's Diner	8/15/1999	Paid	$82.50	$82.50
4697	The Bacchus Tavern	8/22/1999	Paid	$40.50	$40.50
4727	The Bacchus Tavern	10/3/1999	Paid	$40.50	$40.50

Adding Values Across a Group

Another task commonly performed in reports is adding values across a group. In the previous chapter, you saw a simple example of this in a report that used the built-in Sum function. In the Group Contract Status report, you have two levels of grouping: one by group and another by month within group. When you specified sorting and grouping criteria earlier in this chapter, you asked Access to provide group footers. This gives you sections in your report in which you can add unbound controls that use any of the aggregate functions (Sum, Min, Max, Avg, Count, First, Last, StDev, or Var) in expressions to display a calculated value for all the rows in that group. In this example, you can create unbound controls in the GroupName and =[WeekBegin]+6 footers to hold the totals, by group and by month, for commission owed and commission paid, as shown in Figure 18-13. You can also add a line control at the top of each footer section to provide a visual clue that the values that follow are totals. (If you switch to Print Preview at this point, the result should look like that shown in Figure 18-14 on the next page.)

FIGURE 18-13.

Adding summaries by group and by month.

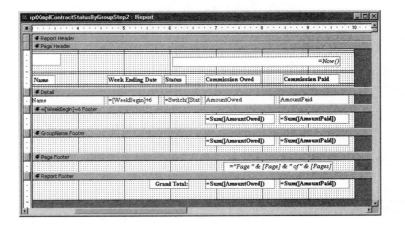

Publishing Information

TIP

An important point to remember about using an aggregate expression in a group section is that the expression cannot refer to any controls in the Detail section. So, you cannot create a calculated field in the Detail section, for example, that multiplies two numbers and then reference that control in the summary expression. You can, however, repeat the calculation expression in the summary. If a detail control named Total has an expression such as =[Quantity] * [Price], you must use an expression such as =Sum([Quantity] * [Price]) in your grouping section, not =Sum([Total]).

You can use a text box control's Running Sum property to calculate extended totals and to tell Access not to reset totals at the end of a group. If you set the Running Sum property to Over Group, Access accumulates the total over all groups at or below the text box control's group level until it encounters a new group value at the next-highest group level. If you set the property to Over All, Access accumulates one total for the entire report and does not reset totals for new groups. *See "Using Running Sum," later in this chapter, for details.*

Creating a Grand Total

Use the Report Footer section to create grand totals for any values across the entire set of records in a report. You can use any of the aggregate functions in the report footer just as you did in the two grouping section footers. Figure 18-13 on the previous page shows you two Sum functions used in controls in the report footer. If you switch to Print Preview, go to the last page in the report, and scroll down, you should see a result similar to that shown in Figure 18-14. You can find this stage of the report design saved as *rptXmplContractStatusByGroupStep2* in the sample database.

FIGURE 18-14.

The grand totals displayed in the report in Print Preview.

The Sourdough Café	6/3/2001	Active	$80.00	$0.00
The Sourdough Café	6/10/2001	Active	$80.00	$0.00
The Sourdough Café	6/17/2001	Active	$80.00	$0.00
The Sourdough Café	6/24/2001	Active	$80.00	$0.00
			$320.00	$0.00
The Sourdough Café	7/1/2001	Active	$80.00	$0.00
The Sourdough Café	7/8/2001	Active	$80.00	$0.00
			$160.00	$0.00
			$3,379.00	$756.00
		Grand Total:	$49,239.16	$12,593.26

Page 44 of 44

If you want to create percentage calculations for any of the groups over the grand total, you must create the control for the grand total in the report footer so that you can reference the total in percentage calculation expressions. *See "Calculating Percentages," later in this chapter.* If you don't want the total to print, set the control's Visible property to No.

Concatenating Text Strings and Hiding Redundant Values

You probably noticed in several of the preceding examples that the GroupName, ContractNo, and ClubName fields print for every detail line. When a particular detail line has values that match the previous line, the report looks less readable and less professional. You can control this by using the Hide Duplicates text box property (which is available only in reports). Switch to the Design view of this report, and set the Hide Duplicates property to Yes for the GroupName text box in the Detail section. The report will now print the group name only once per group or page. When Access moves to a new grouping level or page, it prints the group name even if it matches the previous value displayed.

In this report, you could also set the Hide Duplicates property for both the ContractNo and ClubName fields. Note, however, that Hide Duplicates works on a field-by-field basis. In this database, a couple of the groups have more than one contract in a month for the same club. If you set the Hide Duplicates property to Yes for the two separate fields, you'll find instances in which the new contract number prints but the club name doesn't print because it's the same as the previous line. It would be less confusing to hide duplicates for the *combination* of contract number and club name. To do that, you have to use text string concatenation to display the data in a single control for which you can set Hide Duplicates.

Figure 18-15 shows a text string concatenation as a Control Source property setting. You need to remove both the ContractNo and ClubName text boxes and replace them with a single text box that spans the area covered by the two column heading labels. The ampersand (&) character indicates a concatenation operation of three text strings. The first string derives from the Format function applied to the ContractNo field to return precisely six digits. The second string adds some spaces between the two data fields. The last string is the ClubName field from the record source. You can now set the Hide Duplicates property of this control to Yes to hide redundant data only when both the ContractNo and ClubName fields are the same as on the previous line.

V

Publishing Information

FIGURE 18-15.
The control source expression that allows the Hide Duplicates property to eliminate duplicate ContractNo and ClubName values.

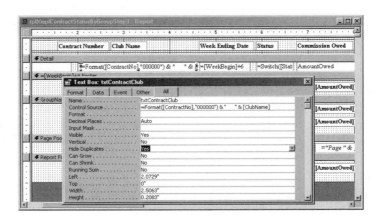

Another good use of string concatenation is to display data that looks like a label but that also includes information from the record source. Sometimes it's useful to combine descriptive text with a value from a text field in the underlying query or table or to combine multiple text fields in one control. In Figure 18-16, you can see a descriptive label (created by a single text box control) on one of the subtotal lines.

FIGURE 18-16.

A text constant and a string derived from a field in the record source are concatenated as a "label" in a text box.

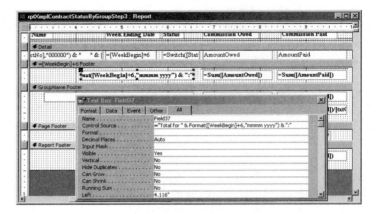

This "label" concatenates the words *Total for* with an expression that uses the Format function—applied here to the week ending date (*[WeekBegin]+6*) to get the name of the month and the year—and an ending string containing a colon, as shown in Figure 18-17. You could certainly define a label followed by a text box followed by another label to create the same display. The advantage of using a single control is that you don't have to worry about lining up three controls or setting the font characteristics. In fact, because the string in the middle, containing the month and the year, will vary in length, you cannot create three separate controls that correctly line up all possible values end-to-end. As you can imagine, you can use the same technique in the group footer to create a "label" that reads *Total for group* followed by the group name and a trailing colon. Set the Text Alignment property of these controls to Right so that they line up correctly next to the summary controls.

When you look at the report in Print Preview, you can see that the duplicate values for GroupName and for the combination of ContractNo and ClubName have been eliminated. You can also see the nice result from using a concatenated string in a text box to generate labels for the total lines.

FIGURE 18-17.

The total lines now have descriptive captions using data from the record source.

Club Name	Week Ending Date	Status	Commission Owed	Commission Paid
				Friday, October 08, 1999
Lucifer's Lighthouse	7/11/1999	Paid	$55.00	$55.00
	7/18/1999	Paid	$55.00	$55.00
	7/25/1999	Paid	$55.00	$55.00
	Total for July 1999:		$165.00	$165.00
Lucifer's Lighthouse	8/1/1999	Paid	$55.00	$55.00
Little Ricky's Diner	8/8/1999	Paid	$82.50	$82.50
	8/15/1999	Paid	$82.50	$82.50
The Bacchus Tavern	8/22/1999	Paid	$40.50	$40.50
	Total for August 1999:		$260.50	$260.50
The Bacchus Tavern	10/3/1999	Paid	$40.50	$40.50
	Total for October 1999:		$40.50	$40.50

Calculating Percentages

In any report that groups and summarizes data, you might want to determine what percentage of an outer group total or the grand total is represented in a particular sum. You can do this in a report because Access makes two passes of the data. On the first pass, it calculates simple expressions in detail lines, sums across groups, sums across the entire report, and calculates the length of the report. On the second pass, it resolves any expressions that reference totals calculated in the first pass. Consequently, you can create an expression in a detail or group summary section that divides by a sum in an outer group or the grand total to calculate percentages.

Figure 18-18 shows an example of a percentage calculation in the GroupName Footer section. The expression divides the sum of the AmountOwed field for this group and then divides it by some value in a field called txtGrandOwed. If you look in the Report Footer section, you'll find that this is the name of the text box containing the grand total for the AmountOwed field.

FIGURE 18-18.

Adding a calculation for a percentage of a grand total.

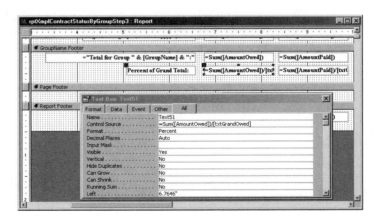

Set the Format property of the text box to Percent, and switch to Print Preview. Scroll down to find a group total, and you'll also see the percent of the grand total, as shown in Figure 18-19. You can find this stage of the report design saved as *rptXmplContractStatusByGroupStep3* in the sample database.

FIGURE 18-19.

A percentage calculation for one group in Print Preview.

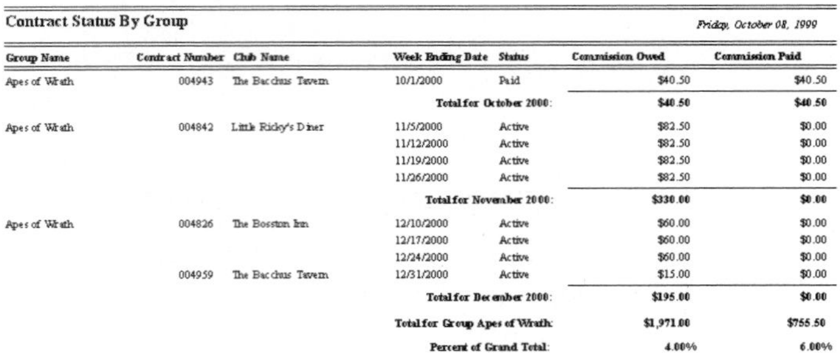

Contract Status By Group   *Friday, October 08, 1999*

Group Name	Contract Number	Club Name	Week Ending Date	Status	Commission Owed	Commission Paid
Apes of Wrath	004943	The Bacchus Tavern	10/1/2000	Paid	$40.50	$40.50
			Total for October 2000:		**$40.50**	**$40.50**
Apes of Wrath	004842	Little Ricky's Diner	11/5/2000	Active	$82.50	$0.00
			11/12/2000	Active	$82.50	$0.00
			11/19/2000	Active	$82.50	$0.00
			11/26/2000	Active	$82.50	$0.00
			Total for November 2000:		**$330.00**	**$0.00**
Apes of Wrath	004826	The Boston Inn	12/10/2000	Active	$60.00	$0.00
			12/17/2000	Active	$60.00	$0.00
			12/24/2000	Active	$60.00	$0.00
	004959	The Bacchus Tavern	12/31/2000	Active	$15.00	$0.00
			Total for December 2000:		**$195.00**	**$0.00**
			Total for Group Apes of Wrath:		**$1,971.00**	**$765.50**
			Percent of Grand Total:		**4.00%**	**6.00%**

Using Running Sum

In addition to producing totals for any group you define, Access lets you create running totals within the Detail section. For any text box that displays a numeric value, you can set the Running Sum property to produce a total that is reset at the start of each group or that continues totaling through the entire report. Let's further refine rptXmplContractStatusByGroupStep3 to see how this works.

First, change the Commission Paid label to read *Cum. Commission Owed* and size it so you can see the entire caption. Remove the AmountPaid text box and all of the Group and Report sum fields based on AmountPaid. Add a text box in the Detail section under the label you just changed. Set its Control Source to AmountOwed, and set the Running Sum property of the text box to Over Group. You can see these steps completed in Figure 18-20.

No, this isn't a second copy of the AmountOwed field. As you'll see in a minute, this produces (as the name of the property implies) a *running sum* of the AmountOwed field within the Detail section. As Access encounters each new row in the Detail section, it adds the current value of AmountOwed to the previous accumulation and displays the result. Because you asked for the sum Over Group, Access resets the accumulating total each time it encounters a new group.

Next, let's use a little trick to generate a line number for each line in the Detail Section. To make room for this line number, shrink the controls that display GroupName and the ContractNo/ClubName expression a bit. Select the Contract Number label, Club Name label, and the

FIGURE 18-20.

Adding a Running Sum calculation on the Amount Owed.

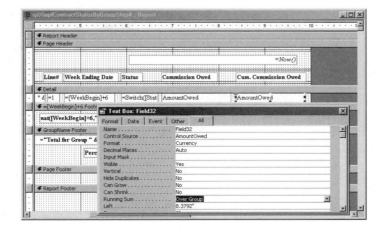

text box displaying ContractNo/ClubName and slide them all to the left about one-half inch. Insert a small text box in the space you just created in the Detail Section. Above this text box, create a label that displays Line#.

Remember that as Access formats each Detail line, it takes the current value of the field (actually, the current value of the text box), adds it to the previous total, and displays the result. If you set the text box equal to any constant numeric value, Access uses that value for each Detail line it produces. So, the "trick" is to set this text box equal to 1 (=1 in the Control Source) and then set Running Sum. If you choose Over All for Running Sum, Access will number the first line 1, add 1 for the second line and display 2, add 1 for the third line and display 3, and so on throughout the report. Note from the settings in Figure 18-21 that I set a format that places a nice decimal point after each displayed value.

FIGURE 18-21.

Using Running Sum to generate a line number.

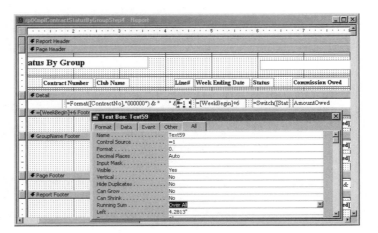

If you switch to Print Preview, you can see the result of using Running Sum, as shown in Figure 18-22. The Commission Owed accumulates over each group, and then resets for the next group. The line numbers start at 1 and continue incrementing for the entire report. You can find this report saved as *rptXmplContractStatusByGroupStep4* in the sample database.

FIGURE 18-22.

The result of using Running Sum to produce a cumulative total for each group and a line number for each detail line in the entire report.

Club Name	Line#	Week Ending Date	Status	Commission Owed	Cum. Commission Owed
Lucifer's Lighthouse	1.	7/11/1999	Paid	$55.00	$55.00
	2.	7/18/1999	Paid	$55.00	$110.00
	3.	7/25/1999	Paid	$55.00	$165.00
		Total for July 1999:		**$165.00**	
Lucifer's Lighthouse	4.	8/1/1999	Paid	$55.00	$55.00
Little Ricky's Diner	5.	8/8/1999	Paid	$82.50	$137.50
	6.	8/15/1999	Paid	$82.50	$220.00
The Bacchus Tavern	7.	8/22/1999	Paid	$40.50	$260.50
		Total for August 1999:		**$260.50**	
The Bacchus Tavern	8.	10/3/1999	Paid	$40.50	$40.50
		Total for October 1999:		**$40.50**	
The Bacchus Tavern	9.	11/7/1999	Paid	$49.50	$49.50
	10.	11/14/1999	Paid	$49.50	$99.00
		Total for November 1999:		**$99.00**	

Taking Advantage of Conditional Formatting

In Chapter 15, you learned how to define conditional formatting for a text box. Access makes a similar facility available to you for reports. Let's say, for example, that you want to highlight any contract amount owed that is more than $50. To do this, open the report from the previous example in Design view, select the text box in the Detail section that displays the AmountOwed field (not the one that has the Running Sum), and choose Conditional Formatting from the Format menu. Access displays the Conditional Formatting dialog box, as shown in Figure 18-23.

FIGURE 18-23.

Setting conditional formatting for a text box.

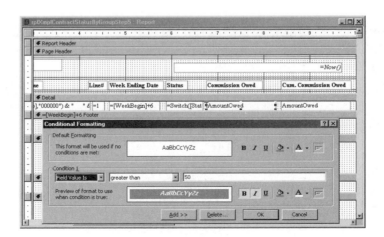

Just like a text box on a form, you can define a test against the current value in the control or enter an expression. In this case, I chose Field Value Is in the first box, Greater Than in the second box, and entered the value 50 in the third box. I could have also chosen Expression Is in the first box and entered *[AmountOwed] > 50* in the second box. Note that in the Detail section, you can reference any other field in the current row to create your expression. When you create a conditional formatting expression in a grouping section, any field reference you use in an expression uses the value of the "current" row. In a Group Footer, for example, the "current" row is the last row displayed in the previous Detail section.

For this example, I asked Access to display values greater than $50 in bold white italic letters on a gray background. If you're using a color printer, you can choose any colors you like to see the result both on the screen and when you print the report. When you switch to Print Preview, you can see the result, as shown in Figure 18-24. You can find this sample saved as *rptXmplContractStatusByGroupStep5*.

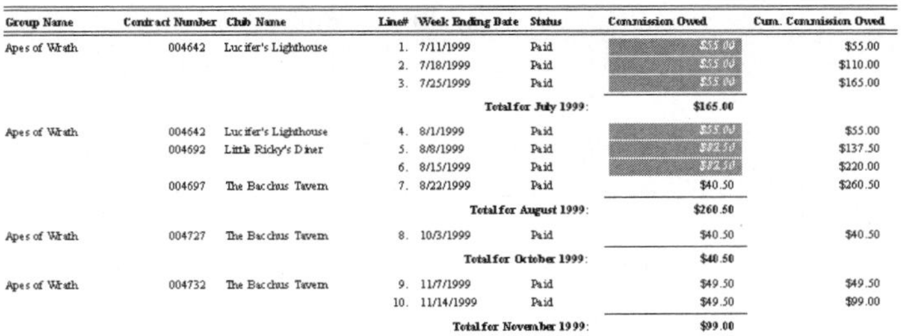

FIGURE 18-24.
The result of setting conditional formatting.

Group Name	Contract Number	Club Name	Line#	Week Ending Date	Status	Commission Owed	Cum. Commission Owed
Apes of Wrath	004642	Lucifer's Lighthouse	1.	7/11/1999	Paid	*$55.00*	$55.00
			2.	7/18/1999	Paid	*$55.00*	$110.00
			3.	7/25/1999	Paid	*$55.00*	$165.00
				Total for July 1999:		**$165.00**	
Apes of Wrath	004642	Lucifer's Lighthouse	4.	8/1/1999	Paid	*$55.00*	$55.00
	004692	Little Ricky's Diner	5.	8/8/1999	Paid	*$82.50*	$137.50
			6.	8/15/1999	Paid	*$82.50*	$220.00
	004697	The Bacchus Tavern	7.	8/22/1999	Paid	$40.50	$260.50
				Total for August 1999:		**$260.50**	
Apes of Wrath	004727	The Bacchus Tavern	8.	10/3/1999	Paid	$40.50	$40.50
				Total for October 1999:		**$40.50**	
Apes of Wrath	004732	The Bacchus Tavern	9.	11/7/1999	Paid	$49.50	$49.50
			10.	11/14/1999	Paid	$49.50	$99.00
				Total for November 1999:		**$99.00**	

Creating and Embedding a Subreport

In many of your reports, you will probably design the Detail section to display a single line of information from the underlying record source. As you learned earlier in this chapter, it's fairly easy to link several tables to get lots of detail across several one-to-many relationships in your database. You also saw how to use the Hide Duplicates property to display a hierarchy across several rows of detail.

However, as with forms and subforms, which you learned about in Chapter 15, "Advanced Form Design," you can embed subreports in the detail section of your report to display multiple detail lines from a table or query that has a "many" relationship to the one current line printed in the detail section. This technique is particularly useful when you want to display information from more than one "many" relationship on a single page. In the Microsoft Press Books database, for example, the rptAuthors report combines the basic author information in the main report with the list of all books the author has written in a subreport. The rptBooks report prints the main book information as the detail, all of the classification categories in one subreport, and all of the authors in another subreport. You could create a very complex query that joins all the information, but you'd get one row for each unique combination of book, book category, and author per book—far more rows than you actually need to solve the problem.

Ray McCann, the owner of RM Productions, presented me with a particularly interesting and challenging problem that I solved with subreports, as you'll see in the following sections. Although an entertainment contract might span several weeks, all of the clubs and groups that Ray deals with like to schedule on a week-to-week basis. He needed a report that would show him, for each of several upcoming weeks, which clubs and groups for which he acts as an agent were not yet booked. Armed with this report, he could easily create a working list of unbooked groups that could be of interest to the open clubs. It would then be a simple matter of calling each club manager to suggest an available group and perhaps book it on the spot. Also, if a club or group for which he is not the usual agent were to call him to request a booking during a certain week, he could quickly generate this report to let the caller know what is available.

As you'll see in the following sections, queries can extract the open club or group information that Ray needs. A creative use of subreports puts all this information on one page per week to make it extremely easy to use.

Building the Subreport Queries

If you read to the end of Chapter 11, "Advanced Query Design—SQL," you already learned about some advanced techniques for wringing information out of the tables in the Entertainment Scheduling database. The queries to solve the "open club or group" problem use some of the same techniques.

What makes this problem difficult is that the tblContracts table contains only one row per contract for a time period that might span several weeks. It doesn't make sense to store one row per week—that would mean a lot of redundant data. But as mentioned earlier, clubs and groups like to book (and take care of payments) on a week-to-week basis. (In Chapter 23, "Automating Your Application with Visual Basic," you'll learn about some special procedures in the frmContracts form that set up the necessary weekly payment records in tblCommissions.) The queries to solve this problem use a "driver" query to separate each contract row into multiple weekly booking rows to perform the necessary analysis.

Since we're trying to find open weeks, we first need a query that generates one row per club or group for each available week on the calendar. You'll use a query that lists all clubs for all weeks in an outer join with a query that lists the booked weeks for each club to determine which weeks are open for the club. There's a companion set of queries that deal with groups.

In the sample database, you can find a table called tblDates that lists all dates from January 1, 1992, through the end of the year 2035. The query named qryMondays creates a row for Monday of each week (the start of the week for most group and club bookings). If you include this query in another query along with either the tblClubs table or the tblGroups table, you can generate one row per club or group for each week. You can see the query for clubs in Figure 18-25. (The query has been optimized by adding a parameter to reference the main report that will include the subreport that uses this query.)

FIGURE 18-25.

A query to return one row for each week for all clubs.

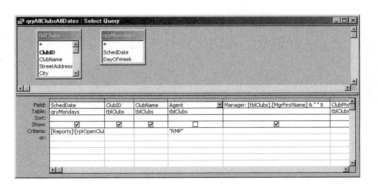

To build the new query, you'll need the ClubID, ClubName, MgrFirstName, MgrLastName, and ClubPhoneNumber fields from the tblClubs table. Because there is no join line between the table and the query, you get the *Cartesian product* of the rows in the two record sources. That is, you get each row in tblClubs matched up with each row in qryMondays. That's a lot of rows. In most cases, Ray will want to look at only a few weeks at a time. Rather than extract all rows every time this query runs, you can restrict the rows returned by the query to only the weeks of interest.

When I built this query, I knew that I was going to use it in a subreport embedded in a main report called rptOpenClubsAndGroups. Furthermore, I knew that the main report would use the SchedDate field from qryMondays to print one week per page. You'll learn more about how to reference open forms and reports in Chapter 21, "Automating Your Application with Macros." For now, it's sufficient to know that the expression *[Reports]![rptOpenClubsAndGroups]![SchedDate]* references the value in the SchedDate field on the current page of the report we're about to build. This limits the query to one week per page so that the report takes a few seconds per page to calculate instead of several minutes. You can find the *qryAllClubsAllDates* and *qryAllGroupsAllDates* queries in the sample database.

Now we need a query to produce one row per booked week for every contract. You can start with a query that joins tblClubs to tblContracts. You can output from this query one row per contract that includes the club name, manager name, club phone number, group name, group leader name, group phone number, contract status, and beginning and ending dates of the contract. To get one row per week, you can add our old friend qryMondays to the mix and use a special type of join to get the required result. Remember, if you don't create a join between qryMondays and the other tables, you'll get one row for all weeks for all contracts. What you want is one row from the join across clubs and contracts linked with each row from qryMondays that represents a week within the span of the contract. As long as the Monday from qryMondays is not more than seven days earlier than the start of the contract and that same date is also less than or equal to the date of the end of the contract, at least part of the contract will fall during that week.

The only way to specify this sort of join is in SQL. You can see the query (which is saved as *qrySchedDates* in the sample database) in Figure 18-26. (This query is also optimized to reference the outer report.) If you studied Chapter 11, "Advanced Query Design—SQL," you know that the list following the SELECT includes all the fields to be output by the query. The FROM clause lists the source tables or queries and specifies how Access should link them. The "magic" part of the query is this phrase:

```
(qryMondays.SchedDate <= tblContracts.EndingDate) AND
(qryMondays.SchedDate > tblContracts.BeginningDate - 7)
```

This states in "SQL-ese" the link criteria necessary to get one row per week. In English, the FROM clause means, "Link the rows from qryMondays with the rows from tblContracts where the week defined by the row in qryMondays spans any part of the contract in tblContracts." As with the qryAllClubsAllDates query, the WHERE clause restricts the output of this query to the date on the current page of the report to get the best performance.

FIGURE 18-26.

A complex query that returns one row per week for each contract (which might span multiple weeks) in the database.

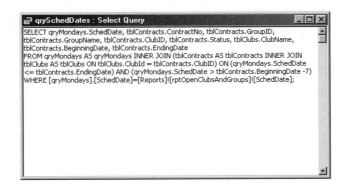

> **NOTE**
>
> You learned in Chapter 15 that Access filters the rows in a subform as you move from row to row in the outer form based on the Link Child and Link Master property settings. Likewise, Access filters a subreport as it formats each related detail row in a report. However, when the query for a subreport is complex (as it is in this case), Access may try to solve the entire query before filtering it for the current row. You can improve performance significantly by embedding a filter within the query for the subreport that directly points to the outer detail row.

The final queries link either qryAllClubsAllDates or qryAllGroupsAllDates with qrySchedDates using an outer join to find the unbooked dates. (Figure 18-27 on the next page shows the final query that returns one row per unbooked week for each club.) As you'll recall from Chapter 8, "Adding Power with Select Queries," you can set the join properties to include all rows from one table or query and any matching rows from the second table or query. When there is no match, Access returns the special Null value in the columns from the second table or query. If you test for Null, the query returns only the unmatched rows—in this case, the weeks for any club or group in which that club or group is not booked.

You can find qryOpenRMPClubs and qryOpenRMPGroups in the sample database; they return the open weeks for clubs and groups, respectively. The next step is to use these queries as the row source for two subreports.

FIGURE 18-27.
A complex query that
returns one row per
unbooked week for
each club.

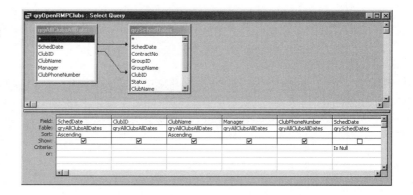

Designing the Subreport

Select either query in the Database window, and select Report from
the New Object toolbar button's drop-down list. Select Design View in
the New Report dialog box, and click OK to open the Report window
in Design view.

Open the View menu, and check that the Page Header/Footer command is not selected. Access won't display page headers and footers in
a subreport. In the final report, the list of open clubs should appear
side-by-side with the list of open groups, so each subreport should be
narrow enough to fit both of them across a standard-width page—about
3 inches will work. You don't need the SchedDate field from the underlying query on the report, but that field will form the link to the main
report, as you'll see in a moment. For clubs, you need the ClubName,
Manager, and ClubPhoneNumber fields, as shown in Figure 18-28.

FIGURE 18-28.
The design of the
subreport to display
unbooked club data.

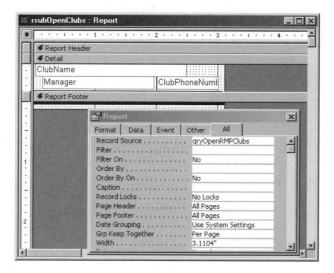

For Groups, you need the GroupName, Leader, and HomePhone fields, as shown in Figure 18-29.

Publishing Information

FIGURE 18-29.

The design of the subreport to display unbooked group data.

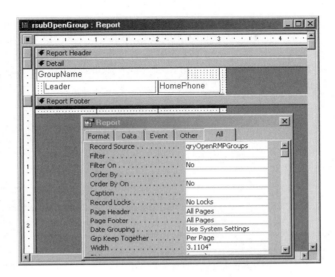

For both subreports, choose Report Header/Footer from the View menu, and shrink the header to a height of 0. Make the report footer about 0.125 inch tall, and place a thick black line control across the top of the section. If the list is long enough to span more than one page, this line will provide a visual indicator of the end of the list. You can find the two subreports saved as *rsubOpenClubs* and *rsubOpenGroup* in the sample database.

Embedding the Subreport

Now comes the payoff. Start a new report on the qryMondays query. Make the report 6.5 inches wide. (This works well with the default 1-inch margins.) Create a title in the Page Header section using a label control, and add a text box to display today's date if you want. Drag the SchedDate field from the field list onto the Page Header section. Change the text box's caption to Week Beginning. Add a label on the left side for clubs and another on the right side for groups. In the Detail section, add two subreport controls next to each other, and make them both about 3 inches wide and 0.5 inch high.

To embed the rsubOpenClubs subreport in the control at the left, enter *Report.rsubOpenClubs* in the Source Object property box of the subreport control, as shown in Figure 18-30 on the next page. Because you can also include a form in the report, the *Report* prefix tells Access to include a report, not a form. As you did with a subform, you need to define linking fields. In this case, the SchedDate field on the main report (which is set in the Link Master Fields property box) matches the SchedDate field on the subreport (which is set in the Link Child Fields property box). You need to set both the Can Shrink and Can Grow properties to Yes to allow the subreport to expand or shrink as necessary.

FIGURE 18-30.

The subreport is linked to the main report.

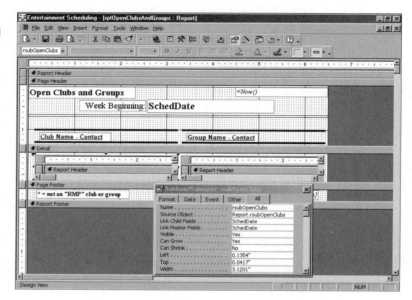

Follow the same procedure to embed the rsubOpenGroup report in the subreport control on the right. Finally, choose the Size command from the Format menu, and then select To Fit from the submenu so that both subreport controls are sized correctly to display all the data in the subreports.

 Access 2000 introduces a new feature that allows you to directly edit your subreport once you have defined it as the source for your subreport control. As you can see in Figure 18-30, the design of both of the subreports is visible in the respective subreport controls. You can click any control in the inner report and change its size or adjust its properties using the property sheet or the Formatting toolbar. You may need to temporarily expand the size of the subreport control in order to work with the inner report easily. Note, however, that you cannot open the inner report in Design view separately from the Database window as long as you have the outer report open. You also cannot use File / Save As to save your changes to a different report definition.

Remember that three of the queries contain references to the main report's SchedDate field to obtain optimum performance. If you want to save your own copy of this report, you must also go to each of the three queries and change the reference to point to your report. You can then open your own report to see how it works. Because your report isn't restricted in any way, you'll see open dates starting with January 1, 1992. If you want to see how this report works in the "live" application, go on to the next section.

Viewing the Embedded Result

To see how this report works in "real life," go to the Database window and open the frmMain form. Click the Reports button on that form to open the Reports switchboard form. On that form, click the Open Clubs And Groups button to open a dialog box in which you can specify a date range, as shown in Figure 18-31.

FIGURE 18-31.

Specifying a date range for the Open Clubs And Groups report.

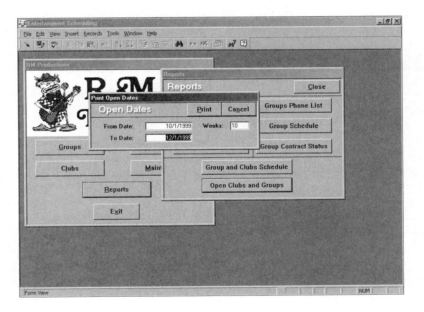

The sample database contains contract data from July 1999 to December 2000. If you specify a date range beginning in late October 1999 and click the Print button in the Print Open Dates dialog box, you should see the result shown in Figure 18-32 on the next page. Do you suppose the No One Wants to Work Here club would be interested in booking Apes of Wrath? Better ask Stephanie first! (You'll recall from Chapter 8 that this is the one club that has never had any bookings.)

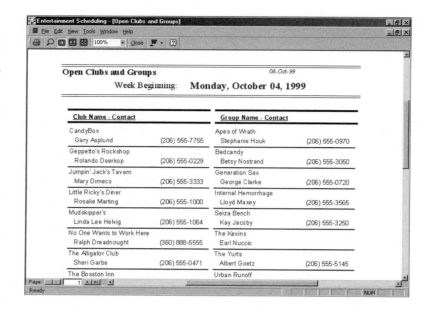

Creating a "Spreadsheet" Report

You can easily create sophisticated reports with totals grouped down the page, like the Group Contract Status report you built in the previous sections. But what if you want a monthly summary of number of contracts, total weeks booked, and total commissions all in one report? Crosstab queries work well for summarizing data by groups and dates, but they can display only a single summarized value.

Building a Summary Query

First you need a query to summarize contract data for the year by group and by month. This query will be very similar to the crosstab query you built in Chapter 8, "Adding Power with Select Queries," but it creates totals for the number of contracts, the number of contract weeks, and total commission on these contracts from the tblContracts table.

You can find the query you need saved as *qryGroupSpreadsheet* in the sample database. This query includes a parameter that prompts the user to enter the year of interest. The query outputs the parameter as a calculated column result and also uses the parameter to restrict which contracts are considered. You can see the query in Figure 18-33 and in Figure 18-34.

FIGURE 18-33.

The first five fields in a query to summarize group contract data by month.

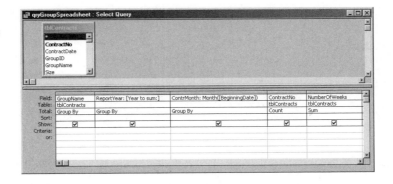

FIGURE 18-34.

The remaining form fields in a query to summarize group contract data by month.

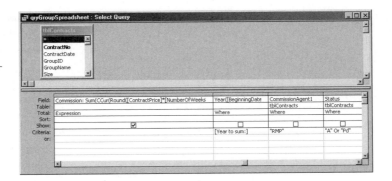

This query groups the data by GroupName, by Year (the parameter field), and by contract Month (using the Month built-in function on the BeginningDate field). In addition, the query counts the contracts, sums the NumberOfWeeks field, and sums an expression that calculates the commission on each contract. The query is restricted to contracts for which RM Productions is the commissioning agent and the contract is marked either Active or Paid.

Designing a "Summaries Only" Report

The report you need in order to display the contract count, number of weeks, and total commission dollars by month in a spreadsheet-like format won't actually have any detail lines. Start by selecting the qryGroupSpreadsheet query, and then select Report from the New Object toolbar button's drop-down list. Open the report in Design view. Start by defining a group on the GroupName field, and set the Group Footer property to Yes. Access will display a GroupName Footer section for you. Your Sorting And Grouping window should look like the one shown in Figure 18-35 on the next page.

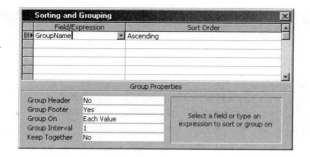

Open the Report Header and Report Footer sections by choosing Report Header/Footer from the View menu. Be sure you also have a page header and a page footer. In the Report Header section, create a text box control to use as a title for the report. In the Control Source property, enter either of the following expressions.

=[ReportYear] & " Contract Commissions By Group"

=[Year to sum:] & " Contract Commissions By Group"

The first expression references the calculated ReportYear field from the query we created above. Remember, the ReportYear field is simply a copy of the [Year to sum:] parameter. The second expression references the parameter directly. Even though the parameter field doesn't show up in the field list, you can reference its value in this way.

In the Page Header section, insert a Group Name label at the left edge. About 1.5 inches to the right, insert labels for each of the month groups. Create a label containing the month name, centered above the three labels for Contracts, Weeks, and Comm. Add a line control on either side of each month group to highlight the "columns" you'll be creating below. Each group of labels should be no more than 1.5 inches wide. Create groups for the months of January through June, extending the report to 10.5 inches wide. Drag the GroupName field from the field list onto the GroupName Footer section, remove its label, and set the control to display Arial 8-point text. Your result should look something like that shown in Figure 18-36.

To create the monthly totals you want, you need three unbound text boxes per month in the GroupName Footer section—one to display the sum of the contract count, one to display the sum of the number of weeks, and one to display the sum of the total commission amount. You want to use the Sum function to total the CountOfContractNo, SumOfNumberOfWeeks, and Commission fields from the query. However, for each month, you want the Sum function to add up only the values for the month in that column. Here's where the IIf function

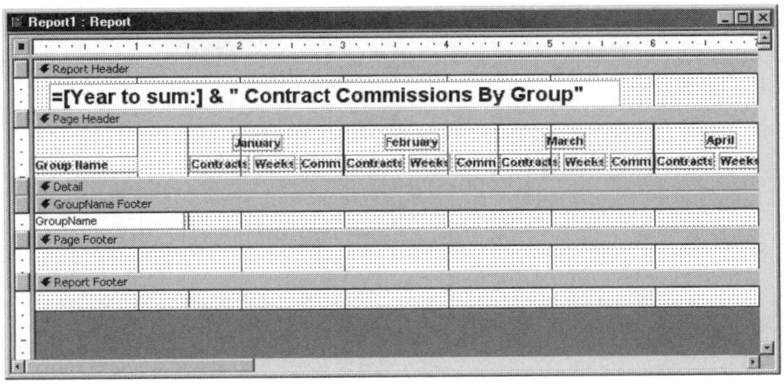

FIGURE 18-36.

A spreadsheet report under construction.

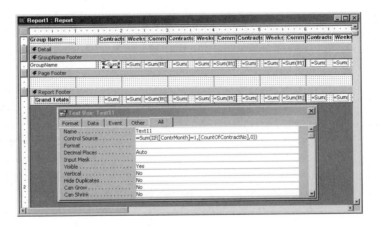

comes in handy. In the unbound text box control for the total contract count in January, test to see whether the month in the "current" row being processed by the Sum function has a month value of 1. If the month is 1, give the Sum function the CountOfContractNo value to work with, as shown in Figure 18-37. If the month is not 1, pass a 0 to the Sum function. The formula in the Control Source property box is as follows.

```
=Sum(IIf([ContrMonth]=1,[CountOfContractNo],0))
```

FIGURE 18-37.

Creating a total of selected month values.

You'll enter a similar formula for the controls that total contract weeks. The formula for January looks like this:

```
=Sum(IIf([ContrMonth]=1,[SumOfNumberOfWeeks],0))
```

And, as you might expect, the formula for the commission text boxes looks like this:

```
=Sum(IIf([ContrMonth]=1,[Commission],0))
```

Publishing Information

For the controls in the other months, change the month number to pick out the total values you want to display in that column. (February is 2, March is 3, and so on.) In the sample report in the Entertainment Scheduling database, lines are drawn on either side of each group of monthly total controls so that they align with the lines in the page header.

You'll notice that the columns for the first six months will fit within a 10.5-inch-wide report, which means that a standard 8.5-inch-wide page would be too narrow. To fix this, choose Page Setup from the File menu, select Landscape mode, and set the left and right margins to 0.25 inch. This gives you a 10.5-inch-wide print area on standard 8.5-by-11-inch paper.

> NOTE

If your default printer doesn't allow margins as small as 0.25 inches, this sample report may not line up correctly for you. If you're following along building this report, you may need to adjust the design to fit within the margins supported by your printer.

To set up the second logical page for the last six months, stretch your report to 21 inches wide. Select all the controls in the first "half" of the report, section by section, and then choose Duplicate from the Edit menu. You can move the duplicated controls to the area between 10.5 and 21 inches. Change the month labels, and change each of the formulas to test for the month in that column.

To create grand totals in the report, copy all the calculation controls from the GroupName Footer section to the Clipboard, click in the Report Footer section, and paste the controls there. You don't have to make any changes to any of the formulas, although you'll need to delete the GroupName controls and add labels for the grand totals. The totals in the GroupName Footer section will be for the rows matching that group. The totals in the Report Footer section will be for all rows returned by the query. Your report in Design view should now look something like that shown in Figure 18-38.

Switch to Print Preview, respond to the year prompt by entering *2000*, and your result should look similar to that shown in Figure 18-39.

You can find this report saved as *rptAnnualSummaryByGroup* in the Entertainment Scheduling database.

FIGURE 18-38.
The completed spreadsheet report in Design view.

2000 Contract Commissions By Group

Group Name	January Contracts	January Weeks	January Comm	February Contracts	February Weeks	February Comm	March Contracts	March Weeks	March Comm	April Contracts	April Weeks	April Comm	Contracts
Apes of Wrath	0	0	$0.00	1	2	$150.00	1	1	$44.00	2	4	$151.50	1
Blind Logwara	1	1	$44.00	0	0	$0.00	2	4	$240.00	0	0	$0.00	0
Bucky and the Fullerenes	2	5	$130.00	0	0	$0.00	0	0	$0.00	1	2	$121.00	0
Cornish Game Hens	0	0	$0.00	0	0	$0.00	0	0	$0.00	0	0	$0.00	0
Generation Sex	0	0	$0.00	1	20	1,300.00	0	0	$0.00	0	0	$0.00	0
Henry and Otis	1	1	$25.00	1	2	$121.00	1	1	$55.00	0	0	$0.00	1
Internal Hemorrhage	1	1	$27.00	0	0	$0.00	1	1	$25.00	0	0	$0.00	0
Jelly Plug	1	5	$0.00	1	1	$27.00	0	0	$0.00	1	4	$36.00	0
King Tut and the Uncommon	0	0	$0.00	0	0	$0.00	0	0	$0.00	1	2	$0.00	2
Life Irritates Art	0	0	$0.00	1	1	$30.00	0	0	$0.00	0	0	$0.00	0
Monk Seal	0	0	$0.00	1	3	$225.00	0	0	$0.00	0	0	$0.00	0
Muddled Thoughts	0	0	$0.00	0	0	$0.00	1	4	$600.00	0	0	$0.00	1
Seiza Bench	0	0	$0.00	0	0	$0.00	0	0	$0.00	0	0	$0.00	0
Shaman's Apprentice	1	1	$40.00	1	2	$130.00	1	2	$0.00	2	3	$30.00	3
Supertube	1	1	$55.00	1	2	$72.00	2	2	$90.00	2	2	$157.00	0
The Beltones	3	4	$166.00	1	1	$33.00	3	3	$100.00	1	2	$0.00	2
The Buddy Love Orchestra	0	0	$0.00	1	7	$123.38	0	0	$0.00	1	2	$150.00	0
The Codpieces	0	0	$0.00	3	3	$87.00	1	1	$22.00	0	0	$0.00	1
The Kevins	0	0	$0.00	0	0	$0.00	1	2	$99.00	0	0	$0.00	2
The Yurts	0	0	$0.00	0	0	$0.00	0	0	$0.00	0	0	$0.00	1
Tiny People	0	0	$0.00	0	0	$0.00	2	2	$58.00	1	1	$25.00	0
Urban Runoff	0	0	$0.00	0	0	$0.00	3	3	$127.00	1	4	$352.00	3

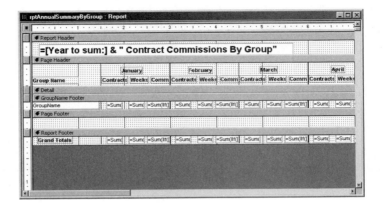

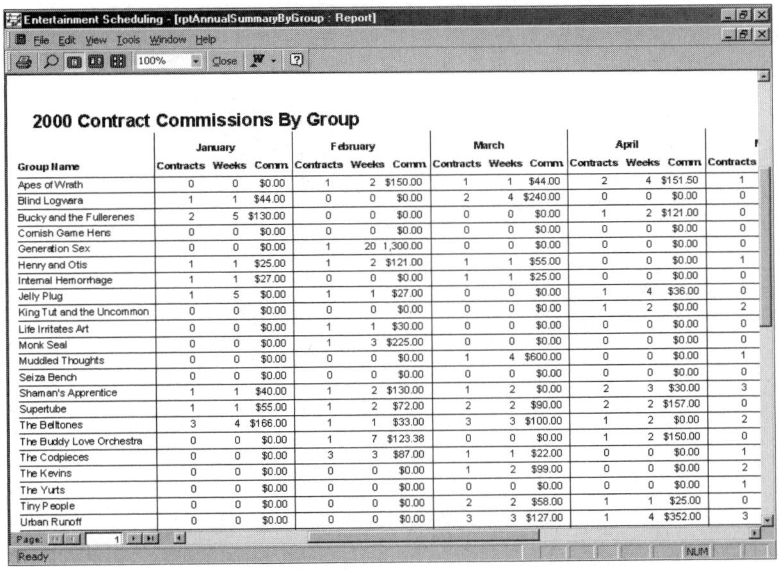

FIGURE 18-39.
The spreadsheet report in Print Preview.

At this point, you should thoroughly understand the mechanics of constructing reports and working with complex formulas. The final part of this book shows you how to bring together all that you've learned to build an application.

CHAPTER 19

Publishing Data on the Web

The World Wide Web, built from simple low-cost servers and universal clients, has revolutionized computing. Not so long ago, the very concept of a common global information network was unthinkable. In fact, even Microsoft was unconvinced that Web technology would ever mature successfully. Originally, The Microsoft Network (MSN) was constructed with proprietary technology, modeled after similar networks such as CompuServe and Prodigy. Today, the concept of living without the Web is just as alien, and all of the formerly proprietary networks (including MSN) have spent millions of dollars to convert to the universal access offered by the Web.

Database applications were among the last to appear on the Web, but today they are arguably the fastest growing type of Web application. The prospect of distributing or collecting data from literally a world of clients, working on disparate computers and operating systems, and not requiring software distribution other than the ubiquitous browser, is simply too compelling to resist for long.

Microsoft Access doesn't provide a complete Web development environment. Nevertheless, it does provide useful tools for developing a variety of Web database applications. This chapter explores the Web, explains how Web capabilities of Access work, and provides pointers to other tools in case Access doesn't satisfy all of your needs.

Working with the Web

Designing and developing Web applications requires a different set of tools, a different approach, and a different mindset than performing the same tasks solely in Access. The Web presents new choices in timeliness (frequency of update and reporting), interactivity (degree of user control), and partitioning (distributed location of application components).

Delivering Static Web Pages

Like all network applications, the World Wide Web defines two roles computers can play: client and server. The client software, called a browser, requests files from the server and displays them. The server software, called a Web server, accepts requests from browsers and transmits the requested files. Figure 19-1 provides a highly simplified diagram of these components.

FIGURE 19-1.

A high-level World Wide Web schematic.

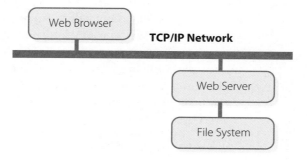

NOTE

TCP/IP stands for Transmission Control Protocol / Internet Protocol. TCP describes a way computers on Internet-style networks can exchange data without loss. The Internet Protocol describes the identification scheme for computers on Internet-style networks.

What Is a Protocol?

When you connect your computer to a network, the communications software on each computer has to send and receive information in a format that all of the computers understand. Think of a computer network as a set of railway tracks. If one "station" can send and receive boxcars but not hopper cars, any other "station" that wants to send cargo to that station must send boxcars only. Similarly, a network protocol defines a specific type of data packaging that can be sent over your network "rails."

In early Microsoft Windows–based systems, Microsoft "packaged" up the data using a protocol called NetBEUI. Systems networked using Novell Netware used a protocol called IPX/SPX. The World Wide Web standardized on the TCP/IP protocol. Today, most computers include software to support multiple protocols, so you can be connected to a local network using IPX/SPX or NetBEUI and also to the World Wide Web using TCP/IP.

TCP/IP is a *transport* protocol that defines the general packaging of the messages sent over the network. What your computer sends within the packaging parameters of a protocol depends on the applications sending and receiving the information—the *application* protocol. (To continue our train analogy, what kind of boxes inside the boxcar is the stationmaster on the other end prepared to unlock?) When you copy a file to a local server using Windows Explorer, Explorer packages up your file information in a format the receiving file system understands. Windows then wraps these packages in an available transport protocol for sending over the network.

When you work on a Web-based network (such as the World Wide Web), your browser uses standardized application protocols to send and receive information. Two of the most common Web protocols are *Hypertext Transport Protocol* (HTTP) for transmitting things like Web pages and pictures, and *File Transfer Protocol* (FTP) for uploading and downloading files.

The key to the explosive success of the World Wide Web is the acceptance and adoption of the transport protocol, application protocols, and page definition language by virtually every computer and software manufacturer. It's these common mechanisms that let you point your Web browser at a Web server halfway around the world to send and receive information. You don't have to worry or care about what kind of computer or operating system is installed for the Web server. For the most part, the folks who program the Web server don't have to worry about what kind of computer you're using or what Web browser you have installed.

Most Web pages are simple text files containing a mix of textual content and formatting codes. Some of these formatting codes control the appearance of the textual content, but others cause display of images, form fields, and all the other kinds of content you see daily on the Web. The overall name for this formatting scheme is *Hypertext Markup Language* (HTML).

Pages stored as simple text files are said to be *static*. Changing a static Web page requires editing or rewriting its HTML file, and Access can publish data to the Web in just this way. Exporting any table, query, form, or report in HTML format creates a Web page that lists the corresponding data. *For details about creating a simple HTML page from Microsoft Access, see "Creating a Static HTML Document," later in this chapter.*

This can be a valuable facility, but it suffers problems of timeliness. Once you've exported Access data as an HTML page, that page won't reflect database updates until you repeat the export process.

Delivering Dynamic Query Results

If, whenever a Web visitor requests a page, you'd rather query the database and create a new Web page on the fly, you're in luck! Figure 19-2 shows the most common network architecture you can build using Access as the database file server to report up-to-the-minute, live database contents. The browser requests a special kind of Web page—an *Active Server Page*—that contains a mixture of HTML and Visual Basic code. The Visual Basic code, running on the server and working through several layers of software, opens the database, runs the query, and formats the results. The Web server then transmits the results to the Web visitor's browser.

As you'll learn a bit later, Access 2000 uses HTML pages linked to ActiveX objects to implement the new data access page feature that delivers "live" data. However, the HTML pages and ActiveX objects for data access pages execute on the client, not the server.

> **NOTE**
>
> The Visual Basic supported in Active Server Pages is Microsoft Visual Basic Scripting Edition (VBScript).

FIGURE 19-2.

A high-level schematic for delivering database queries dynamically.

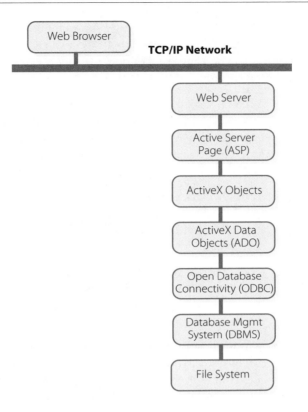

Active Server Pages that are designed to execute on the server only work on Microsoft Web servers, version 3.0 and above. For Windows NT Server 4.0 and Windows 2000 Server, this means Internet Information Server (IIS). For development or small workgroup use on Windows 95, Windows 98, Windows NT Workstation, or Windows 2000 Professional, Microsoft Personal Web Server (PWS) provides most of the same functionality, albeit with license restrictions. If you don't have access to an IIS or don't have permission to publish on an available IIS, you can test your Active Server Pages on your desktop machine by installing PWS on your desktop computer. When you install PWS, your desktop machine becomes both the client and the server.

PWS is part of the Windows NT 4.0 option pack, which you can download from http://www.microsoft.com/Windows/ie/pws/default.htm. Be sure to install PWS *without* the extensions for FrontPage 98 by choosing a Custom setup. Then install FrontPage 2000 (FrontPage is included with Office 2000 Premium) with Server Extensions options. If you installed all of FrontPage 2000 before installing PWS, you can enable the required Web extensions by rerunning Office 2000 Setup and asking it to repair your installation.

Figure 19-2 on the previous page shows the following additional components. Even if you never work with these directly, it's good to know what they are so you can decipher documentation, error messages, and other words of wisdom.

- **ActiveX Objects** are prewritten software modules that provide commonly used functions. Most VBScript code in Active Server Pages works by loading and controlling ActiveX Objects that run on the Web server. The ActiveX objects you need to build most Active Server Pages are included with Microsoft Office.

- **ActiveX Data Objects (ADO)** are a collection of ActiveX objects specially designed to process databases. As you'll learn in Chapter 22, "Visual Basic Fundamentals," the ADO libraries are a standard part of Microsoft Access.

- **Open Database Connectivity (ODBC)** provides a standard interface to many different kinds of database systems. You configure ODBC through Windows Control Panel. *See the Appendix for details about managing ODBC connections.*

- **Database Management System (DBMS)** organizes data into databases, tables, and fields. It also accepts commands (usually coded in SQL) that update or query the database. Microsoft Access and Microsoft SQL Server are typical Database Management Systems you can use to support Active Server Pages.

As you'll learn later in this chapter, Access can export any table, query or form (actually, the data bound to the form, not the form itself) as an Active Server Page. This gives you a Web page that will always retrieve the latest information from the database for display in your browser. If you want to create Web pages that can provide navigation to other pages on your Web or update the data in your database, read on.

Processing "Live Data" with HTML Forms

Among the many objects Web pages can contain are various form elements: text boxes, drop-down lists (similar to combo boxes in Access forms), check boxes, option buttons, push buttons (similar to command buttons in Access forms), and so forth. Web visitors can use these to enter data and submit it to an Active Server Page or other server-based program for processing. Typical database processing includes running customized queries and adding, changing, or deleting records in tables. Processing follows the schematic previously shown in Figure 19-2, except that the server receives form field data from the Web page and the Active Server Page programming is more complex.

HTML forms can't provide nearly as rich nor as helpful an interface as Access forms, but using HTML forms means authorized users anywhere can run your Web application without loading any additional software and regardless of the type of computer. These are important considerations when you need to support many users, many environments, or both.

Unfortunately, Access 2000 can't directly create Active Server Pages that allow you to do more than read "live" data within the architecture shown in Figure 19-2. As you'll learn later in the section titled "Enhancing Your Page with FrontPage," you can customize an exported Active Server Page with graphics and links to other pages on your Web. If you need to also update your data or provide dynamic query capabilities, consider one of the following solutions.

- **Microsoft Access 97.** The previous version of Access, Access 97, has a Publish To Web Wizard that converts tables, queries, forms, and reports of your choosing into Web pages. The same wizard gives all of these pages a common appearance, uniting them with a home page, and publishes them to the Web.

  In retrospect, this feature was probably a bit before its time and never got the notice it deserved. Also, the conversion from Access to HTML is fraught with imperfections and limitations. This is because Access forms are richer than HTML forms, and because the Visual Basic for Applications (VBA) in Access is richer than the VBScript in Active Server Pages. Also, this feature depends on a nonstandard ActiveX HTML Layout control that is not supported under Office 2000.

  In any event, this feature is no longer present in Access 2000. If you have existing applications that depend on this feature, you'll need to start maintaining them by hand or continue using Access 97.

- **Data access pages from Access 2000.** Access 2000 has a new feature that lets you design a special type of HTML form page that can navigate, filter, and update data in your database. As you'll learn in the following section, "Using Data Access Pages," the execution architecture for this type of Web page is quite different from the architecture shown in Figure 19-2. The HTML pages that support data access pages must run on the client, not the server. This means that each user must also have installed Office 2000 ActiveX controls and ADO components. Since many World Wide Web users won't have these components, this solution works well only for local corporate intranets where all users have Office installed. Even so, you can use additional tools like FrontPage 2000 to define navigation and enhance the look of these pages. *See "Enhancing Your Page with FrontPage," later in this chapter, for details.*

 SEE ALSO

For more information about FrontPage 2000, consult *Running Microsoft FrontPage 2000* from Microsoft Press.

- **Microsoft FrontPage 2000.** Although it doesn't provide a complete development environment, FrontPage 2000 has two components that connect HTML forms on the browser to Access databases on the server. The FrontPage Save Results component can collect input from an HTML form and add a record to an Access (or any other ODBC-compliant) database. In addition to creating the necessary HTML and Active Server Page code, this component can also create the necessary Access database and a table with a field corresponding to each form field. FrontPage 2000 also includes a powerful WYSIWYG (What You See Is What You Get) editor for Web pages, additional active components, and a wealth of Web site management features.

  The Database Results component in FrontPage generates HTML and Active Server Page code to query a database. This approach has two advantages over using Access to save a query as an Active Server Page. First, the Database Results component can limit the number of records transmitted to the Web visitor, and then transmit additional or previous records only if the visitor requests them. Second, the Database Results component can accept lookup keys from the Web visitor. This means Web visitors could, for example, enter an order ID and receive a list of items in that order.

SEE ALSO

For more information about Visual InterDev, consult *Inside Microsoft Visual InterDev* from Microsoft Press.

- **Microsoft Visual InterDev.** This is Microsoft's most powerful and most flexible Web development product and, as you might expect, it's also the most difficult to master. It's the 800-pound gorilla of Web development.

  Visual InterDev uses essentially the same user interface as the Visual Basic editor supplied with Access 2000. In addition, it supplies a WYSIWYG HTML editor, design-time ActiveX controls that generate HTML whenever you save a page that contains them, an assortment of database wizards and design tools, and an interactive debugger for both Active Server Pages and scripts that run on the browser. Yet, despite all these aids, Visual InterDev remains at heart a programmer's environment. If you're not comfortable working directly with HTML code, Visual Basic programming, and ActiveX interfaces, this probably isn't the program for you. Otherwise, rest assured that anything you can do in code, you can do in Visual InterDev.

In the Web Pages folder of the samples files included on the companion CD, you can find the files that define an entire Web that demonstrates the various types of pages you can generate using data from Microsoft Access. This Web includes the simple Active Server Pages you can generate directly from Access (in the PlainJane folder), complex forms and Active Server Pages you can build with FrontPage, and data access pages from Access that I enhanced using the themes and navigation tools in FrontPage.

Discovering the Possibilities

Figure 19-3 shows the results of a simple query in the Golf Tournament sample database exported as a simple HTML file. Other than using FrontPage to clean up the page title, add two push buttons to go to lower level pages, and link it into the Web, I didn't do anything else fancy with it.

FIGURE 19-3.

A simple query saved as an HTML result.

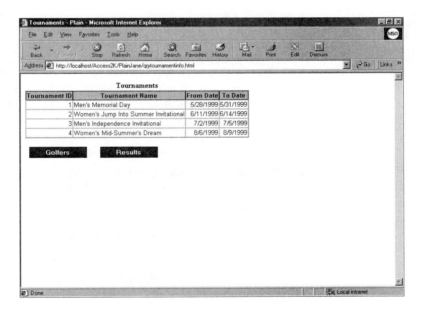

Figure 19-4 on the next page shows the same data in another copy of the page that I significantly enhanced with FrontPage. The formatting comes from a FrontPage theme called Canvas. I also added a title banner bar and navigation buttons to make it easier to move around in the Web.

Figure 19-5 on the next page shows a database page created entirely in FrontPage. You can see this page in FrontPage by opening the

FIGURE 19-4.

Data from a simple query exported from Access and enhanced with FrontPage.

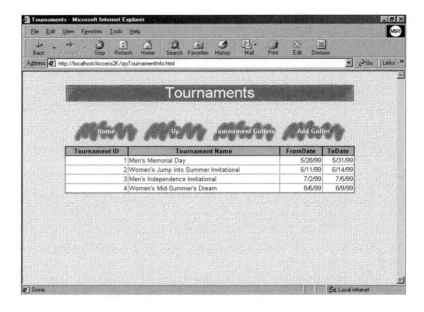

tgolfers.asp sample file. When you run this page from a published Web, you can enter a Tournament ID and click the Submit Query button to ask the page to look up all golfers enrolled in that event, sort them in Last Name sequence, and display the first five records in the result set. The four buttons at the bottom of the page move to the first, previous, next, and last five records, respectively.

FIGURE 19-5.

A Web page that uses the FrontPage Database Results component.

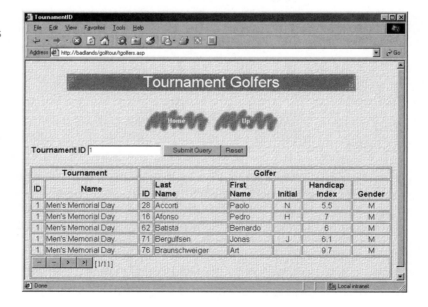

Using Data Access Pages

In place of the Publish To Web Wizard included with Access 97, Access 2000 provides data access pages. A data access page is neither an ordinary Web page nor a regular Access application; it's a special type of Access application, developed with different tools, and implemented using a combination of ActiveX controls and features built into Internet Explorer 5.0 and above.

Figure 19-6 diagrams a typical data access page application that uses a Microsoft Access database as the data source. The Web visitor's browser begins loading the data access page as it does any other Web page, and it loads the data access page ActiveX control in typical ActiveX fashion. The data access page control configures the user display and database connection in accordance with Extensible Markup Language (XML) instructions passed to the control as arguments, initializes the display, opens the database connection, and begins interacting with the user. (XML defines a standard notation for data names, data values, and data descriptions. Its objective is to promote data interchange between disparate systems.)

FIGURE 19-6.

Component diagram of a typical data access page using Microsoft Access as the data source.

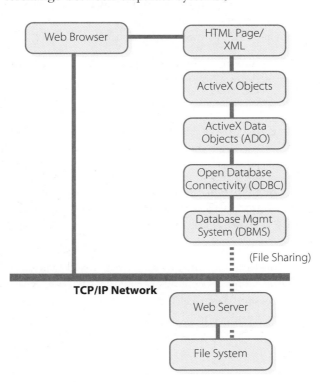

You can see that the major difference between this architecture and that for Active Server Pages (shown in Figure 19-2 on page 647) is that most of the work occurs on the Web browser machine. This means that all the required ActiveX components must be installed (and licensed) on the client machine. In addition, when using Microsoft Access as the database management system, the Web network must be able to support a potentially heavy load of low-level file commands. This works well for an internal corporate intranet, but can be crushingly slow over a typical modem connection to the World Wide Web. The situation improves significantly when using SQL Server as the database management system from an Access project file. In this case, the DBMS component often executes on the same Web server that's responding to requests for Web pages. *See Chapter 25, "After Completing Your Application," for details about working with Access project files.*

The ordinary way of coding data access pages tells the ActiveX control to open an Access database on the user's local disk or a conventional file server. When multiple users share the same data, the database must be on a server—often the same server that's supporting the Web components. To run the data access page, each Web visitor's environment needs to include the following.

- A Win32 operating system—that is, Windows 95 or later, Windows NT, or Windows 2000

- Internet Explorer 5.0 or later

- A copy of Office 2000 installed on the local computer, which provides the ActiveX controls required for the data access page to work

- File-sharing access to the Access database (unless the application uses a database in a known location on each Web visitor's computer)

The advantage of using data access pages lies mostly in software distribution rather than in supporting a wide variety of platform-independent clients. To change a data access page, you just update the necessary pages on the Web server. To change a compiled client/server application (that is, a standard Access application), you need to update each file server or client where it's installed.

Saving Your Data as a Web Page

With concepts firmly established, you're now ready to create some Web pages. The topics that follow explain how to save query results as static or dynamic Web pages, how to upload those pages to a Web server, how to set up database connectivity for dynamic Web pages, how to visually enhance your Web pages, and how to integrate them with the rest of your site.

Creating a Static HTML Document

The simplest way to publish Access information on the Web is to save a table, query, form, or report as a Web page. Here's the procedure.

1 Select the table, query, form, or report you want to export, either by selecting it in the Database window or, if it's already open, by making it the active window.

> When you export a form or report to HTML, Access simply exports the data from the Record Source of the form or report. The resulting page looks like a table datasheet, not like the design of the form or report.

2 Choose Export from the File menu.

3 When the dialog box shown in the foreground of Figure 19-7 appears, specify HTML Documents in the Save As Type box.

FIGURE 19-7.

Exporting a query as a static Web page.

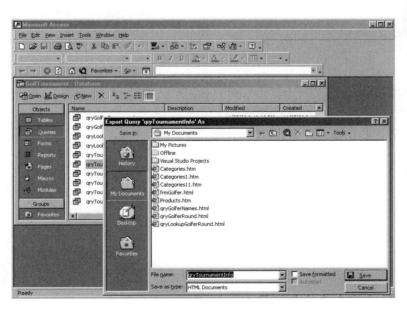

4 Use the Save In combo box at the top of the dialog box to choose a location. Unless you have file-sharing access to a Web server's file system, this should be a temporary work area on your computer.

5 Change the File Name value if you wish. This, plus the htm filename extension, becomes the name of the Web page.

6 Select the Save Formatted check box.

7 Click the Save button.

8 When the HTML Output Options dialog box appears, you can either leave the HTML Template field blank or specify the name of a template file. The sidebar titled "Using HTML Output Templates" explains this feature.

9 Click OK.

Figure 19-8 shows the result of exporting the qryTournamentInfo query as an HTML document with no template. *To transfer the HTML page to a Web server for public viewing, see "Uploading Your Page to a Web Server," later in this chapter.*

FIGURE 19-8.

An Access query exported as a Web page.

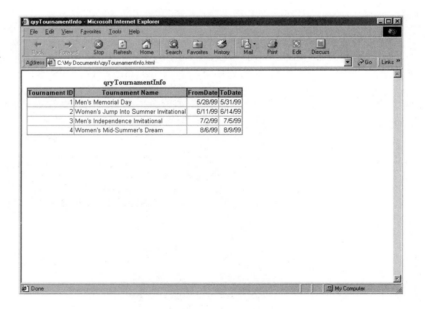

We could have made this page more attractive by using a template, and could still do so after importing it into FrontPage. *For more information, see "Enhancing Your Page with FrontPage," later in this chapter.*

Using HTML Output Templates

When Access exports data as an HTML page or Active Server Page query, the results are simple at best and, to many people, downright unattractive. You can correct this by manually editing the output, but if you repeat the export, you'll have to repeat the manual editing as well.

HTML Output Templates provide at least a partial solution. You can design as complex and artful a Web page as you like, add two special HTML comments, and then export as often as you like without loss of other content. The two comments are:

```
<!--ACCESSTEMPLATE_TITLE-->
```

for the title of the Web page and

```
<!--ACCESSTEMPLATE_BODY-->
```

for the table that displays the data. A simple example appears below.

```
<HTML>
<TITLE><!--ACCESSTEMPLATE_TITLE--></TITLE>
<BODY leftmargin=200 background=grayst.jpg>
<!--ACCESSTEMPLATE_BODY-->
</BODY>
<BR><BR>
<IMG SRC = "msaccess.jpg">
</HTML>
```

(You can find this template saved as Grayst.htm in your sample files.)

If you specify a template that doesn't contain an <!--ACCESSTEMPLATE_BODY--> comment, Access exports its data as the first content on the Web page.

There are two ways to use HTML Output Templates. First, you can make up very simple templates, consisting of formatting instructions only, and use the same template for all related queries (giving them a common appearance). Second, if the exported data is only one portion of a complex page, you can put all the non-Access data in the template and merge in the Access data as often as you like.

Creating a Dynamic Active Server Page

Exporting data as described in the previous section has one big problem: to keep the Web page up to date, you have to repeat the export process every time the database changes. This quickly becomes mundane and downright tedious, especially if the data changes very often. It might even leave you wondering if there's a way to perform the query interactively. Well, there is.

As I explained earlier in the section titled "Delivering Dynamic Query Results," an Active Server Page (ASP) is a special type of Web page that contains scripting code that runs on the Web server. When asked to deliver an Active Server Page, the Web server retrieves it from the file system, interprets and runs the script code, and delivers the results to the Web visitor. If your Access database is accessible to the Web server, code in an Active Server Page can open the database, run a query, format the results, and deliver them as a Web page. (Refer to Figure 19-2 on page 647 for a diagram of how this works.)

Before you can successfully create and test an Active Server Page, you must first define a system link to your database. *See the "Managing ODBC Connections" topic in the Appendix for information about creating a System Data Source Name (DSN).* For the examples shown below, you need a System DSN called "golftour" that points to the sample Golf Tournament database.

Building an Active Server Page

Of course, running Active Server Pages and querying Access databases requires an appropriate collection of software and configurations on the Web server.

- The Web server must be Microsoft Internet Information Server (IIS), version 3.0 or later. This is supplied free with—and only runs under—Windows NT Server 4.0 and Windows 2000 Server. A reduced version of IIS (Personal Web Server, discussed earlier) suitable for development and testing is available for Windows 95, Windows 98, Windows NT Workstation 4.0, and Windows 2000 Professional.

- The Web page must have a filename extension of asp rather than htm.

- The Web page must reside in a folder identified to the Web server as executable. This is something the server administrator must configure. If you're using PWS on your workstation, you can use the Personal Web Manager program to mark the Web as executable. In Personal Web Manager, click the Advanced options, choose the Web you want to publish to, view its Properties, and check the Executable box.

- The Web server must have Microsoft Access ODBC drivers that correspond to the version of Access used to create the database. If you create a database with Access 2000, for example, and the Web server has ODBC drivers for Access 97, the Access 97 drivers won't be able to read the database. If you're using PWS on the machine where you have Office 2000 installed (your machine is both the Web client *and* server), you have the correct drivers installed.

ON THE WEB

To obtain database drivers for Microsoft Web servers, go to http://www.microsoft.com/data/

Here's the procedure for exporting an Access table, query, form, or report as an Active Server Page.

1 Select the table, query, form, or report you want to export, either by selecting it in the Database window or, if it's already open, by making it the active window.

2 Choose Export from the File menu.

3 When the Export dialog box (shown earlier, in the foreground of Figure 19-7 on page 655) appears, specify Microsoft Active Server Pages in the Save As Type box.

4 Use the Save In combo box at the top of the dialog box to choose a location. Unless you have file-sharing access to a Web server's file system, this should be a temporary work area on your computer.

5 Change the File Name value if you wish. This, plus the asp filename extension, will become the name of the Web page.

6 Click Save.

7 When the dialog box shown in Figure 19-9 appears, enter the following data. Note that only one field, Data Source Name, is required.

FIGURE 19-9.

Configuring options when exporting a query as an Active Server Page.

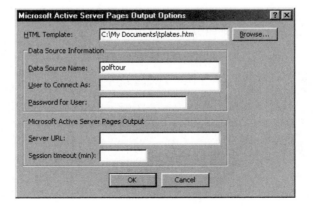

Publishing Information

V

- **HTML Template.** Specify, if desired, the filename of a formatting template as described earlier in this chapter. You can use the sample Grayst.htm file supplied on the companion CD or point to any already saved htm file to use as a template.

- **Data Source Name.** Specify the name of an ODBC System Data Source Name that exists (or will exist) on each Web server where you want the Active Server Page to work. This field is required.

- **User To Connect As.** If accessing the database requires a login name, specify it here.

- **Password For User.** If the login name requires a password, specify it here.

- **Server URL.** If you want Access to publish your page directly to a Web server, specify the URL of the folder where the Active Server Page will reside.

- **Session Timeout (Min).** Specify, if desired, the number of minutes to wait for a database connection to open. Leaving this field blank uses the database driver's default value.

8 Click OK.

Once the page is saved, you have two more jobs to do.

- You must set up an ODBC Data Source Name for the database containing the table, form, or report you just exported. (You don't actually need to build the DSN before you export the page, but you will need the DSN to execute the page on the Web.)

- Transfer the Active Server Page to a Web server. *See "Uploading Your Pages to a Web Server" at the end of this chapter for details about "publishing" your pages.*

Working with Data Access Pages

Access 2000 provides a totally new way to develop and distribute applications accessible by Web visitors: data access pages. This approach avoids the user interface limitations of HTML forms, and it can produce applications that are much more interactive. It requires no special resources on the Web server: no server-side components, no executable folders, no ODBC Data Source Names. What's more, given the high-level tools Access 2000 provides, developing a data access page can be quite easy.

Of course, nothing comes without a price. A data access page isn't so much a Web page as a run-time Access application partially distributed over the Web. In order to work, data access pages require a significant amount of software to be present, installed, and working on the Web visitor's computer.

If the correct software is present and the Web visitor browses a data access page, an <OBJECT> tag in the HTML loads the main data access page ActiveX control and provides the form layout, code, and other specifications (configured in Access) as input. The data access page control then displays the form, opens the database, and runs the application.

Usefulness and Limitations

Unlike traditional HTML forms and server-based processing, data access pages don't provide a general-purpose way to extend applications all across the World Wide Web. The technical requirements (a Windows-based computer and Office 2000 installed) make sure of that. Put more simply, a user on a Macintosh in Paris or user on a Unix system in Sydney won't be able to sign on to your Web over the worldwide network and open your data access page. Nevertheless, data access pages do provide an efficient way of distributing applications to groups of users known to have the correct environment—groups of employees on an intranet, for example, or limited Internet groups such as field service representatives, sales forces, and customers who subscribe to a custom service.

Give careful consideration before deploying data access page applications to users connected by dial-up link. Remember, these users will be reading your Access or SQL Server database directly using file sharing, and this may consume a lot of bandwidth even for well-optimized databases and queries.

Types of Pages You Can Create

Data access pages are a programmable environment, so in one sense they can create any type of page you care to program. Most data access pages, however, work like Access forms or reports. When you open a data access page, you are opening a recordset on your local machine over a network link, and then moving forward and back one record at a time. If your data access page uses a single table as its source, you can create a set of form fields to add, change, or display records. Of course, once you've located a record on an updateable data access page, you can update or delete it.

Data access pages typically feature groups of form fields associated with a record navigation bar. Figure 19-10 shows a typical data access page with a navigation bar at the bottom. Note the filename extension: htm. To the Web server, this is a perfectly ordinary Web page that requires no special processing. The entire application—database drivers and all—loads and executes on the Web visitor's computer.

FIGURE 19-10.

A typical data access page with a record navigation bar.

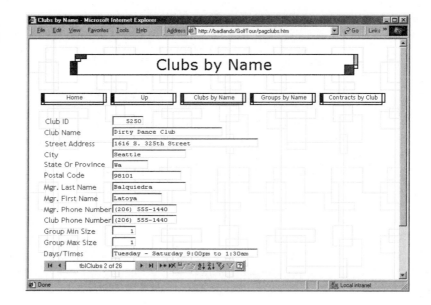

The data access page shown in Figure 19-10 was enhanced with navigation buttons using Microsoft FrontPage 2000. *See "Enhancing Your Pages with FrontPage," later in this chapter, for details.*

Creating Pages Using the Wizards

Access provides three shortcuts to help create and maintain data access pages. These shortcuts are visible when you click the Pages button in the Database window.

- **Create Data Access Page In Design View.** This shortcut initializes the data access page development environment and displays a blank page.

- **Create Data Access Page By Using Wizard.** This option runs a wizard that prompts for specifications and then creates a data access page automatically.

- **Edit Web Page That Already Exists.** This shortcut lets you open an existing data access page that's not linked into your database's Pages list.

The remainder of this section explains how to use the second of these options to create a data access page.

Creating a Page for Query and Update

For this example, you'll create a data access page that queries the Clubs table in the Entertainment Scheduling sample database in name sequence and provides update capability, similar to the page shown in Figure 19-10.

Open the Entertainment Scheduling sample database in Access. It'll be simplest in the long run if you open the database from the same file server that the intended users will use, and open it by specifying a UNC filename (that is, \\<*file server*>\<*sharename*>\<*path*>\Entertain.mdb) instead of specifying a drive letter. When you do this, the connection to the data stored in the data access page will use the network name. In the Open dialog box in Access, you can type the full UNC name directly in the File Name box. Alternatively, you can choose Network Neighborhood from the Look In box at the top, and then navigate to the computer containing your database. The computer must have file sharing enabled for you to be able to do this.

Before you get started, you should know that by default, Access saves data access pages in your default database folder. Choose Options from the Tools menu, and then select the General tab if you want to define a folder other than My Documents. From there, you can copy them to any Web server you want; data access pages require no special services on the Web server. Remember, though, that every user who runs the data access page will try to access the database using the file specification you provided when you opened the database. That's why it's best to avoid drive letters on specific computers or drive letters mapped to network drives. Each Web visitor's drive mappings may be different.

Click the Pages button in the Database window, and then double-click the Create Data Access Page By Using Wizard icon. In the first Page Wizard window, shown in Figure 19-11 on the next page, use the

Tables/Queries combo box to select the table or query that contains the field you want displayed. (In this example, choose tblClubs.) Next, select the desired field from the Available Fields list, and then click the single-right-arrow button. To add all available fields, click the double-right-arrow button. To remove a field from the Selected Fields list, click the single-left-arrow button. To remove all fields, click the double-left-arrow button.

FIGURE 19-11.

Specifying what fields a data access page will display.

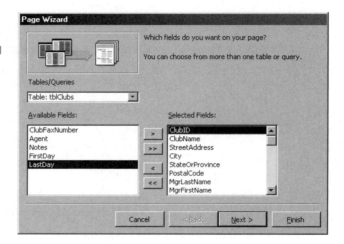

NOTE

You can select fields from any number of tables, but unless those tables have relationships defined, the wizard will fail. In such a case, it's best to quit the wizard, create and save a query, and then rebuild the data access page using the new query.

Click Next to display the wizard's second window, shown in Figure 19-12. Here you can designate one or more fields as a *grouping level*. This is useful when a table can be filtered on multiple fields and you want to allow the user to move through the values in one field at a time. You can, for example, specify grouping on the StateOrProvince field. When you do this, the wizard will move the StateOrProvince field into a separate navigation bar. The user can find the StateOrProvince they want, and then click an expand button to see the details of Clubs in the selected StateOrProvince.

One major drawback to defining grouping levels is that data in a data access page with grouping levels is not updateable! Because we want to be able to change data using this page, do not define any grouping

FIGURE 19-12.

Specifying grouping levels for a data access page.

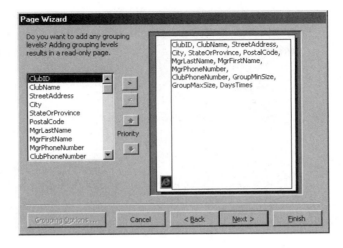

levels. We'll use this feature later to build groups in a page that shows Clubs and their Contracts. Click Next to go on to the next step.

Figure 19-13 shows the third window in the Page Wizard, which controls recordset order. Specify the fields in order, using the drop-down lists provided. To toggle a specified field between ascending and descending order, click the button to its right. For the example, sort the recordset by ClubName.

FIGURE 19-13.

Designating the recordset sort order.

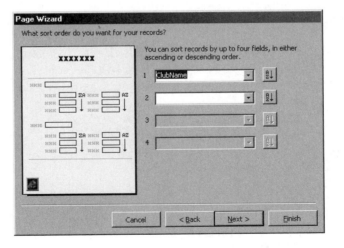

Click Next to display the wizard's last dialog box, shown in Figure 19-14 on the next page, which controls several details of appearance.

In What Title Do You Want For Your Page, enter a descriptive heading for your page. The wizard places this in a banner at the top of your

FIGURE 19-14.

Choosing the final options.

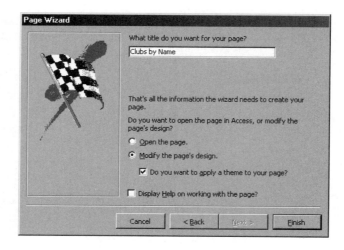

page. You can choose to open your new page in Page view (Open The Page) or in Design view (Modify The Page's Design).

Click the Do You Want To Apply A Theme To Your Page option to see the Theme dialog box shown in Figure 19-15 when you click Finish. In this dialog box, you can select from a variety of themes installed on your machine. (I installed all the available themes from FrontPage and Office Tools.) These themes make it easy to apply a predesigned set of colors, fonts, and graphics to your page. When you click a theme name in the left part of the window, you can see a sample of how the theme will look in the right window. If you want to set a theme as the default for all future pages, choose the theme in the left window, and then click the Set Default button. Once you choose a theme, click OK to apply that theme to your new page.

FIGURE 19-15.

Applying a theme to the data access page.

After you select the theme, Access displays the page in Design view. When you switch to Page view, your finished data access page should look similar to the one shown in Figure 19-10 on page 662. (Remember, I enhanced the data access page you see there with FrontPage—more about that later.) You can click the arrows on the navigation bar at the bottom to move forward or backward in the rows from tblClubs. You can click any field and then click the Sort Ascending or Sort Descending buttons to re-sort the rows based on the values in the field you selected. You can also apply a filter to the rows similar to the way you can in an Access form. Finally, because this data access page is based on a single table, you can update the data by typing in any of the fields. You can also delete the current row (not recommended unless you're working in a copy of the Entertainment Scheduling database!) by moving to the row you want to remove and clicking the Delete button on the navigation bar.

You can find more examples of this type of data access page in the Entertainment Scheduling sample database. The pagClubs and pagGroups pages are simple edit/display pages built using the Citrus theme. The pagClubs_1 and pagGroups_1 pages are additional examples of these pages using the Modular theme and enhanced with FrontPage.

SEE ALSO

For more information about Design view for data access pages, see "Modifying Data Access Pages," later in this chapter.

Let's take another swing through the Page Wizard, but this time we'll build a data access page that uses the grouping features. Go back to the Database window, click the Pages button, and then double-click the Create Data Access Page Using Wizard shortcut to start the wizard again. This time, choose qryContracts in the Table/Queries combo box, and then choose the BeginningDate, ContractNo, ContractDate, GroupName, ContractPrice, ContractDaysTimes, EndingDate, NumberOfWeeks, and ClubName fields, as shown in Figure 19-16.

FIGURE 19-16.

Using the wizard to build a data access page on a query.

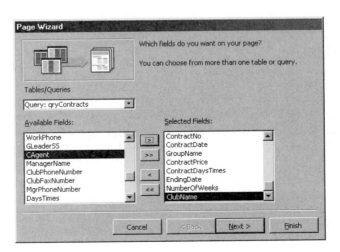

Click Next to go to the next dialog box, shown in Figure 19-17. This time, we want to group all this information by the Club Name. The resulting data access page will open with only the Club Name displayed. Once you navigate to the club you want, you'll be able to click an "expand" button to see the contract details for the selected club. To set up ClubName as a grouping level, click ClubName in the list on the left, and then click the arrow button to set it up as a group, as shown in the figure.

FIGURE 19-17.

Setting a grouping field in the Page Wizard.

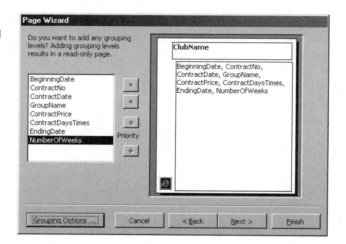

Once you define a group, you can click the Grouping Options button to group the field values within a range. Just like the sorting and grouping options in reports, you can group on the first few characters of a text field, group on a range of dates (by week, month, quarter, and so on), or group a number field on ranges of values. Are you beginning to get the idea that a data access page is a cross-breed of native Access forms and reports?

? SEE ALSO

For more information about grouping, see "Sorting and Grouping Information" in Chapter 17.

In this case, we want to group on the entire Club Name, so you don't need to set grouping options. Click Next to go to the dialog box for specifying additional sorting, as you saw in Figure 19-13 on page 665. In this case, it would be nice to sort the contract data by the BeginningDate field. Click Next again to go to the final dialog box that you saw in Figure 19-14. Select the Do You Want To Apply A Theme To Your Page option, and then click Finish. Pick your theme (I used Citrus Punch and Modular for the sample pages), and then click OK. If you picked the Modular theme, your page in Page view should look something like Figure 19-18. (Again, this example has been enhanced slightly with FrontPage.)

FIGURE 19-18.

A data access page with a grouping level based on the ClubName field.

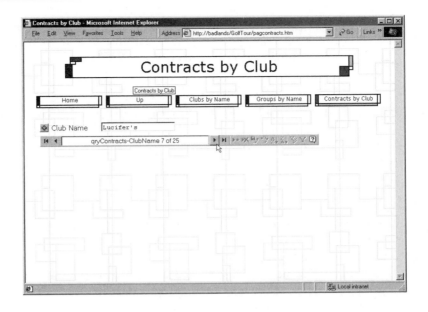

The data access page shown in Figure 19-18 uses the ClubName field as a grouping level. Using this page is a two-step process. First, the Web visitor clicks buttons on the qryContracts-ClubName record navigation bar to locate the club of interest. Then the visitor clicks the expand button (the plus sign), the Web page changes as shown in Figure 19-19, and the visitor uses the qryContracts record navigation bar to locate the desired contract.

FIGURE 19-19.

The data access page of Figure 19-18 expanded to browse contracts for a particular club.

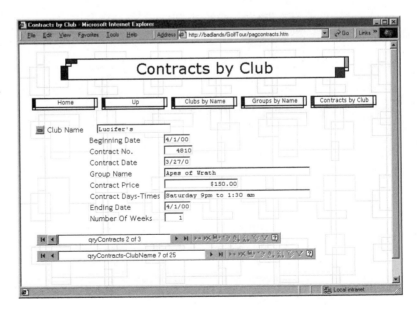

You'll recall that database updates aren't possible when a data access page uses grouping levels. For that reason, the applicable buttons are grayed out on both record navigation bars.

Modifying Data Access Pages

The development environment for data access pages borrows heavily from the rest of Access and from other Microsoft development tools. This can be good or bad. It's good because many tools and features work in familiar ways. It's bad because just when everything starts seeming familiar, the data access page environment does something different.

Figure 19-20 shows a data access page open for editing. The largest window is the Data Access Page window, where you can insert, modify, or delete page elements. To move or resize an element, first select it, and then drag an edge or stretch a corner. To delete an element, first select it, and then press the Delete key. To add an element, first select it in the toolbox and then, in the Data Access Page window, click the spot where you want it to appear.

FIGURE 19-20.

A data access page in Design view.

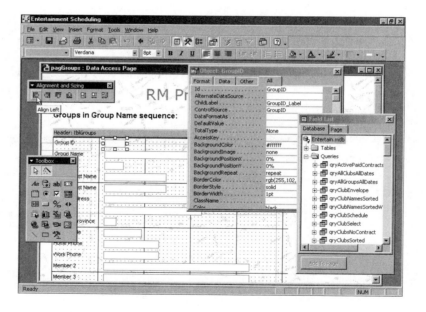

To align elements, you need to learn a procedure completely different from the procedure you learned for Access forms and reports. First, you cannot select multiple elements by holding down the Shift key. If you want to align two text boxes on their left edge, first open the Alignment And Sizing toolbar. Click the first text box, click the Align Left button on the toolbar, and then click the second text box. If you

> **⊗ CAUTION**
>
> In this first version of the data access page editor, there is no Undo facility. If you make a change that you didn't intend, you have to undo it by hand. You may want to save frequently to minimize rework if you make several changes that you need to reverse.

want to align several elements in a row, you can double-click the alignment button to temporarily lock it down. Follow a similar procedure to size two elements using the Size Height and Size Width buttons on the toolbar.

The gray bar titled Header: tblGroups marks the start of the database processing area. A similar bar lower in the page marks the end. Any form fields bound to a database field must reside within this area. To view the data binding for a form field, double-click the form field and then select the Data tab or the All tab on the resulting property sheet. Like controls in forms and reports, the ControlSource property defines the bound field or other data to be displayed in the selected design element. In Figure 19-20, for example, you can see that the GroupID field provides the data for the selected GroupID text box.

The Database tab in the field list (shown at the right side of Figure 19-20) displays a list of all tables and queries in the database, along with the fields they contain. You can add a table or field to the data access page simply by finding it in the field list and dragging it to the database processing area in the Data Access Page window. If no relationships exist between a newly added table and those already present, Access prompts you for one. The Page tab lists database fields already used in the current form. Highlighting a field in the Page tab highlights it in the Data Access Page window as well.

Note that the Entertainment Scheduling database (Entertain.mdb) is the top-level item in the Database tab. Right-clicking this object and choosing Connection displays the dialog box shown in Figure 19-21 on the next page, and permits changing the database to another source or changing connection properties. On the Connection tab in Figure 19-21, note the use of a UNC filename for the Access database. If you didn't open your database using a UNC name, you'll see a drive, path, and filename in this entry. You can change to a UNC name for the connection by typing in the Select Or Enter A Database Name box.

> **⊘ NOTE**
>
> In the sample Entertainment Scheduling database, connections are saved in drive/path format. If you install the sample files to a location other than the Running Access 2000 Samples folder on your C drive, you will need to change the connection property to the correct location in order for the sample pages to work correctly.

FIGURE 19-21.

Data link properties for the data access page.

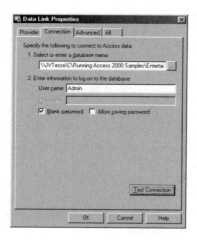

If you want to see the properties for the page itself, open the Properties window, and then click the Data Access Page window's title bar. You can also choose Select Page from the Edit menu. You can see the page properties for the pagGroups sample page in Figure 19-22.

FIGURE 19-22.

Page properties for a data access page.

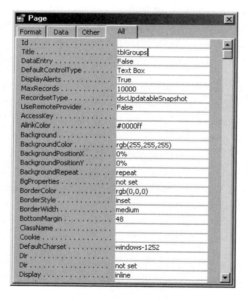

If the properties seem completely unlike the properties for a form or report, remember that you're now in a design environment for Web pages. One of the major differences is that most positioning is expressed in pixels or a relative percentage from the left or top of the design area. The reason for this is you have no control over the size of the Web visitor's browser window. The user's browser will make automatic adjustments based on the size of the user's window. You can, for example, design a data access page to "look best" in a browser window that's 800 by 600 pixels, but you can't control the window size absolutely like you can in an Access form.

Until you've gained experience designing for a Web environment, I recommend you adjust all design elements by moving and sizing them in the design area. Also use the Formatting and Alignment And Sizing toolbars to make adjustments rather than trying to wrestle with the property sheet. The design engine will make appropriate adjustments to the properties for you.

To place elements on a data access page, you can use the Toolbox, which is shown in the lower left corner of Figure 19-20. All of the "controls" you can use as design elements in a data access page are implemented as ActiveX objects. Many of these objects are very similar to the controls you use to design forms and reports. Table 19-1 lists the built-in objects, their Access form and report equivalents, and their specific uses.

TABLE 19-1. Data Access Page Tools

Tool	Form/Report Equivalent	Usage
Aa	Label	**Label.** Display unbound text on the page.
🖼	(None)	**Bound HTML.** Display a bound text or memo field as formatted HTML.
ab|	Text Box	**Text Box.** Display data from a text or memo field.
▤	(None)	**Scrolling Text.** Display text from a field or expression, and scroll the information at a specified rate across the object.
▣	Option Group	**Option Group.** Display a numeric value by highlighting the related option button within the group.
◉	Option Button	**Option Button.** Display a True/False value or an integer value when inside an option group.
☑	Check Box	**Check Box.** Display a True/False value. Unlike Access forms and reports, you cannot place a check box inside an option group.

(continued)

TABLE 19-1. *continued*

Tool	Form/Report Equivalent	Usage
	Combo Box	**Drop-down List.** Display a list of values that opens when the user clicks the drop-down button. Choosing a value in the list sets the value of the Control Source. A wizard is available to help you define the properties for a drop-down list.
	List Box	**List Box.** Display a list of values in a window. Choosing a value in the list sets the value of the Control Source. A wizard is available to help you define the properties for a list box.
	Command Button	**Command Button.** Display an object that can respond to a user click to activate a VBScript action. A wizard is available to help you build script commands for navigation.
	(None)	**Expand.** Display an object that can respond to a user click to expand or contract a grouped display. If you click a bound data field, and then click the Promote button on the toolbar, the design engine creates a grouping level for the field you chose and adds an expand control to facilitate navigation. You won't normally need to use an expand control independently.
	(None)	**Record Navigation.** Display an object that can respond to user clicks to navigate from record to record, sort data, apply filters, and delete rows in an updateable data access page. The design engine adds this control when you first add a field from a table or query to a blank page. You won't normally need to use the record navigation control independently.
	Object Frame, Bound Object Frame	**Office Pivot Table.** Add an Excel pivot table to your page. You can bind the pivot table to data from your database.
	Object Frame, Bound Object Frame	**Office Chart.** Add an Excel chart to your page. You can bind the chart to data from your database.
	Object Frame, Bound Object Frame	**Office Spreadsheet.** Add an Excel spreadsheet to your page. You can bind the spreadsheet to data from your database.
	Text Box bound to a Hyperlink field	**Bound Hyperlink.** Display and edit data from a Hyperlink data type field in your database. The user can click the hyperlink to activate it.

TABLE 19-1. *continued*

Tool	Form/Report Equivalent	Usage
	Label with Hyperlink properties set	**Hyperlink.** Define a static hyperlink on your page. You can set the hyperlink to open another document or go to another page on your Web when the user clicks the link.
	(None)	**Hotspot Image.** Define a picture on your page containing a hyperlink. You can set the hyperlink to open another document or go to another page on your Web when the user clicks the hotspot.
	Object Frame	**Movie.** Display and play a movie file (avi, mov, mpg, or asf filename extension) from your Web.
	Image	**Image.** Display a picture (gif, jpg, jpeg, bmp, xmp, or png filename extension) from your Web.
	Line	**Line.** Draw a line on your page.
	Rectangle	**Rectangle.** Draw a rectangle on your page.

Opening and Saving Data Access Pages

Access remembers any data access pages you create and lists them as components of the database, so the simplest way to open a page is to click Pages in the Database window and then double-click the page name. However, unlike tables, queries, forms, and reports, Access saves data access pages as external files. If you move a data access page and then try to open it from the Database window, you'll get an error message. If you know where the page is, click the Locate button in the error message, navigate to the page, and Access opens the page and thereafter remembers the new location.

You can open a data access page even if its database isn't open. Simply choose Open from the File menu, set Files Of Type to Web Pages (*.html; *.htm), locate the page, and click Open.

The Open dialog box, shown in Figure 19-23 on the next page, has five starting points for locating a file.

- **History** displays shortcuts that point to files recently opened in Office applications.

- **My Documents** displays the contents of your My Documents folder.

V

Publishing Information

FIGURE 19-23.
The full-featured Office 2000 Open dialog box.

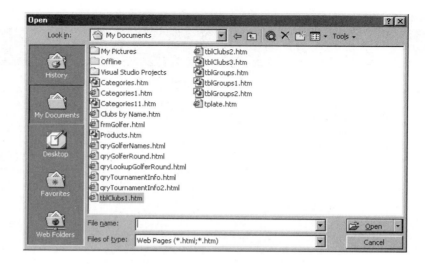

■ **Desktop** displays the same list of starting points as your Windows desktop: My Computer, My Desktop, Network Neighborhood, and so forth.

■ **Favorites** displays the same Web locations as the Favorites menu in Internet Explorer.

? SEE ALSO

For more information about Web folders, see "Uploading Your Page to a Web Server," later in this chapter.

■ **Web Folders** displays the same list of Web servers as the Web Folders icon that Office adds to your My Computer icon.

If you wonder what use the Favorites or Web Folders lists could be, it's this: Access can read data access pages (and other files) directly from a Web server, just as if it were a browser.

If you open a data access page through File Open, the File Save and File Save As commands invoke a dialog box similar to the one shown in Figure 19-23. This permits saving the data access page anywhere you want, including directly to a Web server (subject to security and provided the Web server has the FrontPage Server Extensions installed). If you open a data access page through the Pages list in the Database window, you can save it only to your default database folder. If you want to move or copy it elsewhere, you'll have to do so through Windows Explorer.

Enhancing Your Page with FrontPage

The simple Web page you get when you export data either as plain HTML or as an Active Server Page (such as the example shown in Figure 19-8 on page 656) is functional but hardly attractive. You could enhance such pages somewhat by creating and using an HTML template file, but that assumes you *have* such a file, and using a template doesn't solve another problem: integrating the pages with others in an organization's Web site.

Web pages are just text files, so one approach is to modify them with a text editor. The ever-popular Notepad utility comes to mind, especially if you have a minimalist (and masochistic) frame of mind. However, this requires great care and considerable knowledge of HTML. Consequently, many users turn to specialized editors like FrontPage.

FrontPage can open individual HTML and Active Server Page files directly from your local disk, and save them there as well. Eventually, however, most users start organizing their Web pages into FrontPage Webs. This is an area on your disk or Web server that contains all the files for a specific group of Web pages. Grouping pages into FrontPage Webs lets FrontPage manage them as a set and this, as you'll see shortly, offers several advantages.

Figure 19-24 on the next page shows FrontPage editing a page in a FrontPage Web. The title bar shows the Web's location: in this case, C:\Running Access 2000 Samples\Web Pages—the location of the sample Web included with this book installed in the default location. The Views bar at the left displays the FrontPage Web in various ways. Page view is the one with the WYSIWYG editor. The Folder List to its right displays the files and folders that comprise the Web. The large window at the right shows the default.htm page in edit mode. (Your home page on a Web is usually called Default.htm or Default.asp.)

> **NOTE**
>
> To run the samples in this section on your own computer, first use FrontPage to open the Web Pages folder in the sample files as a Web, and then publish it to your local Web server (Personal Web Server, most likely). If you don't have Personal Web Server, you can follow along in Microsoft FrontPage by choosing Open Web from the File menu and navigating to the Running Access 2000 Samples\Web Pages folder.

I created this "home page" by starting with a new blank page in the FrontPage editor. I applied the Canvas theme by choosing Themes from the Format menu. I added a page banner by choosing Page Banner from the Insert menu, and then typing in the text I wanted. I also added a navigation bar by choosing it from the Insert menu. As you'll see a bit later, FrontPage automatically maintains the "hot spots" on a navigation bar when you define your page structure in Navigation view.

FIGURE 19-24.
FrontPage editing a
Web page.

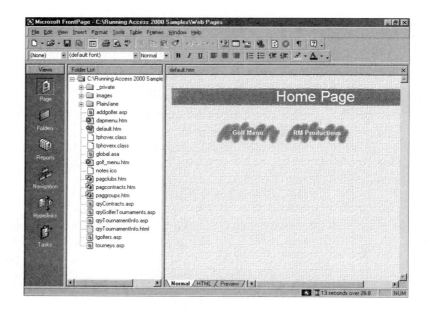

Copying a Web page saved by Access into a FrontPage Web is a
simple matter of dragging the file's icon from Windows Explorer to the
desired folder in the FrontPage Folder List. To edit a Web page flagged
with a FrontPage or generic icon, double-click it. To edit a Web page
flagged with some other icon, such as the one from Access (all data
access pages are originally "owned" by Access), hold down the Shift
key, right-click the file, choose Open With from the shortcut menu,
select FrontPage (frontpg.exe), and then click OK.

> **NOTE**
>
> When an Office application saves a Web page, it marks the file internally with
> the name of the application. In FrontPage, this overrides the file's normal icon
> and determines which program will open the file. Double-clicking a file last
> saved in FrontPage opens it in FrontPage. Double-clicking a file last saved by
> Access opens it in Access.
>
> To open a page last saved by FrontPage in another application, you'll first
> need to add that application to the Open With list. To do this, choose Options
> from the Tools menu, and then click the Configure Editors tab.

FrontPage offers several ways to build hyperlinks among pages in the
same Web, but the most automated involves Navigation view. This
view diagrams the pages in a FrontPage Web as an organization chart.
Figure 19-25 shows the qryTournamentRoundReport.html file being
added to Navigation view. This involves nothing more than dragging

the file name out of the Folder List, positioning it under the desired page, and dropping it.

FIGURE 19-25.

Adding a page to FrontPage's Navigation view.

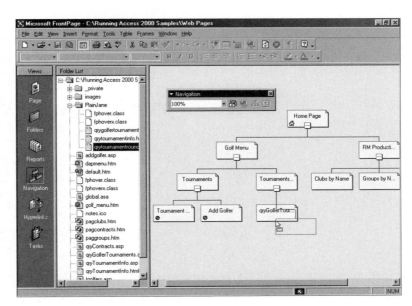

To create this navigation "tree," I first added the default.htm page as the Home page. I then created additional blank pages called golf_menu.htm and DAPMenu.htm. I added page banners and navigation bars to each, and then dragged them under the home page. I continued down the "tree," adding enhanced versions of the three sample data access pages from the Entertainment Scheduling database (off the screen on the right) and both enhanced and "plain jane" versions of HTML and Active Server Pages from the Golf Tournament sample database.

The advantage of recording page relationships in Navigation view is this: FrontPage can use this information to build links among your pages automatically on the navigation bars you include. Here's the procedure.

1   Position the page in Navigation view.

2   Make sure Navigation view displays a useful name for the newly added page. If not, select the page, press F2, and enter a new name.

3   Double-click the page to open it in Normal view in the editor window.

4   Set the insertion point at the top of the Web page.

5   Choose Page Banner from the Insert menu, choose Text in the resulting dialog box, and type in the text you want to appear.

6   Press Enter to insert a paragraph break.

7   Choose Navigation Bar from the Insert menu. When the dialog box shown in Figure 19-26 appears, select the type of menu choices you want, and then click OK.

FIGURE 19-26.

Configuring a navigation bar.

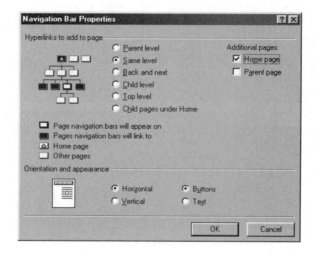

If you start with a plain HTML export of qryTournamentInfo from the Golf Tournament database (see Figure 19-8 on page 656), delete the page heading that Access inserts, and follow along with the steps above, you should have a result similar to the one shown in Figure 19-27. At this point, the title you entered in Navigation view appears as text where you inserted the Page Banner, and the menu bar choices appear as text where you inserted the navigation bar. The navigation bar captions and the Navigation view titles are automatically the same. To change a navigation bar caption, go back to Navigation view.

The page shown in Figure 19-27 is still rather boring, but you can change that by applying a FrontPage theme. Here's the procedure.

1   Make sure the insertion point is in the page you want to enhance.

2   Choose Theme from the Format menu. FrontPage displays a list of available Themes and a preview of each Theme you highlight.

3   Select the Theme you want. For this example, choose Canvas.

4   Click OK.

FIGURE 19-27.

A page banner and navigation bar added in FrontPage.

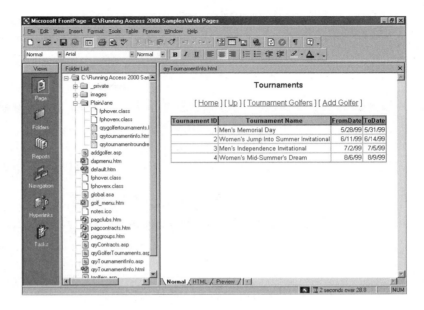

Figure 19-28 shows the results after one additional change: each element on the page—the page banner, the navigation bar, and the table containing the data—was centered.

FIGURE 19-28.

The Web page of Figure 19-8 enhanced using FrontPage.

As you can see, by using a powerful Web editor like Microsoft FrontPage, you can quickly turn your "plain jane" pages created with

Access into works of art and integrate them into an easily navigable Web. For a complete reference, consider *Running Microsoft FrontPage 2000* from Microsoft Press.

Uploading Your Pages to a Web Server

Once you get your Web pages built, they'll really only be useful if you can upload or "publish" them to a Web server. This last section of this chapter describes several ways to accomplish this task.

Copying Pages Using the Office Web Pages Facility

In most cases, the path and filename portions of a Universal Resource Locator (URL) correspond directly to a portion of the Web server's file system, starting at a spot called the HTTP root. For example, if the server's HTTP root is F:\InetPub\wwwroot\, then the URL http://www.theserver.com/default.htm corresponds to F:\InetPub\wwwroot\default.htm on the Web server. Similarly, http://www.theserver.com/veggies/yams.htm points to F:\InetPub\wwwroot\veggies\yams.htm on the Web server.

> **NOTE**
>
> Occasionally, an administrator will break this pattern by defining a *virtual directory*. Web visitors specify the virtual directory normally in a URL, but the Web server translates it to some location outside the normal HTTP root. If, in the second example above, veggies were a virtual directory assigned to G:\plants\edible, the filename corresponding to http://www.theserver.com/veggies/yams.htm would be G:\plants\edible\yams.htm.

If the Web server has a set of programs called the FrontPage Server Extensions installed, the Web Folders feature in Office 2000 makes it very easy to copy files onto the Web server. Here's the procedure.

1 Open the My Computer icon on your Windows desktop.

2 Double-click the Web Folders icon. This is a client component provided with Office 2000.

   The background window shown in Figure 19-29 shows the resulting Web Folders window and some typical contents. If your display doesn't include the Web server you need to use, double-click the Add Web Folder icon, enter the server's URL, give the server a name, and click Finish.

FIGURE 19-29.

The Office 2000 Web Folders feature in action.

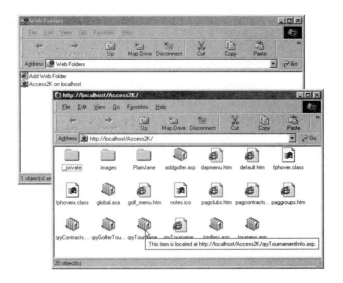

3 Double-click your way through the Web server's folders, just as you would in Windows Explorer, until you see the folder where your Web page should reside. If any folders are protected by passwords, you'll be prompted for them as you attempt to open each protected folder.

4 Open your computer's My Computer or Network Neighborhood icon and locate the file you want to transfer.

5 Drag the file from Windows Explorer to the Web Folders window.

You can also use Web Folders to copy files from the Web server to your local PC, and to rename, delete, or modify files on the Web server. One thing you *can't* do, however, is open an Access database. The Web Folders feature doesn't support all the same operations as a file system on your local disk or file server.

Figure 19-30 on the next page shows Internet Explorer displaying the same Web page as the one shown in Figure 19-8 on page 656, but after I dragged the page to a Web server. Note that the Address field now specifies a URL rather than a file location.

If your Web server doesn't have the FrontPage Server Extensions installed, the HTTP root—or portions of it—may be accessible through Windows file sharing. This is more typical on corporate intranets than on commercial Internet sites. If file sharing is available, the server administrator can tell you what file-sharing location to use and how to construct the corresponding URL. After finding the correct location in

FIGURE 19-30.

A static HTML document displayed via the Web.

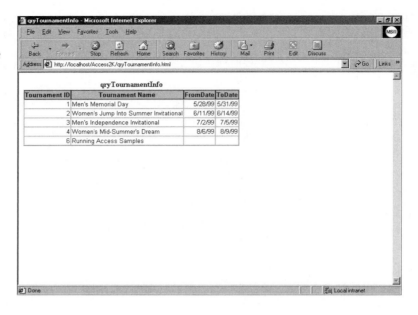

Network Neighborhood, copying files is once again a drag-and-drop process.

Publishing Pages Using File Transfer

If neither the FrontPage Server Extensions nor Windows file sharing is available, you'll probably have to use the Internet's File Transfer Protocol (FTP) for copying files to your Web server. Contact your system administrator or service provider for these details.

- The name of the FTP server to use

- The user name to log in with

- The password to specify

- The directory (folder) to use

The requisite FTP session in an MS-DOS window would then go something like this:

```
ftp <FTP server name>
username: <user name>
password: <password>
cd <directory>
put <local file name> <server file name>
bye
```

You can *put* any number of files before you quit with the *bye* command. Before you transfer any nontextual files—such as images—issue the command *binary*.

Publishing an Entire Web with FrontPage

At the risk of sounding like I'm tooting FrontPage's horn too loudly, the easiest way to publish and maintain all pages in your Web (particularly if you've built the Web with FrontPage) is to use the FrontPage publish facility. Once you're done editing your Web and have saved all your changes, choose Publish Web from the File menu. The resulting dialog box is shown in Figure 19-31.

FIGURE 19-31.

Publishing your Web with FrontPage.

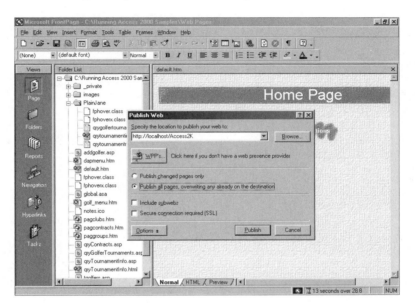

Type in the address of the Web where you want to publish as an HTTP address. In the example, I'm using my local copy of Personal Web Server, and have specified the standard alias of localhost (I could have used my machine network name instead.) I've also asked FrontPage to publish my Web as a subweb called Access2K. Click the Options button to see all the additional options shown in the lower part of the dialog box. As you can see, you can choose to republish your entire Web, or upload only changed pages. When you ask to publish only changed pages, FrontPage lists and compares the pages it finds on the target Web with the pages in your FrontPage Web and sends only the ones needed to update the target Web. If you're operating over a dial-up link, this option can be a real time-saver.

V

Publishing Information

When you publish your Web for the first time and ask to publish to a subweb, FrontPage creates the new Web for you on the server and marks the Web as executable.

At this point, you should understand the basics to get you started publishing your Microsoft Access data to an Internet or intranet Web. It should be clear that you really need a product like Microsoft FrontPage to build professional-looking pages and to link your Web together. In the next section, we'll jump back into Access to learn how to create the code you need to build applications using Microsoft Access alone.

PART VI

Creating an Application

Adding Power with Macros

In Microsoft Access, you can define a macro to execute just about any task you would otherwise initiate with the keyboard or the mouse. The unique power of macros in Access is their ability to automate responses to many types of events without forcing you to learn a programming language. The event might be a change in the data, the opening or closing of a form or a report, or even a change of focus from one control to another. Within a macro, you can include multiple actions and define condition checking so that different actions are performed depending on the values in your forms or reports.

NOTE

Macros are particularly useful for building small, personal applications or for prototyping larger ones. As you'll learn in Chapter 22, "Visual Basic Fundamentals," you probably should use Visual Basic for complex applications or for applications that will be shared by several users over a network. However, even if you think you're ready to jump right into Visual Basic, you should study all the macro actions first. You'll find that you'll use nearly all of the available macro actions in Visual Basic, so learning macros is an excellent introduction to programming in Access in general.

In this chapter, first you'll learn about the various types of actions you can define in macros. Next you'll tour the macro design facility and learn how to build both a simple macro and a macro with multiple defined actions. You'll also learn how to manage the many macros you need for a form or a report by creating a macro group. Finally you'll see how to add conditional statements to a macro to control the actions Access performs. At the end of the chapter, you'll find summaries of the macro actions and of the events that can trigger a macro. You might find these sections useful as a quick reference when you're designing macros for your applications.

Uses of Macros

Microsoft Access provides various types of macro actions that you can use to automate your application.

- You can use macros to open any table, query, form, or report in any available view. You can also use a macro to close any open table, query, form, or report.

- You can use macros to open a report in Print Preview or to send a report directly to the printer. You can also send the output data from a report to a Rich Text Format (rtf) file, a Notepad (txt) file, or a Microsoft Excel (xls) file. You can then open the file in Microsoft Word, Notepad, or Excel.

- You can use macros to execute a select query or an action query. You can base the parameters of a query on the values of controls in any open form.

- You can use macros to base the execution of an action on any condition that tests values in a database, a form, or a report. You can use macros to execute other macros or to execute Visual Basic functions. You can halt the current macro or all macros, cancel the event that triggered the macro, or quit the application.

- You can use macros to set the value of any form or report control. You can also emulate keyboard actions and supply input to system dialog boxes, and you can refresh the values in any control based on a query.

- You can use macros to apply a filter to, go to any record in, or search for data in a form's underlying table or query.

- You can use macros with any form to define a custom menu bar to replace the standard menu bar in Access. You can enable or disable and check or uncheck items on custom menus, including shortcut menus and global menus. You can also open and close any of the standard Access toolbars or your own custom toolbars.

- You can use macros to execute any of the commands on any of the Access menus.

- You can use macros to move and size, minimize, maximize, or restore any window within the Access workspace. You can change the focus to a window or to any control within a window. You can select a page of a report to display in Print Preview.

- You can use macros to display informative messages and to sound a beep to draw attention to your messages. You can also disable certain warning messages when executing action queries.

- You can use macros to rename any object in your database. You can make another copy of a selected object in your database or copy an object to another Access database. You can delete objects in your database. You can use a macro to save an object. With macros, you can also import, export, or attach other database tables, or import or export spreadsheet or text files.

- You can use macros to start an application and exchange data with the application using Dynamic Data Exchange (DDE) or the Clipboard. You can send data from a table, query, form, or report to an output file and then open that file in the appropriate application. You can also send keystrokes to the target application.

Consider some of the other possibilities for macros. For example, you can make moving from one task to another easier by using command buttons that open and position forms and set values. You can create very complex editing routines that validate data entered in forms, including checking data in other tables. You can even check something like the customer

VI

Creating an Application

name entered in an order form and open another form so that the user can enter detailed data if no record exists for that customer.

Creating a Simple Macro

This section explains how to work with the macro design facility in Microsoft Access.

The Macro Window

Open the Wedding List sample database (Wedding.mdb), and close the Wedding List data entry form to return to the Database window. As you'll discover a bit later in this chapter, a special macro called *Autoexec* runs each time you open the database. We'll look at that macro in some detail to see how it hides a few items and opens and maximizes the main data entry form to start the application.

Click the Macros button in the Database window, and then click the New button to open a new Macro window similar to the one shown in Figure 20-1. In the upper part of the Macro window you define your new macro, and in the lower part you enter settings, called *arguments*, for the actions you've selected for your macro. The upper part shows at least two columns, Action and Comment. You can view all four columns shown in Figure 20-1 by clicking the Macro Names and Conditions buttons on the toolbar.

Notice that the area at the lower right displays a brief help message. The message changes depending on where the cursor is located in the upper part of the window. (Remember: you can always press F1 to open a context-sensitive Help topic.)

In the Action column, you can specify any one of the 53 macro actions provided by Access. If you click in any box in the Action column, a down arrow button appears at the right side of the box. Click this button to open a drop-down list of the macro actions, as shown in Figure 20-2.

To see how the Macro window works, select the MsgBox action now. (Scroll down the list to find MsgBox.) You can use the MsgBox action to open a pop-up modal dialog box with a message in it. This is a great way to display a warning or an informative message in your database without defining a separate form.

Assume that this message will be a greeting, and type *Greeting message* in the corresponding box in the Comment column. You'll find the Comment column especially useful for documenting large macros that con-

FIGURE 20-1.

A new Macro window.

Macro Names button

Conditions button

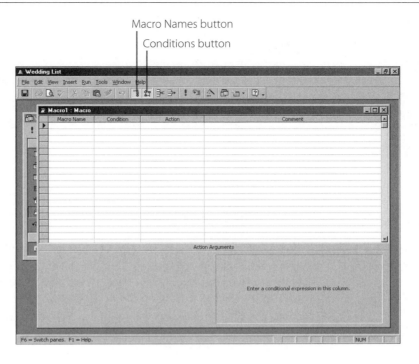

FIGURE 20-2.

The drop-down list of macro actions.

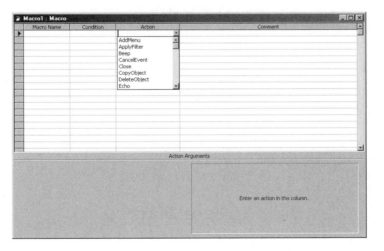

tain many actions. You can enter additional comments in any blank box in the Comment column (that is, any box without an action next to it).

After you select an action such as MsgBox, Access displays argument boxes in the lower part of the window, as shown in Figure 20-3 on the next page, in which you enter the arguments for the action.

VI

Creating an Application

FIGURE 20-3.

Arguments for a MsgBox action that displays a greeting message.

 **TIP**

As you can in the Table and Query windows in Design view, you can use the F6 key to move between the upper and lower parts of the Macro window.

You use the Message argument box to set the message that you want Access to display in the dialog box you're creating. The setting in the Beep argument box tells Access whether to sound a beep when the message is displayed. In the Type argument box, you can set a graphic indicator, such as a red critical icon, that will appear with your message in the dialog box. In the Title argument box, you can type the contents of your dialog box's title bar. Use the settings shown in Figure 20-3 in your macro. (The entire message should read, "Welcome to the Wedding List Database.")

Saving Your Macro

You must save a macro before you can run it. Choose the Save (or Save As/Export) command from the File menu. When you choose Save, Access opens the dialog box shown in Figure 20-4. Enter the name *TestGreeting*, and click OK to save your macro.

FIGURE 20-4.

The Save As dialog box for saving a macro.

Testing Your Macro

You can run some macros (such as the simple one you just created) directly from the Database window or from the Macro window because they don't depend on controls on an open form or report. If your macro does depend on a form or a report, you must link the macro to the appropriate event and run it that way. (You'll learn how to do this later in this chapter.) However you run your macro, Access provides a way to test it by allowing you to single step through the macro actions.

To activate single stepping, switch to the Database window, click the Macros tab, select the macro you want to test, and click the Design button. This opens the macro in the Macro window. Either click the Single Step button on the Macro toolbar or choose the Single Step command from the Run menu. Now when you run your macro, Access opens the Macro Single Step dialog box before executing each step. In this dialog box, you'll see the macro name, the action, and the action arguments.

Try this procedure with the TestGreeting macro you just created. Open the Macro window, click the Single Step button, and then click the Run button. The Macro Single Step dialog box opens, as shown in Figure 20-5.

FIGURE 20-5.

The Macro Single Step dialog box.

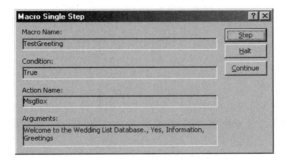

If you click the Step button in the dialog box, the action you see in the dialog box will run and you'll see the modal dialog box with the message you created, as shown in Figure 20-6. Click the OK button in the modal dialog box to dismiss it. If your macro had more than one action defined, you would have returned to the Macro Single Step dialog box, which would have shown you the next action. In this case, your macro has only one action, so Access returns you to the Macro window.

FIGURE 20-6.

The dialog box you created with the TestGreeting macro.

If you encounter an error in any macro during normal execution of your application, Access first displays a dialog box explaining the error it found. You then see an Action Failed dialog box, which is similar to the Macro Single Step dialog box, containing information about the

VI

Creating an Application

action that caused the problem. At this point, you can click only the Halt button. You can then edit your macro to fix the problem.

Before you read on in this chapter, you might want to return to the Macro window and click the Single Step button again so that it's no longer selected. Otherwise you'll continue to single-step through every macro you run until you exit and restart Access or click Continue in one of the Single Step dialog boxes.

Defining Multiple Actions

In Microsoft Access, you can define more than one action within a macro, and you can specify the sequence in which you want the actions performed. The Wedding List database contains several good examples of macros that have more than one action. Open the database (if it is not open already), and close the Wedding List data entry form to return to the Database window. Click the Macros button, and select the macro named Autoexec. Click the Design button to open the Macro window. The macro is shown in Figure 20-7.

FIGURE 20-7.

The Autoexec macro, which defines multiple actions that Access executes when you open the Wedding List database.

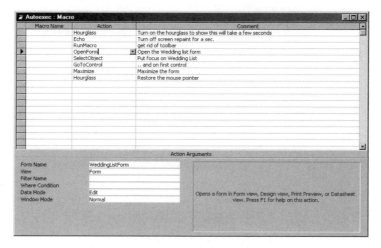

If you create a macro and name it Autoexec, Access runs the macro each time you open the database in which it is stored. You can prevent Access from running this macro if you hold down the Shift key as you open the database. *For details, see Chapter 24, "The Finishing Touches."*

Eight actions are defined in this macro. Access executes each action automatically whenever you open the database. First, the Hourglass action displays an hourglass mouse pointer to give the user a visual clue that the next several steps might take a second or two. It's always a good idea to turn on this visual cue, even if you think the next several actions won't take very long. Next, the Echo command executes (its Echo On argument is set to No) to ask Access not to repaint the screen after any of the succeeding actions. When you plan to execute several actions in a row that can each potentially cause changes to the display, you can turn repainting off to minimize annoying screen flashing. As you'll learn later in Chapter 22, "Visual Basic Fundamentals," a similar command is available in Visual Basic (the Echo method of the Application object).

The next action, RunMacro, runs another macro that hides the standard Form View toolbar. You'll find this technique handy if you use any short series of actions again and again in macros. Create a macro with the repeated commands, and then call that macro from another macro whenever you need to execute those common actions. If you open the Offbars macro that's called from this RunMacro action, you can see that it contains a ShowToolbar action to hide the Form View toolbar.

The next action, OpenForm, opens the WeddingListForm form. As you can see in Figure 20-7, the OpenForm action uses four arguments to define how it should work. The Form Name argument indicates the form you want to open. The View argument tells Access what view you want. (The four choices for the View argument are Form, Design, Print Preview, and Datasheet.) Edit is the default for the Data Mode argument, which allows the user to add, edit, or delete records while using this form. (The choices for this argument are Add, Edit, and Read Only.) The default setting for the Window Mode argument is Normal, which opens the form in the mode set by its design properties. You can override the design property settings to open the form in Hidden mode, as an icon in the Icon mode, or in the special Dialog mode. When you open a form in Dialog mode, Access does not run further actions or Visual Basic statements until you close that form.

Access doesn't always wait for one action to complete before going on to the next one. For example, an OpenForm action merely starts a task to begin opening the form. Particularly if the form displays a lot of data, Access might take several seconds to load all the data and finish displaying the form. Because you're running Microsoft Windows (or perhaps Microsoft Windows NT or Windows 2000), your PC can handle many tasks at once. Access takes advantage of this by going to

VI

Creating an Application

the next task without waiting for the form to completely open. However, because the Autoexec macro is designed to maximize the
WeddingListForm form, the form must be completely open in order for
this to work.

You can force a form to finish opening by telling Access to put the focus
on the form. The Autoexec macro does this by using the SelectObject
action to identify the object to receive the focus (in this case, the
WeddingListForm form), followed by the GoToControl action to put the
focus on a specific control on the form. Once the GoToControl action
puts the focus on the control, the Maximize action sizes the active window (the window containing the object that currently has the focus) to
fit the entire screen. The final action in the Autoexec macro (the Hourglass action again) restores the mouse pointer to let the user know that
the macro is finished.

Learning to define multiple actions within a macro is very useful when
you want to automate the tasks you perform on a day-to-day basis.
Now that you've learned how to do this, the next step is to learn how
to group actions by tasks.

Grouping Macros

You'll find that most of the forms you design for an application require
multiple macros to respond to events—some to edit fields, some to
open reports, and still others to respond to command buttons. You
could design a separate macro saved with its own unique name in the
Database window to respond to each event, but you'll soon have hundreds of macros in your application.

You can create a simpler set of more manageable objects by defining
macro objects that contain several named macros within each object.
(This sort of macro object is called a Macro Group within Microsoft
Access Help.) One approach is to create one saved macro object per
form or report. Another technique is to categorize macros by type of
action—for example, one macro containing all the OpenForm actions
and another containing all the OpenReport actions.

To create a group of named macro procedures within a macro object,
you must open the Macro Names column in the macro design window.
You can create a series of actions at the beginning of the macro definition without a name that you can reference from an event property or
a RunMacro action by using only the name of the macro object. As
you saw earlier in the Autoexec example, naming a macro object in a

RunMacro action (without any qualifier) asks Access to run the un-named actions it finds in that macro object. To create a set of named actions within a macro object, place a name on the first action within the set in the Macro Names column. To execute a named set of actions within a macro object from an event property or a RunMacro action, enter the name of the macro object, a period, and then the name from the Macro Names column.

Figure 20-8 shows the PrintOptions form from the Wedding List data-base in Form view. This form contains two command buttons, each of which triggers a different macro. The two macros are contained within a macro object called DoReport.

FIGURE 20-8.

The Wedding List PrintOptions form.

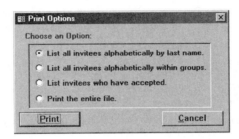

To look at the macro object, switch to the Database window, click the Macros button, and then select DoReport from the list of macro objects in the Database window. Click the Design button to open this macro object in the Macro window. The macro is shown in Figure 20-9.

FIGURE 20-9.

The DoReport macro group.

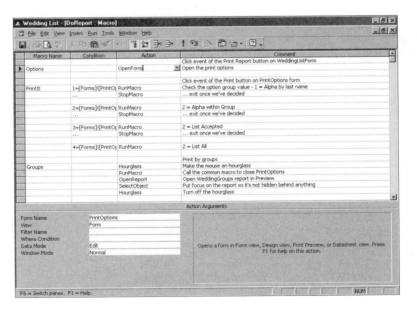

VI

Creating an Application

The DoReport macro object has a Macro Name column. (If you don't see the Macro Name column, click the Macro Names button on the toolbar.) Each of the seven names in this column represents an individual macro within the object. (You have to scroll down to see the other names.) The first macro (triggered by the Print Report button on the WeddingListForm form) opens the PrintOptions form, and the second macro determines which report was selected. The next four macros display the appropriate report in Print Preview mode, based on the result of the second macro. The last macro merely closes the PrintOptions form if the user clicks the Cancel button. As you might have guessed, Access runs a macro starting with the first action of the macro name specified and executes each action in sequence until it encounters a StopMacro action, another macro name, or no further actions. As you'll see a bit later, you can control whether some actions execute by adding tests in the Condition column of the macro.

If you open the PrintOptions form in Design view (see Figure 20-10) and look at the properties for each of the command buttons, you'll see that the On Click property contains the name of the macro that executes when the user clicks the command button. If you open the drop-down list for any event property, you can see that Access lists all macro objects and the named macros within them to make it easy to select the one you want. Remember, the macro name is divided into two parts. The part before the period is the name of the macro object, and the part after the period is the name of a specific macro within the object. So, for the first command button control, the On Click property is set to *DoReport.PrintIt*. When the user clicks this button, Access runs the PrintIt macro in the DoReport macro object. After you specify a macro

FIGURE 20-10.

The On Click property of a command button set to execute a macro.

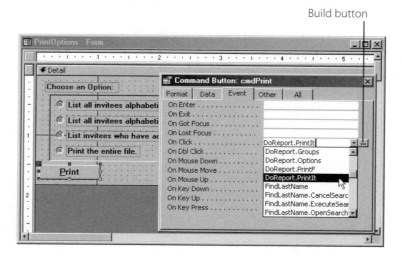

name in an event property, you can click the Build button next to the property and Access opens that macro in a macro design window.

Conditional Expressions

In some macros, you might want to execute some actions only under certain conditions. For example, you might want to update a record, but only if new values in the controls on a form pass validation tests. Or you might want to display or hide certain controls based on the value of other controls.

The PrintIt macro in the DoReport macro group is a good example of a macro that uses conditions to determine which action should proceed. Select DoReport from the list of macros in the Wedding List database, and click the Design button to see the Macro window. Click in the Condition column of the first line of the PrintIt macro, and press Shift+F2 to open the Zoom window, shown in Figure 20-11. If you can't see the Condition column, click the Conditions button on the toolbar.

FIGURE 20-11.

A condition in the DoReport macro group shown in the Zoom edit window.

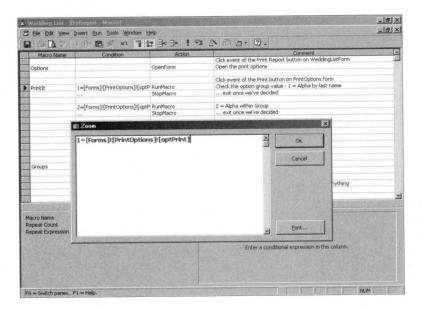

As you saw earlier, this macro is triggered by the On Click property of the Print button on the PrintOptions form. This form allows the user to print a specific report by selecting the appropriate option button and then clicking the Print button. If you look at the form in Design view (see Figure 20-10), you'll see that the option buttons are located within an option group control on the form. Each option button sets a specific numeric value (in this case 1 for the first button, 2 for the second button, 3 for the third button, and 4 for the fourth button) in the option group, which you can test in the Condition column of a macro.

When you include a condition in a macro, Access won't run the action on that line unless the condition evaluates to True. If you want to run a series of actions on the basis of the outcome of a test, you can enter the test in the Condition column on the first action line and enter ellipses (…) in the Condition column for the other actions in the series. This causes Access to evaluate the condition only once and execute additional actions (those with an ellipsis in the Condition column) if the original test evaluated to True.

In this particular example, the condition tests the value of the option group control on the form. You can reference any control on an open form by using the syntax

```
FORMS!formname!controlname
```

where *formname* is the name of an open form and *controlname* is the name of a control on that form. In this case, the direct reference is *[FORMS]![PrintOptions]![optPrint]*. (optPrint is the name of the option group control. You can see this in the Name property on the Other tab of the property sheet for this control.) *For more details about the rules for referencing objects in Access, see Chapter 21, "Automating Your Application with Macros."*

TIP

> If your object names do not contain any embedded blanks or other special characters, you don't need to surround *formname* or *controlname* with brackets when you use this syntax to reference a control on a form; Access inserts the brackets as needed.

Once you understand how to refer to the value of a control on a form, you can see that the PrintIt macro tests for each of the possible values of the option group control. When it finds a match, PrintIt runs the appropriate named macro within the macro object to open the requested report and then stops. If you look at the individual report macros, you'll see that they each run a common macro to close the PrintOptions form (you don't need it after the choice of reports is made) and then open the requested report in Print Preview and put the focus on the window that displays the report.

The rest of this chapter summarizes all the actions you can include in macros and the events that trigger macros. You'll find it useful to browse through these sections to become familiar with the available actions and events before going on to the next chapter, in which you'll see how other parts of the Wedding List database are automated. You'll also find this action and event reference useful as you begin to study how to automate applications with Visual Basic in later chapters.

Summary of Macro Actions

This section summarizes the actions available for you to use in macros. The summaries are organized in the following functional categories.

- Opening and closing Access objects—tables, queries, forms, reports, data access pages, and objects in an Access project file (adp extension)

- Printing data

- Executing a query

- Testing conditions and controlling action flow

- Setting values

- Searching for data

- Building a custom menu and executing menu commands

- Controlling display and focus

- Informing the user of actions

- Renaming, copying, deleting, saving, importing, and exporting objects

- Running another application

Opening and Closing Access Objects

Macro Action	Purpose
Close	Closes either the specified window or the active window for a table, query, form, or report. If the Database window has the focus when you run a Close action with no window specified, Access closes the database. You can also indicate whether to save the object when it's closed.

(continued)

Macro Action	Purpose
OpenDataAccessPage	Opens a data access page in Browse (Page) or Design view.
OpenDiagram	In an Access project file (adp) connected to an SQL Server database, opens a table relationship diagram in the server database in Design view.
OpenForm	Opens a form in Form, Datasheet, or Design view or in Print Preview. You can also apply a filter or a Where condition in Datasheet or Form view or in Print Preview.
OpenModule	Opens a module in Design view and displays the named procedure. To see an event procedure, specify the name of the module in which the procedure is located. This is necessary because event procedures are private and don't appear in the global name space. To open an event procedure of a form or report, the form or report itself must be open.
OpenQuery	Opens a query in Datasheet or Design view or in Print Preview. If you specify an action query, Access performs the updates specified by the query. *(See RunSQL in the "Executing a Query" section, later in this chapter, for information about specifying parameters for an action query.)* You can indicate whether records can be added or modified or whether they should be "read only."
OpenReport	Opens a report in Print Preview (the default), prints the report, or opens the report in Design view. For Print and Print Preview, you can also specify a filter or a Where condition.
OpenStoredProcedure	In an Access project file (adp) connected to an SQL Server database, opens a stored procedure in the server database in Datasheet or Design view or in Print Preview.
OpenTable	Opens a table in Datasheet or Design view or in Print Preview. You can designate whether the data should be "read only" or whether data can be added or modified.
OpenView	In an Access project file (adp) connected to an SQL Server database, opens a view in the server database in Datasheet or Design view or in Print Preview.

Printing Data

Macro Action	Purpose
OpenForm	Optionally opens a form in Print Preview. You can specify a filter or a Where condition.
OpenQuery	Optionally opens a query in Print Preview.
OpenReport	Prints a report or opens a report in Print Preview. You can specify a filter or a Where condition.
OpenStoredProcedure	In an Access project file (adp) connected to an SQL Server database, optionally opens a stored procedure in the server database in Print Preview.
OpenTable	Optionally opens a table in Print Preview.
OpenView	In an Access project file (adp) connected to an SQL Server database, optionally opens a view in the server database in Print Preview.
OutputTo	Outputs the named table, query, form, report, or module to another file format. The formats include HTML (htm), Microsoft Active Server Page (asp), Microsoft Internet Information Server (htx, idc), Microsoft Excel (xls), Rich Text Format (rtf), or text (txt). You can also optionally start the application to edit the file. For forms, the data output is from the form's Datasheet view. For reports, Access outputs all controls containing data (including calculated controls) except ActiveX controls.
PrintOut	Prints the active datasheet, form, module, or report. You can specify a range of pages, the print quality, the number of copies, and collation. Use an "Open" action first if you want to apply a filter or a Where condition.

Executing a Query

Macro Action	Purpose
OpenQuery	Runs a select query and displays the recordset in Datasheet view or in Print Preview. Executes an action query. To specify parameters for an action query, use the RunSQL action.

(continued)

VI

Creating an Application

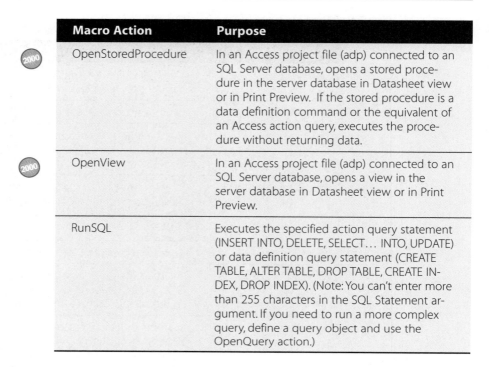

	Macro Action	Purpose
2000	OpenStoredProcedure	In an Access project file (adp) connected to an SQL Server database, opens a stored procedure in the server database in Datasheet view or in Print Preview. If the stored procedure is a data definition command or the equivalent of an Access action query, executes the procedure without returning data.
2000	OpenView	In an Access project file (adp) connected to an SQL Server database, opens a view in the server database in Datasheet view or in Print Preview.
	RunSQL	Executes the specified action query statement (INSERT INTO, DELETE, SELECT... INTO, UPDATE) or data definition query statement (CREATE TABLE, ALTER TABLE, DROP TABLE, CREATE INDEX, DROP INDEX). (Note: You can't enter more than 255 characters in the SQL Statement argument. If you need to run a more complex query, define a query object and use the OpenQuery action.)

Testing Conditions and Controlling Action Flow

Macro Action	Purpose
CancelEvent	Cancels the event that caused this macro to run. You can't use a CancelEvent action in a macro that defines menu commands or in the Close event for a report. CancelEvent can cancel the following events: ApplyFilter, BeforeDelConfirm, BeforeInsert, BeforeUpdate, DblClick, Delete, Exit, Filter, Format, KeyPress, MouseDown, NoData, Open, Print, and Unload.
Quit	Closes all Access windows and exits Access.
RunCode	Executes a Visual Basic function procedure. Other actions following this action execute after the function completes. (Note: To execute a Visual Basic sub procedure, call that procedure from a function procedure.)

Macro Action	Purpose
RunCommand	Executes an Access built-in command. The list of available commands includes all commands you can execute from any of the built-in menus. If you use macros to define a custom menu, you can use a RunCommand action to make selected Access menu commands available on your custom menu.
RunMacro	Executes another macro. Actions following this action execute after the other macro completes.
StopAllMacros	Stops all macros, including any macros that called this macro.
StopMacro	Stops the current macro.

Setting Values

Macro Action	Purpose
Requery	Refreshes the data in a control that is bound to a query (such as a list box, a combo box, a subform, or a control based on an aggregate function such as DSum). When other actions (such as inserting or deleting a row in the underlying query) might affect the contents of a control that is bound to a query, use the Requery action to update the control values. Use Requery without an argument to refresh the data in the active object (form or datasheet).
SendKeys	Stores keystrokes in the keyboard buffer. If you intend to send keystrokes to a modal form or a dialog box, you must execute the SendKeys action before opening the modal form or the dialog box.
SetValue	Changes the value of any control or property that you can update. For example, you can use the SetValue action to calculate a new total in an unbound control or to affect the Visible property of a control (which determines whether you can see that control).

VI

Creating an Application

Searching for Data

Macro Action	Purpose
ApplyFilter	Restricts the information displayed in a table, form, or report by applying a named filter, a query, or an SQL WHERE clause to the records in the table or to the records in the underlying table or query of the form or report.
FindNext	Finds the next record that meets the criteria previously set by a FindRecord macro action or in the Find In Field dialog box.
FindRecord	Finds a record that meets the search criteria. You can specify in the macro action all the parameters available in the Find In Field dialog box.
GoToRecord	Moves to a different record and makes it current in the specified table, query, or form. You can move to the first, last, next, or previous record. When you specify the next or the previous record, you can move by more than one record. You can also go to a specific record number or to the new-record placeholder at the end of the set.

Building a Custom Menu and Executing Menu Commands

Macro Action	Purpose
AddMenu	Adds a drop-down menu to a custom menu bar or to a custom shortcut menu for a form or a report. This is the only action allowed in a macro referenced by a Menu Bar property or Shortcut Menu Bar property. The arguments to AddMenu specify the name of this menu bar and the name of another macro that contains all the named commands for the menu and the actions that correspond to those commands. An AddMenu action can also build submenus by referring to another macro that uses an AddMenu action. (Note: The recommended method for constructing custom menus is to use the Toolbar Customize facility. *For details, see Chapter 24, "The Finishing Touches."*)

Macro Action	Purpose
RunCommand	Executes an Access built-in command. The list of available commands includes all commands you can execute from any of the built-in menus. If you use macros to define a custom menu, you can use a RunCommand action to make selected Access menu commands available on your custom menu.
SetMenuItem	Sets the state of a menu item on a custom menu bar or a custom shortcut menu. Menu items can be enabled or disabled, checked or unchecked.

Controlling Display and Focus

Macro Action	Purpose
Echo	Controls the display of intermediate actions while a macro runs.
GoToControl	Sets the focus to the specified control.
GoToPage	Moves to the specified page in a form.
Hourglass	Changes the mouse pointer to an hourglass icon while a macro runs.
Maximize	Maximizes the active window.
Minimize	Minimizes the active window.
MoveSize	Moves and sizes the active window.
RepaintObject	Forces the repainting of the window for the specified object. Forces recalculation of any formulas in controls on that object.
Requery	Refreshes the data in a control that is bound to a query (such as a list box, a combo box, a subform, or a control based on an aggregate function such as DSum). When other actions (such as inserting or deleting a row in the underlying query) might affect the contents of a control that is bound to a query, use the Requery action to update the control values. Use Requery without an argument to refresh the data in the active object (form or datasheet).

VI

Creating an Application

(continued)

Macro Action	Purpose
Restore	Restores a maximized or minimized window to its previous size.
SelectObject	Selects the specified object. Restores the object's window if it was minimized. If the object is in the process of opening (for example, a form referenced in a previous OpenForm action), SelectObject forces the object to finish opening before performing the next action. Use this action after OpenForm when you need to immediately reference the form, a property of a control on the form, or data in a control on the form.
SetWarnings	When enabled, causes an automatic Enter key response to all system warning or informational messages while a macro runs. For warning messages displayed in a dialog box, pressing the Enter key selects the default button (usually OK or Yes). Does not halt the display of error messages. Use this macro action with the Echo action's Echo On argument set to No to avoid displaying the messages.
ShowAllRecords	Removes any filters previously applied to the active table, query, or form.
ShowToolbar	Shows or hides any of the standard toolbars or any custom toolbars.

Informing the User of Actions

Macro Action	Purpose
Beep	Produces a sound.
MsgBox	Displays a warning or an informational message and optionally produces a sound. You must click OK to dismiss the dialog box and proceed.
SetWarnings	When enabled, causes an automatic Enter key response to all system warning or informational messages while a macro runs. For warning messages displayed in a dialog box, pressing the Enter key selects the default button (usually OK or Yes). Does not halt the display of error messages. Use this macro action with the Echo action's Echo On argument set to No to avoid displaying the messages.

Renaming, Copying, Deleting, Saving, Importing, and Exporting Objects

Macro Action	Purpose
CopyObject	Copies any database object to the current database using a new name, or copies any database object to another Access database using any specified name.
DeleteObject	Deletes any table, query, form, report, macro, or module.
OutputTo	Outputs the named table, query, form, report, or module to a different file format. The formats include HTML (htm), Microsoft Active Server Page (asp), Microsoft Internet Information Server (htx, idc), Excel (xls), Rich Text Format (rtf), or text (txt). You can also optionally start the application to edit the file. For forms, the data output is from the form's Datasheet view. For reports, Access outputs all controls containing data (including calculated controls) except ActiveX controls.
Rename	Renames the specified object in the current database.
Save	Saves any table, query, form, report, macro, or module.
SendObject	Outputs a table datasheet, a query datasheet, a form datasheet, data in text boxes on a report, or a module listing to an HTML (htm), an Excel (xls), a Rich Text Format (rtf), or a text (txt) file and embeds the data in an electronic mail message. You can specify to whom the message is to be sent, the message subject, additional message text, and whether the message can be edited before it is sent. You must have e-mail software installed that conforms to the Messaging Application Programming Interface (MAPI) or Vendor Independent Mail (VIM) standard.
TransferDatabase	Exports data to or imports data from another Access, dBASE, Paradox, Microsoft FoxPro, or SQL database. You can also use this action to attach tables or files from other Access, dBASE, Paradox, FoxPro, or SQL databases, or from text or spreadsheet files.

VI

Creating an Application

(continued)

Macro Action	Purpose
TransferSpreadsheet	Exports data to or imports data from Excel or Lotus 1-2-3 spreadsheet files.
TransferText	Exports data to or imports data from text files.

Running Another Application

Macro Action	Purpose
RunApp	Starts another Windows-based or MS-DOS-based application.

Summary of Form and Report Events

Microsoft Access provides more than 40 event properties on forms and reports that can trigger macros (or Visual Basic procedures). This section summarizes those events and organizes them in the following functional categories.

- Opening and closing forms and reports
- Changing data
- Detecting focus changes
- Detecting filters applied to forms
- Trapping keyboard and mouse events
- Printing
- Activating a custom form, report, or application menu
- Trapping errors
- Detecting timer expiration

The event property names listed on the following pages are the names you will see in the property sheet in form or report Design view. To reference an event property from a macro or a Visual Basic procedure, do not include the blanks in the name. For example, the On Load event property in a form property sheet is the OnLoad property of the form.

Opening and Closing Forms and Reports

Event Property (Event Name)	Description
On Close (Close)	Runs the specified macro or user-defined event procedure when you close a form or a report but before Access clears the screen. You can't use a CancelEvent macro action in the Close event. The Close event occurs after the Unload event.
On Load (Load)	Runs the specified macro or user-defined event procedure when Access loads a form and then displays its records. You can use the event procedure to set values in controls or to set form or control properties. The Load event occurs after the Open event and before the Resize event. You cannot cancel a Load event.
On Open (Open)	Runs the specified macro or user-defined event procedure when you open a form or a report but before Access displays the first record. To gain access to a control on the form or report, the routine must specify a GoToControl action to set the focus on the control. The Open event occurs before Access retrieves the form or report recordset, so you can use the event procedure to prompt the user for parameters and to apply filters.
On Resize (Resize)	Runs the specified macro or user-defined event procedure when a form changes size. This event also occurs when a form opens, after the Load event but before the Activate event. You can use this event to force immediate repainting of the resized form or to recalculate variables that are dependent on the size of the form.
On Unload (Unload)	Runs the specified macro or user-defined event procedure when you close a form but before Access removes the form from the screen. You can cancel an Unload event if you determine that a form should not be closed.

⊗ CAUTION

You must carefully test any routine that can cancel the unloading of a modal form.

Changing Data

Event Property (Event Name)	Description
After Del Confirm (AfterDelConfirm)	Runs the specified macro or user-defined event procedure after a row has been deleted via a

(continued)

Event Property (Event Name)	Description
	form and the user has confirmed the deletion. The AfterDelConfirm event also occurs if the event procedure for the BeforeDelConfirm event cancels the deletion. In a Visual Basic procedure, you can test a status variable to determine whether the deletion was completed, was canceled by the event procedure for the BeforeDelConfirm event, or was canceled by the user. If the deletion was successful, you can use the Requery action within the event procedure for the AfterDelConfirm event to refresh the contents of the form or combo boxes. You can also provide automatic deletion of dependent rows in another table (for example, of all the orders for the customer just deleted) by executing a delete query. You cannot cancel this event.
After Insert (AfterInsert)	Runs the specified macro or user-defined event procedure after a new row has been inserted. You can use this event to requery a recordset after Access has inserted a new row. You cannot cancel this event.
After Update (AfterUpdate)	Runs the specified macro or user-defined event procedure after the data in the specified form or control has been updated. You cannot cancel this event. In the AfterUpdate event of a control, you can, however, use a RunCommand action to choose the Undo command from the Edit menu. This event applies to all forms and to combo boxes, list boxes, option groups, and text boxes as well as to check boxes, option buttons, and toggle buttons that are not part of an option group.
Before Del Confirm (BeforeDelConfirm)	Runs the specified macro or user-defined event procedure after rows have been deleted via a form but before Access displays the standard confirmation dialog box. If you cancel this event, Access replaces the deleted rows and does not display the confirmation dialog box. In a Visual Basic procedure, you can display a custom confirmation dialog box and then set a return parameter to suppress the standard confirmation dialog box.
Before Insert (BeforeInsert)	Runs the specified macro or user-defined event procedure when you type the first character in a new row. This event is useful in providing additional information to a user who is about to add records. If you cancel this event, Access erases any

Event Property (Event Name)	Description
	new data on the form. This event occurs prior to the BeforeUpdate event.
Before Update (BeforeUpdate)	Runs the specified macro or user-defined event procedure before the changed data in the specified form or control has been saved to the database. You can cancel this event to stop the update and place the focus on the updated control or record. This event is most useful for performing complex validations of data on forms or in controls. This event applies to the same controls as the AfterUpdate event.
On Change (Change)	Runs the specified macro or user-defined event procedure whenever you change any portion of the contents of a combo box or a text box control. You cannot cancel this event.
On Delete (Delete)	Runs the specified macro or user-defined function just before one or more rows are deleted. You can use this event to provide a customized warning message. You can also provide automatic deletion of dependent rows in another table (for example, of all the orders for the customer about to be deleted) by executing a delete query. You can cancel this event if you need to stop the rows from being deleted.
On Dirty (Dirty)	Runs the specified macro or user-defined event procedure whenever you first change the contents of a bound control on a bound form (a form that has a record source). This event also occurs if you change the value of a bound control from a macro (SetValue) or a Visual Basic procedure. You can use this event to verify that the current row can be updated. You can cancel this event to prevent the update. After this event occurs, the Dirty property of the form is True until the row is saved.
On Not In List (NotInList)	Runs the specified macro or user-defined event procedure when you type an entry in a combo box that does not exist in the current recordset defined by the Row Source property for the combo box. You cannot cancel this event. You can use this event to allow a user to create a new entry for the combo box (perhaps by adding a row to the table on which the Row Source

(X) CAUTION

You can cause an endless loop if you change the contents of a control within the event procedure for the control's Change event.

2000

VI

Creating an Application

(continued)

Event Property (Event Name)	Description
	property is based). In a Visual Basic procedure, you can examine a parameter passed to the event procedure that contains the unmatched text. You can also set a return value to cause Access to display the standard error message, display no error message (after you've issued a custom message), or requery the list after you've added data to the Row Source property.
On Updated (Updated)	Runs the specified macro or user-defined event procedure after the data in a form's object frame control changes. You cannot cancel this event. In a Visual Basic procedure, you can examine a status parameter to determine how the change occurred.

Detecting Focus Changes

Event Property (Event Name)	Description
On Activate (Activate)	Runs the specified macro or user-defined event procedure in a form or a report when the Form or Report window receives the focus and becomes the active window. You cannot cancel this event. This event is most useful for displaying custom toolbars when a form or a report receives the focus. This event does not occur for pop-up or modal forms. This event also does not occur when a normal Form or Report window regains the focus from a pop-up or modal form unless the focus moves to another form or report.
On Current (Current)	Runs the specified macro or user-defined event procedure in a bound form when the focus moves from one record to another but before Access displays the new record. Access also triggers the Current event when the focus moves to the first record as a form opens. This event is most useful for keeping two open and related forms synchronized. You cannot cancel this event. You can, however, use GoToRecord or other action to move to another record if you decide you do not want to move to the new record.
On Deactivate (Deactivate)	Runs the specified macro or user-defined event procedure when a form or a report loses the focus to a window within the Access application that is not a pop-up or modal window. This event

Event Property (Event Name)	Description
	is useful for closing custom toolbars. You cannot cancel this event.
On Enter (Enter)	Runs the specified macro or user-defined event procedure when the focus moves to a bound object frame, a combo box, a command button, a list box, an option group, or a text box, as well as when the focus moves to a check box, an option button, or a toggle button that is not part of an option group. You cannot cancel this event. This event occurs only when the focus moves from another control on the same form. If you change the focus to a control with the mouse, this event occurs before the GotFocus, MouseDown, MouseUp, and Click events for the control. If you change the focus to a control using the keyboard, this event occurs after the KeyDown event in the control you have left but before the KeyUp and the KeyPress events in the control you have moved to.
On Exit (Exit)	Runs the specified macro or user-defined event procedure when the focus moves from a bound object frame, a combo box, a command button, a list box, an option group, or a text box, as well as when the focus moves from a check box, an option button, or a toggle button that is not part of an option group to another control on the same form. You cannot cancel this event. This event does not occur when the focus moves to another window. If you leave a control using the mouse, this event occurs before the MouseDown and MouseUp events in the new control. If you leave a control using the keyboard, the KeyDown event in this control occurs, and then the Exit, KeyUp, and KeyPress events occur in the new control.
On Got Focus (GotFocus)	Runs the specified macro or user-defined event procedure when an enabled form control receives the focus. If a form receives the focus but has no enabled controls, the GotFocus event occurs for the form. You cannot cancel this event. The GotFocus event occurs after the Enter event. Unlike the Enter event, which occurs only when the focus moves from another control on the same form, the GotFocus event occurs every time a control receives the focus, including from other windows.

(continued)

VI

Creating an Application

Event Property (Event Name)	Description
On Lost Focus (LostFocus)	Runs the specified macro or user-defined event procedure when an enabled form control loses the focus. The LostFocus event for the form occurs whenever a form that has no enabled controls loses the focus. You cannot cancel this event. This event occurs after the Exit event. Unlike the Exit event, which occurs only when the focus moves to another control on the same form, the LostFocus event occurs every time a control loses the focus, including to other windows.

Detecting Filters Applied to Forms

Event Property (Event Name)	Description
On Apply Filter (ApplyFilter)	Runs the specified macro or user-defined event procedure when a user applies a filter on a form from the user interface. (The ApplyFilter action does not trigger this event.) You can examine and modify the form's Filter and Order By properties or cancel the event. Within a Visual Basic procedure, you can examine a parameter that indicates how the filter is being applied.
On Filter (Filter)	Runs the specified macro or user-defined event procedure when the Filter By Form or the Advanced Filter/Sort window is opened. You can use this event to clear any previous Filter or Order By setting, set a default Filter or Order By criterion, or cancel the event and provide your own custom filter form. Within a Visual Basic procedure, you can examine a parameter that indicates whether a user has asked to open the Filter By Form or the Advanced Filter/Sort window.

Trapping Keyboard and Mouse Events

Event Property (Event Name)	Description
On Click (Click)	Runs the specified macro or user-defined event procedure when you click a command button or click an enabled form or control. You cannot cancel this event.

Event Property (Event Name)	Description
On Dbl Click (DblClick)	Runs the specified macro or user-defined event procedure when you double-click a bound object frame, a combo box, a command button, a list box, an option group, or a text box, as well as when you double-click a check box, an option button, or a toggle button that is not part of an option group. The Click event always occurs before DblClick. Access runs the macro before showing the normal result of the double-click. You can cancel the event to prevent the normal response to a double-click a control, such as activating the application for an ActiveX object in a bound control or highlighting a word in a text box.
On Key Down (KeyDown)	Runs the specified macro or user-defined event procedure when you press a key or a combination of keys. You cannot cancel this event. In a Visual Basic procedure, you can examine parameters to determine the key code and whether the Shift, Ctrl, or Alt key was also pressed. You can also set the key code to 0 in Visual Basic to prevent the control from receiving keystrokes. If the form has a command button whose Default property is set to Yes, KeyDown events do not occur when the Enter key is pressed. If the form has a command button whose Cancel property is set to Yes, KeyDown events do not occur when the Esc key is pressed.
On Key Press (KeyPress)	Runs the specified macro or user-defined event procedure when you press a key or a combination of keys. You cannot cancel this event. In a Visual Basic procedure, you can examine the ANSI key value and set the value to 0 to cancel the keystroke.
On Key Up (KeyUp)	Runs the specified macro or user-defined event procedure when you release a key or a combination of keys. You cannot cancel this event. In a Visual Basic procedure, you can examine parameters to determine the key code and whether the Shift, Ctrl, or Alt key was also pressed. If the form has a command button whose Default property is set to Yes, KeyUp events do not occur when the Enter key is released. If the form has a command button whose Cancel property is set

VI

Creating an Application

(continued)

Event Property (Event Name)	Description
	to Yes, KeyUp events do not occur when the Esc key is released.
On Mouse Down (MouseDown)	Runs the specified macro or user-defined event procedure when you press any mouse button. You cannot cancel this event. In a Visual Basic procedure, you can determine which mouse button was pressed (left, right, or middle); whether the Shift, Ctrl, or Alt key was also pressed; and the X and Y coordinates of the mouse pointer (in twips) when the button was pressed. (Note: A *twip* is $1/20$ point or $1/1440$ inch.)
On Mouse Move (MouseMove)	Runs the specified macro or user-defined event procedure when you move the mouse over a form or a control. You cannot cancel this event. In a Visual Basic procedure, you can determine whether a mouse button was pressed (left, right, or middle) and whether the Shift, Ctrl, or Alt key was also pressed. You can also determine the X and Y coordinates of the mouse pointer (in twips) when the button was released.
On Mouse Up (MouseUp)	Runs the specified macro or user-defined event procedure when you release any mouse button. You cannot cancel this event. In a Visual Basic procedure, you can determine which mouse button was released (left, right, or middle); whether the Shift, Ctrl, or Alt key was also pressed; and the X and Y coordinates of the mouse pointer (in twips) when the button was released.

Printing

Event Property (Event Name)	Description
On Format (Format)	Runs the specified macro or user-defined event procedure just before Access formats a report section to print. This event is useful for hiding or displaying controls in the report section based on data values. If Access is formatting a group header, you have access to the data in the first row of the detail section. Similarly, if Access is formatting a group footer, you have access to the data in the last row of the detail section. You can test the value of the Format Count property to determine whether the Format event has

Event Property (Event Name)	Description
	occurred more than once for a section (due to page overflow). You can use the CancelEvent action to keep a section from appearing on the report.
On No Data (NoData)	Runs the specified macro or user-defined event procedure after Access formats a report that has no data for printing and just before the reports prints. You can use this event to keep a blank report from printing.
On Page (Page)	Runs the specified macro or user-defined event procedure after Access formats a page for printing and just before the page prints. In Visual Basic, you can use this event to draw custom borders around a page or add other graphics to enhance the look of the report.
On Print (Print)	Runs the specified macro or user-defined event procedure just before Access prints a formatted section of a report. If you use the CancelEvent action in a macro triggered by a Print event, Access leaves a blank space on the report where the section would have printed.
On Retreat (Retreat)	Runs the specified macro or user-defined event procedure when Access has to retreat past already formatted sections when it discovers that it cannot fit a "keep together" section on a page. You cannot cancel this event.

Activating a Custom Form, Report, or Application Menu

Form Property	Description
Menu Bar	Defines the macro that creates the custom menu or the custom toolbar that defines the custom menu for a form or a report. (Note: The recommended method for constructing custom menus is to use the Toolbar Customize facility. *For details, see Chapter 24, "The Finishing Touches."*) If you use macros to define a menu bar, the macro triggered by the Menu Bar property must contain only named AddMenu actions. Each AddMenu action refers to another macro that defines the individual commands for that menu. You can define

VI

Creating an Application

(continued)

Form Property	Description
	submenus by including additional AddMenu actions in macros referenced by an AddMenu action. From a Visual Basic procedure, you can set the Application.MenuBar property to define a custom menu bar for the application.
Shortcut Menu Bar	Defines the macro that creates the custom shortcut menu or the custom toolbar that defines the custom shortcut menu for a form or a report. (Note: The recommended method for constructing custom shortcut menus is to use the Toolbar Customize facility. *For details, see Chapter 24, "The Finishing Touches."*)

Trapping Errors

Event Property (Event Name)	Description
On Error (Error)	Runs the specified macro or user-defined event procedure whenever a run-time error occurs while the form or report is active. This event does not trap errors in Visual Basic code; use the On Error statement in the Visual Basic procedure instead. You cannot cancel this event. If you use a Visual Basic procedure to trap this event, you can examine the error code to determine an appropriate action.

Detecting Timer Expiration

Event Property (Event Name)	Description
On Timer (Timer)	Runs the specified macro or user-defined event procedure when the timer interval defined for the form elapses. The form's Timer Interval property defines how frequently this event occurs in milliseconds. If the Timer Interval property is set to 0, no Timer events occur. You cannot cancel this event. However, you can set the Timer Interval property for the form to 0 to stop further Timer events from occurring.

You should now have a basic understanding of macros and how you might use them. In the next chapter, you'll see macros in action.

CHAPTER 21

Automating Your Application with Macros

Throughout this book, you've learned how to perform common tasks using menu commands and toolbar buttons. In working with your database, you've probably also noticed that you perform certain tasks repeatedly or on a regular basis. You can automate these tasks by creating macros to execute the actions you perform and then associating the macros with various form or control events, such as the Current event of a form, the Click event of a command button, or the DblClick event of a text box.

In this chapter, you'll use examples from the Wedding List sample database (Wedding.mdb) to understand how macros can help automate your application.

Referencing Form and Report Objects

As you create macros to automate tasks that you repeat frequently, you'll often need to refer to a report, a form, or a control on a form to set its properties or values. The syntax for referencing reports, forms, controls, and properties is described in the following sections.

Rules for Referencing Forms and Reports

You can refer to a form or a report by name, but you must first tell Microsoft Access which *collection* contains the named object. Open forms are in the Forms collection, and open reports are in the Reports collection. To reference a form or a report, you follow the collection name with an exclamation point to separate it from the name of the object to which you are referring. You *must* enclose an object name that contains blank spaces or special characters in brackets ([ ]). If the object name contains no blanks or special characters, you can simply enter the name. However, it's a good idea to always enclose an object name in brackets so that your name reference syntax is consistent.

For example, you refer to a form named WeddingList as:

```
Forms![WeddingList]
```

You refer to a report named WeddingList, as:

```
Reports![WeddingList]
```

Rules for Referencing Form and Report Properties

To reference a property of a form or a report, follow the form or report name with a period and the property name. You can see a list of most property names for a form or a report by opening the form or the report in Design view and displaying the property sheet while you have the form or the report selected. With macros, you can change most form or report properties while the form is in Form view or from the Print and Format events of a report as Access prints or displays it.

You refer to the Scroll Bars property of a form named CityInformation as:

```
Forms![CityInformation].ScrollBars
```

You refer to the Menu Bar property of a report named CityInformation as:

```
Reports![CityInformation].MenuBar
```

> **NOTE**
>
> The names of properties do not contain embedded blank spaces, even though the property sheet shows blanks within names. For example, BackColor is the name of the property listed as Back Color in the property sheet.

Rules for Referencing Form and Report Controls and Their Properties

To reference a control on a form or a report, follow the form or report name with an exclamation point and then the control name enclosed in brackets. To reference a property of a control, follow the control name with a period and the name of the property. You can see a list of most property names for controls by opening a form or a report in Design view, selecting a control (note that different control types have different properties), and opening its property sheet. You can change most control properties while the form is in Design view.

You refer to a control named State on the WeddingListForm form as:

```
Forms![WeddingListForm]![State]
```

You refer to the Visible property of a control named Accepted on a report named WeddingListForm as:

```
Reports![WeddingListForm]![Accepted].Visible
```

Rules for Referencing Subforms and Subreports

When you embed a subform in a form or a report, the subform is contained in a *subform control*. A subreport embedded in a report is contained in a *subreport control*. You can reference a subform control or a subreport control exactly as you would any other control on a form or a report. For example, suppose you have a subform called RelativesSub embedded in the WeddingListForm form. You refer to the subform control on the WeddingListForm form as:

```
Forms![WeddingListForm]![RelativesSub]
```

Likewise, you can reference properties of a subform or a subreport by following the control name with a period and the name of the property. You refer to the Visible property of the RelativesSub subform control as:

```
Forms![WeddingListForm]![RelativesSub].Visible
```

Subform controls have a special Form property that lets you reference the form that's contained in the subform control. Likewise, subreport controls have a special Report property that lets you reference the report contained in the subreport control. You can follow this special property name with the name of a control on the subform or the subreport to access the control's contents or properties. For example, you refer to the LastName control on the RelativesSub subform as:

```
Forms![WeddingListForm]![RelativesSub].Form![LastName]
```

You refer to the FontWeight property of the LastName control as:

```
Forms![WeddingListForm]![RelativesSub].Form![LastName].FontWeight
```

Opening a Secondary Form

As you learned in Chapter 12, "Form Basics," it's easier to work with data by using a form. You also learned in Chapter 15, "Advanced Form Design," that you can create multiple-table forms by embedding subforms in a main form, thus allowing you to see related data in the same form. However, it's impractical to use subforms in situations such as the following.

- You need three or more subforms to see related data

- The main form is too small to display the entire subform

- You need to see the related information only some of the time

The solution is to use a separate form to see the related data. You can open this form by creating a macro that responds to one of several events. For example, you can use a command button or the DblClick event of a control on the main form to give your users access to the related data in the secondary form. This technique helps reduce screen clutter, makes the main form easier to use, and helps to speed up the main form when moving from record to record.

You could make use of this technique in the WeddingListForm form. It would be simple to create a macro that would respond to clicking the City Info button by opening the CityInformation form and displaying all records from the CityNames table, including the best airline to take and the approximate flying time from each city to Seattle. However, if you're talking to Aunt Sara in Boston, it would be even more convenient for the CityInformation form to display only Boston-related data, rather than the data for all cities. In the following section, you'll create a macro that opens the CityInformation form based on the city that's displayed for the current record in the WeddingListForm form.

Creating the SeeCityInformation Macro

Open the Wedding List sample database (Wedding.mdb). Close the Wedding List data entry form to return to the Database window. In the Database window, click the Macros button, and then click the New button. When the Macro window opens, maximize it so that it fills the entire screen. Next click the Macro Names button and the Conditions button on the toolbar to display the Macro Name and Condition columns in the Design window. Although you won't use these columns for this macro, it's a good idea to get in the habit of displaying them because you will use them often when creating new macros.

You can display the Macro Name and Condition columns by default by choosing Options from the Tools menu, clicking the View tab in the Options dialog box, and selecting both options in the Show In Macro Design section. The next time you create a macro, the columns will be displayed automatically.

The macro you are going to create is shown in Figure 21-1. (If you simply want to view the macro, it is saved as *XmplSeeCityInformation* in the sample database.)

FIGURE 21-1.

The Macro window showing the SeeCityInformation macro.

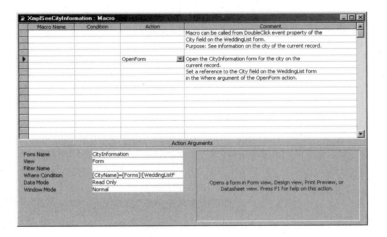

The macro contains only one action, OpenForm. The OpenForm action not only opens the CityInformation form but also applies a filter so that the city that will be displayed matches the city currently displayed in the WeddingListForm form. Click in the Action column, and then choose OpenForm from the drop-down list of actions. In the Action Arguments section of the Macro window, enter the following Where Condition argument.

```
[CityName]=Forms![WeddingListForm]![City]
```

The Where Condition argument causes the OpenForm action to open the CityInformation form showing only the rows in the form's record source whose CityName field equals the value currently shown in the City combo box on the open WeddingListForm form. (A bit later, you'll learn how to create a macro to synchronize these two forms as you move to different rows in the WeddingListForm form.)

Set the rest of the action arguments for the OpenForm action as shown in Figure 21-1 on the previous page. After you finish creating the action for the macro, it's a good idea to use the Comment column to document your macro. Documenting your macro makes it easier to debug, modify, or enhance the macro in the future. It's also easier to read, in English, what each macro action does rather than have to view the arguments for each action line by line. Refer to Figure 21-1, and enter the information displayed in the Comments column. You can see that I've added comments about the macro in general and about the specific action the macro is designed to perform. Choose Save from the File menu, and save the macro as *SeeCityInformation*.

Next you can associate the macro with the City combo box control on the WeddingListForm form. Click the Forms button in the Database window, select WeddingListForm, and open the form in Design view. Click the City combo box control, and then click the Properties button on the toolbar. When the property sheet opens, click the Event tab. You'll want to trigger the SeeCityInformation macro from the DblClick event, so click in the On Dbl Click property box and select the macro from the On Dbl Click event property's drop-down list. You'll find a macro called SeeCityInfo already entered here, as shown in Figure 21-2. I created a slightly different form of the macro and saved it in the form so that the application is fully functional when you first open it. You can change the event property to your macro to test what you've built.

FIGURE 21-2.

The property sheet of the City combo box control.

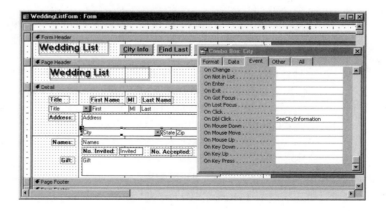

You can also associate the macro with the City Info button by changing the button's On Click event property to point to the macro. Save and close the WeddingListForm form. When you return to the Database window, open the form in Form view, and then maximize it. Scroll down two or three rows, and double-click the City combo box. The CityInformation form opens, and the data displayed should be for the city in the current record in the WeddingListForm form. Your screen should look like the one shown in Figure 21-3.

FIGURE 21-3.

The CityInformation and WeddingListForm forms.

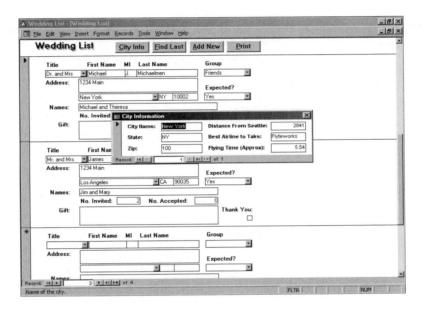

Linking two related forms in this manner is very useful, but what happens to the data displayed in the CityInformation form when you move to a new record in the WeddingListForm form? Try scrolling through the records using the record selector. You'll find that the data in the CityInformation form changes as you move through records in the WeddingListForm form. The data changes because I've set one of the events on WeddingListForm to execute a macro that keeps the data displayed on the two forms synchronized. In the next section, you'll walk through the steps to re-create this macro yourself.

Synchronizing Two Related Forms

In the previous section, you learned how to open a secondary form from a main form based on matching values of two related fields in the two forms. In this section, you'll create a macro that synchronizes the data in the two forms.

Creating the SyncWeddingAndCity Macro

In the Database window, click the Macros button, and then click the New button. When the Macro window opens, maximize it so that it fills the entire screen. The actions and comments you'll create for this macro are shown in Figure 21-4.

FIGURE 21-4.

Actions and comments for the *SyncWeddingAndCity* macro.

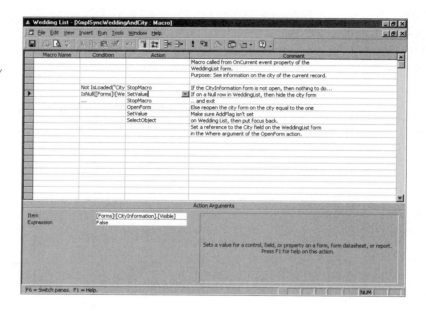

You'll create this macro in the same basic manner that you created the SeeCityInformation macro. Select the actions from the Action column, and type the associated comments in the Comment column. The settings for the actions are shown in Table 21-1. (The SetValue action is explained later in this chapter in the section "Passing Status Information Between Linked Forms.")

Some code and expression examples in this chapter are too long to fit on a single printed line. A line that ends with the ➥ symbol means that the code shown on the following line should be entered on the same line.

This macro has a couple of conditions that determine what parts of the macro execute. The first condition, in plain English, states, "If the CityInformation form is not currently loaded, execute the first action."

TABLE 21-1.   Actions and Settings in SyncWeddingAndCity Macro

Condition	Action	Argument	Setting
Not IsLoaded⬎ ("CityInformation")	StopMacro		
IsNull([Forms]!⬎ [WeddingListForm]!⬎ [City])	SetValue	Item	[Forms]!⬎ [CityInformation].⬎ [Visible]
		Expression	False
...	StopMacro		
	OpenForm	Form Name	CityInformation
		View	Form
		Where Condition	[CityName]=[Forms]!⬎ [WeddingListForm]![City]
		Data Mode	Read Only
		Window Mode	Normal
	SetValue	Item	[Forms]!⬎ [CityInformation]!⬎ [AddFlag]
		Expression	False
	SelectObject	Object Type	Form
		Object Name	WeddingListForm
		In Database Window	No

This condition uses the IsLoaded function, which is included in the modUtility module of the Wedding List database. This function checks to see whether a form (whose name you've provided to the function) is currently open. (The form can be hidden.) The syntax for the function is IsLoaded(*"formname"*), where *formname* is the name of the form in question. You must enclose the name of the form in double quotation marks in order for the function to work. The *Not* before the function expression tells Access to evaluate the converse of the True/False value returned from the function. So this condition will be true only if the form is *not* loaded. If the companion form isn't open, there's nothing to do, so the macro action on this line—StopMacro—executes and the macro ends.

To display the appropriate city information, you could use an ApplyFilter action to refilter the open CityInformation form, but ApplyFilter works only for the form that currently has the focus. A SelectObject action would solve that problem, but why use two macro actions when one would suffice? As it turns out, you can execute

OpenForm again with the same Where condition you used earlier in the SeeCityInformation macro to display the matching row you want. If the form is already open, OpenForm puts the focus on that form (and displays it if it's hidden) and applies any Where condition that you've specified. However, it's a bad idea to reference an "empty" value in a Where condition. In fact, in some cases you'll get an error message. When you move beyond the last row in the WeddingListForm form or choose Go To from the Edit menu and then choose New Record from the submenu, you'll be in a new blank row in which the City field has no value. In this case, OpenForm will show you a blank row in the CityInformation form. It probably makes more sense to test for an "empty," or Null, value and hide the companion form if you're in a new row in the WeddingListForm form. The second line in this macro uses the IsNull built-in function to check for this condition. If City is Null, the macro hides the CityInformation form by setting its Visible property to False. On the third line, the ellipsis (...) in the Condition column tells Access to run this action only if the previous condition is true. This lets you enter the condition only once—and Access tests the condition only once. In this case if the City is Null, Access runs not only the SetValue action on line 2 but also the StopMacro action on line 3—which ends macro execution at this point. Note that the form is *still* open even though you can't see it. If you move back to a row that contains data, the Current event causes this macro to run again and makes the form visible when the OpenForm action runs.

Finally, the OpenForm action in this macro is just like the one you saw earlier in the SeeCityInformation macro. In fact, you could just as well use a RunMacro action here to run that macro again to open the form (or to put the focus on it if it's already open) and apply the filter specified in the Where Condition argument. The SetValue action will be explained later in this chapter in the section "Passing Status Information Between Linked Forms." The SelectObject command ensures that the form has the focus after setting the value of the AddFlag control.

Once you have the synchronization macro you need, save it as SyncWeddingAndCity. The last step is to associate the macro with the Current event of the WeddingListForm form. To do that, click the Forms button in the Database window, and open the WeddingListForm form in Design view. Once you're in Design view, click the Properties toolbar button to open the property sheet for the form, and then click in the On Current property box. Use the drop-down list to select the SyncWeddingAndCity macro. Your screen should look like the one shown in Figure 21-5.

FIGURE 21-5.

Associating the SyncWeddingAndCity macro with the On Current event property of the WeddingListForm form.

When you finish, save and close the form. Open the form in Form view, and double-click the City combo box control. Your screen should look like the one shown earlier in Figure 21-3, assuming that Dr. and Mrs. Michaelmen's record is the current one.

Test the macro by moving through the records in the WeddingListForm form. As you move from record to record, the data in the CityInformation form should change to reflect the city displayed in the current record of the WeddingListForm form. If you move to the blank record at the end of the recordset, the CityInformation form disappears. Move back to a row containing data, and it reappears!

Using a macro to synchronize two forms containing related data is a technique that works well with almost any set of forms, and it can be used in a number of situations. In the next section, you'll learn how to create a more complex macro set of named macros within a macro object, also sometimes referred to as a *macro group*. You can create multiple named macros within a macro object. When you group macros by task, you'll see that this is a good way to organize your work and to keep from cluttering your database with dozens of macro objects.

Validating Data and Presetting Values

Two tasks that you'll commonly automate in your applications are validating data that a user enters in a field and automatically setting values for specific fields. In this section, you'll explore several macro objects saved in the sample database and learn how they perform these tasks on both the WeddingListForm form and the CityInformation form.

VI

Creating an Application

Validating Data

A problem you'll often encounter when you create database applications is ensuring that the data the users enter is valid. Three types of invalid data are unknown entries, misspelled entries, and multiple versions of the same entry.

- **Unknown entries.** A good example of this error is an entry such as *AX* in a state field. No state name is abbreviated as *AX*, but a user who tries to enter *AZ* might accidentally hit the X key instead of the Z key.

- **Misspelled entries.** This sort of error is quite common among users with poor typing or spelling skills and among very fast typists. In this case, you might see entries such as *Settle*, *Seatle*, or *Saettle* for *Seattle*.

- **Multiple versions.** These errors are common in poorly designed databases and in databases that are shared by a number of users. You might see entries such as *ABC Company, Inc.*; *ABC Company, Incorporated*; *ABC Co., Inc.*; or *A B C Company Inc.*

You can use macros to validate data and help reduce errors. In the next section, you'll learn about the macro for the WeddingListForm form that validates the city that the user enters in the City field. If the city doesn't exist in the CityNames table, the macro then executes the following steps.

1 It displays a message indicating that the city is currently unlisted and asks whether the user wants to enter a new city name.

2 If the user wants to create a new city record, another macro runs that opens the CityInformation form in data-entry mode and copies the city name the user just typed.

3 If the user successfully saves a new row, a macro associated with the AfterInsert event of the CityInformation form sets a flag on the WeddingListForm form.

4 Back in the WeddingListForm form, the city name gets revalidated, and, if the city entry is a new one, a macro triggered by the AfterUpdate property of the City field sets the combo box to the new name. When the city name is validated, this macro also automatically enters the state name and the first three digits of the ZIP Code.

Understanding the ValidateCitySetStateAndZip Macro Group

In the Database window, click the Macros button, select the ValidateCitySetStateAndZip macro object, and then click the Design button. Be sure the Macro Name and Condition columns are displayed. The first macro and its associated actions are shown in Figure 21-6.

FIGURE 21-6.

The Macro window for the first two macros in the ValidateCitySet-StateAndZip macro group.

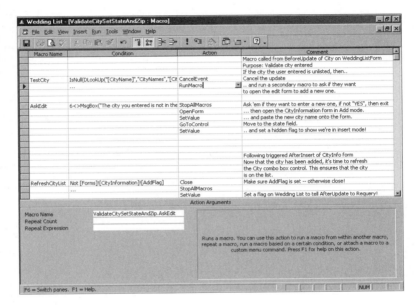

The first three lines of the macro are comments, and *TestCity* is the name of the first macro in the object. You can see the actions for this macro listed in Table 21-2.

TABLE 21-2.   Actions and Settings in the TestCity Macro

Action	Argument	Setting
CancelEvent		
RunMacro	Macro Name	ValidateCitySetStateAndZip.AskEdit

To understand how this macro works, let's take a look at the condition that validates the city name. What we want to do is look up the name just entered in the CityName field to find out if it exists in the CityNames table. If it doesn't exist, the first line of the macro executes a CancelEvent action. The second line then calls another macro that we'll examine a bit later.

To see this condition easily, click the first line of the macro in the Condition column. Press Shift+F2 to open the expression in the Zoom box, as shown in Figure 21-7.

FIGURE 21-7.

The conditional expression used in the TestCity macro.

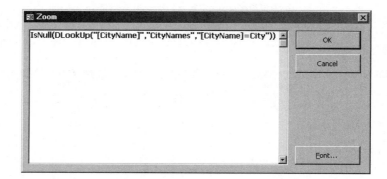

```
IsNull(DLookUp("[CityName]","CityNames","[CityName]=City"))
```

This condition uses two built-in functions: *DLookup* and *IsNull*. The DLookup function looks up the city name in the CityNames table. The IsNull function checks the return value of the DLookup function. If the DLookup function doesn't find the city name, it returns a Null value. This causes the IsNull function to return a True value because the return value of the DLookup function is indeed Null. If no row in the CityNames table matches the current city name in the WeddingListForm form, Access then executes the action associated with this condition because the condition evaluates to True. In this case, the CancelEvent macro action tells Access not to store the new value in the City field. By including an ellipsis (…) in the Condition column of the second action, you tell Access to run the second action only if the previous condition is true. (When you use an ellipsis, you enter the condition only once and Access performs the evaluation only once.) So if the city doesn't exist in the CityNames table, the RunMacro macro action on the second line calls the AskEdit macro, which we'll look at in a moment.

On the other hand, if the DLookup function does find the city name, it returns the city name to the IsNull function. The IsNull function then returns a value of False because the return value of the DLookup function is not Null. Access disregards the action associated with this condition. Because you included an ellipsis on the second condition line, the False evaluation applies there also, so the macro ends without taking any further action.

What's the point of all of this? If you open the WeddingListForm form in Design view, click the CityName text box, and look at its event properties, you'll find this macro "wired" into the Before Update property. If you remember from the previous chapter, you can use the BeforeUpdate event of a form or control to take a look at what's about to be saved. If the data is not valid, you can cancel the event to tell Access not to save the change. This is exactly what the first line of this macro is doing.

When you don't cancel a BeforeUpdate event on a control, Access accepts the changes and gives you a chance to look at the result in the AfterUpdate event. As you'll see a bit later, this application uses AfterUpdate on this control to fill in the correct state and part of the ZIP Code.

So what happens if the user enters a city name that's not yet in the database? The AskEdit macro runs, and the first thing it does is evaluate another condition. As you'll learn in later chapters, this sort of IF…THEN…IF logic testing is much easier to do with procedures written in Visual Basic. With macros, you have to do the first test in one macro, and if that returns a True value, you have to call another nested macro to perform a further test.

The condition on the first line of the AskEdit macro is as follows.

```
6<>MsgBox("The city you entered is not in the →
    database. Do you want to enter a new one?",36)
```

You've seen the MsgBox action before. This condition uses a built-in function called *MsgBox* that's a lot more powerful. The MsgBox function lets you not only display a message but also specify what icon you want displayed, and it provides several options for buttons to display in the message box. You set these options by adding number selections and providing the result as the second argument to MsgBox. In this case, 36 is the sum of 32, which asks for a question icon, and 4, which requests Yes and No buttons. (Intuitive, isn't it?) You can find all the option settings by searching for *MsgBox Function* in Access Help. For your convenience, I've listed all the option settings for the MsgBox function in Table 21-3 on the next page. In addition, the function returns an integer value depending on the button the user clicks in the message box. If you look at the MsgBox Function help topic, you'll find out that when the user clicks Yes, MsgBox returns the value 6. Table 21-4 on the next page shows you the MsgBox return value settings. So if the user *doesn't* click Yes, the first line of this macro—a StopAllMacros action—executes and the macro ends. If the user does click Yes, the rest of the macro executes. All the actions and arguments for this macro are listed in Table 21-5 on the next page.

TABLE 21-3. Option Settings for the MsgBox Function

Value	Meaning
Button settings (choose one)	
0	OK button only
1	OK and Cancel buttons
2	Abort, Retry, and Ignore buttons
3	Yes, No, and Cancel buttons
4	Yes and No buttons
5	Retry and Cancel buttons
Icon settings (choose one)	
0	No icon
16	Critical (red X) icon
32	Warning query (question mark) icon
48	Warning message (exclamation point) icon
64	Information message (letter *i*) icon
Default button settings (choose one)	
0	First button is the default
256	Second button is the default
512	Third button is the default

TABLE 21-4. Return Values for the MsgBox Function

Value	Meaning
1	OK button clicked
2	Cancel button clicked
3	Abort button clicked
4	Retry button clicked
5	Ignore button clicked
6	Yes button clicked
7	No button clicked

TABLE 21-5. Actions and Settings in the AskEdit Macro

Action	Argument	Setting
StopAllMacros		
OpenForm	Form Name View Data Mode Window Mode	CityInformation Form Add Normal
SetValue	Item Value	[Forms]![CityInformation]![CityName] [Forms]![WeddingListForm]![City]
GoToControl	Control Name	State
SetValue	Item Value	[Forms]![CityInformation]![AddFlag] True

This macro contains several actions that Access executes if the user enters the data for a new city name. First Access opens the CityInformation form and copies the city name from the WeddingListForm form to the CityName field of the CityInformation form. It does this for user convenience and to ensure that the user starts with the name just entered. After the macro copies the city name to the CityName field, it tells Access to move the focus to the State field. Finally, the macro sets the value of a hidden text box (called AddFlag) on the CityInformation form to indicate that the user is in data-entry mode. The macro attached to the AfterInsert event checks this flag to determine whether it should notify the AfterUpdate event of the City control on the WeddingListForm form to refresh its list.

Passing Status Information Between Linked Forms

As you just saw, the AskEdit macro sets a special hidden control on the CityInformation form to tell the form's AfterInsert event macro that the WeddingListForm form needs to know whether a new row has been added successfully. Likewise, when a new row is added to the CityInformation form, the macro that runs in response to an AfterInsert event (the event that Access uses to let you know when a new row has been added via a form) needs to check the flag and pass an indicator back to the WeddingListForm form. You'll learn in later chapters that you can do this sort of "status indicator" passing much more easily using variables in Visual Basic procedures than you can by hiding controls on open forms.

VI

Creating an Application

Figure 21-8 shows the macro that responds to the AfterInsert event of the CityInformation form. You may recall from the previous chapter that Access triggers this event right after it has saved a new row. The row could be saved by your choosing Save Record from the Records menu, moving to a new row, or closing the form. The first line has a condition that tests to be sure that the user asked to add a new row. The condition is as follows.

```
Not [Forms]![CityInformation]![AddFlag]
```

FIGURE 21-8.

The RefreshCityList macro.

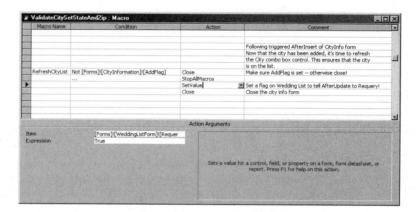

If the flag is not set, the first action closes the form, and the StopAllMacros action causes the macro to end. If the flag is set, the SetValue action sets the flag on the WeddingListForm form (to let it know that it must refresh the list in the City combo box at its earliest opportunity) and then closes the CityInformation form. Remember that the AfterInsert event could be triggered as a result of clicking the form's Close button after entering new data. Normally, you would expect an error if you try to execute a Close command while the form is already in the process of closing (you will get an error in Visual Basic). Because Access assumes that macros are most often used by beginning programmers, it is kind enough not to generate any error from either of the Close actions in this macro if this is the case.

If the user triggers the AfterInsert event by moving to another row, closing the form makes sense after adding the one row you need. If the user closes the form without entering any new data, the AfterInsert event won't happen. The user will be back in the WeddingListForm form with the unmatched city data still typed in the City combo box. As a final touch, the SetValue action in the SyncWeddingAndCity macro that you created in Figure 21-4 (page 730) clears the AddFlag control when you move to a new row on WeddingListForm. When you have just moved to a new row, you clearly aren't worried about adding a new row to the CityNames table. Also, there's a SelectObject action in that macro to make sure the focus is back on the WeddingListForm form after updating the flag.

Presetting Values

Validating data is just one of the many ways you can ensure data integrity in a database. Presetting values for certain fields is another way. Although you can set the Default property of a field, sometimes you'll need to set the value of a field based on the value of another field in a form. For example, you'll want to set the values of the State field and the Zip field in the WeddingListForm form based on the value of the City field. You can accomplish this with a macro.

In this section, you'll examine actions in the ValidateCitySetStateAndZip macro group that set the values of the State and Zip fields in the WeddingListForm form based on the city entered. If you scroll down the Macro window, you can see the additional actions, as shown in Figure 21-9.

FIGURE 21-9.
Data entry actions in the SetStateAndZip macro of the ValidateCitySetStateAndZip macro group.

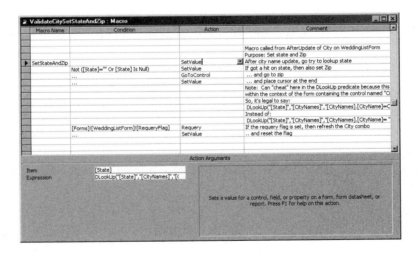

Table 21-6 on the next page lists the actions and arguments in this macro.

TABLE 21-6. Actions and Settings in the SetStateAndZip Macro

Action	Argument	Setting
SetValue	Item	[State]
	Expression	DLookup("[State]","[CityNames]",→ "[CityNames].[CityName]=City")
SetValue	Item	[Zip]
	Expression	DLookup("[Zip]","[CityNames]",→ "[CityNames].[CityName]=City")
GoToControl	Control Name	Zip
SetValue	Item	[Forms]![WeddingListForm]!→ [Zip].SelStart
	Expression	255
Requery	Control Name	City
SetValue	Item	[Forms]![WeddingListForm]!→ [RequeryFlag]
	Expression	False

When the user enters a valid city name, the first SetValue action uses the DLookup function to retrieve the matching State value from the CityNames table. If the value for State isn't blank or Null, the second SetValue action retrieves the first three digits of the ZIP Code from the table, moves the focus to the Zip control with a GoToControl action, and sets the SelStart property of the Zip control to a high value (255) to place the cursor at the end of the data displayed in the control. Pressing the F2 key after you move to a control also places the cursor at the end of the data in the control, so you could use a SendKeys action here instead. However, setting the SelStart property is faster and more reliable. *See Access Help for more information on the SelStart property*. The user can now enter the last two digits of the ZIP Code on the main form before moving on to the Expected field. The Condition column for the second action is as follows.

```
Not ([State]="" Or [State] Is Null)
```

The set of macros in this macro object is now complete. You can see how these macros help to implement data integrity by validating data and presetting specific values. This decreases the likelihood that users will make errors. Now you'll see how these macros are associated with the appropriate events on the WeddingListForm form and the CityInformation form.

Click the Forms button in the Database window, and open the WeddingListForm form in Design view. Click the City combo box control, and then click the Properties toolbar button. After the property sheet opens, click the Event tab. You should see the ValidateCitySetStateAndZip.TestCity macro associated with the BeforeUpdate event of the City combo box. Remember, this is the macro you should run to verify whether the user has entered a valid city name. The After Update event property should be set to ValidateCitySetStateAndZip.SetStateAndZip. This macro automatically sets the matching State and Zip values whenever the user specifies a new City value. Figure 21-10 shows the result.

FIGURE 21-10.

Setting the event properties for the City control on the WeddingListForm form.

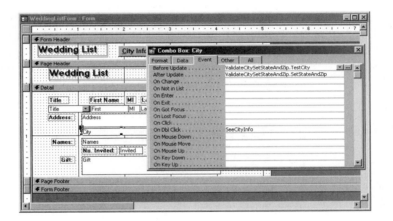

Close the WeddingListForm form. Open the CityInformation form in Design view and click the Properties toolbar button to open the property sheet. The ValidateCitySetStateAndZip.RefreshCityList macro is set in the form's After Insert event property, as shown in Figure 21-11 on the next page. Recall from the previous chapter that you could also use the form's AfterUpdate event to see changed data. However, in this case you don't care about existing rows that change. The AfterInsert event is more appropriate because Access fires this event only when a *new* row is saved, but not when an existing row is saved.

Close the CityInformation form. Now that you've verified that the macros are associated with the appropriate objects and events, you're ready to test how this works. Begin by clicking the Macros button in the Database window and running the Autoexec macro. Move to a new record in the WeddingListForm form, and enter a title, a name,

FIGURE 21-11.

Associating the ValidateCitySetState-AndZip.RefreshCityList macro with the After Insert event property of the CityInformation form.

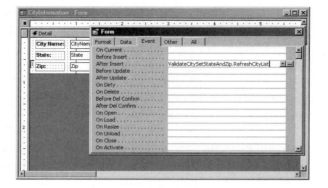

an address, and a group. When the cursor moves to the City combo box, enter *Miami* (a city in the state of Florida). After you press Enter or Tab, Access runs the ValidateCitySetStateAndZip.TestCity macro. Because this city doesn't currently exist in the CityNames table, the AskEdit macro runs, and Access displays the message box shown in Figure 21-12.

FIGURE 21-12.

The message box displayed by the AskEdit macro.

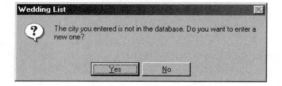

After the user clicks the Yes button, Access executes the remaining actions in the macro. Access opens the CityInformation form in data entry mode, copies the city name to the City field of the form, and moves the cursor to the State field. The result of these actions is shown in Figure 21-13.

FIGURE 21-13.

The result of the remaining actions in the AskEdit macro.

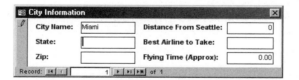

After the user enters information in the remaining fields and closes the CityInformation form, the AfterInsert event of the form triggers the ValidateCitySetStateAndZip.RefreshCityList macro. After the form closes, Access moves the focus back to the WeddingListForm form. When the user finally leaves the now valid City control, the macro triggered by

AfterUpdate requeries the City combo box control and automatically updates the State and Zip fields.

Converting Your Macros to Visual Basic

As you'll learn in the rest of this book, Visual Basic is what you should use to automate any serious applications. If you've spent some time getting familiar with programming in Access in macros but would now like to move to Visual Basic, you're in luck! Access provides a handy tool to convert the "code" in macros called from events on your form to the equivalent Visual Basic statements.

To see how this works, open the WeddingListForm form in Design view. Choose Macro from the Tools menu, and then click Convert Form's Macros To Visual Basic on the submenu, as shown in Figure 21-14.

FIGURE 21-14.

Converting a form's macros to Visual Basic.

In the following dialog box, the Convert Wizard offers you the option to insert error-handling code and to copy the comments from your macros into the new code. You should leave both options checked, and then click Convert to change your macros to Visual Basic. After the wizard is finished, you should see all macro references in event properties changed to [Event Procedure]. Click the On Current event property for the WeddingListForm form, and then click the Build button (...) to the right of the property. You'll see the converted code displayed as shown in Figure 21-15.

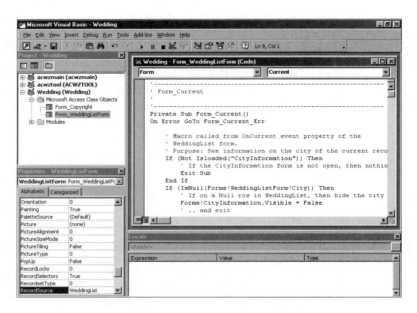

> **NOTE**
>
> Converting your macros to Visual Basic does not delete any of your original macros. Also, the wizard doesn't convert any macros referenced by a RunMacro command—you'll have to do that yourself.

In Chapter 23, I'll introduce you to some enhancements I made to the Wedding List sample database after I converted all the macros to Visual Basic using this wizard. You can find this version of the database saved as WeddingVB.mdb on the companion CD.

In this chapter, you've learned how to validate data and set the values of fields in a form. You've also learned a little more about data integrity in the process. In the next two chapters, you'll learn about the power of Visual Basic.

Visual Basic Fundamentals

Whether you've realized it or not, you've already been using Microsoft Visual Basic procedures. For example, the IsLoaded function you used with macros in the previous chapter is a custom Visual Basic procedure. In this chapter and in the following two, you'll learn more about Visual Basic and how to use it to automate your applications.

Using Visual Basic Instead of Macros

As you saw in previous chapters, you can make lots of magic happen with macros. In fact, as you explore the Northwind Traders, Address Book, Contact Management, and Inventory databases that come with Microsoft Access or the Wedding List database included with this book, you'll discover many additional ways that you can use macros to automate tasks in your database.

However, macros have certain limitations. For example, as you might have noticed when examining the list of available events in Chapter 20, "Adding Power with Macros," many events require or return parameters that can be passed to or read from a Visual Basic procedure but not a macro. Also, even though you can write a macro to handle general errors in forms and reports, you can't really analyze errors effectively within a macro or do much to recover from an error.

When to Use Macros

Use macros in your application in any of the following circumstances.

■ You don't need to trap errors.

■ You don't need to evaluate or set parameters passed by certain events, such as AfterDelConfirm, ApplyFilter, BeforeDelConfirm, Error, Filter, KeyDown, KeyPress, KeyUp, MouseDown, MouseMove, MouseUp, NotInList, and Updated.

■ Your application consists of only a few forms and reports.

■ Your application might be used by nonprogrammers who will want to understand how your application is constructed and possibly modify or enhance it.

■ You're developing an application prototype, and you want to rapidly automate a few features to demonstrate your design.

There are actually a few things that can be done only with macros.

■ Defining alternative actions for certain keystrokes.

■ Creating a startup routine that runs when your database opens. Most of the time, you'll run a startup routine by attaching it to a startup form; however, in some circumstances you might find it useful to create an Autoexec macro startup routine.

You'll learn about most of these specialized tasks for macros in Chapter 24, "The Finishing Touches."

When to Use Visual Basic

Although macros are extremely powerful, a number of tasks cannot be carried out with macros or are better implemented using a Visual Basic procedure. Use a Visual Basic procedure instead of a macro in any of the following circumstances.

■ You need discrete error handling in your application.

■ You want to define a new function.

■ You need to handle events that pass parameters or accept return values (other than Cancel).

- You need to create new objects (tables, queries, forms, or reports) in your database from application code.

- Your application needs to interact with another Windows-based program via ActiveX automation or Dynamic Data Exchange (DDE).

- You want to be able to directly call Windows API functions.

- You want to place part of your application code in a library.

- You want to be able to manipulate data in a recordset on a record-by-record basis.

- You need to use some of the native facilities of the relational database management system that handles your attached tables (such as SQL Server procedures or data definition facilities).

- You want maximum performance in your application. Because modules are compiled, they execute slightly faster than macros. You'll probably notice a difference only on slower processors.

The Visual Basic Development Environment

In Microsoft Access for Windows 95 (version 7.0), Visual Basic replaced the Access Basic programming language included with versions 1 and 2 of Microsoft Access. The two languages are very similar, however; both Visual Basic and Access Basic evolved from a common early design component. In recent years, Visual Basic has become the common programming language for Microsoft Office applications, including Access, Microsoft Excel, Microsoft Word, and Microsoft PowerPoint.

Having a common programming component across applications provides several advantages. You have to learn only one programming language, and you can easily integrate objects across applications by using Visual Basic with ActiveX object automation. Visual Basic provides color-coded syntax, an Object Browser, and other features. It also provides excellent tools for testing and confirming the proper execution of the code you write. Access 2000 uses the Visual Basic Editor common to all Office applications and the Visual Basic programming product.

Modules

You save all Visual Basic code in your database in modules. Access provides two ways to create a module: as a module object or as part of a form or report object.

Module Objects

You can view the module objects in your database by clicking the Modules button in the Database window. Figure 22-1 shows the modules in the Microsoft Press Books sample database. You should use module objects to define procedures that can be used from queries or from several forms or reports in your application. A public procedure defined in a module can be called from anywhere in your application.

FIGURE 22-1.

The module objects in the Microsoft Press Books database.

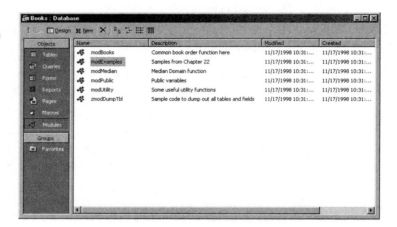

To create a new module, click the New button above the modules list. It's a good idea to name modules based on their purpose. For example, a module that contains procedures to perform custom calculations for queries might be named modQueryFunctions, and a module containing procedures to work directly with Windows functions might be named modWindowsAPIFunctions.

Advanced developers may want to create a special type of module object called a *class module.* A class module defines a custom object in your application, and the Visual Basic procedures you create in a class module define the properties and methods that your object supports. You'll learn more about objects, methods, properties, and class modules later in this chapter.

Form and Report Modules

To make it easy to create Visual Basic procedures that respond to events on forms or reports, Access provides a class module associated with each form or report. Within a form or report class module, you can create specially named event procedures to respond to events, private procedures that you can call only from within the scope of the class module, or public procedures that you can call as methods of the class. *See "Collections, Objects, Properties, and Methods" later in this chapter for more information about objects and methods.* You can edit the module for a form or a report by opening the form or report in Design view and then clicking the Code button on the toolbar or choosing Code from the View menu.

Using form and report modules offers three main advantages over module objects.

- All the code you need to automate a form or a report resides with that form or report. You don't have to remember the name of a separate form-related or report-related module object.

- Access loads module objects into memory when you first reference any procedure or variable in the module and leaves it loaded as long as the database is open. Access loads the code for a form or a report only when the form or the report is open. Therefore, form and report modules consume memory only when you're using the form or the report to which they are attached.

- If you export a form or report, all the code in the form or report module is exported with it.

However, form and report modules have one disadvantage: because the code must be loaded each time you open the form or report, a form or report with a large supporting module will open noticeably more slowly than one that has little or no code. In addition, saving a form or report design can take significantly longer if you have also opened the associated module and changed any of the code. If you have a lot of Visual Basic code in your application, saving, renaming, or deleting a form or report that has a module can take several seconds.

One enhancement that first appeared in Access 97 (version 8.0)—the addition of the HasModule property—makes this slowness even more apparent. Access automatically sets this property to True if you try to view the code for a form or report, even if you don't define any event procedures. If HasModule is False, Access doesn't bother to look for an associated Visual Basic module, so the form or report loads very quickly.

The Visual Basic Editor Window

When you open a module in Design view, Access opens the Visual Basic Editor and asks the Editor to display your code. Open the Microsoft Press Books sample database, click the Modules button in the Database window, select the modExamples module, and then click the Design

VI

Creating an Application

button to see the code for the modExamples module opened in the Visual Basic Editor, as shown in Figure 22-2.

FIGURE 22-2.

The modExamples module in the Visual Basic Editor.

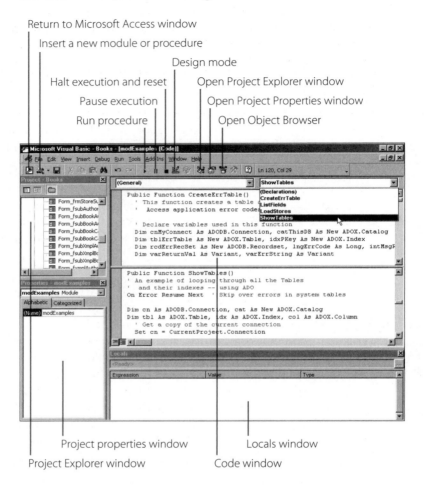

Return to Microsoft Access window

Insert a new module or procedure

Design mode

Halt execution and reset

Open Project Explorer window

Pause execution

Open Project Properties window

Run procedure

Open Object Browser

Project properties window

Locals window

Project Explorer window

Code window

What you see on your screen may differ from Figure 22-2, particularly if you have opened the Visual Basic Editor previously and moved some windows around. In the upper left corner of the figure, you can see the Visual Basic Project Explorer window docked in the workspace. In this window, you can discover all module objects and form and report class modules saved in the database. You can double-click any module to open it in the Code window, which you can see docked in the upper right corner.

Docked in the lower left corner is the Project Properties window. When you have a form or report that has a Visual Basic module open in Design view in Access, you can click that object in the Project

Explorer to see all the properties. If you modify the property in the Properties window, you're changing it in Access. To open a form or report that is not open, you can select it in the Project Explorer, and then choose Object from the View menu.

In the lower right corner you can see the Locals window docked. As you will see a bit later, this window allows you to instantly see the values of any active variables or objects when you pause execution in a procedure.

You can undock any window by grabbing its title bar and dragging it away from its docked position on the edge toward the center of the screen. You can also undock a window by right-clicking anywhere in the window and clearing the Dockable property. As you will see a bit later, you can set the Dockable property of any window by choosing Options from the Tools menu. When a window is set Dockable but not docked along an edge, it becomes a pop-up window that floats on top of other windows—similar to the way an Access form works when its Popup property is set to Yes, as you learned in Chapter 14, "Customizing Forms."

You cannot set the Code window dockable. The Code window always appears in the part of the workspace that is not occupied by docked windows. You can maximize the Code window to fill this remaining space, as shown in Figure 22-2. When you make any other window not Dockable, it shares the space occupied by the Code window.

At the top of the Code window, just below the title bar, you can see two drop-down list boxes.

- **Object list box.** When you're editing a form or report class module, open this list to select the form or the report, a section on the form or the report, or any control on the form or the report that can generate an event. The Procedure list box then shows the available event procedures for the selected object. Select General to view the Declarations section of the module, where you can set options or declare variables shared by multiple procedures. In a Form or Report class module, General is also where you'll see any procedures you have coded that do not respond to events. When you're editing a module object, this list displays only the General option.

- **Procedure list box.** Open this list to select a procedure in the module and display that procedure in the Module window. When you're editing a form or report module, this list shows the available event procedures for the selected object and displays in bold type the event procedures that you have coded and attached to the form or the report. When you're editing a module object, the list displays in alphabetic order all the procedures you coded in the module.

In Figure 22-2, I dragged the divider bar at the top of the scroll bar on the right of the Code window downward to open two edit windows. I clicked in the lower window and chose ShowTables from the Procedure list box. You may find this split window very handy when you're tracing calls from one procedure to another. The Procedure list box always shows you the name of the procedure in which you have currently placed the cursor. In the Code window, you can use the arrow keys to move horizontally and vertically. When you enter a new line of code and press Enter, Visual Basic optionally verifies the syntax of the line and warns you of any problems it finds.

If you want to create a new procedure in a module, you can type in either a *Function* statement or a *Sub* statement on any line above or below an existing procedure and then press Enter, choose Procedure from the drop-down list of the Insert button on the toolbar, or choose Procedure from the Insert menu. Visual Basic creates a new procedure for you (it does not embed the new procedure in the procedure you were editing) and inserts an *End Function* or *End Sub* statement. If you're working in a form or report module, you can select an object in the Object list box and then open the Procedure list box to see all the available events for that object. An event name displayed in bold type means you have created a procedure to handle that event. Select an event whose name isn't displayed in bold type to create a procedure to handle that event.

Visual Basic provides many options that you can set to customize how you work with modules. Choose Options from the Tools menu, and then select the Editor tab to see the settings for these options, as shown in Figure 22-3.

On the Editor tab, some important options to consider are Auto Syntax Check, to check the syntax of lines of code as you enter them; and Require Variable Declaration, which forces you to declare all your variables (you'll see why that's important a bit later). The Auto List Members option displays information about parameters required to complete complex function calls as you type. Auto Quick Info provides drop-down lists where appropriate built-in constants are available to complete parameters in function or subroutine calls. When you're debugging code, Auto Data Tips lets you discover the current value of a variable by hovering your mouse pointer over any usage of the variable in your code.

FIGURE 22-3.

Settings for Visual Basic modules on the Editor tab in the Options dialog box.

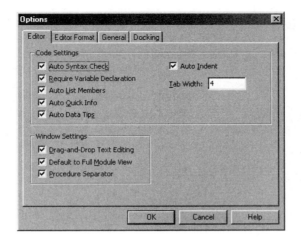

Drag-and-Drop Text Editing allows you to highlight code and drag it to a new location. Full Module View shows all your code for multiple procedures in a module in a single scrollable view. If you clear the Default To Full Module View option, you will see only one procedure at a time and must page up or down or select a different procedure in the Procedure list box to move to a different part of the module. When you're in Full Module View, choosing Procedure Separator asks Visual Basic to draw a line between procedures to make it easy to see where one procedure ends and another begins.

Turning on Auto Indent asks Visual Basic to leave you at the same indent as the previous line of code when you press the Enter key to insert a new line. I wrote all of the sample code you'll see in this book and in the sample databases with indents to make it easy to see related lines of code within a loop or an If...Then...Else construct. You can set the Tab Width to any value from 1 through 32. This setting tells Visual Basic how many spaces you want to indent when you press the Tab key while writing code.

On the Editor Format tab of the Options dialog box, you can set custom colors for various types of code elements and also choose a display font. I recommend using a monospaced font such as Courier New for all code editing.

On the General tab, shown in Figure 22-4 on the next page, you can set some important options that dictate how Visual Basic acts as you enter new code and as you debug your code. You can ignore all the settings under Form Grid Settings because they apply to forms designed in Visual Basic, not Microsoft Access.

VI

Creating an Application

FIGURE 22-4.

Settings for Visual Basic modules on the General tab in the Options dialog box.

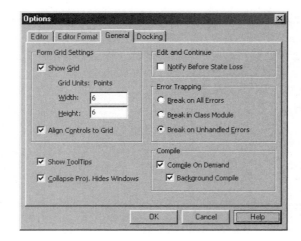

If your code has halted, in many cases you can enter new code or correct problems in code before continuing to test. Some changes you make, however, will force Visual Basic to reset rather than let you continue to run from the halted point. If you check the Notify Before State Loss option, Visual Basic will warn you before allowing you to make code changes that would cause it to reset.

In the Error Trapping section, you can tell Visual Basic how to deal with errors. As you'll discover later in this chapter, you can write statements in your code to attempt to catch errors. If you think you have a problem in your error-trapping code, you can ask Visual Basic to Break On All Errors. If you have written class modules that can be called from other modules, and an untrapped error occurs within a class module, Visual Basic normally halts on the line of code that caused the class module to be invoked. If you want to see the actual error within the class module, you should select Break In Class Module.

The last two important options on this tab are Compile On Demand and Background Compile. With Compile On Demand set, Visual Basic will compile any previously uncompiled new code whenever you run that code directly or run a procedure that calls that code. Background Compile lets Visual Basic use spare machine cycles to silently compile new code as you are working in other areas.

Finally, on the Docking tab you can specify whether the Immediate window, Locals window, Watch window, Project Explorer, properties window, or Object Browser can be docked. We will take a look at the Immediate window and Watch window in the next section. You can use the Object Browser to discover all the supported properties and methods of any object or function defined in Microsoft Access, Visual Basic, or your database application.

Working with Visual Basic Debugging Tools

You may have noticed that the debugging tools for macros are pretty primitive. You can't do much more than run macros in single-step mode to try to find the source of an error. The debugging tools for Visual Basic are significantly more extensive. The following sections describe many of the tools available in Visual Basic. You may want to scan these sections first and then return after you understand Visual Basic in more detail.

Setting Breakpoints

If you still have the modExamples module open, scroll down until you can see all of the ShowTables function, as shown in Figure 22-5. This sample function examines all the table definitions in the current database and displays both the table name and the names of any indexes defined for the table by printing to a special object called *Debug*.

One of the most common ways to test particularly complex code is to open the module you want to examine, set a stopping point in the code (called a breakpoint), and then run the code. As you'll soon see, when Visual Basic stops at a breakpoint, you can examine all sorts of information to help you clean up potential problems. While a

FIGURE 22-5.

Setting a breakpoint in a Visual Basic module.

procedure is stopped, you can look at the values in variables—including all object variables you might have defined. In addition, you can also change the value of variables, single-step through the code, reset the code, or restart at a different statement.

To set a breakpoint, click anywhere on the line of code at which you want Visual Basic execution to halt and either click the Toggle Breakpoint button on the Debug toolbar (open this toolbar by right-clicking any toolbar and choosing Debug on the shortcut menu) or choose Toggle Breakpoint from the Debug menu. You can also press F9 to set or clear a breakpoint. When a breakpoint is active, Access highlights the line of code (in red by default) where the breakpoint is established. After you set a breakpoint, the breakpoint stays active until you close the current database, specifically reset the breakpoint, or choose Clear All Breakpoints from the Debug menu (or press Ctrl+Shift+F9). In the example shown in Figure 22-5 on the previous page, I set a breakpoint to halt the procedure at the bottom of the loop that examines each table. When we run procedure a bit later, you'll see that Visual Basic will halt on this statement just before it executes the statement.

Using the Immediate Window

"Action central" for all troubleshooting in Visual Basic is a special edit window called the Immediate window. You can open the Immediate window while editing a module by clicking the Immediate Window button on the Debug toolbar or choosing Immediate Window from the View menu. Even when you do not have a Visual Basic module open, you can open the Immediate window from anywhere in Access by pressing Ctrl+G.

Executing Visual Basic Commands in the Immediate Window

In the Immediate window, you can type in any valid Visual Basic command and press Enter to have it executed immediately. You can also execute a procedure by typing in the procedure name followed by any parameter values required by the procedure. You can ask Visual Basic to evaluate any expression by typing a question mark character (sometimes called the "what is" character) followed by the expression. Access displays the result of the evaluation on the line below. You might want to experiment by typing *?(5 * 4) / 10.* You should see the answer "2" on the line below.

Because you can type in any valid Visual Basic statement, you can enter an assignment statement to set a variable that you might have forgotten to initialize correctly in your code. For example, there's a global variable (you'll learn more about variables later in this chapter) called gstrWhereBook that the Microsoft Press Books sample application uses to save the latest filter string for the frmBooks form. If you have been running the Microsoft Press Books application and have done any searching in the frmBooks form, you can find out the current value of the string by typing

```
?gstrWhereBook
```

You can set the value of this string by typing

```
gstrWhereBook = "[SuggPrice] < 20"
```

You can verify the value of the variable you just set by typing

```
?gstrWhereBook
```

To have a sense of the power of what you're doing, go to the Database window in Access by clicking the View Microsoft Access button on the left end of the toolbar in the Visual Basic Editor window. Open the frmBooks form in Form view. (Opening this form resets the variable gstrWhereBook.) Then go back to the Visual Basic Editor window, either by using the Windows Alt+Tab feature or by clicking the Visual Basic button on your Windows taskbar. In the Visual Basic Immediate window, set the value of gstrWhereBook again as above. Next, assign the value of the string to the form's Filter property by entering in the Immediate window

```
Forms!frmBooks.Filter = gstrWhereBook
```

If you like, you can ask what the filter property is to see if it is set correctly. Note that nothing has happened yet to the form. Next, turn on the form's FilterOn property by entering

```
Forms!frmBooks.FilterOn = True
```

You should now see the form filtered down to 18 rows—all the books that have a cover price less than $20. If you want to have some more fun, enter

```
Forms!frmBooks.Section(0).Backcolor = 255
```

The background of Section(0), the detail area of the form, should now appear red! Note that none of these changes affect the design of the form. You can close the form, and the next time you open it, it will be back to normal.

Using Breakpoints

You saw earlier how to set a breakpoint within a module procedure. Since the ShowTables procedure is a function that may return a value, you have to ask Visual Basic to evaluate the function in order to run it. The function doesn't require any parameters, so you don't need to supply any. To run the function, type *?ShowTables()* in the Immediate window, as shown in Figure 22-6, and press Enter.

 NOTE

> You can also ask Visual Basic to run any procedure by clicking in the procedure and clicking the Run button on either the Standard or Debug toolbar.

FIGURE 22-6.

Running a module function from the Immediate window.

Visual Basic runs the function you requested. Because you set a breakpoint, the code stops on the statement with the breakpoint, as shown in Figure 22-7.

Note that I chose Locals Window from the View menu to reveal the Locals window you can see across the bottom of Figure 22-7. In the Locals window, Visual Basic shows you all the active variables. You can, for example, click the plus sign next to the word *cat* (a variable set to the currently opened database catalog) to browse through all the property settings for the database and all the objects within the database. *See the section titled "Collections, Objects, Properties, and Methods" later in this chapter for details about all the objects you see in the "tree" under the database catalog.*

The Immediate window displays the output of three Debug.Print statements within the function you're running, as also shown in Figure 22-7.

FIGURE 22-7.
Executing Visual Basic code that stops at a breakpoint.

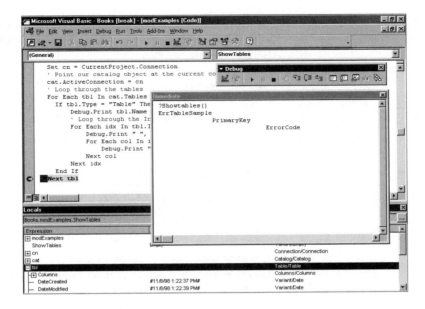

The first line shows the name of the first table the function found in the database. The second (indented) line shows the name of the index for that table.

If you want to see the results of executing the next loop in the code (examining the next table object in the Catalog), click the Run/Continue button on the Debug toolbar. If you want to run the code a single statement at a time, choose Step Into or Step Over from the Debug menu or click the Step Into or Step Over button on the Debug toolbar. Step Into and Step Over work the same unless you're about to execute a statement that calls another procedure. If the next statement calls another procedure, Step Into literally steps into the called procedure so that you can step through the code in the called procedure one line at a time. Step Over calls the procedure without halting and stops on the next statement in the current procedure.

 NOTE

> The Tables collection in the Catalog includes both tables and queries. Because the ShowTables procedure skips over queries, you will need to loop through the code several times until the procedure finds the next object that defines a table.

Working with the Watch Window

Sometimes setting a breakpoint isn't enough to catch an error. You might have a variable that you know is being changed somewhere in your code (perhaps incorrectly). By using the Watch window, you can

VI

Creating an Application

examine a variable as your code runs, ask Visual Basic to halt when the variable changes, or ask Visual Basic to halt when an expression that uses the variable becomes true.

An interesting variable in the Microsoft Press Books sample database is gintIsAdmin (defined in the modPublic module). When this variable is set to True, any form that opens lets you modify any of its data. If the variable is set to False, you'll have read-only access to most forms. To test this, make sure the application has not started (if it has, click Exit on the main switchboard form) and then open the frmBooks form from the Database window. You should not be able to change any of the data on the form. Next set *gintIsAdmin = True* from the Immediate window, and close and reopen frmBooks again. You should now be able to change data on the form.

Suppose you wanted to track down exactly when this powerful variable gets set or reset in the application code. To set a watch for when the value changes, open the Watch window by choosing it in the View menu, right-click in the Watch window, and choose Add Watch from the shortcut menu. If you have a module open, you can also choose Add Watch from the Debug menu. You should see the Add Watch dialog box open, as shown in Figure 22-8.

FIGURE 22-8.

Setting a watch for when a variable's value changes.

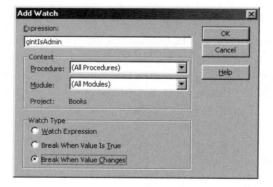

In the Expression text box, enter the name of the variable you want the code to watch. You don't know where the variable is set, so set the Procedure and Module selections to (All Procedures) and (All Modules) respectively. Select the option to Break When Value Changes, and click OK to set the watch. Now start the application by opening the frmCopyright form from the Database window. If you set gintIsAdmin to True, the code execution should halt in the module for the frmSignOn form as shown in Figure 22-9. (I closed the Project

Explorer, Properties window, and Immediate window so I could see the code window without these windows in the way.)

FIGURE 22-9.

Visual Basic code halted immediately after a watch variable has changed.

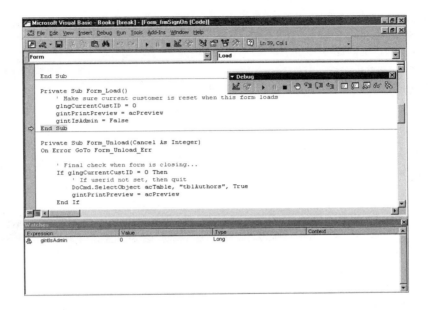

Note that the code halts on the statement immediately after the one that reset the "watched" variable. If you didn't set the variable to True before you started the application, Visual Basic won't halt because the value won't be changing. Proceed to the next section to see where it halts when you exit the application.

Examining the Procedure Call Sequence (Call Stack)

After stopping code that you're trying to debug, it's useful sometimes to find out what started the current sequence of code execution and what procedures have been called by Visual Basic. For this example, you can continue with the watch on the variable gintIsAdmin. Click the Run/Continue button to let the code continue executing. In the Microsoft Press Sign On dialog box, choose my name and enter *password* as the password. Press Enter or click the Sign On button. The procedure halts again, as shown in Figure 22-10 on the next page.

It appears that this code is setting the gintIsAdmin variable to some value from the fourth column (the columns are numbered from zero) in the query for the cmbUserID combo box on the sign on form. If you open frmSignOn in Design view (you can't do this while the procedure is still halted) and examine the row source for the cmbUserID combo box, you'll find that the Admin field in tblCustomers is being returned in the fourth column. Click the Run/Continue button again to let the code finish execution.

FIGURE 22-10.

The gintIsAdmin vari-
able is set to the value
of a form control.

You should now be at the main switchboard form (frmMain) in the application. Click the Exit button to close the application and return to the Database window. The code should halt again in the Close event of the frmMain form. Click the Call Stack button on the toolbar or choose Call Stack from the View menu to see the call sequence shown in Figure 22-11.

The Call Stack dialog box shows the procedures that have executed, with the last procedure at the top of the list, and the first procedure at the bottom. You can see that the code started executing in the Close_Click procedure of the frmMain form. This happens to be the Visual Basic event procedure that runs when you click the Exit button. If you click that line and then click the Show button, you should see the Close_Click procedure with the cursor on the line that executes the form Close command. This line calls the Access built-in Close command (the <Non-Basic Code> you see in the call stack list), which in turn triggered the Close event procedure for the form. It's the Close event that sets the gintIsAdmin variable back to False.

> **NOTE**

Be sure to delete the watch after you are finished seeing how it works by right-clicking it in the Watch window and choosing Delete from the shortcut menu.

FIGURE 22-11.

The call sequence is shown in the Call Stack dialog box.

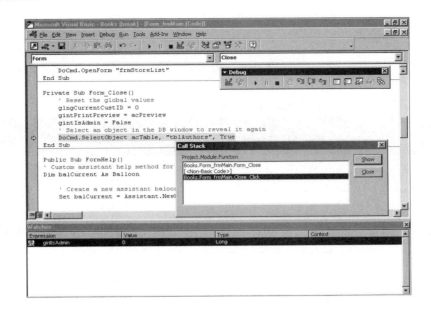

Variables and Constants

In addition to using Visual Basic code to work with the controls on any open forms or reports (as you can with macros), you can declare and use named variables in Visual Basic code for storing values temporarily, calculating a result, or manipulating any of the objects in your database. So instead of defining "hidden" controls on forms to hold data that you want to pass from one procedure to another, you can define a global variable, as you can see in the modPublic module in the Microsoft Press Books sample database.

Another way to store data in Visual Basic is with a constant. A *constant* is a data object with a fixed value that you cannot change while your application is running. You've already encountered some of the "built-in" constants in Microsoft Access—Null, True, and False. Visual Basic also has a large number of "intrinsic" constants that you can use to test for data types and other attributes or that you can use as fixed arguments in functions and expressions. You can view the list of intrinsic constants by searching for the Visual Basic Constants topic in Help. You can also declare your own constant values to use in code that you write.

In the following sections, you'll learn about using variables to store and calculate data and to work with database objects.

VI

Creating an Application

Data Types

Visual Basic supports data types that are similar to the data types you use to define fields in tables. The data types are described in Table 22-1.

TABLE 22-1.   Visual Basic Data Types

Data Type	Size	Data-Typing Character	Can Contain
Byte	1 byte	(none)	Binary data ranging in value from 0 through 255
Integer	2 bytes	%	Integers from −32,768 through 32,767
Long	4 bytes	&	Integers from −2,147,483,648 through 2,147,483,647
Single	4 bytes	!	Floating-point numbers from approximately -3.4×10^{38} through 3.4×10^{38}
Double	8 bytes	#	Floating-point numbers from approximately -1.79×10^{308} through 1.79×10^{308}
Currency	8 bytes	@	A scaled integer with four decimal places from −922,337,203,685,477.5808 through 922,337,203,685,477.5807
String	10 bytes plus 2 bytes per character	$	Any text or binary string up to approximately 2 billion bytes in length, including text, hyperlinks, memo data, and "chunks" from an ActiveX object; a fixed-length string can be up to 65,400 characters long
Boolean	2 bytes	(none)	True or False
Date	8 bytes	(none)	Date/time values ranging from January 1, 100, to December 31, 9999
Object	4 bytes	(none)	Any object reference
Variant	16 bytes through approximately 2 billion bytes	(none)	Any data, including Empty, Null, and date time data (use the VarType function to determine the current data type of the data in the variable)
User-defined	Depends on elements defined	(none)	Any number of variables of any of the above data types

You can implicitly define the data type of a variable by appending a data-typing character, as noted in the table above, the first time you use the variable. For example, a variable named *MyInt%* is an integer variable. If you do not explicitly declare a data variable that you reference in your code and do not supply a data-typing character, Visual Basic assigns the variant data type to the variable. Note that while the variant data type is the most flexible (and, in fact, is the data type for all controls on forms and reports), it is also the least efficient because Visual Basic must do extra work to determine the current data type of the data in the variable before working with it in your code. Variant is also the only data type that can contain the Null value.

TIP

> You can request that Visual Basic generate all new modules with an Option Explicit statement by selecting the Require Variable Declaration check box on the Editor tab of the Options dialog box, as shown in Figure 22-3 on page 755. If you set this option, Visual Basic includes an Option Explicit statement in the Declarations section of every new module. This helps you avoid errors that can occur when you use a variable in your code that you haven't properly declared in a Dim, Public, Static, or Type statement or as part of the parameter list in a Function statement or a Sub statement. (See the next section.) When you specify this option in a module, Visual Basic flags any undeclared variables it finds when you ask it to compile your code. Using an Option Explicit statement helps you find variables that you might have misspelled when you entered your code.

The Object data type lets you define variables that can contain object definitions. *See the section titled "Collections, Objects, Properties, and Methods" later in this chapter for details about objects that you can work with in Visual Basic.* The major object types are AccessObject, Application, Catalog, Column, Command, Connection, Container, Control, Database, Document, Error, Field, Form, Group, Index, Key, Parameter, Procedure, Property, QueryDef, Recordset, Relation, Report, Table, TableDef, User, View, and Workspace.

Variable and Constant Scope

The scope of a variable or a constant determines whether the variable or the constant is known to just one procedure, all procedures in a module, or all procedures in your database. You can create variables or constants that can be used by any procedure in your database (public scope). You can also create variables or constants that apply only to the procedures in a module or only to a single procedure (private scope). You can pass values from one procedure to another using a parameter list, but the values might be held in variables having different names in

VI

Creating an Application

the two procedures. *See the sections on the Function, Sub, and Call statements later in this chapter.*

To declare a public variable, use the *Public* statement in the Declarations section of a module. To declare a public constant, use the Public keyword with a *Const* statement in the Declarations section of a module. To declare a variable or a constant that can be used by all procedures in a module, define that variable or constant in the Declarations section of the module object or the form or report module. To declare a variable or a constant used only in a particular procedure, define that variable or constant as part of the procedure.

Unlike the first two versions of Access, Access for Windows 95, Access 97, and Visual Basic in Access 2000 allow you to use the same name for variables or constants in different module objects or at different levels of scope. In addition, you can declare public variables and constants in form and report modules as well as in module objects.

To use the same name for public variables and constants in different module objects or form or report modules, simply specify the name of the module to which it belongs when you refer to it. For example, you can declare a public variable named intX in a module object with the name modMyModule and then declare another public variable named intX in a second module object, named modMyOtherModule. If you want to reference the intX variable in modMyModule from a procedure in modMyOtherModule (or any module other than modMyModule), you must use:

```
modMyModule.intX
```

You can also declare variables or constants with the same name at different levels of scoping within a module object or a form or report module. For example, you can declare a public variable named intX and then declare a "local" variable named intX within a procedure. (You can't declare a public variable within a procedure.) References to intX within the procedure refer to the local variable, while references to intX outside the procedure refer to the public variable. To refer to the public variable within the procedure, simply qualify it with the name of the module, just as you would refer to a public variable in a different module.

Declaring a public variable or a constant in a form or report module can be useful for variables and constants that are logically associated with a particular form or report but that you might also want to use elsewhere. Like the looser naming restrictions, however, this feature can sometimes create confusion. In general, it's still a good idea to keep common public variables and constants in module objects and to try to give public variables and constants unique names.

Syntax Conventions

The following conventions are used in the syntax descriptions for Visual Basic statements you'll encounter in this chapter.

You must enter all other symbols, such as parentheses and colons, exactly as they appear in the syntax line. Much of the syntax shown in this chapter has been broken into multiple lines. You can format your code all on one line, or you can write a single line of code on multiple lines using the Visual Basic line continuation character (_).

Convention	Meaning
Bold	Bold type indicates keywords and reserved words that you must enter exactly as shown. Microsoft Visual Basic understands keywords entered in uppercase, lowercase, and mixed case type.
Italic	Italicized words represent variables that you supply.
Angle brackets < >	Angle brackets enclose syntactic elements that you must supply. The words inside the angle brackets describe the element but do not show the actual syntax of the element. Do not enter the angle brackets.
Brackets [ ]	Brackets enclose optional items. If more than one item is listed, the items are separated by a pipe character (|). Choose one or none of the elements. Do not enter the brackets or the pipe; they're not part of the element. Note that Visual Basic in many cases requires that you enclose names in brackets. When brackets are required as part of the syntax of variables that you must supply in these examples, the brackets are italicized, as in *[MyTable].[MyField]*.
Braces { }	Braces enclose one or more options. If more than one option is listed, the items are separated by a pipe character (|). Choose one item from the list. Do not enter the braces or the pipe.
Ellipsis …	Ellipses indicate that you can repeat an item one or more times. When a comma is shown with an ellipsis (,…), enter a comma between items.
Underscore _	You can use a blank space followed by an underscore to continue a line of Visual Basic code to the next line for readability. You cannot place an underscore in the middle of a string literal.

Declaring Variables

The following sections show the syntax of the statements you can use to define constants and variables in your modules and procedures.

Const Statement

Use a Const statement to define a constant.

Syntax

```
[Public | Private] Const {constantname [As datatype]
    = <const expression>},...
```

Notes

Include the Public keyword in the Declarations section of a module object or a form or report module to define a constant that is available to all procedures in all modules in your database. Include the Private keyword to declare constants that are available only within the module where the declaration is made. Constants are private by default.

The *datatype* can be Byte, Boolean, Integer, Long, Currency, Single, Double, Date, String, or Variant. Use a separate As type clause for each constant being declared. If you don't declare a type, the constant is given the data type that is most appropriate for the expression provided.

The *<const expression>* cannot include variables, user-defined functions, or Visual Basic built-in functions (such as Chr). You can include simple literals and other previously defined constants.

Example

To define the constant PI to be available to all procedures in all modules, enter the following in the Declarations section of any module object.

```
Public Const PI As Double = 3.14159
```

Dim Statement

Use a Dim statement in the Declarations section of a module to declare a variable or a variable array that can be used in all procedures in the module. Use a Dim statement within a procedure to declare a variable used only in that procedure.

Syntax

```
Dim {[WithEvents] variablename
    [([<array dimension>],... )] [As [New]
    <data type>]},...
```

where *<array dimension>* is

[*lowerbound* **To**] *upperbound*

Notes

If you do not include an *<array dimension>* specification but you do include the parentheses, you must include a ReDim statement in each procedure that uses the array to dynamically allocate the array at run time. You can define an array with as many as 60 dimensions. If you do not include a *lowerbound* value in an *<array dimension>* specification, the default lower bound is 0. You can reset the default lower bound to 1 by including an *Option Base 1* statement in the module Declarations section. The *lowerbound* value must be at least –32,768 and an *upperbound* value cannot exceed 32,767.

Valid *<data type>* entries are Byte, Boolean, Integer, Long, Currency, Single, Double, Date, String (for variable-length strings), String * *length* (for fixed-length strings), Object, Variant, or one of the object types described in the section titled "Data Types" earlier in this chapter. You can also declare a user-defined variable structure using the Type statement and then use the user type name as a data type. Use the New keyword to indicate that a declared object variable is a new instance of an object that doesn't have to be set before you use it.

Use the WithEvents keyword to indicate an object variable within a class module that responds to events triggered by an ActiveX object. Form and report modules that respond to events on the related form and report objects are class modules. You can also define custom class modules to create custom objects. See the Help topic "Event Statement Example" for more information about events in class modules. If you use the WithEvents keyword, you cannot use the New keyword.

Visual Basic initializes declared variables at compile time. Numeric variables are initialized to zero (0), variant variables are initialized to empty, variable-length string variables are initialized as zero-length strings, and fixed-length string variables are filled with ANSI zeros (Chr(0)). If you use a Dim statement within a procedure to declare variables, Visual Basic reinitializes the variables each time you run the procedure. You can use the New keyword only with object variables to create a new instance of that class of object when you first reference it without requiring a Set statement. You can't use New to declare dependent objects, and you can't use WithEvents and New together.

VI

Creating an Application

Examples

To declare a variable named intMyInteger as an integer, enter the following.

```
Dim intMyInteger As Integer
```

To declare a variable named dbMyDatabase as a database object, enter the following.

```
Dim dbMyDatabase As Database
```

To declare an array named strMyString that contains fixed-length strings that are 20 characters long and contains 50 entries from 51 through 100, enter the following.

```
Dim strMyString(51 To 100) As String * 20
```

To declare a database variable, a new table variable, and two new field variables for the table; set up the objects; and append the new table to the Tabledefs collection, enter the following.

```
Sub NewExample()
    Dim tdf As New DAO.TableDef, _
        fld1 As New DAO.Field, _
        fld2 As New DAO.Field
    Dim db As DAO.Database
    ' Initialize the table name
    tdf.Name = "MyTable"
    ' Set the name of the first field
    fld1.Name = "MyField1"
    ' Set its data type
    fld1.Type = dbLong
    ' Append the first field to the Fields
    ' collection of the table
    tdf.Fields.Append fld1
    ' Set up the second field
    fld2.Name = "MyField2"
    fld2.Type = dbText
    fld2.Size = 20
    ' Append the second field to the table
    tdf.Fields.Append fld2
    ' Establish an object on the current database
    Set db = CurrentDb
    ' Create a new table by appending tdf to
    ' the Tabledefs collection of the database
    db.TableDefs.Append tdf
End Sub
```

To declare an object variable to respond to events in another class module, enter the following.

```
Option Explicit
```

```
Dim WithEvents objOtherClass As MyClass

Sub LoadClass ()
    Set objOtherClass = New MyClass
End Sub

Sub objOtherClass_Signal(ByVal strMsg As string)
    MsgBox "MyClass Signal event sent this " & _
        "message: " & strMsg
End Sub
```

In class module "MyClass," code the following.

```
Option Explicit
Public Event Signal(ByVal strMsg As String)

Public Sub RaiseSignal(ByVal strText As String)
    RaiseEvent Signal(strText)
End Sub
```

In any other module, execute the following statement.

```
MyClass.RaiseSignal "Hello"
```

Enum Statement

Use an Enum statement in a module Declarations section to assign long integer values to named members of an enumeration.

Syntax

```
[Public | Private] Enum enumerationname
    <member> [= <long integer expression>]
    ...
End Enum
```

Notes

Enumerations are constant values that you cannot change when your code is running. Include the Public keyword to define an enumeration that is available to all procedures in all modules in your database. Include the Private keyword to declare an enumeration that is available only within the module where the declaration is made. Enumerations are Public by default.

You must declare at least one *member* within an enumeration. If you do not provide a *<long integer expression>* assignment, Visual Basic adds 1 to the previous value or assigns 0 if the *member* is the first member of the enumeration. The *<long integer expression>* cannot include variables, user-defined functions, or Visual Basic built-in functions (such as CLng). You can include simple literals and other previously defined constants or enumerations.

Example

To declare an enumeration for days of the week and use the enumeration in a procedure, enter the following.

```
Option Explicit
Enum WeekDays
     Sunday = 1
     Monday
     Tuesday
     Wednesday
     Thursday
     Friday
     Saturday
End Enum

Sub TestToday ()
'     Select Case Weekday(Date)
         Case WeekDays.Sunday
             MsgBox "Today is Sunday."
         Case WeekDays.Monday
             MsgBox "Today is Monday."
         Case WeekDays.Tuesday
             MsgBox "Today is Tuesday."
         Case WeekDays.Wednesday
             MsgBox "Today is Wednesday."
         Case WeekDays.Thursday
             MsgBox "Today is Thursday."
         Case WeekDays.Friday
             MsgBox "Today is Friday."
         Case WeekDays.Saturday
             MsgBox "Today is Saturday."
     End Select
End Sub
```

Event Statement

Use the Event statement in the Declarations section of a class module to declare an event that can be raised within the module. In another module, you can define an object variable using the WithEvents keyword, set the variable to an instance of this class module, and then code procedures that respond to the events declared and triggered within this class module.

Syntax

```
[Public] Event eventname ([<arguments>])
```

where *<arguments>* is

```
{[ByVal | ByRef] argumentname [As <data type>]},...
```

Notes

An Event must be Public, which makes the event available to all other procedures in all modules. You can optionally include the Public keyword when coding this statement.

You should declare the data type of any arguments in the event's argument list. Note that the names of the variables passed by the triggering procedure can be different from the names of the variables known by this event. If you use the ByVal keyword to declare an argument, Visual Basic passes a *copy* of the argument to your event. Any change you make to a ByVal argument does not change the original variable in the triggering procedure. If you use the ByRef keyword, Visual Basic passes the actual memory address of the variable, allowing the event to change the variable's value in the triggering procedure. (If the argument passed by the triggering procedure is an expression, Visual Basic treats it as if you had declared it by using ByVal.). Visual Basic always passes arrays by reference (ByRef).

Example

To declare an event that can be triggered from other modules, enter the following in the class module MyClass.

```
Option Explicit
Public Event Signal(ByVal strMsg As String)

Public Sub RaiseSignal(ByVal strText As String)
    RaiseEvent Signal(strText)
End Sub
```

To respond to the event from another module, enter the following.

```
Option Explicit
Dim WithEvents objOtherClass As MyClass

Sub LoadClass ()
    Set objOtherClass = New MyClass
End Sub

Sub objOtherClass_Signal(ByVal strMsg As string)
    MsgBox "MyClass Signal event sent this " & _
        "message: " & strMsg
End Sub
```

To trigger the event in any other module, execute the following.

```
MyClass.RaiseSignal "Hello"
```

VI

Creating an Application

Private Statement

Use a Private statement in the Declarations section of a module object or a form or report module to declare variables that you can use in any procedure within the module.

Syntax

```
Private {[WithEvents] variablename
   [([<array dimension>],... )]
   [As [New] <data type>]},...
```

where *<array dimension>* is

```
[lowerbound To ] upperbound
```

Notes

If you do not include an *<array dimension>* specification, you must include a ReDim statement in each procedure that uses the array to dynamically allocate the array at run time. You can define an array with up to 60 dimensions. If you do not include a *lowerbound* value in an *<array dimension>* specification, the default lower bound is 0. You can reset the default lower bound to 1 by including an *Option Base 1* statement in the module Declarations section. The *lowerbound* value must be at least –32,768 and an *upperbound* value cannot exceed 32,767.

Valid *<data type>* entries are Byte, Boolean, Integer, Long, Currency, Single, Double, Date, String (for variable-length strings), String * *length* (for fixed-length strings), Object, Variant, or one of the object types described in the section titled "Data Types" earlier in this chapter. You can also declare a user-defined variable structure using the Type statement and then use the user type name as a data type. Use the New keyword to indicate that a declared object variable is a new instance of an object that doesn't have to be set before you use it.

Use the WithEvents keyword to indicate an object variable within a class module that responds to events triggered by an ActiveX object. Form and report modules that respond to events on the related form and report objects are class modules. You can also define custom class modules to create custom objects. See the Help topic "Event Statement Example" for more information about events in class modules. If you use the WithEvents keyword, you cannot use the New keyword.

Visual Basic initializes declared variables at compile time. Numeric variables are initialized to zero (0), variant variables are initialized to empty, variable-length string variables are initialized as zero-length strings, and fixed-length string variables are filled with ANSI zeros (Chr(0)).

Example

To declare a long variable named lngMyNumber that can be used in any procedure within this module, enter the following.

```
Private lngMyNumber As Long
```

Public Statement

Use a Public statement in the Declarations section of a module object or a form or report module to declare variables that you can use in any procedure anywhere in your database.

Syntax

```
Public {[WithEvents]variablename
    [([<array dimension>],... )]
    [As [New] <data type>]},...
```

where *<array dimension>* is

```
[lowerbound To ] upperbound
```

Notes

If you do not include an *<array dimension>* specification, you must include a ReDim statement in each procedure that uses the array to dynamically allocate the array at run time. You can define an array with up to 60 dimensions. If you do not include a *lowerbound* value in an *<array dimension>* specification, the default lower bound is 0. You can reset the default lower bound to 1 by including an *Option Base 1* statement in the module Declarations section. The *lowerbound* value must be at least –32,768 and an *upperbound* value cannot exceed 32,767.

Valid *<data type>* entries are Byte, Boolean, Integer, Long, Currency, Single, Double, Date, String (for variable-length strings), String * *length* (for fixed-length strings), Object, Variant, or one of the object types described in the section titled "Data Types" earlier in this chapter. Note, however, that you cannot declare a Public fixed-length string within a class module. You can also declare a user-defined variable structure using the Type statement and then use the user type name as a data type. Use the New keyword to indicate that a declared object variable is a new instance of an object.

Use the WithEvents keyword to indicate an object variable within a Class module that responds to events triggered by an ActiveX object. Form and report modules that respond to events on the related form and report objects are class modules. You can also define custom class modules to create custom objects. See the Help topic "Event Statement Example" for more information about events in Class modules. If you use the WithEvents keyword, you cannot use the New keyword.

Visual Basic initializes declared variables at compile time. Numeric variables are initialized to zero (0), variant variables are initialized to empty, variable-length string variables are initialized as zero-length strings, and fixed-length string variables are filled with ANSI zeros (Chr(0)).

Variable Naming Conventions

It's a good idea to prefix all variable names you create with a notation that indicates the data type of the variable, particularly if you create complex procedures. This helps ensure that you aren't attempting to assign or calculate incompatible data types. (For example, the names will make it obvious that you're creating a potential error if you try to assign the contents of a long integer variable to an integer variable.) It also helps ensure that you pass variables of the correct data type to procedures. Finally, including a prefix helps ensure that you do not create a variable name that is the same as an Access or Visual Basic reserved word. The following table suggests data type prefixes that you can use for many of the most common data types.

Data Type	Prefix	Data Type	Prefix
Byte	byt	Database	db
Boolean	bot	Document	doc
Currency	cur	Field	fld
Double	dbl	Form	frm
Integer	int	Index	idx
Long	lng	Key	key
Single	sgl	Parameter	prm
String	str	Procedure	prc
User-defined (using the Type statement)	usr	Property	prp
		QueryDef	qdf
		Recordset	rcd
Variant	var	Report	rpt
Catalog	cat	Table	tbl
Column	col	TableDef	tbl
Command	cmd	View	vew
Connection	cn	Workspace	wks
Control	ctl		

Example

To declare a long variable named lngMyNumber that can be used in any procedure in the database, enter the following.

```
Public lngMyNumber As Long
```

ReDim Statement

Use a ReDim statement to dynamically declare an array within a procedure or to redimension a declared array within a procedure at run time.

Syntax

```
ReDim [Preserve] {variablename
    (<array dimension>,...) [As <data type>]},...
```

where *<array dimension>* is

```
[lowerbound To ] upperbound
```

Notes

If you're dynamically allocating an array that you previously defined with no *<array dimension>* in a *Dim* or *Public* statement, your array can have no more than 8 dimensions. If you declare the array only within a procedure, your array can have up to 60 dimensions. If you do not include a *lowerbound* value in an *<array dimension>* specification, the default lower bound is 0. You can reset the default lower bound to 1 by including an *Option Base 1* statement in the module Declarations section. The *lowerbound* value must be at least –32,768 and an *upperbound* value cannot exceed 32,767. If you previously specified dimensions in a Public or Dim statement or in another ReDim statement within the same procedure, you cannot change the number of dimensions.

Include the Preserve keyword to ask Visual Basic not to reinitialize existing values in the array. When you use Preserve, you can change the bounds of only the last dimension in the array.

Valid *<data type>* entries are Byte, Boolean, Integer, Long, Currency, Single, Double, Date, String (for variable-length strings), String * *length* (for fixed-length strings), Object, Variant, or one of the object types described in the section titled "Data Types" earlier in this chapter. You can also declare a user-defined variable structure using the Type statement and then use the user type name as a data type. You cannot change the data type of an array that you previously declared with a Dim or Public statement. After you establish the number of dimensions for an array that has module or global scope, you cannot change the number of its dimensions using a ReDim statement.

Visual Basic initializes declared variables at compile time. Numeric variables are initialized to zero (0), variant variables are initialized to empty, variable-length string variables are initialized as zero-length strings, and fixed-length string variables are filled with ANSI zeros (Chr(0)). If you use a ReDim statement within a procedure to both declare and allocate an array (and you have not previously defined the array with a Dim or Public statement), Visual Basic reinitializes the array each time you run the procedure.

Example

To dynamically allocate an array named strProductNames that contains 20 strings, each with a fixed length of 25, enter the following.

```
ReDim strProductNames(20) As String * 25
```

Static Statement

Use a Static statement within a procedure to declare a variable used only in that procedure and that Visual Basic does not reinitialize while the module containing the procedure is open. Visual Basic opens all module objects when you open the database containing those objects. Visual Basic keeps form or report modules open only while the form or the report is open.

Syntax

```
Static {variablename [({<array dimension>},...)]
    [As [New] <data type>]},...
```

where *<array dimension>* is

```
[lowerbound To ] upperbound
```

Notes

You can define an array with up to 60 dimensions. If you do not include a *lowerbound* value in an *<array dimension>* specification, the default lower bound is 0. You can reset the default lower bound to 1 by including an *Option Base 1* statement in the module Declarations section. The *lowerbound* value must be at least –32,768 and an *upperbound* value cannot exceed 32,767.

Valid *<data type>* entries are Byte, Boolean, Integer, Long, Currency, Single, Double, Date, String (for variable-length strings), String * *length* (for fixed-length strings), Object, Variant, or one of the object types described in the section titled "Data Types" earlier in this chapter. You can also declare a user-defined variable structure using the Type statement and then use the user type name as a data type. Use the New keyword to indicate that a declared object variable is a new instance of an object.

Visual Basic initializes declared variables at compile time. Numeric variables are initialized to zero (0), variant variables are initialized to empty, variable-length string variables are initialized as zero-length strings, and fixed-length string variables are filled with ANSI zeros (Chr(0)).

Examples

To declare a static variable named intMyInteger as an integer, enter the following.

```
Static intMyInteger As Integer
```

To declare a static array named strMyString that contains fixed-length strings that are 20 characters long and contains 50 entries from 51 through 100, enter the following.

```
Static strMyString(51 To 100) As String * 20
```

Type Statement

Use a Type statement in a Declarations section to create a user-defined data structure containing one or more variables.

Syntax

```
[Public | Private] Type typename
    {variablename [({<array dimension>},...)]
      As <data type>}
    ...
    End Type
```

where *<array dimension>* is

```
[lowerbound To ] upperbound
```

Notes

A Type statement is most useful for declaring sets of variables that can be passed to procedures (including Windows API functions) as a single variable. You can also use the Type statement to declare a record structure. After you declare a user-defined data structure, you can use the *typename* in any subsequent Dim, Public, or Static statement to create a variable of that type. You can reference variables in a user-defined data structure variable by entering the variable name, a period, and the name of the variable within the structure. (See the second part of the example that follows.)

Include the Public keyword to declare a user-defined type that is available to all procedures in all modules in your database. Include the Private keyword to declare a user-defined type that is available only within the module in which the declaration is made.

You must enter each *variablename* entry on a new line. You must indicate the end of your user-defined data structure using an End Type statement. Valid *<data type>* entries are Byte, Boolean, Integer, Long, Currency, Single, Double, Date, String (for variable-length strings), String * *length* (for fixed-length strings), Object, Variant, another user-defined type, or one of the object types described in the section titled "Data Types" earlier in this chapter.

Example

To define a user type structure named MyRecord containing a long integer and three string fields, declare a variable named usrContacts using that user type, and then set the first string to "Jones", first enter the following.

```
Type MyRecord
    lngID As Long
    strLast As String
    strFirst As String
    strMid As String
End Type
```

Within a procedure, enter the following.

```
Dim usrContacts As MyRecord
usrContacts.strLast = "Jones"
```

Collections, Objects, Properties, and Methods

You've already dealt with two of the main collections supported by Microsoft Access—Forms and Reports. The Forms collection contains all the form objects that are open in your application, and the Reports collection contains all the open report objects.

As you'll learn in more detail later in this section, collections, objects, properties, and methods are organized in several object model hierarchies. Objects have *properties* that describe the object and *methods* that are actions you can ask the object to execute. For example, a Form object has a Name property (the name of the form) and a Requery method (to ask the form to requery its Record Source). Many objects also have *collections* that define sets of other objects within the object. For example, a Form object has a Controls collection that is the set of all Control objects (text boxes, labels, and so on) defined on the form.

You don't need a thorough understanding of collections, objects, properties, and methods to perform most application tasks. It's useful, however, for you to know how Access and Visual Basic organize these items so that you can better understand how Access works. If you want to study advanced code examples available in the many sample databases that you can download from public forums, you'll need to understand collections, objects, properties, and methods and how to correctly reference them.

The Access Application Architecture

Access has two major components—the application engine, which controls the programming and the user interface, and the JET DBEngine, which controls the storage of data and the definition of all the objects in your database. As you'll see a bit later, Visual Basic supports two distinct object models for manipulating objects stored by the database engine. Figure 22-12 shows the application architecture of Access.

FIGURE 22-12.

The Access application architecture.

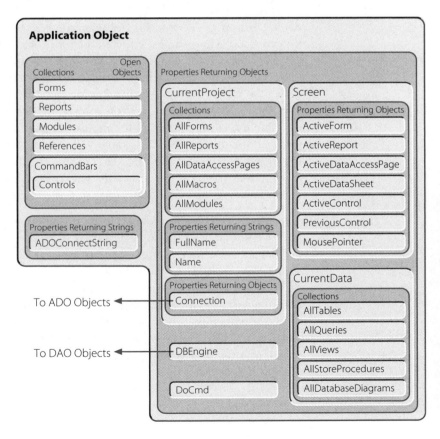

When you open a database, the application engine loads the appropriate object collections from the database and application files to enable it to list the names of all the tables, queries, views, database diagrams, stored procedures, forms, reports, data access pages, macros, and modules to display in the Database window. The application engine establishes the top-level Application object, which contains a Forms collection (all the open forms), a Reports collection (all the open reports), a References collection (all Visual Basic library references), and a Modules collection (all the open modules, including form and report modules). Each form and report, in turn, contains a Controls collection (all of the controls on the form or the report).

The Application object itself has several useful properties that tell you the name of the current command bar, the type of object that currently has the focus, and the name of the object that currently has the focus. The Application object also contains two special objects, the Screen object and the DoCmd object. The Screen object has seven very useful properties: ActiveControl, ActiveDataAccessPage, ActiveDatasheet, ActiveForm, ActiveReport, PreviousControl, and MousePointer. Without knowing the actual names, you can reference the control (if any) that currently has the focus, the data access page (if any) that has the focus, the datasheet (if any) that has the focus, the form (if any) that has the focus, the report (if any) that has the focus, or the name of the control that previously had the focus. You can use the MousePointer property to examine the current status of the mouse pointer (arrow, I-beam, hourglass, and so on) and set the pointer. (Additional details about referencing properties of objects appear later in this chapter.) The DoCmd object lets you execute most macro actions within Visual Basic. *See the section titled "Running Macro Actions" later in this chapter.*

 Two new properties introduced in Access 2000 allow you to directly find out the names of all objects stored in your database without having to call the database engine. In an Access database (mdb file extension), you can find out the names of all your tables and queries via the CurrentData property. In an Access project file (adp file extension) that is connected to SQL Server, you can additionally find out the names of database diagrams, procedures, and views via this same property. In either type of Access file, you can discover the names of all your forms, reports, data access pages, macros, and modules via the CurrentProject property.

The Data Access Objects (DAO) Architecture

The first (and oldest) of the two models you can use to fetch data and examine or create new data objects is the Data Access Object model. This model is best suited for use within Access database applications (mdb file extension) because it provides objects, methods, and properties specifically tailored to the way Access and the JET DBengine work together. To use this model, you must ask Visual Basic to load a reference to the Microsoft DAO 3.6 Object Library. Open any module in Design view, and then choose References from the Tools menu to see which libraries are loaded.

The Application object's DBEngine property serves as a bridge between the application engine and the JET DBEngine. The DBEngine property represents the DBEngine object, which is the top-level object in the Data Access Objects (DAO) hierarchy. Figure 22-13 shows you a diagram of the hierarchy of collections defined in the DAO model.

FIGURE 22-13.

The Data Access Objects (DAO) model.

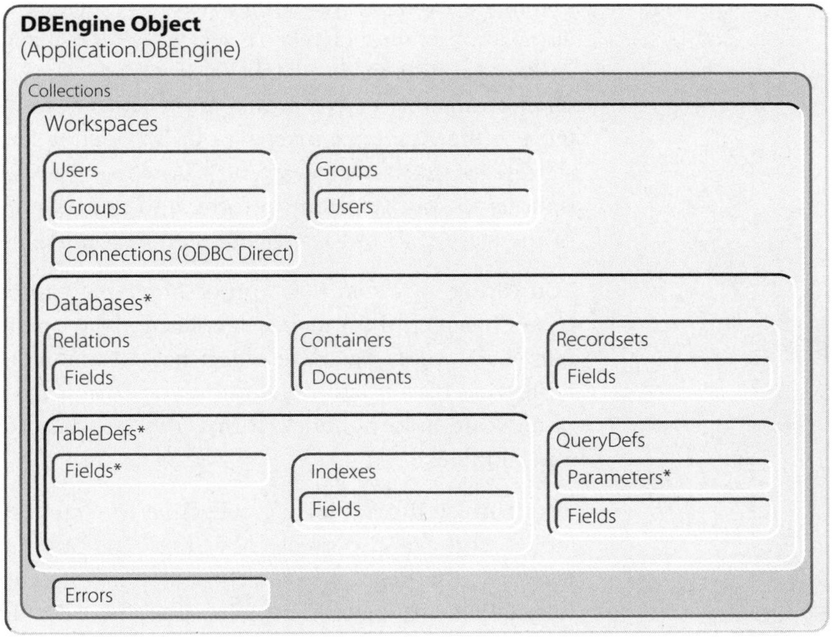

* Default collection of any object contained in the parent collection

VI

Creating an Application

SEE ALSO

See Chapter 25, "After Completing Your Application" for details about security in Microsoft Access. See Chapter 24, "The Finishing Touches," for details on creating an Autoexec macro group.

The DBEngine object controls all the database objects in your database through a hierarchy of collections, objects, and properties. When you open an Access database, the DBEngine object first establishes a Workspaces collection and a default Workspace object. If your workgroup is secured, Access prompts you for a password and a user ID so that the DBEngine can create a User object and a Group object within the default workspace. If your workgroup is not secured, the DBEngine creates a default user called Admin in a default group called Admins.

Finally, the DBEngine creates a Database object within the default Workspace object. The DBEngine uses the current User and/or Group object information to determine whether you're authorized to access any of the objects within the database.

After the DBEngine creates a Database object, the application engine checks the database's startup options to find out whether to display a startup form, menu bar, and title or use one or more of the other startup options. You can set these options by choosing the Startup command from the Tools menu. After checking the startup options, the application engine checks to see whether a macro group named Autoexec exists in the database. If it finds Autoexec, the application engine runs this macro group. In versions 1 and 2 of Access, you'd often use the Autoexec macro group to open a startup form and run startup routines. In Access 2000, however, you should use the startup options to specify a startup form, and then use the event procedures of the startup form to run your startup routines.

You can code Visual Basic procedures that can create additional Database objects in the Databases collection by opening additional mdb files. Each open Database object has a Containers collection that the DBEngine uses to store the definition (using the Documents collection) of all your tables, queries, forms, reports, data access pages, macros, and modules.

You can use the TableDefs collection to examine and modify existing tables. You can also create new TableDef objects within this collection. Likewise, the Relations collection contains Relation objects that define how tables are related and what integrity rules apply between tables. The QueryDefs collection contains QueryDef objects that define all the queries in your database. You can modify existing queries or create new ones. Finally, the Recordsets collection contains a Recordset object for each open recordset in your database.

In one of the examples at the end of this chapter, you'll learn how to create a new TableDef object and then open a Recordset object on the new table to insert rows. All of the code examples that manipulate recordsets or objects in the Entertainment Scheduling sample database use DAO.

The ActiveX Data Objects (ADO) Architecture

Microsoft has introduced a more generic set of data engine object models to provide references not only to objects stored by the JET DBEngine but also to data objects stored in other database products such as Microsoft SQL Server. These models are called the ActiveX Data Objects (ADO) architecture. With Microsoft Access 97 (version 8.0), you could download the Microsoft Data Access Components from the Microsoft Web site to be able to use the ADO model. Access 2000 now provides direct support for ADO with built-in libraries and direct references to key objects in the model from the Access Application object.

Because these models are designed to provide a common set of objects across any data engine that supports the ActiveX Data Objects, they do not necessarily support all of the features you can find in the DAO architecture that was specifically designed for the Microsoft JET DBengine. For this reason, if you are designing an application that will always run with the JET DBengine, you are better off using the DAO model. If, however, you expect that your application might one day "upsize" to an ActiveX data engine such as SQL Server, you are better off using the ADO architecture as much as possible. If you create your Access application as an Access Project (adp file extension) linked to SQL Server, you should only use the ADO models.

When you create a new Access (mdb) database, your Visual Basic project will have a reference to the ADO object model only. If you intend to use the more extensive features of DAO, you must add the reference yourself. Open any module in Design view, and then choose References from the Tools menu and select the Microsoft DAO 3.6 Object Library.

Figure 22-14 on the next page shows you the two major models available under the ADO architecture. The basic ADO model lets you open and manipulate recordsets via the Recordset object and execute action or parameter queries via the Command object. The ADO Extensions for DDL model (ADOX) allows you to create, open, and manipulate

Tables, Views (non-parameter unordered queries), and Procedures (action queries, parameter queries, ordered queries, and Triggers or Procedures) within the data engine Catalog. You can also examine and define Users and Groups defined in the Catalog with ADOX.

FIGURE 22-14.

The ActiveX Data Objects (ADODB) and ActiveX Data Objects Extensions for DDL (ADOX) models.

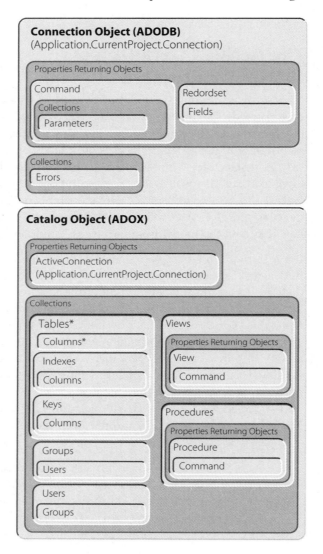

To use the ADODB model, you must ask Visual Basic to load a reference to the Microsoft ActiveX Data Objects Library. For objects in the ADOX model, you need the Microsoft ADO Extensions for DDL and

---

*   Default collection of any object contained in the parent collection

Security library. Note that there are some objects in common between DAO, ADO, and ADOX. If you use multiple models in an application, you must be careful to qualify object declarations. For example, a Recordset object type in the DAO model is a DAO.Recordset, whereas a Recordset in the ADODB model is an ADODB.Recordset.

The link to ADODB and ADOX is via the CurrentProject.Connection property. Once you open an ADODB.Connection object, you can work with other collections, objects, and properties within the ADODB model. Likewise, establishing an ADOX.Catalog object and setting its Connection property, you can work with any collection, object, or property within the ADOX model.

 NOTE

> One of the extensive examples at the end of this chapter uses ADO exclusively to manipulate recordsets in the Microsoft Press Books sample database. Nearly all of the recordset and object manipulation code in the Microsoft Press Books database uses ADO.

For all objects within either DAO, ADODB, or ADOX, you must first establish a base object (database, connection, or catalog, respectively). For example:

```
Dim db As Database, tdf As TableDef
Set db = DBEngine.Workspaces(0).Databases(0)
Set tdf = db.TableDefs![My Table]
```

Or

```
Set tdf = db.TableDefs("My Table")
```

Or

```
Set tdf = db.TableDefs(0)
```

Referencing Collections, Objects, and Properties

In the previous chapter, you learned the most common way to reference objects in the Forms and Reports collections and controls on those objects and their properties. There are two alternative ways to reference an object within a collection. The three ways to reference an object within a collection are as follows.

- **CollectionName![Object Name].** This is the method you used in the previous chapter. For example: *Forms![My Form]*.

VI

Creating an Application

- **CollectionName("Object Name").** This method is similar to the first method but uses a string constant (or a string variable) to supply the object name, as in *Forms("My Form")* or *Forms(strFormName)*.

- **CollectionName(RelativeObjectNumber).** Visual Basic numbers objects within most collections from zero (0) to CollectionName.Count minus 1. For example, you can determine the number of open forms by referring to the Count property of the Forms collection: *Forms.Count*. You can refer to the second open form in the Forms collection as *Forms(1)*.

Forms and Reports are relatively simple because they are top-level collections within the application engine. As you can see in Figure 22-13, when you reference a collection or an object maintained by the DBEngine, the hierarchy of collections and objects is quite complex. If you want to find out the number of Workspace objects that exist in the Workspaces collection, for example, you need to reference the Count property of the Workspaces collection like this:

```
DBEngine.Workspaces.Count
```

(You can create additional workspaces from Visual Basic code.)

Using the third technique described above to reference an object, you can reference the default Workspace object by entering the following.

```
DBEngine.Workspaces(0)
```

Likewise, you can refer to the currently open database by entering the following.

```
DBEngine.Workspaces(0).Databases(0)
```

When you want to refer to an object that exists in an object's default (or only) collection (see Figures 22-13 and 22-14), you do not need to include the collection name. Therefore, because the Databases collection is the default collection for the Workspaces collection, you can also refer to the currently open database by entering the following.

```
DBEngine.Workspaces(0)(0)
```

As you can see, even with this shorthand syntax, object names can become quite cumbersome if you want to refer, for example, to a particular field within an index definition for a table within the current database in the default Workspace object—or a column within an index definition for a table within the current catalog. (Whew!) If for no other reason, object variables are quite handy to help minimize name complexity.

When you use *DBEngine.Workspaces(0).Databases(0)* to set a database object, Visual Basic establishes a pointer to the current database. You can have only one object variable set to the actual copy of the current database, and you must never close this copy. A safer technique is to set your database variable using the CurrentDb function. Using this technique opens a new database object that is based on the same database as the current one. You can have as many copies of the current database as you like, and you can close them when you finish using them.

In particular, you can reduce name complexity by using an object variable to represent the current database. When you set the variable to the current database, you can call the CurrentDb function rather than use the database's full qualifier. For example, you can declare a Database object variable, set it to the current database by using the CurrentDb function, and then use the Database object variable name as a starting point to reference the TableDefs, QueryDefs, and Recordsets collections that it contains. *(See the next page for the syntax of the Set statement.)* Likewise, if you are going to work extensively with Fields in a TableDef or Columns in a Table object, you are better off establishing an object variable that points directly to the TableDef or Table.

When to Use "!" and "."

You've probably noticed that a complex, fully qualified name of an object or a property in Access or Visual Basic contains exclamation points (!) and periods (.) that separate the parts of the name.

Use an exclamation point preceding a name when the name refers to an object that is *in* the preceding object or collection of objects. A name following an exclamation point is generally the name of an object you created (such as a form or a table). Names following an exclamation point must be enclosed in brackets ([ ]) if they contain embedded blank spaces or a special character, such as an underscore (_). To make this distinction clear, you might want to get into the habit of always enclosing in brackets names that follow an exclamation point, even though brackets are not required for names that don't use blank spaces or special characters. Access automatically inserts brackets around names in property sheets, design grids, and action arguments.

Use a period preceding a name that refers to a collection name, a property name, or the name of a method that you can perform against the preceding object. (Names following a period should never contain blank spaces.) In other words, use a period when the following name is *of* the preceding name (as in the TableDefs collection *of* the Databases(0) object, the Count property *of* the TableDefs collection, or the MoveLast method *of* the DAO Recordset object). This distinction is particularly important when referencing something that has the same name as the name of a property. For example, the reference

```
DBEngine.Workspaces(0).Databases(0).TableDefs(13).Name
```

refers to the name of a TableDef object in the current database. In the Entertainment Scheduling database, if you use *Debug.Print* to display this reference, Visual Basic returns the value *tblClubs*. However, the reference

```
DBEngine.Workspaces(0).Databases(0).TableDefs(13)![Name]
```

refers to the contents of a field called Name (if one exists) in the 14th TableDef object in the current database. In the Entertainment Scheduling database, this reference returns an error because there is no Name field in the tblClubs table.

Assigning an Object Variable—Set Statement

Use the Set statement to assign an object or object reference to an object variable.

Syntax

```
Set variablename = [New] objectreference
```

Notes

As noted earlier, you can use object variables to simplify name references. Also, using an object variable is less time-consuming than using a fully qualified name. At run time, Visual Basic must always parse a qualified name to first determine the type of object and then determine which object or property you want. If you use an object variable, you have already defined the type of object and established a direct pointer to it, so Visual Basic can quickly go to that object. This is especially important if you plan to reference, for example, many controls on a form. If you create a form variable first and then assign the variable to point to the form, referencing controls on the form via the form variable is much simpler and faster than using a fully qualified name for each control.

You must first declare *variablename* using a Dim, Private, Public, or Static statement as an AccessObject, Application, ADOX.Catalog, ADOX.Column, ADODB.Command, ADOX.Command,

ADODB.Connection, DAO.Container, Control, DAO.Database, DAO.Document, ADODB.Error, DAO.Error, ADODB.Field, DAO.Field, Form, ADOX.Group, DAO.Group, ADOX.Index, DAO.Index, ADOX.Key, ADODB.Parameter, DAO.Parameter, ADOX.Procedure, ADODB.Property, ADOX.Property, DAO.Property, DAO.QueryDef, ADODB.Recordset, DAO.Recordset, DAO.Relation, Report, ADOX.Table, DAO.TableDef, ADOX.User, DAO.User, ADOX.View or DAO.Workspace object. You can also declare a variable as an instance of the class defined by a class module. The object type must be compatible with the object type of *objectreference*. You can use another object variable in an *objectreference* statement to qualify an object at a lower level. *(See the examples below.)* You can also use an object *method* to create a new object in a collection and assign that object to an object variable. For example, it's common to use the OpenRecordset method of a QueryDef or TableDef object to create a new Recordset object. *See the example in the next section, "Object Methods."*

An object variable is a reference to an object, not a copy of the object. You can assign more than one object variable to point to the same object and change a property of the object, and all variables referencing the object will reflect the change as well. The one exception is that several Recordset variables can refer to the same recordset, but each can have its own Bookmark property pointing to different rows in the recordset. If you want to create a new instance of an object, include the New keyword.

Examples

To create a variable reference to the current database, enter the following.

```
Dim dbMyDB As DAO.Database
Set dbMyDB = CurrentDb
```

To create a variable reference to the tblClubs table in the current database using the dbMyDB variable defined above, enter the following.

```
Dim tblMyTable As DAO.TableDef
Set tblMyTable = dbMyDB![tblClubs]
```

Notice that you do not need to explicitly reference the TableDefs collection of the database, as in dbMyDB.TableDefs![tblClubs] or dbMyDB.TableDefs("tblClubs"), because TableDefs is the default collection of the database. Visual Basic assumes that [tblClubs] refers to the name of an object in the default collection of the database.

VI

Creating an Application

To create a variable reference to the Notes field in the tblClubs table using the tblMyTable variable defined above, enter the following.

```
Dim fldMyField As DAO.Field
Set fldMyField = tblMyTable![Notes]
```

To create a variable reference to the catalog for the current database, enter the following.

```
Dim catThisDB As New ADOX.Catalog
catThisDB.ActiveConnection = _
    CurrentProject.Connection
```

Note that you must use the New keyword because there's no way to open an existing Catalog without first establishing a connection to it. You open a catalog by declaring it as a new object and assigning a connection object to its ActiveConnection property. The above example takes advantage of the existence of the Application.CurrentProject.Connection property rather than first setting a Connection object. If you already have another catalog object open, you can create a copy of it by using

```
Dim catCopy As ADOX.Catalog
Set catCopy = catThisDB
```

To create a variable reference to the tblClubs table in the current database using the catThisDB variable defined above, enter the following.

```
Dim tblMyTable As ADOX.Table
Set tblMytable = catThisDB![tblClubs]
```

Notice that you do not need to explicitly reference the Tables collection of the database, as in catThisDB.Tables![tblClubs] or catThisDB.Tables("tblClubs"), because Tables is the default collection of the catalog. Visual Basic assumes that [tblClubs] refers to the name of an object in the default collection of the catalog.

To create a variable reference to the Notes column in the tblClubs table using the tblMytable variable defined above, enter the following.

```
Dim colMyColumn As ADOX.Column
Set colMyColumn = tblMyTable![Notes]
```

Object Methods

When you want to apply an action to an object in your database (such as open a query as a recordset or go to the next row in a recordset), you apply a *method* of either the object or an object variable that you have assigned to point to the object. In some cases, you'll use a method to create a new object. Many methods accept parameters that you can use to further refine how the method acts on the object. For example, you can tell the DAO OpenRecordset method whether you're creating a recordset against a local table, a dynaset (a query-based recordset), or a read-only snapshot.

> Any table recordset or dynaset recordset based on a table is updateable. (When you ask Access to open a dynaset on a table, Access internally builds a query that selects all columns from the table.) A dynaset recordset based on a query will be updateable if the query is updateable. *See "Limitations on Using Select Queries to Update Data" in Chapter 8 for details.*

Visual Basic supports many different object methods—far more than there's room to properly document in this book. Perhaps one of the most useful groups of methods is the group you can use to create a recordset and then read, update, insert, and delete rows in the recordset.

Working with DAO Recordsets

To create a recordset, you must first declare a Recordset object variable. Then open the recordset using the DAO OpenRecordset method against the current database (specifying a table name, a query name, or an SQL string to create the recordset) or against a DAO.QueryDef, DAO.TableDef, or other DAO.Recordset object. If you're working in ADO, you use the Open method of a New ADODB.Recordset object.

In DAO, you can specify options to indicate whether you're opening the recordset as a local table (which means you can use the Seek method to quickly locate rows based on a match with an available index), as a dynaset, or as a read-only snapshot. For updateable recordsets, you can also specify that you want to deny other updates, deny other reads, open a read-only recordset, open the recordset for append only, or open a read-only forward scroll recordset (which allows you to move only forward through the records).

The syntax to use the OpenRecordset method of a Database object is as follows.

```
Set RecordSetObject =
    DatabaseObject.OpenRecordset(source, [type],
    [options], [lockoptions])
```

RecordSetObject is a variable you have declared as DAO.Recordset, and *DatabaseObject* is a variable you have declared as DAO.Database. *source* is a string variable or literal containing the name of a table, the name of a query, or a valid SQL statement. Table 22-2 describes the settings you can supply for *type*, *options*, and *lockoptions*.

TABLE 22-2.   OpenRecordset Parameter Settings

Setting	Description
Type (Select one.)	
dbOpenTable	OpenRecordset returns a table recordset. You can use this option only when *source* is a table local to the database described by the database object. *Source* cannot be a linked table. You can establish a current index in a table recordset and use the Seek method to find rows using the index. If you do not specify a *type*, OpenRecordset returns a table if *source* is a local table name.
dbOpenDynaset	OpenRecordset returns a dynaset recordset. *Source* can be a local table, a linked table, a query, or an SQL statement. You can use the Find methods to search for rows in a dynaset recordset. If you do not specify a *type*, OpenRecordset returns a dynaset if *source* is a linked table, a query, or an SQL statement.
dbOpenSnapshot	OpenRecordset returns a read-only snapshot recordset. You can use the Find methods to search for rows in a snapshot recordset.
dbOpenForwardOnly	OpenRecordset returns a read-only snapshot recordset that you can move forward through only once. You can use the MoveNext method to access successive rows.
Options (You can select multiple options, adding them together.)	
dbAppendOnly	OpenRecordset returns a table or dynaset recordset that allows inserting new rows only. You can use this option only with the dbOpenTable and dbOpenDynaset types.
dbSeeChanges	Asks Access to generate a run-time error if another user in changes data while you are editing it in the recordset.
dbDenyWrite	Prevents other users from modifying or inserting records while your recordset is open.
dbDenyRead	Prevents other users from reading records in your open recordset.

TABLE 22-2. *continued*

Setting	Description
dbInconsistent	Allows you to make changes to all fields in a multiple table recordset (based on a query or SQL statement), including changes that would be inconsistent with any Join defined in the query. For example, you could change the customer identifier field (foreign key) of an orders table so that it no longer matches the primary key in an included customers table – unless referential integrity constraints otherwise prevent you from doing so. You cannot include both dbInconsistent and dbConsistent.
dbConsistent	Allows you to only make changes to fields in a multiple table recordset (based on a query or SQL statement) that are consistent with the Join definitions in the query. For example, you cannot change the customer identifier field (foreign key) of an orders table so that its value does not match the value of any customer row in the query. You cannot include both dbInconsistent and dbConsistent.
Lockoptions (Select one.)	
dbPessimistic	Asks Access to lock a row as soon as you use Edit method to place the row in an editable state. This is the default if you do not specify a lock option.
dbOptimistic	Asks Access to not attempt to lock a row until you try to write it to the database with an Update method. This generates a run-time error if another user has changed the row after you executed the Edit method.

For example, to declare a recordset for the tblClubs table in the Entertainment Scheduling database and open the recordset as a table so that you can use its indexes, enter the following.

```
Dim dbEntSched As DAO.Database
Dim rcdClubs As DAO.RecordSet
Set dbEntSched = CurrentDb
Set rcdClubs = dbEntSched.OpenRecordSet("tblClubs", _
   dbOpenTable)
```

To open the qryActivePaidContracts query as a dynaset, enter the following.

```
Dim dbEntSched As DAO.Database
Dim rcdAPContracts As DAO.RecordSet
Set dbEntSched = CurrentDb
Set rcdAPContracts = _
   dbEntSched.OpenRecordSet("qryActivePaidContracts")
```

(Note that opening a recordset as a dynaset is the default when the source is a query.)

After you open a recordset, you can use one of the Move methods to move to a specific record. Use recordset.MoveFirst to move to the first row in the recordset. Other Move methods include MoveLast, MoveNext, and MovePrevious. If you want to move to a specific row in the recordset, use one of the Find methods. You must supply a string variable containing the criteria for finding the records you want. The criteria string looks exactly like an SQL WHERE clause *(see Chapter 11, "Advanced Query Design—SQL")* but without the WHERE keyword. For example, to find the first item in the qryActivePaidContracts query's recordset whose AmountOwed entry is greater than $100, enter the following.

```
rcdAPContracts.FindFirst "AmountOwed > 100"
```

To delete a row in an updateable recordset, simply move to the row you want to delete and then use the Delete method. For example, to delete the first row in the qryActivePaidContracts query's recordset whose AmountOwed entry equals 0, enter the following.

```
Dim dbEntSched As DAO.Database
Dim rcdAPContracts As DAO.RecordSet
Set dbEntSched = CurrentDb
Set rcdAPContracts = _
    dbEntSched.OpenRecordSet("qryActivePaidContracts")
rcdAPContracts.FindFirst "AmountOwed = 0"
' Test the recordset NoMatch property for "not found"
If Not rcdAPContracts.NoMatch Then
    rcdAPContracts.Delete
End If
```

If you want to update rows in a recordset, move to the first row you want to update and then use the Edit method to lock the row and make it updateable. You can then refer to any of the fields in the row by name to change their values. Use the Update method on the recordset to save your changes before moving to another row. For example, to increase by 10 percent the AmountOwed entry of the first row in the qryActivePaidContracts query's recordset whose AmountOwed value is greater than $100, enter the following.

```
Dim dbEntSched As DAO.Database
Dim rcdAPContracts As DAO.RecordSet
Set dbEntSched = CurrentDb
Set rcdAPContracts = _
    dbEntSched.OpenRecordSet("qryActivePaidContracts")
rcdAPContracts.FindFirst "AmountOwed > 100"
' Test the recordset NoMatch property for "not found"
If Not rcdAPContracts.NoMatch Then
```

```
      rcdAPContracts.Edit
      rcdAPContracts![AmountOwed] = _
         rcdAPContracts![AmountOwed] * 1.1
      rcdAPContracts.Update
   End If
```

To insert a new row in a recordset, use the AddNew method to start a new row. Set the values of all required fields in the row, and then use the Update method to save the new row. For example, to insert a new club in the Entertainment Scheduling tblClubs table, enter the following.

```
      Dim dbEntSched As DAO.Database
      Dim rcdClubs As DAO.RecordSet
      Set dbEntSched = CurrentDb
      Set rcdClubs = dbEntSched.OpenRecordSet("tblClubs")
      rcdClubs.AddNew
      rcdClubs![ClubName] = "Winthrop Brewing Co."
      rcdClubs![StreetAddress] = "155 Riverside Ave."
      rcdClubs![City] = "Winthrop"
      rcdClubs![StateOrProvince] = "WA"
      rcdClubs![PostalCode] = "98862"
      rcdClubs![ClubPhoneNumber] = "(509) 996-3183"
      rcdClubs.Update
```

Working With ADO Recordsets

Recordsets in ADO offer many of the same capabilities and options as recordsets in DAO, but the terminology is a bit different. Because you will most often use ADO with data stored in a server database such as SQL Server, the options for an ADO recordset are geared toward server-based data. For example, ADO uses the term *cursor* to refer to the set of row returned by the server. Fundamentally, a cursor is a pointer to each row you need to work with in code. Depending on the options you choose (and the options supported by the particular database) server, a cursor may also be read-only, updatable, or forward-only. A cursor may also be able to reflect changes made by other users of the database (a keyset or dynamic cursor), or it may present only a snapshot of the data (a static cursor).

To open an ADO recordset, you must use the Open method of a new ADO Recordset object. The syntax to use the Open method of a Recordset object is as follows.

```
      RecordSetObject.Open [source], [connection],
         [cursortype], [locktype], [options]
```

RecordSetObject is a variable you have declared as a New ADO.Recordset. *Source* is a Command object or a string variable or literal containing the name of a table, the name of a view (query in SQL Server parlance), the name of a stored procedure or a valid SQL

VI

Creating an Application

statement. A stored procedure may be a parameter query or a query that specifies sorting of rows from a table or view. If you supply a Command object as the source, you do not need to supply a *connection* (the connection is defined in the Command object). Otherwise, *connection* must be the name of a Connection object that points to the target database.

Table 22-3 describes the settings you can supply for *cursortype*, *lockoptions*, and *options*.

TABLE 22-3.   RecordSetObject.Open Parameter Settings

Setting	Description
CursorType (Select one.)	
adOpenForwardOnly	Open returns a read-only snapshot cursor (recordset) that you can move forward through only once. You can use the MoveNext method to access successive rows. If you do not supply a CursorType setting, adOpenForwardOnly is the default.
adOpenKeyset	Open returns a Keyset cursor. This is roughly analogous to a DAO dynaset. If you are using ADO to open a recordset against a source in an Access mdb file, you should use this option to obtain a recordset that behaves most like a DAO recordset. In this type of cursor, you will see changes to rows made by other users, but you will not see new rows added by other users after you have opened the cursor.
adOpenDynamic	Open returns a dynamic cursor. This type of cursor lets you see not only changes made by other users but also added rows. Note, however, that certain key properties you may depend on in a DAO recordset such as RecordCount may not exist or may always be zero.
adOpenStatic	Open returns a read-only snapshot cursor. You won't be able to see changes made by other users.
Lock Options (Select one.)	
adLockReadOnly	Provides no locks. The cursor is read-only. If you do not provide a lock setting, this is the default.

TABLE 22-3. *continued*

Setting	Description
adLockPessimistic	Asks the target database to lock a row as soon as you use Edit method to place the row in an editable state.
adLockOptimistic	Asks the target database to not attempt to lock a row until you try to write it to the database with an Update method. This generates a run-time error if another user has changed the row after you executed the Edit method. You should use this option when accessing rows in an Access mdb file.
Options (You can combine one Cmd setting with one Async setting.)	
adCmdText	Indicates that *source* is an SQL statement.
adCmdTable	Indicates that *source* is a table name. In DAO, this is analogous to opening a dynaset recordset on a table.
adCmdTableDirect	Indicates that *source* is a table name. This is analogous to a DAO dbOpenTable.
adCmdStoredProc	Indicates that *source* is a stored procedure. In DAO, this is analogous to opening a dynaset on a sorted query.
adAsyncFetch	After fetching the initial rows to populate the cursor, additional fetching occurs in the background. If you try to access a row that has not been fetched yet, your code will wait until the row is fetched.
adAsyncFetchNonBlocking	After fetching the initial rows to populate the cursor, additional fetching occurs in the background. If you try to access a row that has not been fetched yet, your code will receive an end of file indication.

For example, to declare a recordset for the tblBooks table in the Microsoft Press Books database and open the recordset as a table so you can use its indexes, enter the following.

```
Dim cnThisConnect As ADODB.Connection
Dim rcdBooks As New ADODB.RecordSet
Set cnThisConnect = CurrentProject.Connection
rcdBooks.Index = "PrimaryKey"
rcdBooks.Open "tblBooks", cnThisConnect,
adOpenKeyset, _
    adLockOptimistic, adCmdTableDirect
```

VI

Creating an Application

Note that you must establish the index you want to use before you open the recordset.

To open the qryCustOrderDetails query as a keyset, enter the following.

```
Dim cnThisConnect As ADODB.Connection
Dim rcdODetails As New ADODB.RecordSet
Set cnThisConnect = CurrentProject.Connection
rcdODetails.Open "qryCustOrderDetails", _
   cnThisConnect, adOpenKeyset, adLockOptimistic, _
   adCmdTable
```

After you open a recordset, you can use one of the Move methods to move to a specific record. Use recordset.MoveFirst to move to the first row in the recordset. Other Move methods include MoveLast, MoveNext, and MovePrevious. If you want to search for a specific row in the recordset, use the Find method or set the recordset's Filter property. Unlike the Find methods in DAO, the Find method in ADO is limited to a single simple test on a column in the form "*<column-name> <comparison> <comparison-value>*". Note that to search for a Null value, you must say: "[SomeColumn] = Null", not "[SomeColumn] Is Null" as you would in DAO.

If you want to search for rows using a more complex filter, you must assign a string variable or expression containing the criteria for finding the records you want to the Filter property of the recordset. This limits the rows in the recordset to only those that meet the filter criteria. The criteria string looks exactly like an SQL WHERE clause *(see Chapter 11, "Advanced Query Design—SQL")* but without the WHERE keyword. Note that if you want to use the LIKE keyword, you must use the ANSI wildcards "%" and "_" instead of the Access JET wildcards "*" and "?". Also, ANSI SQL does not support an equivalent to the JET "#" wildcard or range testing.

For example, to find the first item in the qryCustOrderDetails query's recordset whose calculated ExtPrice column is greater than $100, enter the following.

```
rcdODetails.MoveFirst
rcdODetails.Find "[ExtPrice] > 100"
```

To find all rows in qryCustOrderDetails where Quantity is greater than 10 and ExtPrice is greater than $100, enter the following.

```
rcdODetails.Filter = &
   "[Quantity] > 10 AND [ExtPrice] > 100"
If Not rcdODetails.EOF Then
'  Found some rows!
```

To delete a row in a keyset, simply move to the row you want to delete and then use the Delete method. For example, to delete the first row in the qryCustOrderDetails query's recordset whose calculated ExtPrice column is greater than $100, enter the following.

```
Dim cnThisConnect As ADODB.Connection
Dim rcdODetails As New ADODB.RecordSet
Set cnThisConnect = CurrentProject.Connection
rcd0Details.Open "qryCustOrderDetails", _
    cnThisConnect, adOpenKeyset, adLockOptimistic, _
    adCmdTable
rcdODetails.MoveFirst
rcdODetails.Find "[ExtPrice] > 100"
' Test the recordset EOF property for "not found"
If Not rcdODetails.EOF Then
    rcdODetails.Delete
End If
```

If you want to update rows in a recordset, move to the first row you want to update. Although ADO does not require you to use the Edit method to lock the row and make it updateable, you can optionally use the Edit method to signal your intention to the database engine. You can refer to any of the updateable fields in the row by name to change their values. You can use the Update method on the recordset to explicitly save your changes before moving to another row. ADO automatically saves your changed row when you move to a new row. If you need to discard an update, you must use the CancelUpdate method of the recordset object.

For example, to set the Discount column to 15% in the first row in the qryActivePaidContracts query's recordset whose Quantity value is greater than 20, enter the following.

```
Dim cnThisConnect As ADODB.Connection
Dim rcdODetails As New ADODB.RecordSet
Set cnThisConnect = CurrentProject.Connection
rcd0Details.Open "qryCustOrderDetails", _
    cnThisConnect, adOpenKeyset, adLockOptimistic, _
    adCmdTable
rcdODetails.Filter "[Quantity] > 20"
' Test the recordset EOF property for "not found"
If Not rcdODetails.EOF Then
    rcdODetails!Discount = 0.15
    rcdODetails.MoveNext
End If
```

To insert a new row in a recordset, use the AddNew method to start a new row. Set the values of all required fields in the row, and then use the

VI

Creating an Application

Update method to save the new row. For example, to insert a new author in the Microsoft Press Books tblAuthors table, enter the following.

```
Dim cnThisConnect As ADODB.Connection
Dim rcdAuthors As New ADODB.RecordSet
Set cnThisConnect = CurrentProject.Connection
rcdAuthors.Open "tblAuthors", cnThisConnect, _
    adOpenKeyset, adLockOptimistic, adCmdTable
rcdAuthors.AddNew
rcdAuthors![FirstName] = "David"
rcdAuthors![MiddleInit] = "A"
rcdAuthors![LastName] = "Viescas"
rcdAuthors![EmailAddress] = "DavidViescas@msn.com"
rcdAuthors![Bio] = "Son of Access author!"
rcdAuthors.Update
```

Other Uses for Object Methods

As you'll learn later in this chapter in more detail, you must use a method of the DoCmd object to execute the equivalent of most macro actions within Visual Basic. You must use the RunCommand method of either the Application or DoCmd object to execute commands you can find on any of the Access menus.

You can also define a public function or subroutine *(see the next section)* within the module associated with a Form or Report object and execute that procedure as a method of the form or report. If your public procedure is a function, you must assign the result of the execution of the method to a variable of the appropriate type. If the public procedure is a subroutine, you can execute the form or report object method as a Visual Basic statement. *For more information about object methods, find the topic about the object of interest in Help, and then click the Methods hyperlink.*

Functions and Subroutines

You can create two types of procedures in Visual Basic—functions and subroutines (also known as function procedures and sub procedures). Each type of procedure can accept *parameters*—data variables that you pass to the procedure that can determine how the procedure operates. Functions can return a single data value, but subroutines cannot. In addition, you can execute a function from anywhere in Microsoft Access, including from expressions in queries and from macros. You can execute a subroutine only from a function, from another subroutine, or as an event procedure in a form or a report.

Function Statement

Use a Function statement to declare a new function, the parameters it accepts, the variable type it returns, and the code that performs the function procedure.

Syntax

```
[Public | Private] [Static] Function functionname
  ([<arguments>]) [As datatype]
    [<function statements>]
    [functionname = <expression>]
    [Exit Function]
    [<function statements>]
    [functionname = <expression>]
End Function
```

where *<arguments>* is

```
{[Optional][ByVal | ByRef][ParamArray] argumentname
  [As datatype]},...
```

Notes

Use the Public keyword to make this function available to all other procedures in all modules. Use the Private keyword to make this function available only to other procedures in the same module. When you declare a function as private in a module object, you cannot call that function from a query or a macro or from a function in another module.

Include the Static keyword to preserve the value of all variables declared within the procedure, whether explicitly or implicitly, as long as the module containing the procedure is open. This is the same as using the Static statement (discussed earlier in this chapter) to explicitly declare all variables created in this function.

You can use a type declaration character at the end of the *functionname* entry or use the As clause to declare the *datatype* returned by this function. If you do not declare a data type, Visual Basic assumes that the function returns a variant result. You can set the return value in code by assigning an expression of a compatible data type to the function name.

You should declare the *datatype* of any arguments in the function's parameter list. Note that the names of the variables passed by the calling procedure can be different from the names of the variables known by this procedure. If you use the ByVal keyword to declare an argument, Visual Basic passes a *copy* of the argument to your function. Any change you make to a ByVal argument does not change the original variable in the calling procedure. If you use the ByRef keyword, Visual Basic passes the actual memory address of the variable, allowing the procedure to change the variable's value in the calling procedure. (If the argument passed by the calling procedure is an expression, Visual Basic treats it as if you had declared it by using ByVal.) Visual Basic always passes arrays by reference (ByRef).

Use the Optional keyword to declare an argument of the variant data type that isn't required. If you declare an optional argument, all arguments that follow in the argument list must also be declared as optional. Use the IsMissing built-in function to test for the absence of optional parameters. You can also use the ParamArray argument to declare an array of optional elements of the variant data type. When you call the function, you can then pass it an arbitrary number of arguments. The ParamArray argument must be the last argument in the argument list.

Use the Exit Function statement anywhere in your function to clear any error conditions and exit your function normally, returning to the calling procedure. If Visual Basic runs your code until it encounters the End Function statement, control is passed to the calling procedure but any errors are not cleared. If this function causes an error and terminates with the End Function statement, Visual Basic passes the error to the calling procedure. *See the section titled "Trapping Errors" later in this chapter for details.*

Example

To create a function named MyFunction that accepts an integer argument and a string argument and returns a double value, enter the following.

```
Function MyFunction (intArg1 As Integer, strArg2 As _
    String) As Double
    <function statements>
End Function
```

Sub Statement

Use a Sub statement to declare a new subroutine, the parameters it accepts, and the code in the subroutine.

Syntax

```
[Public | Private] [Static] Sub subroutinename
    ([<arguments>]) [As datatype]
    [ <subroutine statements> ]
    [Exit Sub]
    [ <subroutine statements> ]
End Sub
```

where *<arguments>* is

```
{[Optional][ByVal | ByRef][ParamArray]
    argumentname [As datatype]},...
```

Notes

Use the Public keyword to make this subroutine available to all other procedures in all modules. Use the Private keyword to make this procedure available only to other procedures in the same module.

Include the Static keyword to preserve the value of all variables declared within the procedure, whether explicitly or implicitly, as long as the module containing the procedure is open. This is the same as using the Static statement (discussed earlier in this chapter) to explicitly declare all variables created in this subroutine.

You should declare the *datatype* of all arguments that the subroutine accepts in its argument list. Note that the names of the variables that are passed by the calling procedure can be different from the names of the variables as known by this procedure. If you use the ByVal keyword to declare an argument, Visual Basic passes a *copy* of the argument to your subroutine. Any change you make to a ByVal argument does not change the original variable in the calling procedure. If you use the ByRef keyword, Visual Basic passes the actual memory address of the variable, allowing the procedure to change the variable's value in the calling procedure. (If the argument passed by the calling procedure is an expression, Visual Basic treats it as if you had declared it by using ByVal.) Visual Basic always passes arrays by reference (ByRef).

Use the Optional keyword to declare an argument of the variant data type that isn't required. If you declare an optional argument, all arguments that follow in the argument list must also be declared as optional. Use the IsMissing built-in function to test for the absence of optional parameters. You can also use the ParamArray argument to declare an array of optional elements of the variant data type. When you call the subroutine, you can then pass it an arbitrary number of arguments. The ParamArray argument must be the last argument in the argument list.

Use the Exit Sub statement anywhere in your subroutine to clear any error conditions and exit your subroutine normally, returning to the calling procedure. If Visual Basic runs your code until it encounters the End Sub statement, control is passed to the calling procedure but any errors are not cleared. If this subroutine causes an error and terminates with the End Sub statement, Visual Basic passes the error to the calling procedure. *See the section titled "Trapping Errors" later in this chapter for details.*

VI

Creating an Application

Example

To create a subroutine named MySub that accepts two string arguments but can modify only the second argument, enter the following.

```
Sub MySub (ByVal strArg1 As String, ByRef strArg2 _
    As String)
    <subroutine statements>
End Sub
```

Controlling the Flow of Statements

Visual Basic provides many ways for you to control the flow of statements in procedures. You can call other procedures, loop through a set of statements either a calculated number of times or based on a condition, or test values and conditionally execute sets of statements based on the result of the condition test. You can also go directly to a set of statements or exit a procedure at any time. The following sections demonstrate some (but not all) of the ways you can control flow in your procedures.

Call Statement

Use a Call statement to transfer control to a subroutine.

Syntax

```
Call subroutinename [(<arguments>)]
```

or

```
subroutinename [<arguments>]
```

where *<arguments>* is

```
{[ByVal | ByRef] <expression> },...
```

Notes

If the subroutine accepts arguments, the names of the variables passed by the calling procedure can be different from the names of the variables as known by the subroutine. You can use the ByVal and ByRef keywords in a Call statement only when you're making a call to a dynamic link library (DLL) procedure. Use ByVal for string arguments to indicate that you need to pass a pointer to the string rather than pass the string directly. Use ByRef for nonstring arguments to pass the value directly. If you use the ByVal keyword to declare an argument, Visual Basic passes a *copy* of the argument to the subroutine. The subroutine cannot change the original variable in the calling procedure. If you use the ByRef keyword, Visual Basic passes the actual memory address of the variable, allowing the procedure to change the variable's value in the calling procedure. (If the argument passed by the calling procedure is an expression, Visual Basic treats it as if you had declared it by using ByVal.)

Examples

To call a subroutine named MySub and pass it an integer variable and an expression, enter the following.

```
Call MySub (intMyInteger, curPrice * intQty)
```

An alternative syntax is

```
MySub intMyInteger, curPrice * intQty
```

Do...Loop Statement

Use a Do...Loop statement to define a block of statements that you want executed multiple times. You can also define a condition that terminates the loop when the condition is false.

Syntax

```
Do [{While | Until} <condition>]
    [<procedure statements>]
    [Exit Do]
    [<procedure statements>]
Loop
```

or

```
Do
    [<procedure statements>]
    [Exit Do]
    [<procedure statements>]
Loop [{While | Until} <condition>]
```

Notes

The <condition> is a comparison predicate or expression that Visual Basic can evaluate to True (nonzero) or False (zero or Null). The While clause is the opposite of the Until clause. If you specify a While clause, execution continues as long as the <condition> is true. If you specify an Until clause, execution of the loop stops when <condition> becomes true. If you place a While or an Until clause in the Do clause, the condition must be met for the statements in the loop to execute at all. If you place a While or an Until clause in the Loop clause, Visual Basic executes the statements within the loop before testing the condition.

You can place one or more Exit Do statements anywhere within the loop to exit the loop before reaching the Loop statement. Generally you'll use the Exit Do statement as part of some other evaluation statement structure, such as an If...Then...Else statement.

Example

To read all the rows in the tlbClubs table until you reach the end of the recordset, enter the following.

```
Dim dbEntSched As DAO.Database
Dim rcdClubs As DAO.RecordSet
Set dbEntSched = CurrentDb
Set rcdClubs = dbEndSched.OpenRecordSet("tblClubs")
Do Until rcdClubs.EOF
    <procedure statements>
    rcdClubs.MoveNext
Loop
```

For...Next Statement

Use a For...Next statement to execute a series of statements a specific number of times.

Syntax

```
For counter = first To last [Step stepamount]
    [<procedure statements>]
    [Exit For]
    [<procedure statements>]
Next [counter]
```

Notes

The *counter* must be a numeric variable that is not an array or a record element. Visual Basic initially sets the value of *counter* to *first*. If you do not specify a *stepamount,* the default *stepamount* value is +1. If the *stepamount* value is positive or 0, Visual Basic executes the loop as long as *counter* is less than or equal to *last*. If the *stepamount* value is negative, Visual Basic executes the loop as long as *counter* is greater than or equal to *last*. Visual Basic adds *stepamount* to *counter* when it encounters the corresponding Next statement. You can change the value of *counter* within the For loop, but this might make your procedure more difficult to test and debug. Changing the value of *last* within the loop does not affect execution of the loop.

You can nest one For loop inside another. When you do this, you must choose a different name for each *counter*.

Example

To list the names of all the first five queries in the Entertainment Scheduling database, enter the following.

```
Dim dbEntSched As DAO.Database
Dim intI As Integer
Set dbEntSched = CurrentDb
For intI = 0 To 4
    Debug.Print dbEntSched.QueryDefs(intI).Name
Next intI
```

For Each...Next Statement

Use a For Each...Next statement to execute a series of statements for each item in a collection or an array.

Syntax

```
For Each item In group
    [<procedure statements>]
    [Exit For]
    [<procedure statements>]
Next [item]
```

Notes

The *item* must be a variable that represents an object in a collection or an element of an array. The *group* must be the name of a collection or an array. Visual Basic executes the loop as long as at least one item remains in the collection or the array. All the statements in the loop are executed for each item in the collection or the array.

You can nest one For Each loop inside another. When you do, you must choose a different *item* name for each loop.

Example

To list the names of all the queries in the Entertainment Scheduling database, enter the following.

```
Dim dbEntSched As DAO.Database
Dim qdf As DAO.QueryDef
Set dbEntSched = CurrentDb
For Each qdf In dbEntSched.QueryDefs
    Debug.Print qdf.Name
Next qdf
```

GoTo Statement

Use a GoTo statement to jump unconditionally to another statement in your procedure.

Syntax

```
GoTo {label | linenumber}
```

VI

Creating an Application

Notes

You can label a statement line by starting the line with a string of no more than 40 characters that starts with an alphabetic character and ends with a colon (:). A line label cannot be a Visual Basic or Access reserved word. You can also optionally number the statement lines in your procedure. Each line number must contain only numbers, must be different from all other line numbers in the procedure, must be the first nonblank characters in a line, and must contain 40 characters or less. To jump to a line number or a labeled line, use the GoTo statement and the appropriate *label* or *linenumber*.

Example

To jump to the statement line labeled SkipOver, enter the following.

```
GoTo SkipOver
```

If...Then...Else Statement

Use an If...Then...Else statement to conditionally execute statements based on the evaluation of a condition.

Syntax

```
If <condition1> Then
    [<procedure statements 1>]
[ElseIf <condition2> Then
    [<procedure statements 2>]]...
[Else
    [<procedure statements n>]]
End If
```

or

```
If <condition> Then <thenstmt> [Else <elsestmt>]
```

Notes

The *<condition>* is a numeric or string expression that Visual Basic can evaluate to True (nonzero) or False (0 or Null). The *<condition>* can also be the special TypeOf...Is test to evaluate a control variable. The syntax for this test is

```
TypeOf <ControlObject> Is <ControlType>
```

where *<ControlObject>* is the name of a control variable and *<ControlType>* is one of the following: BoundObjectFrame, CheckBox, ComboBox, CommandButton, Chart, CustomControl, Image, Label, Line, ListBox, OptionButton, OptionGroup, PageBreak, Rectangle, Subform, Subreport, TextBox, ToggleButton, or UnboundObjectFrame.

If the *<condition>* is true, Visual Basic executes the statement or statements immediately following the Then keyword. If the *<condition>* is false, Visual Basic evaluates the next ElseIf *<condition>* or executes the statements following the Else keyword, whichever occurs next.

The alternative syntax does not need an End If statement, but you must enter the entire If...Then statement on a single line. Both *<thenstmt>* and *<elsestmt>* can be either a single Visual Basic statement or multiple statements separated by colons (:).

Example

To set an integer value depending on whether a string begins with a letter from *A* through *F*, from *G* through *N*, or from *O* through *Z*, enter the following.

```
Dim strMyString As String, strFirst As String, _
   intVal As Integer
strFirst = UCase$(Mid$(strMyString, 1, 1))
If strFirst >= "A" And strFirst <= "F" Then
    intVal = 1
ElseIf strFirst >= "G" And strFirst <= "N" Then
    intVal = 2
ElseIf strFirst >= "O" And strFirst <= "Z" Then
    intVal = 3
Else
    intVal = 0
End If
```

Select Case Statement

Use a Select Case statement to execute statements conditionally based on the evaluation of an expression that is compared to a list or range of values.

Syntax

```
Select Case <test expression>
    [Case <comparison list 1>
        [<procedure statements 1>]]
    ...
    [Case Else
        [<procedure statements n>]]
End Select
```

where *<test expression>* is any numeric or string expression; where *<comparison list>* is

```
{<comparison element>,...}
```

where *<comparison element>* is

```
{expression | expression To expression |
    Is <comparison operator> expression}
```

and where *<comparison operator>* is

```
{= | <> | < | > | <= | >=}
```

Notes

If the *<test expression>* matches a *<comparison element>* in a Case clause, Visual Basic executes the statements that follow that clause. If the *<comparison element>* is a single expression, the *<test expression>* must equal the *<comparison element>* for the statements following that clause to execute. If the *<comparison element>* contains a To keyword, the first expression must be less than the second expression (either in numeric value if the expressions are numbers or in collating sequence if the expressions are strings) and the *<test expression>* must be between the first expression and the second expression. If the *<comparison element>* contains the Is keyword, the evaluation of *<comparison operator>* expression* must be true.

If more than one Case clause matches the *<test expression>*, Visual Basic executes only the set of statements following the first Case clause that matches. You can include a block of statements following a Case Else clause that Visual Basic executes if none of the previous Case clauses matches the *<test expression>*. You can nest another Select Case statement within the statements following a Case clause.

Example

To assign an integer value to a variable, depending on whether a string begins with a letter from *A* through *F*, from *G* through *N*, or from *O* through *Z*, enter the following.

```
Dim strMyString As String, intVal As Integer
Select Case UCase$(Mid$(strMyString, 1, 1))
    Case "A" To "F"
        intVal = 1
    Case "G" To "N"
        intVal = 2
    Case "O" To "Z"
        intVal = 3
    Case Else
        intVal = 0
End Select
```

RaiseEvent Statement

Use the RaiseEvent statement to signal a declared event in a class module.

Syntax

```
RaiseEvent eventname [(<arguments>)]
```

where *<arguments>* is

```
{ <expression> },...
```

Notes

You must always declare an event in the class module that raises the event. You cannot use RaiseEvent to signal a built-in event (such as Current) of a form or report class module. If an event passes no arguments, you must not include an empty pair of parentheses when you code the RaiseEvent statement. An event can only be received by another module that has declared an object variable WithEvents that has been set to the class module or object containing this class. *See the WeddingVB sample database—described in Chapter 23, "Automating Your Application with Visual Basic"—for an example using RaiseEvent to synchronize two forms.*

Example

To define an event named Signal that returns a text string and then signal that event in a class module, enter the following.

```
Option Explicit
Public Event Signal(ByVal strMsg As String)

Public Sub RaiseSignal(ByVal strText As String)
    RaiseEvent Signal(strText)
End Sub
```

Stop Statement

Use a Stop statement to suspend execution of your procedure.

Syntax

```
Stop
```

Notes

A Stop statement has the same effect as setting a breakpoint on a statement. You can use the Visual Basic debugging tools, such as the Step Into and the Step Over buttons and the Debug window, to evaluate the status of your procedure after Visual Basic halts on a Stop statement.

While...Wend Statement

Use a While...Wend statement to continuously execute a block of statements as long as a condition is true.

Syntax

```
While <condition>
    [<procedure statements>]
Wend
```

Notes

A While...Wend statement is similar to a Do...Loop statement with a While clause, except that you can use an Exit Do statement to exit from a Do loop. Visual Basic provides no similar Exit clause for a While loop. The <condition> is an expression that Visual Basic can evaluate to True (nonzero) or False (0 or Null). Execution continues as long as the <condition> is true.

Example

To read all the rows in the tblClubs table until you reach the end of the recordset, enter the following.

```
Dim dbEntSched As DAO.Database
Dim rcdClubs As DAO.RecordSet
Set dbEntSched = CurrentDb
Set rcdClubs = dbEntSched.OpenRecordSet("tblClubs")
While Not rcdClubs.EOF
    <procedure statements>
    rcdClubs.MoveNext
Wend
```

With Statement

Use a With statement to simplify references to complex objects in code. You can establish a "base" object using a With statement and then use a shorthand notation to refer to objects, collections, properties, or methods on that object until you terminate the With statement.

Syntax

```
With <object reference>
    [<procedure statements>]
End With
```

Example

To use shorthand notation on a recordset object to add a new row to a table, enter the following.

```
Dim rcd As DAO.Recordset, db As DAO.Database
Set db = CurrentDb
Set rcd = db.OpenRecordset("MyTable", _
   dbOpenDynaset, dbAppendOnly)
With rcd
    ' Start a new record
    .Addnew
    ' Set the field values
    ![FieldOne] = "1"
    ![FieldTwo] = "John"
    ![FieldThree] = "Viescas"
    .Update
    .Close
End With
```

Running Macro Actions and Menu Commands

Within Visual Basic, you can also execute most of the macro actions that Access provides and any of the built-in menu commands. Only a few of the macro actions have direct Visual Basic equivalents. To execute a macro action or menu command, use the methods of the DoCmd object, described below.

DoCmd Object

Use the methods of the DoCmd object to execute a macro action or menu command within a Visual Basic procedure.

Syntax

DoCmd.*actionmethod* [*actionargument*],...

Notes

Some of the macro actions you'll commonly execute from Visual Basic include ApplyFilter, Close, DoMenuItem, FindNext and FindRecord (for searching the recordset of the current form and immediately displaying the result), Hourglass, Maximize, Minimize, MoveSize, OpenForm, OpenQuery (to run a query that you don't need to modify), OpenReport, and ShowToolBar. Although you can run the Echo, GoToControl, GoToPage, RepaintObject, and Requery actions from Visual Basic using a method of the DoCmd object, it's more efficient to use the Echo, SetFocus, GoToPage, Repaint, and Requery methods of the object to which the method applies.

To execute a menu command, use the RunCommand method of either the DoCmd or Application object and supply a single action argument that is the numeric code for the command. You can also use one of

VI

Creating an Application

many built-in constants to reference the command you want. For example, acCmdSave executes the Save command from the File menu. When you use RunCommand, you can optionally leave out the DoCmd or Application object.

> **NOTE**
>
> Visual Basic provides built-in constants for many of the macro action and RunCommand parameters. For more information, search on "Microsoft Access Constants" in Help.

Examples

To open a form named Customer in Form view for data entry, enter the following.

```
DoCmd.OpenForm "Customer", acNormal, , , acAdd
```

To close a form named Supplier, enter the following.

```
DoCmd.Close acForm, "Supplier"
```

To open the Find window while the focus is on a form, enter the following.

```
RunCommand acCmdFind
```

Actions with Visual Basic Equivalents

A few macro actions cannot be executed from a Visual Basic procedure. All but one of these actions, however, have equivalent statements in Visual Basic, as shown in Table 22-4.

TABLE 22-4. Visual Basic Equivalents for Macro Actions

Macro Action	Visual Basic Equivalent
AddMenu	No equivalent
MsgBox	MsgBox statement or function
RunApp	Shell function
RunCode	Call subroutine
SendKeys	SendKeys statement
SetValue	Variable assignment (=)
StopAllMacros	Stop or End statement
StopMacro	Exit Sub or Exit Function statement

Trapping Errors

One of the most powerful features of Visual Basic is its ability to trap all errors, analyze them, and take corrective action. To enable error trapping, you use an On Error statement.

On Error Statement

Use an On Error statement to enable error trapping, establish the procedure to handle error trapping (the error handler), skip past any errors, or turn off error trapping.

Syntax

```
On Error {GoTo lineID | Resume [Next] | GoTo 0}
```

Notes

Use a GoTo *lineID* statement to establish a code block in your procedure that handles any error. The *lineID* can be a line number or a label. In your error handling statements, you can examine the built-in Err variable to determine the exact nature of the error. You can use the Error function to examine the text of the error message associated with the error. If you use line numbers with your statements, you can use the built-in Erl function to determine the line number of the statement that caused the error. After taking corrective action, use a Resume statement to retry execution of the statement that caused the error. Use a Resume Next statement to continue execution at the statement immediately following the statement that caused the error. You can also use an Exit Function or Exit Sub statement to reset the error condition and return to the calling procedure.

Use a Resume Next statement to trap errors but skip over any statement that causes an error. You can call the Err function in a statement immediately following the statement that you suspect might have caused an error to see whether an error occurred. Err returns 0 if no error has occurred.

Use a GoTo 0 statement to turn off error trapping for the current procedure. If an error occurs, Visual Basic passes the error to the error routine in the calling procedure or opens an error dialog box if there is no previous error routine.

VI

Creating an Application

Examples

To trap errors but continue execution with the next statement, enter the following.

```
On Error Resume Next
```

To trap errors and execute the statements that follow the MyError: label when an error occurs, enter the following.

```
On Error GoTo MyError
```

To turn off error trapping in the current procedure, enter the following.

```
On Error GoTo 0
```

Some Complex Visual Basic Examples

A good way to learn Visual Basic techniques is to study complex code that has been developed and tested by someone else. In the Microsoft Press Books and Entertainment Scheduling sample databases, you can find dozens of examples of complex Visual Basic code that perform various tasks. The following sections describe two of the more interesting ones in detail.

A Procedure to Randomly "Sell" Books

You might have noticed that there's a lot of sample "sales" data in the Microsoft Press Books database. No, I didn't sit at my keyboard for hours entering sample data! Instead, I built a Visual Basic procedure that accepts some parameters entered on a form. The form is saved in the database as *zfrmSellBooks*. If you open this form from the Database window, you'll see that you use it to enter a beginning date, a number of days, and some maximum values for orders per day, books per order, and copies of any one book in an order. Figure 22-15 shows this form with the values I used to load the database. I used a high maximum number of copies so that you could see several types of discounts in the sample.

FIGURE 22-15.
The zfrmSellBooks form in Form view.

Sell some books...		
Sell Some Books...	**Sell!**	**Cancel**
Beginning Date:	7/2/1999	
Number of Days:	180	
Max orders per day:	8	
Max books per order:	10	
Max copies per book:	12	

As you might expect, when you click the Sell button, my procedure examines the values entered and loads some sample data into tblOrders and tblOrderDetails. If you want to run this code, you should either pick a date starting after July 1, 1999, or delete the data in tblOrderDetails and tblOrders first.

To look at the code, which is associated with the cmdSell_Click event procedure that runs when you click the Sell button, select the form in the Database window and click the Code button on the toolbar. The code and a line-by-line explanation follow. I've added line numbers to some of the lines in this code listing so that you can follow along with the line-by-line explanations in the table that follows the listing. As with most procedures in the Microsoft Press Books database, this procedure uses the ADO object model.

```
1  Private Sub cmdSell_Click()
2    Dim cn As ADODB.Connection, _
       rcdO As New ADODB.Recordset, _
       rcdOD As New ADODB.Recordset
3    Dim rcdC As New ADODB.Recordset, _
       rcdB As New ADODB.Recordset
4    Dim varBeginDate As Variant, _
       intNumDays As Integer, _
       varCurrentDate As Variant
5    Dim intNumOrders As Integer, _
       intNumBooks As Integer, _
       intNumCopies As Integer
6    Dim intCountCustomers As Integer, _
       intCountBooks As Integer
7    Dim intOrdersToday As Integer, _
       intBooksThisOrder As Integer
8    Dim intO As Integer, intOD As Integer, _
       intCust As Integer
9    Dim intBook As Integer, intBookIncr As Integer
10   Dim lngOrderID As Long, varRtn As Variant

11   ' Capture values from the form
12   varBeginDate = Me!BeginDate
13   intNumDays = Me!NumDays
14   intNumOrders = Me!NumOrders
15   intNumBooks = Me!NumBooks
16   intNumCopies = Me!NumCopies

     ' Initialize the randomizer on system clock
17   Randomize

     ' Set the current connection and
     ' open all recordsets
```

(continued)

```
18    Set cn = CurrentProject.Connection
19    rcdO.Open "tblOrders", cn, adOpenKeyset, _
         adLockOptimistic
20    rcdOD.Open "tblOrderDetails", cn, adOpenKeyset, _
         adLockOptimistic
21    rcdC.Open "tblCustomers", cn, adOpenKeyset, _
         adLockOptimistic
22    rcdB.Open "Select * From tblBooks " & _
         "Where Not [OutOfPrint];", _
         cn, adOpenKeyset, adLockOptimistic
      ' Find out how many customers and books
      ' we have to work with
23    rcdC.MoveLast
24    intCountCustomers = rcdC.RecordCount
25    If intCountCustomers = 0 Then
26      MsgBox "Can't generate any orders - " & _
           "no customers in this database!", vbCritical, _
           "Microsoft Press"
27      Exit Sub
28    End If

29    rcdB.MoveLast
30    intCountBooks = rcdB.RecordCount
31    If intCountBooks = 0 Then
32      MsgBox "Can't generate any orders -" & _
           " no books in this database!", vbCritical, _
           "Microsoft Press"
33    Exit Sub
34    End If
35    If intCountBooks < intNumBooks Then
36      MsgBox "You have asked for more books per " & _
           "order than there are books in the data" & _
           "base. Books per order must not exceed " & _
           intCountBooks & ".", vbExclamation, _
           "Microsoft Press"
37      Exit Sub
38    End If

      ' Set up to bail if something funny happens
      ' (it shouldn't)
39    On Error GoTo BailOut
      ' Protect everything with a transaction
40    cn.BeginTrans
      ' Turn on the hourglass
41    DoCmd.Hourglass True

      ' Initialize the status bar
42    varRtn = SysCmd(acSysCmdInitMeter, _
         "Creating orders...", intNumDays)

      ' Set up the outside loop on dates
```

```
43    For varCurrentDate = varBeginDate To _
        (varBeginDate + intNumDays)
        ' Figure out max orders for today
44      intOrdersToday = Int((intNumOrders * Rnd) + 1)
        ' Loop to create orders
45      For intO = 1 To intOrdersToday
          ' Start a new order
46        rcdO.AddNew
          ' Randomly grab a customer record
47        intCust = Int(intCountCustomers * Rnd)
48        rcdC.MoveFirst
49        If intCust > 0 Then rcdC.Move intCust
          ' Move customer info to the order record
50        rcdO!CustomerID = rcdC!CustomerID
51        rcdO!OrderDate = varCurrentDate
52        rcdO!ShipName = rcdC!FirstName & " " & _
            rcdC!LastName
53        rcdO!ShipAddress = rcdC!Address
54        rcdO!ShipCity = rcdC!City
55        rcdO!ShipStateOrProvince = rcdC!StateOrProvince
56        rcdO!ShipPostalCode = rcdC!PostalCode
57        rcdO!ShipCountry = rcdC!Country
58        rcdO!ShipPhoneNumber = rcdC!PhoneNumber
59        rcdO!PayBy = rcdC!PayBy
60        rcdO!CCNumber = rcdC!CCNumber
61        rcdO!Printed = True
          ' Save the generated order number for detail
          ' lines
62        lngOrderID = rcdO!OrderID
          ' Add the master order row
63        rcdO.Update

          ' Calculate number of books for this order
64        intBooksThisOrder = _
            Int((intNumBooks * Rnd) + 1)
          ' Randomly grab a book record
65        intBook = Int(intCountBooks * Rnd)
66        rcdB.MoveFirst
67        If intBook > 0 Then rcdB.Move intBook
          ' Calculate the "jump" interval to the next
          ' book using integer divide here to always get
          ' a truncated result
68        intBookIncr = intCountBooks \ intBooksThisOrder
          ' Make sure result is at least 1
69        If intBookIncr = 0 Then intBookIncr = 1
          ' Loop to add books
70        For intOD = 1 To intBooksThisOrder
            ' Add a detail row
71          rcdOD.AddNew
```

(continued)

```
72              rcdOD!OrderID = lngOrderID
73 TryAgain:
74              rcdOD!ISBNNumber = rcdB!ISBNNumber
75              rcdOD!Quantity = _
                  Int((intNumCopies * Rnd) + 1)
                ' Set max possible discount based on quantity
76              Select Case rcdOD!Quantity
77                Case Is < 5
78                  rcdOD!Discount = 0
79                Case Is < 11
80                  rcdOD!Discount = 0.05
81                Case Is < 21
82                  rcdOD!Discount = 0.1
83                Case Else
84                  rcdOD!Discount = 0.15
85              End Select
                ' Set a specific trap for duplicate record
86              On Error Resume Next
87              rcdOD.Update
88              If Err <> 0 Then
89                If Err <> -2147217887 Then GoTo BailOut
                  ' Ooops -- we must have looped around --
                  ' ... move one more to avoid the duplicate
                  ' and go try again
90                rcdB.MoveNext
91                If rcdB.EOF Then rcdB.MoveFirst
92                On Error GoTo BailOut
93                GoTo TryAgain
94              End If
                ' Reset the generic error trap
95              On Error GoTo BailOut
                ' Skip forward to "next" book
96              rcdB.Move intBookIncr
                ' If bounced past the end, then start over
                '  with first book
97              If rcdB.EOF Then rcdB.MoveFirst
98            Next intOD
99          Next intO
            ' Update the status bar
100        varRtn = SysCmd(acSysCmdUpdateMeter, _
              Int(varCurrentDate - varBeginDate))
          ' Loop to the next date value
101      Next varCurrentDate
        ' Done - commit all updates
102      cn.CommitTrans
        ' Clear the status bar
103      varRtn = SysCmd(acSysCmdClearStatus)
        ' Done with error trapping, too
104      On Error GoTo 0
        ' Be nice and close everything up
105      rcdO.Close
```

```
106    rcdOD.Close
107    rcdB.Close
108    rcdC.Close
       ' Turn off the hourglass
109    DoCmd.Hourglass False
110    DoCmd.Close acForm, Me.Name
111    Exit Sub

112 BailOut:
113    MsgBox "Unexpected error: " & Err & ", " & Error
114    cn.RollbackTrans
       ' Turn off the hourglass
115    DoCmd.Hourglass False
116    varRtn = SysCmd(acSysCmdClearStatus)
117    Exit Sub

118 End Sub
```

Table 22-5 lists the statement line numbers and explains the code on each line in the preceding Visual Basic code example.

TABLE 22-5.   Explanation of Example to "Sell" Books

Line	Explanation
1	Declares the beginning of the subroutine. The subroutine has no arguments.
2	Declares local variables for a Connection object, a Recordset object for Orders, and a Recordset object for Order Details.
3	Declares local variables for a Recordset object for Customers and a Recordset object for Books.
4	Declares local variables for a Variant that is used to store the beginning date you entered on the form, an Integer for number of days, and another Variant to hold the "current" date value within the loop that builds orders.
5	Declares local variables for an Integer to hold the maximum number of orders from the form, an Integer for the maximum number of books per order, and an Integer for the maximum number of copies per book.
6	Declares local Integer variables to hold the current number of customers in the database and the current number of books that aren't out of print.
7	Declares local Integer variables to hold the result of a randomizer calculation for number of orders to be generated for the current day and number of books to be generated for the current order.
8	Declares local Integer variables to control the record generation loops for Orders and Order details and a random offset for the Customer for the current order.

(continued)

TABLE 22-5. *continued*

Line	Explanation
9	Declares local Integer variables to hold the random offset to the first book and a random increment to loop to the "next" book to sell.
10	Declares a local Long Integer variable to hold the number of the current order just added and a local Variant to receive the return value from some system function calls.
11	You can begin a comment anywhere on a statement line by preceding the comment with a single quotation mark. You can also create a comment statement using the Rem statement.
12–16	Initialize some of the local variables declared above with values from the form. Since this code is running in the form module, you can refer to the form using the shorthand "Me" object instead of "Forms!zfrmSellBooks". It's more efficient to use declared variables within Visual Basic rather than references to the controls on the form.
17	Initializes the built-in randomizer. Executing a Randomize statement with no arguments uses the current system clock as the "seed" value. This means you will get different results every time you run this subroutine even though you use the same input values.
18	Initializes the local connection object by setting it to the CurrentProject.Connection object. You must use a Set statement to initialize an object variable not declared as New.
19	Opens a recordset on tblOrders that we'll use to append new rows.
20	Opens a recordset on tblOrderDetails that we'll use to append new rows.
21	Opens a recordset on the tblCustomer table.
22	Opens a recordset on a query statement that retrieves only books that are in print.
23	Moves to the last row in the Customer recordset to get an accurate record count. You could also retrieve the RecordCount property directly from the table, which might be more efficient.
24	Sets a variable equal to the number of records in the Customer recordset.
25	Checks to be sure there are some customers in the database.
26	Uses the MsgBox statement to tell you if there are no customers. The code will halt here until you dismiss the message box by clicking the OK button.
27	Exits the subroutine since we found a problem. This also closes the open recordsets.
28	End If statement that matches the If on line 25.
29	Moves to the last row in the Books recordset to get an accurate record count.
30	Sets a variable equal to the number of records in the Books recordset.
31	Checks to be sure there are some books in the database.
32	Uses the MsgBox statement to tell you if there are no books.

TABLE 22-5. *continued*

Line	Explanation
33	Exits the subroutine since we found a problem.
34	End If statement that matches the If on line 31.
35	Checks to be sure the number of books available to sell is at least as large as the maximum books per order that you specified.
36	Uses the MsgBox statement to tell you if there are insufficient books.
37	Exits the subroutine since we found a problem.
38	End If statement that matches the If on line 35.
39	Sets an error trap that will branch to the BailOut label on line 112 if an error is raised.
40	Starts a database transaction. This ensures that either all orders are generated or none are saved if an error occurs. Statements within a transaction are treated as a single unit. Changes to data are saved only if the transaction completes successfully with a CommitTrans method. Using transactions when you're updating records can speed performance by reducing disk access.
41	Turns the mouse pointer into an hourglass to let you know the transaction is underway and may take a while. You could also set the Screen.MousePointer property to 11 (busy).
42	Calls the built-in SysCmd function to open a progress meter on the status bar. The meter will show percentages based on the total number of days requested. Statement number 100 updates the meter at the end of creating orders for each day.
43	Begins the main outer loop to create orders, starting with the first day, incrementing by one until we reach the start date plus number of days. This works because the integer portion of a date/time variable is the day number. The code uses varCurrentDate within the loop to set the order date.
44	Calls the Rnd function (which returns a Single value greater than or equal to zero but less than one). This value is then used to generate a random integer between 1 and the maximum number of orders per day.
45	Generates orders based on the random number calculated in line 44.
46	Uses the AddNew method of the orders recordset to start a new row.
47	Calculates a random offset into the customers recordset to find a customer for this order.
48	Uses the MoveFirst method of the customer recordset to move to the first customer record.
49	If the random calculation in line 47 generated an offset greater than zero, uses the Move method of the customer recordset to move forward that number of rows.
50–61	Initializes fields in the new row in the Orders table using the date loop variable and data from the Customers recordset.

(continued)

TABLE 22-5. *continued*

Line	Explanation
62	Saves the value of the tblOrders recordset's OrderID field for use in generating related order detail rows. Since the primary key of the tblOrders table is an AutoNumber, Access sets the next available value when the code makes any assignment to a field in the new record.
63	Uses the Update method of the orders recordset to save the new row. Congratulations! You've just created your first new record in the database using Visual Basic code.
64	Calculates a random number for the number of books to place in this order.
65	Computes a random offset into the books recordset as a starting point, based on the random maximum number of books just calculated.
66	Moves to the first row in the books recordset.
67	Checks the offset just calculated, and moves forward if it's greater than zero.
68	Uses an integer divide to calculate a jump forward on each loop based on the total number available divided by the number we want for this order.
69	Makes sure the jump forward is at least 1.
70	Starts the loop to add order detail rows.
71	Uses AddNew to set up a new row in the order details recordset.
72–85	Initializes the order details fields based on the saved OrderID and the fields from the current book row. The Select Case…End Select sequence generates a valid discount based on the randomly generated quantity of books for this order details line.
86	Sets a local error trap to check for a duplicate record error code. We can sometimes get a duplicate ISBNNumber for this order because we loop around at the end of the recordset if we fall off the end. (See statements 68, 96, and 97.) This statement lets us avoid this error.
87	Attempts to insert the new order detail row using Update.
88	If we had an error, the Err system variable will not equal zero.
89	Checks whether the error was an ADO duplicate record error (-2147217887).
90	We had a duplicate book in this order, so try moving forward one row to avoid it using a different book.
91	If moving forward one row got us to the end of the books recordset, then go back to the first one.
92	Resets the error trap.
93	The GoTo statement loops back up to try again with a different book. In general, use GoTo only in cases like this, where the only way to restart is with a specific branch after an error. Using lots of GoTo statements in code makes it hard to understand and debug.

TABLE 22-5. *continued*

Line	Explanation
94	End If statement that matches the If on line 88.
95	Resets the error trap outside the If nest started on line 88.
96	Uses the calculated skip forward value to move to another book.
97	If we fell off the end, then goes back to the first one. (This means the first book may show up in orders slightly more often than the others, but it makes the code simpler!)
98	Next statement that closes the For statement in line 70.
99	Next statement that closes the For statement in line 45.
100	Calls the built-in SysCmd function to update the status bar progress meter based on the number of days processed thus far.
101	Next statement that closes the For statement in line 43.
102	Commits all the updates—everything finished successfully.
103	Calls SysCmd one last time to clear the status bar.
104	Turns off error trapping.
106–108	Closes all open recordsets.
109	Restores the mouse pointer.
110	Closes the form we're running in—we're all done.
111	Exits just before the error handling code.
112	Label that indicates the start of the error handling code.
113	Displays the error code (Err) and the current error message (Error).
114	Makes sure any updates started thus far aren't saved.
115	Resets the hourglass.
116	Clears the status bar.
117	Bails out! (Using an Exit statement here resets any pending errors.)
118	End of the subroutine.

A Procedure to Examine All Error Codes

In the Entertainment Scheduling database, I created a function that dynamically creates a new table and then inserts into the table (using DAO) a complete list of all the error codes used by Microsoft Access and the text of the error message associated with each error code. You can find a partial list of the error codes in Help, but the table in the

VI

Creating an Application

Entertainment Scheduling sample database provides the best way to see a list of all the error codes. You might find this table useful as you begin to create your own Visual Basic procedures and set error trapping in them.

The name of the function is CreateErrTable, and you can find it in the modExamples module. The function statements are listed below. You can execute this function by entering the following in the Immediate window.

```
? CreateErrTable
```

Again, I've added line numbers to some of the lines in this code listing so that you can follow along with the line-by-line explanations in the table that follows the listing.

```
1 Function CreateErrTable ()
2   ' Declare variables used in this function
3   Dim dbMyDatabase As DAO.Database, tblErrTable As _
      DAO.TableDef, fldMyField As DAO.Field
4   Dim rcdErrRecSet As DAO.Recordset, lngErrCode As _
      Long, intMsgRtn As Integer
5   Dim varReturnVal As Variant, varErrString As _
      Variant, ws As DAO.Workspace
    ' Create Errors table with Error Code and Error
    ' String fields
    ' Initialize the MyDatabase database variable
    ' to the current database
6   Set dbMyDatabase = CurrentDb
7   Set ws = DBEngine.Workspaces(0)
    ' Trap error if table doesn't exist
    ' Skip to next statement if an error occurs
8   On Error Resume Next
9   Set rcdErrRecSet = _
      dbMyDatabase.OpenRecordset("ErrTable")
10  Select Case Err   ' See whether error was raised
11    Case 0   ' No error--table must exist
12      On Error GoTo 0   ' Turn off error trapping
13      intMsgRtn = MsgBox("ErrTable already " & _
        "exists. Do you want to delete and " & _
        "rebuild all rows?", 52)
14      If intMsgRtn = 6 Then
          ' Reply was YES--delete rows and rebuild
          ' Run quick SQL to delete rows
15        dbMyDatabase.Execute_
          "DELETE * FROM ErrTable;", dbFailOnError
16      Else                  ' Reply was NO--done
17        rcdErrRecSet.Close   ' Close the table
18        Exit Function        ' And exit
19      End If
```

```
20      Case 3011, 3078            ' Couldn't find table,
                                   ' so build it
21        On Error GoTo 0   ' Turn off error trapping
          ' Create a new table to contain error rows
22        Set tblErrTable = _
            dbMyDatabase.CreateTableDef("ErrTable")
          ' Create a field in ErrTable to contain the
          ' error code
23        Set fldMyField = tblErrTable.CreateField( _
            "ErrorCode", dbLong)
          ' Append "ErrorCode" field to the fields
          ' collection in the new table definition
24        tblErrTable.Fields.Append fldMyField
          ' Create a field in ErrTable for the error
          ' description
25        Set fldMyField = _
            tblErrTable.CreateField("ErrorString", _
            dbText)
          ' Append "ErrorString" field to the fields
          ' collection in the new table definition
26        tblErrTable.Fields.Append fldMyField
          ' Append the new table to the TableDefs
          ' collection in the current database
27        dbMyDatabase.TableDefs.Append tblErrTable
          ' Set text field width to 5" (7200 twips)
          ' (calls sub procedure)
28        SetFieldProperty _
            tblErrTable![ErrorString], _
            "ColumnWidth", dbInteger, 7200
          ' Set recordset to Errors Table recordset
29        Set rcdErrRecSet = _
            dbMyDatabase.OpenRecordset("ErrTable")

30      Case Else
          ' Can't identify the error--write message
          ' and bail out
31        MsgBox "Unknown error in CreateErrTable " & _
            Err & ", " & Error$(Err), 16
32        Exit Function

33    End Select

      ' Initialize progress meter on the status bar
34    varReturnVal = SysCmd(acSysCmdInitMeter, _
        "Building Error Table", 32767)
      ' Turn on hourglass to show this might take
      ' a while
35    DoCmd.Hourglass True
```

(continued)

```
       ' Start a transaction to make it go fast
36     ws.BeginTrans

       ' Loop through Microsoft Access error codes,
       ' skipping codes that generate
       ' "Application-defined or object-define error"
       ' message
37     For lngErrCode = 1 To 32767
38       varErrString = AccessError(lngErrCode)
39       If Not IsNothing(varErrString) Then
40         If varErrString <> "Application-" & _
             "defined or object-defined error" Then
             ' Add each error code and string to
             ' Errors table
41           rcdErrRecSet.AddNew
42           rcdErrRecSet("ErrorCode") = lngErrCode
             ' Some error messages are longer
             ' than 255--truncate
43           rcdErrRecSet("ErrorString") = _
               Left(varErrString, 255)
44           rcdErrRecSet.Update
45         End If
46       End If
         ' Update the status meter
47       varReturnVal = SysCmd(acSysCmdUpdateMeter, _
           lngErrCode)
         ' Process next error code
48     Next lngErrCode

49     ws.CommitTrans

       ' Close recordset
50     rcdErrRecSet.Close
       ' Turn off the hourglass--we're done
51     DoCmd.Hourglass False
       ' And reset the status bar
52     varReturnVal = SysCmd(acSysCmdClearStatus)
       ' Select new table in the Database window
       ' to refresh the list
53     DoCmd.SelectObject acTable, "ErrTable", True
       ' Open a confirmation dialog box
54     MsgBox "Errors table created."
55 End Function
```

Table 22-6 lists the statement line numbers and explains the code on each line in the preceding Visual Basic code example.

TABLE 22-6.   Explanation of Example to Examine Error Codes

Line	Explanation
1	Declares the beginning of the function. The function has no arguments.
2	You can begin a comment anywhere on a statement line by preceding the comment with a single quotation mark. You can also create a comment statement using the Rem statement.
3	Declares local variables for a Database object, a TableDef object, and a Field object.
4	Declares local variables for a Recordset object, a Long Integer, and an Integer.
5	Declares local variables for a Variant that is used to accept the return value from the SysCmd function, a Variant that is used to accept the error string returned by the AccessError function, and a Workspace object.
6	Initializes the Database object variable by setting it to the current database.
7	Initializes the Workspace object by setting it to the current workspace.
8	Enables error trapping but executes the next statement if an error occurs.
9	Initializes the Recordset object variable by attempting to open the ErrTable table. If the table does not exist, this generates an error.
10	Calls the Err function to see whether an error occurred. The following Case statements check the particular error values that interest us.
11	The first Case statement that tests for an Err value of 0, indicating no error occurred. If no error occurred, the table already existed and has opened successfully.
12	Turns off error trapping because we don't expect any more errors.
13	Uses the MsgBox function to ask whether you want to clear and rebuild all rows in the existing table. The value 52 asks for an exclamation-point Warning icon (48) and Yes/No buttons (4). The statement assigns the value returned by MsgBox so that we can test it on the next line.
14	If you click Yes, MsgBox returns the value 6.
15	Runs a simple SQL statement to delete all the rows in the error table.
16	Else clause that goes with the If statement on line 14.
17	Closes the table if the table exists and you clicked the No button on line 13.
18	Exits the function.
19	End If statement that goes with the If statement on line 14.
20	Second Case statement. Error code 3011 is "object not found."
21	Turns off error trapping because we don't expect any more errors.

(continued)

VI

Creating an Application

TABLE 22-6. *continued*

Line	Explanation
22	Uses the CreateTableDef method on the database to start a new table definition. This is the same as clicking the Tables button in the Database window and then clicking the New button.
23	Uses the CreateField method on the new table to create the first field object—a long integer named ErrorCode.
24	Appends the first new field to the Fields collection of the new Table object.
25	Uses the CreateField method to create the second field—a text field named ErrorString.
26	Appends the second new field to the Fields collection of the new Table object.
27	Saves the new table definition by appending it to the TableDefs collection of the Database object. If you were to halt the code at this point and repaint the Database window, you would find the new ErrTable listed.
28	Calls the SetFieldProperty subroutine in this module to set the column width of the ErrorString field to 7200 twips (5 inches). This ensures that you can see most of the error text when you open the table in Datasheet view.
29	Opens a recordset by using the OpenRecordset method on the table.
30	This Case statement traps all other errors.
31	Shows a message box with the error number and the error message.
32	Exits the function after an unknown error.
33	End Select statement that completes the Select Case statement on line 10.
34	Calls the SysCmd function to place a "building table" message on the status bar and initializes a progress meter. The CreateErrTable function will look at 32,767 different error codes.
35	Turns the mouse pointer into an hourglass to indicate that this procedure will take a few seconds.
36	Uses the BeginTrans method of the Workspace object to start a transaction. Statements within a transaction are treated as a single unit. Changes to data are saved only if the transaction completes successfully with a CommitTrans method. Using transactions when you're updating records can speed performance by reducing disk access.
37	Starts a For loop to check each error code from 1 through 32,767.
38	Assigns the error text returned by the AccessError function to the variable varErrString.
39	Calls the IsNothing function in the modUtility module of the sample database to test whether the text returned is blank. We don't want blank rows, so don't add a row if the AccessError function for the current error code returns a blank string.

TABLE 22-6. *continued*

Line	Explanation
40	Lots of error codes are defined as "Application-defined or object-defined error." We don't want any of these, so this statement adds a row only if the AccessError function for the current error code doesn't return this string.
41	Uses the AddNew method to start a new row in the table.
42	Sets the ErrorCode field equal to the current error code.
43	Some error messages are very long. We want to save only the first 255 characters, so sets the ErrorString field equal to the first 255 characters of error text. The text is stored in the varErrString variable.
44	Uses the Update method to save the new row.
45	End If statement that completes the If statement on line 40.
46	End If statement that completes the If statement on line 39.
47	After handling each error code, updates the progress meter on the status bar to show how far we've gotten.
48	Next statement that completes the For loop begun on line 37. Visual Basic increments lngErrCode by 1 and executes the For loop again until lngErrCode is greater than 32,767.
49	CommitTrans method that completes the transaction begun on line 36.
50	After looping through all possible error codes, closes the table.
51	Changes the mouse pointer back to normal.
52	Clears the status bar.
53	Puts the focus on the ErrTable table in the Database window.
54	Displays a message box confirming that the function has completed.
55	End of the function.

 **NOTE**   You can find the ADO equivalent of the above example in the modExamples module in the Microsoft Press Books sample database.

You should now have a basic understanding of how to create functions and subroutines using Visual Basic. In the final chapters of this book, you'll use what you've learned to complete major parts of the Microsoft Press Books and Entertainment Scheduling applications.

VI

Creating an Application

Automating Your Application with Visual Basic

N ow that you've learned the fundamentals of using Microsoft Visual Basic, it's time to put this knowledge into practice. In this chapter, you'll learn how to automate many of the tasks you saw in Chapter 21, "Automating Your Application with Macros," but this time you'll use Visual Basic in form modules.

You can find dozens of examples of automation in the Microsoft Press Books, Entertainment Scheduling, and Wedding List – Visual Basic sample databases. As you explore the databases, whenever you see something interesting, open the form or report in Design view and take a look at the Visual Basic code behind the form or report. This chapter walks you through a few of the more interesting examples in these databases.

Assisting Data Entry

You can do a lot to help make sure the user of your application enters correct data by defining default values, input masks, and validation rules. But what can you do if the default values come from a related table? What can you do if the input mask should change depending on the value in a related field? How can you assist a user if they need to enter a value that's not in the row source of a combo box? You can find the answers to these questions in the following sections.

Filling In Related Data

If you remember from Chapter 4, "Designing Your Database Application," the tblContracts table in the Entertainment Scheduling database has fields that duplicate the "current" data from the related tblGroups record when a contract is created. Similarly, the tblOrders table in the Microsoft Press Books database has the customer name and address information that's used as the "default" data for the shipping fields. When you're working in either of these databases and creating a new contract or order, you shouldn't have to manually enter this "default" information from one table to another. Unfortunately, the DefaultValue property can't refer to a field in another table. However, it's easy to write code in your data-entry forms to take care of this.

Let's look at the Contracts form in the Entertainment Scheduling database. Start by opening the sample database and allowing the application to start. Click the Contracts button on the main switchboard form, and then click Edit All in the Select Contracts window to open the form. Click the Add New button on the form to start a brand new contract record, as shown in Figure 23-1.

FIGURE 23-1.

Starting a new contract record in the Entertainment Scheduling database.

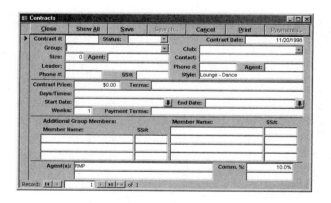

When you choose a new group on this form, you would like all the related "point in time" data that needs to be stored with the contract (leader name, phone number, group size, group members, and payment terms) to be copied from the selected group record. If some of the group members will be different for this particular engagement, it's a simple matter to change the information in the new record. If the basic information is correct, you avoid potential errors due to rekeying. Likewise, when you choose a club for the contract, you would like the current manager name, phone number, and usual booking hours to be copied. Let's try this by choosing a group. In the contract you just started, choose Bucky And The Fullerenes from the Group list. You should see the group size, agent code, leader name, leader phone number, group members, and payment terms "magically" appear on the form, as shown in Figure 23-2.

FIGURE 23-2.

Default group information copied to a new contract when a group has been selected.

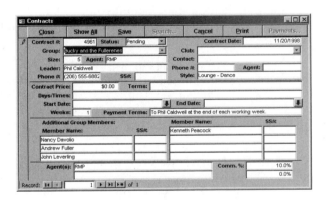

To make this work, you must have the fields from the related Group and Club records available in the record source of the form. You learned how to do this in Chapter 15, "Advanced Form Design," when you saw how to build a "many-to-one" form that allows you to edit data in the table on the "many" side of a relationship (in this case, Contracts) but show related data from the table on the "one" side (in this case, both Groups and Clubs). For this example, you won't display fields from the "one" side tables on the form; however, you need to be able to copy values from these fields into related fields in the contract using Visual Basic code. If you look at the query that is the record source of the frmContracts form, you'll see that it includes both the tblClubs and tblGroups tables, even though the main purpose is to edit rows in tblContracts. You can see qryContracts in Figure 23-3 on the next page. Note that many of the fields from the tblGroups table have been given alias names to make it easy to reference them independently of the similarly named fields in the tblContracts table.

FIGURE 23-3.

The record source for frmContracts that includes two tables on the "one" side of the relationship.

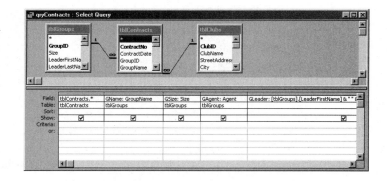

To fill in the Group information, you need an event procedure that runs as soon as the GroupID combo box is updated. Here's the sample code that does this.

```
Private Sub GroupID_AfterUpdate()
    GroupIDSetValue
    ' Make sure club data is filled in
    If Not IsNothing(Me!ClubID) Then ClubIDSetValue
End Sub

Private Sub GroupIDSetValue()
    ' Called by both Group and Club ID After Update
    Me!GroupName = Me!GName
    Me!Size = Me!GSize
    Me!GroupAgent = Me!GAgent
    Me!Leader = Me!GLeader
    Me!LeaderHomePhone = Me!HomePhone
    Me!LeaderSS = Me!GLeaderSS
    Me!LeaderWorkPhone = Me!WorkPhone
    Me!Member2 = Me!GMember2
    Me![Member2SS#] = Me!Member2SS
    Me!Member3 = Me!GMember3
    Me![Member3SS#] = Me!Member3SS
    Me!Member4 = Me!GMember4
    Me![Member4SS#] = Me!Member4SS
    Me!Member5 = Me!GMember5
    Me![Member5SS#] = Me!Member5SS
    Me!Member6 = Me!GMember6
    Me![Member6SS#] = Me!Member6SS
    Me!Member7 = Me!GMember7
    Me![Member7SS#] = Me!Member7SS
    Me!Member8 = Me!GMember8
    Me![Member8SS#] = Me!Member8SS
    Me!PaymentTerms = "To " & Me!Leader & _
        " at the end of each working week."
End Sub
```

The AfterUpdate event procedure first calls a sub procedure named GroupIDSetValue, also shown. The procedure then checks to see whether a value is set in the ClubID combo box. If the ClubID has a value, the procedure calls the ClubIDSetValue sub procedure to make sure club information is also copied. I know you're thinking, "If a ClubID is already set, won't the ClubID's AfterUpdate event have already filled in the club information?" There's some additional code in the form's Current event to try to help you even more. If, when you start a new contract, you have either the frmClubs or frmGroups form (or both) open, the form's Current event procedure sets the default value of ClubID and/or GroupID for you. Setting the default value doesn't cause Access to start creating the new record; that doesn't happen until you set some other value somewhere on the new row. If, however, the default value is set for ClubID and you choose a GroupID on a new record, Access sets the ClubID value but does *not* trigger the AfterUpdate event. So this extra test in both the ClubID and GroupID AfterUpdate procedures makes sure they both copy default values automatically whenever either one is set.

If you want to test how this works, open the Clubs form and select a club for which you want to book a new contract. Click the New Contract button on the Clubs form to open the Contracts form on a new record. You'll notice that the club name appears on the form, but none of the related information is set yet. Pick a group for the contract, and you should see default information pasted in for both the club and the group. As you can imagine, this little bit of code saves Ray McCann lots of keystrokes.

Setting a Custom Input Mask

For this next example, switch to the Microsoft Press Books sample database. Open the database and let the application start, sign on (the password for all the protected accounts is "password"), click the Orders button on the main switchboard, and then click one of the Review Open Orders buttons (button 2 or button 5) in the Order Options dialog box. I loaded at least one "open" (not printed) order for every customer, which you can edit if you're signed on as that customer. If you've already printed this order, click the Add New button on the Orders form to start a new order.

As you might know, the major credit card companies use different patterns and numbers of digits for their card numbers. If you're working on an order entry form that has a field for a credit card number, it would be nice to have an input mask on that field to help enter the number correctly. If you've ever wondered why you're asked what type of credit card you'll be using when you place an order on the phone, it could be that the seller is using an application with a pattern-matching feature like this sample.

To see how this works, choose Cash as the payment method for the order. This hides and clears the credit card field. Next choose Visa as the payment type. Click in the Credit Card # text box. Your screen should now look something like Figure 23-4. Tab to the Credit Card field, and you should see an input mask that is a series of four sets of four spaces separated by dashes, which is the pattern for this type of credit card.

FIGURE 23-4.

The application has set an appropriate input mask for a Visa credit card.

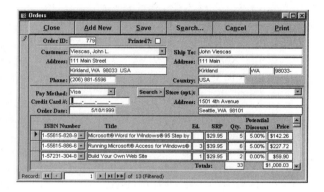

Next click the Pay Method combo box again, and choose American Express. When you tab to the Credit Card field and begin typing, you'll see the four-six-five digit pattern needed for that type of credit card, as shown in Figure 23-5.

FIGURE 23-5.

The input mask for a credit card has changed to match the American Express pattern.

As you might have guessed, an event procedure runs in the AfterUpdate event of the PayBy combo box. Here's the code.

```
Private Sub PayBy_AfterUpdate()
    ' Reveal CCNumber and set Input Mask based
    '    on payment method
    Select Case Me!PayBy
        Case 1, 2
            Me!CCNumber = Null
            Me!CCNumber.Visible = False
        Case 3
```

```
                    Me!CCNumber.Visible = True
                    Me!CCNumber.InputMask = _
                        "0000\-000000\-00000;0;_"
                Case Else
                    Me!CCNumber.Visible = True
                    Me!CCNumber.InputMask = _
                        "0000\-0000\-0000\-0000;0;_"
            End Select
        End Sub
```

As you can see, if the payment method is Cash or Check (codes 1 or 2), the procedure clears the credit card number and hides the text box for editing it. If PayBy is 3 (American Express), the procedure checks that the CCNumber field is visible and sets its Input Mask property to the special pattern for that credit card. In all other cases, the Input Mask is set to the more common four-four-four-four pattern. If you take a look at the form's Current event procedure, you'll also see code to hide or show the CCNumber text box, based on what's in PayBy, as you move from order to order.

Handling the "NotInList" Event

In almost every data entry form you'll ever build, you'll need to provide a way for the user to set the foreign key of the edited record on the "many" side of a relationship to point back to the correct "one" side record—for example, to set the CustomerID in an Order table or the AuthorID in the Book-Author linking table. In the Microsoft Press Books database, the frmOrders form forces you to create new orders for the currently signed-on customer by setting the Default Value of the CustomerID for tblBooks. (You can find a NotInList event procedure for the CustomerID combo box in frmOrders, but it has no effect because the BeforeUpdate event forces you to use only the current CustomerID.)

Suppose you are one of the application data administrators at Microsoft Press. You need to add an author for a book, but the author isn't defined in the database yet. You don't want to find this out while editing the book information, have to stop what you're doing to add the author record, and then come back to the book form to enter the correct data again. It would be great to be able to add the author record without having to stop what you're doing in the book form.

To see how this works, either sign on to the application as me (Viescas, John L.; password is "password") or open the Immediate window (press Ctrl+G) and set the global gintIsAdmin variable to True. This flag gives you the authority to edit book and author information in the database by using the sample forms. Next open the frmBooks

VI

Creating an Application

form by clicking the Books button in the main switchboard, and then click the Edit All button in the Select Books dialog box. (Or simply open frmBooks from the Database window.) Click the Authors tab in the form to see the authors defined for any book.

In this case, I decided to give my son equal credit for helping me build the College.mdb sample database featured in *Running Microsoft Access 97*. I used the Book Search dialog box to find the book I wanted (more about how this dialog box works later in this chapter), clicked the Authors tab, and started to enter my son's name on a new record of the subform, as shown in Figure 23-6.

FIGURE 23-6.

Entering an author name for a book written by an author who isn't defined in the database.

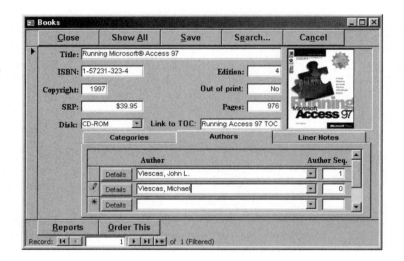

When you tab out of the Author field, what had been typed in the combo box was not in the list of records returned by the record source of the combo box. The NotInList event procedure defined for this combo box first confirms that you want to define a new author, as shown in Figure 23-7. (You might have mistyped the name of an existing author.)

FIGURE 23-7.

The NotInList procedure for the Author combo box responds with a confirmation message.

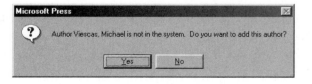

If you click Yes to confirm that you do want to add this author, the event procedure opens the frmAuthorAdd form in Dialog mode to let you enter the new data, as shown in Figure 23-8. Opening a form in Dialog mode forces the user to respond before the application resumes execution. You can see that the author name you entered has been "parsed" (last name and first name separated) and default values have been set for those fields. You still might change your mind at this point, so the data isn't actually set into the new record—that would require another AuthorID in the AutoNumber primary key of the tblAuthors table.

FIGURE 23-8.
The frmAuthorAdd form open and ready to define the missing author.

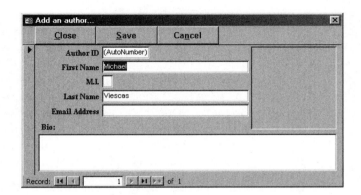

To see how this works, open the fsubBookAuthors form in Design view, click the AuthorID combo box, find the NotInList event in the field Properties list, and click the Build button to open the code. The code for the procedure is shown below.

```
Private Sub AuthorID_NotInList(NewData As String, _
    Response As Integer)
    Dim strAuth As String, strLast As String, _
        strFirst As String, intComma As Integer
    Dim intReturn As Integer, varName As Variant
    strAuth = NewData
    intComma = InStr(strAuth, ",")
    If intComma = 0 Then
        strLast = strAuth
    Else
        strLast = Left(strAuth, intComma - 1)
        strFirst = Mid(strAuth, intComma + 2)
    End If
    intReturn = MsgBox("Author " & strAuth & _
        " is not in the system." & _
        "   Do you want to add this author?", _
        vbQuestion + vbYesNo, "Microsoft Press")
    If intReturn = vbYes Then
        DoCmd.OpenForm FormName:="frmAuthorAdd", _
            DataMode:=acAdd, _
            WindowMode:=acDialog, _
            OpenArgs:=strAuth
```

(continued)

```
                             If IsNull(DLookup("AuthorID", _
                                 "tblAuthors", _
                                 "[LastName] = """ & _
                                 strLast & """")) Then
                                 Response = acDataErrContinue
                             Else
                                 Response = acDataErrAdded
                             End If
                             Exit Sub
                     End If
                     Response = acDataErrDisplay
             End Sub
```

As you can see, Access passes two parameters to the NotInList event. The first parameter (NewData) contains the string you typed in the combo box. You can set the value of the second parameter (Response) before you exit the sub procedure to tell Access what you want to do. You wouldn't have access to these parameters in a macro, so you can see that this event requires a Visual Basic procedure to handle it properly.

The procedure first uses the InStr built-in function to look for a comma in the string you typed. If it finds a comma, it assumes that what you typed to the left of the comma is the author last name and that everything to the right of the comma is the first name. Next the procedure uses the MsgBox function to ask whether you want to add this author to the database (the result shown in Figure 23-7). If you've ever looked at the MsgBox function help topic, you know that the second parameter is a number that's the sum of all the options you want. Fortunately, Visual Basic provides named constants for these options, so you don't have to remember the number codes. In this case, the procedure asks for a question mark icon and for the Yes and No buttons to be displayed.

If you respond Yes in the message box, the procedure opens the frmAuthorAdd form in Dialog mode and passes it the name you entered in the form's OpenArg property. Note the use of the named parameter syntax in the call to DoCmd.OpenForm to make it easy to set the parameters you want. You must open the form in Dialog mode. If you don't, your code will continue to run while the form opens. Whenever a dialog box form is open, Visual Basic code execution stops until the dialog box closes, which is critical in this case because you need the record to be saved before you can continue with other tests.

After the frmAuthorAdd form closes, the next statement calls the DLookUp function to verify that you really did add the author to the database. In this example, the test isn't very specific because it checks for only the author last name. That should work even if the addition of

Michael Viescas is canceled because an author with the last name of Viescas is already in the database, so the procedure sets the response to indicate that it thinks the missing record has been added. Access requeries the combo box and attempts a new match. This will fail if you didn't actually save a new matching row for Michael. If Access doesn't find a match, setting Response to acDataErrContinue avoids the extra Access error message. Finally, if you reply No in the message box shown in Figure 23-7, the procedure sets Response to acDataErrDisplay to tell Access to display its normal error message.

The other bit of "magic" happens in the Load event for the frmAuthorAdd form. The code is as follows.

```
Private Sub Form_Load()
    Dim strAuth As String, intComma As Integer
    ' Check for an open argument - exit if none
    If IsNothing(Me.OpenArgs) Then Exit Sub
    ' Parse out first and last names -
    '   set default values for a new row
    strAuth = Me.OpenArgs
    intComma = InStr(strAuth, ",")
    If intComma = 0 Then
        Me![LastName].DefaultValue = """" & _
            strAuth & """"
        Else
        Me![LastName].DefaultValue = """" & _
            Left(strAuth, intComma - 1) & """"
        Me![FirstName].DefaultValue = """" & _
            Mid(strAuth, intComma + 2) & """"
    End If
End Sub
```

If you remember, the AuthorID NotInList event procedure passes the original string entered as the OpenArgs parameter to the OpenForm method. This sets the OpenArgs property of the form being opened. The Form_Load procedure checks that property and again parses the first and last name fields and uses them to set the DefaultValue property of the appropriate text boxes. It could simply set the field values, but that would cause Access to create a new record and use up another AutoNumber value in the AuthorID, even if the user immediately cancels the new record. Note that you can't merely set the DefaultValue property to the string value. This property is a string, but Access treats the property's value as an expression to evaluate. If you set *Me![LastName].DefaultValue = "Viescas"*, Access looks for a command or subprocedure called *Viescas*. There isn't one, so you'll end up with a #Name error in the text box. The code adds quotation marks around the name, so Access sees a string expression in the property (*"Viescas"* instead of *Viescas*) and returns a correct value.

Controlling Tabbing on a Multiple-Page Form

In Chapter 15, "Advanced Form Design," you learned how to create a multiple-page form as one way to handle displaying more data than will fit on one "page" of a form on your computer screen. You also learned how to control simple tabbing on the form by setting the form's Cycle property to Current Page. One disadvantage of this approach is that the user can no longer use Tab or Shift+Tab to move to other pages or other records. They must use the Page Up and Page Down keys or the record selector buttons to do that. You can set Cycle to All Records to give the user this capability again, but some strange things happen if you don't add code to handle page alignment.

To see what happens, open frmAuthorsBadTab in the Microsoft Press Books sample database from the Database window. Move to the last record using the record selector buttons, and press Page Down to move to the Bio field for the last author. Next press Shift+Tab once (back tab). Your screen should look something like Figure 23-9.

FIGURE 23-9.

The form page doesn't align correctly when you back-tab from the Bio field in frmAuthorsBadTab.

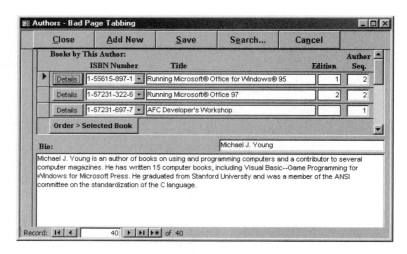

If you leave the Cycle property set to All Records or Current Record, tabbing across page boundaries causes misalignment unless you add some code to fix it. What happens is that Access moves the form display only far enough to show the control you just tabbed to. (In this example, you're tabbing to the fsubAuthorBooks subform control.)

To allow tabbing across a page boundary while providing correct page alignment, you need event procedures in the Enter event for the first and last controls on each page that can receive the focus. In this case, the second page of the frmAuthors form has only one control that can receive the focus (Bio), so you'll find three event procedures defined in the module for this form. Here they are.

```
Private Sub AuthorID_Enter()
    ' The following GoToPage realigns the page
    ' when you tab forward from the previous
    ' record. It has no effect otherwise.
    Me.GoToPage 1
End Sub

Private Sub Bio_Enter()
    ' The following GoToPage realigns the page
    ' when you tab backward from the next record.
    ' It is also activated when you press PgDn
    ' in the subform control on the previous page.
    ' The KeyDown event puts the focus here, and
    ' this event procedure aligns the page
    ' correctly.
    Me.GoToPage 2
End Sub

Private Sub fsubAuthorBooks_Enter()
    On Error Resume Next
    ' If tabbing into fsubAuthorBooks from the
    ' control named "Bio".
    If Screen.PreviousControl.Name = "Bio" Then
        ' Do some funny stuff to align the "page"
        ' correctly.
        Application.Echo False
        Me!AuthorID.SetFocus
        Me.GoToPage 1
        Me!fsubAuthorBooks.SetFocus
        Application.Echo True
    End If
End Sub
```

You can test this code by opening the frmAuthors form to display multiple records and then tabbing around on the form. Remember from Chapter 12, "Form Basics," that to tab out of a subform control you have to hold down the Ctrl key while pressing either Tab (forward) or Shift+Tab (backward). As you can see, the code for the AuthorID and Bio text boxes is really very simple. In the case of AuthorID, you don't care which direction you came from—you simply need to be sure that the form is set to the top of page 1 by using the GoToPage method on the form. For Bio, since it's the only control on the page that can receive the focus, a simple GoToPage works well here as well.

The fsubAuthorBooks control is another matter. First, because it's a subform control, focus is actually on the form inside the control, so using the GoToPage method will cause an error. You need to turn off screen flashing, move the focus to a control on page 1 of the main form (because you're doing this in code, moving to a control won't fire the Enter event for that control), align on page 1, and then put the focus back in the subform. This is a lot of work if you're already on page 1, so there's also a test to see if, in fact, you just tabbed to fsubAuthorBooks from the Bio control on page 2—a handy use of the PreviousControl property of the Screen object. Only if you just tabbed from page 2 do you need to do the fancy stuff to align page 1.

Automating Data Selection

One of the most common tasks to automate in a database application is filtering data. Particularly when a database contains thousands of records, users will rarely need to work with more than a few records at a time. If your edit forms always display all of the records, performance can suffer greatly. So it's a good idea to enable the user to easily specify a subset of records. This section examines three ways to do this.

Working with a Multiple-Selection List Box

You work with list boxes all the time in Microsoft Windows and in Microsoft Access. For example, the file list in Windows Explorer is a list box, and the List view in the Access Database window is a list box. In the Database window, you can select only one object from the list at a time. If you click a different object, the previous object is deselected. This is a simple list box. In Windows Explorer, you can select one file, select multiple noncontiguous files by holding down the Ctrl key and clicking, or select a range of files by holding down the Shift key and clicking.

Suppose a customer using the Microsoft Press Books database is interested in looking at the details for several books at one time but will rarely want to look at the entire list. If you open the application and click the Books button on the main switchboard form, the application opens the frmBookList form.

As shown in Figure 23-10, the frmBooklist form contains a multiple-selection list box. (If you're signed on as an admin user, you'll see Edit buttons on this form; otherwise, the form displays View buttons.)

FIGURE 23-10.

Selecting multiple book records to edit.

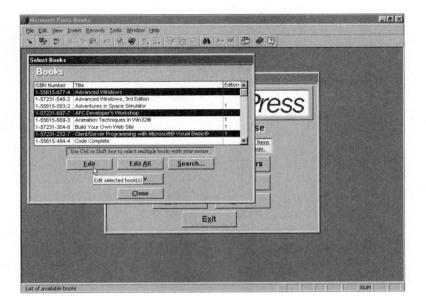

In this list box, the books are shown in alphabetic order by title, and the list is bound to the book ISBN number field in the underlying table. You can move the highlight up or down by using the arrow keys. (In the frmAuthorList form, the author names are displayed in the first column by last name. You can type the first letter of an author last name to jump to the first author whose last name begins with that letter.) You can hold down the Shift key and use the arrow keys to extend the selection to multiple names. Finally, you can hold down either the Shift key or the Ctrl key and use the mouse to select multiple names.

Figure 23-10 shows three books selected using the Ctrl key and the mouse. When you click the Edit (or View) button, the application opens the frmBooks form with only the records you selected. As shown in Figure 23-11 on the next page, the caption to the right of the record number box indicates three available records and that the recordset is filtered.

To see how this works, you need to go behind the scenes of the frmBookList form. Click Exit on the main switchboard form to return

FIGURE 23-11.
Editing a selected
book record from the
filtered list of books.

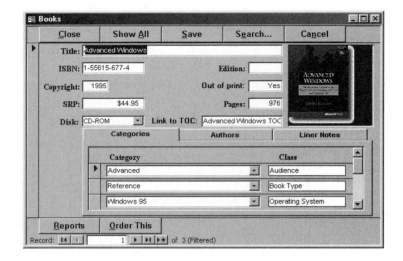

to the Database window. Select frmBookList, and open the form in
Design view, as shown in Figure 23-12. Click the list box control, and
open its property sheet to see how the list box is defined. The list box
uses three columns from the qryBooksForCombo query, displaying the
book ISBN number (the primary key that will provide a fast lookup) in
the first column, the book title in the second column, and the book
edition number in the third column. The key to this list box is that its
Multi Select property is set to Extended. Using the Extended setting
gives you the full Ctrl+click or Shift+click features that you see in most
list boxes in Windows. The default for this property is None, which
lets you select only one value at a time. You can set it to Simple if you
want to select multiple noncontiguous values using the mouse.

FIGURE 23-12.
The multiple-selection
list box on the
frmBookList form and
its property sheet.

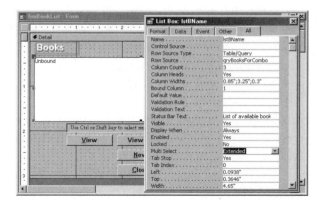

If you scroll down to the Event properties, you'll find an event procedure defined for On Dbl Click. The code for this event procedure (which is called when you double-click an item in the list box) runs only the cmdSome_Click procedure. Right-click the cmdSome command button (the one whose caption says *View*), and choose Build Event from the shortcut menu to jump to the cmdSome_Click procedure that does all the work, as shown below.

```
Private Sub cmdSome_Click()
    Dim strWhere As String, varItem As Variant
    ' If no items selected, then nothing to do
    If Me!lstBName.ItemsSelected.Count = 0 Then
        Exit Sub
    End If
    ' Loop through the items selected collection
    For Each varItem In Me!lstBName.ItemsSelected
        ' Grab the ISBN for each selected item
        strWhere = strWhere & Chr$(34) & _
            Me!lstBName.Column(0, varItem) & _
            Chr$(34) & ","
    Next varItem
    ' Throw away the extra comma on the IN string
    strWhere = Left$(strWhere, Len(strWhere) - 1)
    ' Open the books form filtered on the
    ' selected books
    gstrWhereBook = "[ISBNNumber] IN (" & _
        strWhere & ")"
    DoCmd.OpenForm FormName:="frmBooks", _
        WhereCondition:=gstrWhereBook
    ' Hide the Add New button, but show the
    ' Show All button
    Forms!frmBooks!cmdAddNew.Visible = False
    Forms!frmBooks!cmdShowAll.Visible = True
    DoCmd.Close acForm, Me.Name
End Sub
```

When you set the Multi Select property of a list box to something other than None, you can examine the control's ItemsSelected collection to determine what (if anything) is selected. In the cmdSome_Click procedure, the Visual Basic code first checks the Count property of the control's ItemsSelected collection to determine whether anything is selected. If the Count is 0, there's nothing to do, so the procedure exits.

The ItemsSelected collection is composed of variant values, each of which provides an index to a highlighted item in the list box. The For Each loop asks Visual Basic to loop through all the available variant values in the collection, one at a time. Within the loop, the code uses

VI

Creating an Application

the value of the variant to retrieve the ISBN number from the list. List boxes also have a Column property, and you can reference all the values in the list by using a statement such as

```
Me!ListBoxName.Column(ColumnNum, RowNum)
```

where *ListBoxName* is the name of your list box control, *ColumnNum* is the relative column number (the first column is 0, the second is 1, and so on), and *RowNum* is the relative row number (also starting at 0). The variant values in the ItemsSelected collection return the relative row number. This Visual Basic code uses column 0 and the values in the ItemsSelected collection to append each selected book ISBN number to a string variable, separated by commas. You'll recall from studying the IN predicate in Chapter 8, "Adding Power with Select Queries," and Chapter 11, "Advanced Query Design—SQL," that a list of values separated by commas is ideal for an IN clause.

After retrieving all of the book ISBN numbers, the next statement removes the trailing comma from the string. The final Where clause is saved in a global variable for later use (in the frmBookPrintParms form). The DoCmd.OpenForm command uses the resulting string of comma-separated values to create a filter clause as it opens the form. The last two statements set up the Add New and Show All buttons on the frmBooks form. Since you're looking at a filtered list, it doesn't necessarily make sense to be able to add new rows. (You can do that directly from the New button on the frmBookList form anyway if you're an admin user.) However, you might be interested in looking at all rows, so this code hides the Add New button and reveals the Show All button. If you look at the Form Header section of the frmBooks form in Design view, you'll find the Show All button stacked on top of the Add New button.

Providing a Custom Query By Form

Suppose you want to do a more complex search on the frmBooks form—using criteria such as price, author name, or book type rather than simply using book title. You could teach your users how to use the Filter By Form features to build the search, or you could use Filter By Form to easily construct multiple OR criteria on simple tests. But if you want to find, for example, all books that are about either Microsoft Access or Microsoft Excel, there's no way to construct this request using standard filtering features. The reason for this is when you define a filter for a subform (such as the Categories subform in frmBooks) using Filter By Form, you're filtering only the subform rows. You're not finding books that have only a matching subform row.

The only solution, then, is to provide a custom Query By Form that provides options to search on all the important fields and then build the Where clause to solve the category search problem using Visual Basic code. To start, open the Microsoft Press Books application. (If you have exited to the Database window, you can start the application by opening frmCopyright.) Sign on, click the Books button on the main switchboard form, and then click the Search button in the Select Books dialog box. You should see the frmBookSearch form, as shown in Figure 23-13.

FIGURE 23-13.

Using a custom Query By Form to perform a complex search.

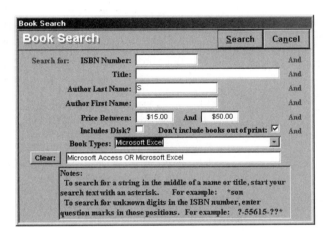

Try selecting authors whose last name begins with the letter *S*, books priced between $15 and $50, and books about Microsoft Access or Microsoft Excel (from the Book Types drop-down list). When you click the Search button, you should see the frmBooks form open, displaying four books.

To see how this works, you need to explore the design of the frmBookSearch form. Switch to the Database window, and open the form in Design view. You should see a window like that shown in Figure 23-14 on the next page. Notice that the form is not bound to any record source. The controls must be unbound so they can accept any criteria values that a user might enter.

VI

Creating an Application

FIGURE 23-14.

The frmBookSearch form in Design view.

Part of the secret of this form is the TypeList combo box and its AfterUpdate event. Whenever you select a new type classification in the combo box, the following event procedure executes.

```
Private Sub TypeList_AfterUpdate()
    ' Selected a new type code, so add it to
    ' the search list
    If IsNothing(Me!TypeCodes) Then
        Me!TypeCodes = Me!TypeList
        Me!Types = Me!TypeList.Column(0)
    Else
        Me!TypeCodes = Me!TypeCodes & _
            ", " & Me!TypeList
        Me!Types = Me!Types & " OR " & _
            Me!TypeList.Column(0)
    End If
End Sub
```

This code creates an IN clause that contains the matching type codes. Note that this code does not check to see whether you selected the same classification twice; you could add this feature to enhance the way the code works. This code stores the IN string in a hidden text box control on the form called TypeCodes. (Its Visible property is set to No.) To see how this works, select the TypeCodes control in the Object drop-down box on the Formatting toolbar, set its Visible property to Yes, and switch to Form view. When you select a new classification, you can see the contents of both controls get updated. Another approach would be to declare a Static string variable within the event procedure for storing the list of codes. If you do so, the variable has to be Static or it will be reset every time this procedure is called.

The bulk of the work happens when you click the Search button. The code for the event procedure for the Click event of the Search button is shown below. (I added a few comments to the code listed in the book to make it easier for you to identify the various segments of the code described after the code listing.)

```
Private Sub cmdSearch_Click()
    Dim db As DAO.Database, rcd As DAO.Recordset
    Dim lngCount As Long, intRtn As Integer, _
        strANameComp As String
    Dim intI As Integer, strISBN As String
    ' Search parameters entered (we hope)...
    ' Clear the global book filter string
    gstrWhereBook = ""
    ' .. and parse out a new one:
    If Not IsNothing(Me!ISBNNumber) Then
    ' **** Clean up the ISBN number
        strISBN = Me!ISBNNumber
        ' The ISBN has an input mask to help the
        ' user out, but they could enter all sorts
        ' of dashes and numbers. The following
        ' code does an additional "parse" to clean
        ' it up.
        ' First, replace all blanks in the ISBN with
        ' question marks
        intI = 1
        Do Until intI > Len(strISBN)
          If Mid$(strISBN, intI, 1) = " " Then
            If intI = 1 Then
              strISBN = "?" & Mid$(strISBN, 2)
            Else
              strISBN = Left$(strISBN, intI - 1) & _
                "?" & Mid$(strISBN, intI + 1)
            End If
          End If
          ' Look for dashes in the right/wrong places
          If intI = 2 Or intI = 8 Or intI = 12 Then
            ' A dash is OK in position 2, 8, or 12
            If Mid$(strISBN, intI, 1) <> "-" Then
              ' Move it down
              strISBN = Left$(strISBN, intI - 1) & _
                "?" & Mid$(strISBN, intI)
            End If
          Else
            ' Not position 2, 8, or 12, so should
            ' not be a dash
            If Mid$(strISBN, intI, 1) = "-" Then
              If intI = 1 Then
                strISBN = "?" & strISBN
              Else
                ' Watch out for too many dashes!
```

(continued)

```
                  If intI > 12 Then
                     ' Replace the dash
                     strISBN = Left$(strISBN, intI - 1) _
                        & "?" & Mid$(strISBN, intI + 1)
                  Else
                     ' Shove the dash down
                     strISBN = Left$(strISBN, intI - 1) _
                        & "?" & Mid$(strISBN, intI)
                  End If
               End If
            End If
         End If
         intI = intI + 1
      Loop
      Me!ISBNNumber = Left$(strISBN, 13)
      ' Result at this point should be a nice ISBN
      ' in the form ?-?????-???-? where the user
      ' may have specified digits for any one
      ' or more of the question marks.
      gstrWhereBook = "[ISBNNumber] LIKE " & _
         Chr$(34) & Me!ISBNNumber
      ' Add "*" on the end for good measure...
      If Right$(Me!ISBNNumber, 1) = "*" Then
         gstrWhereBook = gstrWhereBook & Chr$(34)
      Else
         gstrWhereBook = gstrWhereBook & _
            "*" & Chr$(34)
      End If
   End If

   ' **** Check for a Title
   If Not IsNothing(Me!Title) Then
      If IsNothing(gstrWhereBook) Then
         gstrWhereBook = "[Title] LIKE " & _
            Chr$(34) & Me!Title

      Else
         gstrWhereBook = gstrWhereBook & _
            " AND [Title] LIKE " & _
            Chr$(34) & Me!Title
      End If
      If Right$(Me!Title, 1) = "*" Then
         gstrWhereBook = gstrWhereBook & Chr$(34)
      Else
         gstrWhereBook = gstrWhereBook & _
            "*" & Chr$(34)
      End If
   End If

   ' **** Check for Author first name or last name
   If Not IsNothing(Me!LastName) Then
```

```
        strANameComp = "[LastName] LIKE " & _
          Chr$(34) & Me!LastName
        If Right$(Me!LastName, 1) = "*" Then
          strANameComp = strANameComp & Chr$(34)
        Else
          strANameComp = strANameComp & "*" & Chr$(34)
        End If
      End If

      If Not IsNothing(Me!FirstName) Then
        If IsNothing(strANameComp) Then
          strANameComp = "[FirstName] LIKE " & _
            Chr$(34) & Me!FirstName
        Else
          strANameComp = strANameComp & _
            " AND [FirstName] LIKE " & _
            Chr$(34) & Me!FirstName
        End If
        If Right$(Me!FirstName, 1) = "*" Then
          strANameComp = strANameComp & Chr$(34)
        Else
          strANameComp = strANameComp & "*" & Chr$(34)
        End If
      End If

      ' Did we build any author compares?
      If Not IsNothing(strANameComp) Then
        'Yes - build a special author subquery
        If IsNothing(gstrWhereBook) Then
          gstrWhereBook = "[ISBNNumber] IN " & _
            "(SELECT ISBNNumber FROM " & _
            "qryBookAuthors WHERE " & strANameComp & ")"
        Else
          gstrWhereBook = gstrWhereBook & _
          " AND [ISBNNumber] IN " & _
          "(SELECT ISBNNumber FROM  " & _
          "qryBookAuthors WHERE " & strANameComp & ")"
        End If
      End If

      ' **** Set up price comparisons
      If Not IsNothing(Me!LowPrice) Then
        If IsNothing(gstrWhereBook) Then
          gstrWhereBook = "[SuggPrice] >= " & _
            Me!LowPrice
        Else
          gstrWhereBook = gstrWhereBook & _
            " AND [SuggPrice] >= " & Me!LowPrice
        End If
      End If
```

(continued)

```
      If Not IsNothing(Me!HighPrice) Then
        If IsNothing(gstrWhereBook) Then
          gstrWhereBook = "[SuggPrice] <= " & _
            Me!HighPrice
        Else
          gstrWhereBook = gstrWhereBook & _
          " AND [SuggPrice] <= " & Me!HighPrice
        End If
      End If

      ' **** Set up "has disk" test
      If Me!Disk Then
        If IsNothing(gstrWhereBook) Then
          gstrWhereBook = "([Disk] Is Not Null)"
        Else
          gstrWhereBook = gstrWhereBook & _
              " AND ([Disk] Is Not Null)"
        End If
      End If

      ' **** Set up out of print Test
      If Me!OutOfPrint Then
        If IsNothing(gstrWhereBook) Then
          gstrWhereBook = "(Not [OutOfPrint])"
        Else
          gstrWhereBook = gstrWhereBook & _
            " AND (Not [OutOfPrint])"
        End If
      End If
      ' **** Build IN string for type codes
      If Not IsNothing(Me!TypeCodes) Then
        If IsNothing(gstrWhereBook) Then
          gstrWhereBook = "[ISBNNumber] IN " & _
            "(SELECT ISBNNumber FROM " & _
            "qryBookCategories WHERE " & _
            "CategoryID IN (" & Me!TypeCodes & "))"
        Else
          gstrWhereBook = gstrWhereBook & _
            " AND [ISBNNumber] IN " & _
            "(SELECT ISBNNumber FROM  " & _
            "qryBookCategories WHERE " & _
            "CategoryID IN (" & Me!TypeCodes & "))"
        End If
      End If

      ' If no criteria, then nothing to do!
      If IsNothing(gstrWhereBook) Then
        MsgBox "No criteria specified.", _
          vbExclamation, "Microsoft Press"
        Exit Sub
      End If
```

```
' **** Search based on the string we've built
' Hide myself and turn on Hourglass
Me.Visible = False
DoCmd.Hourglass True
If IsLoaded("frmBooks") Then
  ' If books form already open,
  ' then just filter it
  Forms!frmBooks.SetFocus
  DoCmd.ApplyFilter , gstrWhereBook
  If Forms!frmBooks.RecordsetClone.RecordCount _
     = 0 Then
    ' If no records found,
    ' reset the books form and try again ...
    DoCmd.Hourglass False
    MsgBox "No Books meet your criteria", _
       vbExclamation, "Microsoft Press"
    DoCmd.ShowAllRecords
    If gintIsAdmin Then
       Forms!frmBooks!cmdAddNew.Visible = True
    Else
       Forms!frmBooks!cmdAddNew.Visible = False
    End If
    Forms!frmBooks!cmdShowAll.Visible = False
    Me.Visible = True
    Exit Sub
  End If

  ' If we didn't search for categories,
  ' but did do a name search
  If IsNothing(Me!TypeCodes) And _
     (Not IsNothing(strANameComp)) Then
     ' Turn on the author display option
     Forms!frmBooks!tabDisplay = 1
  End If

  Forms!frmBooks!cmdAddNew.Visible = False
  Forms!frmBooks!cmdShowAll.Visible = True
  DoCmd.Hourglass False
Else  ' Matches the IsLoaded("frmBooks") test
  ' Do any books satisfy the WHERE clause?
  Set db = CurrentDb
  Set rcd = db.OpenRecordset( _
    "SELECT DISTINCTROW " & _
    "tblBooks.ISBNNumber " & _
    "FROM tblBooks " & _
    "WHERE " & gstrWhereBook & ";")
  ' If none found, then tell the user
  ' and make me visible to try again
```

(continued)

VI

Creating an Application

```
                  If rcd.RecordCount = 0 Then
                    DoCmd.Hourglass False
                    MsgBox "No Books meet your criteria", _
                      vbExclamation, "Microsoft Press"
                    gstrWhereBook = ""
                    Me.Visible = True
                    rcd.Close
                    Exit Sub
                  End If
                  ' Move to last row to get an accurate
                  ' record count
                  rcd.MoveLast
                  lngCount = rcd.RecordCount
                  DoCmd.Hourglass False
                  ' If more than 10 records matched, then ask if
                  ' the user wants to see only a summary
                  If lngCount > 10 Then
                    intRtn = MsgBox("More than 10 books meet " & _
                      "your criteria.  Click Yes to see a " & _
                      "summary list for all " & lngCount & _
                      " books found, " & _
                      "No to see complete data on all that " & _
                      "match, or Cancel to try again.", _
                      vbInformation + vbYesNoCancel, _
                      "Microsoft Press")
                    Select Case intRtn
                      Case vbCancel    ' Cancel - Try again
                        Me.Visible = True
                        Exit Sub
                      Case vbYes       ' Yes - show summary form
                        DoCmd.OpenForm _
                          FormName:="frmBookSummary", _
                          WhereCondition:=gstrWhereBook
                        DoCmd.Close acForm, Me.Name
                        Forms!frmBookSummary.SetFocus
                        Exit Sub
                    End Select
                  End If
                  ' Replied NO or not more than 10, show full
                  ' details
                  DoCmd.OpenForm FormName:="frmBooks", _
                    WhereCondition:=gstrWhereBook
                  Forms!frmBooks!cmdAddNew.Visible = False
                  Forms!frmBooks!cmdShowAll.Visible = True
                  If IsNothing(Me!TypeCodes) And _
                    (Not IsNothing(strANameComp)) Then
                      ' If not book categories, but did do a name
                      ' search, turn on the author display option
                      Forms!frmBooks!tabDisplay = 1
                  End If
                End If
              End If
```

```
            ' Close me, and we're done
            DoCmd.Close acForm, Me.Name
        End Sub
```

The first part of the procedure works with the data entered in the ISBNNumber field to make sure it has a correct format. Although there's an input mask defined for this field to help the user out, the mask has to be defined to allow the user to enter the "?" wildcard character anywhere in the string. This also lets them enter extra dashes and other characters. Also, since the text box is unbound, there's no easy way to limit the user to entering no more than 13 characters. (You could limit it by writing a KeyDown event procedure that throws away any keystrokes entered after the 13th position.) This code examines what was entered one character at a time. If it finds a dash in an inappropriate place, it shoves the text to the right and inserts a question mark wildcard. If it finds anything other than a dash in positions 2, 8, and 12, it moves the string to the right and inserts a dash. Finally, it grabs the first 13 characters and adds an asterisk (*) wildcard to the end.

The next several segments of code "build up" a WHERE string by looking at the unbound controls one at a time. If the corresponding field is a string, the code builds a test using the LIKE predicate so that whatever the user enters can match any part of the field in the underlying table, but not all the fields are strings. For the two price fields, the code builds a simple ">=" or "<=" comparison. If there's no disk included with the book, the [Disk] field will be Null. To determine whether a book is out of print, a simple True/False test suffices. When the function adds a clause as it builds the WHERE string, it inserts the AND keyword between clauses if other clauses already exist.

Because the underlying record source for the frmBooks form does not include either author or category information directly, the procedure has to build a predicate using a subquery if you ask for a search by either author name or category. In the first case, the procedure looks at both last name and first name and builds two separate comparison clauses to extract the ISBN number. The subquery finds the list of ISBN numbers from a query that joins tblBookAuthor (which has ISBNNumber) with tblAuthors (where the author name fields can be found). For a search by category, the subquery uses a query that joins tblBookCategories (which has ISBNNumber) with tblCategories (which has the CategoryID field).

The final part of the procedure builds a simple recordset on the tables used in both the frmBooks and frmBookSummary forms, applying the WHERE clause built by the code in the first half of the procedure. If it finds no records, it uses the MsgBox function to inform the user and then gives the user a chance to try again. When you first open a recordset object in code, its RecordCount property is 0 if the recordset is empty and is some value greater than 0 if the recordset contains some qualifying records. The RecordCount property of a Recordset object contains only a count of the number of rows visited and not the number of rows in the recordset. So if it finds some rows, the procedure moves to the last row in the temporary recordset to get an accurate count. When the record count is greater than 10, the procedure lets the user view a summary of the records found in the frmBookSummary form, view all data in the full frmBooks form, or try again. This is a good example of using the MsgBox function to not only display some variable data but also respond to a user choice. We'll examine how the frmBookSummary form works in the next section.

Selecting from a Summary List

As you saw in the cmdSearch_Click procedure in the previous section, the user gets to make a choice if more than 10 rows meet the entered criteria. To examine this feature in more detail, ask for a search of books with a Book Type of Advanced in the frmBookSearch form. The result should look like that shown in Figure 23-15, in which 13 books are categorized as Advanced.

FIGURE 23-15.

The message box that appears when the cmdSearch_Click procedure returns more than 10 rows.

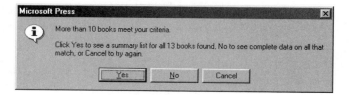

When you click Yes, the cmdSearch_Click procedure opens the frmBookSummary form, as shown in Figure 23-16. You can scroll down to any row, put the focus on that row (be sure the row selector indicator is pointing to that row), and then click the View Details button to open the frmBooks form and view the details for the one book you selected. You can see that this is a very efficient way to help the user narrow a search down to one particular book.

FIGURE 23-16.

Selecting a specific book from a search summary.

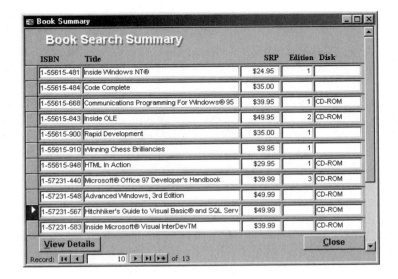

Linking to Related Data in Another Form or Report

Now that you can see how to build a filter to limit what the user sees, you can probably surmise that using a filter is a good way to link to displaying either details about data in the same table or related data from another table. This section shows you how to do this for both forms and reports. Later in the section, you will learn how to use events in class modules to build sophisticated links.

Linking Forms Using a Filter

Behind the View Details button on the form shown in Figure 23-16 is a simple Visual Basic procedure, shown below, that uses the current value of the ISBNNumber field on the form to build a filter for the OpenForm method.

```
Private Sub Details_Click()
    ' Picked one from the list, so open books
    ' filtered... (also activated if user
    ' double-clicks anywhere on the row)
    gstrWhereBook = "[ISBNNumber] = """ & _
        Me!ISBNNumber & """"
    DoCmd.OpenForm FormName:="frmBooks", _
        WhereCondition:=gstrWhereBook
    DoCmd.Close acForm, Me.Name
    Forms!frmBooks.SetFocus
```

(continued)

```
                    Forms!frmBooks!cmdAddNew.Visible = False
                    Forms!frmBooks!cmdShowAll.Visible = True
          End Sub
```

Another way to handle additional related data is to display the details of that data in another form. The fsubAuthorBooks subform has a command button on each row to link the user to the full details of the book listed on that row. When you click this button, Visual Basic code opens the frmBooks form for the book selected in the subform, as shown in Figure 23-17. This provides an easy way to view the full details of a specific book when reviewing author data. You can find a similar Details button on the fsubBookAuthors form that lets you view details about an author when you're working with book data.

FIGURE 23-17.

Using a second form to edit data related to one of the Author subforms.

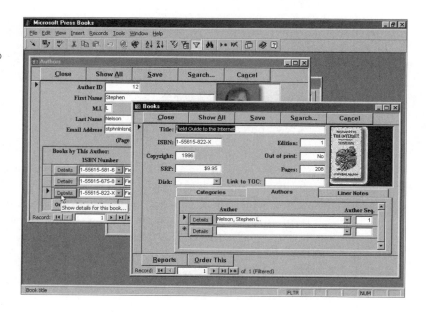

The code behind the Details button also uses a filter, but against a set of rows from a related table, as shown below.

```
          Private Sub cmdDetails_Click()
          Dim frm As Form
             If Not IsNothing(Me!ISBNNumber) Then
                ' Open the books form filtered on this book
                gstrWhereBook = "[ISBNNumber] = """ & _
                   Me!ISBNNumber & """"
                DoCmd.OpenForm FormName:="frmBooks", _
                   WhereCondition:=gstrWhereBook
                ' Set up an object variable for efficiency
                Set frm = Forms!frmBooks
                ' Hide the New button, but
```

```
                          ' show the Show All button
                          frm!cmdAddNew.Visible = False
                          frm!cmdShowAll.Visible = True
                          ' Turn on the author display option
                          frm!tabDisplay = 1
                End If
        End Sub
```

In this case, the code uses the ISBNNumber field from tblBookAuthor to "link" to the related data in tblBooks displayed in the frmBooks form. Because we have just filtered the frmBooks form, the code also hides the add a new record button and reveals the show all (remove the filter) button. Since we're linking to author information, setting the value of the tabDisplay control to 1 reveals that tab (the Authors tab) on the frmBooks form.

Linking to a Report Using a Filter

Now let's take a look at using the Filter technique to link to related information in a report. Open the frmOrders form in the Microsoft Press Books database and move to an order that looks interesting. Click the Print button as shown in Figure 23-18. This button opens form frmOrderPrintParms that gives you the option to see the order formatted in a report, print a mailing label for the customer, or, if the order has a store specified, print a mailing label for the store. Choose the Print the Current Order option and click Print again to see the order in a report.

FIGURE 23-18.

The result of asking to print the current order in the Microsoft Press Books database.

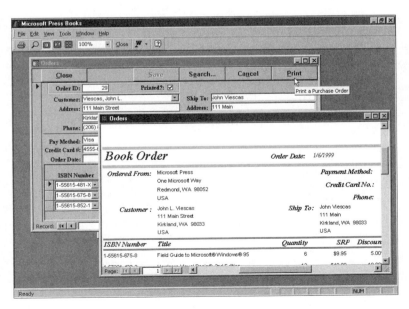

VI

Creating an Application

The code from the Click event of the Print button in frmOrderPrintParms is shown below.

This first thing this procedure does is set an object reference to the frmOrders form to make it easy to grab either the OrderID (for the order invoice report), the CustomerID (for the customer mailing label), or the StoreID (for the store mailing label). The Select Case statement examines which option button you selected on frmOrderPrintParms and prints the appropriate report. You set the variable gintPrintPreview when you sign on to the application in frmSignon. If you selected the option to see all reports in print preview, you will see the report on the screen; otherwise, the report prints directly. You can see in each DoCmd.OpenReport statement, the code uses the WhereCondition clause to filter the report based on the current order.

```
Private Sub cmdPrint_Click()
On Error GoTo Print_Err
  ' Print what they asked for...
  Dim frmO As Form, cn As ADODB.Connection, _
    strSQL As String
  Set frmO = Forms!frmOrders
  Select Case Me!optPrtOptions
    Case 1
      ' Print the current order --
      Me.Visible = False
      DoCmd.OpenReport ReportName:="rptOrders", _
        View:=gintPrintPreview, _
        WhereCondition:="[OrderID] = " & frmO!OrderID
      ' If this user has print preview option set,
      If gintPrintPreview = acPreview Then
        ' Then make sure focus goes to the report window
        DoCmd.SelectObject acReport, "rptOrders"
      End If
      If Not (frmO!Printed) Then
        ' If not marked printed, then do so
        strSQL = "UPDATE tblOrders SET " & _
          "[Printed] = True WHERE [OrderID] = " & _
          frmO!OrderID
        Set cn = CurrentProject.Connection
        cn.Execute strSQL
        ' and call the orders form sub
        ' to lock all controls
        ' NOTE: The PUBLIC sub in frmOrders
        ' is like an object METHOD!
        frmO.SetLocked True
      End If
      DoCmd.Close acForm, Me.Name
    Case 2
      ' Customer Label
```

```
          DoCmd.OpenReport ReportName:="rptCustLabels", _
            View:=gintPrintPreview, _
            WhereCondition:="[CustomerID] = " & _
            frmO!CustomerID
          DoCmd.Close acForm, Me.Name
          ' If this user has print preview option set,
          If gintPrintPreview = acPreview Then
            ' Then make sure focus goes to the report window
            DoCmd.SelectObject acReport, "rptCustLabels"
          End If
        Case 3
          ' Store label --
          DoCmd.OpenReport ReportName:="rptStoreLabels", _
            View:=gintPrintPreview, _
            WhereCondition:="[StoreID] = " & frmO!StoreID
          DoCmd.Close acForm, Me.Name
          ' If this user has print preview option set,
          If gintPrintPreview = acPreview Then
            ' Then make sure focus goes to the report window
            DoCmd.SelectObject acReport, "rptStoreLabels"
          End If
      End Select
      Exit Sub

  Print_Err:
      MsgBox "Error: " & Err & ", " & Error
      Exit Sub
  End Sub
```

Synchronizing Two Forms Using a Class Event

Sometimes it's useful to give the user an option to open a pop-up form that displays additional details about some information displayed on another form. As you move from one row to another in the main form, it would be nice if the additional information form stayed in sync.

Of course, the Current event of a form lets you know when you move to a new row. In the Wedding List sample database built with macros (see Chapter 21, "Automating Your Application with Macros"), the macros do some elaborate filtering to keep a pop-up form with additional city information in sync with the main form. You can see these two forms in action in Figure 23-19 on the next page.

I created a special version of the Wedding database called WeddingVB that has all the macro code converted to Visual Basic. Because I used Visual Basic, I was able to declare and use a custom event in the WeddingListForm form to "signal" the CityInformation form if it's open

VI

Creating an Application

FIGURE 23-19.

The CityInformation form popped up over the main WeddingListForm to display additional information about the invitee's home city.

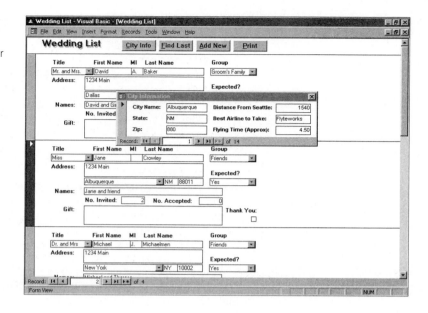

and responding to the events. In the Current event of WeddingListForm, I didn't have to worry about whether the companion form is open. The code simply signals the event and lets the CityInformation form worry about keeping in sync with the main form.

Here's the code from the WeddingListForm class module.

```
Option Compare Database
Option Explicit

Public Event NewCity(varCityName As Variant)

Private Sub Form_Current()
On Error GoTo Form_Current_Err
    ' Signal the city form to move to this city
    RaiseEvent NewCity(Me!City)

Form_Current_Exit:
    Exit Sub

Form_Current_Err:
    MsgBox Error$
    Resume Form_Current_Exit

End Sub
```

In the Declarations section of the module, I declared an event variable and indicated that I'm going to pass a parameter (the city name) in the event. In the Form_Current event procedure, the code uses RaiseEvent to pass the current city name to any other module that's "listening." The code doesn't have to worry about whether any other module is interested in this event—it just signals when appropriate and then ends. Note that the variable passed is declared as a Variant to handle the case when you move to the new row at the end—the City control will be Null in that case.

The CityInformation form does all the work (when it's open) to respond to the event signaled by WeddingListForm and move to the correct row. The code is shown below.

```
Option Compare Database
Option Explicit

Dim WithEvents frmWedding As Form_WeddingListForm

Private Sub Form_Load()
On Error GoTo Form_Load_Err
    ' If the wedding list form is open
    If IsLoaded("WeddingListForm") Then
        ' Then set to respond to the NewCity event
        Set frmWedding = Forms!WeddingListForm
    End If

Form_Load_Exit:
    Exit Sub

Form_Load_Err:
    MsgBox Error$
    Resume Form_Load_Exit
End Sub

Private Sub frmWedding_NewCity(varCityName As Variant)
    ' The Wedding List form has asked us to move to a
    ' new city via the NewCity event
    On Error Resume Next
    If IsNothing(varCityName) Then
        ' Hide me if city name is empty
        Me.Visible = False
    Else
        ' Reveal me if there's a city name, and go
        ' find it
        Me.Visible = True
        Me.Recordset.FindFirst "[CityName] = """ & _
            varCityName & """"
    End If
End Sub
```

In the Declarations section, you can find an object variable called frmWedding that has a data type equal to the class module name of WeddingListForm. The WithEvents keyword indicates that code in this class module will respond to events signaled by any object assigned to this variable. When the form opens, the Form_Load procedure checks to see that WeddingListForm is open (just in case you opened this form by itself from the Database window). If WeddingListForm is open, it "hooks" the NewCity event in that form by assigning it to the frmWedding variable.

The frmWedding_NewCity procedure responds to the NewCity event of the frmWedding object. Once the Load event code establishes frmWedding as a pointer to WeddingListForm, this procedure runs whenever code in the class module for that form signals the NewCity event with RaiseEvent.

The code in the event procedure is pretty simple. If the CityName parameter passed by the event is "nothing" (Null or a zero length string), the procedure hides the form because there's nothing to display. If the event passes a valid city name, the procedure uses the FindFirst method of the Recordset object of this form to move to the correct city. Pretty cool, huh?

 NOTE

> The Recordset property of a form in an Access database (mdb file) returns a DAO recordset in Access 2000. For this reason, you should use a DAO FindFirst method, not an ADO Find method to locate rows in a form recordset.

Creating Meaningful Messages and Help

If you're an advanced programmer, you can use Microsoft Word or one of many products available to build rich text format (rtf) files that you can use with the Windows Help Compiler to build a full-blown help system for your application. You can set properties in your database to point to a custom help file. You can also set a Help Context ID property in forms, reports, and many controls to jump to a specific topic within your help file. However, if your application needs only a few message boxes and some simple help instructions for your forms, Access has several easy-to-use features that you can use to add a professional feel to your application.

Creating Informative MsgBox Messages

You have already seen how to use the MsgBox function to display information and ask the user to provide a response. You can make your error messages appear even more professional by taking care to insert the Visual Basic vbCrLf constant to break your message into separate header, problem description, and suggested solution sections.

To see how you can do this, open the Microsoft Press Books database but hold down the Shift key so the application doesn't start. If you have already started the application, click Exit on the main switchboard form to return to the Database window. Find the form frmMain in the Database window, and try to open it directly from the window. You should see a formatted message box, as shown in Figure 23-20.

FIGURE 23-20.

A formatted message box with header, problem description, and solution lines.

The Open event procedure of the form generates this message when it discovers you haven't signed on yet. The code for the procedure is listed here.

```
Private Sub Form_Open(Cancel As Integer)
    If glngCurrentCustID = 0 Then
        ' The following is a good example of a MsgBox that
        ' formats the instructions on separate lines
        If vbOK = MsgBox("No customer is currently " & _
            "'signed on' to this application." & _
            vbCrLf & vbCrLf & _
            "Are you sure you want to continue?" & _
            vbCrLf & vbCrLf & _
            "Click OK to continue without signing " & _
            " on -- you won't be able to create any " & _
            " new orders." & _
            vbCrLf & vbCrLf & _
            "Click Cancel to return to the database " & _
            "window.  " & vbCrLf & _
            "Start the application and sign on by " & _
            "opening 'frmSignon'.", _
```

(continued)

VI

Creating an Application

```
                    vbQuestion + vbOKCancel, "Microsoft Press") Then
                   gintPrintPreview = acPreview
                   Exit Sub
               End If
               Cancel = True
               DoCmd.SelectObject acTable, "tblAuthors", True
           End If
       End Sub
```

The secret is to use the vbCrLf constant within the text of your message to force new lines as appropriate. The only limitation is that the total length of the message string must be less than 1024 characters.

 **NOTE**

> The Visual Basic implemented in Microsoft Access 2000 no longer supports the special "@" segment indicator used by Windows to separate header, problem description, and suggested solution sections that you see in many Windows error messages. If you used this feature in Microsoft Access 97, you will need to change your code to do your own formatting.

Using the Office Assistant and Custom Balloon Help

Introduced in Office 97 was the Office Assistant. This interface might seem a bit whimsical, but you can actually program the Assistant by creating a "balloon" object (the help messages that the Assistant spouts are called balloons), setting its properties, and using a Show method to display it.

In many of the forms in the Microsoft Press Books database, you can find a public procedure called FormHelp that defines and activates custom balloon help for that form. (The reason for declaring these as public will become apparent in a moment.) If you want to see one of these procedures in action, open most any form (the frmBookList form is used in the following example), and press the F1 key (the universal Help key) while the form has the focus. You should see a result something like the one shown in Figure 23-21.

If you have the Microsoft Press Books database open, you can also click the Office Assistant button on the toolbar or choose Help Assistant from the Help menu. Both of these require custom command bars that you'll learn how to create in the next chapter.

FIGURE 23-21.

Custom balloon help for the frmBookList form displayed in the Office Assistant. This example shows the Assistant called Links.

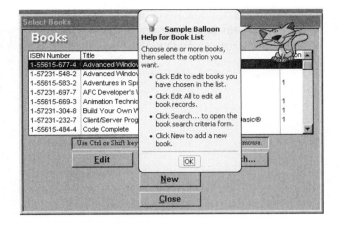

The F1 key works because this database has a special macro named *AutoKeys*. You can use this macro to intercept any function key; the Insert and Delete keys; and the Ctrl key used in combination with any letter, number, or function key, or the Ins or Del key. The commands you program in the macro replace the normal action of these keystrokes. You can see the AutoKeys macro for the Microsoft Press Books database in Figure 23-22.

FIGURE 23-22.

The AutoKeys macro in the Microsoft Press Books database.

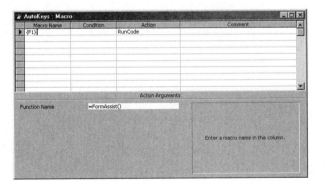

The concept is really quite simple. In the Macro Name column, enter the special code for the key you want to intercept. The key list is shown in Table 23-1 on the next page. You can add tests in the Condition column, and, of course, you should have at least one macro action defined in the Action column. In this case, the macro intercepts only the F1 function key and calls a function named FormAssist.

TABLE 23-1. AutoKeys Macro Key Codes

AutoKeys Macro Name	Key Intercepted
^*letter* or ^*number*	Ctrl+*[the named letter or number key]*
{F*n*}	The named function key (F1–F12)
^{F*n*}	Ctrl+*[the named function key]*
+{F*n*}	Shift+*[the named function key]*
{Insert}	Insert
^{Insert}	Ctrl+Insert
+{Insert}	Shift+Insert
{Delete} or {Del}	Delete
^{Delete} or ^{Del}	Ctrl+Delete
+{Delete} or +{Del}	Shift+Delete

You can find the FormAssist function in the modUtility module. The code is listed below.

```
Public Function FormAssist()
    ' Generic function to respond to OnAction on
    ' custom menu or toolbar help command
    ' Function checks for an active form, then
    ' looks for a "FormHelp" handler subroutine
    ' on that form
    Dim frm As Form

    ' Set an error trap
    On Error Resume Next

    ' Try to locate a form that has the focus
    Set frm = Screen.ActiveForm
    If Err <> 0 Then
        ' Error means no active form,
        ' so open standard Office Assistant
        Application.Assistant.Help
        Exit Function
    End If

    ' No error, so try to call the FormHelp
    ' method of the active form
    frm.FormHelp
    If Err <> 0 Then
        ' Error means no FormHelp method for
        ' the current form,
        ' so open standard Office Assistant
```

```
        Application.Assistant.Help
    End If
End Function
```

This function first checks to see whether some form has the focus in form view. If it finds a form, it checks to see whether the form has a public procedure called FormHelp, which it calls as a method of the form object. If you recall, Access builds all functions and procedures in form and report modules as private, which means they can normally be called only from other procedures within the same module. You'll see in the sample code that follows that FormHelp is defined as a public procedure so that it can be called from this external function, FormAssist. If no form is active or the form has no help procedure, the function defaults to calling the Help method of the Assistant object.

> To call the Office Assistant directly, you must add a reference to the Office Visual Basic library to your database. You can do this by opening any module, choosing References from the Tools menu, and then selecting Microsoft Office 9.0 Object Library.

The real action happens in each form's FormHelp procedure. The procedure for the frmBookList form is shown below.

```
Public Sub FormHelp()
    ' Custom assistant help method for this form
    Dim balCurrent As Balloon

    ' Create a new assistant balloon
    Set balCurrent = Assistant.NewBalloon

    With balCurrent
        ' Set balloon type to bullets
        .BalloonType = msoBalloonTypeBullets
        ' Set mode to auto-close as soon as
        ' the user clicks anywhere else
        .Mode = msoModeAutoDown
        ' Add an OK button just for looks
        .Button = msoButtonSetOK
        ' Define the balloon title
        .Heading = "Sample Balloon Help for Book List"
        ' This is a tip, so use the proper icon
        .Icon = msoIconTip
        ' Show help based on Admin status
        If gintIsAdmin Then
            ' Use labels to display helpful hints
```

(continued)

```
                              .Labels(1).Text = "Click Edit to edit" & _
                                  " books you have chosen in the list."
                              .Labels(2).Text = "Click Edit All to" & _
                                  " edit all book records."
                              .Labels(3).Text = "Click Search... to" & _
                                  " open the book search criteria form."
                              .Labels(4).Text = "Click New to add a" & _
                                  " new book."
                        Else
                              .Labels(1).Text = "Click View to view" & _
                                  " books you have chosen in the list."
                              .Labels(2).Text = "Click View All to" & _
                                  " view all book records."
                              .Labels(3).Text = "Click Search... to" & _
                                  " open the book search criteria form."
                        End If
                        ' Set up title text inside the balloon
                        .Text = "Choose one or more books," & _
                            " then select the option you want."
                        ' Activate the balloon
                        .Show
                        ' Code stops here until user dismisses the
                        ' balloon
                  End With
            End Sub
```

After you have added a reference to the Microsoft Office 9.0 object library, you can use the object browser to explore the properties and methods of the Balloon object. The sample code above uses the With statement to make it easy to reference properties and methods of the established Balloon object. The code sets up the balloon as a simple bulleted list. You can define text in as many as five built-in labels. Setting the Mode to msoModeAutoDown means that the balloon closes as soon as the user clicks anywhere, including on the OK button that is displayed in the balloon. As you can see in Figure 23-21 on page 875, the text defined for Heading appears in bold at the top of the balloon and the text defined for the labels appears in normal font just below that.

Automating Complex Tasks

The most complex Visual Basic code we've examined thus far in this chapter is the procedure to build a search clause from the data you enter in the frmBookSearch form. Trust me, we've only started to scratch the surface!

Triggering a Data Task from a Related Form

One of the more complex pieces of code in the Microsoft Press Books sample database can be triggered from either the frmBooks form or the fsubAuthorBooks form that's part of the frmAuthors form. Once you have signed on correctly to the application, you can click the Order This button while reviewing any book to add that book to your current "open" order, as shown in Figure 23-23. An "open" order is defined as the most current order that has not yet been printed. If no "open" order exists, the code called by this button builds a brand new order and adds the book to that order.

FIGURE 23-23.

Ordering a book by clicking the OrderThis button on the frmBooks form.

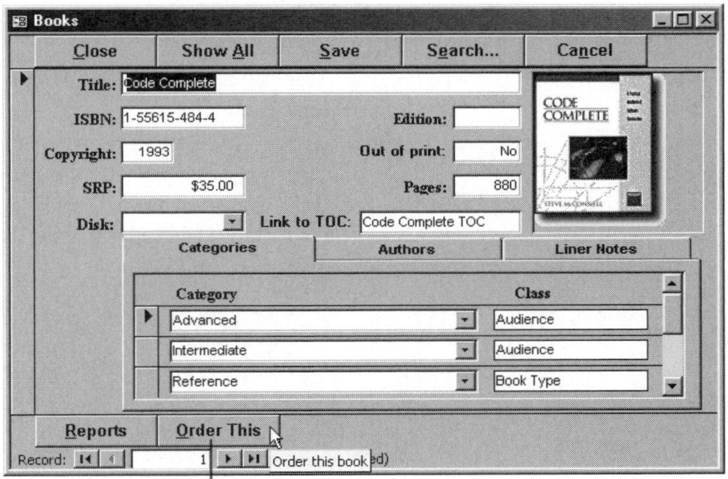

Click to add this book to the current order.

If you look behind either the frmBooks form or the fsubAuthorBooks form, you'll find event procedures that call a function named OrderThis and pass the ISBN number of the current book to the function. You can find this function in the module modBooks. The code is listed below. (Note: Like most of the object procedures in the Microsoft Press Books database, this procedure uses the ADO model objects.)

```
Public Function OrderThis(strISBN As String) _
    As Integer
  Dim cn As ADODB.Connection
  Dim rcdC As New ADODB.Recordset, _
    rcdO As New ADODB.Recordset, _
    rcdOD As New ADODBRecordset
```

(continued)

```
Dim strSQL As String, intTrans As Integer, _
   lngOrderID As Long
On Error GoTo OrderThis_Err
' Make sure they're signed on
If glngCurrentCustID = 0 Then
   If vbYes = MsgBox("You must be signed on" & _
      " to order a book.  Would you like to "&_
      " sign on now?", vbQuestion + vbYesNo, _
      "Microsoft Press") Then
      ' Try to sign them on - tell signon
      ' form to not go to frmMain
      DoCmd.OpenForm FormName:="frmSignon", _
         WindowMode:=acDialog, _
         OpenArgs:="NotMain"
      ' If still not signed on, then bail out
      If glngCurrentCustID = 0 Then Exit Function
   Else
      Exit Function
   End If
End If

' Get a copy of the current connection
Set cn = CurrentProject.Connection
cn.BeginTrans
intTrans = True
' Set up to find the latest open order
' for this customer
strSQL = "SELECT * FROM tblOrders" & _
   " WHERE [CustomerID] = " & _
      glngCurrentCustID & _
   " AND [Printed] = False" & _
   " AND [OrderDate] = " & _
   "(Select Max([OrderDate]) From "&_
   " tblOrders As tblO2" & _
   " WHERE tblO2.[CustomerID] = " & _
      glngCurrentCustID & _
   " AND tblO2.[Printed] = False);"

rcdO.Open strSQL, cn, adOpenKeyset,
adLockOptimistic
   ' If no open order found, then...
   If rcdO.RecordCount = 0 Then
      ' Go find customer record and add a new order
      strSQL = "SELECT * FROM tblCustomers" & _
         " WHERE [CustomerID] = " & _
            glngCurrentCustID

   rcdC.Open strSQL, cn, adOpenKeyset,
adLockOptimistic
      If rcdC.RecordCount = 0 Then
         Err.Raise 9001, , "Unexpected error. " & _
            "Customer record for customer number " & _
            glngCurrentCustID & " not found."
```

```
            End If
            rcdO.AddNew
            rcdO!CustomerID = glngCurrentCustID
            rcdO!OrderDate = Date
            rcdO!ShipName = rcdC!FirstName & _
              IIf(IsNull(rcdC![MiddleInit]), "",_
                " " & rcdC![MiddleInit] & ".") & _
                " " & rcdC!LastName
            rcdO!ShipAddress = rcdC!Address
            rcdO!ShipCity = rcdC!City
            rcdO!ShipStateOrProvince = _
              rcdC!StateOrProvince
            rcdO!ShipPostalCode = rcdC!PostalCode
            rcdO!ShipCountry = rcdC!Country
            rcdO!ShipPhoneNumber = rcdC!PhoneNumber
            rcdO!PayBy = rcdC!PayBy
            rcdO!CCNumber = rcdC!CCNumber
            rcdO!Printed = False
            ' Save generated order number for detail lines
             lngOrderID = rcdO!OrderID
            ' Add the master order row
            rcdO.Update
            rcdC.Close
          Else
             lngOrderID = rcdO!OrderID
          End If
          rcdO.Close
          ' See if this book already in this order
          strSQL = "SELECT * FROM tblOrderDetails" & _
            " WHERE [OrderID] = " & lngOrderID & _
            " AND [ISBNNumber] = """ & strISBN & """;"

      rcdOD.Open strSQL, cn, adOpenKeyset, adLockOptimistic
          If rcdOD.RecordCount = 0 Then
            ' Nope, add a new row
            rcdOD.AddNew
            rcdOD![OrderID] = lngOrderID
            rcdOD![ISBNNumber] = strISBN
            ' Yes, edit it!
          Else
            rcdOD.Edit
          End If
          rcdOD![Quantity] = rcdOD![Quantity] + 1
          rcdOD.Update
          rcdOD.Close
          cn.CommitTrans
          intTrans = False
          OrderThis = True
          Exit Function
```

(continued)

VI

Creating an Application

```
OrderThis_Err:
  MsgBox "Unexpected error: " & Err & ", " & Error
  If intTrans Then Rollback
  Exit Function

End Function
```

The first part of this function checks to see whether a valid customer is signed on. If no user is signed on, the function gives the user a chance to do so by calling the frmSignOn form with a special parameter to let the form know that it should not open the standard main switchboard form (frmMain) if it completes sign-on successfully. If you are signed on properly, the code builds a query to find the latest order that is also not yet printed for your customer ID. If it finds no "open" order, it builds a new record in tblOrders and saves the new OrderID.

Next the function looks for an order detail row for the book ISBN number passed to it by the calling procedure. If it finds one, it edits the row and simply adds one to the quantity ordered. If no row for this book exists in the order, the function adds a new row with an order quantity of 1. Note that the function does not recalculate any potential discount if the total quantity ordered exceeds any of the discount thresholds. The function also starts a transaction before beginning any updates so that either all rows (both in tblOrders and in tblOrderDetails) are added or none are added if there's an error.

Linking to a Related Task

Let's switch to the Entertainment Scheduling database and take a look at the frmContracts form that is "action central" for this application. RM Productions' business centers on booking groups into clubs, issuing contracts, and tracking commission payments. This section explores a few of the tasks that are automated in the frmContracts form.

Earlier in this chapter, you learned one technique for using a command button to link to a related task. One of the key tasks in the main frmContracts form, shown in Figure 23-24, is tracking commission payments for active contracts. As you move from contract to contract in this form, the Payments button will either be available or unavailable depending on the status of the particular contract. The form's Current event procedure (Form_Current) examines the contract status field and sets the Enabled property of the button accordingly.

FIGURE 23-24.

The frmContracts form in the Entertainment Scheduling database.

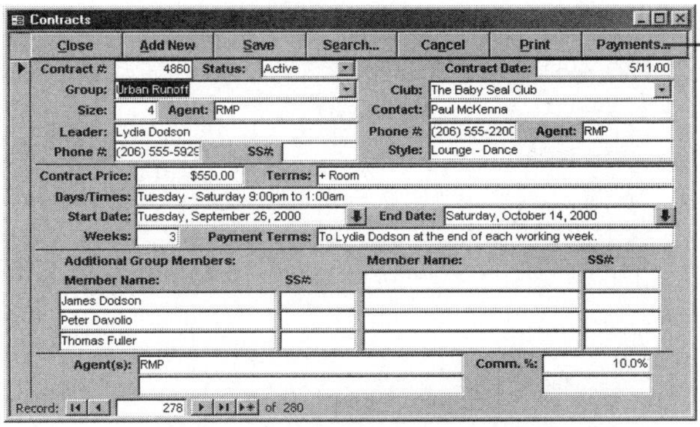

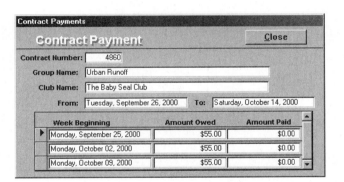

Click to enter contract payment data.

Move to an active contract, and click the Payments button. You should see the frmPayments form open, as shown in Figure 23-25. This form, in which you enter payments for the current contract, opens as a modal form so that the user must enter all payments before moving to another contract.

FIGURE 23-25.

Posting a payment for a specific contract.

If you open the frmPayments form in Design view, as shown in Figure 23-26 on the next page, you'll discover that it has no record source! So how does this form work? Because we know that this form will always be used for editing data for exactly one contract, there's no point in incurring the overhead to open another recordset on the tblContracts table, especially because you don't need to edit the contract data in the Payments form. The subform *is* bound to the tblCommissions table, and its subform control's Link Master Fields property references the unbound ContractNo control on the main form. The other controls on the form are there merely to confirm the contract data and are in locked (not updateable) controls.

VI

Creating an Application

FIGURE 23-26.

The property settings for the frmPayments form, which has no record source.

This form is opened and filled in by the OnClick event procedure for the Payment button on the main frmContracts form. The code for the procedure is shown below.

```
Private Sub cmdPayment_Click()
    Dim frm As Form
    ' Check for unsaved data on this form
    If Me.Dirty Then
        ' If so, then must have a valid GroupID
        ' and ClubID
        If IsNothing(Me!GroupID) Or _
            IsNothing(Me!ClubID) Then
            MsgBox "You can't save a contract " & _
                "without a Group Name and Club Name.", _
                vbCritical, "Payments"
            Me!GroupName.SetFocus
            Exit Sub
        End If
        ' Save the "dirty" data
        DoCmd.RunCommand acCmdSaveRecord
    End If
    ' Open the related payments form, hidden
    DoCmd.OpenForm "frmPayments", _
        acNormal, , , acHidden
    ' Set a form variable for efficiency
    Set frm = Forms!frmPayments
    ' Plug in the unbound data on payments
    ' ... the ContractNo is what makes the
    ' subform work
    frm!ContractNo = Me!ContractNo
    frm!GroupName = Me!GroupID.Column(0)
    frm!ClubName = Me!ClubID.Column(0)
    frm!BeginningDate = Me!BeginningDate
```

```
        frm!EndingDate = Me!EndingDate
        ' Move the focus to the subform
        frm!fsubPayments.SetFocus
        ' and make the form visible
        frm.Visible = True
    End Sub
```

After checking to be sure that any changes are saved, the code opens frmPayments as a hidden form (so you won't see it pasting in the contract data), copies the display data to the form, and then makes the form visible. Note that there are no forms to enter new commission rows in the database. The commission rows are created automatically by another Visual Basic procedure that runs each time an update is completed on the frmContracts form (in the AfterUpdate event). The code is as follows.

```
Private Sub Form_AfterUpdate()
    Dim db As DAO.Database, rcd As DAO.Recordset, _
       qd As DAO.QueryDef
    Dim varMonday As Variant, curOwed As Currency
    Dim intWeeks As Integer, intI As Integer
    On Error GoTo LoadComBail
    DoCmd.Hourglass True
    Set db = CurrentDb
    ' If not an active or pending RMP contract,
    ' then make sure Commissions file is clean
    If IsNothing(Me!Status) Or Me!Status = "D" _
      Or Me!Status = "SB" Or _
        Me!CommissionAgent1 <> "RMP" _
      Or IsNull(Me!CommissionAgent1) Then
        ' Create a temporary querydef to delete
        ' commission rows
        Set qd = db.CreateQueryDef("",_
          "Delete * From qryCommissions;")
        ' Fill in the parameter required by
        ' qryCommissions
        qd![Forms!frmContracts!ContractNo] = _
          Me!ContractNo
        qd.Execute
        qd.Close
        DoCmd.Hourglass False
        Exit Sub
    End If
    ' Active, Pending or Paid RMP contract --
    ' make sure commissions are correct
    ' Open a recordset on tblCommissions
    Set qd = db.QueryDefs("qryCommissions")
    ' Point to contract on this form
```

(continued)

```
qd![Forms!frmContracts!ContractNo] = _
  Me!ContractNo
Set rcd = qd.OpenRecordset(dbOpenDynaset)
' Calculate the weekly commission amount
curOwed = CCur(CLng(Me!ContractPrice * _
  Me![Commission1%] * 100) / 100)
' Figure out the Monday previous to
' Beginning Date
varMonday = Me![BeginningDate] - _
  WeekDay(Me![BeginningDate], 2) + 1
' If contract terms span a Monday,
' then adjust first billing week day
If Me![ContractLastDay] > 7 Then
  varMonday = varMonday + 7
EndIf
' Calculate number of weeks
intWeeks = CInt(Me!EndingDate - _
  varMonday + 7) \ 7
' Set up an array containing all the
' valid weeks for this contract
ReDim varWeekBeginning(1 To intWeeks + 1) _
  As Variant
ReDim intHit(1 To intWeeks + 1) As Integer
For intI = 1 To intWeeks
  varWeekBeginning(intI) = varMonday
  varMonday = varMonday + 7
Next intI
' Insert a dummy "high" date
varWeekBeginning(intWeeks + 1) = #1/1/2099#
intI = 1
' Find the matching commission records
' and make sure they're updated
Do Until rcd.EOF
  Do Until varWeekBeginning(intI) >= _
    rcd!WeekBeginning
    intI = intI + 1
  Loop
  If varWeekBeginning(intI) = _
    rcd!WeekBeginning Then
    rcd.Edit
    rcd!AmountOwed = curOwed
    If Me!Status = "Pd" Then
      rcd!AmountPaid = curOwed
    End If
    ' Mark this week found in the weekly array
    intHit(intI) = True
    rcd.UPDATE
  Else
    ' If it's not a week in the array, delete it
    rcd.Delete
  End If
```

```
        rcd.MoveNext
    Loop
    ' Now add in any missing ones
    For intI = 1 To intWeeks
      If Not intHit(intI) Then
        rcd.AddNew
        rcd!ContractNo = Me!ContractNo
        rcd!WeekBeginning = varWeekBeginning(intI)
        rcd!AmountOwed = curOwed
        If Me!Status = "Pd" Then
          rcd!AmountPaid = curOwed
          End If
          rcd.UPDATE
        End If
      Next intI
    rcd.Close
    DoCmd.Hourglass False
    Exit Sub
LoadComBail:
    MsgBox "Unexpected Error. " & Err & " " & _
      Error, 16
    Exit Sub
End Sub
```

In a nutshell, this procedure does the following.

1 It verifies that this is an active contract for which RM Productions is the main commissioning agent. If the contract is not active, the routine checks that no rows exist for this contract in the tblCommissions table and exits.

2 Based on the contract BeginningDate and EndingDate values, the procedure builds an internal array containing the date of Monday in a contract week and another array containing a flag to indicate whether that week already exists in the tblCommissions table. The procedure also calculates the weekly commission amount.

3 The procedure loops through any existing rows for this contract, looking for matching weeks. If it finds a week that doesn't match, it deletes the row. If it finds a matching week, it sets the "found" flag and makes sure the commission amount is correct.

4 For any weeks in the calculated array that it doesn't find in the tblCommissions table, the procedure builds a new row.

Validating Complex Data

Visual Basic is a powerful language that includes many built-in functions that you can use to test and validate data. Although most of the time you will handle data validation by using simple validation rule expressions in tables and forms, you can, when needed, create a validation procedure to parse and validate complex data.

An example of data validation in the Entertainment Scheduling database is the Days/Times text string, which exists in both the tblClubs and tblContracts tables. In a club record, the string defines the "default" days and times for which the club normally books entertainment. When you select a new club in the frmContracts form, a procedure in the AfterUpdate event of the ClubID combo box copies this information to the contract. However, for any particular contract, the days and times that the booked group is to perform might change from the club default. Since this is a field that ends up in the club and group booking contract, it needs to be validated for correct days of the week. Also, the beginning and ending dates of the contract need to match the Days/Times text. You can open a contract and try to enter an invalid day name in the Days/Times string. When you enter an invalid string and tab out of the field, you should see an error message like the one shown in Figure 23-27.

FIGURE 23-27.

The error message that appears when you try to enter an invalid day name in the frmContracts form.

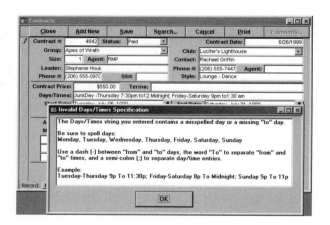

In the module named modRMP, the ValDaysTimes function provides this validation. It not only checks for valid spellings of days of the week but also makes sure the string has the following form:

> *dayname [- dayname] [booking times]*
> *[; dayname [- dayname] [booking times]]...*

That is, the string must begin with a valid day name. A range of days for the same booking times can be specified by including a hyphen and a second day name. Any subsequent set of booking days must be delimited with a semicolon. Also, the ValDaysTimes function calculates the day of the week of both the first day it finds in the booking string and the last day, and it then returns the values based on Monday as the first day of the week. If the "last" day falls earlier in the week than the "first" day, the function assumes that the booking dates span a weekend and adds 7 to the ending date to indicate this. The Visual Basic code in the BeforeUpdate event procedure of the Days/Times string is shown below.

```
Private Sub ContractDaysTimes_BeforeUpdate( _
    Cancel As Integer)
    Dim intReturn As Integer, intFirst As Integer
    Dim intLast As Integer
    intReturn = ValDaysTimes( _
      Me!ContractDaysTimes, intFirst, intLast)
    If Not intReturn Then
        DoCmd.OpenForm "frmDaysTimesError"
        Cancel = True
    End If
    Me!ContractFirstDay = intFirst
    Me!ContractLastDay = intLast
End Sub
```

Note that this procedure passes local variables called intFirst and intLast to the function rather than passing the fields from the contract. Visual Basic passes form control variables by value, so they can't be updated directly by the called function. If the string is successfully parsed, the procedure updates the first and last contract days in the underlying contract recordset. As you'll see in the final section of this chapter, these beginning and ending day of week values are used by other Visual Basic procedures to validate the beginning and ending days of the contract.

Using the Calendar Custom Control

If you open the frmContracts form in Form view, you'll see down arrow buttons next to both the Start Date and End Date fields on the form. If you click one of these buttons, you'll see a graphical calendar displayed, as shown in Figure 23-28 on the next page.

This calendar display is part of the custom calendar control that comes with Access. If you open the frmContracts form in Design view, as shown in Figure 23-29 on the next page, you'll see two calendar controls overlaid on the form just below the Start Date and End Date fields.

FIGURE 23-28.

Using one of the calendar custom controls on the frmContracts form.

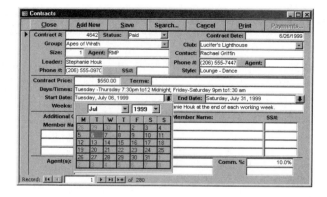

FIGURE 23-29.

The embedded calendar controls on the frmContracts form.

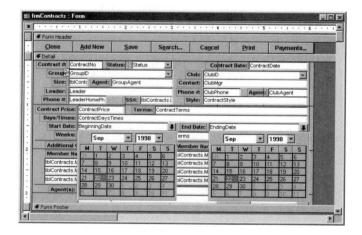

To place a calendar control on a form, you can open the form in Design view and then click the More Controls button in the Toolbox. Choose Calendar Control 9.0 from the pop-up list.

 TIP

> Custom controls use ActiveX technology, which means you can purchase additional controls from various software vendors. Office 2000 Developer (see Chapter 25, "After Completing Your Application," for more information) contains additional custom controls that you can use in your applications.

You can bind the calendar control to data in the record source of your form. When you select a new date on the calendar, the control updates the field. However, there's a number of important points you need to know to work with ActiveX controls and two controls bound to the same field.

- When you have more than one form control bound to a field in the underlying recordset, it's a good idea to give each control a unique name so that you can reference the field and each of the controls independently. In this case, the BeginningDate field is bound to a text box named txtBeginningDate and to an ActiveX calendar control named acxCalBegin. Likewise, the EndingDate field is bound to a text box named txtEndingDate and to an ActiveX calendar control named acxCalEnd.

- Access generates On Updated, On Enter, On Exit, On Got Focus, and On Lost Focus event properties in the property sheet for all ActiveX controls. Some controls, however, do not support all of these events (for example, the Calendar ActiveX control does not support the On Updated event).

- Most ActiveX controls support additional useful events such as BeforeUpdate and AfterUpdate. Aside from checking documentation for a particular control, the only way to discover which events a control supports is to open the form's module, choose the ActiveX control from the Object list (if the control has no event procedures, this generates the "default" Updated event procedure), and then examine the available list of events in the Procedure list.

- In some cases, you must refer to the Value property of the object inside an ActiveX control to discover its current value. As you'll see below, you must use this syntax in the calendar control's BeforeUpdate event to find out what value has just been chosen.

If you look at the code attached to the txtBeginningDate and txtEndingDate text boxes, you'll find BeforeUpdate procedures that call a common routine to validate the day of the week chosen. If the ContractDaysTimes string indicates the opening day is a Wednesday (see the ValDaysTimes procedure in the previous example), you want to be sure that the BeginningDate is always a Wednesday. Similarly, the acxCalBegin calendar control has a BeforeUpdate event procedure to call the same ValBegin function, as shown below. Remember, you won't find the Before Update event property in this control's property list. You can either choose the control and then choose BeforeUpdate in the Procedure list, or you can type in the Private Sub statement in the form module exactly as shown to define this event procedure. Note that this code looks at the Value property of the object inside the calendar control to find the value about to be set.

VI

Creating an Application

```
Private Sub acxCalBegin_BeforeUpdate(_
    Cancel As Integer)
    If Not ValBegin(Me!acxCalBegin.Object.Value) _
        Then
        Cancel = True
    End If
End Sub
```

If the new beginning or ending date is valid, you need to add code in the AfterUpdate event of both calendar controls to recalculate the NumberOfWeeks field. It would also be nice to automatically close the calendar because you probably don't need it in the way after you've chosen a new date. Below is the AfterUpdate code for the acxCalBegin calendar control that does this. Note that at this point the bound control will have updated the underlying fields, so you can refer directly to the field names in the calculation of the new number of weeks.

```
Private Sub acxCalBegin_AfterUpdate()
    ' Move the focus off this control so we
    ' can hide it
    Me!txtBeginningDate.SetFocus
    ' Close the calendar after picking a new
    ' valid date
    Me!acxCalBegin.Visible = False
    Me!tglBegin = False
    If IsNothing(Me!BeginningDate) Or _
        IsNothing(Me!EndingDate) Then Exit Sub
    Me!NumberOfWeeks = _
        DateDiff("ww", Me!BeginningDate, _
        Me!EndingDate) + 1
End Sub
```

The Current event procedure for the form also closes both calendar controls automatically when you move to a new record. Finally, there's a Click procedure for each of the toggle buttons you see next to each calendar control. (On the companion CD, you can find a bitmap named Down Arrow Small.bmp for the image that's on these buttons.) The procedure for the tglBegin button next to the acxCalBegin control is shown below.

```
Private Sub tglBegin_Click()
    ' Reset the visibility of the calendar
    Me!acxCalBegin.Visible = Me!tglBegin
    ' If opened the calendar
    If Me!tglBegin Then
        ' and beginning date not set yet
        If IsNothing(Me!BeginningDate) Then
            ' Set date to today as a default
            Me!acxCalBegin.Year = Year(Date)
            Me!acxCalBegin.Month = Month(Date)
```

```
            End If
        End If
    End Sub
```

The first thing this procedure does is set the Visible property of the related calendar control equal to its own value. If the toggle button is "pressed" (its value is True), the calendar control must be displayed. Next, if we're displaying the calendar but no date is set in BeginningDate, the procedure sets the calendar to today's date. When you open the calendar control by clicking the down arrow button, you can use the two combo boxes at the top of the control to select a different month or year.

As you've seen in this chapter, Visual Basic is an incredibly powerful language, and the tasks you can accomplish with it are limited only by your imagination. In the next chapter of this book, you'll learn how to set startup properties, create custom menus, and build a main switchboard form for your application.

The Finishing Touches

You're in the home stretch. You have almost all the forms and reports you need for the tasks you want to implement in your application, but you need some additional forms to make it easier to navigate and to provide a jumping-off place for all your tasks. Your application could also use a custom menu bar and a custom toolbar for most forms (and perhaps for some reports) to add a professional touch. Finally, you need to set the startup properties of your database to let Microsoft Access know how to get your application rolling, and you need to perform a final compile of your Visual Basic code to achieve maximum performance.

Creating a Custom Form Toolbar

When your application is running, you probably won't want or need some of the Access design features. However, you might want some additional toolbar buttons on your form toolbar that provide direct access to commands such as Save Record and Find Next. For example, if you open the Microsoft Press Books sample database, open the frmBooksPlain form (which uses the standard Form View toolbar), and then right-click the toolbar and open the Book Form Bar, you can see some useful differences between the two toolbars, as shown in Figure 24-1 on the next page. As you can see, buttons the user won't need, such as Form

View, Save, Print, Print Preview (none of the forms in the Microsoft Press Books database are designed to be printed), Format Painter, and New Object, aren't available on the custom toolbar. However, the Book Form Bar does have Close and Save Record buttons added at the left end. In the Microsoft Press Books application, all forms (except frmBooksPlain and a few other example forms) have their Toolbar property set to use the custom Book Form Bar.

FIGURE 24-1.

Comparing the standard Form View toolbar and the custom Book Form Bar from the Microsoft Press Books sample database.

Defining a New Toolbar

To begin defining a new toolbar, open the Customize dialog box by choosing Toolbars from the View menu and then choosing Customize from the submenu. (You can also click with the right mouse button on any open toolbar to open the toolbar shortcut menu and then choose Customize from that menu.) The Customize dialog box with the Toolbars tab selected is shown in Figure 24-2.

FIGURE 24-2.

The Toolbars tab of the Customize dialog box.

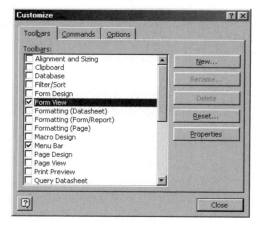

On the left side of the Customize dialog box, you can see the names of all the built-in toolbars in Access. You can make any of the toolbars visible by selecting the check box next to the toolbar name.

NOTE

If you look about a third of the way down the Toolbars list in the Customize dialog box, you can find an entry for the standard built-in menu bar. As you'll learn later in this chapter, you can also build custom menus using this customize facility.

Near the end of the list, you'll see three special built-in toolbars that Access displays only if you select them in this dialog box: Utility 1, Utility 2, and Shortcut Menus. The two utility toolbars are empty, so you can add buttons of your choice to them to create custom toolbars that are available in all the databases you open. The Shortcut Menus toolbar is a "placeholder" for any custom shortcut menus that you need to build. When the Customize dialog is open, you can't right-click to open any of the usual Access shortcut menus. You can find and customize all the Access shortcut menus on this special toolbar. In the Microsoft Press Books sample database, you can see a custom form toolbar, a custom menu bar, and a custom print preview toolbar already defined at the bottom of the list.

NOTE

If you open one of the built-in toolbars in a context in which the toolbar would not normally be open, the toolbar remains open until you close it. For example, if you open the Customize dialog box while the focus is on the Database window and then open the Form Design toolbar, the toolbar remains open no matter what you are doing in Access. Likewise, if you close a toolbar in a context in which that toolbar is normally open (for example, if you close the Formatting toolbar in a Form window in Design view), that toolbar will remain closed until you open it again within the usual context or from the Customize dialog box.

Customize Dialog Box Options

If you click the Options tab in the Customize dialog box, you can find check boxes that you can use to select large buttons, to display ScreenTips, and to display shortcut keys on ScreenTips. If you're working on a large monitor at a high resolution (1024×768 or 1280×1024), you might find the larger toolbar buttons easier to work with. The large buttons are approximately 50 percent wider and taller than the standard buttons. There's also an option on this tab to "animate" your menus when you open them—an interesting effect if you have a fast graphics card on your PC.

VI

Creating an Application

If you have made changes to one of the built-in toolbars or menu bars, you can select it in the Customize dialog box and click the Reset button to return the toolbar to its default. Access prompts you to confirm this action so that you don't inadvertently erase any custom changes you've made.

Any new toolbar that you define is available only in the database that you had open at the time you created the toolbar. If you want to define a custom toolbar that is available in all the databases that you work with on your computer, you must modify one of the built-in toolbars. You can use the two "blank" toolbars—Utility 1 and Utility 2—to create a custom set of toolbar buttons that is available in any database. For example, you might want to build a "standard" custom form toolbar for all your databases using either Utility 1 or Utility 2. The only drawback to these two toolbars is that you cannot give them custom names. Note, however, that any change you make to a built-in toolbar is effective only for your workstation.

> **NOTE**

If you want to build a custom toolbar to use with one or more of your forms, it's a good idea to first open one of the target forms in Form view because this makes the built-in form menu and toolbar available. As you'll see below, it's often easiest to copy the command or toolbar button you want from built-in menus or toolbars rather than build them from scratch. In all of the examples in this section, I have the frmBooksPlain form in the Microsoft Press Books database open in Form view.

Click the New button in the Customize dialog box to begin defining a new toolbar. Access will prompt you for a name to use for your new toolbar. If you want to follow the example in this section, create a new toolbar in the Microsoft Press Books sample database and give it a name like *Sample Books Toolbar*. You'll see the name appear at the bottom of the Toolbars list, and an empty toolbar in the form of a tiny, gray window will open in the Access workspace. Select your new toolbar in the Toolbars list, and click the Properties button to open the dialog box shown in Figure 24-3.

In the Toolbar Properties dialog box, you can select any toolbar from the Selected Toolbar drop-down list. If you select a custom toolbar (not a built-in one), you can rename it and set its type. Because we're building a toolbar, be sure Type is set to Toolbar. If you want to, you can position your toolbar and then restrict where the user can move it. For example, you can dock the toolbar at the bottom of your screen and then set Docking to either Can't Change or No Vertical. For cus-

FIGURE 24-3.

The Toolbar Properties dialog box.

tom toolbars, you can check Show On Toolbars Menu to make the toolbar available on the list of toolbars displayed from the View menu's Toolbars command or when the user right-clicks any toolbar or menu bar. You can't change this option for built-in toolbars. You can pick from additional options that determine whether this toolbar can be customized, resized, moved, or hidden. Finally, for built-in toolbars, you can click the Restore Defaults button to undo any changes you made. (This button is grayed in Figure 24-3 because a custom toolbar is selected.) Close this dialog box to go to the next step.

Click the Commands tab in the Customize dialog box to display the list of available commands, shown in Figure 24-4. On the left side of the dialog box is a list of all the command categories that Access provides. The buttons for that category of commands appear on the right side of the dialog box. If you want to see details about a command, select it in the Commands list and click the Description button. Access pops open a description of the command you chose over the bottom of the dialog box.

FIGURE 24-4.

The Customize dialog box and command category buttons; the custom toolbar under construction is open at the left.

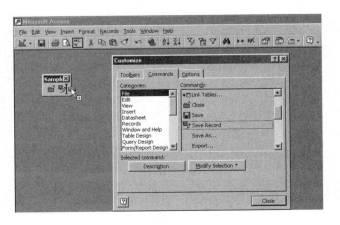

VI

Creating an Application

The custom toolbar in the Microsoft Press Books sample database starts with a Close button and a Save Record button at the left end of the toolbar. You can find the Close command partway down the list in the File category. As you can see, the Save Record command is located two down from Close. When you find the command you want in the Commands list, drag it onto your new toolbar.

The next several buttons for the Microsoft Press Books custom toolbar are all available on the built-in Form View toolbar. You can "steal" them from this toolbar rather than hunt for them in the Commands list. You can drag buttons from one toolbar to another, but when you do that, you're *moving* the button. In other words, you're deleting the button from the built-in toolbar and adding it to your custom toolbar. To copy a button from an existing toolbar, press the Ctrl key and hold it down while you drag the button. When you're copying a button, Access displays a small plus sign in a white box next to your mouse cursor, as shown in Figure 24-4 on the previous page. A large I-beam appears on the receiving toolbar to indicate where you're dropping the new command.

If you want to duplicate the custom toolbar in the Microsoft Press Books database, you need to copy the following buttons from the built-in Form View toolbar in this order: Spelling, Cut, Copy, Paste, Undo, Insert Hyperlink, Sort Ascending, Sort Descending, Filter By Selection, Filter By Form, Apply/Remove Filter, Find, New Record, Delete Record, and Database Window. (You won't see these buttons on the Form View toolbar unless you also have a form open.) You can find the Web Toolbar command in the Web category. Insert this command just to the right of Insert Hyperlink.

To complete the right end of the toolbar, go to the Window And Help category on the Commands tab of the Customize dialog box and copy the Microsoft Access Help button. The Book Form Bar includes a custom Contents And Index help command that for some unexplained reason is no longer directly available in Access 2000. This command provides a direct jump to the index of help, bypassing the Office Assistant. I was able to retain this button by importing the toolbar from the Access 97 version of the Microsoft Press Books database. If you want this button on your toolbar, open the Book Form Bar and copy it to the left of the Office Assistant button (it has a closed book icon on it).

If you didn't open a form before starting to build your toolbar, you can also force open the built-in Form View toolbar in the Toolbars list. Unless you're building the toolbar while a form is open in Form view, some buttons will appear gray (disabled) and some buttons will not be visible. As soon as you open a form in Form view, the appropriate buttons will become available. If you force the Form View toolbar open, remember to close it before exiting the customize facility or it will stay open all the time.

Customizing Your New Toolbar

After you build a toolbar, you can rearrange the buttons and add dividing lines between them. You can also change the button image, the label in the ScreenTip, and the button style. Finally, and perhaps most importantly, you can define a custom macro or function that you want Access to execute when you click the toolbar button. If you're not still in customize-toolbar mode, choose Toolbars from the View menu and then choose Customize from the submenu to open the Customize dialog box, shown in Figure 24-2 on page 896.

When you open the Customize dialog box, all toolbar buttons become editable. You can:

- Remove any button from any open toolbar (including any built-in toolbar) by clicking the button and dragging it off its toolbar.

- Move any button by clicking it and dragging it to a new location on its toolbar or another toolbar.

- Copy a button from one toolbar to another by holding the Ctrl key while you drag.

- Add a button by dragging it from the Commands list to any toolbar.

- Right-click a button to open a pop-up list of properties that you can modify to change the look of the toolbar button.

- Right-click a button and choose Properties from the pop-up list to define a custom action for a toolbar button.

Creating Button Images

To make your custom toolbar look just like the Book Form Bar in the Microsoft Press Books database, the first thing you need to do is change the Close button to show a different image. If there's another button that has an image you want to use, you can right-click that button to drop down the shortcut menu and choose Copy Button Image to place that button's bitmap on the Clipboard. (See Figure 24-5.) Move to the button you want to change, right-click, and choose Paste Button Image.

FIGURE 24-5.

Pasting a custom button image onto a toolbar button.

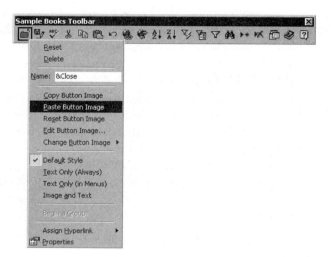

If you're good at visualizing button images by setting individual pixel colors on a 16-by-16-pixel square, choose Edit Button Image from the shortcut menu to open a simple design window for the bitmap image. Finally, if you have a 16-by-16-pixel bitmap or icon file that you want to use as a button image, open that file in an image-editing program (for example, Microsoft Paint in the Windows Accessories menu of the Start button), copy the bitmap to the Clipboard, and then choose Paste Button Image from the shortcut menu. In this case, I used an arrow that angles down from upper left to lower right. You can find this image on the companion CD, saved as *Close Arrow.bmp*.

Arranging Buttons

To make buttons easier to use, it's often useful to "cluster" buttons that perform similar functions by adding a dividing line between those clusters. To create a dividing line to the left of any button, right-click the button and turn on the Begin A Group property for the button near the bottom of the shortcut menu.

Assigning Custom Actions

Last, but not least, you can define a custom macro or function that you want Access to run instead of the built-in action. If you remember from the previous chapter, many of the forms in the Microsoft Press Books database have a public custom help procedure that can be called from the FormAssist function in modUtility. I designed the function this way so that both the AutoKeys F1 macro and any toolbar button could call this one function that subsequently figures out what form is active and specifically calls that form's FormHelp subprocedure.

To define a custom action for a toolbar button, right-click that button to open the shortcut menu and then choose Properties. You'll see the Toolbar Control Properties window, as shown in Figure 24-6.

FIGURE 24-6.

The Toolbar Control Properties window, where you can define a custom action for the control.

In the Toolbar Control Properties window, you can choose any control on the toolbar from the drop-down list at the top of the window. As you can see, you can redefine the caption for controls that display text and for the ScreenTip text if you have ScreenTips enabled. The Short-cut Text property applies only to controls you define on menus. *See the next section for details.* You can also change the style of the control and define a help file and help context for the command. (If you've copied a built-in command as shown in Figure 24-6, you probably want to leave the help pointers set as they are for the built-in help topic.) The Parameter and Tag properties are advanced settings for programmers who build their own command bars and commands using Visual Basic, which is not covered in this book.

The critical setting in this window is the On Action property. You can set this property to a macro name or specify an expression by preceding the expression with an equal sign (=). This works exactly like the event properties in forms and controls. In this case, you want to call the FormAssist function, and the function requires no parameters, as shown in Figure 24-6 on the previous page.

Once you have finished building your toolbar, set the Toolbar property of any form that you want to open with this toolbar displayed to point to this custom toolbar instead of to the built-in Form View toolbar. You can also set the Toolbar property for reports to specify the toolbar you want to display when you open the report in Print Preview.

Creating a Custom Form Menu Bar

After you build a custom form toolbar, it would be helpful (and consistent) to replace the built-in form menu bar with a custom menu bar. You can then set the Menu Bar property of your forms to point to the custom menu bar's macro. For example, the Book Menu Bar in the Microsoft Press Books sample database, as shown in Figure 24-7, has a limited set of commands that matches the functionality of the custom toolbar described in the previous section. When you open the File menu, you can see that the commands that a user shouldn't need, such as New Database, aren't available on the custom menu.

> If you or your user choose to leave adaptive menus turned on (enter customize mode, and then choose Menus Show Recently Used Commands First on the Options tab), this won't affect the design of your custom menus. You can still design full menus for your application. With this option turned on, Access shows only the "most recently used" options first on your custom menus.

FIGURE 24-7.
The custom File menu on the Book Menu Bar eliminates unneeded commands, such as Open Database, New Database, Save, Export, and Database Properties.

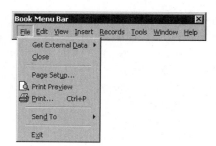

Defining a New Menu Bar

Prior to Microsoft Access 97 (version 8), the only way you could define a custom menu bar was to construct a complex series of macros. You needed one macro consisting of AddMenu actions to define the basic menu bar. You also needed an additional macro for each drop-down menu or submenu in that menu bar. You might have used as many as a dozen macros just to define one custom menu bar.

Access 2000 still supports AddMenu macros for backward compatibility, but you can now define a menu using the customize facility described in the previous section. For several of the standard menus, such as Edit, Insert, Records, and Window, you can copy the built-in menu "as is."

One of the advantages of copying built-in menus is that you automatically get any additional commands that appear on these menus in particular situations. For example, if you copy the built-in Edit menu, when the focus is on an OLE object, you will see OLE object editing commands at the bottom of the Edit menu on your custom menu bar. If you were to build these menus "by hand," you would first have to place the focus on a control that activates these commands before opening the Customize dialog box and then copy the commands from the built-in Access menus. (No, you can't find these commands in the Edit category on the Commands tab.) If you take that approach, you still get the desired effect of having the commands appear only when the focus is on an appropriate object. As another example, if you copy the built-in Window menu, you get the built-in list of open windows at the bottom of your custom Window menu.

To start building a custom menu, make sure you have the frmBooksPlain form open in Form view (this reveals all the built-in commands on the built-in menu bar). Right-click any menu bar or toolbar, and select Customize from the shortcut menu. Click the New button on the Toolbars tab, and name the menu bar *Book Menus* in the New Toolbar dialog box. Click the Properties button, and set the Type to Menu Bar.

Next click the Commands tab in the Customize dialog box, and scroll to the bottom of the Categories list. The custom menu bar in the Microsoft Press Books database (Book Menu Bar) uses the original Edit, Insert, Records, and Window menus, but it has customized File, View, Tools, and Help menus. To make your new menu match, select the New Menu category, which provides one special entry that allows you to start a new menu on the menu bar. Drag the New Menu command from the Commands list to your menu bar four times, once for each of the custom menus you need to build. Right-click each New Menu item, and change its name to reflect the menu name you want, as shown in Figure 24-8 on the next page. Adding an ampersand (&) before one of the letters in the menu name establishes the "access key" for that menu item, much like using an ampersand in the Caption

FIGURE 24-8.

Using the New Menu command to set up custom menus on your custom menu bar.

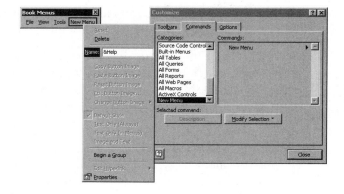

property of a form label or command button. *See the section titled "Designing a Switchboard Form" later in this chapter for details.*

You don't want to customize the built-in Edit, Insert, Records, or Windows menus in this exercise. You can copy them either from the built-in menu bar named Menu Bar (it's probably docked right above the built-in toolbar) or from the Built-In Menus category on the Commands tab of the Customize dialog. Be sure you place the menus in the same order as the standard Access menu bar (File, Edit, View, Insert, Records, Tools, Window, Help) so that your application is consistent with what a user is familiar with seeing in other applications. When you copy the menus, be sure to hold down the Ctrl key! If you don't hold down the Ctrl key, you will remove them from the built-in menu bar and place them only on your custom menu bar.

NOTE

When you copy a built-in menu (either from an available menu bar or from the Built-In Menus category), Access does *not* make an independent copy of the original. So, if you copy a menu and then change some of its properties (for example, you delete one of the commands from the menu), you're also affecting the built-in menu. This is why you must use the New Menu command to build the custom File, View, Tools, and Help menus in this example. If you were to copy the originals and delete unwanted commands from the copies, you'd be deleting them from the built-in menus as well.

Now you can add the commands you want to your four custom menus. You can copy commands either from the Commands list or from another menu bar. Remember to hold down the Ctrl key when you copy a command from another menu bar so that you do copy the command, not move it. When you drag a command to a menu bar and hover over one of the menu commands, Access drops down the current list of commands. You can then move the cursor down the list. Access shows you a horizontal bar on the drop-down menu where it will place your command if you release the mouse button at that point. It takes a bit of hand-eye coordination, but it's not too difficult. You can always grab a command and move it if you drop it in the wrong place. Figure 24-9 shows adding the Zoom command to the View menu just below the Subform Datasheet command.

FIGURE 24-9.

Adding the Zoom command to a custom View menu.

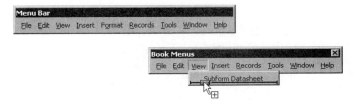

 TIP

When you copy a command from one menu to another, Access resets the command's Begin A Group property. You might want to turn this property back on for commands that normally begin a group, such as the Zoom command on the View menu.

To create the custom menu bar in the Microsoft Press Books sample database, you'll need the Get External Data, Close, Page Setup, Print Preview, Print, Send To, and Exit commands on the File menu; the Subform Datasheet, Zoom, and Pages commands on the View menu; and the Spelling, AutoCorrect, Office Links, and Options commands on the Tools menu.

On the custom Help menu on the Book Menu Bar menu bar, you can find commands for Help Assistant, About MS Press Books (which opens the frmAbout form), and About Microsoft Access. To make your new menu match, go to the All Forms category on the Commands tab of the Customize dialog box, and drag the frmAbout form onto the drop-down portion of your Help menu. You can set up the Help Assistant command by copying the Microsoft Access Help command from the built-in menu bar, or you can scroll to the File category on the Commands tab and choose the Custom command you find at the top of the list. If you choose the Custom command, you can then go to the Microsoft Access Help command to copy its image and paste it as described earlier in this chapter in the section "Customizing Your New Toolbar." This will paste the icon from the built-in menu command. You will still need to change the text for your menu command. To further customize the Help Assistant command, right-click it and choose Properties from the bottom of the shortcut menu to display the Control Properties dialog box, as shown in Figure 24-10. Set the On Action property to point to the FormAssist function so that the menu command works just like the custom toolbar button you created earlier.

FIGURE 24-10.

Customizing the Help Assistant command on your custom menu bar.

For the frmAbout command, you need to change its caption to read "About &MS Press Books." You can find a small bitmap on the companion CD called *Book Button.bmp*, which you can use to set the command image. Be sure to right-click the About Microsoft Access command and set it to Begin a Group on the popup menu. When you're finished, you can place the name of your custom menu bar in the Menu Bar property of each form that you want to open with your custom menu bar displayed instead of the built-in menu bar. Open a form in Form view, and you can see both the custom menu bar and custom toolbar, as shown in Figure 24-11.

FIGURE 24-11.

A form that has both a custom menu bar and a custom toolbar.

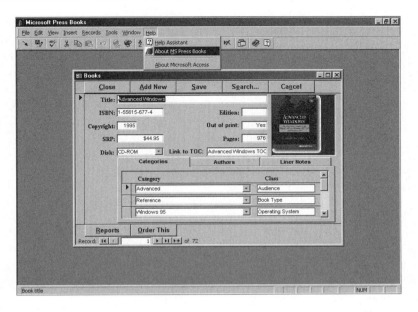

Fine-Tuning with the Performance Analyzer Wizard

Even the most experienced database designers (including me) don't always take advantage of all the techniques available to improve performance in an Access application. Fortunately, Access provides a Performance Analyzer Wizard to help you do a final analysis after you build most of your application. In this section, we'll let the wizard analyze the Entertainment Scheduling sample database. To start the wizard, switch to the Database window, choose Analyze from the Tools menu, and then choose Performance from the submenu. Access opens the window shown in Figure 24-12.

FIGURE 24-12.

The main selection window of the Performance Analyzer Wizard.

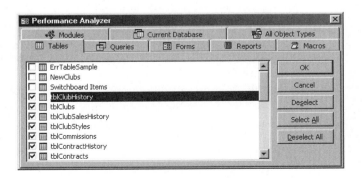

You can select a specific category of objects to analyze—Current Database (which lets you analyze table relationships), Table, Query, Form, Report, Macro, Module, or All Object Types. Within a category, you can click the check box next to an object name to select it for analysis. You can click the Select All button to ask the wizard to examine all objects or click Deselect All if you made a mistake and want to start over. In this example, I chose the All Object Types tab, clicked Select All, and then clicked on sample tables, queries, forms, and reports that aren't part of the actual application (all the extra examples I built for the book) to deselect them.

Click OK to run the wizard. The wizard will open a window that shows you its progress as it analyzes the objects you selected. When it is finished, the wizard displays the results of its analysis, similar to those shown in Figure 24-13.

FIGURE 24-13.

Analysis results from the Performance Analyzer Wizard.

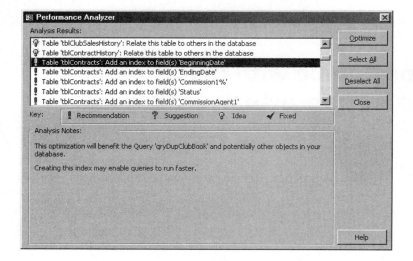

You can scan the list of recommendations, suggestions, and ideas displayed by the wizard. (Notice the key below the Analysis Results list.) Click any recommendation or suggestion that you like, and then click the Optimize button to have the wizard implement the change on the spot. After the wizard implements a change, you'll see a check mark next to the item. If you like, you can click the Select All button to highlight all the recommendations and suggestions and then click Optimize to implement the fixes.

You can't implement ideas directly from the wizard. Most ideas are changes that could potentially cause a lot of additional work. For example, changing a data type of a field in a table might improve performance slightly, but it might also cause problems in dozens of queries, forms, and reports that you've already built using that table field. Other ideas are fixes that the wizard isn't certain will help; they depend on how you designed your application.

⓿ Disabling Form Design View

You might have noticed as you built new forms in your Access 2000 databases that Access sets the new Allow Design Changes property to "All Views" by default. This is a handy feature while you build forms because it allows you to change any form or control property directly from Form view and see the results immediately. Figure 24-14 shows you one of the sample forms from the Entertainment Scheduling database opened in Form view. You can see that Access shows you the Form Design toolbars and menus and lets you open the property sheet to make changes.

FIGURE 24-14.

The sample frmXmplClub1 form from Chapter 13 opened in Form view.

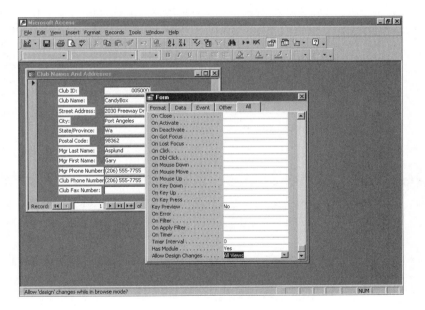

When you're ready to put your application "in production," however, you need to reset this new property to "Design View Only" for all your forms so the users see your forms as you intended. You could open every form in Design view, change the property, and save the form. Why do it the hard way? You can also code a simple Visual Basic procedure to open all of your forms and reset the property for you.

VI

Creating an Application

To help you out, I included a sample procedure in the modExamples module in both the Microsoft Press Books and Entertainment Scheduling sample databases. You can copy this code into your database to take care of this tedious process. Here's the procedure.

```
Sub FixAllowDesign()
Dim objFrm As AccessObject, frm As Form
   For Each objFrm In CurrentProject.AllForms
      DoCmd.OpenForm FormName:=objFrm.Name, _
         View:=acDesign
      Set frm = Forms(objFrm.Name)
      If frm.AllowDesignChanges = True Then
         frm.AllowDesignChanges = False
         DoCmd.RunCommand acCmdSave
      End If
      DoCmd.Close acForm, objFrm.Name
   Next objFrm
End Sub
```

This procedure takes advantage of the new AllForms collection to find the names of all your forms. To examine a form property or modify a property, you have to open the form in Design view. Although the Allow Design Changes property setting in the form design properties window shows "All Views" and "Design View Only," these actually correspond to "True" and "False" internal property values, respectively. So, if AllowDesignChanges is True, the procedure sets the value to False and saves the result. The code closes the current form before moving on to the next one.

Defining the Main Switchboard Form

Usually the last form that you need to build is a main switchboard form that gives the user direct access to the major tasks in your application.

Designing a Switchboard Form

Your main switchboard form should be a simple form with a logo, a title, and perhaps as many as eight command buttons. The command buttons can be used to open the forms that you defined in the application. Figure 24-15 shows the main switchboard form for the Entertainment Scheduling database in Design view.

One feature worth mentioning here is the use of the ampersand (&) character when setting each control's Caption property. You can use the ampersand character to define a shortcut key for the control. In the Caption property for the Groups command button, for example, the

FIGURE 24-15.

The main switchboard form for the Entertainment Scheduling database.

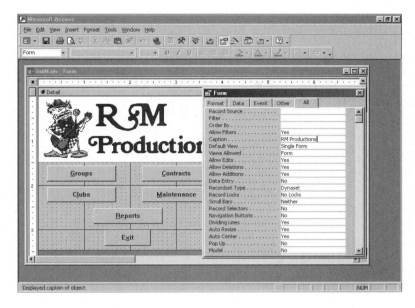

ampersand precedes the letter *G*. The letter *G* becomes the shortcut key, which means that you can choose the Groups button by pressing Alt+G as well as by more traditional methods such as clicking the button with the mouse or tabbing to the button and pressing the Spacebar or the Enter key. You must be careful, however, not to duplicate another shortcut key letter. For example, the shortcut key for the Clubs command button in this example is *L,* to avoid conflict with the *C* access key for the Contracts command button.

You can use a shortcut key to make it easier to select any control that has a caption. For command buttons, the caption is part of the control itself. For most other controls, you can find the caption in the attached label. For example, you can define shortcut keys to select option buttons or toggle buttons in an option group by including an ampersand in the caption for each button in the group.

For each command button, you need a simple event procedure to handle the Click event and to open the appropriate form. Here is the procedure for the Groups button.

```
Private Sub cmdGroups_Click()
    DoCmd.OpenForm "frmGroups"
End Sub
```

If you have a custom form menu bar, you should set the Menu Bar property of your switchboard form to point to the name of the custom menu bar. If you also have a custom form toolbar, you should set the form's Toolbar property. In the Microsoft Press Books and Entertainment Scheduling applications, a single custom form toolbar is used for all forms.

If this form "starts" your application *(see the section "Setting Startup Properties for Your Database" for details about startup properties)*, you may want to hide the Database window. The frmMain Load event in the Entertainment Scheduling database uses the following procedure.

```
Private Sub Form_Load()
    ' Halt screen flashing
    Application.Echo False
    ' Select an object in the Database window
    DoCmd.SelectObject acForm, "frmMain", True
    ' And hide the window
    DoCmd.RunCommand acCmdWindowHide
    ' Show 'em what we've done
    Application.Echo True
End Sub
```

Note that the procedure hides the Database window (although you'll see later that you can also set startup properties to hide this window) by selecting a known object in the Database window to give the Database window the focus and then executing the WindowHide command. This particular application is designed to "close" when this main form closes, so there's also a procedure to handle the Close event.

```
Private Sub Form_Close()
    DoCmd.SelectObject acForm, "frmMain", True
End Sub
```

Note that this code again selects a known object in the Database window, which has the effect of displaying the Database window if it's currently hidden.

Using the Switchboard Manager

If your application is reasonably complex, building all the individual switchboard forms you need to provide navigation through your application could take a while. Access has a Switchboard Manager utility that helps you get a jump on building your switchboard forms. This utility uses a creative technique to handle all switchboard forms by using a single form. It uses a driver table named Switchboard Items to allow you to define any number of switchboard forms with up to eight command buttons each.

To start the Switchboard Manager, choose Database Utilities from the Tools menu and then choose Switchboard Manager from the submenu.

The utility will check to see whether you already have a switchboard form and a Switchboard Items table in your database. If you don't have these, the Switchboard Manager displays the message box shown in Figure 24-16, which asks you if you want to build them.

> The Entertainment Scheduling Database already has a Switchboard Items table. If you want to follow along with this procedure to build an entirely new switchboard in this database, first rename the Switchboard Items table.

FIGURE 24-16.

The message box that appears if the Switchboard Manager does not find a valid switchboard form and table in your database.

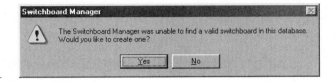

After the Switchboard Manager builds a skeleton switchboard form and a Switchboard Items table (or after it establishes that you already have these objects in your database), it displays the main Switchboard Manager window. To build an additional switchboard form (called a "page" in the wizard), click the New button and enter a name for the new switchboard form in the resulting dialog box, as shown in Figure 24-17. Click OK to create the form.

FIGURE 24-17.

Adding an additional switchboard form to the main switchboard form.

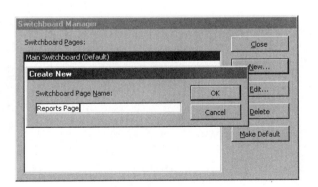

After you create the additional switchboard forms that you need, you can select one in the main Switchboard Manager window and click the Edit button to begin defining actions on the form. You'll see a window similar to the one shown in the background in Figure 24-18 on the next page. Use this window to create a new action, edit an existing action, or change the order of actions. Figure 24-18 shows a new action being created. The Switchboard Manager can create actions such as moving to another switchboard form, opening a form in add or edit mode, opening a report, switching to Design view, exiting the application, or running a macro or a Visual Basic procedure. When you create a new action, the Switchboard Manager places a command button on the switchboard form to execute that action.

FIGURE 24-18.

Creating a new action on a switchboard form.

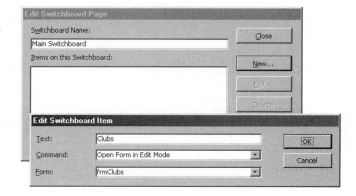

On the main switchboard form, you should create actions to open other forms. You should also consider creating an action to exit the application. On each subsequent form, you should always provide at least one action to move back through the switchboard-form tree or to go back to the main switchboard form, as shown in Figure 24-19.

FIGURE 24-19.

Creating an action to return to the main switchboard form from another switchboard form.

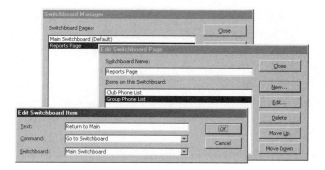

After you finish, the Switchboard Manager saves the main switchboard form with the name *Switchboard*. You can rename this form if you'd like to. If you want to rename the Switchboard Items table, be sure to edit the Visual Basic procedures stored with the switchboard form so that they refer to the new name. You'll also need to change the record source of the form.

Figure 24-20 shows an example switchboard form for the Entertainment Scheduling database. I edited the form design to add the RM Productions logo.

FIGURE 24-20.

The resulting main switchboard form.

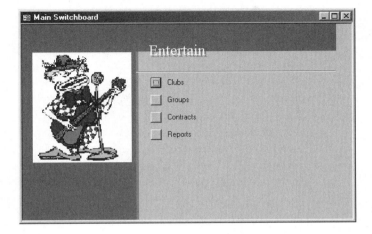

Setting Startup Properties for Your Database

At this point, you know how to build all the pieces you need to fully implement your database application. But what if you want your application to perform a task automatically when you open your database? If you create a macro named *Autoexec*, Microsoft Access will always run it when you open the database (unless you hold down the Shift key when you open the database). However, a better way to start your application is to specify an opening form in the startup properties for the database. You can set these properties by switching to the Database window and then choosing Startup from the Tools menu. Access opens the Startup dialog box. Click the Advanced button to see the entire dialog box, as shown in Figure 24-21.

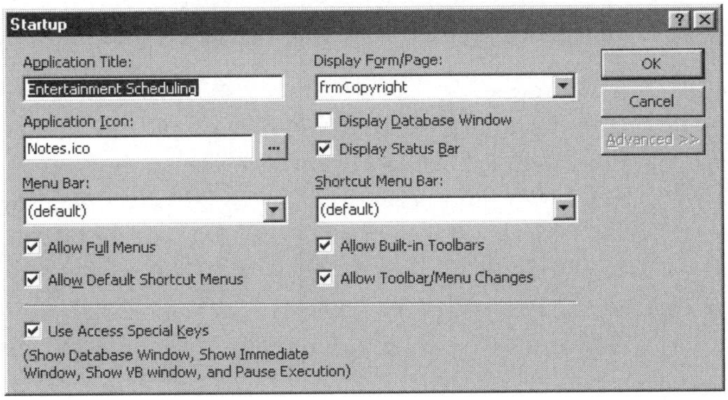

FIGURE 24-21.

Setting startup properties for your database.

You can specify which form or data access page opens your database by selecting a form from the Display Form/Page drop-down list. You can also specify a custom title for the application, an icon for the application, a default menu bar, and a default shortcut menu bar to override the standard menus for all forms. If you always open the database with its folder set to the current directory, you can simply enter the icon file name, as shown in the figure. If you're not sure what folder will be current when the application opens, you should enter a fully qualified filename location. If you clear the Display Database Window check box, Access hides the Database window when your application starts. You can also hide the status bar if you want to by clearing the Display Status Bar check box. Access has a set of condensed built-in menus that don't provide, for example, access to design commands. If you clear the Allow Full Menus check box, Access provides these shortened menus as the default. You can also hide all the built-in toolbars (you should provide your own custom toolbars in this case), disallow toolbar changes, and disallow the default shortcut menus.

Finally, you can disable some of the special keys—such as F11 to reveal the Database window, Ctrl+G to open the Debug window, or Ctrl+Break to halt code execution. As you can see, you have many powerful options for customizing how your application starts and how it operates.

Performing a Final Visual Basic Compile

The very last task you should perform before placing your application "in production" is to compile and save all of your Visual Basic procedures. When you do this, Access stores a compiled version of the code in your database. Access uses the compiled code when it needs to execute a procedure you have written. If you don't do this, Access has to load and interpret your procedures the first time you reference them, each time you start your application. For example, if you have several procedures in a form module, the form will open more slowly the first time because Access has to also load and compile the code.

To compile and save all the Visual Basic procedures in your application, open any module—either a module object or a module associated with a form or report. Choose Compile from the Debug menu, as shown in Figure 24-22. If your code compiles successfully, be sure to save the result by choosing Save from the File menu or by clicking the Save button on the toolbar. Close your database, and compact it as described in Chapter 6, "Modifying Your Database Design." In Access for Windows 95, renaming your database always "decompiled" your code.

This meant that if you changed the database name, you would have to compile your code again. With Access 97 and Access 2000, you don't have to recompile the code after renaming the database file.

FIGURE 24-22.

Choose the Compile And Save All Modules command from the Debug menu to compile all the Visual Basic procedures in your database.

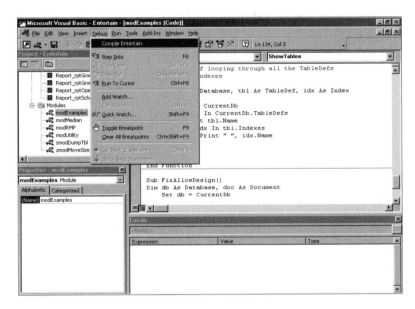

I hope you're as impressed as I am by the power and simplicity of Microsoft Access as an application development tool. As you've seen in this book, you can quickly learn to build complex applications for the Windows 95, Windows 98, Windows NT, and Windows 2000 operating systems. You can use the relational database management system in Access to store and manage your data locally or on a network, and you can access information in other popular database formats or in any server-hosted or mainframe-hosted database that supports the Open Database Connectivity (ODBC) standard. You can get started with macros to become familiar with event-oriented programming and to prototype your application. With a little practice, you'll soon find yourself writing Visual Basic event procedures like a pro. In the final chapter in this book, you can learn about some additional features you might want to use—security, replication, client/server databases, and the Office Developer Edition—to further enhance the way your application works or to prepare it for distribution to many users.

CHAPTER 25

After Completing Your Application

I f you've worked through the previous chapters in this book, you've created all the components and have all the knowledge necessary to produce a fully functioning application in Microsoft Access. If you've built an application for your personal use, you may never need to learn more about "advanced" Access features. But the first time you want to take your database "on the road," share the application with other users, or create a version of your application that links directly to Microsoft SQL Server, you'll need to become familiar with one or more of the features discussed in this chapter. Read on.

Taking Advantage of Replication

Replication allows you to make copies of a "master" database that you can later synchronize by using utilities provided in Access. Once you've set up a database for replication, one copy becomes the *Design Master,* and this is the only copy in which you can make changes to the design of any tables, queries, forms, reports, macros, and modules. You can make one or more replicas either from the Design Master or from

921

another replica. The replicas can reside on the same machine, on another machine connected through a local area network (LAN), or on a remote machine that can connect over the Internet or over a modem to the local network. You can make changes in the Design Master and use synchronization utilities to send the changes to each replica. You can change data in any replica and use the same synchronization utilities to exchange updates between copies. When different changes have been made to the same record in two different copies, Access provides a conflict resolution utility to help you decide which version of the record to keep.

You might find replication useful in the following ways.

- You can create a replication copy on a laptop computer that you take on the road and use synchronization utilities when you return to update your master copy. You can also dial in from a remote location to save changes to the master copy in your office.

- Remote users who need to run the same application but who need to share updates only periodically (for example, sales representatives who have distinct territories) can be given replicas. Design updates can be broadcast periodically from the Design Master, and data updates can be retrieved as needed by the remote users.

- You can use replication for a large and complex database to maintain one or more backup copies. As you make changes in the Design Master, you can synchronize copies periodically to maintain several generations of backup data. Synchronization is often faster than making full copies.

Replication Considerations

When you convert a database to be used with replication, Access makes several changes to the database. Access adds a number of system tables to track both design and data changes. If you make only a few changes between each synchronization, these tables remain relatively small.

For tables that do not have an AutoNumber field as a primary key, Access adds a hidden Replication ID field to ensure that it can uniquely identify new rows in any replica. When the primary key of a table is an AutoNumber field, Access changes the New Values property of the field to Random. Note that Random values include very large positive and negative numbers. If you display the primary key value (for example, as a customer ID on an invoice), you might want to add a Visual Basic procedure to your application's customer-entry form to generate a new Long Integer value as the primary key and let Access create a separate Replication ID field.

Finally, Access generates additional fields to track changes to memo fields and OLE object fields. The net result is that large databases might grow by 10 to 20 percent, but small databases might double in size to support replication.

Creating a Replica

CAUTION

Anyone with exclusive access to an Access database can convert it to a Design Master. Unless you save a backup copy, changes are difficult to reverse. Never replicate a database that you do not own without first checking with your system administrator or the owner of the database.

Before you convert a database to a Design Master, you might want to create a backup copy of the database in another folder. Once you convert a database to a Design Master, you can't easily change it back to a "plain" database. If you use the Create Replica utility in Access, as you'll see below, the utility offers to create a backup copy with the file extension bak. You must have permission to open the database exclusively. You must also have full access to any folder in which you want to create a replica.

For users on the road, Access replication also works with the Windows 95/98 Briefcase. You can connect your portable computer to your network, find the "master" copy in a shared folder, and drag it to your Briefcase to create a replica. If the database in the shared folder is not yet a Design Master, Access offers to convert it for you. When you create a replica using the Briefcase, you'll see many of the same dialog boxes and messages that are shown in this section.

NOTE

> You must install Microsoft Briefcase Replication using the Microsoft Office 2000 Setup program in order to use Access replication with the Windows Briefcase feature.

To convert a database to a Design Master and create a replica is quite simple. In the following example, I first made a copy of the Wedding List database and named it Wedding Repl. I then converted Wedding Repl to a Design Master and created a replica named Replica Of Wedding Repl. Finally I made a few changes to the data in the replica for the synchronization example that follows. You can find these additional files on the companion CD, or you can create them yourself as follows.

First you should open the database that you want to replicate. Choose Replication from the Tools menu, and choose Create Replica from the submenu, as shown in Figure 25-1 on the next page. Note that the

VI

Creating an Application

other options on the Replication submenu are grayed out, indicating that the current database is not yet part of a replica set.

FIGURE 25-1.
Choose Create Replica to begin converting the current database to a Design Master and creating a replica copy.

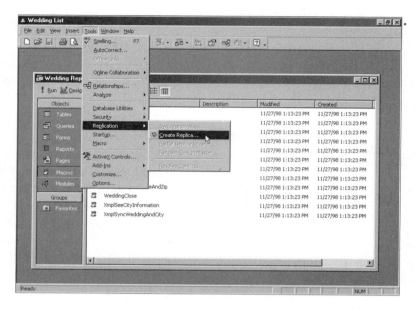

When you choose Create Replica, Access informs you that it needs to close and reopen the current database before it can proceed. It does this to ensure that it can open the database in exclusive mode so that no one else can change the database while Access converts it. Next Access displays the dialog box shown in Figure 25-2. You'll see that Access strongly recommends that you create a backup copy because changes necessary to implement replication are difficult to undo. If you haven't already made a backup copy, you should accept the offer to create a copy with the bak filename extension. Click Yes to create a backup or No to proceed without creating a backup. Click Cancel to exit without creating a Design Master or replica.

FIGURE 25-2.
The replication utility strongly recommends that you create a backup copy before converting a database to a Design Master.

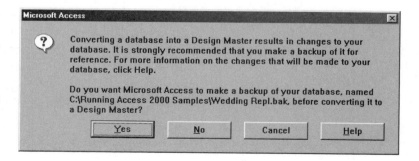

If you tell Access to proceed, it creates a backup (if you clicked Yes) and then converts the database you had open to a Design Master. Access adds several hidden system tables to the database, adds some tracking fields to your tables, and in each table either converts the AutoNumber primary key field or inserts a Replication ID field. Next Access asks you to identify a folder and filename for your replica. If you click Cancel at this point, Access does not create a replica. If you identify a folder and filename, Access creates a replica and confirms successful completion by displaying the message shown in Figure 25-3.

FIGURE 25-3.

Access confirms creation of your Design Master and one replica.

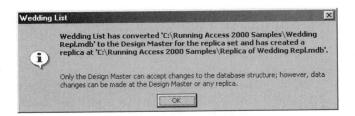

If you want to create additional replicas, you must open either the Design Master or any of the replicas and then use the Create Replica command again. When you open any replicated database, the title in the Database window gives you a clear indication of whether you've opened the Design Master or one of the replicas. Objects that were replicated appear with special symbols next to the object's name, as shown in Figure 25-4. If you've opened the Design Master, you can open any object in Design view and change it. The next time you synchronize with any of the replicas (see the next section), Access copies only the changed objects to the replica.

FIGURE 25-4.

The Database window in a Design Master with special symbols next to all replicated objects.

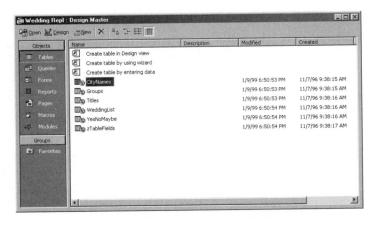

VI

Creating an Application

NOTE

If you move a Design Master database to a different folder or to a different computer (even though the folder name is the same), Access will continue to recognize that the database is replicated, but it will no longer identify it as a Design Master. For this reason, when you first open Wedding Repl (after you copy it from the companion CD), Access will not recognize that it is a Design Master. To identify this database as a Design Master (or to convert any replica to a Design Master if your original master copy becomes corrupted or lost), choose Replication from the Tools menu and then choose Recover Design Master from the submenu. Access will prompt you to first synchronize the database with all other replicas. This is important only if there are design changes that have not yet been incorporated into a replica that you are converting to a Design Master.

When you open a replica, you can open replicated objects in Design view, but Access warns you that it will open a read-only copy. If you make any design changes to a replicated object in a replica, you can save the changes only as a new object. You can create new objects in a replica, but these objects will not participate in synchronization. (You can use this technique if you need to replicate only a few tables.)

Synchronizing Replicas

To give you an idea of how synchronizing replicas works, I opened the Replica Of Wedding Repl database and made a few changes to the data, as shown in Figure 25-5. I added a new invitee to the WeddingList table, and, in the process, I added a new city in the CityNames table. If you open either of the sample replica databases, you'll find this data missing. Open one of them and add a new invitee and city, and then follow along to synchronize the data in both.

To synchronize a replica with either the Design Master or another replica in the set, open either database, switch to the Database window, choose Replication from the Tools menu, and then choose Synchronize Now from the submenu. If any objects are open in the database, Access will prompt you to close them. Access displays the Synchronize Database dialog box, shown in Figure 25-6.

Access displays all the known replicas in the replica set in the Synchronize With drop-down list. (If you created another replica by copying an existing replica, Access won't know about the copy, but you can still synchronize the copy with any legitimate replica.) If you have moved the replica with which you want to synchronize, click the Browse button to locate the folder and file. Click OK to complete the

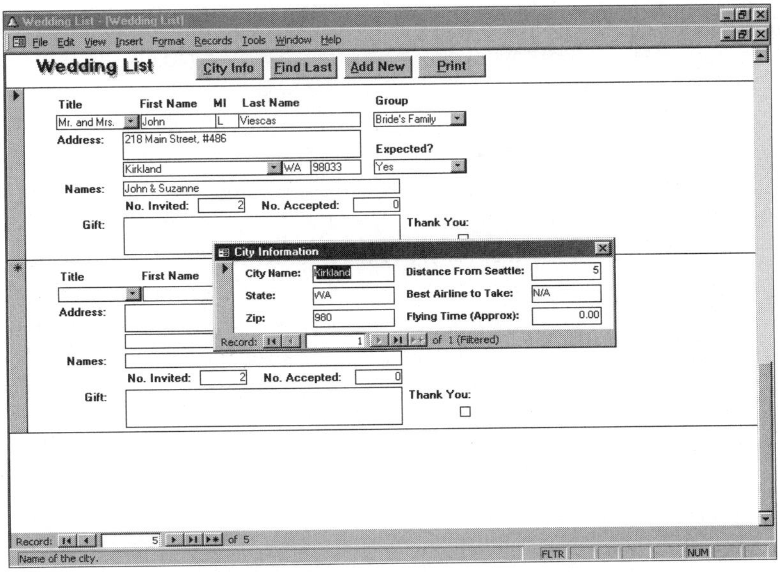

FIGURE 25-5.

New data entered in tables in a replica.

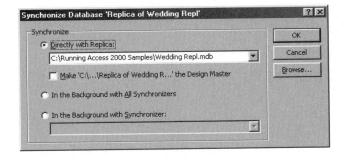

FIGURE 25-6.

Use the Synchronize Database dialog box to identify the replica or Design Master that you want to synchronize with the current database.

synchronization. Note that there's an option to convert the current database to the Design Master as you do this.

If you perform synchronization between the Wedding Repl and Replica Of Wedding Repl databases, you will find that the missing invitation and city records now appear in the Wedding Repl.

If Access has any problems synchronizing the databases (for example, if it finds two different changes to the same record), it saves the conflicts in a special internal table. Choose Replication from the Tools menu, and then choose Resolve Conflicts from the submenu to review and resolve any conflicts. Access shows you the conflicting results in two side-by-side windows and gives you the chance to choose which update "wins."

Securing Your Database

If you explore any of the main editing forms in the Microsoft Press Books database, you'll discover lots of code in the form Load and Current event procedures that enables and disables various controls and features on the form depending on the "sign-on" status of the user. Also, when you start the application, a sign-on form opens and asks you to identify yourself and enter a password if you're logging on to an account that either has "admin" status (you can change book and author information) or has a credit card number defined.

These measures may keep the casual user "locked out" of features they shouldn't be allowed to use, but they don't prevent anyone who has a retail copy of Access from opening the database with the Shift key held down (so that the application doesn't start) and then rummaging around in the code to figure out how to break through this security. If you really want to prevent unauthorized access to the objects in this database, you must implement the security features built into Access.

> **NOTE**
>
> Few, if any, computer security systems are completely impenetrable. Although the security facilities in Access are state-of-the-art for personal computer desktop systems, a very knowledgeable person, given enough time, could probably break into your properly secured Access database. If you require utmost security for your data, you should consider moving it to a database system such as Microsoft SQL Server.

Access Security Architecture

If you have had any experience with security on server or mainframe systems, the security architecture in Access will seem familiar to you. You can set up individual users who can be authorized or denied permission to various objects in your database. You can also define groups of users and assign permissions at the group level to make it easy to set up security for a large number of users. A user must be a member of the group to acquire the permissions of the group.

Access stores its security information in two separate locations. When you install Access, the setup program creates a default workgroup file (System.mdw) in your \Program Files\Microsoft Office\Office folder that contains the definition of all users and groups. When you create a database, Access stores within the database (mdb) file the permissions granted to individual users or groups of users. You can see this architecture depicted in Figure 25-7.

FIGURE 25-7.

The general architecture of the Access security system. User and Group Profiles are stored in a workgroup file. Individual object permissions are stored in each database file.

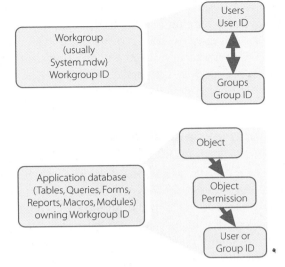

The location of your current workgroup file is stored in your Windows registry. As you'll see a bit later, you can use a special utility program called Wrkgadm.exe to change your current workgroup or to define a new workgroup file. You can also pick a different workgroup file at run time by specifying a parameter on the command line of a startup shortcut. *See "Creating an Application Shortcut" later in this chapter for details about run-time options.* If you frequently run a shared, secured application over a network, your system administrator might set up your default workgroup as a shared file in a network folder.

Each workgroup has a unique internal identifier that Access creates when you define a workgroup file. Any database created under the workgroup is "owned" by the workgroup as well as by the user who created the database. Each user and group also has a unique internal identifier, and, as you'll see a bit later, you can duplicate the same user and group ID in several different workgroups. When you assign a permission to an object in your database, Access stores the internal ID of the user or group along with the permission in the database. In this way, the permissions that you grant move with the database file if you move the file to another folder or computer.

Users, Groups, and Permissions

In general, a computer security system is either *open* or *closed*. In an open security model, access is granted to all users (even users not identified to the system) unless specifically denied. In a closed model, no access is granted to anyone unless specifically defined. At first blush, the Access security model seems open because you can start Access without logging on, create databases, and give them to other users who have Access to run or modify them as they please. You don't have to interact with security at all. In truth, the security model in Access is closed, but it appears open because your default workgroup always defines certain built-in user and group IDs that are universal to all installations of Access.

Built-In Users and Groups

All Access workgroup files installed anywhere in the world contain one built-in user ID and two built-in groups. The user ID is called *Admin,* and if there's no password defined for this user, Access automatically logs you on with the Admin ID and grants you all the rights and privileges of this user ID. Whenever you create a new database or an object within a database, your current user ID becomes the owner of the object and is granted full permissions to the object by default. Because most users of Access never "turn on" security, they always log on to Access as Admin, so anything they create is owned by the universal Admin ID.

The first built-in group is Users. By default, all users (even new ones you create) become members of the Users group and cannot be removed from it. In addition, the internal ID for the Users group is universal and identical in every workgroup. Access by default grants the Users group full permissions to any new database or object you create. Unless in your database you explicitly remove permissions from the Users group, even if a user is logged on with a user ID other than Admin, he or she still has full access to your databases and the objects within them because the user is always a member of the universal Users group!

The second built-in group is Admins. The internal ID of the Admins group is unique for each workgroup file, depending on the information you supplied to the workgroup administrator program when you created the workgroup file. Only the Admin user is, by default, a member of the Admins group. However, as you'll see a bit later, you can define another user, add that user to the Admins group, and remove the default Admin user ID. You must always have at least one user in the Admins group.

The Admins group has a couple of key properties. First, only members of the Admins group may define or modify user and group profiles and reset passwords. (You can always reset your own password.) Second, members of the Admins group that matches the Admins group in use when you created the database have full authority to grant permissions to objects in the database. This means that members of Admins can grant themselves permission to secured objects, even if they initially have no permission. The key thing to understand is that any database you create while connected to a particular workgroup file inherits the ID of that workgroup. Someone can be a member of Admins in another workgroup, but unless the workgroup IDs match, that person won't have security permissions to your database.

Object Permissions

Table 25-1 lists the various permissions you can assign to a database or to the objects within a database. Note that the owner of an object might not have any specific permissions, but because of owner status he or she can grant any or all of the permissions to any user or group, including to his or her own user ID.

 NOTE

> Because data access pages are stored outside your mdb file, Access cannot secure them.

TABLE 25-1.   Permissions You Can Grant Using Access Security

Permission	Applies To	Meaning
Open/Run	Database, Form, Report, Macro	Grants permission to open or run the object. (All users have permission to run procedures in modules.)
Open Exclusive	Database	Grants permission to open the database and lock out other users.
Read Design	Table, Query, Form, Report, Macro, Module	Grants permission to open the object in Design view. For tables and queries, granting any access to the data also implies Read Design permission because the design must be available in order to correctly open a recordset.
Modify Design	Table, Query, Form, Report, Macro, Module	Grants permission to change the design of an object. If your application has Visual Basic code that changes the definition of queries while executing, you must grant Modify Design permission to all users for those queries.
Administer	Database, Table, Query, Form, Report, Macro, Module	Grants permission to assign permissions to the object, even though the user or group might not own the object.

VI

Creating an Application

(continued)

TABLE 25-1. *continued*

Permission	Applies To	Meaning
Read Data	Table, Query	Allows the user or group to read the data in the table. Also implies Read Design permission. For a query, the user must also have Read Data permissions on all tables or queries used in the query.
Update Data	Table, Query	Grants permission to update data in the table or query. Also implies Read Data and Read Design permissions. For a query, the user must also have Update Data permissions on the tables being updated through the query.
Insert Data	Table, Query	Grants permission to insert data in the table or query. Also implies Read Data and Read Design permissions. For a query, the user must also have Insert Data permissions on the tables or queries being updated through the query.
Delete Data	Table, Query	Grants permission to delete data in the table or query. Also implies Read Data and Read Design permissions. For a query, the user must also have Delete Data permissions on the tables being updated through the query.

Explicit and Implicit Permissions

As implied earlier, you can gain access to an object either by permissions assigned to your user ID or through permissions granted to any group to which you belong. Access uses a "least restrictive" permissions model, which means you have the highest permissions granted either to your user ID or to any group of which you are a member. Figure 25-8 shows a hypothetical set of users and groups and the permissions granted explicitly to each user or group for a Table object. Note that individual users might implicitly inherit additional permissions or ownership rights because of their membership in one or more groups. David has at least Read Data, Update Data, Insert Data, and Delete Data permissions because of his membership in the Marketing group. If he is the owner because he created the Table object, he will also have Modify Design and Administer permissions because Access assigns those permissions when you create an object. On the other hand, if someone else created the object and later transferred ownership to David or to a group of which David is a member, David can directly grant himself any missing permissions.

FIGURE 25-8.
An example showing explicitly assigned permissions and the permissions implicit for each user either directly or by group membership.

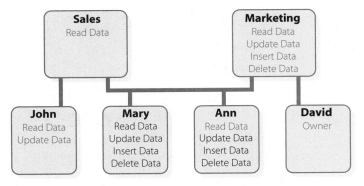

Key: Explicit permissions
         Inherited permissions

Explicit permissions:
   Sales has Read Data permission
   Marketing has Read Data, Update Data, Insert Data, and Delete Data permissions
   John has Read Data and Update Data permissions
   Mary has no explicit permissions
   Ann has Read Data permission
   David owns the object

Actual permissions:
   John has Read Data and Update Data permissions (even though Sales has only Read Data permission)
   Mary has Read Data, Update Data, Insert Data, and Delete Data permissions (through Marketing)
   Ann has Read Data, Update Data, Insert Data, and Delete Data permissions (through Marketing)
   David has full permissions, can assign permissions, and can delete the object (because he owns the object)

You can see why a user other than Admin might still have full permissions to all your objects—all users are always members of the Users group, which is, by default, granted full permissions to any new object. To check the permissions for any user or group, first open the database in which you want to review permissions. (You can do this for all the sample databases on the companion CD except Books Secured.mdb.) You must either be the owner of the database and of all the objects you want to check or have Administer permission on the database and objects. Choose Security from the Tools menu, and then choose User And Group Permissions from the submenu. Access opens the window shown in Figure 25-9 on the next page.

In the upper portion of the window, in the User/Group Name list, you can see the list either of users or of groups defined in the database. Choose either the Users or the Groups option button to switch from one list to the other. In the Object Name list, you can see a list of objects. Use the drop-down box below the list to select the type of objects you want to review. Click the object of interest to see the explicitly defined permissions in the check boxes in the lower half of the window. If you select Groups and then select the Users group, you

VI

Creating an Application

FIGURE 25-9.

Some of the permissions for the Users group in the Microsoft Press Books sample database.

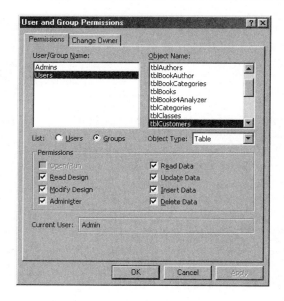

can wander around all the objects and see that this group has full permissions for all objects. As you'll see a bit later, you can select one or more objects to which you have Administer permission and change the permissions for any user or group.

If you click the Change Owner tab, you can peruse lists of the various objects and see what ID (either a user or a group) currently owns the object. In most cases, the Admin user owns all the objects. You can select one or more objects, choose a different user or group, and click the Change Owner button to assign a new owner. Never give away ownership of an object unless you fully understand the implications of doing so. You might first want to be sure that you know how to log on as the potential new owner before assigning ownership to that new owner. If you own an object, you can always give ownership away (or back) to another user or group ID.

⊗ CAUTION

Do not attempt to change permissions or ownership of any object until you fully understand all the implications of doing so. As you first start to learn about security facilities in Access, it's a good idea to always work in a backup copy of your database. You might end up denying yourself permission and not be able to recover!

Using the Security Wizard

Now that you understand a little bit about how Access security works, it should be obvious to you that making Access security "transparently open" means you have a lot of work to do to actually secure a database. The typical setup builds your default workgroup from your Windows user and company name information—something that anyone who has access to your computer can figure out and duplicate. So, for starters you need a unique workgroup so that it's difficult to reproduce the workgroup ID that gives all members of the Admins group authority to change permissions. Next you need a user ID other than Admin to own your database and all the objects in it. You also need to remove all permissions from the Users group for all objects. To make sure no one can peruse your data and code with a disk-editing utility, you should also encrypt your database.

You could perform all these steps "by hand," but fortunately Microsoft has provided a User-Level Security Wizard to help you out. The Security Wizard performs all the repetitious work involved in the above steps. Before you can use the wizard, however, you need to make a few preliminary preparations.

Preliminary Preparations

Before the wizard can successfully perform its task, you must be logged on as the owner of the database that you want to secure, or you must be logged on to the same workgroup file you used when you created the database and you must be a member of the Admins group in that workgroup. Remember that one of the key steps is creating a new workgroup with a unique workgroup ID; this probably won't match the workgroup you used to create the database. Also, you were probably logged on as user Admin when you created the database. You can't make a database owned by Admin secure, so you need to assign a new owner as well.

As you'll see a bit later, the Security Wizard in Access 2000 lets you secure your database even when you're logged on as user Admin in the original workgroup. When you try to use the wizard in this situation, the wizard forces you to create a new workgroup. The wizard transfers ownership of your database to the new user ID in the new workgroup—but you must be the owner of the database for it to be able to do so. You can also create a new workgroup and a new non-Admin user ID in the Admins group of that workgroup before you start the wizard, but your new user ID must own the database, or the wizard will fail when it tries to reassign ownership.

I think it helps you understand Access security better if you first create a new workgroup, define at least one new user ID, and remove the Admin user from the Admins group. To create a new workgroup, you need to find the Wrkgadm.exe program on your computer. Setup normally installs this program in a subfolder of your Microsoft Office installation folder. To help you out, I created a shortcut called Workgroup Administrator that you can copy from the companion CD. If you installed Office on your C drive in the Program Files folder, the shortcut should work for you without modification. If Office is in another location, you can right-click the shortcut in Windows Explorer, select Properties from the shortcut menu, and click the Shortcut tab to change the Target and Start In settings. Double-click the shortcut to start Workgroup Administrator, shown in Figure 25-10.

FIGURE 25-10.

The opening dialog box in Workgroup Administrator.

The Access 2000 version of Workgroup Administrator no longer displays your name and company information in its opening dialog box. However, you can find out this information by opening any Office application on your machine and choosing About from the Help menu. This makes it easy to obtain this key information. You can also see the full pathname of the workgroup file to which you are currently attached. As shown in Figure 25-10, your default file is called System.mdw, which can be found in your Office folder. If you have a different workgroup file already built, you can click the Join button to open a dialog box in which you can specify the location of that file. A Browse button on the resulting dialog box makes it easy to locate the file.

To create and join a new workgroup, click the Create button. Workgroup Administrator displays a second dialog box, as shown in Figure 25-11. Enter a Name, Organization name, and a pattern of letters and numbers up to 20 characters long as the Workgroup ID. Workgroup Administrator uses the information in these three fields to generate a unique 64-bit internal ID. To create another workgroup file with an identical ID, you must enter the information in these three fields in *exactly* the same manner, including the same pattern of uppercase and lowercase letters. You should record this information and keep it in a safe place so that you can rebuild your workgroup file should it ever be deleted or become unusable. The information you can see in Figure 25-11 is the exact data I used to create the Secured.mdw workgroup file that you can find on the companion CD.

You'll need either the sample Secured.mdw file or one created with the same parameters to open the Books Secured sample database successfully. You can either create your own workgroup file with the settings shown in Figure 25-11 or use Workgroup Administrator to join the Secured.mdw workgroup you'll find in the sample files.

FIGURE 25-11.

Entering the information that Workgroup Administrator uses to create a unique ID in your new workgroup file.

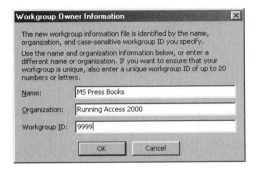

Click OK to go on to a dialog box where you can specify the location and name of your new workgroup file. If you're creating the file in the same folder as the existing workgroup file, be sure to give the new file a different name—something like *secured.mdw*. Click OK in that dialog box to create the new workgroup file. Workgroup Administrator also changes your registry settings to "join" you to the newly created workgroup. Click OK in the confirmation dialog boxes, and then click Exit in the first dialog box to close Workgroup Administrator. If Access is already running on your computer, you must exit and restart Access in order to run in the new workgroup.

After you start Access in the new workgroup, you need to add a new user, make that user an Admin user, define a password for Admin, and remove the default Admin user from the Admins group. You don't need to open a database to do any of this. Once you have Access open, choose Security from the Tools menu and then select User And Group Accounts from the submenu. (Because you don't yet have a password defined for Admin, Access silently logs you on as Admin, the only member of the Admins group in your new workgroup.) Access shows you the User And Group Accounts maintenance window that you can see in Figure 25-12 on the next page.

If you drop down the Name list in the User area of the Users tab, you'll see there's only one user defined in this workgroup—Admin. In the lower part of the window, the two available groups appear on the left.

VI

Creating an Application

FIGURE 25-12.

Creating a new user in the User And Group Accounts maintenance window.

The right side shows that Admin belongs to both groups. You'll see how to add and remove groups just a bit later. The top of the Users tab contains the buttons you use to define a new user, to delete the user currently selected in the Name list (but Access won't ever let you delete the Admin user), and to clear the password for the currently selected user.

In this case, you need a new user who will both own all the objects and be a member of the Admins group. Click the New button to display the New User/Group dialog box, also shown in Figure 25-12. In the Secured.mdw workgroup file, I created a user named JohnV with a Personal ID of 9999, as shown. The Personal ID (this is *not* the user's password) must contain at least 4 and no more than 20 characters and numbers. If you enter this exact information in another workgroup file, you will have a JohnV user ID identical to this one. Note that the combination of uppercase and lowercase letters is important. In other words, entering JOHNV and 9999 creates a user ID that has an entirely different internal identification code. As you'll discover later, the name is not case sensitive in the Logon dialog box, so you can't create a JohnV and a JOHNV user in the same workgroup.

> **NOTE**
>
> The Books 2B Secured database is owned by user JohnV as described in this section. You must either use the Secured.mdw sample workgroup file and log on as JohnV or create an identical user in your workgroup and log on as that user to be able to use the Security Wizard in the examples later in this chapter.

Click OK to add the user. You should see the new user selected in the Name drop-down box. In the Available Groups list, select the Admins group and click the Add button to make the new user a member of the Admins group. You can see that the new user is already a member of the Users group, which gives it full permissions to all objects in any unsecured database. You cannot remove any user from the Users group.

Next select your current ID (Admin) in the Name drop-down box. Select the Admins group in the Member Of list, and click Remove to remove Admin from the Admins group. Note that if you try to do this before you create the new user ID and add it to Admins, Access won't let you because at least one user must be a member of the Admins group. Finally, click the Change Logon Password tab, and enter a password in both the New Password and Verify boxes. In the Secured.mdw file, I set a password of "books" for the Admin user. Click Apply to set the password for the Admin user ID. Setting a password for Admin forces Access to ask you for a name and password the next time you start Access in this workgroup.

Once you create the new user ID, you need to close Access once again, and then restart. As soon as you try to open any database, Access prompts you for a user name and password because the default user ID, Admin, now is secured with a password. Because you haven't logged on as JohnV yet and assigned a password to that account, you should be able to enter JohnV and no password in the Logon dialog box.

If you want to use the Security Wizard to secure a database other than the sample Books 2B Secured database, you must first create a copy of the database that is owned by JohnV or another user in the Admins group other than Admin. (Remember that you must be the owner of the database you want to secure.) To do that, follow these steps.

1 Log on as the new (non-Admin) user.

2 Create a new blank database. *See "Creating a New Empty Database" in Chapter 5 for details.*

3 Import all the objects from the database you want to secure by choosing Get External Data from the File menu, and then choosing Import from the submenu. Point to the original database, and then be sure to select all objects in the Import dialog box.

    If your old database contains any custom menus, toolbars, or import/export specifications, be sure to click the Options tab and select the options to import these objects. *See "Importing Access Objects" in Chapter 10 for details.*

4 Once the import is complete, you should compile and save the Visual Basic project and compact the database.

To compile the project, open any module in Design view. If the code you imported from the old database used either Data Access or Office objects, you should choose References from the Tools menu and include those libraries. Choose Compile from the Debug menu, and if the project compiles successfully, choose Save from the File menu.

To compact the database, close it, choose Database Utilities from the Tools menu, and then choose Compact And Repair Database from the submenu.

You should now have a new copy of your database that is owned by the new user ID you created in a new workgroup.

Running the Wizard

Now you're ready to run the Security Wizard. Be sure you're logged on as the owner of the database that you want to secure. If you have followed along with the steps thus far, you can open the Books 2B Secured database that's in your sample files folder. (Hold down the Shift key when you open the database so the application doesn't start.) If you prefer, you can open any other database you want to secure as long as you're the owner. The Security Wizard will secure the open database, so it's a good idea to have a backup copy (although the wizard will offer to create one for you).

To start the Security Wizard, choose Security from the Tools menu and then choose User-Level Security Wizard from the submenu. The wizard starts and displays the dialog box shown in Figure 25-13.

The first dialog box explains a bit about what the wizard does and gives you two options. If you choose the first option, the wizard will create a new workgroup file, create a new (not Admin) user ID in that workgroup, and then secure the database using that workgroup and user ID. If you choose the second option (if you're logged on as user Admin, the Wizard won't let you pick this option), the wizard will secure the database using your current workgroup file and user ID. Because we just built a new workgroup and user ID, in this example you should choose the second option, and then click Next to display the dialog box shown in Figure 25-14.

FIGURE 25-13.

The opening dialog box in the User-Level Security Wizard.

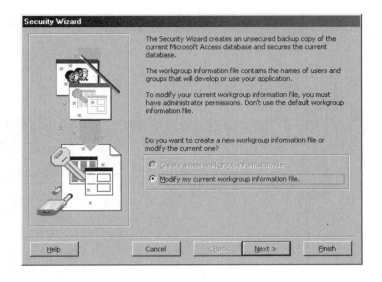

FIGURE 25-14.

Choosing the objects that you want the wizard to secure.

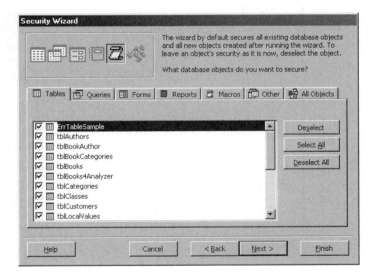

In the dialog box shown in Figure 25-14, the wizard gives you the option to secure only selected objects. By default, the wizard selects all objects. (Note that you cannot secure data access pages with Access security because these objects are stored in files external to Access.) You might want to deselect certain objects. (Click the check box next to an object name to change the object's selection status.) For example, perhaps you don't need to secure certain forms and reports, but you do want to assign permissions to tables and queries. Click Next to continue.

Exploring the Wizard's First Option

If you're curious how the first option in the Security Wizard's opening dialog box works, select it and click Next. The wizard displays a workgroup setup dialog box as shown below.

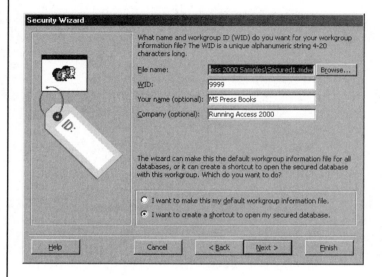

Note that the Wizard asks you for the same bits of information as Workgroup Administrator, which you used earlier, but in a slightly different sequence. You must also specify the location and name of your new workgroup file. You can click an option to make this new workgroup the default once the wizard has finished—I don't recommend this option because it's too easy to forget that the wizard has switched workgroups on you if you want to work with or secure other databases. The best option is to let the wizard create a shortcut on your desktop that will specifically ask for the new workgroup to be used when you open the secured database. See later in this chapter about the options you can use in an Access application shortcut.

In the following dialog box (shown in Figure 25-15), the wizard offers to set up one or more optional groups for you. You can click the name of each group in the box on the left to display a description of the permissions that the wizard will set up for the group in the Group Permissions box. If, for example, you want to set up a group of users who have only read and execute permissions to all objects, select the Read-Only Users check box to ask the wizard to create this group.

FIGURE 25-15.

Choosing additional optional Groups in the Security Wizard.

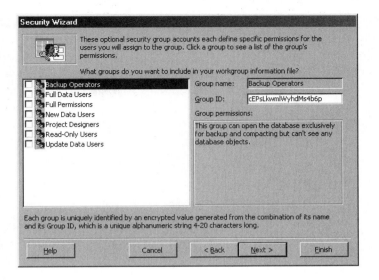

You can accept the randomly generated Group ID that the wizard displays or type in your own ID. In either case, I recommend that you write down the exact Group Name and Group ID information, because you will need this information (like the Workgroup ID and the Personal ID, the Group ID is case sensitive) if you ever need to rebuild the group. As you'll see a bit later, the wizard gives you the option to also define users and assign them to the groups you choose.

As you'll learn later in this section, Visual Basic code in the Books 2B Secured database checks for the existence of two special groups named AppAdmin and NotAdmin to determine the permissions of users within the application. We'll build these groups after the wizard has finished doing its job. We'll also examine this special Visual Basic code in detail later.

Since we don't need any of the groups that the wizard offers, you can leave them all unchecked. Click Next to go to the next dialog box, shown in Figure 25-16 on the next page.

In this dialog box, the wizard offers to leave some permissions intact for the universal Users group. Normally, you will want to let the wizard to remove all permissions from this group (the default) to fully secure your database. If you have tried to open the Books Secure database—a database that is a copy of the result you should obtain if you complete all the steps in this section—you probably discovered that you can look at all the data and the design of all objects, but you can't change anything. I accomplished this by granting to the Users

FIGURE 25-16.
Allowing some permissions to the default Users group.

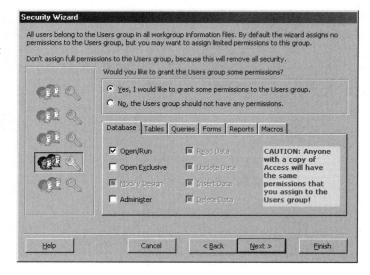

group Open/Run permission on the database, and either Read Design or Read Data permission on all other objects. You can duplicate this by first selecting Yes, I Would Like To Grant Some Permissions To The Users Group, and then setting the appropriate permissions for each of the object types. Note that the wizard cautions you about granting access once you do this! Click Next to go on to the next dialog box, shown in Figure 25-17.

FIGURE 25-17.
Defining additional users in your Workgroup.

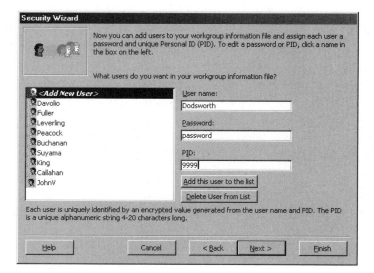

You can save a lot of time later if you take advantage of the wizard's offer to create new users. For Books 2B Secured, you will eventually need one user ID for each customer. I used this panel to set up all the customers and gave them a PID (Personal ID) of 9999. I assigned a password of "password" to Davolio, Fuller, Suyama, and Dodsworth to match the information in tblCustomers. These users are required to have passwords by the application because their customer records contain credit card information.

To add a user to the list, click the <Add New User> entry at the top of the list, enter the information required for User Name, Password (optional), and PID, and then click Add This User To The List to move the information to the list.

Note that the wizard also displays existing users in the list (JohnV in this case). The wizard indicates new users you have defined in this dialog box by displaying an asterisk next to the person icon. If you think you made a mistake, you can select any of the new users in the list to see the data you specified. You can click Delete User From List to remove one you added by mistake.

Click Next to go to the next dialog box, in which the wizard allows you to assign users to groups. Since we didn't select any additional groups (in the dialog box shown earlier in Figure 25-15), click Next to go to the wizard's final dialog box, shown in Figure 25-18.

FIGURE 25-18.

Telling the User-Level Security Wizard where to make a backup copy of your database.

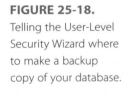

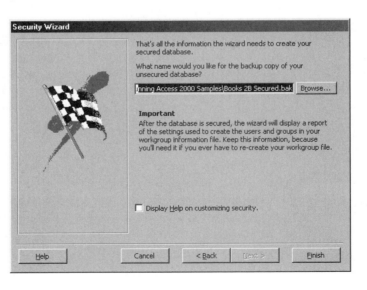

VI

Creating an Application

In the last dialog box, you can specify the name of the backup copy of your database file. Note that the wizard suggests using the original name of the database with a bak extension. Click Finish to let the wizard do its work.

When the wizard is done securing your objects, it produces a report that lists the workgroup parameters it used if you asked it to create a new workgroup, and the information you'll need to re-create any users and groups the wizard built for you. When you close the report window, the wizard offers to save the report as a Snapshot file (snp extension) for later reference. You should accept the wizard's offer so that you don't lose this critical information. The wizard then closes your newly secured database, encrypts it, and then reopens it. If there's a Startup form defined in the database (there is in Books 2B Secured), you should hold down the Shift key during this process to prevent the application from starting when the wizard reopens the database.

If you didn't get the result you wanted, you can always delete the newly secured database and rename the backup file that the wizard created back to its original name. In your sample files, you'll find Books Secured.mdb that is the result of running the wizard following the steps noted above on the Books 2B Secured database.

Setting Up Your Secured Database

Once you have a secured database, you may need to define some new users and groups to make it easy to grant the permissions you need. You could create only new users, but you would have to assign the permissions for each user individually. It's much easier to define one group for each level of access you intend to grant, and then define users and add them to the appropriate groups. In the Secured.mdw sample workgroup file, I created one group, called AppAdmin, that has full permissions over all objects. I created another group, called NotAdmin, to define normal execute-only or read-only status to most objects.

Open the newly secured database (hold down the Shift key if you're opening your secured copy of the Books 2B Secured database) while you are still using the Secured.mdw workgroup file. Choose Security from the Tools menu, and then choose User And Group Accounts from the submenu to open the User And Group Accounts dialog box. Click the Groups tab, and click the New button to open the New User/ Group dialog box, as shown in Figure 25-19. Defining a new group works just like defining a new user—the generation of the internal identifier is case sensitive for the name and personal ID that you enter. In Secured.mdw, I created both group names with an initial capital let-

FIGURE 25-19.
Creating a new security group.

ter and a capital letter A for Admin and used a Personal ID of 9999. Click OK to add the new group.

Next you need to define and add users to these groups. If you let the wizard define all the users we need for the secured version of the Microsoft Press Books database, you won't need to define them now. *See the instructions on page 938 (Figure 25-12) if you need to set up additional users.*

To define a user as a member of a group, choose Security from the Tools menu and choose User And Group Accounts from the submenu. On the Users tab, select the User that you want to assign to one or more groups. The lower part of this dialog box shows the list of available groups on the left and the list of groups to which the user is assigned on the right. In this case, you need to assign all the new users you created with the wizard to the NotAdmin group. Figure 25-20 on the next page shows that I've just added Buchanan to this group. Also be sure to assign JohnV to the AppAdmin group.

Next you need to set up permissions for the groups. Close the User And Group Accounts dialog box. Open the Tools menu again, choose Security, and then choose User And Group Permissions to see the dialog box shown in Figure 25-21 on the next page. Click Groups in the List options to see the list of groups. You can start by granting full permissions to the AppAdmin group. Select that group in the User/Group Name list, and then select each type of object in the Object Type drop-down list. Start with the database itself, and select Administer in the Permissions area. Click Apply before selecting a new object type.

FIGURE 25-20.

Assigning users to groups.

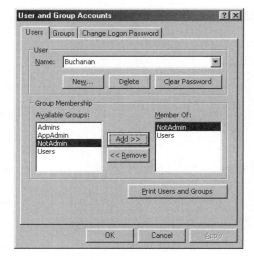

When you get to Tables in the Object Type drop-down list, choose the top entry in the list, scroll down to the bottom, press and hold the Shift key, and click the last item in the list to select them all. Make sure Administer appears with a black check mark (not a gray check mark), and then click Apply. Do the same for queries, forms, reports, macros, and modules.

FIGURE 25-21.

Set restricted permissions for the NotAdmin group.

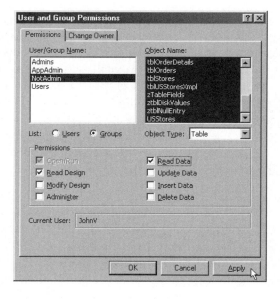

Next select the NotAdmin group in the User/Group Name list. Grant only Open/Run permission on the database. Grant Read Data for all tables and queries. Grant Open/Run for all forms, reports, and macros. Because users need to be able to "log on" internally to the application and create new orders for themselves, go back to the tblLocalValues table (used by the application sign-on form), the tblOrderDetails table, and the tblOrders table and grant Update Data, Insert Data, and Delete Data permissions. Also grant these permissions to the qryOrderBooks and qryOrdersSorted queries.

In the Books 2B Secured database (and its companion, the Books Secured database), I made a few changes to the frmSignon, frmMain, frmCustomer, and frmOrders forms so that they would work more smoothly with security implemented. For example, the frmSignon form no longer asks you to select a user ID. It examines your current logon ID (by using the built-in CurrentUser function) and sets your "admin" status in the application based on whether you are a member of the AppAdmin group. Then it merely asks you to confirm your ID. If you're not running with Secured.mdw as your workgroup file or if the file doesn't have the correct groups defined, the application closes the database. Also, if the application cannot find your Access user name in the tblCustomers table (there's an added Access User ID field), it won't let you continue.

The frmMain form makes additional checks to be sure you're signed on correctly, just in case you try to open the application by opening this form. It also quits Access when you close the form rather than returning you to the Database window. The frmCustomer form has some special code added that recognizes when you've changed an existing customer or added a new one. Because you must have "admin" status to change a customer in this application, that also means you are a member of the Admins group in the workgroup. This lets the code directly modify the Users and Groups collections in the workgroup file to match any changes you make to the customers table. The code to do this is shown here.

```
Private Sub Form_AfterUpdate()
  Dim ws As DAO.Workspace, usr As DAO.User, _
    grpA As DAO.Group, grpN As DAO.Group, _
    grpU As DAO.Group
  Set ws = DBEngine.Workspaces(0)
  Set grpA = ws.Groups("AppAdmin")
  Set grpN = ws.Groups("NotAdmin")
```

(continued)

VI

Creating an Application

```
        On Error Resume Next   ' Local trap all errors
        ' Check to see if we need to adjust Workgroup
        ' security profiles
        ' Did the logon ID change?
        If varLogon = Me![LogonID] Then
          ' No change - but make sure Admin flag
          ' matches group membership
          Set usr = ws.Users(varLogon)
          ' Check for error trying to find this user
          If Err <> 0 Then
            ' Yup, reset the error and go add 'em
            Err = 0
            GoTo AddUser
          End If
          If Me!Admin Then
            For Each grpU In usr.Groups
              If grpU.Name = "AppAdmin" Then Exit Sub
            Next grpU
            ' Didn't find the AppAdmin group for this
            ' user, so add it
            Set grpU = usr.CreateGroup("AppAdmin")
            usr.Groups.Append grpU
            Set grpU = usr.CreateGroup("Admins")
            usr.Groups.Append grpU
            Exit Sub
          Else
            ' Not admin, so make sure user isn't in
            ' that group
            For Each grpU In usr.Groups
              If grpU.Name = "AppAdmin" Then
                usr.Groups.Delete "AppAdmin"
                usr.Groups.Delete "Admins"
                Exit Sub
              End If
            Next grpU
            Exit Sub
          End If
        Else
          ' User has changed - make sure old ID (if
          ' any) is NotAdmin
          If Not IsNothing(varLogon) Then
            Set usr = ws.Users(varLogon)
            If Err = 0 Then
              ' Found the user, now check group
              ' membership
              ' The following may generate errors, but
              ' we previously set Resume Next, so should
              ' blow by them
              Set grpU = usr.CreateGroup("NotAdmin")
              usr.Groups.Append grpU
              usr.Groups.Delete "AppAdmin"
```

```
                    usr.Groups.Delete "Admins"
                    ' Reset any errors
                    Err = 0
                End If
            End If
            ' Now make sure new ID exists
            Set usr = ws.Users(Me!LogonID)
            If Err <> 0 Then
AddUser:
                Err = 0
                Set usr = ws.CreateUser(Me!LogonID, "9999")
                ws.Users.Append usr
                ' Make sure new user is at least a
                ' member of the Users group
                 Set grpU = usr.CreateGroup("Users")
                usr.Groups.Append grpU
                 Err = 0
            End If
            ' Force "old" status to Null so we check below
            varAdminStat = Null
        End If
        ' Check to see if admin status changed
        If varAdminStat = Me![Admin] Then
            ' No change - done
        Else
            ' Check this user's group membership to be sure
            ' it matches the application admin status
            Set usr = ws.Users(Me!LogonID)
            If Err <> 0 Then
                MsgBox ("Unexpected error trying to " & _
                    "locate user = " & Me!LogonID)
                Exit Sub
            End If
            ' All users in this app should at least
            ' belong to the NotAdmin group
            Set grpU = usr.CreateGroup("NotAdmin")
            usr.Groups.Append grpU
            Err = 0
            If Me!Admin Then
                Set grpU = usr.CreateGroup("AppAdmin")
                usr.Groups.Append grpU
                Set grpU = usr.CreateGroup("Admins")
                usr.Groups.Append grpU
            Else
                usr.Groups.Delete "AppAdmin"
                usr.Groups.Delete "Admins"
            End If
            Exit Sub
        End If
    End Sub
```

X CAUTION

Before leaving this section, be sure you rejoin your standard workgroup file using the Workgroup Administrator program. You can find System.mdw in the C:\Program Files\ Microsoft Office\ Office folder.

Sharing Your Application with Multiple Users

Unless you're building database applications only for your own personal use, you're probably going to need to set up your application so that it can be run by several people at the same time. This section discusses various ways to accomplish this, with a focus on ultimately "upsizing" your application to run in a true client/server mode using Microsoft SQL Server.

Sharing an MDB File

The simplest way to share an Access database (mdb) file is to place the database on a network share, and secure it so that most users cannot edit the design of any object or open the database exclusively. This will work just fine if only a few users need to share the database. Note that performance may suffer because Access must run on each user's workstation and load any part of the application that it needs to execute over the network.

Another way to set up a shared application is to separate out all (or most) data tables into a separate mdb file (a "data" database), place that file on a network share, and then link these tables into a copy of your database that otherwise contains only the queries, forms, reports, data access pages, macros, and modules needed for your application (a "code" database). You could do this "by hand" by first creating a new empty database *(see Chapter 5)*, and then importing all your tables into that database using the techniques described in Chapter 10. Next, go back to your original database and delete all the tables. Finally, move the "data" database (the one containing the tables) to a network share, and then link these tables into your original "code" database, again using the techniques you'll find in Chapter 10.

Fortunately, there's an easier way to do this in one step using the Database Splitter utility. Open your original database, choose Database Utilities from the Tools menu, and then choose Database Splitter. The utility displays the dialog box shown in Figure 25-22.

When you click the Split Database button, the utility opens a window where you can define the name and location of the back-end, or data-only, database. Be sure to choose a location for this database on a network share that is available to all potential users of your application. Click the Split button in that window, and the utility exports all your tables to the new data-only database, deletes the tables in your original database, and creates links to the moved tables. You can now give

FIGURE 25-22.
The Database Splitter utility.

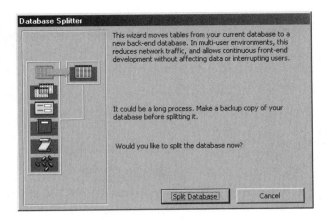

each user a copy of the "code" database containing the table links to enable them run your application using a shared set of tables.

The new data-only database you create using the Database Splitter is owned by the user ID that you used to log on to Access. Even if the "code" database is secured, the data-only database will not be. You must run the Security Wizard *(see "Using the Security Wizard," earlier in this chapter)* against the new data-only database to secure it.

The main advantage to this technique over simply sharing your data is that your application needs to retrieve only the data from the tables over the network. Because each user will have a local copy of the queries, forms, reports, data access pages, macros, and modules, Access running on each user workstation will be able to load the "working" parts of your application quickly from the local hard drive. Particularly if you have secured your application, you should have each user log on to the same workgroup file that you copy to a network share. *See "Creating an Application Shortcut," later in this chapter, for details about setting up a shortcut for each user that points not only to the local copy of your application database but also specifies the location of the shared workgroup file.*

Although splitting a database application makes it easier for multiple users to share your application, this technique works well only for applications requiring a moderate amount of data (under 200 megabytes is a good guideline) with up to 20 simultaneous users. Remember that Access is fundamentally a desktop database system. All of the work—including solving complex queries—occurs on the client machine, even when you have placed all the data on a network share. Each

VI

Creating an Application

copy of Access on each client machine uses the file sharing and locking mechanisms of the server operating system. When many users share the same application accessing large volumes of data, many simple tasks can start taking minutes instead of seconds to complete.

If you need more simultaneous users or large amounts of data, what can you do? For a solution, read the next section.

"Upsizing" Your Application to Microsoft SQL Server

As you learned in Chapter 10, Access has the ability to link to tables in Microsoft SQL Server (or, for that matter, any ODBC-compliant database) instead of tables in an mdb file on a network share. When the data is stored in a true server database management system, nearly all of the queries are solved directly on the server. This can greatly reduce network traffic and the locking overhead associated with accessing shared files.

You can export your tables to SQL Server and create links in your "code" database similar to splitting an mdb file that originally contains all the application code and data. In fact, Access has an Upsizing Wizard that helps you split your application in this way. *For details about the wizard, see "Upsizing Your Access Application," later in this chapter.* One benefit of exporting to SQL Server and linking into your original mdb file is you don't have to worry about how your queries are constructed or how your code is written. The downside is this technique might require Access to open multiple connections (perhaps dozens, depending on the complexity of your form designs) to SQL Server to get the job done under the covers for you.

 The best technique is to use the new "project file" feature of Access. With this new feature, you store not only your tables but also your queries (known as views or stored procedures) directly in SQL Server. The major advantage is the server does more of the work and your application requires only a single connection to the server.

You could build a new project file (adp filename extension) from scratch by opening Access, choosing New from the File menu, and then requesting that Access build a new project file connected to an existing SQL Server database or a new project file with a new database in SQL Server. Perhaps one of the best ways to "get your feet wet" in this new technology, however, is to use the Upsizing Wizard to convert an existing database into an SQL Server database and an associated Access project file.

Preparing to Upsize an Access Application to Client/Server

Although you can upsize just about any Access application, you will get a better end result if you take some preparatory steps. Since part of the end result is a new SQL Server database, you must either:

■ Have access to an SQL Server version 6.5 or later server, and you must have full create and modify permissions, or

■ Have installed the Microsoft Data Engine (MSDE) that comes with Microsoft Office 2000 on your desktop machine. *See the Appendix for details about installing MSDE.*

Your database will convert most easily if all the code uses the ADO model rather than DAO. *See Chapter 22, "Visual Basic Fundamentals," for information about ADO and DAO.* You cannot use DAO in a project file to access the data in your tables that will be converted to MSDE or SQL Server, so you must change any code that uses DAO either before or after you convert. (You can use DAO to fetch data from an Access [mdb] file in your Visual Basic procedures.) You should also consider the following points.

■ Queries that use features unique to Access will not convert. This includes queries containing expressions that call Access built-in functions and crosstab queries. In many cases where an expression using Access functions creates an output column, you can move the expression to the form or report controls that reference the query column and remove the column from the query.

As an alternative, you can remove the expression from the query before you upsize it, and then replace the expression with the SQL Server equivalent in the view or stored procedure that the Upsizing Wizard creates. For example, I removed the following expression for the field ExtPrice from qryOrderBooks.

> Round(CCur(NZ(([Quantity]*[SuggPrice])*
> (1-[Discount]),0)),2)

I replaced it with the following expression after I upsized the database.

> ROUND(CONVERT(money, ISNULL(tblOrderDetails.Quantity
> * tblBooks.SuggPrice * (1 - tblOrderDetails.Discount), 0)), 2)

■ Although most multiple-table views created from joined queries in Access will be updateable, you can update information only in the "most-many" table. For example, a form based on a query joining Customers and Orders will be able to update the fields only in the Orders table after conversion.

- Queries that contain an Order By clause will not be updateable. You must change any form based on a query that contains sorting information. You can either remove the sorting specification from the query or use a table directly as the Record Source for the form.

- Queries or filters you build in Visual Basic code must comply with SQL Server syntax. String literals must be enclosed in single, not double, quotation marks. Date literals must be enclosed in single quotation marks, not pound signs (#). In a LIKE predicate, you must use a percent sign (%) instead of an asterisk (*) and an underscore (_) instead of a question mark (?).

- Forms in an Access mdb database use DAO recordsets, and you can build filters on these recordsets using native Access rules. Forms in an Access project file use ADO recordsets. You can apply a filter to ADO recordsets, but the filter cannot contain an IN clause or a subquery. You may have to recode any Visual Basic procedures that apply filters after you convert the application.

- The Upsizing Wizard might not successfully upsize certain types of UNION queries or queries containing a sort on an expression. You will have to rebuild these in SQL Server after running the wizard.

In the following sections, I show you how to upsize a special version of the Microsoft Press Books sample database called Books 2B Upsized. In this database, I corrected many of the problems noted above. For example, frmBooks uses the table directly as a Record Source rather than using a query that's sorted. I also changed all code that uses string literals for queries to use a single quotation mark rather than a double quotation mark.

Upsizing Your Access Application

Let's take a look at upsizing the Books 2B Upsized sample database. The upsize process does not alter the original database in any way. It creates a new project file that contains the converted forms, reports, macros, and modules, and converts the tables and queries to an SQL Server database.

Before you begin, you must be sure you can connect to an SQL Server database system that lets you create a new database and tables, views, and stored procedures in that database. If you installed the Microsoft

Data Engine (MSDE) on your desktop machine, you should be sure the server service is running. With MSDE, you can double-click the SQL Server Service Manager icon in your system tray (the group of icons at the right end of the taskbar) to open the manager, which is shown in Figure 25-23.

FIGURE 25-23.

SQL Server Service Manager.

In the top box, enter the name of your computer. (If you don't know the name of your computer, open Windows Control Panel, double-click the Network icon, and then click the Identification tab in the re-sulting display.) Be sure the Services box shows MSSQLServer. Click the Start/Continue button to start the server and wait until the message in bottom of the window shows that the server is running. You can click the window's close button to dismiss SQL Server Service Man-ager; this won't stop SQL Server.

Next start Access and open the Books 2B Upsized sample database. Choose Database Utilities from the Tools menu, and then choose Upsizing Wizard from the submenu. The wizard may take several sec-onds to initialize, and then it displays the opening dialog box shown in Figure 25-24.

FIGURE 25-24.

The opening options dialog box in the Upsizing Wizard.

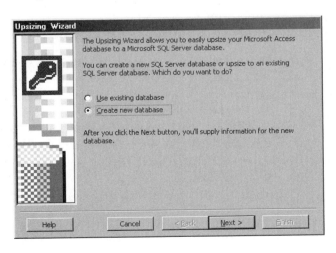

VI

Creating an Application

Your first choice is to upsize your tables to an existing SQL Server database or to create a new database. Unless you are upsizing a database application that's part of a larger application system, I recommend you ask the wizard to create a new database for the exclusive use of this application. Click Next to display the second dialog box, shown in Figure 25-25.

FIGURE 25-25.

Specifying the SQL Server for your database and the name of the database to create on the server.

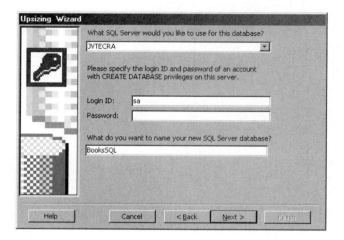

The wizard asks you for the parameters it needs to connect to the SQL Server where it will create your new tables, views, and stored procedures. If you are using MSDE, enter the name of your computer in the top box, type *sa* (the built-in System Administrator user ID) in the Login ID box, and leave the password blank. If you are connecting to an SQL Server on a network, ask your server administrator for the information you should enter for these three values.

In the last box, enter the name of the database you want to create. I chose BooksSQL for this example. Click Next to display the next dialog box, shown in Figure 25-26.

The wizard now asks you to choose the tables you want to upsize. The wizard also upsizes any queries that reference these tables. In most cases, you will click the double right arrow to select all of the tables. Because USStores is a linked text file in the sample, you don't need to upsize it; if you leave USStores in the list, the wizard copies the data from the linked text file and creates a new table in your server database. After you have chosen the tables you need by moving them to the list on the right, click Next to go on. The wizard displays the dialog box shown in Figure 25-27.

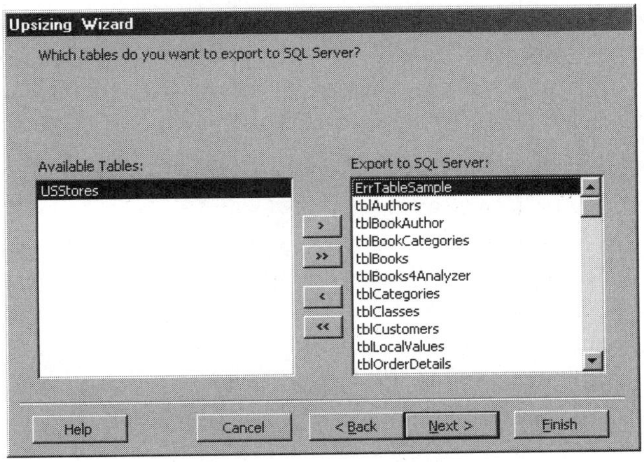

FIGURE 25-26.

Choosing the tables to define on the server.

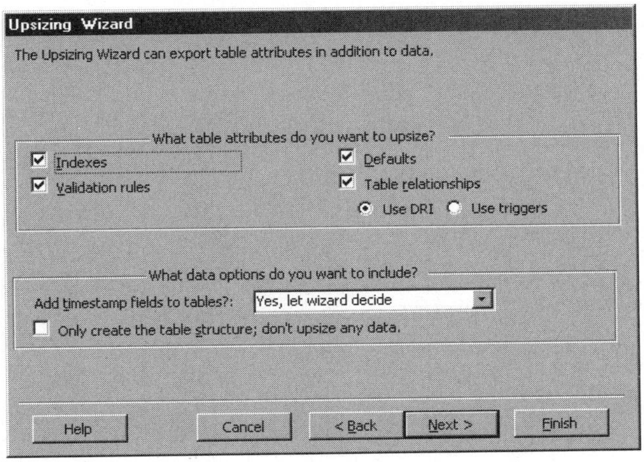

FIGURE 25-27.

Choosing the table options for upsizing.

In this dialog box, you can tell the wizard to not upsize some of the properties of your Access tables. For example, you might have defined a large number of indexes on some tables to aid searching in Access. You might want to upsize your tables without additional indexes and then later define appropriate indexes in SQL Server.

In most cases, you will want to let the wizard upsize all your indexes, validation rules, default values, and relationships. If you are using SQL Server version 7.0 or later or MSDE, you can choose to define relationships between tables using the REFERENCES keyword in the Create Table statements the wizard sends to the server by selecting Use DRI under Table References. The one drawback is this facility does not support any cascading deletes or updates you may have defined on your Access tables. If your application depends on cascading features in Access, you should choose the Use Triggers options. The wizard defines update and delete triggers in SQL Server that duplicate any cascading rules you have defined in Access.

Under Data Options, you can ask the wizard to add a timestamp field to no tables, all tables, or "let the wizard decide." When a table includes a timestamp field, SQL Server updates this field whenever any user makes a change to any other field in the table. Without the timestamp field, when your application needs to update a row Access has to refetch the row you are about to update and compare the value of each field to the value that existed before your application requested the update. When the table contains only text and simple numeric values, this task is simple. If your table contains memo, OLE Object, or floating-point data (Single or Double), the comparison can take a long time and might incorrectly assume that someone else has updated the row. If you let the wizard decide, it adds a timestamp field to any table that contains a memo, OLE Object, or floating-point numeric field. In most cases, you should either let the wizard decide or add a timestamp field to all tables.

You also have an option to upsize the table structures, but not export the existing data to SQL Server. If you are upsizing a prototype application that doesn't really contain any live data, upsizing only the table structure should work just fine. In the case of Books 2B Upsized, I let the wizard decide about timestamp fields and asked it to upsize the data also. Click Next to display the next dialog box, shown in Figure 25-28.

FIGURE 25-28.

Asking the Upsizing Wizard to convert the application to an Access Project File (adp).

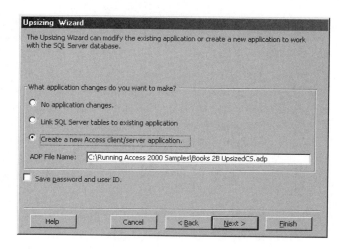

In the wizard's penultimate dialog box, you have three options.

- Only upsize your tables but not change your application (No Application Changes)

- Upsize your tables, remove them from the existing application, and create links to the new SQL Server tables (Link SQL Server Tables To Existing Application)

- Build a new Access project file containing your forms, reports, data access pages, macros, and modules, and connect it to the tables, views, and stored procedures upsized in SQL Server (Create A New Access Client/Server Application)

To see how the new Access project file feature works, choose the third option. Note that in all three cases, you can ask the wizard to save the connection user ID and password with the connection or table link information. If you ask the Wizard to save the password and user ID and this information is critical to maintaining security in SQL Server, you should also be sure to secure and encrypt your Access file to prevent unauthorized use.

When you click Next, the wizard displays a dialog box informing you that it has all the information it needs to proceed. Click the Finish button to let the wizard upsize your database. Depending on the speed of your machine, the speed of your connection to the server, and the complexity of your database, the upsizing process could take several minutes—maybe a good time to go get a fresh cup of coffee! When the wizard is done, it displays a report of what it upsized and any problems it encountered. Particularly if you're also upsizing all your queries and moving your application to an Access project file, you might find a number of queries that the wizard failed to successfully convert.

> **NOTE**   Your sample files include SQL Server files for the upsized BooksSQL database that include views and stored procedures that the wizard fails to upsize, as well as corrections to expressions using SQL Server built-in functions. To connect this database to your desktop version of SQL Server, run the Attach Books.bat file.

Once the wizard completes its task, you can open Access, and then open either your new adp file or the sample BooksCS.adp file. You should see a result similar to the one shown in Figure 25-29 on the next page.

FIGURE 25-29.
The resulting client portion (Access project file) of your new Client/Server application.

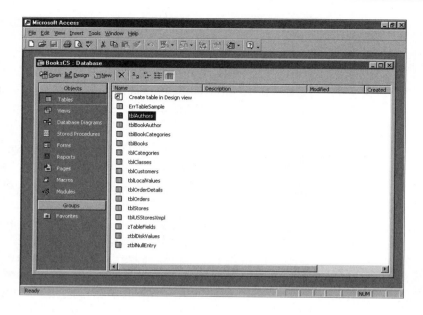

The wizard exported all your tables to SQL Server, and then created a connection in the resulting project file. The tables, views, database diagrams, and stored procedures you see in your project file Database window are all objects stored in SQL Server.

Table Design in an Access Project

You can create a new table or edit the structure of an existing table just like you can in a regular Access database file. The table editor looks a bit different, however, because your table is now stored in SQL Server. Figure 25-30 shows you the tblOrders table from the BooksCS project file in Design view.

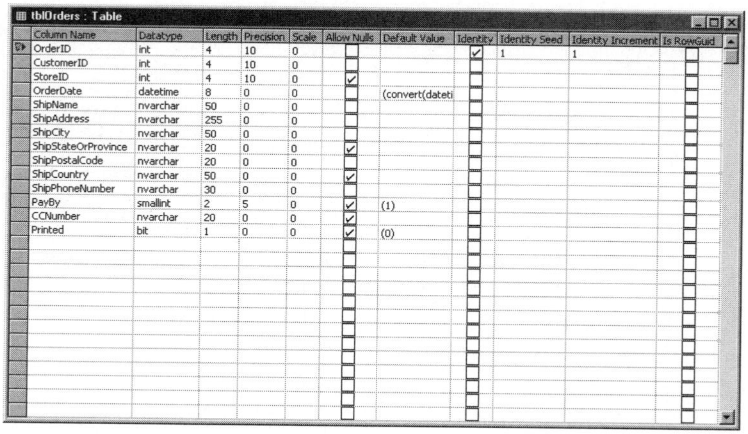

FIGURE 25-30.
The tblOrders table (now stored in SQL Server) in Design view.

Rather than showing you properties of individual fields in the bottom part of the window as you click each field, this design interface displays all the available SQL Server properties horizontally in a datasheet view. You can move fields around by selecting and then moving them with the row selector on the left. To remove a field, select it and then press the Delete key. When you want to add a field, you can click the field following the point where you want to insert a new one and choose Row from the Insert menu. You can also choose a blank row below the existing fields. Table 25-2 lists the SQL Server data types you can choose for fields, along with their Access equivalent data types.

TABLE 25-2.   SQL Server Data Types

Data Type	Length (bytes)	Description	Access
binary	Fixed, up to 8000	Fixed-length binary data	(No equivalent)
bit	1	True/false values	Yes/No
char	Fixed, up to 8000	Non-Unicode fixed-length character values	(No equivalent)
datetime	8	Date/time value from January 1, 1753, to December 31, 9999, precise to 0.03 seconds	Date/Time
decimal	9	Fixed-precision numeric data from -10^{38} to $+10^{38}$	Number, Decimal
float	8	Floating-precision numeric data from -1.79×10^{308} to $+1.79 \times 10^{308}$	Number, Double
image	16 plus length of the image	OLE Object data	OLE Object
int	4	Fixed-point integer from −2,147,483,648 to +2,147,483,647	Number, Long Integer
money	8	Currency data from −922,337,203,685,477.5808 to +922,337,203,685,477.5807	Currency
nchar	Fixed, up to 8000 (4000 characters)	Unicode fixed-length character values	(No equivalent)

(continued)

VI

Creating an Application

TABLE 25-2. *continued*

Data Type	Length (bytes)	Description	Access
ntext	16 plus length of the text (maximum 1 billion characters)	Varying length Unicode character values	Memo
numeric	9	An alias for decimal	Number, Decimal
nvarchar	Varying, up to 8000 (4000 characters)	Varying length Unicode character values	Text
real	4	Floating-precision numeric data from -3.4×10^{38} to $+3.4 \times 10^{38}$	Number, Single
smalldatetime	4	Date/time value from January 1, 1900 to June 6, 2079, precise to one minute	(No equivalent)
smallint	2	Fixed-point integer from $-32,768$ to $+32,767$	Number, Integer
smallmoney	4	Currency data from $-214,748.3648$ to $+214,748.3647$	(No equivalent)
text	16 plus length of the text (maximum 2 billion characters)	Varying length non-Unicode character values	Memo
timestamp	8	Database-wide unique number that changes each time a row is updated	(No equivalent)
tinyint	1	Fixed-point integer from 0 to 255	Number, Byte
uniqueidentifier	16	Globally-unique identifier	Number, GUID
varbinary	Varying, up to 8000	Varying length binary data	(No equivalent)
varchar	Varying, up to 8000	Varying length non-Unicode character values	Text

In most cases, the length will be the default length for the data type you choose. For nvarchar and varchar, you can set the maximum length of the field, just as you can for the Text data type in Access. For decimal and numeric data types, you can set the Precision and Scale values similar to the Decimal data type in Access.

You can specify whether a field can contain nulls (the opposite of the Required property in Access). You can also specify a default value for the field in new rows as a constant or as an expression using SQL Server built-in functions. *You can open Help and enter the keywords "Transact SQL" to find details about available SQL Server functions.*

The Identity attribute is similar to AutoNumber in Access, but you can specify that any numeric value is an identity. An identity field cannot be null and cannot have a default value. In addition, you can specify the starting value (Seed) and Increment value for an Identity. Finally, for a unique identifier field, you can check the Is RowGUID attribute to indicate the field is the identifier for replication.

Where are properties like Caption, Format, and Input Mask? These properties have no equivalent in SQL Server tables, but you can still define these properties in form controls that edit the fields.

Query Design in an Access Project

The wizard converts all the queries you had defined in your Access application to either an SQL Server view or stored procedure, as appropriate. Figure 25-31 shows the qryBookAuthors query converted to an SQL Server view.

FIGURE 25-31.
The query qryBookAuthors converted to an SQL Server view.

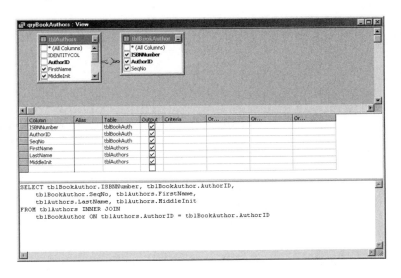

To get Figure 25-31, I opened the view in Design view, and then chose Show Panes from the View menu and selected the SQL pane to

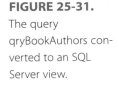

display not only the table diagram and design grid, but also the under-lying SQL. In an SQL Server view, the table diagram looks and works much like the top part of a query design in Access. You can add a field to the design grid by selecting the check box next to the field name in the table field list. The design grid lists the fields or expressions vertically rather than horizontally, as in Access. You can use the Alias column to assign an alternate name to a field or expression. The Table column is just like the Table Name row in Access query design. The Output column works just like the Show box in Access. Note that you cannot specify sorting criteria. In SQL Server, you must use a stored procedure to sort rows—and the result is not updateable.

Figure 25-32 shows a typical stored procedure. In the original Books 2B Upsized database, the qryCustomerSorted query selects certain columns from tblCustomers and then sorts the result by last name, first name, and middle initial. If you look in BooksCS, you'll find a view named qryCustomerSortedView that is the original query without the sort. The qryCustomerSorted stored procedure then alters this view and adds the sorting criteria.

FIGURE 25-32.

The query qryCustomerSorted converted to an SQL Server stored procedure.

For the Books 2B Upsized database, the wizard fails to completely convert qryAuthForCombo, qyrCustForCombo, qryCustForSignon-Combo, qryOrderReport, and qryStoresForComboWNull (a UNION query). In all cases except the UNION query, the final query needs to be a stored procedure that sorts the companion view. In the first three cases, the wizard fails to convert the query completely because there's a sort specified on an expression. In the fourth case, the wizard fails because qryOrderReport is a query on another query that is sorted. For the last case (the UNION query), the wizard just doesn't handle UNION queries at all.

For the first three queries, you need to create a stored procedure based on the view of the same name (the wizard appends "View" to the original query name) and specify a sort. For example, you can create the equivalent of qryAuthForCombo by clicking the Stored Procedures button in the Database window, and then clicking New to start a new procedure. Enter the following SQL.

```
Create PROCEDURE qryAuthForCombo
AS
Select * From qryAuthForComboView ORDER BY Aname
return
```

Click the Save button, type *qryAuthForCombo* in the resulting Save As dialog box, and click OK.

To create the more complex qryOrderReport stored procedure, you need to start another new procedure and enter the following SQL.

```
Create Procedure qryOrderReport
As
SELECT qryOrdersSorted.LastName,
qryOrdersSorted.FirstName,
qryOrdersSorted.MiddleInit, qryOrdersSorted.Address,
qryOrdersSorted.City,
qryOrdersSorted.StateOrProvince,
qryOrdersSorted.PostalCode, qryOrdersSorted.Country,
qryOrdersSorted.PhoneNumber, qryOrdersSorted.PayBy AS
CustPayBy, qryOrdersSorted.CCNumber AS CustCCNumber,
qryOrdersSorted.OrderID, qryOrdersSorted.CustomerID,
qryOrdersSorted.StoreID, qryOrdersSorted.OrderDate,
qryOrdersSorted.ShipName,
qryOrdersSorted.ShipAddress,
qryOrdersSorted.ShipCity,
qryOrdersSorted.ShipStateOrProvince,
qryOrdersSorted.ShipPostalCode,
qryOrdersSorted.ShipCountry,
qryOrdersSorted.ShipPhoneNumber,
qryOrdersSorted.PayBy, qryOrdersSorted.CCNumber,
qryOrdersSorted.Printed, qryOrdersSorted.StoreName,
qryOrdersSorted.StAddress, qryOrdersSorted.StCity,
qryOrdersSorted.StPostalCode,
qryOrdersSorted.StStateOrProvince,
qryOrdersSorted.StCountry,
tblOrderDetails.ISBNNumber, tblBooks.Title,
tblBooks.EditionNumber, tblOrderDetails.Quantity,
tblBooks.SuggPrice, tblOrderDetails.Discount
FROM tblBooks INNER JOIN (qryOrdersSorted INNER JOIN
tblOrderDetails ON qryOrdersSorted.OrderID =
tblOrderDetails.OrderID) ON tblBooks.ISBNNumber =
tblOrderDetails.ISBNNumber
ORDER BY qryOrdersSorted.LastName,
qryOrdersSorted.FirstName, qryOrdersSorted.OrderDate
return
```

VI

Creating an Application

Again, click the Save button, type *qryOrderReport* in the Save As dialog box, and then click OK. (Aren't you glad you studied Chapter 11?)

Finally, for the qryStoresForComboWNull query, start another new stored procedure. Enter the following SQL.

```
Create Procedure "qryStoresForComboWNull"
As
SELECT NullLongID As StoreID, '<No specific store>'
As StoreName, Null As CityState, Null As State From
ztblNullEntry
UNION
SELECT StoreID, StoreName, City + IsNull(', ' +
StateOrProvince,'') AS CityState, StateOrProvince As
State
FROM tblStores
ORDER BY State, CityState, StoreName
```

Click Save again, type *qryStoresForComboWNull* in the Save As dialog box, and click OK.

As you might guess, a stored procedure can do much more than simply sort a view or define a UNION query. SQL Server supports a very powerful language called *Transact-SQL* that contains hundreds of built-in functions and supports IF – THEN – ELSE processing. You can get your feet wet in this language by exploring the extensive help topics that come with MSDE.

Special Considerations for Forms in an Access Project

For the rest of your Access client/server application, you can design forms, reports, data access pages, macros, and modules just like you would in a native Access application. Forms, however, have a few new data properties that you must set in certain cases so that the form works correctly with your SQL Server tables and views.

In the BooksCS database, click the Forms button, and open the fsubOrderBooks form in Design view. Open the Properties window, and click the Data tab. Figure 25-33 shows the result.

This particular form is based on a view that links tblOrderDetails with tblBooks. To make the form updateable, you must set the Unique Table property to the table that the form needs to update. In this case, the form "looks up" data from tblBooks (to show the relevant title and edition number), but it's updating tblOrderDetails. The Recordset Type property indicates we want to have an updateable recordset in this form. If the form might retrieve many thousands of rows, you can set the Max Records property to limit how many rows Access retrieves from the server before showing any results.

FIGURE 25-33.

Setting form properties unique to a project file.

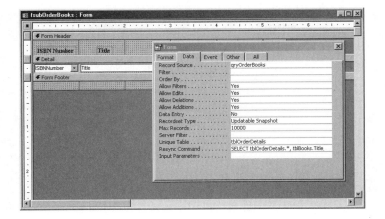

If you've worked with the Orders form in the Microsoft Press Books sample database, you might have noticed that the subform automatically displays the book title and edition information when you pick a book's ISBN. This is a handy little feature in Access called AutoLookup; Access fetches the related "one"-side information from tblBooks when you enter a new ISBN in the "many"-side table—tblOrderDetails. However, SQL Server doesn't support this feature. You can have the form emulate this feature by entering the appropriate SELECT statement in the Resync Command property of the form.

Note that Resync Command must be an SQL statement, *not* a query. To let SQL Server know what key fields need to be resynchronized, you need to add a WHERE clause that includes the key fields of the Unique Table. In addition, you must enter the key field names in the exact same sequence as they are defined in the underlying table. Here's the Resync Command for frmOrderDetails.

```
SELECT tblOrderDetails.*, tblBooks.Title,
tblBooks.EditionNumber,  tblBooks.SuggPrice
FROM tblBooks INNER JOIN  tblOrderDetails ON
tblBooks.ISBNNumber = tblOrderDetails.ISBNNumber
WHERE tblOrderDetails.OrderID = ?
And tblOrderDetails.ISBNNumber = ?
```

You can see two additional new properties at the bottom of the property sheet shown in Figure 25-33. The Server Filter property is similar to the normal Access form Filter property. The difference is Access applies any filter defined in the Filter property on the client machine. When you define a filter in Server Filter, Access sends that filter to the server for execution, which can be more efficient. You can define a Filter or Server Filter only on forms bound to a table or query. Access

VI

Creating an Application

ignores these properties when the record source is a stored procedure. You can activate the Server Filter in code by setting the ServerFilterByForm property to True.

Use the Input Parameters property to define parameter values when the record source is a stored procedure. If you do not set this property and you use a stored procedure as the record source for a subform, the subform displays *all* the rows in the record source; the Link Child and Link Master properties of the subform control are ignored. For example, suppose you want to display order details sorted by book title in a stored procedure (this will make the subform not updateable). You'll need to build a stored procedure to sort the rows, and you'll need to add a parameter in the procedure that you can set in the Input Parameters property. Your stored procedure might look like the following.

```
Alter PROCEDURE qryOrderBooks @parmOrderID int
AS
SELECT * FROM "qryOrderBooks"
WHERE qryOrderBooks.OrderID = @parmOrderID
ORDER BY "qryOrderBooks".Title
```

In the Input Parameters property, you should enter the following to automatically filter the rows in the stored procedure on the current OrderID.

```
@parmOrderID = Forms!frmOrders!OrderID
```

Accessing SQL Server Data with ADO

To complete the upsizing process, you must convert any remaining DAO code in your database to exclusively use ADO. You must also change any code that creates SQL commands to the equivalent SQL Server syntax. In the Microsoft Press Books database, the code that has to change is in the various custom search forms (frmAuthorSearch, frmBookSearch, frmCustSearch, and frmStoreSearch). Here's the modified code from frmBookSearch that you can compare with the same code in the section titled "Providing a Custom Query By Form" in Chapter 23, "Automating Your Application with Visual Basic."

```
Private Sub cmdSearch_Click()
Dim rcd As New ADODB.Recordset, cn As ADODB.Connection
Dim lngCount As Long, intRtn As Integer, strANameComp As String
Dim intI As Integer, strISBN As String
    ' Search parameters entered (we hope)...
    ' Clear the global book filter string
    gstrWhereBook = ""
    ' .. and parse out a new one:
    If Not IsNothing(Me!ISBNNumber) Then
        strISBN = Me!ISBNNumber
```

```
' The ISBN has an input mask to
' help the user out, but they could
' enter all sorts of dashes and numbers.
' The following code does an
' additional "parse" to clean it up!
' First, replace all blanks in ISBN with question marks
intI = 1
Do Until intI > Len(strISBN)
    If Mid$(strISBN, intI, 1) = " " Then
        If intI = 1 Then
            strISBN = "_" & Mid$(strISBN, intI + 1)
        Else
            strISBN = Left$(strISBN, intI - 1) _
              & "_" & Mid$(strISBN, intI + 1)
        End If
    End If
    ' Watch out for dashes in the right/wrong places
    If intI = 2 Or intI = 8 Or intI = 12 Then
        ' If position 2, 8, or 12, then a dash is OK
        If Mid$(strISBN, intI, 1) = "-" Then
        Else
        ' Otherwise, move it down
            strISBN = Left$(strISBN, intI - 1) _
              & "_" & Mid$(strISBN, intI)
        End If
    Else
        ' Not position 2, 8, or 12, so should be no dash
        If Mid$(strISBN, intI, 1) = "-" Then
            If intI = 1 Then
                strISBN = "_" & strISBN
            Else
                ' Watch out for too many dashes!
                If intI > 12 Then
                ' Replace the dash if beyond position 12
                    strISBN = Left$(strISBN, intI - 1) _
                      & "_" & Mid$(strISBN, intI + 1)
                Else
                ' Shove the dash down if position <=12
                    strISBN = Left$(strISBN, intI - 1) _
                      & "_" & Mid$(strISBN, intI)
                End If
            End If
        End If
    End If
    intI = intI + 1
Loop
Me!ISBNNumber = Left$(strISBN, 13)
```

(continued)

VI

Creating an Application

```
                              ' Result at this point should be a nice ISBN in the form:
                              ' __-_____-___-_
                              ' Where the user may have specified
                              ' digits for any one or more of the
                              ' question marks.
                              gstrWhereBook = "[ISBNNumber] Like " & _
                                  Chr$(39) & Me!ISBNNumber
                              ' Add "%" on the end for good measure...
                              If Right$(Me!ISBNNumber, 1) = "%" Then
                                  gstrWhereBook = gstrWhereBook & Chr$(39)
                              Else
                                  gstrWhereBook = gstrWhereBook & "%" & Chr$(39)
                              End If
                          End If

                          If Not IsNothing(Me!Title) Then
                              If IsNothing(gstrWhereBook) Then
                                  gstrWhereBook = "[Title] Like " & Chr$(39) & Me!Title
                              Else
                                  gstrWhereBook = gstrWhereBook & _
                                      " AND [Title] Like " & Chr$(39) & Me!Title
                              End If
                              If Right$(Me!Title, 1) = "%" Then
                                  gstrWhereBook = gstrWhereBook & Chr$(39)
                              Else
                                  gstrWhereBook = gstrWhereBook & "%" & Chr$(39)
                              End If
                          End If

                          If Not IsNothing(Me!LastName) Then
                              strANameComp = "[LastName] Like " & _
                                  Chr$(39) & Me!LastName
                              If Right$(Me!LastName, 1) = "%" Then
                                  strANameComp = strANameComp & Chr$(39)
                              Else
                                  strANameComp = strANameComp & "%" & Chr$(39)
                              End If
                          End If

                          If Not IsNothing(Me!FirstName) Then
                              If IsNothing(strANameComp) Then
                                  strANameComp = "[FirstName] Like " & _
                                      Chr$(39) & Me!FirstName
                              Else
                                  strANameComp = strANameComp & _
                                      " AND [FirstName] Like " & Chr$(39) & Me!FirstName
                              End If
                              If Right$(Me!FirstName, 1) = "%" Then
                                  strANameComp = strANameComp & Chr$(39)
                              Else
                                  strANameComp = strANameComp & "%" & Chr$(39)
```

```
            End If
        End If

        If Not IsNothing(strANameComp) Then
        ' Did we build any author compares?
            If IsNothing(gstrWhereBook) Then
                gstrWhereBook = "[ISBNNumber] IN " & _
                    "(Select ISBNNumber From [qryBookAuthors]" & _
                    " Where " & strANameComp & ")"
                Else
                gstrWhereBook = gstrWhereBook & _
                    " AND [ISBNNumber] IN (Select ISBNNumber" & _
                    " From [qryBookAuthors] Where " & _
                    strANameComp & ")"
            End If
        End If

        If Not IsNothing(Me!LowPrice) Then
            If IsNothing(gstrWhereBook) Then
                gstrWhereBook = "[SuggPrice] >= " & Me!LowPrice
                Else
                gstrWhereBook = gstrWhereBook & _
                    " AND [SuggPrice] >= " & Me!LowPrice
            End If
        End If

        If Not IsNothing(Me!HighPrice) Then
            If IsNothing(gstrWhereBook) Then
                gstrWhereBook = "[SuggPrice] <= " & Me!HighPrice
                Else
                gstrWhereBook = gstrWhereBook & _
                    " AND [SuggPrice] <= " & Me!HighPrice
            End If
        End If

        If Me!Disk Then
            If IsNothing(gstrWhereBook) Then
                gstrWhereBook = "([Disk] Is Not Null)"
                Else
                gstrWhereBook = gstrWhereBook & _
                    " AND ([Disk] Is Not Null)"
            End If
        End If

        If Me!OutOfPrint Then
            If IsNothing(gstrWhereBook) Then
                gstrWhereBook = "([OutOfPrint] = 0)"
                Else
```

(continued)

VI

Creating an Application

```
            gstrWhereBook = gstrWhereBook & _
                " AND ([OutOfPrint] = 0)"
        End If
    End If

    If Not IsNothing(Me!TypeCodes) Then
        If IsNothing(gstrWhereBook) Then
            gstrWhereBook = "[ISBNNumber] IN " & _
                "(Select ISBNNumber From [qryBookCategories]" & _
                " Where CategoryID IN (" & Me!TypeCodes & "))"
        Else
            gstrWhereBook = gstrWhereBook & _
                " AND [ISBNNumber] IN (Select ISBNNumber" & _
                " From [qryBookCategories] Where CategoryID IN (" _
                & Me!TypeCodes & "))"
        End If
    End If

    ' If no criteria, then nothing to do!
    If IsNothing(gstrWhereBook) Then
        MsgBox "No criteria specified.", vbExclamation, _
            "Microsoft Press"
        Exit Sub
    End If

    ' Hide myself and turn on Hourglass
    Me.Visible = False
    DoCmd.Hourglass True
    If IsLoaded("frmBooks") Then
        ' If books form already open,
        ' Then just filter it
        Set cn = CurrentProject.Connection
        rcd.Open "Select * From tblBooks Where " & _
            gstrWhereBook, cn, adOpenKeyset, adLockOptimistic
        If rcd.RecordCount = 0 Then
            DoCmd.Hourglass False
            MsgBox "No Books meet your criteria", _
                vbExclamation, "Microsoft Press"
            rcd.Close
            Me.Visible = True
            Exit Sub
        End If

        Forms!frmBooks.SetFocus
        Set Forms!frmBooks.Recordset = rcd
        rcd.Close
```

```
        If IsNothing(Me!TypeCodes) And _
          (Not IsNothing(strANameComp)) Then
        ' If not book categories, but did do a name search,
            ' Turn on the author display option
            Forms!frmBooks!tabDisplay = 1
        End If

        Forms!frmBooks!cmdAddNew.Visible = False
        Forms!frmBooks!cmdShowAll.Visible = True
        DoCmd.Hourglass False
    Else
        ' Find out if any books satisfy the Where clause
        Set cn = CurrentProject.Connection
        rcd.Open "Select * From tblBooks Where " & _
            gstrWhereBook, cn, adOpenKeyset, adLockOptimistic
        ' If none found, then tell them and
        ' make me visible to try again
        If rcd.RecordCount = 0 Then
            DoCmd.Hourglass False
            MsgBox "No Books meet your criteria", _
                vbExclamation, "Microsoft Press"
            gstrWhereBook = ""
            Me.Visible = True
            rcd.Close
            Exit Sub
        End If
        ' Move to last row to get an accurate record count
        rcd.MoveLast
        lngCount = rcd.RecordCount
        DoCmd.Hourglass False
        ' If more than 10, then ask if they
        ' want to only see a summary
        If lngCount > 10 Then
            intRtn = MsgBox("More than 10 books meet " & _
                "your criteria. " & vbCrLf & vbCrLf & _
                "Click Yes to see a summary list for all " & _
                lngCount & _
                " books found, " & _
                "No to see complete data on all that match, " & _
                "or Cancel to try again.", vbInformation + _
                vbYesNoCancel, "Microsoft Press")
            Select Case intRtn
                Case vbCancel   ' Cancel - Try again
                    Me.Visible = True
                    Exit Sub
                Case vbYes      ' Yes - show summary form
                    Application.Echo False
                    DoCmd.OpenForm FormName:="frmBookSummary"
                    DoCmd.Close acForm, Me.Name
```

(continued)

VI

Creating an Application

```
                          Forms!frmBookSummary.SetFocus
                          Set Forms!frmBookSummary.Recordset = rcd
                          Application.Echo True
                          rcd.Close
                          Exit Sub
                   End Select
            End If
            ' Replied NO or not more than 10, show full details
            Application.Echo False
            DoCmd.OpenForm FormName:="frmBooks"
            Forms!frmBooks!cmdAddNew.Visible = False
            Forms!frmBooks!cmdShowAll.Visible = True
            Set Forms!frmBooks.Recordset = rcd
            If IsNothing(Me!TypeCodes) And _
               (Not IsNothing(strANameComp)) Then
            ' If not book categories, but did do a name search,
            ' Turn on the author display option
                Forms!frmBooks!tabDisplay = 1
            End If
            Application.Echo True
            rcd.Close
        End If
        ' Close me, and we're done
        DoCmd.Close acForm, Me.Name
End Sub
```

In addition to changing the SQL, the code now also uses ADO recordsets to see if any records were found. This code takes advantage of the fact that you can now assign a recordset object built in code and assign it directly to the new Recordset property of an open form. (You can also do this with a DAO recordset in a form in a standard Access database.)

Creating an Execute-Only Database

Even if you have secured your database, you might still want to be sure that no one can examine the Visual Basic procedures you created. Once a database is fully compiled, Access no longer needs the original text of your Visual Basic statements. You can create a special "execute-only" copy of your database by using one of the utilities supplied with Access. An additional advantage of an execute-only database is that it might be significantly smaller than the "full code" copy—particularly if you have written many Visual Basic procedures.

To create an execute-only copy of any completed database application, open that database and go to the Database window. Choose Database Utilities from the Tools menu, and then choose Make MDE File from the submenu for a standard Access mdb file, or Make ADE File from the submenu for an Access project (adp) file. The utility asks you for a location and name for your new database. It then makes sure the current database is fully compiled and saved, copies the database to a new file with an mde or ade extension, removes the Visual Basic source code, and compacts the new file.

If you open the mde file (you can find a file called Entertain.mde on the companion CD), you'll find that you can't open any form or report module or any module object. You also won't be able to open a form or a report in Design view. Figure 25-34 shows the Modules list in the Entertain.mde database file. Notice that the Run, Design, and New buttons are grayed out, indicating that you can neither create a new module nor view the source code of an existing module, and that the only way to run code is through the database application's interface.

FIGURE 25-34.
You can't edit any modules in the Entertain.mde database file.

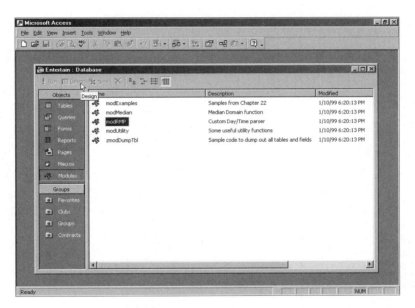

Creating an Application Shortcut

When you're all done, you might need to create a way for users to easily start your application. If your users all have a copy of Access, you could give them your database application files and simply instruct them to open the appropriate file. But what if you've secured your database, requiring the user to be a member of a specific workgroup? What if the user doesn't have Access, so you have to set them up to execute your application with the run-time version of Access? (You can distribute your application to users who do not own Access provided you have set up your application with the Office 2000 Developer tools. See the sidebar for details) What if you want to also define certain utility functions that the user may need to execute from time to time? The answer is a shortcut.

Understanding Microsoft Office 2000 Developer

You can purchase a version of Office called Microsoft Office 2000 Developer. With Office Developer, you get a host of additional utilities, ActiveX controls, documentation, and, most importantly, an unlimited run-time license to let you distribute your applications to users who don't have a full copy of Access. An Access database designed to execute with the run-time version of Access must have the following.

- All features of the application must be implemented with forms and reports. The user will not have access to the Database window to execute queries or to open tables.

- The application must have a startup form or an Autoexec macro that opens a startup form.

- All forms and reports must have custom toolbars. No built-in toolbars are available in the run-time version.

- All (or nearly all) code must be written in Visual Basic and must implement error trapping. Any untrapped errors cause the application to exit.

- The application should execute the Quit method of the Application object to terminate. If you simply close the final form, the user will be left staring at an empty Access workspace.

As you might expect, the run-time version also blocks access to all design views and hides the Database window. Also, many undesirable commands (such as Save or Save As) are eliminated from the built-in menus. Finally, many keystrokes are disabled, such as pressing F11 to show the Database window or Ctrl+Break to halt Visual Basic code execution.

To create a shortcut on your Windows desktop for your Access application, right-click the desktop, choose New from the shortcut menu, and then choose Shortcut. You can also create a shortcut in a folder by opening Windows Explorer, navigating to the folder you want, choosing New from the File menu, and then choosing Shortcut from the submenu. Windows opens a dialog box to help you find the program you want the shortcut to execute. Click the Browse button and find C:\Program Files\Microsoft Office\Office\MSAccess.exe. Click the Next button, give your shortcut a name, and then click Finish.

Right-click your new shortcut and choose Properties from the shortcut menu. You'll see a dialog box similar to the one shown in Figure 25-35.

FIGURE 25-35.
Modifying the command line in a WIndows shortcut.

Immediately following the name of the Access program on the Target line, enter a space followed by the database you want to open (with its full path) enclosed in quotation marks. Follow the name of the database with the options you need to perform the task you want. For example, you might need to specify the location of the workgroup file your application requires.

Table 25-3 on the next page summarizes the shortcut command-line options you can use.

VI

Creating an Application

TABLE 25-3.   Access Shortcut Command-Line Options

Option	Description
database	Opens the specified database. Must appear immediately after the folder and file location for Msaccess.exe.
/cmd	Specifies a program parameter that can be retrieved by a Visual Basic procedure using the Command built-in function. Must be the last option on the command line.
/compact	Compacts the specified database but does not open the database.
/convert *target*	Converts the specified version 8 or earlier database to version 9 format and stores it in the *target* file.
/excl	Opens the specified database with exclusive access. Only one user at a time can open a database exclusively.
/nostartup	Opens the specified database without displaying the standard Access splash screen.
/profile *userprofile*	Specifies the name of a user profile in the Windows registry. You can use a profile to override Database Engine settings and specify a custom application title, icon, or splash screen.
/pwd *password*	Specifies the password for the specified user in the current workgroup.
/repair	Repairs the specified database but does not open the database.
/ro	Opens the specified database in read-only mode.
/runtime	Specifies that Access will execute with run-time version options.
/user *userid*	Specifies the logon user ID.
/wrkgroup *workgroupfile*	Uses the specified workgroup file.
/x *macroname*	Runs the specified macro after opening the specified database.

Installing
Microsoft Office

T his book assumes you are installing Microsoft Access as part of the Microsoft Office 2000 Professional or Premium suite. To install Microsoft Office for a single user, you need a Microsoft Windows–compatible computer configured as follows.

- A Pentium or higher microprocessor (Pentium-75 recommended as a minimum)

- Windows 95, Windows 98, Microsoft Windows NT version 4.0, or Microsoft Windows 2000

- At least 16 megabytes (MB) of RAM for the operating system (32 MB for Windows NT or Windows 2000) plus 4 MB of RAM for each concurrently executing application (8 MB for Access and Outlook)

- A hard drive with at least 190 MB of free space for a minimum installation (390 MB for a full Premium installation)

- A CD-ROM drive (not required if you are installing over a network)

- A mouse or other pointing device

- A VGA or higher display (800 × 600 SVGA recommended as a minimum)

Other options required to use all features include:

- A multimedia computer for sound and other multimedia effects

- A 9600 baud or higher modem (28,800 recommended)

- Microsoft Mail, Microsoft Exchange, Internet SMTP/POP3 service, or other MAPI-compliant messaging software for e-mail

- Microsoft Exchange Server for advanced collaboration functions

- Connection to an Internet service provider with updated FrontPage extensions for Web publishing features, or a local copy of Personal Web Server 4.0 or later installed

To run Access as a server on a network, you need:

- User workstations configured as specified above for each user

- Network software that supports named pipes, such as Microsoft Windows NT Server, Microsoft Windows 2000 Server, Microsoft LAN Manager, Novell NetWare, or Banyan VINES

- A Windows-compatible computer to act as the server with at least 190 MB of free disk space for the Office software plus additional space for user files

Before you run the Office setup program, be sure that no other applications are running on your computer and then start Windows.

TIP

If you have previous versions of Microsoft Office programs (including Microsoft Outlook and Microsoft FrontPage) installed that you do not want to keep, I recommend that you run those programs' setup to remove the programs before running Microsoft Office 2000 setup. This is especially true if you want to keep some previous versions (for example, previous versions of Microsoft Access to support older applications), but not all. Office 2000 setup offers options to keep all or remove all previous versions, but it is not able to selectively keep or remove only some programs.

If you're installing from the Microsoft Office Professional or Microsoft Office Premium CD-ROM, insert the first CD-ROM. On most systems, Office Setup starts automatically. If Setup does not start automatically, choose the Run command from the Windows Start menu. In the Run dialog box, type *x:\setup.exe* (where *x* is the drive letter of your CD-ROM drive).

To install from a network drive, use Windows Explorer to connect to the folder in which your system manager has placed the Office setup files. Run Setup.exe in that folder.

Appendix

If you're running Windows 95, Windows 98, or Windows NT version 4.0, the setup program states that it is updating your "Windows Installer Program." This is a new program that Office must install to continue. Once it completes this installation, it may ask you to reboot your computer and restart setup. After you reboot your computer, start Office setup again. Note that the setup program might take several minutes after it displays its opening screen to examine your machine and determine what programs you have currently installed. Be patient! The setup program then asks for your name and your company name (and the CD key from your installation package if you're installing from a CD).

Next, setup asks you to confirm that you accept the license agreement. If you do not have any previous versions of Office programs installed, the following screen lets you choose to either Install Now with default options or Customize the setup to specify an installation folder and options. If this screen appears, I recommend you select the Customize option. If setup detects that you have previous versions of Office programs installed, or you choose the Customize option, setup lets you select the folder in which you want to install the Office files, as shown in Figure A-1.

FIGURE A-1.

Selecting the location to install Microsoft Office 2000.

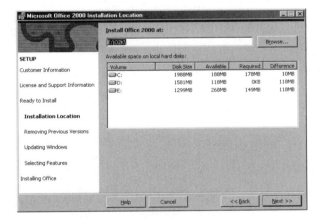

If you have chosen an installation location other than the default, the setup program next asks you if you want to keep the earlier versions it has found on your machine, as shown in Figure A-2 on the next page. Click the Keep These Programs check box to instruct setup not to remove old versions. If you want to keep only older versions of Microsoft Access but remove other Office applications, you must run Office setup separately from your original installation disks to remove previous versions of Microsoft Excel, Microsoft PowerPoint, or Microsoft Word. If you have an earlier version of Microsoft FrontPage installed (as I did on my machine), you may also want to run FrontPage setup to remove it. I recommend that you perform these removal steps before continuing Office 2000 setup. You can safely exit Office 2000 setup at this point and restart it after you have removed old versions.

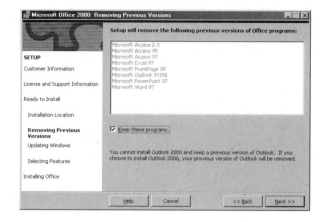

Next, setup asks you if you want to upgrade to Internet Explorer version 5.0, as shown in Figure A-3. You can choose to not upgrade, install the standard edition (the default), or perform a minimal install of Internet Explorer.

> **NOTE**
>
> If you want to be able to view data access pages you create in Access in your Web browser, you must upgrade to Internet Explorer 5.0 standard edition.

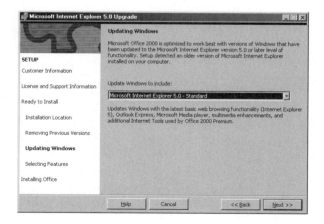

Finally, Office 2000 setup asks you which options to install, as shown in Figure A-4. Most features let you choose an option to Run From My Computer, Run All From My Computer (which includes all options in the selection tree below the selected option), Run From CD, Run All From CD (which sets all options in the selection tree below the selected option), Installed On First Use (you must have your installation CD available if you try to use a feature that requires this option), or Not Available. Because the examples in this book rely on all of the options for Microsoft Access being installed, I recommend you click the arrow next to the disk icon for Microsoft Access and choose Run All From My Computer as shown in Figure A-4. I also recommend that you install all of the items under the Office Tools category except the language options you don't need.

FIGURE A-4.

Selecting the option to install all of Microsoft Access.

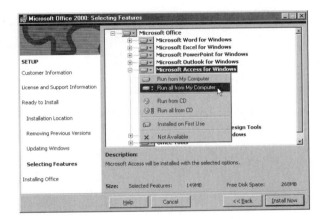

If you don't want to install all options, you will have to select additional components to follow along with some of the examples in this book. (You can rerun the setup program to add these components if you have already run Office 2000 setup and accepted the defaults.) The additional components needed are:

- For the Entertainment Scheduling sample database, install the calendar control item from the Microsoft Access options (installed by default unless you deselect it).

- For Chapter 19, "Publishing Your Data on the Web," install all of the options in Office Server Extension support under Office Tools. If you have Office 2000 Premium, I also recommend that you install all of FrontPage 2000.

- For Chapter 25, "After Completing Your Application," install the Database Replication item under Microsoft Access. You will also need to install the Microsoft Data Engine as described in the next section.

Click Install Now to complete the installation.

Installing the Microsoft Data Engine (MSDE)

If you intend to build Microsoft Access project files (adp filename extension) that link directly to a database defined in Microsoft SQL Server, you should install the Microsoft Data Engine (MSDE) on your desktop machine to facilitate building and testing your application. MSDE is a special version of Microsoft SQL Server configured to run on any Windows 95, Windows 98, Windows NT 4.0, or Windows 2000 desktop. With MSDE installed, you can use a Microsoft Access project file to create databases and define tables, views, diagrams, and stored procedures that you can later move to SQL Server on a network. You will normally install MSDE on your desktop machine. However, you can also install MSDE on a server. If you need to install MSDE on a server, you must install from that server's console.

MSDE has its own setup program; you can't install MSDE using Office 2000 setup. To start MSDE setup, insert the first of your Office 2000 setup disks. If Office 2000 setup starts, cancel it. Choose Run from the Windows Start menu, enter the following, and click OK.

```
x:\SQL\X86\SETUP\SetupSQL.exe
```

(Replace *x* with the drive letter of your CD-ROM drive.) MSDE setup then displays its first dialog box, as shown in Figure A-5.

FIGURE A-5.

Establishing the installation locations for MSDE.

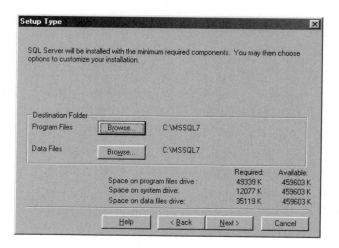

You can click the Browse buttons to select an alternate installation location for either the program files or data files for MSDE. If you choose an alternate location for data files, the setup program creates a Data folder in the location you choose. Click Next to go on to the next step, as shown in Figure A-6.

FIGURE A-6.

Choosing character set, sort order, and Unicode options in MSDE setup.

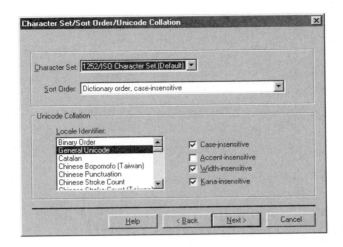

You shouldn't normally need to change any of the options shown on this second dialog box. If you want to be able to work directly with the sample BooksSQL database, you must leave the options set as shown in Figure A-6. If you plan to move your databases to a full version of SQL Server later, you should check with your database administrator to verify that the options you choose match those on the production server. If the options are different, you will have to import your database to the new server rather than simply attach it.

Click Next to go on to the next dialog box, shown in Figure A-7.

FIGURE A-7.

Choosing Network Library options in MSDE setup.

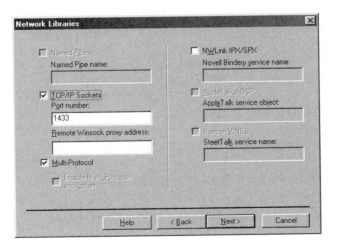

Again, you should not normally need to change any of the networking options. If you are installing on your local machine, you should leave TCP/IP enabled and not change the default Port Number. If you are installing MSDE on a server that uses Novell protocols, you might need to check the NWLink IPX/SPX option.

When you click Next, MSDE setup shows you a final dialog box informing you that it has all the information it needs to install. Click Finish to install MSDE. Once you have MSDE installed, a new icon for SQL Service Manager appears in your system tray (at the right end of the Windows taskbar). Double-click this icon to open the manager. Click the Start button to activate MSDE on your machine. You can also choose an option in the manager to automatically start MSDE each time you start your machine.

Managing ODBC Connections

When you need to connect to your Microsoft Access database tables (in an mdb or mde file) from any Office application or on a Web server, you must first define an Open Database Connectivity (ODBC) Data Source Name (DSN) on the system from which you want to make the connection. You don't need to define a connection to your database for links from another Access database—Access uses its own internal drivers to make the connection.

If you want to use Microsoft Access to connect to SQL databases that support the ODBC standard, you must install both the ODBC driver for that database and define a connection in the Microsoft ODBC administrator program. The ODBC driver for Microsoft SQL Server is included with Access.

ODBC is a technique that isolates applications from differences among database systems. If your application performs all its database processing through ODBC interfaces you can, in theory, change database systems at will without changing your application.

Given that objective, it really doesn't make sense to code things like the filename of your Access or SQL Server database—or specify the type of database—within your application. If you did and then changed the database system to some other product, you'd have to change the connection information inside the application, and that would be counter to the design of ODBC.

To avoid this problem, you can define a DSN. The DSN defines—once—the database's type, physical location, physical name, and any other configuration details. The application then opens the DSN by name and doesn't need to know (or be configured with) all database-specific details.

There are three kinds of ODBC Data Source Names.

- **User DSN.** This type of DSN stores its information in the system registry on a user-by-user basis. User DSNs are available only when the corresponding user is logged on to the computer.

- **System DSN.** A System DSN also stores its information in the registry, but it's available no matter who's currently logged on (or even if no one is currently logged on).

- **File DSN.** Like a System DSN, a File DSN is available no matter who's currently logged on. A File DSN isn't stored in the system registry, though; it's stored in an ordinary text file. The advantage of a File DSN is that setting it up doesn't require use of the ODBC administrator program. If you know the format of the parameters for the kind of database file you'll be connecting to, you can create a File DSN with Notepad. You can find a sample File DSN named "SQL Server Example.dsn" in the sample files included on the companion CD.

Creating an ODBC System Data Source Name for Microsoft Access

The most "universal" type of DSN is a System DSN. The ODBC manager creates registry entries for this type of DSN that can be used by all applications, no matter what user is signed on. You must use a System DSN, for example, to define the database connections on a Web server. You can create a System DSN for a Microsoft Access database by following these steps.

1 Log on to the computer whose applications require a connection to your database. If you're creating a System DSN on a Web server, you must be logged on at the Web server's console.

2 Open Windows Control Panel.

3 Double-click the ODBC icon. Depending on the version of ODBC installed, this may be titled 32bit ODBC, ODBC Data Sources, or ODBC Data Sources (32bit). It looks like this.

4 The ODBC Data Source Administrator dialog box appears, as shown in Figure A-8. To create a System DSN, first click the System DSN tab and then click the Add button.

New versions of ODBC usually appear with each new version of any Microsoft database product, operating system, or Web server, and at other times as well. As a result, the screens on your computer may differ somewhat from those shown here.

FIGURE A-8.

ODBC Data Source Administrator dialog box, which is accessible from Control Panel.

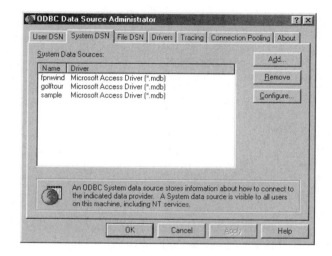

5 When the dialog box shown in Figure A-9 appears, choose Microsoft Access Driver, and then click Finish.

FIGURE A-9.

Telling ODBC which database driver to use for a data source.

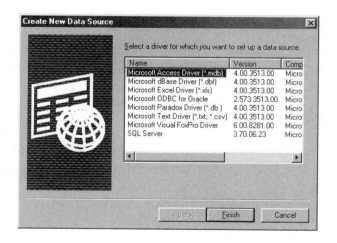

6 Make the following settings in the dialog box that configures the ODBC Microsoft Access Driver, shown in Figure A-10. Only the Data Source Name and Database entries are required; the others are optional.

FIGURE A-10.

Defining an ODBC Data Source Name for a Microsoft Access database.

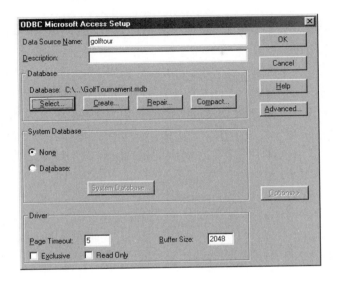

- **Data Source Name.** Give the data source a name that applications will use to identify it.

- **Database.** Click the Select button, locate your Access database, and click OK.

  If the database resides on another computer, be sure to specify its location in Universal Naming Convention (UNC) format. Network locations mapped to drive letters might change depending on who's logged on to the computer, and disappear completely when no one is logged on. A UNC filename has this form.

  `\\<server name>\<share name>\<folder path>\<filename>`

> **NOTE**
>
> To specify a UNC name, you must enter the entire server, share, path, and file name in the Database Name field of the dialog box that appears when you click the Select button.

Entries in the remaining fields, described on the next page, are optional.

- **Description.** Enter one line of documentation regarding the DSN.

- **System Database.** If your application requires a specific workgroup file for security *(see Chapter 25)*, select the Database option button and then click the System Database button to locate the workgroup file.

- **Page Timeout.** Specify a time limit for completing ODBC operations. The default value is normally adequate.

- **Buffer Size.** Specify the number of bytes available for ODBC buffering. The default value is normally adequate.

- **Exclusive.** Turn this option on if the application requires exclusive use of the database.

- **Read Only.** Turn this option on if the application requires read-only use of the database.

- **Advanced.** Click this button if using the database requires additional settings, such as a user name and password.

7   When all your entries are correct, click OK to create the System DSN.

If you have several applications that use the same database, you should use the same System DSN for all of them. That way, if you ever have to move, rename, or reconfigure the database, you have only one System DSN to update.

If you need to establish a System DSN on a Web server and you don't have access to your Web server's console, whoever *does* have access will need to set up the System DSN for you. On a corporate intranet, contact your departmental administrator or MIS department. For Internet service providers, contact the support staff or system administrator.

Using ODBC for Connecting to Microsoft SQL Server

Like Access, Microsoft SQL Server is an ODBC-compliant database. If SQL Server drivers are available on your PC, you can use ODBC for opening SQL Server databases in Access. If SQL Server drivers are available on your Web server, Active Server Pages can read SQL Server databases via ODBC. Here's the procedure for defining an ODBC System DSN for a SQL Server database.

1 Follow steps 1 through 4 as described in the previous section for setting up a Microsoft Access DSN.

2 When you get to step 5 (Figure A-9) select SQL Server and then click Finish.

3 At this point, older versions of the ODBC administrator program display a single dialog box containing all available SQL Server options. Newer versions run a wizard that presents several dialog boxes in sequence. Although we'll look at the wizard here, all the essential fields appear—with the same titles—in the older dialog box.

Figure A-11 shows the first dialog box in the SQL Server wizard. Enter the following fields.

FIGURE A-11.

The first step in defining an ODBC DSN for SQL Server.

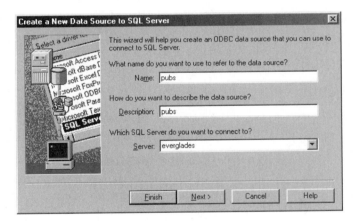

• **Name.** Give the data source a name that applications will use to identify it. This field and the Data Source Name field that ultimately appears in the dialog box shown in Figure A-8 must contain the same value.

• **Description.** Specify one line of documentation regarding the DSN. This field is optional.

• **Server.** Specify the computer where the SQL Server software is running. If the computer name doesn't appear in the drop-down list, type it.

4 Click Next to display the dialog box shown in Figure A-12. You may need to ask the SQL Server administrator how to fill in these values.

FIGURE A-12.

Settings related to SQL Server communication and security.

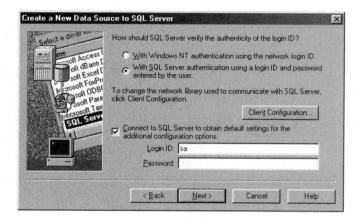

- **How Should SQL Server Verify The Authenticity Of The Login ID?** Select With Windows NT Authentication if SQL Server is set up to use the same login IDs and passwords that are used for logging on to a Windows NT network. Select With SQL Server Authentication if SQL Server uses its own built-in security; choose this option if you're defining a link to MSDE on your own computer.

- **Client Configuration.** Click this button to select the type of network communication. You don't need to change the default settings for MSDE.

- **Connect To SQL Server To Obtain Default Settings.** To obtain defaults from the server specified in the previous dialog box, turn this check box on and specify a Login ID and Password acceptable to SQL Server. To connect to your local MSDE, type *sa* in the Login ID box and leave the Password box empty.

5 The wizard's next two dialog boxes, shown in Figure A-13 and Figure A-14, seldom require configuration. Unless your SQL Server administrator has instructed you differently, click Next and then Finish to bypass them. For more information on these settings, click the Help button.

FIGURE A-13.

Advanced settings that seldom require configuration.

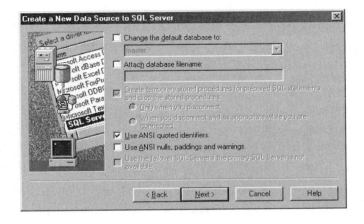

FIGURE A-14.

More advanced settings.

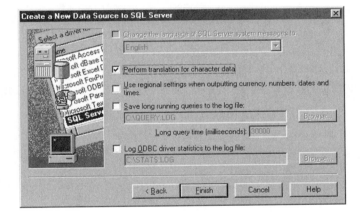

6 After you click Finish in the dialog box shown in Figure A-14, the ODBC administrator program displays the informational screen shown in the background of Figure A-15 on the next page. Clicking the Test Data Source button gives the new DSN a brief workout. If you get the message "TESTS COMPLETED SUCCESSFULLY," your System DSN is ready to use. If you don't get the confirmation message, recheck your entries and perhaps consult your SQL Server administrator.

You might recall from Chapter 10, "Importing, Linking, and Exporting Data," that ODBC provides a way to import or link to SQL Server tables from Microsoft Access. *For details about the procedure to link a table from SQL Server into a Microsoft Access database, see the section titled "Linking SQL Tables" in Chapter 10.* Remember, the DSN must exist on the same machine that's going to use it.

FIGURE A-15.

Testing an SQL Server DSN.

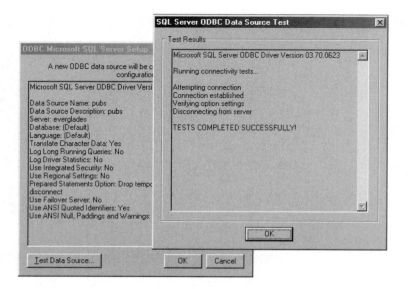

Converting from a Previous Release

Although Microsoft Access 2000 (version 9 of Access) can work with the data and tables in a database file created by Access version 1.x, version 2, version 7 (Access for Windows 95), or version 8 (Access 97), you cannot use version 9 to modify the queries, forms, reports, macros, or modules in a database created in an earlier version. You might be able to run your earlier version database application using version 9, but your application will fail if it attempts to modify queries, forms, or reports as part of its normal execution.

You can easily convert a version 1.x, version 2, version 7, or version 8 database file to version 9. First, make sure all Access Basic or VBA (Visual Basic for Applications) modules are compiled in your earlier version database. For version 2 databases, this means you must open each form and report module individually and compile and save the module. Start Access 2000, and click Cancel in the opening choices dialog box. Choose Database Utilities from the Tools menu, choose Convert Database from the submenu, and then choose To Current Access Database Version. (Access 2000 also includes a utility to convert a version 9 database back to version 8.) In the Database To Convert From dialog box, select the earlier version file that you want to convert. Access opens the Convert Database Into dialog box. You must specify a different filename for your version 9 database because Access won't let you replace your previous version file directly.

If you open an earlier version database in Access 2000, you will see a dialog box that offers to convert the database to the current version or attempt to modify the database for shared use between versions. You can also convert an earlier version database by creating a new version 9 database, and then importing all the objects from the older version database.

Conversion Issues

Access 2000 (version 9) reports any objects or properties that it is unable to convert by creating a table called Convert Errors in your converted database. The most common problems you're likely to encounter are field validation rules that reference another field, an Access built-in function, or a user-defined function. Because field and table validation rules are enforced by the JET Database Engine *(see Chapter 22, "Visual Basic Fundamentals," for a discussion of the Access 2000 architecture),* you cannot use functions to validate data in Access 2000 as you could in version 1.*x*. This means, however, that the validation rules you define are always enforced in Access 2000, regardless of whether your data is being accessed from the Access application environment or from another application environment, such as Word, Excel, or Visual Basic.

Other changes that might affect the conversion of your application code or how your converted application runs include the following.

- Access version 1.*x* allows you to perform a Save Record menu command on a form even if the data in the form has not changed. Versions 2, 7, 8, and 9 generate an error. Be sure to check the Dirty property of the form before using Save Record.

- Version 1.*x* supports a CancelEvent action in the Close event handler of a form. Beginning with version 2, you must use CancelEvent in the Unload event handler. The Close event no longer supports a cancel. The conversion utility correctly changes Close to Unload in most cases.

- Version 1.*x* allows you to specify the default value of a text field without including double quotation marks. Beginning with version 2, you must enclose all text default values in double quotation marks. The conversion utility adds double quotation marks in most cases.

- Many more query fields are updateable in versions 2, 7, 8, and 9. For example, if you do not want to allow certain fields on the "one" side of a query to be updateable in a form, you must set the Locked property of the form controls to Yes in version 2 or later.

- You could use the fourth parameter in the Format function in versions 1.*x* and 2 to test for a Null value in a string variable or field. In versions 7 and later, you must use the IIf function to test for the special Null case. The Format function can handle Null in both arithmetic and date values in all versions.

- You had to use macros to construct custom menus in versions 7 and earlier. Access version 9 continues to support macros for custom menus, but you might want to rebuild custom menus using the custom command bar facility in version 9. *For details, see Chapter 24, "The Finishing Touches."*

- DoMenuItem is no longer supported as of version 8. The conversion utility replaces this command in all macros and Access Basic or VBA code with the equivalent RunCommand action or method.

- In version 8, you could create a formatted Windows dialog box with the MsgBox action or function, separating the sections of the message with the "@" character. Version 9 no longer supports this feature.

- If you convert a database by importing its objects, your new database might not compile or execute properly. Access version 9 sets the default data objects library to ActiveX Data Objects (ADO) in a new database. Most databases created with earlier versions require the Data Access Objects (DAO) library. You can correct this by opening any module in the Visual Basic Editor, and then choosing References from the Tools menu.

Index

About the Author

John Viescas When John Viescas isn't exploring the latest intricacies of Microsoft Access, you're likely to find him surfing the Internet or zipping around town helping one of his many database clients. Or you might run into him as he flies in to teach a developer seminar on Access or to speak at one of several major conferences or regional user group meetings. If you hang out on the Web, you can find him answering questions about Access in the newsgroups or on the CompuServe forums. John has been named a "Microsoft MVP" every year since 1993 for his continuing help to Access users online.

Born in Texas, John got started in computing long before many of the current employees at Microsoft were "knee high to a grasshopper." He likes to comment to students that the laptop he carries with him on the road has more than 5000 times the memory, has ten times the disk space, and is many times faster than the first so-called "mainframe" computer he used to teach himself Autocoder (a computer language spoken by the ancients). John has been working with database systems for most of his career. He began by building large database application systems for El Paso Natural Gas Company in his hometown in the early 1970s. From there, he went to Applied Data Research in Dallas, where he managed the development of database and data dictionary systems for mainframe computers and became involved in the evolution of the SQL database language standard. Before forming his own company a few years ago, he helped market and support NonStop SQL for Tandem Computers in California. Somewhere along the way (would you believe 1991?), he got involved in the early internal testing of a Microsoft product code-named "Cirrus." The first edition of *Running Microsoft Access* was published in 1992.

In addition to frequent business travel, John enjoys cashing in his frequent flier miles to go winging somewhere with his wife, Suzanne, just for fun. Between them, John and Suzanne have seven children and (at last count) six grandchildren. When they're not visiting their far-flung family, they like to spend at least part of the Seattle winter in sunnier places like Hawaii or more romantic places like Paris (no, not Texas).

You can reach John on The Microsoft Network at: **JohnV@msn.com**

Colophon

The manuscript for this book was prepared and submitted to Microsoft Press in electronic form. Text files were prepared using Microsoft Word 2000. Pages were composed using Adobe PageMaker 6.52 for Windows, with text in Garamond and display type in Myriad. Composed pages were sent to the printer as electronic prepress files.

Cover Designer
Tim Girvin Designs, Inc.

Interior Graphic Designers
Kim Eggleston
Amy Peppler Adams,
designLab

Illustrators
Blake Wesley Whittington
Thomas Williams

Layout Artist
Paula J. Kausch

Editors
Carl Siechert
Stan DeGulis

Technical Editor
Blake Wesley Whittington

Indexer
Carl Siechert

Editorial Assistant
Kristen Weatherby

up! Step

STEP BY STEP books provide quick and easy self-training—to help you learn to use the powerful word processing, spreadsheet, database, presentation, communication, and Internet components of Microsoft® Office 2000—both individually and together. The easy-to-follow lessons present clear objectives and real-world business examples, with numerous screen shots and illustrations. Put Office 2000 to work today, with STEP BY STEP learning solutions, made by Microsoft.

- MICROSOFT OFFICE PROFESSIONAL 8-IN-1 STEP BY STEP
- MICROSOFT WORD 2000 STEP BY STEP
- MICROSOFT EXCEL 2000 STEP BY STEP
- MICROSOFT POWERPOINT® 2000 STEP BY STEP
- MICROSOFT INTERNET EXPLORER 5 STEP BY STEP
- MICROSOFT PUBLISHER 2000 STEP BY STEP
- MICROSOFT ACCESS 2000 STEP BY STEP
- MICROSOFT FRONTPAGE 2000 STEP BY STEP
- MICROSOFT OUTLOOK 2000 STEP BY STEP

mspress.microsoft.com

See clearly—
now!

Here's the remarkable, *visual* way to quickly find answers about the powerfully integrated features of the Microsoft® Office 2000 applications. Microsoft Press AT A GLANCE books let you focus on particular tasks and show you, with clear, numbered steps, the easiest way to get them done right now. Put Office 2000 to work today, with AT A GLANCE learning solutions, made by Microsoft.

- MICROSOFT OFFICE 2000 PROFESSIONAL AT A GLANCE
- MICROSOFT WORD 2000 AT A GLANCE
- MICROSOFT EXCEL 2000 AT A GLANCE
- MICROSOFT POWERPOINT® 2000 AT A GLANCE
- MICROSOFT ACCESS 2000 AT A GLANCE
- MICROSOFT FRONTPAGE® 2000 AT A GLANCE
- MICROSOFT PUBLISHER 2000 AT A GLANCE
- MICROSOFT OFFICE 2000 SMALL BUSINESS AT A GLANCE
- MICROSOFT PHOTODRAW® 2000 AT A GLANCE
- MICROSOFT INTERNET EXPLORER 5 AT A GLANCE
- MICROSOFT OUTLOOK® 2000 AT A GLANCE

Microsoft®

mspress.microsoft.com

Microsoft Press offers *comprehensive* **learning solutions** to help new users, power users, and professionals get the most from ***Microsoft technology.***

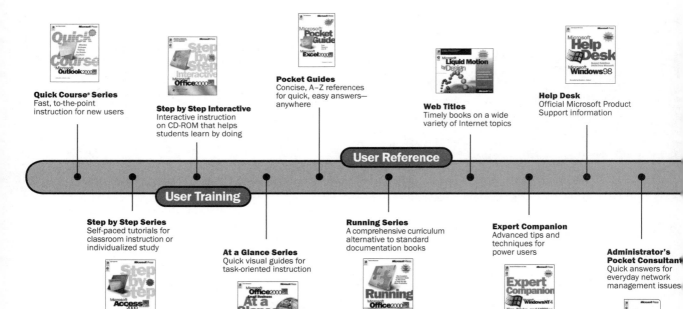

Quick Course® Series
Fast, to-the-point instruction for new users

Step by Step Interactive
Interactive instruction on CD-ROM that helps students learn by doing

Pocket Guides
Concise, A–Z references for quick, easy answers—anywhere

Web Titles
Timely books on a wide variety of Internet topics

Help Desk
Official Microsoft Product Support information

User Reference

User Training

Step by Step Series
Self-paced tutorials for classroom instruction or individualized study

At a Glance Series
Quick visual guides for task-oriented instruction

Running Series
A comprehensive curriculum alternative to standard documentation books

Expert Companion
Advanced tips and techniques for power users

Administrator's Pocket Consultant
Quick answers for everyday network management issues

Microsoft Press® products are available worldwide wherever quality computer books are sold. For more information, contact your book or computer retailer, software reseller, or local Microsoft Sales Office, or visit our Web site at mspress.microsoft.com. To locate your nearest source for Microsoft Press products, or to order directly, call 1-800-MSPRESS in the U.S. (in Canada, call 1-800-268-2222).

Prices and availability dates are subject to change.

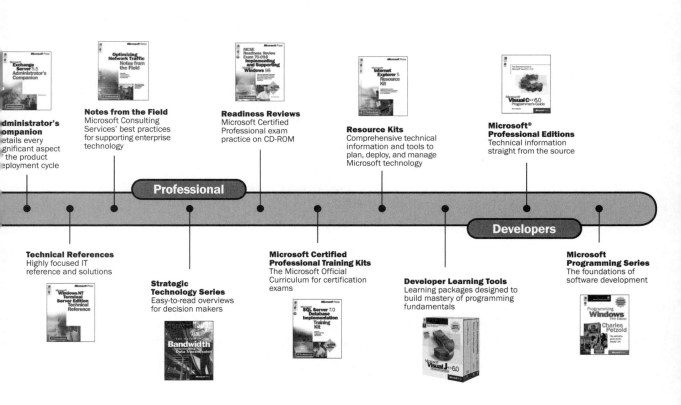

Get a **Free**
e-mail newsletter, updates,
special offers, links to related books,
and more when you
register on line!

Register your Microsoft Press® title on our Web site and you'll get a FREE subscription to our e-mail newsletter, *Microsoft Press Book Connections.* You'll find out about newly released and upcoming books and learning tools, online events, software downloads, special offers and coupons for Microsoft Press customers, and information about major Microsoft® product releases. You can also read useful additional information about all the titles we publish, such as detailed book descriptions, tables of contents and indexes, sample chapters, links to related books and book series, author biographies, and reviews by other customers.

Registration is easy. Just visit this Web page and fill in your information:

http://www.microsoft.com/mspress/register

Microsoft·

Proof of Purchase

Running Microsoft® Access 2000
1-57231-934-8

CUSTOMER NAME

Microsoft Press, PO Box 97017, Redmond, WA 98073-9830

MICROSOFT LICENSE AGREEMENT

Book Companion CD

IMPORTANT—READ CAREFULLY: This Microsoft End-User License Agreement ("EULA") is a legal agreement between you (either an individual or an entity) and Microsoft Corporation for the Microsoft product identified above, which includes computer software and may include associated media, printed materials, and "online" or electronic documentation ("SOFTWARE PRODUCT"). Any component included within the SOFTWARE PRODUCT that is accompanied by a separate End-User License Agreement shall be governed by such agreement and not the terms set forth below. By installing, copying, or otherwise using the SOFTWARE PRODUCT, you agree to be bound by the terms of this EULA. If you do not agree to the terms of this EULA, you are not authorized to install, copy, or otherwise use the SOFTWARE PRODUCT; you may, however, return the SOFTWARE PRODUCT, along with all printed materials and other items that form a part of the Microsoft product that includes the SOFTWARE PRODUCT, to the place you obtained them for a full refund.

SOFTWARE PRODUCT LICENSE

The SOFTWARE PRODUCT is protected by United States copyright laws and international copyright treaties, as well as other intellectual property laws and treaties. The SOFTWARE PRODUCT is licensed, not sold.

1. **GRANT OF LICENSE.** This EULA grants you the following rights:

   a. **Software Product.** You may install and use one copy of the SOFTWARE PRODUCT on a single computer. The primary user of the computer on which the SOFTWARE PRODUCT is installed may make a second copy for his or her exclusive use on a portable computer.

   b. **Storage/Network Use.** You may also store or install a copy of the SOFTWARE PRODUCT on a storage device, such as a network server, used only to install or run the SOFTWARE PRODUCT on your other computers over an internal network; however, you must acquire and dedicate a license for each separate computer on which the SOFTWARE PRODUCT is installed or run from the storage device. A license for the SOFTWARE PRODUCT may not be shared or used concurrently on different computers.

   c. **License Pak.** If you have acquired this EULA in a Microsoft License Pak, you may make the number of additional copies of the computer software portion of the SOFTWARE PRODUCT authorized on the printed copy of this EULA, and you may use each copy in the manner specified above. You are also entitled to make a corresponding number of secondary copies for portable computer use as specified above.

   d. **Sample Code.** Solely with respect to portions, if any, of the SOFTWARE PRODUCT that are identified within the SOFTWARE PRODUCT as sample code (the "SAMPLE CODE"):

      i. **Use and Modification.** Microsoft grants you the right to use and modify the source code version of the SAMPLE CODE, *provided* you comply with subsection (d)(iii) below. You may not distribute the SAMPLE CODE, or any modified version of the SAMPLE CODE, in source code form.

      ii. **Redistributable Files.** Provided you comply with subsection (d)(iii) below, Microsoft grants you a nonexclusive, royalty-free right to reproduce and distribute the object code version of the SAMPLE CODE and of any modified SAMPLE CODE, other than SAMPLE CODE, or any modified version thereof, designated as not redistributable in the Readme file that forms a part of the SOFTWARE PRODUCT (the "Non-Redistributable Sample Code"). All SAMPLE CODE other than the Non-Redistributable Sample Code is collectively referred to as the "REDISTRIBUTABLES."

      iii. **Redistribution Requirements.** If you redistribute the REDISTRIBUTABLES, you agree to: (i) distribute the REDISTRIBUTABLES in object code form only in conjunction with and as a part of your software application product; (ii) not use Microsoft's name, logo, or trademarks to market your software application product; (iii) include a valid copyright notice on your software application product; (iv) indemnify, hold harmless, and defend Microsoft from and against any claims or lawsuits, including attorney's fees, that arise or result from the use or distribution of your software application product; and (v) not permit further distribution of the REDISTRIBUTABLES by your end user. Contact Microsoft for the applicable royalties due and other licensing terms for all other uses and/or distribution of the REDISTRIBUTABLES.

2. **DESCRIPTION OF OTHER RIGHTS AND LIMITATIONS.**

   - **Limitations on Reverse Engineering, Decompilation, and Disassembly.** You may not reverse engineer, decompile, or disassemble the SOFTWARE PRODUCT, except and only to the extent that such activity is expressly permitted by applicable law notwithstanding this limitation.

   - **Separation of Components.** The SOFTWARE PRODUCT is licensed as a single product. Its component parts may not be separated for use on more than one computer.

   - **Rental.** You may not rent, lease, or lend the SOFTWARE PRODUCT.

   - **Support Services.** Microsoft may, but is not obligated to, provide you with support services related to the SOFTWARE PRODUCT ("Support Services"). Use of Support Services is governed by the Microsoft policies and programs described in the user manual, in "online" documentation, and/or in other Microsoft-provided materials. Any supplemental software code provided to you as part of the Support Services shall be considered part of the SOFTWARE PRODUCT and subject to the terms and conditions of this EULA. With respect to technical information you provide to Microsoft as part of the Support Services, Microsoft may use such information for its business purposes, including for product support and development. Microsoft will not utilize such technical information in a form that personally identifies you.

- **Software Transfer.** You may permanently transfer all of your rights under this EULA, provided you retain no copies, you transfer all of the SOFTWARE PRODUCT (including all component parts, the media and printed materials, any upgrades, this EULA, and, if applicable, the Certificate of Authenticity), **and** the recipient agrees to the terms of this EULA.

- **Termination.** Without prejudice to any other rights, Microsoft may terminate this EULA if you fail to comply with the terms and conditions of this EULA. In such event, you must destroy all copies of the SOFTWARE PRODUCT and all of its component parts.

3. **COPYRIGHT.** All title and copyrights in and to the SOFTWARE PRODUCT (including but not limited to any images, photographs, animations, video, audio, music, text, SAMPLE CODE, REDISTRIBUTABLES, and "applets" incorporated into the SOFTWARE PRODUCT) and any copies of the SOFTWARE PRODUCT are owned by Microsoft or its suppliers. The SOFTWARE PRODUCT is protected by copyright laws and international treaty provisions. Therefore, you must treat the SOFTWARE PRODUCT like any other copyrighted material **except** that you may install the SOFTWARE PRODUCT on a single computer provided you keep the original solely for backup or archival purposes. You may not copy the printed materials accompanying the SOFTWARE PRODUCT.

4. **U.S. GOVERNMENT RESTRICTED RIGHTS.** The SOFTWARE PRODUCT and documentation are provided with RESTRICTED RIGHTS. Use, duplication, or disclosure by the Government is subject to restrictions as set forth in subparagraph (c)(1)(ii) of the Rights in Technical Data and Computer Software clause at DFARS 252.227-7013 or subparagraphs (c)(1) and (2) of the Commercial Computer Software—Restricted Rights at 48 CFR 52.227-19, as applicable. Manufacturer is Microsoft Corporation/One Microsoft Way/Redmond, WA 98052-6399.

5. **EXPORT RESTRICTIONS.** You agree that you will not export or re-export the SOFTWARE PRODUCT, any part thereof, or any process or service that is the direct product of the SOFTWARE PRODUCT (the foregoing collectively referred to as the "Restricted Components"), to any country, person, entity, or end user subject to U.S. export restrictions. You specifically agree not to export or re-export any of the Restricted Components (i) to any country to which the U.S. has embargoed or restricted the export of goods or services, which currently include, but are not necessarily limited to, Cuba, Iran, Iraq, Libya, North Korea, Sudan, and Syria, or to any national of any such country, wherever located, who intends to transmit or transport the Restricted Components back to such country; (ii) to any end user who you know or have reason to know will utilize the Restricted Components in the design, development, or production of nuclear, chemical, or biological weapons; or (iii) to any end user who has been prohibited from participating in U.S. export transactions by any federal agency of the U.S. government. You warrant and represent that neither the BXA nor any other U.S. federal agency has suspended, revoked, or denied your export privileges.

DISCLAIMER OF WARRANTY

NO WARRANTIES OR CONDITIONS. MICROSOFT EXPRESSLY DISCLAIMS ANY WARRANTY OR CONDITION FOR THE SOFTWARE PRODUCT. THE SOFTWARE PRODUCT AND ANY RELATED DOCUMENTATION ARE PROVIDED "AS IS" WITHOUT WARRANTY OR CONDITION OF ANY KIND, EITHER EXPRESS OR IMPLIED, INCLUDING, WITHOUT LIMITATION, THE IMPLIED WARRANTIES OF MERCHANTABILITY, FITNESS FOR A PARTICULAR PURPOSE, OR NONINFRINGEMENT. THE ENTIRE RISK ARISING OUT OF USE OR PERFORMANCE OF THE SOFTWARE PRODUCT REMAINS WITH YOU.

LIMITATION OF LIABILITY. TO THE MAXIMUM EXTENT PERMITTED BY APPLICABLE LAW, IN NO EVENT SHALL MICROSOFT OR ITS SUPPLIERS BE LIABLE FOR ANY SPECIAL, INCIDENTAL, INDIRECT, OR CONSEQUENTIAL DAMAGES WHATSOEVER (INCLUDING, WITHOUT LIMITATION, DAMAGES FOR LOSS OF BUSINESS PROFITS, BUSINESS INTERRUPTION, LOSS OF BUSINESS INFORMATION, OR ANY OTHER PECUNIARY LOSS) ARISING OUT OF THE USE OF OR INABILITY TO USE THE SOFTWARE PRODUCT OR THE PROVISION OF OR FAILURE TO PROVIDE SUPPORT SERVICES, EVEN IF MICROSOFT HAS BEEN ADVISED OF THE POSSIBILITY OF SUCH DAMAGES. IN ANY CASE, MICROSOFT'S ENTIRE LIABILITY UNDER ANY PROVISION OF THIS EULA SHALL BE LIMITED TO THE GREATER OF THE AMOUNT ACTUALLY PAID BY YOU FOR THE SOFTWARE PRODUCT OR US$5.00; PROVIDED, HOWEVER, IF YOU HAVE ENTERED INTO A MICROSOFT SUPPORT SERVICES AGREEMENT, MICROSOFT'S ENTIRE LIABILITY REGARDING SUPPORT SERVICES SHALL BE GOVERNED BY THE TERMS OF THAT AGREEMENT. BECAUSE SOME STATES AND JURISDICTIONS DO NOT ALLOW THE EXCLUSION OR LIMITATION OF LIABILITY, THE ABOVE LIMITATION MAY NOT APPLY TO YOU.

MISCELLANEOUS

This EULA is governed by the laws of the State of Washington USA, except and only to the extent that applicable law mand: governing law of a different jurisdiction.

Should you have any questions concerning this EULA, or if you desire to contact Microsoft for any reason, please contact Microsoft subsidiary serving your country, or write: Microsoft Sales Information Center/One Microsoft Way/Redmond, W 98052-6399.

PN 097-0002296